MW01258732

The Mystery of Marriage
of Marriage
A Theology of the Body and the Sacrament

Perry J. Cahall, PHD

Hillenbrand Books®

Chicago / Mundelein, Illinois

Nihil Obstat
Reverend Daniel A. Smilanic, JCD
Vicar for Canonical Services
Archdiocese of Chicago
October 28, 2014

Imprimatur
Very Reverend Ronald Hicks, DMIN
Vicar General
Archdiocese of Chicago
October 28, 2014

To Marisa

Contents

Acknowledgements

There are many people who have made contributions to this book. First of all, I would like to thank the undergraduate students who took the Theology of Marriage course that I taught at Ohio Dominican University in my time there as assistant professor of theology. This course served as the remote origin of the present book, and I am indebted to the students who took this course for their interest in the material, as well as for their questions and insights that helped me to refine my teaching. I would also like to thank the seminarians at the Pontifical College Josephinum who have taken the Pastoral Care of Marriage and the Family course for their desire to learn how to serve married couples and families as ministers in Christ's Church. In addition, I would like to thank Deacon James Keating, director of theological formation at the Institute for Priestly Formation in Omaha, Nebraska, for suggesting to me that I consider writing an accessible book on the theology of marriage.

More proximate to the publication of this book, I would like to thank those who provided me the time I needed to complete this project. Thanks to the members of the Faculty Advisory Committee at the Pontifical College Josephinum and Msgr. Christopher Schreck, rector/president of the Pontifical College Josephinum, for approving and arranging for my sabbatical during the spring 2013 semester throughout which I completed most of the work on this project. I could not have completed this book without having the time to devote my efforts to it in a focused manner. I am also incredibly grateful to Msgr. Kevin McMahon, professor of moral theology at the Pontifical College Josephinum, for agreeing to serve as interim dean of the School of Theology so I could take my sabbatical.

Finally, there are several people who made more immediate contributions to this work. I am grateful to Mrs. Beverly Lane, assistant librarian at the Pontifical College Josephinum, and Mr. Peter Veracka, director of library services at the Pontifical College Josephinum, for assisting me with the research for this book. I could not have completed this project without your assistance. I owe a debt of gratitude to Mrs. Gina Switzer for reading the first draft of each chapter as I completed it, and for providing me with invaluably helpful comments that improved the text. Thank you for all of the time you spent thoughtfully reading these early drafts. I also owe thanks to Dr. Michael Dougherty, Sr. Mary Ann Fatula, Mrs. Katie Jones, Sr. Elizabeth McDonough, Msgr. Kevin McMahon, Msgr. Dennis Lyle, Msgr. Robert J. Dempsey, and my wife, Dr. Marisa Cahall. Each of you generously devoted your time to reading a complete draft of the manuscript of this book and provided me with comments that greatly improved the quality of the work. I am sincerely grateful to each of you. Finally, I would like to thank Kevin Thornton, editor of Hillenbrand Books. Thank you for your thoughtful and careful reading of several drafts of this project, and for your suggestions that helped to shape and improve the final product. Thank you also for your enthusiastic support of this project. With input from so many thoughtful readers, I take full responsibility for any deficiencies that remain in the text.

Quite apart from the direct contributions to the text of this book, I would like to thank my parents who will have been married for forty-five years by the time this book is published. Mom and Dad, your unwavering fidelity to each other has taught your children and grandchildren more about married love than any book I could ever write.

Finally, I would like to thank my wife and children for their loving support during the entire time I was working on this project. Andrew and Claire, thanks for being interested in Dad's project, even if it is about "that marriage stuff," and for sharing in the excitement of making this book a reality. Marisa, thank you for your unwavering encouragement and support during the process of writing this book, especially when my own enthusiasm wavered and when I began to doubt my ability to finish what I had started. More than that, thank you for entering into the mystery of marriage with me and for giving me the privilege of calling myself your husband and the father of your children. It is truly a joy to go through life with you, and the privilege of loving you and receiving your love is a gift that is humbling beyond words. I dedicate this book to you.

Introduction

Everyone is interested in marriage. This is a conclusion I reached when I taught at a Catholic liberal arts college and offered an undergraduate elective course called "Theology of Marriage." Each year I taught this course it would fill up with the maximum of thirty-five students and have a waiting list of students who hoped to take it. Each time I taught the course, I found the students to be open and eager to learn about the Catholic view of marriage. Although at the end of the course not all of the students accepted every Catholic teaching on marriage, they grew in their understanding of why the Church teaches what it does, and they at least respected the Church's positions even if they disagreed with them. Regardless of the disposition or background of the students taking the course, I am convinced that the popularity of the course evidenced how central marriage is to human existence. I am convinced that what prompted the students to enroll in the course is the deep desire each of us has to experience nuptial love, a desire to know and be known, a desire to give ourselves to another in love and receive the other in turn as a gift. Everyone has a natural inclination for marriage and everyone desires to know more about the mystery that marriage is.

Most people understand intuitively that the vocation of marriage provides the opportunity to experience deep joy and happiness in this life. There is joy in finding someone with whom you can go through life, facing whatever "ups and downs" life may bring. There is a joy in knowing that someone loves you enough to pledge his or her life to you, that someone has found you loveable enough to bind himself or herself to you for life. There is joy in knowing that someone is there to support and encourage you even when you feel unworthy of support and encouragement. There is joy in being able to offer the same life-long support and encouragement to your beloved in return, feeling a deep sense of privilege that you have the opportunity, for however long the both of you are alive, to be such an intimate part of someone else's existence. There is the happiness of simply enjoying each other's presence, delighting in each other without having to say a word. There is the joy of realizing that your lives are inextricably bound together, and that this bond has provided the love-structured framework that shapes your life. There is joy, and a deep sense of peace and security, in being able to come home at the end of a day to a person who is in every way your life's companion. There is a simple joy and delight to be found in just being there for each other.

The opportunity for still more joy is available in the blessing of having and raising children together. The conjugal act itself can be a time of deep personal encounter that provides spouses with the opportunity to delight in each other. When a child is conceived through this act of mutual self-giving, spouses experience a completely new joy together. As husband and wife you rejoice in the mystery of the life that develops in the womb. Then, the birth of the child is life-changing and transformative as the child reveals aspects of each of you that neither of you knew before. Instead of knowing each other as husband and wife, you now also know each other as father and mother, and you begin to understand the awesome privilege and responsibility of these titles. You revel in the opportunity to care for your children and for each other in a new way. Your heart nearly explodes with joy to watch your children grow and experience the world, providing you the opportunity to experience anew the joy of the "everydayness" of life that you had perhaps begun to take for granted. As your children grow you rejoice in the privilege to assist them in developing into virtuous adults, hopefully enabling them to live happy, productive lives even when you are gone. And, seeing yourself and your beloved in your children, you are constantly aware that your children are living embodiments of your love for each other. How can you not be joyful?

However, marriage is not without its frustrations, difficulties, and even tragedies, realities which are often ignored by those who ponder marriage. Nevertheless, there is also a joy that can be experienced in marriage even in the face of hardship and suffering. Knowing that you are there for each other in the face of the uncertainties of life, like severe financial difficulty or unemployment, provides a security that is priceless. Having the opportunity to hold your beloved in your arms when he or she is stricken by a life-threatening illness, or supporting each other when a child dies prematurely, presents unexpected opportunities for intimacy amidst a sadness and grief that no one would ever hope to have to endure. Bearing suffering together, you realize what a gift your beloved is and what a gift it is to be given the opportunity to suffer with your spouse. You realize what a gift it is to be there for each other, supporting each other through the worst. The preciousness of your beloved and the preciousness of the love you share become more apparent in these times of suffering; even amidst this suffering, there is a deep sense of peace, consolation, and even joy in knowing that you are in this together.

Married life is full of daily opportunities to experience joy, even amidst difficulties. Yet, too often it is the difficulties and the tragedies that blind couples to the daily blessings and simple joys of life together. This is why the grace that Christ offers to spouses in the Sacrament of Marriage is so important. In the Sacrament of Marriage Jesus offers spouses the assistance they need to love with his love. Empowered by the Holy Spirit in a way that is particular to married life, spouses have all the resources they need to deal with the daily irritations and more acute sufferings of marriage. There is peace and security in knowing that as spouses you do not have to rely upon your own feeble efforts for your marriage to succeed. You have the greatest ally of all in Jesus Christ, *the* Bridegroom, who will ensure that nothing you experience in life will extinguish your love for each other as long as you turn to him. The grace of the Sacrament of Marriage also allows you to appreciate more deeply the daily joys of married life, lifting up every aspect of your life together as the joint worship that you offer to God. In a sacramental marriage there are times in your life together when you become acutely aware that there is a Love at work in your lives that is beyond the both of you. You become aware that this Love is seeking to make you a better person, a holier person, in service to your spouse. You become aware that the love you share with each other as spouses is a ray of Christ's love that is drawing you toward your ultimate destination—resting in God's love.[1] Knowing that God has put you in each other's lives and has allowed you to journey together toward this ultimate destination can increase the joy of marriage in an immeasurable way.

---

1. See Pope Francis' comments on our human loves containing rays of Christ's love in his encyclical letter *Lumen Fidei*, no. 32, June 29, 2013, www.vatican.va/holy_father/francesco /encyclicals/documents/papa-francesco_20130629_enciclica-lumen-fidei_en.html, accessed July 13, 2013.

However, the joys of marriage are only open to spouses if they embrace the reality of marriage that God offers them. This book is designed to enable the reader to see and appreciate God's original plan for marriage and how this plan was restored, elevated, and incorporated into the "great mystery" of Christ's spousal offering of himself to his Church. These pages attempt to facilitate "a conversion to the real"[2] by helping readers to see that marriage, both as a reality present in nature and as a sacrament of the Church, points to the divine, and to a reality for which the human person was made. This book serves as an accurate and helpful means, for all those who are interested, to understand the Catholic vision of marriage, which is nothing more than God's plan for marriage.

The role of marriage in the order of creation is ingrained in nature itself, and this design for marriage that comes to us from our loving Creator is unalterable. This plan is also one that responds to the deepest desires of the human heart, safeguards the dignity of the human person, and both promotes and safeguards the well-being of society. This plan has often been obscured by the lack of clear vision that results from human sinfulness. However, in the fullness of time, Jesus Christ came to reaffirm and restore God's original plan for marriage, calling us to see reality. Jesus even elevated the natural bond of husband and wife to the level of a grace-giving sacrament that helps us to see and experience his own salvific love for us. Therefore, this book will help readers see and understand the wonder of the mystery of marriage, and grasp the significance of marriage as a reality central to human existence.

This book presents a comprehensive Catholic theology of marriage, without claiming to be exhaustive. I have attempted to present a theology of marriage that incorporates biblical, historical, and systematic perspectives. However, some aspects of married life that are addressed within these pages could be elaborated further. For instance, more reflections could be offered on the daily joys and "ordinary" blessings of married life. In addition, much more attention could be devoted to discussing the rearing of children and daily family life. Addressing these topics and others in more depth would take at

---

2. Angelo Scola, *The Nuptial Mystery*, trans. Michelle K. Borras (Grand Rapids, MI: William B. Eerdmans Publishing Company, 2005), 90.

least another whole volume. However, within these pages I have tried to address all of the essential aspects of a theology of marriage.

The theology of marriage presented here draws upon Scripture and Tradition, with particular attention given to the *Theology of the Body* of St. John Paul II. While there is certainly much scholarship on marriage, there is currently no book available in English that attempts to present a comprehensive theology of marriage from a Catholic perspective. Also, while there is a great deal of scholarly literature dealing with different aspects of marriage, and while there is an increasing amount of scholarship emerging on St. John Paul II's *Theology of the Body*, there does not yet exist a book that attempts to show the implications of the *Theology of the Body* for a comprehensive theology of marriage. This book represents a fresh approach to presenting the sacramental theology of marriage with a broad scope and incorporates the invaluable insights of the *Theology of the Body* given to us by St. John Paul II. This approach should make this book attractive to professors and students, as well as anyone interested in learning about the Catholic vision of marriage.

I envision this book being used primarily as a resource for undergraduate, seminary, religious formation, deaconate formation, and lay education audiences. It will also be of interest to those preparing for marriage and spouses who desire a more complete understanding of the vocation to which God has called them. In fact, I hope that those who read this book will be better able to assist those called to marriage to understand and live out their vocation. This book will not presuppose any background knowledge of the Catholic view of marriage, but instead will present a theology of marriage that treats marriage both as a natural institution and as one of the Seven Sacraments of the Church. Thus the content of this book should be accessible to Catholics and non-Catholics alike. The goal is that this book, while representing sound scholarship, will be accessible to as wide an audience as possible.

Part 1 begins with a discussion of mystery, inviting readers to see the beautiful reality of the mystery of marriage. I explain how St. John Paul II's *Theology of the Body* helps us to understand the mystery of marriage, and how his insights have contributed to developing the theology of marriage itself. Part 2 explains marriage in the natural order. This part deals with aspects of theological anthropology, the unique nature of conjugal love, and marriage as a natural reality with objective features that are ascertainable to all. Thus, the focus of part 2 is "to explain properly the reasons for the Church's position [on the nature of marriage], stressing that it is not a case of imposing on nonbelievers a vision based on faith, but of interpreting and defending the values rooted in the very nature of the human person" (NMI, 51). A treatment of marriage in the Bible follows in part 3, highlighting marriage as a unifying theme in salvation history, and tracing the history of the institution of marriage in both the Old and New Testaments. In a summary fashion, but also providing sufficient detail, part 4 of the book succinctly traces the development of the theology of marriage from the early Church up through the present day, especially focusing on the contributions of Pope St. John Paul II. Part 5 of the book presents a systematic sacramental theology of marriage. Part 6 engages the reader in a presentation of Christian married spirituality informed by a sacramental understanding of marriage, an explanation of sexual morality with a particular focus on the practice of responsible parenthood, and a concluding chapter discussing the relationship between marriage and consecrated celibacy. In presenting a theology of marriage, throughout the book I used the current *Order of Celebrating Matrimony*, illustrating how the Church's theology of marriage is expressed through the rite.[3] A unique feature of this book is that from beginning to end it incorporates insights from John Paul II's *Theology of the Body*, as well as his other writings in which he addressed marriage. Attention is also given to the *Catechism of the Catholic Church* and other recent magisterial texts pertaining to marriage so that the reader is presented with the Catholic Church's most fully developed doctrine on marriage. Through this approach, and with each of its chapters, I hope that this book assists the reader in seeing and understanding more completely the wonderful mystery of marriage, a mystery that forms the very basis of human existence and that is central to understanding our relationship to God.

---

3. Thus, *The Order of Celebration Matrimony* demonstrates the principle that the law of praying (*lex orandi*) illustrates the law of believing (*lex credendi*) in the life of the Church.

List of Abbreviations

ACW   *Ancient Christian Writers*. Edited by J. Quasten and J. C. Plumpe. New York, NY / Mahwah, NJ / Westminster, MD: Newman Press.

ANF   *The Ante-Nicene Fathers: The Writings of the Fathers Down to A.D. 325*. Edited by Alexander Roberts and James Donaldson. 10 vols. 1885. Reprint, Peabody, MA: Hendrickson Publishers, 1995.

BB   *Book of Blessings*. Study Edition. Collegeville, Minnesota: The Liturgical Press, 1989.

CC   Pius XI. *Casti Connubii* (*On Christian Marriage*). Encyclical Letter. December 31, 1930. www.vatican.va/holy_father /pius_xi/encyclicals/documents/hf_p-xi_enc_31121930 _casti-connubii_en.html.

CCC   *Catechism of the Catholic Church*. 2nd ed. Washington, DC: Libreria Editrice Vaticana-United States Conference of Catholic Bishops, 2000.

CIC   *Code of Canon Law: Latin-English Edition: New English Translation* (*Codex Iuris Cononici* [CIC]). Washington, DC: Canon Law Society of America, 1998.

DCE   Benedict XVI. *Deus Caritas Est* (*God is Love*). Encyclical Letter. December 25, 2005. www.vatican.va/holy_father /benedict_xvi/encyclicals/documents/hf_ben-xvi_enc _20051225_deus-caritas-est_en.html.

DS   *Enchiridion Symbolorum, Definitionum et Declarationum de Rebus Fidei et Morum. Compendium of Creeds, Definitions, and Declarations on Matters of Faith and Morals*. Edited by Heinrich Denzinger and Adolphus Schönmetzer. 43rd ed. edited by Peter Hünerman. Latin-English edition edited by Robert Fastiggi and Anne Englund Nash. San Francisco: Ignatius Press, 2012.

EG   Francis. *Evangelii Gaudium* (*The Joy of the Gospel*). Apostolic Exhortation. November 24, 2013. Washington, DC: United States Conference of Catholic Bishops, 2013.

EV   John Paul II. *Evangelium Vitae* (*The Gospel of Life*).
        Encyclical Letter. March 25, 1995. Boston: Pauline Books
        and Media, 1995.

FC   John Paul II. *Familiaris Consortio* (*The Role of the Christian
        Family in the Modern World*). Apostolic Exhortation.
        November 22, 1981. Boston: Pauline Books and Media,
        1981.

FOC   *The Fathers of the Church.* Edited by R. J. Deferrari.
        New York: Father of the Church Inc.; Washington, DC:
        Catholic University of America Press.

GS   Second Vatican Council. *Gaudium et Spes* (*Pastoral
        Constitution on the Church in the Modern World*). In *The Basic
        Sixteen Documents: Vatican Council II; Constitutions, Decrees,
        Declarations.* Edited by Austin Flannery, OP. Northport,
        NY: Costello Publishing, 1996.

HV   Paul VI. *Humanae Vitae* (*Of Human Life*). Encyclical
        Letter. July 25, 1968. www.vatican.va/holy_father/paul_vi
        /encyclicals/documents/hf_p-vi_enc_25071968_humanae
        -vitae_en.html.

LF   John Paul II. *Gratissimam Sane (Letter to Families).*
        February 2, 1994. Boston: Pauline Books and Media, 1994.

LG   Second Vatican Council. *Lumen Genitum* (*Dogmatic
        Constitution on the Church*). In *The Basic Sixteen Documents:
        Vatican Council II; Constitutions, Decrees, Declarations.*
        Edited by Austin Flannery, OP. Northport, NY: Costello
        Publishing, 1996.

MD   John Paul II. *Mulieris Dignitatem* (*The Dignity of Woman*).
        Apostolic Letter. August 15, 1988. Boston: Pauline Books
        and Media, 1988.

ND   *The Christian Faith in the Doctrinal Documents of the Catholic
        Church.* Edited by J. Neuner and Jacques Dupuis. 7th ed.
        New York: Alba House, 2001.

NMI   John Paul II. *Novo Millenio Ineunte* (*The Coming of the New
        Millenium*). Apostolic Letter. January 6, 2001. Boston:
        Pauline Books and Media, 2001.

NPNF *A Select Library of Nicene and Post-Nicene Fathers of the Christian Church.* Edited by Philip Schaff and Henry Wace, 1894. Reprint, Peabody, MA: Hendrickson Publishers, 1995.

OCM *The Order of Celebrating Matrimony.* Washington, DC: United States Conference of Catholic Bishops, 2014.

RH John Paul II. *Redemptor Hominis (The Redeemer of Man).* Encyclical Letter. March 4, 1979. Boston: Pauline Books and Media, 1979.

RM *The Roman Missal.* English translation according to the Third Typical Edition, 2011.

SC Second Vatican Council. *Sacrosanctum Concilium (Constitution on the Sacred Liturgy).* In *The Basic Sixteen Documents: Vatican Council II; Constitutions, Decrees, Declarations.* Edited by Austin Flannery, OP. Northport, NY: Costello Publishing, 1996.

SCG Thomas Aquinas. *Summa contra Gentiles.* Translated by Vernon Bourke. 4 vols. Notre Dame, IN: University of Notre Dame Press, 1956.

ST Thomas Aquinas. *Summa Theologica.* Translated by Fathers of the English Dominican Province. 5 vols. Reprinted, Allen, TX: Christian Classics, 1981.

TOB John Paul II. *Man and Woman He Created Them: A Theology of the Body.* Translation and introduction by Michael Waldstein. Boston: Pauline Books and Media, 2006.

VS John Paul II. *Veritatis Splendor (The Splendor of Truth).* Encyclical Letter. August 6, 1993. Boston: Pauline Books and Media, 1993.

WSA *The Works of Saint Augustine: A Translation for the 21st Century.* Edited by J. E. Rotelle. New York: New City Press.

Part I

Seeing Reality through the Lens of the Theology of the Body

Part 1 invites readers to open their eyes to seeing mystery, and in particular the mystery of marriage. The first chapter invites readers to see the mystery of marriage that was part of God's original created order and which was renewed and infused with new significance by Jesus Christ. Chapter 2 highlights the importance of Pope St. John Paul II's *Theology of the Body* for helping us to see and understand the mystery of marriage, and for presenting a comprehensive theology of marriage.

Chapter 1

Seeing the Mystery of Marriage

UNDERSTANDING MYSTERY

Many people misunderstand the meaning of "mystery." To call something a "mystery" is not to imply that the reality in question is completely unintelligible. Mysteries are not things that we cannot know
anything about; instead, mysteries are realities about which we cannot
know everything. This distinction makes a huge difference for human
life. Mysteries are not vast, incomprehensible enigmas upon which we
gaze in utter confusion and insoluble ignorance leading to complete
befuddlement and absolute frustration, hopelessness, and despair.
Instead, a "mystery" is a glorious reality about which we can know
something, but it is a reality so rich and deep that regardless of how
much we understand there is still more to learn.

We are able to understand more about some mysteries than
others. Faced with some mysteries we may be able to comprehend
very little, but what we can comprehend allows us to be captivated by
the mystery, to be drawn into it in utter amazement. Thus, far from
detracting from human existence, the fact that we cannot understand everything about a mystery gives meaning to human existence.
In fact it is mystery that makes life exciting and worth living!
Yet, the excitement that we experience when faced with a mystery is
not ultimately the result of finding or pursuing the "solution" to the
mystery. Mysteries are not puzzles to be put together or riddles to be
solved. Instead, a mystery is a beautiful reality within which we are
invited to live and into which we are beckoned to enter.

What we can know about mysterious realities is not meaningless. In fact, what we are able to comprehend about a mystery enables
us to accept and enter into it. What we can know about a mystery

leads us to be enthralled by and grateful for its existence. What we can know about mystery eventually leads to fascination and gratitude for our own existence. Therefore the reality of mystery and our ability to know something about mystery is important and essential for human existence.

One need only think of the reality of the human person to confirm the existence of mystery. Every human person is a finite mystery, and his or her depths can never be fully plumbed. In a real way, every human person is a mystery to him or herself. On a basic level each of us marvels at, and is even sometimes confounded by, our own personalities—why we have the interests we do, why we think the way we do, why we react to things the way we do, etc. Even though we might not ever fully understand ourselves, deep down each of us realizes that we have yearnings and desires that we cannot fulfill by ourselves. No matter how much each of us likes to pretend that we are self-sufficient, we realize that we are not. We realize that we need other persons. Ultimately, we long to transcend ourselves and seek fulfillment in relationship, in communion with other persons. Furthermore, the more we take the time to learn about another human person the more we realize that we will never be able to unravel the mystery of his or her unique and unrepeatable identity, just as we cannot unravel our own. Yet, there comes a point when we realize that we need not "solve" the mystery of the other person or the mystery of ourselves in order to experience joy in life. Instead, we need only cultivate the disposition of gratitude for our own lives and the lives of others, welcoming, affirming, and marveling at the mystery of personal existence.

Additionally, one need only think about the relationship of love that can exist between persons to verify the importance of mystery for human existence. Love involves a fascination with the mystery of another person. It is an ecstatic experience that enables us to come out of ourselves in relationship to another.[1] The true lover can never adequately respond to the question, "Why do you love your beloved?" There may be qualities of the other person that initially attracted us to him or her, but ultimately it is the person, a finite

---

1. Thomas Aquinas, ST I-II, q. 28, a. 3.

mystery, whom we love.[2] However, we cannot love the other person without knowing something about him or her, and the more we come to know about the mystery of the beloved the more our love grows.[3] As love grows, lovers desire deeper intimacy with each other, they desire to dwell within each other, to enter into each other's finite mystery.[4] Love between persons is a reality that defies the attempts of philosophers and poets to exhaustively explain it, and regardless of how much will be said and written about this reality throughout the ages, there will always be more to say. Yet, even though love is a mystery, it is a reality about which we can understand something, a reality that gives meaning to life, and a reality which the human person needs in order to live.

The mystery of love helps to reveal something about the mystery of the beloved and something about ourselves. When we love another we recognize in him or her a good beyond measure and we seek union with the beloved.[5] As love unites the lover and the beloved, love brings with it a vision and a knowledge of the other person that is beyond purely intellectual knowledge.[6] True lovers "know" each other in a manner that is beyond words, and in this knowledge they cease trying to unravel the riddle of each other's mystery. In fact, to do so would be seen as a desecration of the other's mysterious beauty. Instead, love allows the lover to marvel at the mystery of the beloved and to simply and profoundly proclaim, "It's good that you are here; how wonderful that you exist!"[7]

Affirming the existence of the beloved in this way is the very essence of love.[8] When we love someone we acknowledge that he or she is a gift and a mystery who makes life more worth living. We are grateful for the beloved's existence and we want to serve the good of

---

2. A helpful reflection on the uniqueness and unrepeatability of every human person can be found in John F. Crosby, "The Incommunicability of Human Persons," *The Thomist* 57 (1993): 403–442.

3. ST I-II, q. 27, a.2, ad 2.

4. ST I-II, q. 28, a. 2.

5. ST I-II, q. 28, a. 1.

6. ST I-II, q. 28, a, 1, ad 3.

7. Josef Pieper, *Faith, Hope, Love* (San Francisco: Ignatius Press, 1997), 170. Josef Pieper (1904–1997) was one of the most important Catholic Thomistic philosophers of the twentieth century. His treatise on love is incredibly lucid and helpful in exploring the nature of love.

8. Ibid., 163–186.

the one we love, because we recognize that the beloved is an irreplaceable good whom we are privileged to know and experience. Furthermore, each of us realizes that we need to be the recipient of this type of affirmation as well, and that we cannot live without it.[9] We need to know that it is wonderful that we exist. In fact, receiving this type of affirmation is essential for human flourishing. In truth, love is life giving, and it is only in receiving love that we blossom and become more ourselves.[10]

Ultimately, the love we give to and receive from each other and the intimacy we experience in our human relationships is a sign and a reflection of the love of our Creator.[11] God is love (1 Jn 4:8).[12] He creates out of love and with his love he continues to affirm our existence as "very good" (Gen 1:31). The mystery of the person and the mystery of personal love are both signs of the ultimate mystery who is God, a Trinitarian communion of Persons whose essence is love. We have been made in the image of this God of love (Gen 1:27) and we are invited to share in his life (2 Pet 1:4). God wants us to experience the intimacy of mutual indwelling, he in us and us in him.[13] Our human vocation is to journey deeper and deeper into the reality of this love, continually growing in our knowledge of this mystery without ever fully exhausting it. Even when we abide in this mystery of love in eternity we will never exhaust it. Moreover, the fact that we cannot ever exhaust the mystery of infinite love is not a problem that should frustrate us, but instead it is the most beautiful reality of all—a reality that every human person, whether he or she is conscious of it or not, longs to enter! We are designed to spend eternity in communion with the ultimate lover, the one who is *the* mystery of personal love, the one who alone can affirm and fulfill our own personal mystery. Thus mystery is truly what makes life worth living!

The reality and the mystery of marriage are central to revealing the meaning of the human person as a being who is destined to be united to the infinite mystery of the Triune God of love. As we shall

---

9. Ibid., 176.

10. Ibid., 174.

11. Ibid., 193.

12. Unless otherwise noted, all scriptural citations in this book are taken from the Revised Standard Version (RSV) of the Bible.

13. ST I-II, q. 28, a. 2.

see throughout this book, our natural desire for nuptial union reveals something to us about our ultimate destiny to be joined to the God of love. The Catholic Church holds that marriage was instituted by God at the beginning of creation and was re-created in Christ's work of redemption to be a sign that makes present the love to which all of us are ultimately called. In short, the Catholic Tradition holds:

> The relationship between a man and a woman—a mutual and total bond, unique and indissoluble—is part of God's original plan, obscured throughout history by our "hardness of heart," but which Christ came to restore to its pristine splendor, disclosing what had been God's will "from the beginning" (Mt 19:8). Raised to the dignity of a sacrament, marriage expresses the "great mystery" of Christ's nuptial love for His Church (cf. Eph 5:32). (NMI, 47)

Thus the mystery of marriage is a sign, a sacrament, of the mystery of God's love for us, a love that is unique, total, and indissoluble, a love that is made fully manifest in the Person of Jesus Christ, a love for which we all long in the deepest recesses of our hearts.

Developing a Sacramental Vision

In his book *The Spirit of the Liturgy*, Cardinal Joseph Ratzinger, later Pope Emeritus Benedict XVI, commented on the problem of knowing in the modern world. He addressed the situation of modern people who often restrict themselves to acknowledging only empirically verifiable reality, closing themselves off to the transcendent. Addressing this disposition, Ratzinger spoke of the human person's need for "an interior opening-up . . . that enables him to see more than what can be measured or weighed, to perceive the reflection of divine glory in creation."[14] Thus we need the ability to see that creation itself points to something, someone, beyond itself. Commenting on the ability of creation to reveal the divine, Ratzinger emphasized that "God has acted in history and entered into our sensible world, so that it may become transparent" to us.[15] He noted, "God is the Wholly Other, but he is powerful enough to be able to show himself. And

---

14. Joseph Cardinal Ratzinger, *The Spirit of the Liturgy*, trans. John Saward (San Francisco: Ignatius Press, 2000), 122.

15. Ibid., 131.

he has so fashioned his creature that it is capable of 'seeing' him and loving him."[16] The problem is that, preoccupied by worldly pursuits, we have impaired vision and have often allowed our sight to be obscured. In order to acknowledge the fullness of reality, what we need is "a new kind of seeing,"[17] one that "perceives the Invisible in the visible."[18]

Cardinal Angelo Scola has stated that only in "a conversion 'to the real' . . . will it be possible to grasp the mystery of which reality itself is always a *sign*."[19] One reality which the reader must be willing to acknowledge in order to fully benefit from this book is the "sacramental principle" of reality. In brief, the sacramental principle is the understanding that visible, material creation can be a sign of something beyond itself, pointing to invisible, spiritual realities. More precisely, the sacramental principle holds that the material universe is a sign that points to the invisible God who created it.[20] St. Paul attests to this sacramental reality of creation when he tells us that "ever since the creation of the world his [God's] invisible nature, namely, his eternal power and deity, has been clearly perceived in the things that have been made" (Rom 1:20). Thus, in reality, the whole of material creation is sacramental, a sign of something beyond itself because God intends it to be so. As the *Catechism of the Catholic Church* states: "God speaks to man through visible creation. The material cosmos is so presented to man's intelligence that he can read there traces of the Creator" (CCC, 1147). Or, as the Jesuit poet Gerard Manley Hopkins (1844–1889) so eloquently wrote in his poem, "God's Grandeur," "The world is charged with the grandeur of God." We just need the eyes to see this mystery.

For the Christian, the central sign or sacrament in all of history through which God speaks to man is the Incarnation, the event of God becoming man, which shows beyond a shadow of a doubt the value of material creation in revealing the mystery of God. The divine

---

16. Ibid., 124.

17. Ibid., 135.

18. Ibid., 133.

19. Angelo Scola, *The Nuptial Mystery*, trans. Michelle K. Borras (Grand Rapids, MI: Eerdmans, 2005), 90.

20. William E. May, *Theology of the Body in Context: Genesis and Growth* (Boston: Pauline Books and Media, 2010), 80.

and human mystery of the God-man Jesus Christ is continued in the visible and spiritual reality of the Catholic Church and in the Seven Sacraments that Christ himself gives to the Church. Thus the reality that God uses matter, concrete "stuff," to convey himself and his gifts to humanity is central to the worship life of the Church. In her worship the Church "expresses and perceives spiritual realities through physical signs and symbols" (CCC, 1146) that were given to her by Christ himself to make these realities truly present (CCC, 1131).

The sacramental principle is central to a theology of marriage because, from the beginning, marriage was meant to be a unique sign of the mystery of God and his love for humanity. Christ himself confirms this divine reference of marriage and elevates the natural reality of marriage to one of the Seven Sacraments of the Church that convey divine grace (CCC, 1617). Thus marriage truly is a "great mystery" (Eph 5:32; *mega mysterion* in Greek; *magnum sacramentum* in Latin), a sign and a cause of something much greater and more sublime than many people realize—God's permanent, faithful, and life-giving love. Perhaps more than anyone in recent history, Pope St. John Paul II has helped us to realize that seeing and understanding the mystery of marriage is essential for human flourishing. We will discuss John Paul II's insights, and in particular his *Theology of the Body*, in the next chapter.

Chapter 2

Theology of Marriage and Theology of the Body

From September 5, 1979, to November 28, 1984, Pope St. John Paul II delivered a series of Wednesday general audiences, the impact of which is only beginning to be felt in the life of the Church and the world. In the final audience of his approximately five-year-long series of reflections, John Paul II said he had presented a catechesis that can be called "Human Love in the Divine Plan . . . The Redemption of the Body and the Sacramentality of Marriage."[1] In this same final audience, he explained that the term "theology of the body" is a "working" term that was used throughout the series "to set the topic 'The Redemption of the Body and the Sacramentality of Marriage' on a wider basis" (TOB 133:1).[2] In the English speaking world, these monumental audiences on human love have thus been referred to as the *Theology of the Body*. The title of the definitive English edition of these audiences is *Man and Woman He Created Them: A Theology of the Body*, an alternative title taken from a manuscript that John Paul II produced before being elevated to the papacy in 1978.[3] After becoming

---

1. John Paul II, *Man and Woman He Created Them: A Theology of the Body*, trans. Michael Waldstein (Boston: Pauline Books and Media, 2006), 133:1. Henceforth, this second English edition of the collected audiences will be referred to as the *Theology of the Body*. Citations of this work will be abbreviated TOB, followed by an audience number and a section number found in this edition. Italicized words appear in the original text, unless otherwise indicated.

2. John Paul II noted that his series of "reflections do not include many problems belonging, with regard to their object, to the theology of the body (e.g., the problem of suffering and death, so important in the biblical message). One must say this clearly" (TOB 133:1). Thus, John Paul II himself pointed to further implications of a theology of the body, for which he laid the foundation.

3. For a discussion of different titles given to the audiences see Michael Waldstein, "Introduction," in *Man and Woman He Created Them: A Theology of the Body*, 4. The first one-volume English edition of the full text of the general audiences was published under the title *The Theology of the Body: Human Love in the Divine Plan* (Boston: Pauline Books and Media, 1997). The

pope, John Paul II adapted this manuscript which he delivered in 129 general audiences,[4] in preparation for the 1980 Synod of Bishops which was on the topic of marriage and the family (TOB 133:4). He finished delivering these audiences after the publication of his apostolic exhortation *Familiaris Consortio* (On the Role of the Christian Family in the Modern World) which was the fruit of the synod (TOB 133:4). Before becoming pope, as Cardinal Archbishop Karol Wojtyla of Krakow, Poland, John Paul II had already written *Love and Responsibility* which is a philosophical exploration of human sexuality.[5] Dealing with some of the same issues transposed into a theological key, in the *Theology of the Body* John Paul II provided us with an extended catechesis explaining the good news that Jesus has revealed about the human person, sexuality, marriage, and family.

The importance of the *Theology of the Body* is being recognized on a progressively wider scale. George Weigel has said, "John Paul's *Theology of the Body* has ramifications for all of theology,"[6] claiming that in it the pontiff "proposed one of the boldest reconfigurations of

---

second one-volume English edition, translated by Michael Waldstein, *Man and Woman He Created Them: A Theology of the Body*, is an improvement over the first edition for several reasons. First of all, the original English edition was translated by several different translators in the editorial office of *L'Osservatore Romano* (the official newspaper of the Vatican) from the Italian text that was delivered orally by John Paul II in his general audiences (see Waldstein, "Introduction," 11–14). The second edition, instead, was translated by Michael Waldstein from the original Polish manuscript that John Paul II produced before becoming pope. Waldstein compared this Polish text to the Italian version that John Paul II delivered in his general audiences, thus providing for a unified and consistent text. Also, in the first English edition the organizational structure, headings, and subheadings were provided by the editors of the Italian version (see Waldstein, "Introduction," 6–9). In the second edition, the organizational structure, headings, and subheadings came from John Paul II's original Polish manuscript, making it more obvious how the parts relate to the whole.

4. In his series of general audiences, which numbered 129, John Paul II did not deliver some reflections that were part of his original Polish manuscript. Also, in revising his Polish work for the format of general audiences, John Paul added some text. *Man and Woman He Created Them: A Theology of the Body* contains all of the delivered and undelivered texts from John Paul II's project. For an explanation of the different numbers of audiences in the original Polish and in different Italian editions see Michael Waldstein, "Introduction," 5, 10–11 and "Systems of Reference to TOB," 731–35.

5. For a newly updated translation of *Love and Responsibility* see Karol Wojtyla, *Love and Responsibility*, trans. Grzegorz Ignatik (Boston: Pauline Books and Media, 2013). For a brief description of the evolution of and the influences on John Paul II's thought leading up to the *Theology of the Body*, see Waldstein, "Introduction," 23–94.

6. George Weigel, *Witness to Hope: The Biography of John Paul II* (New York: HarperCollins, 1999), 343.

Catholic theology in centuries."[7] I agree with George Weigel's statement that John Paul II's *Theology of the Body* is a "theological time bomb set to go off with dramatic consequences, sometime in the third millennium of the Church. When that happens perhaps in the twenty-first century, the theology of the body may well be seen as a critical moment not only in Catholic theology, but in the history of modern thought."[8] The importance of the *Theology of the Body* lies in the fact that it is about what it means to be and act as a human person (see TOB 58:5). Thus it is a project with a message that is pertinent to everyone. In fact, to understand the *Theology of the Body* affords the opportunity to experience "the rediscovery of the meaning of the whole of existence, of the meaning of life" (TOB 46:6).

One example of the theological importance of the *Theology of the Body* is found in John Paul II's reflections on what it means for the human person to be made in the image and likeness of God (Gen 1:26–27). In his reflections, he emphasized an understanding of the communal or relational dimension of the image of God (*imago Dei*) which incorporates the human body, representing a development of the theological tradition of the Church. Throughout Church history the focus has typically been on the image of God as it resides in the rational soul.[9] Cardinal Marc Ouellet has noted: "The predominant tradition in the West, in the wake of St. Augustine and St. Thomas Aquinas and under the influence of the Greek heritage, confined the image of God in man to his purely spiritual dimension, overlooking the human being's body and sexuality."[10] While John Paul II did not contradict previous reflections, he articulated a more robust understanding of the image of God which made explicit what previous reflections often implied. As John Paul II noted in one of his reflections that was not part of the *Theology of the Body*:

> The conviction that man is the "image of God" because of the soul has frequently been expressed. But traditional doctrine does not lack the

---

7. Ibid., 336.

8. Ibid., 343.

9. See Augustine, *The Trinity*, translated by Edmund Hill, WSA I.5 (1991), XIV; ST I, Q. 93, a. 6.

10. Marc Cardinal Ouellet, *Divine Likeness: Toward a Trinitarian Anthropology of the Family*, translated by Philip Milligan and Linda M. Cicone, (Grand Rapids, MI: Herder, 2006), 180.

conviction that the body also participates in the dignity of the "image of God" in its own way, just as it participates in the dignity of the person.[11]

In addition to articulating how the human body participates in the "image of God," John Paul also broadened the notion of the *imago Dei* to include the capacity of man and woman for interpersonal communion. This teaching articulated in the *Theology of the Body* is presented with even more clarity in John Paul's apostolic letter *Mulieris Dignitatem* (On the Dignity of Women), 6–8. Angelo Scola goes so far as to call this insight of John Paul II "an original development of the notion of the *imago Dei*," noting:

> John Paul II does not limit himself, in the footsteps of the Judeo-Christian tradition, which continues to leave its mark even on secularized Western thought, to identifying the content of the image of God with the human being's rational and free nature. The pope highlights the communal *qualitas* of the image. Man and woman are the image of God not only as individuals, but also insofar as they are capable of interpersonal communion.[12]

These insights of John Paul II pertaining to the image of God are clearly important for a theology of marriage and they are incorporated into the next chapter which deals with theological anthropology.

While the *Theology of the Body* can be seen to have pertinence to many areas of theology, it is most certainly important because it provides a context for understanding Catholic teaching on marriage, family, and sexuality. The twofold purpose of the *Theology of the Body* is to defend the reality and the truth of the human body (including sexual differentiation) and to defend the teaching of Pope Paul VI in *Humanae Vitae* on the intrinsic immorality of contraception.[13]

John Paul II explicitly stated that the Church's teachings on marriage and the family must be reread in light of the theology and pedagogy of the body that he finds in Christ's words (TOB 59:5). John Paul even went so far as to say, " . . . the theology of the body . . . is quite indispensable for an adequate understanding of the

11. John Paul II, *God, Father and Creator: A Catechesis on the Creed* (Boston: Pauline Books and Media, 1998), 228.

12. Angelo Scola, *The Nuptial Mystery*, trans. Michelle K. Borras (Grand Rapids, MI: Eerdmans, 2005), 386–87.

13. William E. May, *Theology of the Body in Context: Genesis and Growth* (Boston: Pauline Books, 2010), 67–68.

magisterial teaching of the contemporary Church" (TOB 59:7). An example of this is that toward the end of his five-year-long series of audiences, John Paul applied his theology of the body to the Church's teaching on contraception (TOB 118–132), explaining in his very last audience that he had envisioned this treatment at the beginning of the project (133:4).

It is no secret that most non-Catholics, and many Catholics, do not understand the Church's teachings on sexual morality, and especially her opposition to contraception.[14] John Paul II himself pointed this out in his 1994 *Letter to Families* when he stated:

> The Church's magisterium is often chided for being behind the times and closed to the promptings of the spirit of modern times, and for promoting a course of action which is harmful to humanity, and indeed to the Church herself. By obstinately holding to her positions, it is said, the Church will end up losing popularity, and more and more believers will turn away from her. (LF, 12)

Thus, John Paul was aware that many people see the Church as "out of touch" when it comes to sex. He was aware that there are some who see the Church's teachings as limiting or preventing intimacy between couples, and that many think the Church impinges upon their freedom because of what it teaches about sex. In reality, the teachings of John Paul II show that the world knows far less about sex than it realizes. In truth, the modern world has drained the body and sexuality of meaning. The sexual difference and complementarity between man and woman are no longer viewed as determining the way in which people may legitimately enter into a one-flesh union with another person. Instead, sexual intercourse is viewed as a pastime that is pursued for personal pleasure, evidenced by the fact that references to "casual" or "recreational" sex are part of our cultural vocabulary.

Amidst this sexual banality neither John Paul II nor the Catholic Church intends to win a popularity contest. However, John Paul wanted to make it clear that the Catholic Church teaches what it does about sex, not because it thinks sex is bad or because it wants to do away with erotic love, but because through her teachings it preserves God's plan for sex. John Paul wanted to make it clear that in reality it

---

14. The following three paragraphs are adapted from Perry J. Cahall, "Preaching, Teaching, and Living the Theology of the Body," *Linacre Quarterly* 73.3 (Aug. 2007): 213–16.

is the Catholic Church's teachings on human sexuality that will lead us to realize true intimacy, true freedom, and true happiness. As such, contrary to popular belief, the Catholic Church's teachings on sex are part of the good news of Jesus Christ.[15] Since everyone should have access to this good news, John Paul II offered his reflections in the *Theology of the Body*.

Faced with a culture that reacts to Catholic teaching on sex with incredulity at best and with vehement and violent rejection at worst, in his *Theology of the Body* John Paul II tried to give us the means to explain this part of the good news of Jesus Christ to a world that so desperately needs to hear it. Make no mistake that Catholic sexual morality is a set of teachings that many will react to by saying, "This is a hard teaching; who can listen to it?" (Jn 6:60). However, if we approach proclaiming God's plan for human sexuality by using the insights of the *Theology of the Body*, those who have open ears and open hearts will be more likely to heed these "words of eternal life" (Jn 6:68). All of us long to live out God's design for our sexuality, even if we do not realize this is what we are longing for. The *Theology of the Body* is such an attractive work because it appeals to these deepest desires of the human heart. John Paul II invited people to be honest with themselves, to listen to their hearts, and to open themselves up to the Trinity's plan of love for their lives—a plan of ultimate happiness.

While there is an ever-increasing number of studies dealing with John Paul II's *Theology of the Body*,[16] this book is not intended as an addition to these studies. Nor is it intended to be a guide to or an explanation of the *Theology of the Body*.[17] Instead this book seeks to integrate John Paul II's insights into human love in the divine plan into a comprehensive theology of marriage. John Paul II divided *The Theology of the Body* into two major parts composed of six chapters:

---

15. See the popular book by Christopher West, *Good News About Sex and Marriage: Answers to Your Honest Questions about Catholic Teaching* (Ann Arbor, MI: Servant Publications, 2000).

16. Michael Waldstein provides a bibliography of studies of the *Theology of the Body* in *Man and Woman He Created Them: A Theology of the Body*, 665–76.

17. In addition to the guides and explanations of the *Theology of the Body* listed in the bibliography of *Man and Woman He Created Them*, see also Carl Anderson and Jose Granados, *Called to Love: Approaching John Paul II's Theology of the Body* (New York: Doubleday, 2009), and William E. May, *Theology of the Body in Context: Genesis and Growth*. As the title connotes, William May's book provides a brief synthesis of the origins and development of John Paul II's insights contained in the *Theology of the Body*.

Part 1: The Words of Christ

Chapter 1: Christ Appeals to the "Beginning" [TOB 1–23, focusing on Mt 19:8]

Chapter 2: Christ Appeals to the Human Heart [TOB 24–63, focusing on Mt 5:28]

Chapter 3: Christ Appeals to the Resurrection [TOB 64–86, focusing on Mt 22:30]

Part 2: The Sacrament [of Marriage, focusing on Eph 5:22–33]

Chapter 1: The Dimension of Covenant and Grace [TOB 87–102]

Chapter 2: The Dimension of Sign [TOB 103–117]

Chapter 3: He Gave Them the Law of Life as Their Inheritance [TOB 118–133]

In the three chapters of part 1, John Paul II articulated the fundamental components of his theology of the body, commenting on what he calls the "three words" of Jesus that pertain to a theology of the body.[18] The three chapters of the second part then apply the theology of the body from part 1 to the Sacrament of Marriage.[19] The insights from the first part of the *Theology of the Body* are incorporated into parts 2 and 3 of this book, dealing with marriage in the order of creation and marriage in the Bible, while the insights from the second part of the *Theology of the Body* are integrated into parts 5 and 6 of this book, which address a systematic treatment of the Sacrament of Marriage and how the sacrament is lived out. In addition, part 4 of this book, which provides an overview of the history of the development of the theology of marriage, will highlight the insights of John Paul II that have helped to develop and refine a sacramental theology of marriage.

However, because it is true that, "No pope ever wrote as deeply, or as much, on human love as has John Paul II,"[20] incorporating his thought into a theology of marriage means including his insights not only from the *Theology of the Body*, but also from other

---

18. See Waldstein, "Introduction," 110–111.

19. Waldstein, "Introduction," 111.

20. Mary Healy, *Men and Women are from Eden: A Study Guide to John Paul II's Theology of the Body* (Cincinnati, OH: St. Anthony Messenger Press, 2005), 3.

documents in which he articulated or developed his teachings on the human person, marriage, family, and sexuality. This necessitates incorporating insights from John Paul II's apostolic exhortation *Familiaris Consortio* from 1981, in which he synthesized some of his key insights from the *Theology of the Body* (see especially FC, 11–16). Attention will also be given to John Paul's apostolic letter *Mulieris Dignitatem* (On the Dignity of Women) written on the occasion of the Marian Year in 1988, in which he further developed some of his insights contained in the *Theology of the Body*. In addition, John Paul's *Letter to Families*, written on the occasion of the United Nations International Year of the Family in 1994, synthesizes in very readable language some of his central insights into marriage and family (see especially LF, 6–12, 19). Additionally, several of John Paul II's teachings on the human person, marriage, family, and sexuality have been incorporated into the official summary of the Catholic faith contained in the *Catechism of the Catholic Church*. All of these documents, as well as other writings of John Paul II, are integrated into this study.

Cardinal Angelo Scola has noted that in the face of the need for an intellectual and moral conversion "to the real,"[21] oftentimes "Christian thought has been at a loss to propose an organic, unified reflection on the person, marriage, and the family."[22] What John Paul II has done, especially in the *Theology of the Body*, is to provide such a reflection. If the Second Vatican Council placed "'the appreciation of the dignity of marriage and the family' among the most urgent problems of the Church in the contemporary world" (TOB 59:5), in the *Theology of the Body* and his other writings John Paul II has given the world a means by which to recover that dignity. In fact, if we are to realize the dignity of marriage, sexuality, and ourselves, we should embrace the teaching contained in the *Theology of the Body* (TOB 59:7).

Embracing this teaching is essential because although John Paul II's *Theology of the Body* expresses truths about man, marriage, and sexuality in a new mode, John Paul II himself made it clear that he was not presenting new teaching, in the sense that it is unprecedented. In fact, while the expressions contained in the *Theology of the Body* may be new, its content is as old as the Christian faith.

---

21. Scola, *The Nuptial Mystery*, 90.
22. Ibid., 193.

Throughout, the *Theology of the Body* is a profoundly biblical theology. Furthermore, John Paul II insists that Christ himself outlines a theology of the body that instructs us in "the ways that lead to . . . fulfillment" (TOB 59:2). As Michael Waldstein noted, "John Paul II intends to present a theology of the body that is built on Scripture, above all on the words of Christ (see TOB 86:4)."[23]

It is instructive to note that the entire *Theology of the Body* starts with the Pharisees' question to Jesus about divorce in Matthew's Gospel:

> And Pharisees came up to him and tested him by asking, "Is it lawful to divorce one's wife for any cause?" He answered, "Have you not read that he who made them from the beginning made them male and female, and said, 'For this reason a man shall leave his father and mother and be joined to his wife, and the two shall become one flesh'? So they are no longer two but one flesh. What therefore God has joined together, let not man put asunder." (Mt 19:3–6)

John Paul II noted that in Jesus' response to the Pharisees' question Jesus takes them, and us, back to "the beginning," citing Genesis 2:24. Thus John Paul followed Christ back to Genesis, to the way in which man and woman were formed in the mystery of creation, in order to allow Jesus to teach us about God's intention for marriage and what it means to be male and female (TOB 1:4).

While the content of the *Theology of the Body* is not new, it does give us a new language with which to present the Gospel again to a world that is in desperate need of it. As such, the *Theology of the Body* is one facet of the "new evangelization" to which John Paul II called the Church from the beginning of his pontificate during his historic pastoral visit to Poland in 1979.[24] This "new evangelization" is not new in content, but new in the "ardor, methods, and expressions" used to transmit the Gospel.[25] In the *Theology of the Body*, John Paul II has given us a new language that can be employed in new methods with new ardor in order to proclaim God's design for human love. As

---

23. Waldstein, "Introduction," 18.

24. Noted by Benedict XVI, Address to the Bishops of the Polish Episcopal Conference on Their *ad Limina* Visit, December 3, 2005, accessed November 12, 2010, www.vatican.va /holy_father/benedict_xvi/speeches/2005/december/documents/hf_ben_xvi_spe_20051203 _adlimina-polonia-ii_en.html.

25. John Paul II, *Ecclesia in America*, Apostolic Exhortation (Boston: Pauline Books and Media, 1999), 66.

Mary Healy has said, John Paul II has given us "a new vocabulary to make the church's teaching compelling and attractive, to unveil the radiance of truth."[26] In a culture in which marriage, family, and sexuality have been trivialized and banalized, the *Theology of the Body* helps to remove the blinders from secularized eyes, helping people to see the dignity and sacredness of these realities in God's design. The rest of this book employs this new language in a comprehensive theology of marriage, to enable men and women to see the awesome importance of the mystery of marriage in God's plan for humanity.

I undertook the endeavor of integrating John Paul II's thought into a comprehensive theology of marriage because my own eyes were opened to seeing the mystery of marriage when I first read John Paul II's *Theology of the Body*. I was introduced to this work in a class I took as part of my graduate studies, and the experience of reading this book was life-changing. I remember taking three months to read the text, digesting small portions of it every day, often rereading a single paragraph several times. On a few occasions I had to pause and set the book down because I felt so wonderfully overwhelmed by what I was reading. It was as if John Paul II was showing me the truth of the human person, the truth of human sexuality, the truth of marriage, and the truth of myself, for the first time. I remember discussing what I was reading with my girlfriend, whom I am now blessed to call my wife, and telling her that whatever I ended up doing in life I knew I needed to help expose other people to the beautiful insights contained in John Paul's *Theology of the Body*. I truly believe that John Paul's *Theology of the Body*, as well as the teachings on human sexuality, marriage, and the family contained in his other writings, are gifts that God in His providence has given to the world at a juncture in human history when this gift is sorely needed. My hope is that by integrating John Paul's insights into a theology of marriage, this book will enable others to see more clearly the beautiful mystery of marriage and married love.

---

26. Mary Healy, *Men and Women are from Eden*, 3.

Part II

Marriage in the Order of Creation

Marriage is a created reality. However, before discussing the nature of marriage it is important to understand the nature of the human person and the nature of married or conjugal love. Therefore, the chapters of part 2, relying primarily upon natural law reasoning but also on Sacred Scripture, present truths about the human person, married love, and marriage that are ascertainable to all people. These chapters focus on what it means to proclaim that the human person is made in the "image of God." Chapter 6 also introduces the understanding of natural marriage as the "primordial sacrament" of God's love for humanity.

Chapter 3

Marriage and the Human Person

INTRODUCTION

In order to see and understand the full beauty of the nature and mystery of marriage, it is first necessary to understand certain basic truths about human nature, including the essential place that human sexuality holds in the understanding of the human person. Unfortunately, this is a highly controversial issue today. There exists a widespread confusion regarding the nature of the human person, made male and female, and this confusion is leading to a proliferation of moral quandaries on many issues, including the issue of marriage. John Paul II attested to this pervasive confusion when he noted, "At its roots, the contemporary crisis of moral culture is a crisis of understanding of the nature of the human person."[1] What he meant was that as we develop a personal and cultural "amnesia" about who and what we are, the more confused we become about how we should act. Thus, any attempt to set forth the Catholic understanding of marriage and the act of getting married is an attempt to address one of the most acute moral crises of our time.

Explaining marriage must begin by addressing the nature of the human person. The crisis of a lack of understanding of marriage is directly related to the lack of understanding of the human person as an embodied spirit who is made either male or female. In turn, "doubt or error in the field of marriage or the family involves obscuring to a serious extent the integral truth about the human person" (FC, 31).

---

1. Pope John Paul II, *Ad Limina* Address to the US Bishops of Texas, Oklahoma, and Arkansas, June 27, 1998, in John Paul II, *Springtime of Evangelization* (San Francisco: Ignatius Press, 1999), 112.

Thus, to forget about our most fundamental identity as men and women leads to a forgetfulness regarding marriage, and, in turn, to obscure the meaning of marriage leads to a further confusion regarding ourselves. The purpose of this chapter, therefore, is to explain some basic and fundamental truths of theological anthropology (the study of the human person taking into account divine revelation), without which we cannot understand marriage (see TOB 23:3). These truths will allow us to see more clearly the nature of married love and marriage, topics which will be dealt with in greater detail in the next two chapters. Due to space limitations, I will not attempt to present a comprehensive theological anthropology, which would include more in-depth discussion of topics like the nature of the rational soul and the relationship between nature and grace. I will limit myself to addressing central truths about the human person that are essential for understanding marriage.

The Unique Dignity of the Human Person Made in the Image of God

Some of the fundamental texts for the Christian understanding of the human person are found in the first pages of the Bible in the opening chapters of the book of Genesis:

> Then God said, "Let us make man in our image, after our likeness; and let them have dominion over the fish of the sea, and over the birds of the air, and over the cattle, and over all the earth, and over every creeping thing that creeps upon the earth." So God created man in his own image, in the image of God he created him; male and female he created them. And God blessed them, and God said to them, "Be fruitful and multiply, and fill the earth and subdue it; and have dominion over the fish of the sea and over the birds of the air and over every living thing that moves upon the earth."
>
> And God saw everything that he had made, and behold, it was very good. (Gen 1:26–28, 31)

> [T]hen the Lord God formed man of dust from the ground, and breathed into his nostrils the breath of life; and man became a living being. And the Lord God planted a garden in Eden, in the east; and there he put the man whom he had formed. And out of the ground the Lord God made to grow every tree that is pleasant to the sight and good for food, the tree

of life also in the midst of the garden, and the tree of the knowledge of good and evil. . . . And the Lord God commanded the man, saying, "You may freely eat of every tree of the garden; but of the tree of the knowledge of good and evil you shall not eat, for in the day that you eat of it you shall die." Then the Lord God said, "It is not good that the man should be alone; I will make him a helper fit for him." So out of the ground the Lord God formed every beast of the field and every bird of the air, and brought them to the man to see what he would call them; and whatever the man called every living creature, that was its name. The man gave names to all cattle, and to the birds of the air, and to every beast of the field; but for the man there was not found a helper fit for him. So the Lord God caused a deep sleep to fall upon the man, and while he slept took one of his ribs and closed up its place with flesh; and the rib which the Lord God had taken from the man he made into a woman and brought her to the man. Then the man said, "This at last is bone of my bones and flesh of my flesh; she shall be called Woman, because she was taken out of Man." Therefore a man leaves his father and his mother and cleaves to his wife, and they become one flesh. And the man and his wife were both naked, and were not ashamed. (Gen 2:7–9, 16–25)

The starting place for the Christian vision of the human person is the dignity which man and woman possess by being created in the image and likeness of God (Gen 1:26–27).[2] This truth is rich and multifaceted, opening up new venues for our understanding of the human person. Through the use of reason we can see that the human being is the most highly developed creature in the visible world. However, knowing that we are made in God's image (*imago Dei*) reveals the unique dignity that we possess in the created order. No other being bears this mark (LF, 6), and both of the creation narratives of Gen 1–2[3] highlight the fact that the human person occupies a unique place in creation (CCC, 355) as "the highpoint of the whole order of

---

2. John Paul II called the "image and likeness" of God the "immutable *basis of all Christian anthropology*" (MD, 6).

3. The creation narratives in the book of Genesis do not attempt to provide an historical or scientific account of how the world came to be, but instead provide a rich theology of creation, a cosmology, explaining the ultimate origin and purpose of creation. In other words, the inspired writers of the creation narratives were not primarily concerned with "how" creation occurred, but "why." Gen 1:1a–2:4a is the creation narrative structured around the seven days of creation, and stems from around the fifth century BC. Gen 2:4b–2:24 is focused more precisely on the creation of man, and is the older creation narrative, written as early as the ninth century BC. See TOB 2:2 for more on these two creation narratives.

creation in the visible world" (MD, 6). The moment of divine self-deliberation, "Let us make . . . " (Gen 1:26), in the first creation narrative presents us with a dramatic pause in God's creative action just before he creates the human person. This pause in the first creation account is unique in the account of God's creative activity, emphasizing and highlighting the unique dignity of the human person in the whole created order (TOB 2:3; LF, 6).

The human person's uniqueness and exalted status in creation is also evidenced when God grants humanity dominion over all of visible creation (Gen 1:26, 28), giving the human race the responsibility to exercise God's loving care in the created order (Gen 2:15).[4] Thus, the human person is "the only creature on earth that God willed for its own sake" (CCC, 356; see also GS, 24, and LF, 9), meaning, as is highlighted in the second creation narrative, that everything else was created for humanity's sake (see Gen 2:5). The human person alone is called to walk as a friend of God and share in God's life as a "partner of the Absolute" (TOB 6:2). The Genesis creation narratives show us that before sin enters the world everything is ordered to the human race's well-being (see Gen 1:29). It is only after the creation of humanity that God states that everything is "very good" (Gen 1:31). Creation thus finds its focal point in the human person. "God created everything for man, but man in turn was created to know and love God and to offer all of creation back to him" (CCC, 358). The human person stands above the rest of the visible created order as God's representative. In the beginning, all of creation was ordered to God through humanity since the human race was given dominion and stewardship over creation, and it is through the human person, made in God's image, that all of creation is destined for the glory of God (CCC, 373).

Made in the Image of God, Soul and Body

Having the breath of life breathed into him by God (Gen 2:7), the human person unites the spiritual and material worlds in his or her very being (CCC, 355, 362). Possessing a rational and immortal soul, a human person is the only being on earth who begins to exist in time but is destined to live for all eternity (CCC, 1703). "What makes man

---

4. CCC, 373, points out that humanity's dominion over creation is not "arbitrary and destructive domination," but responsible stewardship.

like God is the fact that—unlike the whole world of other living creatures, including those endowed with senses (*animalia*)—man is also a rational being (*animal rationale*)" (MD, 6). It is in fact the human person's rational soul that gives one the dignity of a *person*, with the faculties of reason and will that enable the person to know and love. Only persons possess rational souls. "Of all visible creatures only man is 'able to know and love his creator.' . . . and he alone is called to share, by knowledge and love, in God's own life" (CCC, 356). Non-rational animals cannot know and love as persons can. Human beings alone in the visible created order can compose symphonies and make noble sacrifices out of love for others. The reason animals do not do these things is not because they lack interest, but because they are incapable of these actions, lacking rational souls. With a unique dignity and destiny it is true to say that a single human person has more intrinsic value than the rest of material creation. This does not give human beings the right to abuse the rest of nature. However, not to acknowledge our proper place in the created order is itself a disservice to the rest of creation.

Throughout Christian history the majority of theological reflection on the *imago Dei* has focused on the human person's likeness to God found in the rational soul, giving him or her the capacities to know and to love. Yet, the human person is an intimate unity of soul *and* body. There are other persons in the universe who possess rational souls, but do not have bodies; we call these persons angels. The human person is a body that is animated by a rational soul, and because of this his or her body possesses a unique dignity among all bodies in creation (CCC, 365). As John Paul II said: "The body can never be reduced to mere matter: it is a *spiritualized body*, just as a man's spirit is so closely united to the body that he can be described as *an embodied spirit*" (FC, 19). In fact, so intimate is the union between the body and the soul that, "The human body shares in the dignity of the 'image of God'" (CCC, 364).

Our society acts as if this were not so, driving a wedge between the human body and the human soul. In the modern world, and throughout history, the body has been drained of its meaning in one of two ways. First, there is a dualistic view of the human person which sees the human spirit as "the real me" while relegating the body to the position of a tool of the spirit, disconnecting it from the person.

Second, there is a materialistic vision of the person that ignores the soul and reduces the person to the body, treating the body's desires as directives which must be followed. As John Paul II noted: "The separation of spirit and body in man has led to a growing tendency to consider the human body, not in accordance with the categories of its specific likeness to God, but rather on the basis of its similarity to all the other bodies present in the world of nature, bodies which man uses as raw material in his efforts to produce goods for consumption" (FC, 19). John Paul's comments point to the fact that whether the body is undervalued or idolized, the result is the same: an impoverished and bifurcated view of the human person that results in the degradation of human dignity and the use of the body as a type of raw data or pleasure device. In this situation the human person "*ceases to live as a person and a subject* . . . [and instead] . . . becomes merely an *object*" (FC, 19). As Cardinal Angelo Scola has noted, in the development of modernity, "One's own body and the body of others were reduced to a mechanism that must keep the fire of pleasure burning."[5]

In response to this anemic view of the human person, the Christian tradition continues to uphold the nature of the human person as a unity of body and soul. In fact, since the nature of a human being is that of a body-soul unity, it is even possible to say that the "image of God" in which we are made is reflected in and expressed through the human body, because it is through our bodies that we express our persons (TOB 7:2; 12:4). Because the body "reveals man" (TOB 9:4) and because the human person expresses himself or herself through a body, we can even say that the human person "is" a body (TOB 55:2), which highlights how central the body is to a proper understanding of the human person.[6] In some way, we can even say that the human body is a sign or "sacrament" of the soul, in the sense that the body is a "visible manifestation of an invisible reality."[7]

---

5. Angelo Scola, *The Nuptial Mystery*, trans. Michelle K. Borras (Grand Rapids, MI: William B. Eerdmans Publishing Company, 2005), 216.

6. The necessity of the body for understanding the human person is pointed out by Thomas Aquinas when he says that human souls separated from bodies at death cannot properly be called persons until they are reunited with their bodies in the resurrection (see ST I, q. 29, a. 1, ad 5; see also Suppl., q. 69, a. 1, where Aquinas is careful not to call separated souls "persons").

7. Livio Melina, *Building a Culture of the Family: The Language of Love* (Staten Island: Alba House, 2011), 77.

The important point that must not be forgotten is that the human person is a unity of soul and body, and it is in this totality that he or she images God. As William May has said, "What is needed today is a 're-evangelization,' a proclamation that helps men and women, blinded by the culture of death that has come about as a result of a denigration of the reality of the human body, to realize that they are in fact living *bodies* of a unique kind."[8]

"In the Image of God He Created Him; Male and Female He Created Them"

For the human person, there are two ways of "being a body" (TOB 8:1). Genesis 1:27 states: "God created man in his image; in the divine image he created him; male and female he created them." This Scripture verse makes it clear that both man and woman are made fully in God's image (LF, 6; MD, 6). This means that both male and female humanity possess equal personal dignity (CCC, 369, 2334) at the pinnacle of the hierarchy of being in the visible created order. The second creation narrative in Genesis depicts the first woman as being fashioned from the rib of the first man (Gen 2:21). Not only does this show the common nature that they possess, but also the fact that the rib (and not the foot, or the elbow, etc.), which guards the heart, is chosen as the basis for forming the woman evidences the intimacy that is supposed to exist between the man and the woman.[9]

Yet, while possessing the same nature and equal dignity, man and woman are obviously not identical (CCC, 369). Equal dignity does not mean sameness. "Each of the two sexes is an image of the power and tenderness of God, with equal dignity though in a different way" (CCC, 2335). The God-given differences between men and women are not intended to promote competition between the sexes, but instead are supposed to complement each other in their one shared humanity.[10] In fact, man and woman each reflect the image of God in

---

8. William E. May, *Theology of the Body in Context: Genesis and Growth* (Boston: Pauline Books and Media, 2010), 87.

9. See ST I, q. 92, a. 3.

10. For a beautiful discussion of the complementarity of male and female see Dietrich Von Hildebrand, *Man and Woman: Love and the Meaning of Intimacy* (Manchester, NH: Sophia Institute Press, 1992), esp. 35–38.

their own unique and complementary way.[11] This distinction without inequality is another way in which man and woman are made in the image of God who is three Persons, coequal, coeternal, but distinct in their relations to each other. As two complementary aspects of a unified image of love, man and woman only discover who they are through each other (more on this later in this chapter).

This means that sexual difference or gender is a gift which the human person receives as an essential aspect of the gift of his or her humanity. Human sexual difference has a meaning beyond that of animal sexual differentiation because human sexuality participates in the life of a person.[12] Hence, human sexuality is not merely a biological reality. Our sexuality tells each of us who we are and how we can relate interpersonally and how we can form bonds of love (CCC, 2332). Being made male or female determines our "affectivity, [and our] capacity to love and procreate" (CCC, 2332). What is more, "sexuality affects all aspects of the human person in the unity of his body and soul" (CCC, 2332). Human sexuality "is not something simply biological, but concerns the innermost being of the human person as such" (CCC, 2361; citing FC, 11). Thus, one's sexuality constitutes an essential, undeniable, and unchangeable aspect of who a person is.

Sexuality is not simply "part" of the person in an external sense, nor is a person's sexuality a mere matter of psychological or emotional preference. Human sexuality specifies the fundamental identity of the human person and therefore it is not malleable. This truth challenges a culture that treats gender not as a given, but as a purely subjective construct.[13] As Cardinal Scola has noted, "The contemporary world is confused; with incredible speed, it has moved . . . to claiming to abolish sexual difference itself, to erase it in favor of a culture of androgynism and pervasive eroticism."[14] However, the reality is that "the identity of the human person is expressed in and through the

---

11. Peter J. Elliott, *What God Has Joined: The Sacramentality of Marriage* (New York: Alba House, 1990), xxvii.

12. See John F. Crosby, "Karol Wojtyla's Personalist Understanding of Man and Woman," in *Personalist Papers* (Washington, DC: Catholic University of America Press, 2004), 253.

13. I am aware of the movement to use the terms "gender" and "sexuality" as if they can refer to separate realities; gender referring to one's physical characteristics, and "sexuality" referring to one's choice of "identity." In this book, the two terms are used interchangeably to refer to the reality of a person being made either male or female.

14. Angelo Scola, *The Nuptial Mystery*, 401–402.

body with its sexuality."[15] This means that every man and woman should accept his or her sexual identity (CCC, 2333) as part of the Creator's gift to him or her. This acceptance may pose difficulties for particular individuals. However, because sexuality is so central to one's proper self-understanding, it would be unjust and unloving to allow or encourage someone to deny, change, or act in a way that is contrary to this objective and defining aspect of their personhood.[16]

In fact, the sexual difference of male and female bodies reveals the nuptial foundation of reality. This means that human sexuality is a sign of a profound truth. In the second Genesis creation narrative, before the woman is created, the man experiences a state of "original solitude" (TOB 5–7; MD, 6) when he looks at other animal bodies and realizes that he does not have a suitable helpmate in any of the creatures of the garden (Gen 2:19–20). It is through the experience of his body that the first man realizes that none of the animals provides the opportunity for him to exist in a relationship of self-giving (TOB 14). There is no one like himself with whom he can exist in personal communion because none of the bodies he sees are the bodies of persons. Conversely, the man fully realizes who he is called to be when he gazes upon the body of the newly formed woman and utters his nuptial cry, "This at last is bone of my bone and flesh of my flesh . . . " (Gen 2:23). John Paul II refers to this utterance as the "the first 'wedding song' of the first man" (TOB 8:4, fn. 15). It is, in fact, the complementarity of the male and female bodies that reveals to all of us, not just to the first man, that we are made to be gift, to express love for one another, to exist for someone. Without both genders in the world, one gender isolated unto itself is simply

---

15. J. Brian Bransfield, *The Human Person According to John Paul II* (Boston: Pauline Books and Media, 2010), 103.

16. A lack of acceptance of one's sexuality is obviously exhibited in transgender operations. Additionally, homosexual activity is opposed to the proper orientation of human sexuality. It should be noted that experiencing same-sex attraction does not make someone guilty of a moral fault (CCC, 2358). However, if a person chooses to act out on these disordered desires, instead of striving to live chastely (see CCC, 2357, 2359), he or she is acting in a way that is not consistent with his or her sexual identity as a man or a woman. For a good treatment of same-sex orientation see John Harvey, *The Homosexual Person: New Thinking in Pastoral Care* (San Francisco: Ignatius Press, 1987), and *The Truth about Homosexuality: The Cry of the Faithful* (San Francisco: Ignatius Press, 1996). Also see Congregation for the Doctrine of the Faith, *Letter to the Bishops of the Catholic Church on the Pastoral Care of Homosexual Persons*, October 1, 1986, accessed June 5, 2013, www.vatican.va/roman_curia/congregations/cfaith/documents/rc_con_cfaith_doc _19861001_homosexual-persons_en.html.

unintelligible. The body's ability to reveal the person's capacity for self-giving love is what John Paul II referred to as the "spousal meaning of the body" (TOB 13:1).[17] It is the human body, with its sexual differentiation, that reveals to human persons that we are not created to be isolated individuals, isolated thinking and acting selves. Instead, the gendered human body reveals that the human person is meant to be a gift, to express love for another, to exist for someone. In short, the "spousal meaning of the body" is seeing the body as a gift-sign. Remember: the body itself is a visible sign that points to a deeper truth and an invisible reality. In this sense, the body itself is a sacrament.

The concept of "gift" is thus key to understanding human sexuality (TOB 13:2).[18] God creates man and woman as gifts for each other, gifting them with their masculine or feminine identities. It is in realizing the "spousal meaning of the body" through a life of "self-gift" for each other that man and woman come to a full understanding of their humanity (MD, 7). Thus among all bodies, the gendered human body, because it is the body of a rational creature, has the unique capacity to express love and make love visible in the world (TOB 15:1). Animal bodies, though gendered, cannot donate themselves to each other in acts of love. With our bodies, men and women express self-giving love in a myriad of ways, from friendly embraces and kisses, to gentle caresses and healing touches, to the marital act which, among all embodied expressions of love, has the capacity to bring forth new life, enfleshing the love of a husband and a wife. Only human sexual union is a union of persons that can express spousal love.[19] While animal sexual union serves to reproduce a species, human sexual union is an encounter of persons that serves not only to create with God (procreate) another unrepeatable human person, but also to express the self-donation of personal love. It is because the body, made male or female, reveals and expresses the person-as-gift that John Paul II said the "spousal meaning of the body . . . constitutes the fundamental component of human existence in the world" (TOB 15:5). Unless we acknowledge and live in accord with this fundamental component of human existence it is impossible to understand marriage.

---

17. The concept of "gift" is a key concept that recurs throughout the *Theology of the Body*.

18. In his theology of the body John Paul II speaks of the "hermeneutics of the gift" as key to understanding the human person (see TOB 13:2; 16:1).

19. See John F. Crosby, "Karol Wojtyla's Personalist Understanding of Man and Woman," 245.

Masculinity and Femininity and the Communal Dimension of the *Imago Dei*

The Christian tradition sees the "Let us make . . . " of Genesis 1:26 as a veiled revelation of the Trinity, and the fact that the human person is made in the image of the Triune God of love (LF, 6). God, who is love (1 Jn 4:8) and exists as an infinite communion of Persons has created human persons, male and female, in his image so that we may form a *communio* that reflects God's life (MD, 7). John Paul II explained: "This union merits the name communion (*communio*) which signifies more than community (*communitas*). The Latin word *communio* denotes a relationship between persons that is proper to them alone; and it indicates the good that they do to one another, giving and receiving within that mutual relationship." [20] Thus, "because man is made in God's image, he resembles him in both his spiritual *and* social nature."[21] When Genesis 2:18 states, "The Lord God said: 'It is not good for the man to be alone,'" it shows that men and women were not intended to be "solitary beings" (GS, 12), but instead were made to exist in relationship. "Being a person in the image and likeness of God thus also involves existing in a relationship, in relation to the other 'I'" (MD, 7).

In fact, when we look into our hearts it is apparent that we only find ourselves by making a sincere gift of ourselves (GS, 24; TOB 15:3). In order to realize our humanity, every person must break out of his or her solipsism and self-centeredness and offer himself or herself in loving service to others. Being made in the image of God who is a Trinity of Persons, man and woman are distinct and coequal persons called to exist as gifts for another (MD, 7).[22] It is through this giving that the human person enters into communion with others and with God. Thus from "the beginning" we are called to

---

20. John Paul II, *Sources of Renewal: The Implementation of the Second Vatican Council* (San Francisco: Harper & Row, 1980), 61.

21. Mary Shivanandan, *Crossing the Threshold of Love: A New Vision of Marriage in the Light of John Paul II's Anthropology* (Washington, DC: Catholic University of America Press, 1999), 79.

22. The fact that as human persons we fully realize ourselves by making a sincere gift of ourselves does not compromise the fact that a person is incommunicable; in other words, each individual person is unrepeatable, inviolable, and unique. John Paul II (as Karol Wojtyla) explained that the giving of the person does not take place on the natural or metaphysical plane, but "in the order of love and in the moral sense" (*Love and Responsibility*, trans. Grzegorz Ignatik [Boston: Pauline Books & Media, 2013], 79).

live in communion with God, and we are meant to image the communion of God in our personal relations. Indeed, "the Lord Jesus, when praying to the Father, 'that they may all be one . . . even as we are one' (John 17:21–22), has opened up new horizons closed to human reason by indicating that there is a certain similarity between the union existing among the divine persons and the union of God's children in truth and love" (GS, 24). This means that while the divine image is present in every human person as a rational being, it "shines forth in the communion of persons, in the likeness of the union of the divine persons among themselves" (CCC, 1702). "Man's resemblance to God finds its basis, as it were, in the mystery of the most holy Trinity. Man resembles God not only because of the spiritual nature of his immortal soul but also by reason of his social nature" realizing himself "in an act of pure self-giving" to form a communion of persons.[23] This means that, "Man becomes an image of God not so much in the moment of solitude as in the moment of communion. He is, in fact, 'from the beginning' not only an image in which the solitude of one Person, who rules the world, mirrors itself, but also and essentially the image of an inscrutable divine Communion of Persons" (TOB 9:3). In all of our personal relations—spousal relations, familial relations, ecclesial relations, and societal relations—we are called to form a communion of persons that images God.

However, it is crucial to note that in God's creative plan the "partnership of man and woman constitutes the first form of communion between people" (GS, 12) and serves as a foundation for all human communion. John Paul II highlighted this when he wrote: "God is love and in himself he lives a mystery of personal loving communion. Creating the human race in his own image . . . , God inscribed in the humanity of man and woman the *vocation*, and thus the capacity and responsibility, *of love* and communion" (FC, 11; cited in CCC, 2331). John Paul noted, "The first communion is the one which is established and which develops between husband and wife" (FC, 19), and elsewhere he stated:

> Man is the image of God not only as male and female, but also because of the reciprocal relation of the two sexes. The reciprocal relation constitutes

---

23. Karol Wojtyla, *Sources of Renewal: The Implementation of the Second Vatican Council* (San Francisco: Harper & Row, 1980), 61.

the soul of the "communion of persons" which is established in marriage and presents a certain likeness with the union of the three Divine Persons.[24]

Before sin entered the world, man and woman existed in a state of "original unity" (TOB 8) constituting a communion of persons in marriage based on a lucid understanding of the spousal meaning of the body (TOB 17). Being two aspects of a unified image of love, man and woman fully found themselves through each other (TOB 17:6). As will be discussed later in this chapter, it is sin that distorted this original communion between the first husband and wife.

In God's design, man and woman are made for each other (CCC, 371), and their physical and spiritual differences are oriented toward complementarity (CCC, 2333), allowing them to form a "communion of persons" (TOB 9:2; LF, 6; GS, 12). In fact, we can say that the sexual differentiation of male and female is a part of what it means to be made in the image and likeness of God (MD, 7).[25] In other words, it is gender that allows the human person to enter into a body-soul communion of love in the visible, created order that mirrors the communion of love, who in the invisible, supernatural order is the Trinity. While the divine nature itself is not gendered (CCC, 370), and while there is always more "non-likeness" than likeness between Creator and creature (MD, 8), the life of the Trinity is an infinite communion of Persons that humanity is meant to image in a finite way.[26] It is sexuality or gender that governs the fundamental way in which we form bonds of communion with other persons, and also makes communion possible (CCC, 2332). Since the human person is "an incarnate spirit . . . called to love in his unified totality" (FC, 11), it is only in the distinction between masculinity and femininity that a

---

24. John Paul II, *God, Father and Creator: A Catechesis on the Creed* (Boston: Pauline Books and Media, 1998), 232.

25. See also Angelo Scola, *The Nuptial Mystery*, 9, 33, 335. Scola points out that because human sexual difference is part of the image of God, human sexuality transcends the level of mere animal sexuality (333).

26. It is important to note that John Paul II does not "apply spousal language directly to the Trinity. It is the father-son relation, not the bride-bridegroom relation, that is the normative image for the Trinity, in agreement with the teaching of Jesus. Yet, it is clear . . . that the archetype and source of spousal love lies in the Trinity: 'All that is mine is yours, and yours is mine'" (Michael Waldstein, "Introduction," in *Man and Woman He Created Them: A Theology of the Body* (Boston: Pauline Books, 2006), 33). Thus it is the self-giving love of husband and wife that provides the analog to the life of love of the Trinity.

communion of persons can be realized *through the body* and that the love within the Trinity can be fully imaged through the body.

This means that the "image of God" was not complete without the creation of woman, but with the distinction between man and woman our bodies *can* express and reflect the image of the Trinity. As was already pointed out, the "nuptial cry" uttered by the man in Genesis 2:23, "This at last is bone of my bones and flesh of my flesh; she shall be called woman (*'issah*), because she was taken out of man (*'is*),"[27] shows that man and woman are called to exist as a "communion of persons" (CCC, 372). This "cry of wonder, [is] an exclamation of love and communion . . . [in which] . . . man discovers woman as another 'I,' sharing the same humanity" (CCC, 371). Thus the "image" in which humanity is fashioned is completed in personal relationship and self-giving love.[28] Therefore, the body and the duality of the sexes that allows us to enter fully into interpersonal communion is a revelation of God inscribed in creation. As John Paul II said: "Man, whom God created 'male and female,' bears the divine image impressed in the body 'from the beginning'; man and woman constitute, so to speak, two diverse ways of 'being a body' that are proper to human nature in the unity of this image" (TOB 13:2).

It is sexual difference that allows man and woman to unite in marriage and imitate "in the flesh the Creator's generosity and fecundity" (CCC, 2335). In fact, "awareness of the body includes awareness of its procreative capacity,"[29] and the ability to participate in giving life to another person shows forth fully the unique complementarity of masculinity and femininity (CCC, 372). God's command to the first married couple to "increase and multiply" (Gen 1:28) shows that man and woman are called to share in God's creative work, populating the world with more little images and likenesses of God. The "image of God" is thus realized in a particular way in a communion of love and

---

27. John Paul II notes regarding the original Hebrew text of Gen 2:23: "In biblical language this name indicates her essential identity with regard to man—*'is-'issah*—something which unfortunately modern languages in general are unable to express" (MD, 6).

28. Peter J. Elliott, *What God Has Joined*, 8.

29. Mary Shivanandan, *Crossing the Threshold of Love*, 122.

life, between a husband and a wife,[30] and they are called to extend the communion of persons in the family.[31] In fact, John Paul II stated:

> It is possible to discern how *the primordial model of the family is to be sought in God himself*, in the Trinitarian mystery of life. The divine "We" is the eternal pattern of the human "we," especially of that "we" formed by the man and the woman created in the divine image and likeness. (LF, 6)

We can extend John Paul's thought to point out that the "we" formed by a man and a woman in marriage is the fundamental human "we" without which there would be no other forms of "we." This means that the complementarity of the sexes oriented toward a communion of persons in marriage is so central to human existence that in reality, "The harmony of the couple and of society depends in part on the way in which sexual complementarity, needs, and mutual support between the sexes are lived out" (CCC, 2333). God instituted marriage, the one-flesh union of husband and wife (Gen 2:24), at the beginning of creation to serve as the basis for all of human existence and to serve as the foundation for imaging the self-giving love of the Trinity.

At this point it is important to note that in God's creative design, the gendered human body with its spousal meaning has a "sacramental" quality that reveals the meaning of the human person and all of created reality. Pertaining to this sacramental quality, John Paul II stated:

> Man appears in the visible world as the highest expression of the divine gift, because he bears within himself the inner dimension of the gift. And with it he carries into the world his particular likeness to God, with which he transcends and also rules his "visibility" in the world, his bodiliness, his masculinity and femininity, his nakedness. A reflection of this likeness is also the primordial awareness of the spousal meaning of the body pervaded by the mystery of original innocence.
>
> Thus, in this dimension, a primordial sacrament is constituted, understood as a sign that efficaciously transmits in the visible world the

---

30. See also Francis Martin, "Male and female he created them: A summary of the teaching of Genesis chapter one," *Communio* 20 (1993): 240–65.

31. See Angelo Scola, *The Nuptial Mystery*, 285, where he supports speaking of the human family as an aspect of the *imago Dei*. Also in support of this thesis see Marc Cardinal Ouellet, *Divine Likeness: Toward a Trinitarian Anthropology of the Family*, trans. Philip Milligan and Linda M. Cicone (Grand Rapids, MI: William B. Eerdmans Publishing Company, 2006), especially chapter 2, "The Family, Image of the Trinity," 20–37.

invisible mystery hidden in God from eternity. And this is the mystery of Truth and Love, the mystery of divine life, in which man really participates. . . . The sacrament, as a visible sign, is constituted with man, inasmuch as he is a "body," through his "visible" masculinity and femininity. The body, in fact, and only the body, is capable of making visible what is invisible: the spiritual and the divine. It has been created to transfer into the visible reality of the world the mystery hidden from eternity in God, and thus to be a sign of it.

In man, created in the image of God, the very sacramentality of creation, the sacramentality of the world, was thus in some way revealed. In fact, through his bodiliness, his masculinity and femininity, man becomes a visible sign of the economy of Truth and Love, which has its source in God himself and was revealed already in the mystery of creation. (TOB 19:3–5)

This rather long but beautiful passage means that the masculinity and femininity of human persons are meant to be visible signs or "sacraments" of the human person as gift, creation as gift, and God as gift. Made male or female, the human body with its "spousal meaning" is a visible sign of who the human person is called to be—namely gift. The human body as a gift-sign is also the preeminent sign of the loving gift that creation itself is, having its origin in the life of the God of self-giving love. Finally, masculinity and femininity are meant to be signs of the very inner life of God, enabling man and woman to form a communion of persons in marriage that images God who is *the* communion of Persons. John Paul II stated:

The body in its masculinity and femininity has been called "from the beginning" to become the manifestation of the spirit. It becomes such a manifestation also through the conjugal union of man and woman when they unite with each other so as to form "one flesh. . . . This unity, through which the body in its masculinity and femininity takes on the value of a sign, [is] in a certain sense a sacramental sign." (TOB 45:2)

Thus, in God's design human sexual difference enables man and woman to enter into a spousal communion of love that is an analog to the dynamic of the total gift of self among the Father, Son, and Holy Spirit. Each person, male and female, possesses a specific dignity according to how God has made him or her and only by accepting, reverencing, and giving as gift what is uniquely theirs can they contribute to the communal aspect of God's image (MD, 10).

In God's creative plan neither sexual difference nor marriage are accidental or malleable. This is a challenge to our current cultural climate which tends to regard human sexuality "more as an area *for manipulation and exploitation* than as the basis of that *primordial wonder* which led Adam on the morning of creation to exclaim before Eve: 'This is at last bone of my bones and flesh of my flesh' (Gen 2:23)" (LF, 19). This manipulation and exploitation of human sexuality strikes at the dignity of the human person because it refuses to accept masculinity and femininity as part of the mystery of the human person. However, it remains a fundamental fact of human existence that God created humanity male and female (TOB 18:4). "Man, whom God created 'male and female,' bears the divine image impressed in the body 'from the beginning'" (TOB 13:2). In God's plan gender is a visible sign that the human person is meant to be self-gift and it is gender that enables us to form a communion of persons that images the Trinity, the fundamental instance of which is marriage (MD, 7). The reality is that everyone, whether married or unmarried, is called to make a gift of self in accord with his or her masculinity or femininity and thereby enter into the communion of persons that is the human family, and to enter into communion with God.[32] However, as John Paul II said: "The divine 'We' is the eternal pattern of the human 'we,' *especially* of that 'we' formed by the man and the woman created in the divine image and likeness" (LF, 6, emphasis added). Thus to maintain that only a man and a woman can enter into the matrimonial state is not to discriminate against other human relationships, but is merely to point out the distinct, irreplaceable, and unchangeable nature of marriage as a fundamental revelation and sign, the "primordial sacrament" (TOB 19:4) of God's life-giving love. We will address marriage as the primordial sacrament in more detail in chapter 5.

The Many Facets of the *Imago Dei*

Based on the preceding discussion, it is easy to see that being made in the "image and likeness of God" has many facets. The human person acts as God's representative in the visible order, exercising dominion over the rest of material creation. Man and woman have a particular

---

32. We will address how those who are not called to marriage can realize themselves as self-gift and enter into a communion of persons in the concluding chapter of this book.

likeness to God through their spiritual, immortal, and rational souls. With their souls' capacities of reason and free will, man and woman are capable of self-knowledge and self-determination, thus making him or her a person—a "someone" (CCC, 357) instead of a "something." It is the human person's rational nature that also gives us the capacity for interrelation and interpersonal communion (LF, 6). Man and woman can freely give themselves to others, entering into a communion of persons, in preparation for communion with God who is the ultimate end or purpose of the human person's existence. Since the human person is a body-soul unity, he or she is made in God's image in his or her totality, and it is through the body that a man or woman recognizes and actualizes the call to self-gift and communion. This self-gift can be realized through the body only because the body is sexually differentiated, possessing a spousal meaning that reveals the meaning of human existence and the very foundation of reality. However, due to sin it is often difficult for us to see the spousal meaning of the body and to recognize and live out our dignity as persons made in God's image.

SIN AND THE DISTORTION OF THE *IMAGO DEI*

The account of the entrance of sin into the world and its effects on the human person are found in the Book of Genesis, chapter three. As we saw in the first two chapters of the Genesis creation narratives, before sin man and woman would have experienced complete harmony within themselves, between each other, with creation, and with God (CCC, 374). Original man and woman existed in this state of "original holiness and justice" by being given a participation in God's life which we call sanctifying grace (CCC, 376). This special gift of God's love allowed them to order themselves completely, body and soul, to God, while existing in self-giving communion with each other. While they remained in God's loving friendship, our first parents would retain this gift of grace and exist in a state of original harmony (CCC, 375).

Before the Fall of man from grace, the "spousal meaning of the body" would have been readily apparent, and through their bodies man and woman would have been able to express themselves in total, reciprocal self-giving, which imaged the self-giving of the Trinity.

They would have had an experience of "original unity" (TOB 8–10; MD, 6) that resolved the original man's experience of "original solitude" prior to the creation of the woman. That the body aided their personal communion, and did not hinder it, is evident in the Genesis reference to them being "naked without shame" (Gen 2:25). Thus they had an experience of "original nakedness" in which they understood fully the spousal meaning of each other's bodies and in which the body was transparent to the meaning of the person (TOB 11–13), as "an unquestionable sign of the 'image of God'" (TOB 27:3).

However, instead of journeying into deeper friendship and communion with God and each other, and thereby continuing to exist in a state of harmony, our first parents abused their freedom and fell from grace.[33] Succumbing to the temptation of the serpent (Gen 3:1–5) Adam[34] and Eve[35] ate from the "tree of knowledge of good and evil" (Gen 2:9), an act which is symbolic of them wanting to decide for themselves what is right and wrong without reference to their loving Creator (MD, 9). In this choice of self over God they evidenced a lack of trust in God's goodness, and a prideful lack of willingness to accept their dependence on God (CCC, 396–397) in their relationship to him as their Creator (MD, 9). With this choice, our first parents rejected God's love and lost the grace that allowed them to exist in a state of integration and harmony. The Genesis reference to their eyes being opened to realize that they were naked (Gen 3:7) shows a drastic departure from the experience of "original nakedness" before sin.

Rather than being a transparent revelation of the meaning of the person, the body now poses an obstacle to their communion (TOB 29:3). The body's spousal meaning is now obscured by sin

---

33. Throughout history there have been aberrant interpretations of the account of Original Sin that have blamed the woman for sin. Sometimes these interpretations have been based on what St. Paul says about Original Sin in his First Letter to Timothy: "For Adam was formed first, then Eve; and Adam was not deceived, but the woman was deceived and became a transgressor" (1 Tim 2:13-14). Regarding this, John Paul II has said: "But there is no doubt that, independent of this 'distinction of roles' in the biblical description, *that first sin is the sin of man,* created by God as male and female. It is also *the sin of the 'first parents,'* to which is connected its hereditary character" (MD, 9.4). Thus, whatever their individual roles were in the commission of the first sin, *both* members of the first couple were culpable of rebelling against God.

34. In Hebrew there is a play on words between the word for "man" (*adam*) and the word for "ground" (*adama*) out of which the man was formed (see Gen 2:7).

35. In Hebrew the name "Eve" (*hawwa*) is derived from the word for "living" (*hay*) (see Gen 3:20).

(TOB 27:4), and the body itself is affected by sin, destined now for suffering and death (Gen 3:16, 19). Experiencing a rupture in the innermost core of their being, the first couple's interior harmony, signified by being "naked without shame" (Gen 2:25), is also ruptured (TOB 26:5; 28). No longer masters of their own desires (testified to by Rom 7:22–23) they experience a lack of integration that prompts them to cover themselves with loincloths (Gen 3:7). Through sin, man and woman have in some way become alienated from their own bodies (TOB 28:4).[36] The rest of the account of the Original Sin evidences a loss of communion with God (Gen 3:8), of communion with creation (Gen 3:17–18), and of the communion of persons they experienced with each other (Gen 3:12, 16; CCC, 400; MD, 9).

The devil, under the guise of a serpent, has indeed struck a blow to the nuptial bond between the man and the woman.[37] Where once there was harmony and mutual self-giving, now there is a tendency toward domination and possession (Gen 3:16; MD, 10). Yet, God did not withdraw from the first man and his wife the blessing of being able to participate in his creative activity (Gen 3:20; 4:1). However, due to their attempt to decide for themselves what was right and wrong and thus attempting to become gods unto themselves, the first couple transmitted a human nature deprived of original holiness and wounded by Original Sin (CCC, 404). Human nature is not deprived of the dignity of being created in God's image, but the image is disfigured (MD, 9). Humanity, existing in a fallen state, now has to bear the wounds of ignorance, suffering, and death and is inclined to sin through desires that are disordered and tend to escape the control of reason (CCC, 405). This inclination to sin, due to disordered desires, is referred to as concupiscence (CCC, 377, 1264; MD, 10), which is not sin itself, but it does lead to sin and therefore must be struggled against in a fallen world.

Concupiscence, in general, refers to disordered desires, whether spiritual or carnal, and should not be simply equated with sexual lust. In fact, carnal concupiscence itself can refer to any disordered desire based in bodily passions. Scripture refers to a three-fold concupiscence:

---

36. For further helpful comments on how we have become alienated from our own bodies, see John F. Crosby, "The Estrangement of Persons from Their Bodies," in *Personalist Papers* (Washington, DC: Catholic University of America Press, 2004), 113–127.

37. Peter J. Elliott, *What God Has Joined*, 9.

the lust of the body, the lust of the eyes, and the pride of life (1 Jn 2:16–17; see TOB 26:1). However, a particular form of concupiscence, sexual lust, poses a danger to the man-woman relationship. The fact that the body is no longer easily subject to the spirit as in the case of original innocence (TOB 28:1) can threaten the one-flesh union of husband and wife. Instead of seeing the other as a gift to be reverenced and loved, lust prompts us to look upon each other as objects of gratification (TOB 32:5). In a fallen world, "The heart has become a battlefield between love and concupiscence" (TOB 32:3). In addition, "The more concupiscence dominates the heart, the less the heart experiences the spousal meaning of the body" (TOB 32:3). The movement of lust in the heart violates the person as gift and distorts the spousal meaning of the body. Apprehension and even fear of relationships results from this distortion, as is evidenced when Adam and Eve cover themselves (Gen 3:7). This lust can even exist between spouses, causing them to become "less sensitive . . . to the gift of the person" (TOB 32:3), and eroding their communion of persons (TOB 42:7), which is a task they must now strive to achieve (see TOB 29).

HUMAN FREEDOM AND THE *IMAGO DEI*

The enticing nature of the serpent's deception (see Gen 3:6) shows that the temptation to create our own morality and be "gods" unto ourselves is always seductive. Existing in a fallen state, there is a struggle between good and evil within human society and every human person (CCC, 1732, 1707). In this struggle it is the free choices we make that determine whether we experience true freedom or the slavery of sin (Jn 8:34). In order to understand the nature and purpose of marriage, it is necessary to have a correct understanding of human freedom.

There is a conflict today between a misconception of freedom that proposes a radical "freedom" to do whatever one wants, which is tantamount to license, and true freedom, which is the capacity to become perfected in our human nature by choosing what is true and good.[38] In this conflict it is necessary to explain that freedom is not

---

38. For an extended discussion of these opposing views of freedom see Servais Pinckaers, *Sources of Christian Morality* (Washington, DC: Catholic University of America Press, 1995), 327–378.

simply the capacity to choose, and human dignity is not found by merely exercising free choice. Contrary to popular opinion, freedom is not merely self-will; it is not simply the ability to do whatever one wants to do, whenever one wants to do it. Simply *choosing* something does not guarantee that the object of that choice will promote human flourishing and fulfillment. Certainly if we are honest with ourselves we will acknowledge times in life when choosing what we wanted did not lead to anywhere happy. Instead, the experience of freedom is contingent upon making choices that are in accord with the truth that comes from God. True freedom is found in the ability to choose wisely and to live according to what is good and true. The account of the Fall in Genesis 3 illustrates that when we choose evil we fall into the slavery of sin. The first couple failed by freely sinning and thereby freely refusing God's plan of love. "From its outset, human history attests to the wretchedness and oppression" that man suffers as the result of an abuse of our freedom (CCC, 1739). However, even while living in a fallen world and struggling with the effects of Original Sin on human nature, we can still choose what is good and true and thus grow in freedom and perfection (CCC, 1733). The more we do what is good and build positive and constructive habits, the freer we become and the more we realize that there is no freedom apart from the truth (VS, 34, 84).

In all of creation only human beings, made in God's image and likeness, can choose reflectively. Freedom of choice is a power rooted in reason and free will, which are faculties of the rational soul. Through reason the human person can understand "the order of things established by the Creator" (CCC, 1704), and through free will we are able to choose what we perceive to be good (CCC, 1704). The power to perform deliberate actions on one's own responsibility (CCC, 1731) through freedom of choice is an "outstanding manifestation of the divine image" (CCC, 1705, citing GS, 17). In fact, the greatness of the human being is found precisely in being a creature of a loving God, who gave us the capacity to know the good and freely choose it. By exercising freedom of choice we shape our own lives. These free choices lead to maturity and perfection of our nature if we choose what is true and good (CCC, 1704), and thereby direct our choices toward God who is our ultimate fulfillment and beatitude. Mastering ourselves and acting in accord with the truth that comes from God forms us more completely in God's image and allows us to experience deeper, more lasting joy.

Ultimately freedom is the fundamental characteristic of the person that allows us to live out our "being-gift" (see VS, 87). God gave us freedom so that we would be capable of loving and entering into communion with him and each other (CCC, 387; VS, 86). As John Paul II noted, before sin our first parents were "free with the freedom of the gift" (TOB 15:1). This freedom is evidenced by being "naked without shame" (Gen 2:25). In this state, our first parents were in the presence of each other's naked bodies, but instead of being tempted to look upon each other as objects of use, they existed *for* each other, giving to and receiving each other instead of taking for selfish gratification. Every human person is created in God's image with the capacity to act as his representative through self-consciousness (reason) and self-determination (free will). We become more like God to the extent that we master ourselves according to reason and will, with the help of God's grace, and exercise our dominion through self-giving. We are only truly free if we accept who we are and give ourselves totally in love to God and to others. Thus a human being is defined by his or her ability to freely be a gift for another: human person = a being who is made to give himself/herself (EV, 49). This means that *true freedom* is the ability to realize our full potential as persons who are made to be gifts, *not* doing whatever we want.

When people are told that if they want to be free they cannot do whatever they want, the reaction may be one of dismay, confusion, or outright rejection of the claim. I have experienced these reactions from students in my years at the front of a classroom. However, the reality is that freedom is not simply doing whatever we want to do. True freedom is paradoxically found in abandoning oneself to God's will, a will which always desires what is best for us. In fact, what may help people get over the difficulty of accepting that true freedom coincides with abandoning the desire to do whatever we want to do, is to point out to them that the God to whom we belong and to whom we submit our wills knows better than we do what will make us happy. Additionally, God desires this happiness for us more than we desire it for ourselves. Thus we have nothing to fear, and everything to gain, by abandoning a false view of radical freedom and embracing a freedom that coincides with choosing the truth that comes from God.

Probably one of the greatest mysteries regarding the human person is that God has given us the ability to freely accept or reject the dignity of the image in which we were made. The God of love (1 Jn 4:8) has created us out of love and has called us into loving communion with himself. Yet, God will only accept a free response to this loving invitation. Love cannot be demanded or programmed. We are only truly free if we accept what and who we are as a gift from the God who loves us more than we love ourselves, and who wants our happiness more than we want it. True freedom is therefore contingent upon the truth that comes from God about our nature and can never be separated from it (VS, 31–34). It is the truth that sets us free (Jn 8:32)! Yet, human freedom misconstrued as radical indeterminate choice leads to a lack of understanding, or even a rejection, of the nature of the human person, human sexuality, and marriage.[39] What is rampant in our day is "a corruption of the idea and the experience of freedom, conceived not as a capacity for realizing the truth of God's plan for marriage and the family, but as an autonomous power of self-affirmation, often against others, for one's own selfish well-being" (FC, 6). This concept of freedom that claims to be radically absolute (i.e., doing whatever one wants) ends up dominating nature, or denying it altogether, and treats the human body as manipulable "raw datum" (VS, 48). Misconstrued freedom leads to the denigration of the human person, the denigration of human sexuality, and the denigration of marriage as the fundamental communion of persons.

THE RESTORATION OF THE *IMAGO DEI*

The good news is that the grace won for us by Jesus Christ's sacrifice on the Cross has made it possible for us to experience the liberation of our freedom (VS, 86). By his Cross, Christ has redeemed all of humanity and saved us from the sin that held us in bondage (CCC, 1741). Christ delivered us from Satan and sin and he came to give us new life in the Holy Spirit. "For freedom Christ has set us free" (Gal 5:1). In Christ we have communion with the fullness of "truth that makes us free" (Jn 8:32). This means that the grace of Christ does not limit our

---

39. For a very helpful discussion of how radical, autonomous, absolute freedom opposes, or even replaces, nature leading to the quest to redefine marriage and sexuality see George Cottier, "Reflections on Marriage and the Family," *Nova et Vetera*, English ed., 1.1 (2003): 19–22.

freedom when freedom aims toward the true and the good (CCC, 1742). Jesus sends the Holy Spirit who seeks to educate us in freedom so that we may be collaborators in his work of our sanctification. Thus, with the help of the grace of Christ, we can grow in freedom (VS, 107) and respond to his challenge to be perfect as our heavenly Father is perfect (Mt 5:48; see VS, 16–18).

Coming to make us truly free, Christ came to fully reveal us to ourselves (GS, 22), teaching us of our exalted vocation as children of God, and trying to convince us to trust our Father and his loving plan for us. Believing in Christ and being baptized into him we become sons of God, and this adoption transforms us into new creatures (CCC, 1709). "The victory that Christ won over sin has given us greater blessings than those which sin had taken away from us: 'where sin increased, grace abounded all the more' (Rom 5:20)" (CCC, 420).

Coming to reveal us to ourselves (GS, 22) Christ came to restore the image of God in us. "His grace restores what sin had damaged in us" (CCC, 1708). "It is [ultimately] in Christ, 'the image of the invisible God,' that man has been created 'in the image and likeness' of the Creator" (CCC, 1701). "He who is 'the image of the invisible God' (Col 1:15), is himself the perfect man who has restored in the children of Adam that likeness to God which had been disfigured ever since the first sin" (GS, 22). Thus through Christ, "the divine image, disfigured in man by the first sin, has been restored to its original beauty and ennobled by the grace of God" (CCC, 1701).

Moreover, in the work of redemption "the entire person is inwardly renewed, even to 'the redemption of the body' (Rom 8:23)" (GS, 22). As part of the project of renewing the whole man from within, Jesus addressed sexual concupiscence or lust. Jesus speaks of sexual concupiscence as a disorder of the human heart when he identifies it with "adultery of the heart" (Mt 5:27–28), and he exhorts us to overcome this disorder in our relationships (see TOB 38–43). Jesus is telling us that we must master ourselves, by practicing virtue to control our desires, instead of letting our desires control us (TOB 49). Regarding this exhortation of our Lord, John Paul II asked, "Should we *fear* the severity of these words [Mt 5:27–28], or rather *have confidence* in their salvific content, in their power?" (TOB 43:7). Responding to this question, John Paul encouraged us not to fear but to have confidence that through an ongoing conversion of heart we *can* experience the redemption of our sexuality, rediscover the spousal meaning of the body, and live out the true meaning of masculinity and femininity to form a communion of persons (TOB 46:6).

Christ came to restore God's original plan for human love in the world, and because of this, Christ wants to redeem *all* of us, soul and body (TOB 46:4; 56:4). Every man and woman can recover the "freedom of the gift" if they rely upon God's grace and put forth effort to overcome concupiscence and master their desires (TOB 32:6; 43:6; VS, 103). Growing in self-mastery through the practice of virtue allows us to become self-giving gifts and experience true love and true freedom (TOB 58:7). This is not a return to "the beginning" before sin (because concupiscence will always be with us in a fallen world), but it is a perspective opened through redemption to exist as the "new man" spoken of by St. Paul (TOB 49:4; see Eph 4:24).

Christ seeks to redeem our love by incorporating us into his spousal union with his Church (Eph 5:21–33), nourishing us through the sacraments. It is precisely through the Sacrament of Marriage that Christ restores and elevates marriage and married love, allowing husbands and wives to realize God's original plan for these realities and enabling spouses to form a true communion of persons. Now, seeing the dignity of man and woman made in the image and likeness of God, let us turn to seeing the nature of love and marriage.

Chapter 4

Marriage and Conjugal Love

INTRODUCTION

The opening chapter addressed the centrality of the mystery of love to human existence. As St. John Paul II said, "God created man in His own image and likeness: calling him to existence *through* love, He called him at the same time *for love*" (LF, 11). As human beings we instinctively know that love is the meaning of life. We know that neither power nor fame nor fortune will provide us with ultimate satisfaction. Instead we intuit that "love is . . . the fundamental and innate vocation of every human being" (FC, 11). We know that "the meaning of life is found in giving and receiving love" (EV, 81). John Paul II was right when he said:

> Man cannot live without love. He remains a being that is incomprehensible for himself; his life is senseless, if love is not revealed to him, if he does not encounter love, if he does not experience it and make it his own, if he does not participate intimately in it. (FC, 18; citing RH, 10)

This desire to love and be loved is ingrained in our "DNA." We are like giant sponges that cannot soak up enough love. Ultimately, we have this desire to love and be loved because we have been created by the God of love, who has created us in his image to realize ourselves as gifts and thereby enter into loving communion with him and with others. God has created us out of love and has called us to love (CCC, 1605). We have been built to indwell God's life of love and to allow him to indwell us, and nothing short of entering into this communion of love with him will fill the deepest yearnings of our hearts. As St. Augustine famously wrote about the human heart's yearning for God, "you have made us for yourself, and our heart is restless until it rests in you."[1]

However, even though love is our ultimate destiny, "love" may be one of the most misused or even abused words in the English language.[2] Often times we conceive of love as some sort of instinct residing in the realm of intense emotion, having little to do with reason or will. Emotions are part of our experience of love, just not the essence of love. Many times we use the term *love* when in reality what we mean is desire or even lust. In reality, love that is proper to the human person is an act of the will whereby we affirm that it is good that something exists, we will the good of that reality, and we desire to experience some sort of communion with that reality.[3] As love is the result of a free choice, this means that love has its origin in the rational soul, and therefore only persons, possessing reason and will, have the capacity to love. It also means that as persons we can experience different forms of love depending on the good that is the object of our love.

Even when the word *love* is not misused it can be employed in different contexts with vastly different meanings. We can rightly say, "I love ice cream, I love my dog, I love my country, I love my work, I love my friend, I love my parents, I love my siblings, I love my wife, I love my children, and I love God." However, the meaning of "love" in each of these instances is obviously different. As we continue to outline a theology of marriage, it is important that we see clearly the unique type of love that can lead to marriage. This is especially important in a time when many people claim the right to marry anyone they want, simply because they "love" that person. First, relying largely upon the insight of C.S. Lewis we will outline the different kinds of love that the human person is capable of giving and receiving—affection, friendship, eros, and charity.[4] Then we will focus on explicating the unique form of love that is shared between spouses—conjugal love.

---

1. Augustine, *Confessions*, trans. Henry Chadwick (New York: Oxford University Press, 1991), 1.1.

2. Benedict XVI notes the many semantic uses of the word *love* in DCE 2.

3. See Josef Pieper, *Faith, Hope, Love* (San Francisco: Ignatius Press, 1997), 162–163; and ST I-II, q. 26, a. 4; q. 28, a. 1; II-II, q. 27, a. 2, ad 2.

4. To provide an outline of different types of love I have utilized C.S. Lewis, *The Four Loves* (New York: Harcourt, Brace and Co., 1988). Lewis's treatment of love is incredibly lucid and

AFFECTION

We often speak of the "love" that we have for things other than persons. This is actually love understood as taking pleasure in something, and is more akin to liking,[5] or to desire.[6] This love of pleasure arises out of the need to fulfill a desire (like eating when one is hungry) or out of appreciation for the goodness of an object (like a beautiful flower).[7] These nonpersonal types of love (like love of nature, love of country, love of one's work, etc.) are good if properly ordered, ultimately by our love for God, but if they are not properly ordered they can become gods unto themselves.[8] With a little thought, we can probably all identify someone who is obsessed with a thing, like a pet, or an activity, like a sport, and has allowed the appreciative love for a particular good, like food or a job, to become the center of his or her life, thus becoming a god. To love a nonpersonal reality in this disordered way simultaneously elevates the reality to a dignity it does not deserve, and denigrates the dignity of the person who offers the nonpersonal reality a reverence that cannot provide the fulfillment he or she seeks.

Of the forms of love that can be directed towards persons, but not exclusively to persons, affection, a love which the ancient Greeks called *storge*, is the least discriminating and most instinctive of loves.[9] The love we have for things other than persons, mentioned above, can be qualified as a form of affection.[10] However, affection is also the instinctive love that a parent has for a child and that children have for parents. Affection also goes beyond the bounds of family ties. In reality, affection is the "most widely diffused of loves," and almost anyone or anything can become on object of affection.[11] Since the

---

I recommend this book for anyone who desires a more in-depth description of the types of love that are briefly covered here.

5. Ibid., 10.

6. Thomas Aquinas said a love of concupiscence is that according to which "we do not wish good to what we love, but wish its good for ourselves, (thus we are said to love wine, or a horse, or the like)" (ST II-II, q. 23, a. 1; see also ST I-II, q. 26, a. 4).

7. C.S. Lewis, *The Four Loves*, 10–14.

8. Ibid., 17–30.

9. Ibid., 32.

10. I differ here from C.S. Lewis who in *The Four Loves* distinguishes likings and loves for the subhuman from affection.

11. Ibid., 31.

object of affection is someone or something familiar to us,[12] it is hard to pinpoint a moment when it begins.[13] As its name denotes, this type of love has its roots in human affect and as such affection can permeate other types of love.[14] The benefit of affection is that it can lead to appreciation for and affirmation of the goodness of its object.[15] Thus affection can open our eyes to the goodness of persons and things that surround us. However, affection is also ambivalent and can be good or bad depending on whether or not it is in accord with reason.[16] In other words, one's affection for someone or something may be inordinate (like loving a pet as if it were human).[17] Also, because it is based on familiarity with its object, "Change is a threat to Affection."[18] In fact, a change in the object of one's affection may lead to a waning interest in that object, be it a person or a thing. In addition, the same familiarity that is required for affection to arise can also give rise to disinterest in that same thing (hence the saying "Familiarity breeds contempt").[19] Thus, while affection is truly a good natural love, and affection may be "responsible for nine-tenths of whatever solid and durable happiness there is in our natural lives,"[20] the ambivalence of affection means that it must ultimately be purified by a higher love.

FRIENDSHIP

A form of love that can be shared only among persons is friendship, or *philia* in Greek. Following Aristotle, Thomas Aquinas saw friendship as the highest form of love that can be shared between persons, a love which is a sign of the love that God offers humanity.[21] Friendship is

---

12. Ibid., 33.

13. Ibid., 40.

14. Ibid., 34.

15. Ibid., 37.

16. Ibid., 38.

17. See ibid., 52–53.

18. Ibid., 45.

19. Ibid., 40.

20. Ibid., 53.

21. ST II-II, q. 23, a. 1. For an excellent treatment of Aquinas' understanding of friendship-love, see Mary Ann Fatula, *Thomas Aquinas, Preacher and Friend* (Collegeville, MN: The Liturgical Press, 1993).

essentially a relationship between individuals and is selective[22] because it is based on sharing a common interest. By its nature, friendship is the least jealous of loves,[23] since a circle of friends can expand to include those who share the same interest, with each additional friend revealing new aspects of the common interest as well as new aspects of the other friends in the circle.[24] Thus, while it is selective, friendship is not exclusively between two persons. While lovers stand face-to-face "absorbed in each other," gazing into each other's eyes, friends stand side-by-side "absorbed in some common interest."[25] The truest of friendships are formed around a truth that is shared in common,[26] and the higher the shared truth the more profound the friendship. Yet, because friendship is based on the interests that are held in common among friends, there is an ambivalence about friendship giving it the potential to be a school of virtue or of vice,[27] depending on what is shared in common. There is also the possibility that friends may be guilty of corporate pride, becoming cliquish, exclusivist, and condescending towards those who do not share their interest.[28] So, like affection, friendship needs to be purified by a higher love to keep it humble and centered on what is truly good.

Eros

The form of personal love that can be shared only between a man and a woman is erotic love or *eros*. *Eros* can be thought of as "being in love,"[29] or romantic love. The essence of sharing erotic love is that a man and a woman desire personal union with each other.[30] John Paul II noted that in its origin *eros* "signifies the inner power that 'attracts' man to the true, the good, and the beautiful" (TOB 47:5) found in another. This type of love can be shared only between a man and a woman,

---

22. C.S. Lewis, *The Four Loves*, 60.
23. Ibid., 61.
24. Ibid., 62.
25. Ibid., 61.
26. Ibid., 66, 70.
27. Ibid., 80.
28. Ibid., 82–83.
29. Ibid., 91.
30. Ibid., 94.

because only a man and a woman complement each other in a way that allows the two lovers to achieve the full personal union that they desire. There cannot be true personal union without the requisite body-soul complementarity present between a man and a woman. Male bonding and female bonding are good, but they are types of friendship-love (*philia*) according to which the friends experience communion around their common interests. As a result of living in a fallen world and struggling with the disordered desires of concupiscence, sometimes the energy involved in male or female bonding can be misdirected into erotic love. However, when two men or two women attempt to share erotic love there will ultimately be frustration because they cannot achieve the personal communion that erotic love seeks.

As was discussed in the previous chapter, due to the reality of concupiscence, sexual desire can seek physical union and sensual pleasure from someone without reference to the *person* to whom one is attracted.[31] However, *eros* is improperly conceived of as simply sensual or concupiscible desire (TOB 47).[32] As C.S. Lewis said, "Sexual desire, without Eros, wants *it*, the *thing in itself*; Eros wants the Beloved."[33] *Eros* does include sexual desire, but sexual desire itself does not constitute eros.[34] Benedict XVI noted: "*Eros*, reduced to pure 'sex', has become a commodity, a mere 'thing' to be bought and sold, or rather, man himself becomes a commodity" (DCE, 5). Sadly, however, sexual lust is the common misunderstanding of erotic love in our day. While *eros* certainly includes physical attraction, it has a spiritual element that seeks intimacy *with a particular person*. This spiritual aspect of *eros* can integrate sexual desire (which tends to be focused on a desire for pleasure and thus on the self) into a desire to appreciate and experience body-soul personal intimacy with the beloved.[35] This desire for personal union with the beloved has the ability to foster selflessness and a disregard for one's own happiness in

---

31. Ibid., 92–94. Lewis referred to the carnal aspect of *eros* as Venus. Before becoming pope, John Paul II provided an in-depth analysis of sexual desire in *Love and Responsibility*, trans. Grzegorz Ignatik (Boston: Pauline Books & Media, 2013), "Chapter I: The Person and the Drive."

32. The entirety of TOB 47 is a wonderful explanation of the ancient understanding of *eros* and how *eros* is improperly conceived of as simply sensual or concupiscible desire.

33. Lewis, *The Four Loves*, 94.

34. Ibid., 91.

35. Ibid., 95.

order to preserve this union.[36] Thus true "being in love" is not infatua-
tion or illusion,[37] nor is it, even at a superficial level, sensual desire.[38]
Real "being in love" helps us overcome self-centeredness and fosters a
tenderness towards the beloved.[39]

Experiencing true *eros* means loving another, body and soul.
Pope Benedict XVI pointed out: "Man is truly himself when his body
and soul are intimately united; the challenge of *eros* can be said to be
truly overcome when this unification is achieved" (DCE, 5). Created
as an embodied spirit, the human person must not ignore either body
or soul in seeking personal union with his or her beloved. For, "it is
neither the spirit alone nor the body alone that loves: it is man, the
person, a unified creature composed of body and soul, who loves. Only
when both dimensions are truly united, does man attain his full stature.
Only thus is love—*eros*—able to mature and attain its authentic
grandeur" (DCE, 5). This holistic understanding of *eros* should make
it clear why *eros* can be shared only between a man and a woman.

Yet, we must note that there are dangers of *eros* corresponding
to its sensual *and* spiritual elements. While the carnal element presents the danger of sexual lust and an objectification and instrumentalization of the person, the spiritual element of *eros* presents the danger
of possessiveness or domination.[40] John Paul II pointed out that while
eros does not shy away from the greatest effort in order to reach the
ecstasy of union; it is . . . an egocentric love" (TOB 22:4, fn. 35). *Eros*
therefore has a grasping, possessive quality about it that can tend
towards self-centeredness. Also, because it grasps for ecstatic union
eros presents the additional danger of turning the desire for union
with the beloved into a god in itself.[41] Because *eros* has an "ecstatic"
quality that tends "to lead us beyond ourselves" in an ascent to the

---

36. Ibid., 107.

37. Dietrich von Hildebrand, *Marriage: The Mystery of Faithful Love* (Manchester, NH: Sophia Institute Press, 1991), 15–17. Von Hildebrand was an important Catholic philosopher of the mid-twentieth century who will be discussed more in chapter 13. In addition to the work cited here, von Hildebrand also provided a helpful philosophical analysis of the love that can be uniquely shared between a man and a woman in *Man and Woman: Love and the Meaning of Intimacy* (Manchester, NH: Sophia Institute Press, 1992).

38. Dietrich von Hildebrand, *Marriage*, 17.

39. Ibid.

40. C.S. Lewis, *The Four Loves*, 102–103.

41. Ibid., 111.

divine (DCE, 5), in ancient cults *eros* was celebrated as a type of divine intoxication or power that offered "fellowship with the Divine" (DCE, 4). Thus *eros*, without purification, has a grasping tendency that not only grasps at the beloved for oneself, but also grasps at divine status. Therefore, like affection (*storge*) and friendship (*philia*), erotic love (*eros*) also needs to be purified by a higher love if it is to maintain its own integrity. It "needs to be disciplined and purified if it is to provide not just fleeting pleasure, but a certain foretaste of the pinnacle of our existence, of that beatitude for which our whole being yearns" (DCE, 4). In order to foster true, personal communion *eros* needs to surpass itself in order *"to reach . . . the very nucleus of the gift of person to person"* (TOB 113:3). It needs to reach the point where: "No longer is it self-seeking, a sinking in the intoxication of happiness; instead it seeks the good of the beloved: it becomes renunciation and it is ready, and even willing, for sacrifice" (DCE, 6).

CHARITY

Up to this point the loves that have been discussed are natural loves that we are capable of giving and receiving on our own efforts. However, as has been pointed out, each of these human loves needs to be purified by a higher love if it is to avoid dangers inherent to it. Especially in a fallen world wounded by sin, natural loves need to be transformed by supernatural love, or grace, if they are to maintain their own integrity.[42] This transformation does not distort, destroy, or harm the natural loves, but instead, as an example of grace building upon nature, supernatural love ennobles and liberates natural loves to be fully what they are.[43] This supernatural love that is needed to purify natural loves is the love of *agape* or charity. *Agape* has its origin in God who is love (1 Jn 4:8, 16). Since this love is proper to God's life, it lies beyond the human capacity to exercise without it first being gifted to us. Thus the love of *agape*, or charity, is a theological virtue infused into our souls by God,[44] a gift that adapts our "faculties for participation in the divine nature" (CCC, 1812). Although God can give people a share in his life of love in many ways, he guarantees us

---

42. Ibid., 119.
43. Ibid., 133-134; ST I, q. 1, a. 8, ad 2.
44. ST II-II, q. 24, a. 2.

a share in this love through the Seven Sacraments of the Church (CCC, 1212), pouring it into our hearts in Baptism and increasing it through the reception of the other sacraments.

The essence of *agape* is loving as God loves. It is loving "God above all things for his own sake, and our neighbor as ourselves for the love of God" (CCC, 1822). *Agape* is an altruistic and utterly selfless love whereby the lover seeks the good of the beloved without counting the cost to himself or herself. It is a love that needs nothing and seeks only to give, even to the point of sacrifice. The noblest aspects of all the natural loves are images of this divine love, but the ultimate "diagram" of agapic love is the Crucifix.[45] Sharing in God's love, exemplified in Jesus Christ's self-oblation on the Cross, we are empowered to love with a love that goes beyond the capacities of our natural loves. We are empowered to seek the good of the other for the other's sake in a disinterested fashion, even if the other is, according to natural calculations, unlovable.[46] *Agape*, or charity, allows us to offer ourselves as gifts to God and others, thus realizing ourselves as person-gifts in accord with the "spousal meaning of the body" and enabling us to form a communion of persons. Receiving the love of God and allowing this love to transform our natural ability to love is truly the fulfillment of the deepest desires of our hearts and the realization of the meaning of life. We need now to discuss how this transformation of love applies to the particular type of love shared between spouses.

The Characteristics of Conjugal Love

The distinct form of love that is experienced in marriage is conjugal love. From the Latin word *coniungere* meaning "to yoke together," conjugal love can also be called married love, spousal love, or nuptial love. The essence of conjugal love is that it seeks a total mutual donation of persons. Like all personal loves, conjugal love wills the good of the other and desires communion with the other. Conjugal love itself is also a natural love that includes aspects of all the natural loves: affection, friendship, and erotic love. Benedict XVI explained: "Fundamentally, 'love' is a single reality, but with different dimensions; at different

---

45. C.S. Lewis, *The Four Loves*, 127.
46. Ibid., 128.

times, one or other dimension may emerge more clearly" (DCE, 8).
In *Love and Responsibility*, John Paul II (then Karol Wojtyla), treating
conjugal love under the title of "spousal love," noted, "Although
spousal love itself differs by its essence from all the forms of love
previously analyzed, it nonetheless cannot be formed in separation
from them."[47] Conjugal love can arise between a man and a woman
who first experience affection for or friendship with each other, after
which they experience a romantic or erotic love that includes both its
sensual and spiritual aspirations. Conjugal love can also develop out of
the sensual attraction of *eros* if this attraction progresses to include the
spiritual desire of *eros* for union with the person. Once this desire for
union with the person is present, one would assume that affection and
friendship would also enter into the relationship. As conjugal love
develops there is the realization that the other represents a good for
me and that I desire the good of the other.[48] Thus conjugal love, as it
matures, not only desires the beloved with the love of *eros*, but it also
desires to give oneself to the beloved.

It should be noted that true conjugal love cannot develop where
there is merely sexual desire. Contrary to popular belief, conjugal love
is not unique because it involves intense desire or because it is sensual.[49] Conjugal love is "a far cry from mere erotic attraction [under-
stood as mere sensual desire], which is pursued in selfishness and soon
fades away in wretchedness" (GS, 49). While the mere sensual aspect
of erotic love fades away when the sensual desire is fulfilled, conjugal
love does not fade because it seeks union with the mystery of the other
person who can never be exhausted. Although a married couple
sharing conjugal love does experience friendship, conjugal love should
also not be thought of as friendship with the addition of sensuality,[50]
since to introduce sensuality would be a distortion of friendship's focus
on the commonly shared interest. Conjugal love should instead be
conceived of as a distinct form of love that seeks a complete and total

---

47. Karol Wojtyla, *Love and Responsibility*, 82–83. The entirety of "Chapter II: The Person
and Love" in *Love and Responsibility* is a detailed analysis of love that can be shared between
a man and a woman in its metaphysical, psychological, and ethical dimensions.

48. Angelo Cardinal Scola, *The Nuptial Mystery*, trans. Michelle K. Borras (Grand Rapids,
MI: William B. Eerdmans, 2005), 381.

49. Dietrich von Hildebrand, *Marriage*, 7.

50. Ibid., 19.

mutual giving of the self. [51] In *Love and Responsibility*, John Paul II (then Karol Wojtyla) said of spousal love: "It consists in giving one's own person. The essence of spousal love is giving oneself, giving one's 'I'".[52] While it is true that every form of love involves giving, only conjugal love is a complete and ultimate giving that involves a mutual handing over of the entire person, body and soul, one to the other.[53] In short, conjugal love is a love of complete mutual self-donation.

Since the distinguishing character of conjugal love is a *total* reciprocal giving and receiving of the entire self, conjugal love can only be experienced between a man and a woman, and only within the context of marriage. As was discussed in the previous chapter, there is a unique physical and spiritual complementarity between man and woman made in the image and likeness of God. It is precisely this unique complementarity that enables a man and a woman to enter into a relationship of reciprocal self-donation that includes both the spiritual and physical aspects of their personhood. Two men and two women do not possess the requisite complementarity that allows them to receive each other's personal gift and enter into a body-soul personal communion. Thus any attempt to experience conjugal love with someone of the same sex will ultimately be frustrated by the lack of personal complementarity.

This unique love of total mutual self-donation between a husband and a wife has further defining characteristics. John Paul II noted these characteristics when he wrote:

> Conjugal love involves a totality, in which all the elements of the person enter—the body and instinct, power of feeling and affectivity, aspiration of the spirit and of will. It aims at a *deeply personal* unity, a unity that, beyond union in one flesh, leads to forming one heart and soul; it demands *indissolubility* and *faithfulness* in definitive mutual giving; and it is open to *fertility*. (FC, 13; quoted in CCC, 1643)[54]

Thus one characteristic of conjugal love is that it is imminently personal or "fully human" (HV, 9). It includes all aspects of the

---

51. Ibid., 7.

52. Karol Wojtyla, *Love and Responsibility*, 78. This giving of the self is on the moral plane, and therefore does not contradict the incommunicability of the mystery of the human person.

53. Dietrich Von Hildebrand, *Marriage*, 8.

54. In this passage, John Paul II is summarizing the characteristics of conjugal love mentioned by Paul VI in HV, 9.

person, and aims at a deeply personal unity in body and soul. As Benedict XVI noted, love "engages the whole man" (DCE, 17). As a deeply personal love that seeks the good of the other and that involves all of one's person, conjugal love must involve a free choice. As Dietrich von Hildebrand noted, conjugal love involves a definitive decision to love a particular person expressed by, "I love you."[55] Thus, unlike affection which may arise almost unnoticed, conjugal love involves a conscious choice.

Once a couple has decided to exist for each other in conjugal love, their love is necessarily marked by the quality of exclusivity and fidelity (see CCC, 1646–1651). By definition, this giving of themselves *to each other* is exclusive; it is a closed relationship where each person has handed himself/herself totally over to the other.[56] Thus, unlike friendship which is open to including others who share the common interest of the friends, conjugal love, because it is focused on the giving and receiving of a particular man and a particular woman to each other, is by its very nature exclusive. The nature of conjugal love excludes polygamy because it is by its nature directed toward only one person in an act of complete, mutual, and exclusive self-giving.[57] It is therefore impossible for a man to love more than one woman, or a woman to love more than one man, conjugally at the same time.[58] This exclusiveness of conjugal love is not possessiveness, which would have its origins in egoism, but instead arises out of the awareness that this unique love can exist only between these two people.[59] Again, conjugal love yearns for "*I* love *you*."

Another hallmark of conjugal love is that it longs for permanence. Alice von Hildebrand said that "a person truly in love wants to bind himself forever to his beloved."[60] This is why, she noted, that "love without unqualified commitment betrays the very essence of love."[61] True "being in love" has the intention and the hope of not

55. Dietrich von Hildebrand, *Marriage*, 10–11.
56. Ibid., 8.
57. Ibid., 20.
58. Ibid.
59. Ibid., 20–21.
60. Alice von Hildebrand, "Introduction," in *Marriage: The Mystery of Faithful Love* (Manchester, NH: Sophia Institute Press, 1991), ix–x. Alice von Hildebrand, a philosopher in her own right, is the widow of Dietrich von Hildebrand.
61. Ibid., x.

only exclusiveness, but also permanence.[62] Hardly anyone would deny conjugal love's aspiration for permanence. As Cardinal Angelo Scola stated:

> I never tire of repeating to young people: When you are really in love, I challenge you to say to your boyfriend or girlfriend, "I love you," without adding the "forever." You might even be intimately convinced that you do not know how to avoid falling short of this affirmation, but when the heart says in truth, "I love you," to someone, the "forever" comes naturally.[63]

Total mutual self-giving implies a desire for unity and indissolubility (CCC, 1644), for fidelity and permanence. Love songs do not contain lyrics that aspire to loving for a delineated or limited period of time, but forever. "Love seeks to be definitive; it cannot be an arrangement 'until further notice'" (CCC, 1646). "In freedom the lover desires to commit his whole future to the beloved;"[64] and, to be unwilling to hand oneself over to one's beloved for the indefinite future means that there is not really an offering of true love. As John Paul II has noted, "By its very nature the gift of the person must be lasting and irrevocable" (LF, 11).

The last aspiration or yearning of conjugal love is its desire for superabundance or fruitfulness. Msgr. Livio Melina has well described conjugal love's orientation towards fruitfulness when he stated:

> By its very nature, love is oriented toward bearing fruit that transcends it. In order to avoid self-absorption and self-consumption, love must open itself up to a further fruitfulness, of which procreation is naturally the most obvious aspect. . . . Unity in love is always fruitful and the body's fruitfulness, which in the sexual act opens itself to the possibility of procreation, is the sign of the spiritual fruitfulness of the marital act of love.[65]

Thus true conjugal love is life-giving and a couple sharing conjugal love longs "to give and receive new life" (LF, 11). As the *Catechism* points out, "A child does not come from outside as something added on to the mutual love of the spouses, but springs from the very heart of that mutual giving, as its fruit and fulfillment" (CCC,

---

62. Dietrich von Hildebrand, *Marriage*, 18.

63. Cardinal Angelo Scola, *The Nuptial Mystery*, 377.

64. Ibid., 267.

65. Livio Melina, *Building a Culture of the Family: The Language of Love* (Staten Island, NY: Society of St. Paul / Alba House, 2011), 84.

2366). This desire for fruitfulness is both spiritual and biological, as a couple who shares true conjugal love seeks not only to have children but also to raise and educate them (CCC, 1653). A couple who shares true conjugal love seeks to leave a legacy together, a legacy which is most evident in and through their children.

MARRIAGE MAKES CONJUGAL LOVE POSSIBLE

Conjugal love is the form of love that can be experienced only in marriage, for it is only in marriage that the couple has joined themselves together by formally handing themselves over to each other. As Dietrich von Hildebrand pointed out, the one right motive for entering into marriage is the desire to share conjugal love with each other.[66] By this he means that a couple must discern, through consideration of the intellect, whether they really do desire to share a love that is faithful, permanent, and open to children, seeking the good of each other through a sincere mutual gift of self (more will be said about this discernment in chapter 17). However, it should be noted that even if a couple should discern that they desire to share this type of love, this desire itself does not make them married. The desire to share conjugal love anticipates the meaning of marriage but is not yet marriage.[67] Marriage is more than conjugal love, because what constitutes marriage is a solemn act of the will by which the couple hands themselves over to each other.[68] Through a formal and public act of the will the couple exchanges their consent to enter into a relationship of life-long mutual surrender,[69] thus pledging to form a communion of persons. Marriage is not a private agreement, but the formation of an interpersonal communion that has social consequences. It is a "*conscious and free choice*' which gives rise to marriage," a choice that only persons are capable of making (LF, 8). As the Second Vatican Council noted, "Married love is an eminently human love

---

66. Dietrich von Hildebrand, *Marriage*, 67–69. John Paul II affirmed this insight of von Hildebrand when he stated: "A man and a woman whose love has not thoroughly matured, has not crystallized as a fully-mature union of persons, should not marry, for they are not prepared for the life test of marriage" (*Love and Responsibility*, 215).

67. Dietrich von Hildebrand, *Marriage*, 21.

68. Ibid.

69. Ibid., 22.

because it is an affection between two persons rooted in the will and it embraces the good of the whole person" (GS, 49).

Following upon this consent the spouses fully actualize their union by consummating their mutual self-surrender through sexual intercourse.[70] In this way they really do hand over the entirety of their persons to each other. As John Paul II stated:

> As an incarnate spirit, that is a soul which expresses itself in a body and a body informed by an immortal soul, man is called to love in his unified totality. Love includes the human body, and the body is made a sharer in spiritual love. (LF, 11)

In the act of consummation, therefore, the body expresses, in a very particular way and according to its spousal meaning, self-giving love and the person as gift. As Dietrich von Hildebrand explained, the conjugal act makes the partners' loving union "*objectively real in the fullest sense*, and no other earthly communion of love can become objective to such a degree. Both partners now belong wholly to each other. An objective bond unites them: they are no longer *two*, but *one*."[71] After exchanging consent and consummating their union, a bond has been formed which is a "communion of objective validity."[72] This means that a new objective reality has come into being according to which the two spouses have joined their lives to become one. Once established, this objective union remains, "regardless of the sentiments or attitudes of the partners."[73] As Dietrich von Hildebrand stated, "the act of voluntary surrender of one's own person to another with the intention of forming a permanent and intimate union of love, creates an objective bond which, once established, is withdrawn from the sphere of arbitrary decision of the persons concerned."[74] Once established, this union is a public reality that "imposes specific obligations" and makes demands on the spouses.[75]

Thus the desire to share conjugal love may lead to marriage, and conjugal love itself permeates and gives marriage meaning, but

70. Ibid.
71. Ibid., 23.
72. Ibid., 22.
73. Ibid.
74. Ibid., 23.
75. Ibid., 22.

conjugal love does not itself establish the objective bond of marriage.[76] What causes the objective bond of marriage to come into being is a free act of the will. What is more, this decision to permanently bind oneself to another is an act of true freedom. It is a free decision to live in accord with the truth of conjugal love, and fulfill the longings of that love. As Benedict XVI pointed out: "It is part of love's growth towards higher levels and inward purification that it now seeks to become definitive, and it does so in a twofold sense: both in the sense of exclusivity (this particular person alone) and in the sense of being 'forever'" (DCE, 6). It is failing to give oneself irrevocably that leads to isolation because "love by its very essence longs for infinity and eternity. Therefore, a person truly in love wants to bind himself forever to his beloved—which is precisely the gift that marriage gives him."[77] In fact, it is marriage that allows a couple to fully realize and experience conjugal love.

The relationship between conjugal love and marriage is evidenced in the *Order of Celebrating Matrimony* in the Catholic Church. Before exchanging their consent, the couple is asked to respond to three questions. The questions are as follows:

> N. and N., have you come here to enter into Marriage
> *without coercion,*
> *freely and wholeheartedly?*
> Are you prepared, as you follow the path of Marriage,
> *to love and honor each other*
> *for as long as you both shall live?*
> Are you prepared *to accept children lovingly from God*
> *and to bring them up*
> *according to the law of Christ and his Church?* (OCM, 60, emphasis added)

By responding positively to these questions the couple is stating that they are freely ("without coercion, freely and wholeheartedly") pledging to enter into a relationship that is faithful ("love and honor each other"), life-long ("for as long as you both shall live"), and open to bearing fruit both biologically and spiritually ("accept children lovingly from God, and bring them up according to the law of Christ and his Church"). Thus, the couple is pledging to form a communion

---

76. Ibid.
77. Alice von Hildebrand, "Introduction," ix–x.

of persons that is structured by conjugal love. Only after promising conjugal love to each other does the couple exchange their consent:

> I, N., take you, N., to be my husband/wife.
> I promise to be faithful to you,
> in good times and in bad,
> in sickness and in health,
> to love you and to honor you
> all the days of my life. (OCM, 62)

The essence of the above consent is a total and irrevocable giving of self to the beloved, consistent with the nature of conjugal love. It should be noted that, in accord with the most admirable aspirations of conjugal love, there is nothing in the consent that says anything about what one hopes to get from one's spouse, but only what one promises to give; and what one gives is one's very self for the good of one's spouse. As Pope Paul VI noted, "Whoever really loves his partner loves not only for what he receives, but loves that partner for the partner's own sake, content to be able to enrich the other with the gift of himself" (HV, 9).

Thus, it is marriage alone that allows conjugal love to be realized with its aspirations of a free, faithful, forever, and fruitful gift of self to one's beloved. As John Paul II stated:

> The only "place" in which this self-giving [of conjugal love] in its whole truth is made possible is marriage, the covenant of conjugal love freely and consciously chosen, whereby man and woman accept the intimate community of life and love willed by God Himself, which only in this light manifests its true meaning. The institution of marriage is not an undue interference by society or authority, nor the extrinsic imposition of a form. Rather it is an interior requirement of the covenant of conjugal love which is publicly affirmed as unique and exclusive, in order to live in complete fidelity to the plan of God, the Creator. A person's freedom, far from being restricted by this fidelity, is secured against every form of subjectivism or relativism and is made a sharer in creative Wisdom. (LF, 11)

What John Paul II highlighted in the above passage is that far from being "just a piece of paper," by nature marriage is required by the desire to share true conjugal love. To choose marriage is to make a free choice to realize the aspirations of conjugal love, and in this way it is through the binding of marriage that the lovers are truly liberated.

CONJUGAL LOVE, MARRIAGE, AND SEXUAL INTERCOURSE

It should also be noticed that even though conjugal love desires sexual union as part of the fulfillment of the longing for mutual self-giving, it is marriage alone that justifies sexual intercourse. Sexual intercourse makes sense only in a communion of conjugal love wherein spouses truly give themselves to each other completely. Consummation enacts a true surrender, not just "passing intimacy."[78] The total surrender of sexual intercourse, the two becoming one, can only logically come as a result of the free and irrevocable decision to give oneself to the beloved for a lifetime.[79] Thus sexual intercourse enacts the promises already spoken. As John Paul II noted, "The choice is what establishes the conjugal covenant between the persons, who become 'one flesh' only based on this choice" (TOB 10:3). After this choice of marriage is made, "the physical intimacy of the spouses becomes a sign and pledge of spiritual communion" (CCC, 2360).

Through this one-flesh union, the husband and wife "reveal themselves to one another" and "know" one another as unrepeatable persons through the gift of their masculinity and femininity (TOB 20:4).[80] Since the act of consummation is a *complete* self-gift, implying absolute fidelity and permanence, it cannot be repeated with another as long as the person to whom one has surrendered oneself is alive.[81] The act of sexual intercourse solidifies the reality that the spouses really do belong to each other. The problem with sexual activity outside of marriage is seen when one understands that extramarital sex turns an act that should be an act of complete and total surrender and self-giving into a source of fleeting sensual gratification.[82]

I once entered into a conversation with a man who wanted to discuss Catholic teaching on sexual morality. As the discussion progressed, he revealed to me that he was living a rather promiscuous lifestyle. As he kept hurling one objection after another at the Church's

---

78. Dietrich von Hildebrand, *Marriage*, 24.

79. Ibid., 32.

80. In TOB 20:4, John Paul II explained beautifully the biblical language of "knowledge" of another that takes place through sexual intercourse (see Gen 4:1–2).

81. Dietrich von Hildebrand, *Marriage*, 25.

82. Ibid., 31.

teaching, hardly listening to my responses, an idea came to me. I said, "I am willing to continue this discussion as long as you would like in order to help you understand why the Catholic Church teaches what it does, but I think we need to agree to something first. I think we need to agree to be honest with each other and honest with ourselves. I am honest when I tell you that I have found liberation in the Catholic Church's teachings on sexual morality. Can I ask you to be honest with yourself and with me?" When he responded that he could, I then decided to ask him another question. I said, "I want you to be honest with yourself. After your sexual encounters with the young women you just spoke of, did you feel happy, content, and free; or, as you lay in bed, or sat on the edge of the bed, did you feel like some part of you had died?" I do not know what prompted me to ask this question, and I attribute it to a movement of the Holy Spirit, but the man's reaction was also a movement of the Spirit. In response to my question, he said nothing. He simply began weeping. This is in fact the horror of extramarital sex. Somewhere deep down inside this man knew that the lifestyle he was involved in was a lie, and all of his resistance to the Church's teaching was simply an attempt to avoid and deny the awful isolation and deep loneliness that he experienced by misusing the gift of the marital act.

Engaging in sexual intercourse outside of marriage violates the very meaning of sexual intercourse as an expression of total self-giving love, and thereby it violates the "spousal meaning of the body." As John Paul II said:

> Consequently, sexuality, by means of which man and woman give themselves to one another through the acts which are proper and exclusive to spouses, is by no means something purely biological, but concerns the innermost being of the human person as such. It is realized in a truly human way only if it is an integral part of the love by which a man and woman commit themselves totally to one another until death. The total physical self-giving would be a lie if it were not the sign and fruit of a total personal self-giving, in which the whole person, including the temporal dimension, is present: if the person were to withhold something or reserve the possibility of deciding otherwise in the future, by this very fact he or she would not be giving totally. (FC, 11; partially quoted in CCC, 2361)

In his *Theology of the Body*, John Paul II explained more fully why it is a lie to attempt to engage in total physical self-giving outside of the context of marriage. Based upon the truth that as human persons we express ourselves through our bodies, he observes that in the act of sexual intercourse the body expresses a particular truth. He pointed out that the body speaks a "language" in sexual intercourse. In short, this "language of the body" (TOB 103:4–6) is a language of self-gift that is consistent with the "spousal meaning of the body," which reveals to us that we have a capacity for communion, that we are meant to be self-giving gifts. In the act of sexual intercourse, spouses communicate their persons and speak a language of total, mutual self-gift, surrendering themselves completely to each other. This language can only be "read in truth" within the context of marriage (see TOB 105–106), because only in marriage can the act of sexual intercourse objectively "speak" the language of complete mutual self-donation. Outside of the context of marriage (even during the engagement period), the body is forced to speak a lie in sexual intercourse because there is always something that is being held back in what is supposed to be a complete communication of oneself that pledges permanence, fidelity, and an openness to children. Thus only within the context of marriage can the truth of conjugal love be "spoken" through the body, and only in marriage can sexual union enable spouses to enter into a body-soul communion of persons.

When discussing the immorality of premarital sexual activity with people, I have often heard the rationalization that if two people love each other they should be able to express it. While it is true that people should be able to express love, the real question is what expressions of love are appropriate to the relationship and therefore actually coincide with the objective nature of the love that is shared and the objective good of the couple. Certainly we cannot have sexual intercourse with anyone we want. In fact, the only people who have a right to sexual intercourse are married couples. John Paul II's discussion of the "language of the body" provides an easy way to help couples who are not married, even if they are engaged, to understand why sexual intercourse does not make sense for their relationship. Unmarried couples cannot argue that they are truly giving themselves completely and irrevocably to each other in their acts of intercourse, because they know, even if they are engaged, that the possibility exists for them to walk away from the relationship. They have not yet, through a solemn act of their wills, publicly expressed in a mutual exchange of consent, handed themselves over to each other completely and irrevocably to bring into being a new objective reality. There is a world of difference between solemnly and unconditionally pledging to hand one's self over to another, and simply agreeing to a relationship of mutual convenience.

When discussing this point with a group of students, one young man revealed that he and his girlfriend had been dating for a couple of years and loved each other, and he did not see anything wrong with them having sex. I responded that I was not questioning that they loved each other, but I maintained that having sex was not the right way to express the type of love that they shared at this point in their relationship. I explained that conjugal or married love is a love of complete, mutual self-surrender, and that in the context of marriage where conjugal love can be shared sexual intercourse makes sense, but that outside of the context of marriage sexual intercourse can severely confuse a couple's motives. I pointed out that because sexual intercourse involves intense biochemical and emotional actions and reactions, it can confuse a couple's accurate assessment of their relationship. The young man responded that he and his girlfriend loved each other and that sex was not the focus of their relationship. I then asked this young man, "How do you know whether or not your relationship is overly focused on sex, unless you are willing to give it up?" This young man was incredibly honest, and after a long pause he responded, "I don't; you've got me." I went on to explain that if he and his girlfriend were not willing to sacrifice what rightfully belongs only to married couples, namely sexual intercourse, how could they know if they were willing to undertake greater sacrifices for each other to form a life-long union in which they truly hand their lives over to each other? This is precisely the point. Outside of marriage sexual intercourse, or more properly the marital act, cannot speak the "language" God intends it to speak—a language of free, faithful, fruitful, and forever—because the couple has not truly handed their lives over to each other.

The Role of Conjugal Love in Marriage

Since the desire to share conjugal love is what leads to marriage, and since conjugal love is what spouses pledge to offer each other throughout their married life, conjugal love must be nourished in every marriage as a task and a duty.[83] As Paul VI noted, the conjugal love that spouses pledge to each other

> is not, then, merely a question of natural instinct or emotional drive. It is also, and above all, an act of the free will, whose trust is such that it is meant not only to survive the joys and sorrows of daily life, but also to grow, so that husband and wife become in a way one heart and one soul, and together attain their human fulfillment. (HV, 9)

This means, firstly, that one's spouse, and only one's spouse, has a right to conjugal love.[84] But, it also means that spouses must struggle not to become complacent in their love.[85] They must be vigilant not to let their love "die" as is so often talked about in marriages gone bad. They need to realize that the love they have pledged to offer each other is not based in how they "feel" for each other on any given day or over a span of days, but instead is based in a free act of their wills that has bound them to live faithfully and fruitfully for each other for life. On their wedding day a couple is not able to say how they will *feel* for each other ten, or twenty, or fifty years into the future, but they are able to say that they will *love* each other ten, or twenty, or fifty years into the future, precisely because this is what they have vowed to do. Love is an act of the will, and as such this commitment perdures regardless of the vicissitudes of changing emotions.

However, the task of nurturing love differs depending on the particular character of the marriage.[86] All spouses must strive to form a communion of persons "within the limits of the possibilities of their individual case."[87] Even in "unhappy" marriages, where love is lacking on one side or when suffering is caused to one spouse by another, the obligation to live up to the objective bond of marriage through sacrifice

---

83. Ibid., 32.
84. Ibid., 33.
85. Ibid., 34.
86. Ibid.
87. Ibid., 36.

and self-renunciation still exists.[88] What is universally true is that no love is free from difficulties, and because of this spouses must fight to save their love amidst these difficulties.[89] John Paul II noted quite frankly "that *true conjugal love . . . is a difficult love*" (TOB 83:3). Even if one spouse proves to be unloving, or unfaithful, the other spouse must seek to remain faithful to the promises he or she made on their wedding day. While this may involve suffering, there is also a peace in knowing that one is doing everything in one's power to live up to the objective reality of the bond they have forged.

I once taught a class in which I was discussing the permanence of the marriage bond, and I started receiving objections from some students in the class regarding the permanence of the marital commitment. The students stated that it seemed unfair for a faithful spouse to have to live alone while his or her unfaithful spouse did not suffer the same fate. I responded in part by stating that the unfaithful spouse was really not in a better situation than the faithful spouse because to be unfaithful is a betrayal not only of one's spouse, but of oneself. After class, one of the older students approached me to say that she understood from personal experience the truth of what I was saying. She went on to relate that for several years she had been living as a single mother with her children after her husband had left them. She explained that many of her friends were encouraging her to get a divorce and to start dating, potentially to find another husband. Her response to them was quite emphatic. She stated, "I tell my friends, 'I *am* married, and regardless of what my husband has chosen to do, I intend to live up to the promises I made on our wedding day. I pray every day that my husband will come to his senses and that we can live as a family again. But whether or not that ever happens, I made promises to my husband and to God, and I intend to keep them.'" I will never forget this moment in the classroom. This woman, who was not Catholic, understood better than most people the nature of married love and the fact that living up to the demands of this love, even if it involves suffering, is worth it. She understood the importance of living as a person of integrity, being true to one's word, and

---

88. Ibid., 36–37. This is not to imply that one spouse should subject himself or herself to abusive behavior perpetrated by the other spouse. In these situations, separation may be necessary to preserve one's safety.

89. Alice von Hildebrand, "Introduction," xi.

being faithful to the truth of conjugal love. If spouses are not willing to endure suffering to remain faithful to their vows, at a certain point we will be forced to ask if the words of consent mean anything anymore. The woman in my class was taking a stance that the promises spouses make must mean something.

The reality is that the main struggle a spouse must undertake to preserve conjugal love in marriage is a struggle with the self. Spouses must fight against themselves for the sake of their beloved—they must win a victory over self.[90] In his *Letter to Families*, John Paul II commented on the demanding nature of love and the fact that these demands primarily entail overcoming selfishness in all of its forms (LF, 14). Every spouse must overcome an individualism that "remains egocentric and selfish," an individualism that refuses to tolerate demands from the beloved based in objective truth, an individualism that attempts to "establish the truth" based on personal choice, and refuses to be a "sincere gift" (LF, 15). True love always involves effort and sacrifice, especially to overcome all forms of concupiscence in one's heart to be able to be a giver rather than a taker (TOB 127:4). This effort and sacrifice lasts a lifetime. John Paul noted that part of accepting the demands of love entails understanding and accepting who we are as persons who only find ourselves by making sincere gifts of ourselves (LF, 14). Accepting who we are as person-gifts also entails realizing that freedom does not mean "license to do *absolutely anything*," but instead "means a *gift of self*" in accord with the truth (LF, 14). By exercising the power of self-giving in love of the truth, spouses can form a true "communion of persons" (LF, 14). Thus it is the demanding nature of love that makes love beautiful, building up "the true good of man," and serving as "the truly firm foundation of the family" to build a "civilization of love" (LF, 14). John Paul II noted how dangerous the concept of "free love" is, which tells us to follow our instincts or emotions, tells us that love can exist without commitment, demands, or responsibilities, and attempts to "'soothe' consciences by creating 'moral alibi.'" He pointed out how this love is not "free" but instead enslaves us to our passions, exploits human weakness, represents a form of utilitarianism that only seeks pleasure for

---

90. Ibid., xii. More will be said about suffering in marriage and in particular about suffering the struggle with oneself in chapter 18.

selfish gratification, and is ultimately destructive of love, marriages, and families, making children *"orphans of living parents"* (LF, 6–8).

Conjugal Love and Charity

John Paul II called the thirteenth chapter of St. Paul's First Letter to the Corinthians the *"Magna Carta* of the civilization of love" (LF, 14), a passage that points out the demanding nature of true love. In 1 Corinthians 13:4–8 St. Paul states:

> Love is patient and kind; love is not jealous or boastful; it is not arrogant or rude. Love does not insist on its own way; it is not irritable or resentful; it does not rejoice at wrong, but rejoices in the right. Love bears all things, believes all things, hopes all things, endures all things.

This hymn to love contained in the writings of St. Paul certainly entails an exhortation to submit to a death to self in an effort to give life to one's beloved. It is a call to love the beloved "not for any qualities that he or she possesses, but for his or her inherent and unrepeatable value as a person."[91] Ultimately the love that "endures all things" is the love of *agape*, a love that is willing to accept the full demands of love by being willing to sacrifice oneself to the point of suffering for the good of one's beloved. True love wills the good of the other no matter what must be endured and no matter what the cost to self might be. The measure of true love is sacrifice—a sacrificial giving of oneself—a love that is willing to suffer, even when the suffering is caused by the beloved. In short, this love is Christ-like, and this love is not possible without God's help.

When the love of *eros* (accompanied by affection and friendship) is transformed by *agape* it is rightly called conjugal charity. Benedict XVI pointed out that far from being opposed to each other, *agape* enters into the noble desires of *eros* to keep it from becoming impoverished and losing its own nature (DCE, 7). He even claimed that God's love for humanity is simultaneously *eros* and *agape* (DCE, 9), a love seeking personal union with the beloved that desires nothing but the beloved's true good. Benedict XVI noted:

---

91. Peter J. Elliott, *What God Has Joined: The Sacramentality of Marriage* (New York: Alba House, 1990), 189.

Eros and *agape*—ascending love and descending love—can never be completely separated. The more the two, in their different aspects, find a proper unity in the one reality of love, the more the true nature of love in general is realized. Even if *eros* is at first mainly covetous and ascending, a fascination for the great promise of happiness, in drawing near to the other, it is less and less concerned with itself, increasingly seeks the happiness of the other, is concerned more and more with the beloved, bestows itself and wants to "be there for" the other. The element of *agape* enters into this love, for otherwise *eros* is impoverished and even loses its own nature. (DCE, 7)[92]

This type of selfless love is hard for many to understand, especially in a world that is focused on "*utilitarian happiness*,' seen only as pleasure or as immediate gratification for the exclusive benefit of the individual, apart from or opposed to the objective demands of the true good" (LF, 14). However, in our heart of hearts all of us desire the love described by St. Paul and not the counterfeit love offered by the world.

John Paul II noted that at work in the love that endures all things "is the power and the strength of God himself, who 'is love' (1 Jn 4:8, 16)" (LF, 14). Thus we see the need for grace, a participation in the life of God (CCC, 1997),[93] to purify and elevate our natural ability to love. We need charity to transform natural conjugal love, the love between a husband and a wife, into conjugal charity. *Gaudium et Spes* states that married love "bringing together the human and the divine, leads the partners to a free and mutual self-giving, experienced in tenderness and action, and permeating their whole lives" (GS 49). It is grace that allows the love that a married couple shares to experience "an ongoing exodus out of the closed inward-looking self towards its liberation through self-giving, and thus towards authentic self-discovery and indeed the discovery of God. 'Whoever seeks to gain his life will lose it, but whoever loses his life will preserve it' (Lk 17:33), as Jesus says throughout the Gospels (cf. Mt 10:39; 16:25; Mk 8:35; Lk 9:24; Jn 12:25)" (DCE, 6). John Paul II pointed to the fact that

---

92. Joseph Pieper offered some beautiful insights into the unity of love and the relationship between *eros* and *agape* [*Faith, Hope, Love* (San Francisco: Ignatius Press, 1997), 246–271].

93. The *Catechism* also defines grace as "the free and undeserved help that God gives us to respond to his call to become children of God, adoptive sons, partakers of the divine nature and of eternal life" (CCC, 1996). It goes on to say that grace "introduces us into the intimacy of Trinitarian life" (CCC, 1997).

with grace, "conjugal love reaches that fullness to which it is interiorly ordained, conjugal charity, which is the proper and specific way in which the spouses participate in and are called to live the very charity of Christ who gave Himself on the Cross" (FC, 13). It is only this type of love that can heal wounds through forgiveness and reconciliation (LF, 14), a love that is willing to undergo a death to self and to accept the demands of serving the good of one's beloved. It is this love alone that truly satisfies. The good news is this love is possible! Christ has given us the Sacrament of Marriage that guarantees husbands and wives the grace to allow them to experience this conjugal charity in their spousal communion.

Chapter 5

The Nature of Marriage

MARRIAGE AND NATURAL LAW

The previous two chapters discussed the nature of the human person and the nature of conjugal love. This chapter discusses the nature of marriage as it is ingrained in human nature. When we discuss the nature of a reality we are looking at it through the lens of natural law. Natural law is not the same thing as the laws of nature, which are scientific principles that govern the physical universe. Instead, natural law is the human person's ability to participate in eternal law, which is the wisdom by which God orders creation (CCC, 1954; see also VS, 36). Natural law allows us to see the ordered nature of reality. St. Paul attests to the reality of natural law when he speaks of those who deny and suppress the truth, saying: "For what can be known about God is plain to them, because God has shown it to them. Ever since the creation of the world his invisible nature, namely, his eternal power and deity, has been clearly perceived in the things that have been made" (Rom 1:19–20). Thus St. Paul testifies to the fact that the human person can understand "the order of things established by the Creator" (CCC, 1704). In fact, natural law is called "natural" because reason, which perceives and dictates this law, is part of human nature (CCC, 1955; VS, 42; ST I-II, q. 90, a. 1). Thus it is a law that is natural to us. God's truth is planted in our hearts (CCC, 1958)[1] in such a way that we can grasp it naturally.

---

1. Robert Sokolowski points out that when St. Thomas Aquinas says that natural law is written in the hearts of men (see ST I-II, q. 94, a. 6) Thomas means "that we are able to acknowledge, rationally, what the good is" (in "What is Natural Law? Human Purposes and Natural Ends." *The Thomist* 68 [2004]: 525). Therefore, saying that the natural law is written in the human heart does not mean it is a matter of sentiment, but an achievement of reason.

There are certain things that we "can't not know."[2] We know these things through natural law. Natural law provides us with a way of understanding the nature of things (what things are) by discerning what their proper ends are (what they are for). Being able to identify the end for which something exists means identifying its *telos* or goal, or in other words, where it finds its perfection. The end of a thing (traditionally called the *finis operis*, or "the end of the work"), is the objective end of something, which exists regardless of the subjective ends/intentions/purposes (traditionally called the *finis operantis*, or the "end of the one performing a work") someone may have for that thing.[3] Right reason applied to reality to see the ends of things (*finis operis*) allows us to derive principles of natural law that should be acceptable to everyone and that can provide the basis for a common morality (see CCC, 1957), apart from subjective intentions (*finis operantis*).

Ideally the subjective intention (*finis operantis*) of an acting agent coincides with the objective end (*finis operis*) of a reality in question. For example, a physician may choose to practice medicine with the subjective intention of healing people, which is also the objective end of medical practice. However, a person can have many subjective intentions that are distinct from but consistent with (or at least do not contradict) the objective end of a reality, thus still preserving the nature of the reality. For instance, a physician can choose to practice medicine to provide for his or her family, but still intend to heal people. Even if the physician is guilty of greed by practicing medicine for the purpose of getting rich, he or she can do so while preserving the nature of medical practice itself. It is possible though for a person to hold a subjective intention which contradicts the objective end of a reality, and thus perform an act which is intrinsically disordered and immoral according to the nature of things. An example of this would be a sadistic physician who practices "medicine" not for the purpose of healing, but for the purpose of causing patients pain.[4]

---

2. See, J. Budziszewski, *What We Can't Not Know* (Dallas: Spence Publishing Company, 2003).

3. For a good discussion of the distinction of ends vs. purposes see Robert Sokolowski, "What is Natural Law?," 508–512.

4. For a discussion of how ends and purposes relate to each other, which includes the example of the physician used here, see Sokolowski, "What is Natural Law?," 512–514.

Even though natural law is accessible to everyone of right reason, it is possible to ignore it or reject it. St. Paul notes as much when he says of those who deny the truth: "for although they knew God they did not honor him as God or give thanks to him, but they became futile in their thinking and their senseless minds were darkened. Claiming to be wise, they became fools" (Rom 1:21–22). Many people attempt to deny the reality of natural law and they attempt to deny that it is possible to speak of "truth" or the "nature" of things in a way that would dictate moral principles. Ultimately, the denial of "truth" and "nature" is rooted in the aforementioned distorted view of "freedom" that claims the ability to create our own truth or to change nature and conquer it (see VS, 46, 48). We all tend to want to disagree with the natural law when it is not convenient to follow because it conflicts with our subjective purposes.[5] We have not only reason, but will, and sometimes what we desire does not coincide with what we know to be true. Due to the fact that we are wounded by sin, at times what is natural does not come naturally.[6] At times we find that our purposes (intentions, desires) conflict with the objective ends of things. When this occurs, we must realize that it is the objective end of a thing and not our subjective purposes that determines what a thing is. Ends, which determine natures, exist independent of our wishes and feelings. So, regardless of how difficult the struggle may be, we should not allow our subjective intentions to override the ends of things. In the final analysis, practicing natural law means giving priority to ends (*finis operis*) over individual purposes (*finis operantis*). "Natural law is shown to us when we recognize that there are ends in things and that our purposes and choices must respect that priority."[7]

Even though we can deny or suppress the natural law, we can never fully destroy the truth of natural law in our hearts and consciences (CCC, 1958). In reality, all natures, including human nature, are dependent upon God. We receive ourselves as gifts and we cannot redefine our nature to be other than what God has made us. As we discussed in the chapter on anthropology, we are persons made body and soul, male or female, in the image and likeness of God.

---

5. Mark Lowery, *Living the Good Life: What Every Catholic Needs to Know About Moral Issues* (Cincinnati, OH: Servant, 2003), 65.

6. Ibid.

7. Robert Sokolowski, "What Is Natural Law?," 521.

Furthermore, we have also seen that "the vocation to marriage is written in the very nature of man and woman as they came from the hand of the Creator" (CCC, 1603). It is appropriate to point out with Cardinal Jorge Medina Estevez that

> no human institution is so deeply rooted in nature and in the heart of man and of woman as marriage and family. Prior to any philosophical reasoning, men and women know that they are made for each other, that they need each other, and that there exists between them a sort of relationship that is different from all the other relationships found in human society.[8]

In the order of nature, man and woman are created for marriage (TOB 18:5; see Gen 2:24) and have a natural inclination to marriage, an institution which itself has a specific nature. The nature of marriage, and the ends that help define it, are ascertainable to everyone of right reason. Committing ourselves to prioritizing the objective nature of marriage and its ends over any subjective desires or purposes we may have for marriage will lead to true freedom and happiness, because it is in maintaining this priority that we are following the design of the God of love.

This means that while marriage is a natural institution, it "is not a purely human institution" (CCC, 1603). "God himself is the author of marriage" and he has endowed marriage "with its own proper laws" (CCC, 1603, citing GS, 48). As Pope Pius XI pointed out, "matrimony was not instituted or restored by man but by God," and therefore the "laws [of marriage] cannot be subject to any human decrees or to any contrary pact even of the spouses themselves" (CC, 5). He also stated that "the nature of matrimony is entirely independent of the free will of man, so that if one has once contracted matrimony he is thereby subject to its divinely made laws and its essential properties" (CC, 6). The laws of marriage are ascertainable through human reason, and because marriage is instituted in the natural order by God, spouses must choose what marriage is, and not what they might want it to be.[9] It is important to stress that "the natural laws of marriage are not an imposition of the blind forces of

---

8. Jorge Cardinal Medina Estévez, *"Male and Female He Created Them": On Marriage and the Family* (San Francisco: Ignatius Press, 2003), 13.

9. Thus the Code of Canon Law states: "If, however, either or both of the parties by a positive act of the will exclude marriage itself, some essential element of marriage, or some essential property of marriage, the party contracts invalidly" (CIC, c. 1101 §2).

nature but the norms meant to lead the human person to his or her own perfection."[10] Thus the laws of marriage are not arbitrarily imposed from without as a burden, but they are laws of freedom; freedom understood, not as the ability to do whatever we want, but as the ability to grow in perfection, happiness, and fulfillment by embracing the truth that comes from God. Marriage possesses "common and permanent characteristics" regardless of culture or certain cultural distortions (CCC, 1603), and it is by living in accord with the unchanging nature of marriage that the well-being of individuals, couples, and society will be preserved (CCC, 1603). In this chapter we explore these unchanging characteristics of marriage.

THE DEFINITION OF MARRIAGE

Canon law, which is quoted in the *Catechism of the Catholic Church*, defines marriage as a "covenant, by which a man and a woman establish between themselves a partnership of the whole of life and which is ordered by its nature toward the good of the spouses and the procreation and education of offspring" (CIC, c. 1055 §1; CCC, 1601). This concise definition of marriage represents an understanding of the nature, characteristics, and ends of marriage according to natural law. A clearer understanding of marriage in the order of nature can be arrived at by examining this definition in detail. We will begin by explaining marriage as a covenant, and then progress to discussing the essence, goods, ends, and properties of marriage as an institution of nature.[11]

---

10. Ignatius Gramunt, "The Essence of Marriage and the *Code of Canon Law*," *Studia Canonica* 25 (1991): 367. This brief article is incredibly helpful at delineating the essence, ends, properties, and goods of marriage.

11. There are different ways of explaining how the goods, properties, and ends of marriage relate to each other in an integral understanding of marriage. In what I present here I am indebted to the insights of Ignatius Gramunt, "The Essence of Marriage and the *Code of Canon Law*," and also to Mark Lowery, "The Nature and Ends of Marriage: A New Proposal," *The Jurist* 65 (2005): 98–118. However, this chapter also contains insights of my own regarding the goods of marriage.

Marriage as a Covenant

Marriage is a covenantal relationship. A covenant is a particular and solemn type of contractual agreement.[12] Contracts are agreements which normally govern the exchange of goods and services, granting rights and imposing obligations and duties on the parties involved in the agreement. Contracts can be entered into for a specified period of time, and depending on the terms of the agreement, there can be circumstances under which the contract is rendered null and void. However, a covenantal relationship, which grants rights and imposes duties on the parties involved, encompasses more than an exchange of goods and services. Although covenants can involve personal duties,[13] what is essentially involved in a covenant is a mutual exchange of persons.[14] As the person, whose dignity far exceeds that of any good or service, is what is being given and received, the duration of a covenant is for life. There are no qualifying terms of the agreement that allow for the breaking of a personal covenant once it has been validly contracted.

The covenant of marriage is forged by the spouses' "irrevocable personal consent" by which they "give themselves definitively and totally to one another" (CCC, 2364; GS, 48)[15] to form a communion

---

12. It is true that in the history of the Church marriage has often been approached and explained as a "contract," and only recently in the Church's history has there been more of an emphasis on explaining marriage with the more biblical language of "covenant." Part 4 of this book will address this development. However, it remains true that all covenants imply a form of juridical contract. While the 1983 *Code of Canon Law* refers to marriage primarily as a "matrimonial covenant" (CIC, c. 1055 §1) it also refers to the "matrimonial contract" (CIC, c. 1055§ 2). Therefore, one should not see a contradiction or a "substantial change" in the emphasis of covenant over contract (see Gramunt, 372). Peter Elliott provides a good discussion of the choice of the word "covenant" instead of "contract" as it is used in the Second Vatican Council document *Gaudium et Spes* in *What God Has Joined: The Sacramentality of Marriage* (New York: Alba House, 1990), 176–180.

13. Peter J. Elliott, *What God Has Joined*, 170. Elliott stated: "To assert that contracts deal with things and covenants deal with people is a naïve simplification of reality." Yet, he goes on to say that the biblical notion of covenant was derived from treaties between groups of peoples and ultimately dealt with the "relationship between God and his People" (171). While I do not discount the fact that the word "covenant" is sometimes used to refer to nonpersonal agreements, Scripture reveals to us the full meaning of "covenant" as an exchange of persons.

14. John S. Grabowski comments on the biblical understanding of a covenant as an exchange of persons in *Sex and Virtue: An Introduction to Sexual Ethics* (Washington, DC: Catholic University of America Press), 29.

15. The exchange of consent is thus the efficient cause (that which produces existence or change) of marriage. It is possible to speak of the moment of the exchange of consent (that constitutes the covenant of marriage) as marriage in the process of becoming (*matrimonium in*

of persons.[16] The consent that spouses exchange is "an act of the will by which a man and a woman mutually give and accept each other through an irrevocable covenant in order to establish marriage" (CIC, c. 1057 §2). Thus through their consent, which we discussed in the previous chapter when dealing with conjugal love, the couple freely chooses to mutually and irrevocably give and receive each other to form a marriage (see CIC, c. 1057 §2). After entering into this solemn agreement in which they swear a mutual oath to hand themselves over completely to each other, they then seal the covenant through conjugal intercourse, enacting their pledge.[17] From this point the spouses, "are no longer two; from now on they form one flesh" (CCC, 2364). "The covenant they freely contracted imposes on the spouses the obligation to preserve it as unique and indissoluble" (CCC, 2364). As a result of their exchange of consent to form one life together, the spouses have given each other the right to those things that pertain to marriage (CIC, c. 1135). Through their consent, and now "joined by a holy covenant,"[18] each spouse has the *right* to receive conjugal love, a love that is faithful, permanent, and open to having and raising children together, which includes the right to sexual intercourse.[19]

---

fieri), which brings about the permanent partnership of the spouses' lives, or marriage in fact (*matrimonium in facto esse*). See Gramunt, "The Essence of Marriage and the *Code of Canon Law*," 369, 372.

16. Understanding marriage as a covenant helps us understand the communion of persons that spouses form in marriage, as John Paul II pointed out when he stated, "The family originates in a marital communion described by the Second Vatican Council as a 'covenant,' *in which man and woman 'give themselves to each other and accept each other'*" (LF, 7).

17. For comments on sexual intercourse as the sealing of the marital covenant see, John Grabowski, *Sex and Virtue*, 24. Grabowski points out that in the Bible covenants were contracted through the exchange of an oath *and* the sealing of the oath through a ceremonial act (31–32). For the marital covenant it is sexual intercourse that enacts or seals the covenant oath between the married couple (37–38). More will be said about sexual intercourse as the sealing of the marital covenant in chapter 19 of this book dealing with sexual morality.

18. RM, "Nuptial Blesssing A."

19. As Mark Pilon noted, "Marriage is without question a kind of legal agreement, a legal contract with serious moral consequences, including the exchange of important, fundamental rights and duties related to the essential matter of the contract." He goes on to explain that "the vows of marriage involve a surrender of one's whole person to the partner, at least in so far as the specific purpose of marriage is concerned. This mutual gift of the whole self entails, at a minimum, that the partners exchange a strict moral right to the marriage act. . . . Indeed, it is in this act that they actually surrender their whole person to the other, for this act morally and physically demands the total gift of both body and soul. Moreover, this strict moral right established by the vows implies a corresponding strict moral duty of each partner to respond to the reasonable request of the other spouse for his or her marriage rights" (*Magnum Mysterium: The Sacrament of Matrimony* [Staten Island: Alba House, 2010], 30). This right and duty to

Each of the spouses has also promised to fulfill the *obligation* of offering faithful, permanent, and fruitful conjugal love, supporting his or her spouse body and soul, in the communion of persons that they have formed.

The Essence of Marriage

The essence of something is that which makes it what it is.[20] The essence of marriage, or marriage in fact (*matrimonium in facto esse*), consists of a man and a woman establishing between themselves "a partnership of the whole of life".[21] The *Catechism of the Catholic Church* and *Gaudium et Spes* express the essence of marriage as an "intimate community of life and love" (CCC, 1603, quoting GS, 48). Another way of expressing this essence of marriage is as a "communion of persons" (*communio personarum*). It has already been explained in the preceding chapters why this particular communion of persons can only be entered into by a man and a woman; only a man and a woman possess the full personal complementarity to allow them to surrender themselves to each other completely. Further, in the previous chapter we discussed the unique form of love, conjugal love, that spouses pledge to each other through their consent to form a communion of persons. It is therefore appropriate to define the essence of marriage as a communion of persons based in conjugal love, or simply a conjugal communion.[22]

---

engage in sexual intercourse is traditionally referred to as the "conjugal debt," based on the text of 1 Cor 7:3 in which St. Paul says, "The husband should give to his wife her conjugal rights, and likewise the wife to her husband." While the language of "conjugal debt" highlights the contractual and legal aspects of the marital covenant, including the responsibility spouses have to support each other body and soul through sexual intercourse, it lacks a personalist approach to marital intercourse. It should always be understood that the right and duty to request and render the conjugal debt presupposes that it is exercised reasonably, in accord with conjugal love that seeks the good of the other.

20. James P. Lyons, *The Essential Structure of Marriage: A Study of the Thomistic Teaching on the Natural Institution*, Dissertation, Studies in Sacred Theology No. 40 (Washington, DC: Catholic University of America Press, 1950), 9.

21. CCC, 1601.

22. Ignatius Gramunt noted: "Canonists have often asked whether love is of the essence of marriage. As the term is analogical and the meaning most often used is that of an 'affective inclination', they have either answered the question negatively or have been opposed to include a term that is ambiguous in the language of the law. But if marriage is a *union of persons* sustained by the mutual habit of the will to seek the good of the spouse by virtue of a commitment, then love is of the very essence of marriage, for the same *habit of the will* is a habit of love and justice" ("The Essence of Marriage and the *Code of Canon Law*," 75).

Dietrich von Hildebrand explained that a communion of love is the deepest meaning and the very core of marriage.[23] He noted that no human relationship (friendship, parent-child, family relations, etc.) is based exclusively on mutual love except for marriage.[24] As was discussed in the previous chapter on conjugal love, marriage is unique among all human relationships because it is the most intimate of earthly unions in which a man and a woman give themselves totally to each other without reserve. As John Paul II explained:

> By virtue of the covenant of married life, the man and woman 'are no longer two but one flesh' and they are called to grow continually in their communion through day-to-day fidelity to their marriage promise of total mutual self-giving.
>
> This conjugal communion sinks its roots in the natural complementarity that exists between man and woman, and is nurtured through the personal willingness of the spouses to share their entire life-project, what they have and what they are: for this reason such communion is the fruit and the sign of a profoundly human need. (FC, 19)

Thus marriage is rooted in human nature and the couples' irrevocable personal consent that is the covenant of marriage establishes a communion of conjugal love, which is the essence of marriage. Marriage is a community of life and love that finds its life-giving principle in the conjugal love that the couple has pledged to give and receive.[25] This is why Thomas Aquinas referred to the "bond of mutual affection that cannot be sundered" as the "form" of marriage, or that which makes marriage what it is.[26] However, the lack or even absence of conjugal love in the conjugal communion of persons does not destroy

---

23. Dietrich von Hildebrand, *Marriage: The Mystery of Faithful Love* (Manchester, NH: Sophia Institute Press, 1991), 32, 4–5. Von Hildebrand made the distinction between love as the primary *meaning* of marriage and procreation as the primary *end* of marriage (xxv, 7). In making this distinction he was responding to a situation in which many theologians were stressing the primary end of procreation without saying much about the role of love in marriage (xxvi). While acknowledging the value of von Hildebrand's insight, I think the word "meaning" lacks a certain clarity, and I think that it is more precise to speak about a communion of persons based in conjugal love, or conjugal communion, as the *essence* of marriage.

24. Dietrich von Hildebrand, *Marriage*, 6.

25. Ramón García de Haro, *Marriage and the Family in the Documents of the Magisterium: A Course in the Theology of Marriage*, 2nd ed., trans. William E. May (San Francisco: Ignatius Press, 1993), 248.

26. ST III, q. 29, a. 2.

the marital covenant.[27] Spouses can choose to deprive married life of conjugal love, but this does not change the essence of marriage as a communion of persons in which conjugal love is owed.[28] Just because a spouse refuses to live in accord with the essence of the life he or she has committed to, this does not change the essence of the life that they are obliged to live. The essence of marriage as a communion of conjugal love is a reality that the spouses agreed to when freely forging their covenant, and this reality is not subject to fluctuating dispositions. Spouses have chosen to subject themselves to the essence of marriage, and they must strive to live up to this choice (just like a doctor who chooses to practice medicine).

The Goods of Marriage

As was explained in our discussion of the relationship between conjugal love and marriage in the previous chapter, by freely consenting to form a communion of persons structured by conjugal love, a husband and a wife freely pledge to offer each other a love that is faithful, permanent, and open to having and raising children.[29] Thus the three aspirations of conjugal love—fidelity, indissolubility, and fruitfulness—are the goods (*bona*) that marriage allows the spouses to realize in their relationship.[30] The rite of marriage asks that God help the married couple to realize these three goods when it states: "O God, who in creating the human race / willed that man and wife should be *one*, / join, we pray, in a bond of *inseparable love* / these your servants who are to be united in the covenant of Marriage, / so that, as you make their love *fruitful*, / they may become, by your grace, witnesses to charity itself. . . . "[31] Although the goods of marriage are sometimes treated as "blessings or gifts that accrue to the spouses,"[32] or are seen to relate to and overlap with the properties and ends of marriage

---

27. Ramón García de Haro, *Marriage and the Family in the Documents of the Magisterium*, 248.

28. Ibid., 250.

29. Thus the *Code of Canon Law* states: "For matrimonial consent to exist, the contracting parties must be at least not ignorant that marriage is a *permanent* partnership *between a man and a woman* ordered to the *procreation of offspring* by means of some sexual cooperation" (CIC, c. 1096 §1, emphasis added).

30. In Scripture the good of offspring is clearly attested to in Gen 1:28, the good of fidelity in Gen 2:24, and the good of indissolubility in Mt 19:6.

31. RM, "Collect A"; emphasis added.

32. Ignatius Gramunt, "The Essence of Marriage and the *Code of Canon Law*," 380.

in various ways,[33] it is most accurate to view the three goods of marriage in relation to the essence of marriage. Since the essence of marriage is a communion of persons founded in conjugal love, it is the three goods of marriage that provide a further description of the essence of marriage and actually provide the very structure of the communion that the spouses form through their exchange of consent.

In fact, so essential to the essence of marriage are the three goods of fidelity, indissolubility, and fruitfulness that it is not possible to withhold consent to one of these goods and still have a marriage. Fidelity, indissolubility, and fruitfulness are inseparably woven together in the fabric that is marriage. If a potential spouse would exclude any one of the three goods of fidelity, indissolubility, or fruitfulness in the exchange of consent, he or she would not be pledging what conjugal love aspires to and would not want what marriage offers (see CIC, c. 1096 §1; 1101 §2).[34] In this way, the three goods of marriage are so intrinsic to marriage that it is possible to view them not as three separable goods, but as three distinct but inseparable aspects of the one threefold good that is the essence of the conjugal communion of marriage.[35] By entering marriage spouses are pledging to form a communion of persons that is by its very nature faithful, permanent, and procreative. Thus to want marriage means to want the threefold good that defines the communion of persons of marriage. The threefold good of marriage, which structures and further specifies the conjugal communion of persons that is the essence of marriage, in turn implies ends and properties that are constitutive of marriage.

The Ends of Marriage

The definition of marriage in the *Catechism of the Catholic Church* states that marriage "is by its nature ordered toward the good of the spouses and the procreation and education of offspring" (CCC, 1601, citing

---

33. See Mark Lowery, "The Nature and Ends of Marriage," 99.

34. Excluding one of the three goods of marriage through a formal act of the will of one of the spouses invalidates the consent and thus renders the marital contract null, meaning that the marriage never actually existed.

35. I have argued that St. Augustine, who began reflection on the three goods of marriage in Christian theology, saw the goods of marriage not as three separable goods but as one threefold good in Perry J. Cahall, "The Trinitarian Structure of St. Augustine's Good of Marriage," *Augustinian Studies* 34:2 (2003): 223–232.

CIC, c. 1055 §1). This part of the definition points out the objective ends (*finis operis*) of marriage that can be perceived by natural law reasoning and which dictate the *telos* of marriage, where marriage finds its fulfillment and perfection. In other words, everyone should be able to agree that marriage is, by its nature, objectively designed for and ordered toward the procreation and education of children and the good of the spouses. These ends are so central to a proper understanding of marriage that "it is impossible to conceive of the essence [of marriage] without them."[36] As this twofold end of marriage defines the *telos* of the conjugal communion of persons, we need to comment extensively on what each of the ends of marriage encompasses.

First of all, by freely surrendering themselves to each other in the conjugal covenant of marriage, a man and a woman agree to form a communion of persons with each other that is by its very nature potentially procreative. It has already been pointed out that conjugal love "naturally tends toward motherhood and fatherhood" (LF, 7; see also CCC, 2366). The spousal meaning of the body that reveals the capacity of the person to be self-gift (that we discussed in chapter 3) also carries with it a generative meaning (TOB 23:5). A child is the visible fruit of the total gift of self of a husband and a wife, a living sign of their love for each other (FC, 28). Thus a true desire to give oneself completely to one's spouse entails being open to children because the communion of the spouses reaches greater fulfillment in the family (LF, 7). As John Paul II noted:

> In its most profound reality, love is essentially a gift; and conjugal love, while leading the spouses to the reciprocal "knowledge" which makes them "one flesh," does not end with the couple, because it makes them capable of the greatest possible gift, the gift by which they become cooperators with God for giving life to a new human person. Thus the couple, while giving themselves to one another, give not just themselves but also the reality of children, who are a living reflection of their love, a permanent sign of conjugal unity and a living and inseparable synthesis of their being a father and a mother. (FC, 14)

Thus giving oneself totally to one's spouse entails giving one's procreative capacity. Natural law reasoning confirms that "by its very nature the institution of marriage and married love is ordered to the

---

36. James P. Lyons, *The Essential Structure of Marriage*, 30.

procreation and education of the offspring and it is in them that it finds its crowning glory" (CCC, 1652). This is why the rite of marriage states that God has established marriage "for the increase of the human race"[37] and prays that the newly married couple "be blessed with children."[38]

God himself calls married love to be fruitful (Gen 1:28), and precisely because a natural end of marriage is to procreate, the covenant of marriage can only be contracted by a man and a woman who are capable of forging a one-flesh union through sexual intercourse.[39] This underlines the fact, hotly contested by many today, that we do not have the right to marry anyone we love. A person can only marry someone of the opposite sex because only the complementarity of a man and a woman allows for the possibility of procreation, an objective end of marriage and a constitutive element of conjugal love. Also, the fact that marriage can only be contracted by a man and a woman capable of engaging in sexual intercourse shows that in order to contract a marriage a couple must be able to surrender themselves to each other in bodily union.[40] Marriage is more than very deep friendship; it is the mutual handing over of one's entire person to another, a handing over which is fully actualized through sexual intercourse. Thus an inability to consummate marriage through sexual intercourse renders a person incapable of forming a body-soul communion of persons and incapable of entering into and sealing the marital covenant. In addition, sexual intercourse is properly understood as a union of

---

37. RM, "Collect A."

38. RM, "Nuptial Blessing A."

39. Thus the current *Code of Canon Law* states that a marriage is consummated when "the spouses have performed between themselves in a human fashion a conjugal act which is suitable in itself for the procreation of offspring, to which marriage is ordered by its nature and by which the spouses become one flesh" (CIC, c. 1061 §1). The code further specifies, "Antecedent and perpetual impotence to have intercourse, whether on the part of the man or the woman, whether absolute or relative, nullifies marriage by its very nature " (CIC, c. 1084 §1).

40. Jesus himself affirms the necessity of being able to engage in sexual intercourse in order to enter marriage in Mt 19:12 when he points out that there are those who are "eunuchs" from birth, those who are made eunuchs by others, and those who make themselves eunuchs for the kingdom of heaven. A eunuch is a man who is incapable of sexual intercourse either through some type of physical impairment or, in the case of those who have been made eunuchs by others, through mutilation or castration. While the third type of eunuch Jesus mentions refers to those who voluntarily embrace a life of celibacy (which will be discussed in a later chapter) and thereby willingly forego marriage, the first two types of eunuchs that Jesus mentions represent those who are incapable of marrying because they are incapable of sexual intercourse.

sexual organs or genital union. Sexual activity between two people of the same gender is not true sexual intercourse because there is no sexual union, and therefore no personal union, due to a lack of personal complementarity.

To consent freely to marriage is simultaneously to consent to the possibility of becoming a parent. In God's design he calls spouses "to cooperate with the Creator in giving life," populating the world with more little images and likenesses of God (LF, 8) and renewing *"the mystery of creation"* (TOB 21:6). "Begetting is the continuation of creation" (LF, 9), and "the fundamental task of marriage and family is to be at the service of life" (CCC, 1653). By freely choosing marriage, spouses simultaneously choose to be open to the great gift and the great responsibility of procreation (LF, 9). For this reason, anyone who attempts to enter into marriage but simultaneously intends never to have a child is not really married. Although raising children can present challenges, spouses should not see children as burdens or intrusions into their relationship (LF, 11), but instead they should want children for their own sakes (LF, 9) as the "crowning glory" of their love (CCC, 1652). The mutual giving and reception of self by spouses creates the space within which children are to be received as person-gifts (LF, 11). In this way the self-gifting love of the spouses is embodied in the newborn child (LF, 11).

It is important to note that marriage is ordered toward *procreation and education* of offspring, not just biological procreation. Thus, "the fruitfulness of conjugal love is not restricted solely to the procreation of children . . . it is enlarged and enriched by all those fruits of moral, spiritual and supernatural life which the father and mother are called to hand on to their children" (FC, 28). This is why in one of the nuptial blessings the rite of marriage asks God that the couple will "prepare their children / to become members of your heavenly household / by raising them in the way of the Gospel" (RM, "Nuptial Blessing B"). Natural law reasoning dictates that spouses have the obligation and the right to nurture and educate any children that they have.[41] This right and duty is "primordial and inalienable" (CCC, 2221). The fecundity of marriage "extends to the fruits of the moral,

---

41. Thus the *Code of Canon Law* states: "Parents have the most grave duty and the primary right to take care as best they can for the physical, social, cultural, moral and religious education of their offspring" (CIC, c. 1136).

spiritual, and supernatural life" of their children for whom parents serve as the "principal and first educators" (CCC, 1653, 2221). Educating itself is a form of spiritual begetting (LF, 16). Thus, "fatherhood and motherhood represent a *responsibility which is not simply physical but spiritual in nature*" (LF, 10). Those who freely enter into the covenant of marriage are also freely accepting the responsibility of educating children in truth and love, enabling them to experience the fullness of their humanity through a sincere gift of self (LF, 16; CCC, 2223). "The 'communion of persons,' expressed as conjugal love at the beginning of the family, is thus completed and brought to fulfillment in raising children" (LF, 16).

By begetting children, both physically and spiritually, a married couple forms a family which is the "fundamental 'cell' of society" (LF, 13; see also CCC, 2207). "Since marriage by its own natural function transcends the individual interests of the parties involved, it is not to be treated as a private affair but as a social institution of the greatest importance."[42] Thus it is patently false to try to claim that marriage is a "private" agreement. It is not only appropriate, but necessary that a society should codify some of the natural laws pertaining to marriage in positive law, in order to safeguard the good of the spouses, the children, and the community.[43] It is likewise appropriate, and in some ways necessary, for couples to exchange their consent publicly. For ages, societies have recognized the necessity of codifying laws regarding the institution of marriage because marriages have the ability to give societies more citizens. In creating humanity God intended that the first and basic human society would be a natural communion in which a man and a woman would come together as husband and wife, giving the gifts of love and life. The family, understood as a "man and a woman united in marriage, together with their children" is therefore an institution that "is prior to any recognition by public authority, which has an obligation to recognize it" (CCC, 2202). As the family is the first human society (LF, 7) and the basis of all society (GS, 52), only true marriages, out of which the family grows, should be recognized and supported by society (LF, 17; GS, 52). As the family is the foundation of society, if this foundation is healthy

---

42. Ignatius Gramunt, "The Essence of Marriage and the *Code of Canon Law*," 368.
43. Ibid.

then society will be healthy. Likewise, marriage and family cannot be redefined without endangering the rest of society (LF, 17). It is therefore profoundly true to say: "*The future of humanity passes by way of the family*" (FC, 86). The family is thus a "sovereign" society, preceding the state, a society that must be served and supported by the state (LF, 17). True marriages and families have rights, the most fundamental of which are the rights of spouses to the procreation and education of children (LF, 17), a natural end of marriage.

It should be noted that even if the end of procreation is not attainable due to the inability of one or both spouses to produce children, a man and a woman can still be married.[44] "Marriage does not exist solely for the reproduction of another member of the species, but for the creation of a communion of persons;"[45] and regardless of their ability to procreate, by virtue of their male-female complementarity, a husband and a wife have formed a communion of persons that is the essence of marriage. Furthermore, a couple who is unable to produce children can still form the type of union that is by its nature ordered towards procreation. In general, ends (*finis operis*) of a thing should be aspired to and should not be contradicted by the acting agent who chooses what the thing is designed for. However, the ends of a thing may not be able to be realized by the agent. For instance, a physician who chooses to practice medicine in accord with the end (*finis operis*) of healing his or her patients, may not be able to heal a particular patient because there is no known cure for a disease, or because of a lack of expertise. Likewise, the reality that a particular married couple may not be able to procreate, due to factors beyond their control, does not change the fact that by its nature their union is the type of union that is ordered toward having babies.

It is also essential to point out that every marriage filled with conjugal love is truly fruitful.[46] "The fact that the closest communion of love between two people" can produce a child shows that by its nature love is fruitful.[47] This fruitfulness, which flows from male-female

---

44. Thus the *Code of Canon Law* states: "Sterility neither prohibits nor nullifies marriage," (CIC, c. 1084 §3).

45. United States Conference of Catholic Bishops, Pastoral Letter, "Marriage: Love and Life in the Divine Plan," (Washington, DC: USCCB Publishing, 2009), 10.

46. Dietrich von Hildebrand, *Marriage: The Mystery of Faithful Love*, 30.

47. Ibid.

complementarity, is spiritual as well as biological. True conjugal love possesses a spiritual fruitfulness that fosters spiritual and moral growth.[48] Love, by its nature is life giving. Thus even a marriage that is childless due to the inability to procreate serves a communion of love while a sexual union outside of marriage that produces a child does not.[49] Even a man and a woman who are incapable of generating biological progeny, and thus incapable of realizing the end of procreation and education of children, can still experience true fruitfulness through conjugal communion. Such a couple can also achieve the other end of marriage, which is the promotion of the good of the spouses.

Just as we have discussed what is encompassed by the end of procreation and education of children, it is also important to understand what is included in the end of *the good of the spouses* or the mutual assistance (*mutuum adiutorium*) which marriage has as an end. First of all, the "good of the spouses" as an objective end of marriage is *not* to be equated with the conjugal love that the spouses pledged to each other and which is the essence of their conjugal communion.[50] Making this false equation would result in mistakenly separating and perhaps even dissociating the end of procreation from conjugal love. In contrast to this misperception Karol Wojtyla stated that "the interior and essential *raison d'être* of marriage is not only to become a family, but above all to constitute a durable personal union of a man and a woman based on love. First and foremost, marriage serves existence . . . but is based on love."[51] As "the love of husband and wife . . . pervades all the duties of married life and holds pride of place in Christian marriage" (CC, 23), both the end of procreation and the mutual assistance of the spouses take place within the context of conjugal love. Conjugal love is of the essence of marriage, it is not an end.

Secondly, speaking of the "good of the spouses" as an objective end of marriage is not to be understood as coterminous with the subjective "happiness" of the spouses. It is simply the case that one or

48. Ibid.

49. Ibid., 31.

50. Ramón García de Haro, *Marriage and the Family in the Documents of the Magisterium*, 100, 200. In *Love and Responsibility*, trans. Grzegorz Ignatik (Boston: Pauline Books & Media, 2013), 52, John Paul II (Karol Wojtyla) also made the point that the love should not be confused with an end of marriage.

51. Karol Wojtyla, *Love and Responsibility*, 202.

the other spouse in a marriage will not always be subjectively "happy." While a man and a woman contemplating marriage may have a reasonable expectation of finding subjective happiness together, the purpose of marriage is not the subjective individual "fulfillment" of each spouse. Ultimately no human relationship is capable of providing absolute subjective fulfillment. Couples who get married because they think they have found the person who has the ability *to make* them happy will soon be disappointed and disenchanted. These unrealistic expectations for one's spouse and for marriage are perhaps why many couples get divorced. I often tell students that I am convinced that the reason why many couples get divorced is precisely because they entered into marriage with the unrealistic expectation that their spouse had the ability or perhaps even the obligation *to make* them happy. Once the couple experiences difficulties or disenchantment in their marriage, which will inevitably happen, they blame marriage, or their spouse, for not providing what they thought they were owed. They buy into the fallacy of thinking, "If I had just married the right person I would be happy, but because I am not happy I must have married the wrong person." One spouse placing the responsibility on the other spouse of fulfilling their heart's desire for happiness is ultimately unjust. It is placing a burden on one's spouse that he or she cannot bear and that will ultimately crush him or her. God is the only one who can fill the deepest desires of the human heart, providing for our happiness and fulfillment in every respect.

As was noted in the chapter on conjugal love, there is nothing in the wedding vows about what one hopes to get from marriage, only what one promises to give. "The words of consent . . . express what is essential to the common good of the spouses" (LF, 10), namely, "love, fidelity, honor, the permanence of their union until death" (LF, 10). The essence of marriage, as a faithful, permanent, and fruitful communion of persons, offers the structure that provides for the objective good of the spouses as persons who are made in the image and likeness of God called to be self-gifts. Even if one spouse proves to be disagreeable or contentious, thus detracting from the subjective happiness of the other spouse, marriage still provides the opportunity for the "unhappy" spouse to progress in the good. As was pointed out in the chapter on conjugal love, through self-sacrificial love in fidelity to the vows of the marital covenant, even an "unhappy" spouse can still grow in human perfection. By its nature marriage provides the context within which spouses can assist each other to grow in virtue and in their humanity by growing in their ability to live as gift for each other. This can happen even in "unhappy" marriages.[52] Feelings do not constitute the essence of love or marriage. The essence of marital consent is the handing over of oneself to form a communion of persons in service to the good of one's spouse in a permanent, faithful, and fruitful relationship, *no matter what*. Thus by forging a marital covenant spouses become life partners, pledging to assist each other come what may. Even if unintentionally, or in spite of himself or herself, a disagreeable spouse can assist his or her partner in growing in the good (more will be said about this in the chapters dealing with married spirituality).

Part of providing for the good of the spouses means that marriage provides a "remedy for concupiscence" (*remedium concupiscentiae*).[53] This does not mean that marriage provides a definitive cure for the disordered desires of concupiscence against which we will always have to struggle in a fallen world, but marriage as a "remedy for concupiscence" does mean that marriage helps to ameliorate and redirect these disordered desires. Marriage as a "remedy for concupiscence" has sometimes been misunderstood as marriage providing the opportunity for sexual satisfaction, or marriage providing some type of outlet for indulging in sexual lust. Far from providing some type of excuse for sexual indulgence, providing a "remedy for concupiscence" means that marriage provides the context in which the couple can direct and

---

52. By referring to "unhappy" marriages this is not referring to situations of abuse. Anyone has the right, and the obligation, to remove herself or himself from an abusive situation. In the case of spousal abuse this would necessarily entail separation.

53. Throughout Church history, oftentimes the "remedy for concupiscence," a concept based on the Pauline texts found in 1 Cor 7:2, 3, 5, 9, has been presented as a distinct end of marriage (see Mark Lowery, *Living the Good Life*, 99). In *Love and Responsibility* John Paul II (Karol Wojtyla) commented on the primary end (*procreatio*), the secondary end (*mutuum adiutorium*), and the tertiary end (*remedium concupiscentiae*) of marriage that have been commented on in traditional teachings on marriage (*Love and Responsibility*, 50–53). However, more recently neither the documents of Vatican II, the 1983 *Code of Canon Law*, nor the *Catechism of the Catholic Church* refer to the *remedium concupiscentiae* as a distinct end of marriage. In "The Essence of Marriage and the *Code of Canon Law*," Ignatius Gramunt noted, "Traditional theology has included the *remedium concupiscentiae* among the ends of marriage in order to emphasize both the goodness of sexual acts within marriage and the evil of those acts outside of marriage or contrary to it" (378). However, I would argue that it is better to treat the *remedium concupiscentiae* as part of the mutual support and good of the spouses, since this is one aspect of the overall support that the spouses provide to each other.

order their sexual desire in accord with conjugal love, thus growing in virtue and struggling against the selfish inclinations of sexual concupiscence.[54] "Marriage, precisely as a channel for chaste sexuality, remains a prime opportunity to avoid the disordered use of that sexuality."[55] Thus, pledging to offer one's life in service to the good of one's spouse means striving to master oneself through chastity in order to give oneself as a gift (more will be said about this in the chapter on sexual morality). Marriage provides a remedy for concupiscence by providing the structure in which spouses can mutually assist each other to grow in chastity.

Traditionally, the *primary* end of marriage has been referred to as the end of procreation and education, or life, while the *secondary* end has been referred to as the good and mutual support of the spouses.[56] This distinction, while helpful, is often misunderstood and needs to be explained.[57] First of all, to designate a hierarchy of ends of marriage is not to establish a hierarchy of value pertaining to those

---

54. Contextualizing the *remedium concupiscentiae* with respect to the mutual assistance spouses provide each other can mitigate against inappropriately misconstruing the phrase "remedy for concupiscence."

55. Mark Lowery, *Living the Good Life*, 10.

56. St. Thomas affirmed the primary and secondary ends of marriage (ST Suppl., q. 41, a. 1). The 1917 *Code of Canon Law* explicitly mentioned the primary and secondary ends of marriage (c. 1013 §1). Pius XI affirmed the distinction between primary and secondary ends of marriage in *Casti Connubii* (see CC, 59). Pius XII reaffirmed this distinction in several addresses (see Charles A. Schleck, *The Sacrament of Matrimony: A Dogmatic Study* [Milwaukee: Bruce, 1964], 30–34), and during his pontificate the Holy Office affirmed the primary and secondary ends of marriage, making it clear that the secondary end is subordinate to the primary end (DS, 3838). However, much has been written about the fact that neither Vatican II, the 1983 *Code of Canon Law*, nor the *Catechism of the Catholic Church* refers to primary or secondary ends of marriage. Mark Lowery discusses the debate that has ensued since Vatican II about whether the language of *primary* and *secondary* ends should be maintained. I agree with Lowery's position in *Living the Good Life* "that the traditional hierarchy of ends remains intact" (98). John Haas reaches the same conclusion in "The Contemporary World," *Christian Marriage: A Historical Study*, ed. Glenn W. Olsen (New York: Crossroad, 2001), 340–352. This position is confirmed, as will be noted, by the fact that John Paul II has supported the traditional hierarchy of ends (TOB 20:3; 30:3; 127:3). I will attempt to explain why this distinction, if understood properly, is not only helpful but necessary for understanding marriage.

57. Mark Lowery pointed out that while *Gaudium et Spes* did not use the language of primary and secondary ends, it did affirm the reality that this traditional terminology expressed, rightly understood. Lowery, and others cited by Lowery, have pointed out that the abandonment of the traditional philosophical terminology of primary and secondary ends in *Gaudium et Spes* was a choice by the bishops at Vatican II not to use terms which are easily misunderstood (*Living the Good Life*, 105).

ends.[58] It is not saying that the good of the spouses is somehow of less value than the procreation and education of children. It is also not saying that the good of the spouses as a secondary end only has value as a means to attain the primary end of procreation.[59] If this were the case, then by definition it would turn the good of the spouses into a means instead of an end. Far from attempting to designate a hierarchy of value, the "ranking" of the primary and secondary ends of marriage is meant to point out what distinguishes marriage from other relationships which could also serve the good of the persons in these relationships, through some type of mutual assistance they provide to each other.[60] In other words, to say that the procreation and education of children is the *primary* end of marriage is to point out what is most distinctive about this type of relationship, and what makes it unique among all types of human relationships.[61] As Mark Lowery has aptly noted, "If one eliminates the primary end of children, one loses the distinctiveness of the marital relationship as compared to other types of relationships, and thereby loses a prime *reason* for the permanence and exclusivity of marriage, not to mention heterosexuality."[62] Thus, while mutual support of the spouses is essential to marriage as an end (*finis operis*) that determines the very nature of marriage, it is a secondary end that is "subordinate" to the primary end of procreation and education of offspring. This is not in terms of value or as a means to an end, but in terms of defining the distinctiveness of marriage.[63]

58. Mark Lowery, *Living the Good Life*, 104.

59. John C. Ford and Gerald Kelly, "The Essential Subordination of the Secondary Ends of Marriage," in *Marriage*, Readings in Moral Theology No. 15, ed. Charles E. Curran and Julie Hanlon Rubio (New York: Paulist Press, 2009), 23; originally published in *Contemporary Moral Theology*, vol. 2: Marriage Questions (Westminister, MD: Newman, 1963).

60. Mark Lowery, *Living the Good Life*, 104.

61. To call procreation and education of offspring the primary end of marriage is to identify philosophically "the final cause of marriage, that is, the cause or purpose that specifies marriage as a distinct reality" (Mark Pilon, *Magnum Mysterium*, 245). Thus John Haas rightly pointed out that the understanding of the primary and secondary ends of marriage is a matter of metaphysics (see Haas, "The Contemporary World," 349–352).

62. Mark Lowery, *Living the Good Life*, 111.

63. While Ford and Kelly were correct with regard to the subordination, rightly understood, of the mutual help of spouses to the procreation and education of children ("The Essential Subordination of the Secondary Ends of Marriage," 23–24), they discussed secondary ends of marriage delineated as "mutual help, conjugal love, and the remedy for concupiscence" (24). I think Ford and Kelly were incorrect in listing conjugal love as a secondary end of marriage, since conjugal love is of the essence of marriage. The other secondary ends listed by Ford and Kelly are consistent with the language of Pius XI in *Casti Connubii*, who spoke of the "cultivation of

Now that we have presented the proper understanding of procreation and education as the *primary* end of marriage and the good of the spouses as the *secondary* end, we need to stress that neither end can be separated from the other in a proper understanding of marriage. Marriage is essentially ordered to *both* ends, and as the twofold end of marriage, neither end is in competition with the other. It is not possible to choose either one end or the other. In fact, the two ends mutually interpenetrate each other in the dynamic reality of conjugal love. The primary end of procreation and education of children implies the secondary end of the good of the spouses. "The good of the spouses is implied in, and inseparable from, the procreative/educative end, for the work of procreation and education requires that the spouses give each other those goods needed to fulfill their role as parents."[64] Not only does the good of the spouses help to fulfill the procreative/educative end, but the procreative/educative end also serves to realize the good of the spouses. Part of the "mutual inward molding" that takes place in marriage to perfect the spouses takes place in and through the procreation and education of children (see CC, 24). "Indeed children are the supreme gift of marriage and greatly contribute to the well-being of the parents themselves" (GS, 50) helping to sanctify them (GS, 48). Welcoming children into a marriage refines the love of the spouses for each other and causes them to mature. Children increase the need for selfless loving because there are new needs for the spouses to put before their own individual needs. Procreation also brings about the possibility of a husband and wife "knowing" each other through their child (TOB 21:3–4). New aspects of the husband and wife, now become a father and a mother, are revealed, and the couple tend to each other in a new way as they together tend to the needs of their offspring. In this way, children

---

mutual love" and not conjugal love itself as a secondary end of marriage (CC, 59). However, speaking of secondary ends is less helpful than speaking about the one secondary end of the good or mutual support of the spouses that includes different dimensions. Also, Ford and Kelly spoke of the secondary ends of marriage as essential to marriage but as less "important" or less "fundamental" than procreation (23). The designation of the secondary end(s) of marriage as less important or less fundamental can be confusing. Procreation can be seen as more important and more fundamental than the good of the spouses with respect to the larger social implications of marriage and its necessity for perpetuating the human race. Also, procreation is more important and more fundamental to understanding the uniqueness of marriage, since the good of the persons can be achieved in other relationships.

64. Ignatius Gramunt, "The Essence of Marriage and the *Code of Canon Law*," 378.

"consolidate" the marriage covenant, "enriching and deepening the conjugal communion of the father and mother" (LF, 7).[65] Thus the two ends of marriage relate in such a way that the "good of the spouses is infused into the mutual aid for the children," and "procreativity, without losing its own autonomy, is infused into the good of the spouses."[66] Therefore, John Paul II aptly stated that "the traditional teaching on the ends of marriage (and on their hierarchy) is confirmed and at the same time deepened from the point of view of the interior life of the spouses, of conjugal and familial spirituality" (TOB 127:3).[67]

Just as neither the procreation and education of children nor the good of mutual support of the spouses can be separated from marriage as natural ends of conjugal communion, neither can either of these ends be separated from that act which is properly the right of spouses, the conjugal act. In sexual intercourse, "the spouses' union achieves the twofold end of marriage; the good of spouses and the transmission of life" (CCC, 2363). Natural law reasoning should enable people to see "the fundamental structure of the conjugal act" as an expression of spousal love that has a unique life-giving potential, and thereby to understand "the inseparable connection . . . between the unitive significance and the procreative significance which are both inherent to the conjugal act" (HV, 12). The inseparability of these two ends of sexual intercourse is the "relevant principle of conjugal morality" (TOB 121:6). Engaging in the conjugal act, "it is not enough to take only the good intention and the evaluation of motives [the *finis operantis*] into account: objective criteria [*finis operis*] must be used"

---

65. John Paul II noted: "When this [enriching and deepening of the conjugal communion] does not occur [with the presence of children], we need to ask if the selfishness which lurks even in the love of man and woman as a result of the human inclination to evil is not stronger than this love. Married couples need to be well aware of this. From the outset they need to have their hearts and thoughts turned toward God 'from whom every family is named,' *so that their fatherhood and motherhood will draw from that source the power to be continually renewed in love*" (LF 7; (italics in original).

66. Mark Lowery, *Living the Good Life*, 101.

67. John Paul II affirmed the hierarchy of the ends of marriage elsewhere when he commented on God's original intention for marriage stating: "This communion had been intended to make man and woman mutually happy through the search of a simple and pure union in humanity, through a reciprocal offering of themselves, that is, through the experience of the gift of the person expressed with soul and body, with masculinity and femininity—'flesh of my flesh' (Gen 2:23)—and finally through the *subordination* of such a union to the blessing of fruitfulness with 'procreation'" (TOB 30:3; emphasis added).

(GS, 51; CCC, 2368). This means that one spouse cannot use another as a "baby-making instrument" and disregard or oppose the good of the spouse and the loving union that is an end of the conjugal act. Likewise, because "the unitive significance and the procreative significance . . . are both inherent to the marriage act" (HV, 12; CCC, 2366), this also means that "each and every marital act must of necessity retain its intrinsic relationship to the procreation of human life" (HV, 11; CCC, 2366). Thus spouses cannot express love for each other in sexual intercourse and deliberately oppose the procreative potential of that act without simultaneously undermining the good of each other and their communion of love. As the *Catechism* states: "A child does not come from outside as something added on to the mutual love of the spouses, but springs from the very heart of that mutual giving, as its fruit and fulfillment" (CCC, 2366). Spouses, therefore, cannot seek to totally hand themselves over to each other in the marital act and simultaneously seek to withhold the gift of their fertility from each other. This denies the body-soul unity of the person and thus wounds the dignity of the person and the personal act of sexual inter-course as an expression of total self-giving. More will be said about this in the chapters on sexual morality and responsible parenthood. For now, it is sufficient to draw attention to the inseparability of procreation and the good of the spouses as ends of marriage and ends of the marital act.

The Properties of Marriage

The definition of marriage found in the *Code of Canon Law* and the *Catechism* states that in forging a marital covenant "a man and a woman establish between themselves a partnership of the whole of life" (CIC, c. 1055 §1; CCC, 1601). That the partnership of marriage is established between one man and one woman refers to the unity of marriage, and that this partnership is for the whole of life refers to the indissolubility of marriage. These characteristics of unity and indis-solubility are traditionally referred to as "essential properties of marriage" (CIC, c. 1056). A property of something is a necessary characteristic for the thing to be what it is and to achieve the ends for which it is designed. The properties of unity and indissolubility are attested to in Scripture when Genesis affirms that "a man leaves his father and his mother and cleaves to his wife, and they become one flesh" (Gen 2:24). These properties are reaffirmed by Jesus when he quotes Gen 2:24 stating, "So they are no longer two but one flesh. What therefore God has joined together, let not man put asunder" (Mt 19:6). These same properties are attested to in the rite of marriage in one of the nuptial blessings with the following lines: "O God, who . . . making the woman an inseparable helpmate to the man, that they might no longer be two, but one flesh, and taught that what you were pleased to make one must never be divided . . . " (RM, "Nuptial Blessing A"). Natural law requires both of the properties of unity and indissolubility as they pertain to marriage. These properties are consistent with the nature of conjugal love as faithful and permanent, as well as with the corresponding goods of marriage. These same properties also serve the ends of marriage, the procreation and education of children as well as the good and mutual support of the spouses.

"Unity means that marriage by its nature consists of the union of one man and one woman."[68] Thus by its nature marriage is monogamous and exclusive, excluding polygamy or polyandry. This property is implied by the good of fidelity as an exclusive gift of one spouse to the other. The unity and fidelity of marriage respects the dignity of each spouse who is treated as a unique and unrepeatable gift. The unity of marriage also provides for the mutual support of the spouses as they embrace the common project of raising children. Therefore both the good of the spouses and the good of the children require absolute fidelity (CCC, 1646), and thus the property of unity.

Indissolubility means that the union *cannot be dissolved* by the parties themselves or by any human power. Only death dissolves the marriage bond, and for that reason it is said to be permanent. An "unbreakable union of their two lives" is formed in the two spouses becoming one (CCC, 1605). The covenant in which a man and a woman give themselves totally to each other is the source of the indissolubility of marriage. "By its very nature the gift of the person must be lasting and irrevocable" (LF, 11). The indissolubility of the marital covenant serves the good of the spouses and children and is *the basis of the common good of the family*" (LF, 7). This permanence also provides for

---

68. Ignatius Gramunt, "The Essence of Marriage and the *Code of Canon Law*," 379.

mutual support of spouses throughout life. The indissolubility of marriage means that each spouse can fully give himself or herself to the other without being anxious about the future prospects of their gift being rejected. The objective, irrevocable bond of marriage thus helps love grow by giving it the stability it needs to perfect itself. The permanence of marriage also provides a stable environment for children, and the firm foundation for society that rests upon the family.

Together, the properties of unity and indissolubility allow spouses to be truly vulnerable to each other, baring themselves to each other. Without these properties it would be too risky to be vulnerable in a relationship that could end at any moment and in which one's gift was not valued as exclusive and unrepeatable. The essential properties of unity and indissolubility respect the full dignity of the persons united in marriage, mitigating against one spouse treating the other spouse as "an object of use."[69] Thus the properties of marriage make it possible to pursue the ends of marriage. These properties are in fact necessary qualities for realizing the ends of marriage, because a union that lacks unity and is temporary or transitory is not truly capable of procreating *and* educating children, nor of respecting and serving the true good of the spouses. These properties are essential characteristics of the reality that a couple chooses when they choose to get married.

---

69. Karol Wojtyla, *Love and Responsibility*, 195. Wojtyla comments on the properties of unity (under the heading of monogamy) and indissolubility on pages 195–200.

Chapter 6

Choosing Marriage: The Primordial Sacrament

CHOOSING MARRIAGE

The preceding discussion of the covenant, essence, goods, ends, and properties of marriage allows us to understand the nature of marriage and thus to answer the question, "What is marriage?" This is a question about which our contemporary culture is very confused.[1] Pope Francis has noted, "Marriage now tends to be viewed as a form of mere emotional satisfaction that can be constructed in any way or modified at will" (EG, 66). In reality, a man and a woman enter into the state of marriage as a result of forging a covenant. In this covenant they freely hand themselves over to each other through the mutual exchange of irrevocable consent in order to form a communion of persons. This communion is faithful, permanent, and fruitful. Furthermore, the couple pledges to serve the primary end of procreation and education of children as well as the secondary end of the good of each other, the attainment of which requires the properties of unity and indissolubility. This understanding of marriage is part of natural law and is ascertainable to all people.

---

1. Several recent books that have tried to engage the larger culture regarding the nature of marriage from philosophical, historical, and sociological perspectives include: Sherif Girgis, Ryan T. Anderson, and Robert P. George, *What is Marriage? Man and Woman: A Defense* (New York: Encounter Books, 2012); Elizabeth Fox-Genovese, *Marriage: The Dream That Refuses to Die*, ed. Sheila O'Connor-Ambrose (Wilmington, DE: ISI Books, 2008); Dale O'Leary, *One Man, One Woman: A Catholic's Guide to Defending Marriage* (Manchester, NH: Sophia Institute Press, 2007); Robert P. George and Jean Bethke Elshtain, eds., *The Meaning of Marriage: Family, State, Market, and Morals* (Dallas: Spence Publishing Co., 2006); and Linda J. Waite and Maggie Gallagher, *The Case for Marriage: Why Married People are Happier, Healthier, and Better Off Financially* (New York: Doubleday, 2000).

This natural law understanding of marriage used to be common knowledge and "part of the air that people breathed." In generations past, when the average marrying age was much younger, teenage prospective spouses knew that marriage involved handing themselves over to each other to form a union that was intrinsically faithful, fruitful, and forever. They understood that they were entering into a relationship that was potentially procreative, a goal they sought, and that in this relationship they were supposed to support each other in the unity and the permanence of their marital relationship. Any man and woman exchanging mutual consent with this understanding of the conjugal communion, to which they are committing themselves, contract a valid marriage. Furthermore, they forge a marital covenant regardless of the abundance or lack of emotion and sentiment that is present at the time they exchange their vows. The objective covenant remains regardless of the vicissitudes of their subjective emotional states. We must remember that *marriage (like love) is not based on feelings; it is based on a free commitment to an objective reality—a reality with ascertainable characteristics to which the couple surrenders themselves when they exchange their consent.*

Consider the example of arranged marriages, which can be valid marriages if freely consented to by the couple. The idea of arranged marriages seems bizarre to most people in Western culture, and I am not advocating a return to them. However, I am using them to make a point about the nature of marriage. In an arranged marriage a couple may have minimal feelings for each other before they exchange their mutual consent. Yet, understanding the nature of marriage they can pledge conjugal love to each other, trusting that the feelings of love will come later. I once heard a couple from India, whose marriage had been arranged, speak of their situation. They explained that while Americans think a couple must feel deeply in love with each other before getting married, in their culture couples choose to get married and then learn how to love each other. It is possible for a couple in an arranged marriage to contract a marriage with subjective purposes (like marrying for wealth, or to solidify a treaty between two families or two nations) alongside the ends, goods, and properties of marriage, but as long as their purposes do not contradict the natural ends, goods, and properties of marriage, they are married. However, if a couple intends to form a union that is not faithful, or permanent, or open to children, or in which they intend to sadistically thwart the good of each other, then they are not committing to the reality that is marriage.[2]

Today there is nothing in the "air that we breathe" that allows a young person to know exactly what the objective reality of marriage is. The term "marriage" is sometimes used equivocally to refer to different types of civilly sanctioned relationships. Often, and sadly, marriage is reduced to a relationship of convenience in which the spouses seek personal satisfaction and subjective, self-defined "happiness," often understood as emotional well-being. With this deficient and flawed understanding of marriage, if either one of the spouses reaches the subjective conclusion that this "happiness" cannot be attained, he or she seeks to end the relationship. One can raise the legitimate question as to whether some couples understand enough about the reality of marriage to be able to contract a marital covenant (this question will be dealt with in chapter 16 when we briefly discuss annulments granted by the Church). However, because the nature of marriage *can* be understood by natural reason it will always be possible for a man and a woman to commit themselves to the reality of marriage. When they do so, a couple is committing themselves to an institution created by God, and they become in some way a sign of God's love.

MARRIAGE AS THE PRIMORDIAL SACRAMENT

As we come to see the nature of marriage we can also see that marriage is the primordial sacrament, or first sign, of the love that God offers to humanity. Marriage is created by God, who endows it with its essence, goods, ends, and properties. Therefore, marriage is a *created reality*, always bearing some reference to God, and is never a merely "secular reality."[3] "Marriage, then, is far from being the effect of chance or the result of the blind evolution of natural forces. It is in

---

2. This is why St. Thomas Aquinas, regarding the goods of fidelity and offspring said, "They are caused in matrimony by the marriage pact itself, so that if anything contrary to these were expressed in the consent which makes a marriage, the marriage would be invalid" (ST Suppl., q. 49, a. 3). He also said in the same article that "there is no matrimony without inseparability."

3. Peter J. Elliott, *What God Has Joined*, 10–11. This is a critique of Edward Schillebeeckx, who throughout *Marriage: Human Reality and Saving Mystery*, trans. N.D. Smith, 2 vols. (New York: Sheed and Ward, 1965) refers to marriage as a "secular" reality.

reality the wise and provident institution of God the Creator, whose purpose was to effect in man His loving design." (HV, 8). In his design the Triune God offers spouses "a way of sharing as creatures in his own union and communion, through the created reality of gender, through sexuality and procreation, through the community of life and love that is the family."[4] Thus, one of the Prefaces in the Rite of Marriage states:

> For you willed that the human race,
> created by the gift of your goodness,
> should be raised to such high dignity
> that in the union of husband and wife
> you might bestow a true image of your love. (RM, "Preface C")

This image can be seen in the covenant of marriage, its essence, goods, ends, and properties, thus making marriage the primordial sign or sacrament of God's love in the created order.

The *covenant* of marriage is supposed to be a sign of God's covenantal love for humanity. In the rite of marriage, one of the nuptial blessings states:

> O God, who, to reveal the great design you formed in your love,
> willed that the love of spouses for each other
> should foreshadow the covenant you graciously made with
>   your people . . . (RM, "Nuptial Blessing B")

This blessing claims that in God's plan, the mutual love of husband and wife is a sign of his covenantal love for his people. Thus in God's design married love is "an image of the absolute and unfailing love with which God loves man" (CCC, 1605). As John Paul II said:

> The communion of love between God and people, a fundamental part of the Revelation and faith experience of Israel, finds a meaningful expression in the marriage covenant which is established between a man and a woman.
>
> For this reason the central word of Revelation, "God loves His people," is likewise proclaimed through the living and concrete word whereby a man and a woman express their conjugal love. Their bond of love becomes the image and the symbol of the covenant which unites God and His people. (FC, 12)

---

4. Ibid., 41. Although Elliott made this comment specific to the Sacrament of Marriage in the Church, this statement applies to all natural marriages.

The Triune God of the covenant who created freely out of love allows his creative freedom to be imaged in the free choice of the marital covenant.[5] Only persons, who image the Triune God, are capable of this type of conscious and free choice (LF, 8). The free choice that a man and a woman make to get married and to live out the truth of married love is meant to be, in God's design, a reflection of the free offering of love that God makes of himself to humanity in the very gift of creation. Entering into the covenant of marriage, a man and a woman choose to make a sincere and irrevocable gift of themselves. This is meant to be a sign of the covenant that God forges with his people when he makes the irrevocable pledge, "I will be your God, and you will be my people" (see Ex 6:7; Lev 26:12; Jer 30:22; Ez 36:28; Hos 2:23).

The *essence* of marriage as a conjugal communion of persons "shows forth in this world something of the love of the Father, Son and Holy Spirit."[6] *"Only persons are capable of living 'in communion'"* (LF, 7), and as was discussed in the chapter on theological anthropology, by creating humanity male and female in his image and likeness, God enables spouses to form a communion of persons that images the divine communion of Persons. As was also pointed out, this communion of persons is expressed through the spouses' bodies as they solidify their conjugal covenant by becoming one flesh (LF, 8). The family, founded on the marital covenant and issuing forth from the one-flesh union of husband and wife, also exists as a "communion of persons" capable of reflecting the divine communion of Persons (LF, 7). The "family is a communion of persons, a sign and image of the communion of the Father and the Son and the Holy Spirit" (CCC, 2205). Thus the "communion of persons" of marriage and the family "is drawn in a certain sense from the Mystery of the Trinitarian 'We'" (LF, 8). "The family, which originates in the love of man and woman, ultimately derives from the mystery of God" (LF, 8; see Eph 3:14–16),[7] the infinitely intimate communion of Persons.

---

5. Peter J. Elliott, *What God Has Joined*, 41.

6. Ibid., 39.

7. We need to exercise caution in presenting the family as an analogy to the Trinity without qualification. I agree with Peter Elliott when he stated: "Such an analogy is not wholly satisfactory, not only because it depends on our understanding of 'person,' in human terms leading to tritheism, but also because it raises the problem of appropriation. To whom in a family do you assign the terms 'Son' and 'Holy Spirit'? But, if the family can only give us a faint or inaccurate

All marriages in which the spouses pledge to realize the three *goods of marriage*, are signs of God's love, however faint. The three goods of marriage, that provide the very structure of the conjugal communion of persons, help us to understand the covenantal love that God offers to humanity. The *faithful* love of spouses is supposed to be a sign of the fidelity of God's love (CCC, 1648). The *indissoluble* love of spouses is intended by God to reflect His irrevocable offering of self to his people: "I will be your God" (Ex 6:7). Finally, spousal love opens the spouses up to creating with God (procreating) a new image and likeness of God, thus imaging God's superabundant, *fruitful* love. Therefore, "in the procreation and education of children [marriage] reflects the Father's work of creation" (CCC, 2205). In addition, marriage as a communion of persons structured by conjugal love reflects something of God's inner life. The three distinct, but inseparable aspects of the one threefold good of marriage provide an analogy to the Triune life of God. The essence of marriage is a communion of conjugal love with the three distinct but inseparable aspects of fidelity, permanence, and fruitfulness. It seems reasonable to see in the Triune good of married love a trace or vestige of the Trinity that St. Augustine said can be found throughout creation.[8]

The three inseparable goods of marriage imply the *ends* and *properties* of the conjugal communion of persons, which can also be seen to refer to God. By endowing marriage with procreation and education of children as an end, God calls spouses "to a special sharing in His love and in His power as Creator and Father, through their free

---

analogy of God the Trinity, moving in the opposite direction, from God, we can see something of the Holy Trinity given to Marriage and the family" (*What God Has Joined*, 39–40). Elliott was pointing out that it would be inappropriate to try to match up the Persons of the Trinity with the persons of the human family, because God is a Trinity and not a tri-unity or triplicity (ST I, q. 31, a. 1, ad 3). We cannot reverse the polarity of the principle of analogy and project human realities onto the inner life of God. We should never allow ourselves to forget "the radical dissimilarity between the triune God and the reality of the human family" (Scola, *The Nuptial Mystery*, 285). Cardinal Marc Ouellet discussed the familial analogy to the Trinity extensively; he pointed out that the basis of the analogy between the human family and the Trinity should not be sought in "the correspondence between the persons" of the family and the Persons of the Trinity [trying to match up person to Person], but in the correspondence between the "communion of persons" of the family and the communion of Persons of the Trinity (*Divine Likeness: Toward a Trinitarian Anthropology of the Family*, trans. Philip Milligan and Linda M. Cicone [Grand Rapids, MI: Eerdmans, 2006], 34). Thus, it is the dynamic of interpersonal love and the mutual giving and receiving of persons in the family that provides us with an analogy to the Trinity (ibid.). This is precisely the analogy that John Paul II presented in his *Theology of the Body* and in other writings.

8. Augustine, *The Trinity*, trans. Edmund Hill, WSA I.5 (1991), VI.2.12.

and responsible cooperation in transmitting the gift of human life" (FC, 28). "Thus the fundamental task of the family is to serve life, to actualize in history the original blessing of the Creator—that of transmitting by procreation the divine image from person to person" (FC, 28). The secondary end of mutual support of the spouses shows God's loving care for human persons, always seeking our good, our restoration, and our renewal. The properties of unity and indissolubility that are intrinsic to marriage in order to provide for the good of the couple and children are also willed by God as a sign of his indelibly faithful love for man (FC, 20). Thus the communion of life and love that is marriage is a primordial sign of the life and love that God offers to humanity.

The preceding discussion should help to explain why John Paul II called marriage the "primordial sacrament." John Paul II pointed out that "man appears in the visible world as the highest expression of the divine gift, because he bears within himself the inner dimension of the gift" (TOB 19:3). Since man, as a person-gift made in the image and likeness of God, is the highest expression of the divine gift, John Paul II said:

> A primordial sacrament is constituted, understood as a sign that efficaciously transmits in the visible world the invisible mystery hidden in God from eternity. . . . The sacrament, as a visible sign, is constituted with man, inasmuch as he is a "body," through his "visible" masculinity and femininity. The body, in fact, and only the body, is capable of making visible what is invisible: the spiritual and the divine. It has been created to transfer into the visible reality of the world the mystery hidden from eternity in God, and thus to be a sign of it. (TOB 19:4)

So humanity made male and female, is the primordial sign of God's love. Marriage, to which man and woman are naturally inclined, is created by God to be the first and constant reminder of his love for humanity. What is more, in the beginning the primordial sacrament of marriage was an efficacious sign, truly effecting what it signified. This is because, as John Paul II explains:

> *The institution of marriage* . . . was to serve not only to extend the work of creation, or procreation, but also to spread the same sacrament of creation to further generations of human beings, that is, to spread the supernatural

fruits of man's eternal election by the Father in the eternal Son, the fruits man was endowed with by God in the very act of creation." (TOB 96:7)

Thus, before sin entered the world, marriage was intended to transmit to successive generations the grace which God gifted to our first parents.

John Paul II explained that the primordial sacrament of marriage was created to be a sign of the "mystery hidden from ages in God" (TOB 95b:6). This mystery "is God's intention for mankind to participate in divine Trinitarian life for all eternity."[9] From the beginning, marriage was created to be a sign of this mystery. As marriage was created to be a sign of God's love and his intention to draw humanity into his infinite communion of love, it was also created to be a sign of the "great mystery" (Eph 5:32) of Christ's relationship with the Church. John Paul II calls this the "sacrament of redemption" (TOB 97:2). It is this "great mystery" that "constitutes the fulfillment and concretization" of God's intention to draw humanity into his own divine life (TOB 95b:7). Moreover, the great mystery of "the sacrament of redemption clothes itself, so to speak, in the figure and form of the primordial sacrament" (TOB 97:2). John Paul II explained, "The Mystery hidden from all eternity in God—a mystery that in the beginning in the sacrament of creation became *a visible reality through the union* of the first man and the first woman in the perspective of marriage—becomes in the sacrament of redemption *a visible reality in the indissoluble union of Christ with the Church*, which the author of Ephesians presents as the spousal union of the two, husband and wife" (TOB 97:4).

When Adam and Eve sinned and lost the grace of original innocence, "marriage, as the primordial sacrament, was deprived of . . . supernatural efficaciousness" (TOB 97:1). "Nevertheless . . . in the state of man's hereditary sinfulness, *marriage never ceases to be the figure of the sacrament, about which we read in Ephesians 5:22–33* and which the author of the same letter does not hesitate to call a 'great mystery'" (TOB 97:1). As John Paul II explained, "marriage has remained the platform for the realization of God's eternal plans, according to which the sacrament of creation had come near to human

---

9. Mary Shivanandan, *Crossing the Threshold of Love: A New Vision of Marriage in Light of John Paul II's Anthropology* (Washington, DC: Catholic University of America Press, 1999), 132.

beings and prepared them for the sacrament of redemption" (TOB 97:1). This means that even after sin entered the world, marriage was still intended by God to be a sign of his love for humanity, a sign that would prepare us for the full manifestation of God's love. A nuptial blessing that I have already quoted from the rite of marriage states:

> O God, who, to reveal the great design you formed in your love,
> willed that the love of spouses for each other
> should foreshadow the covenant you graciously made
>   with your people,
> so that, by fulfillment of the sacramental sign,
> the mystical marriage of Christ with his Church
>   might become manifest
> in the union of husband and wife among your faithful;
>   (RM, "Nuptial Blessing B")

This prayer proclaims that even after the Fall, marriage remained a sign of God's covenantal love, a love which is made fully visible in the spousal union of Christ for the Church. Thus the "great mystery" of Christ's self-donating love for his Church (Eph 5:21–33) that accomplishes our redemption is foreshadowed in the mystery of creation by the primordial sacrament of marriage.

Furthermore, in the mystery of redemption the natural institution of marriage is renewed and elevated to be one of the Seven Sacraments of the Church. Sacramental Marriage is no longer just a sign of God's love, but is now an efficacious sign that makes God's love present in the union of the couple. In addition, Marriage itself provides *"the foundation of the whole sacramental order"* (TOB 95b:7) because "all the sacraments find their prototype in some way in marriage as the primordial sacrament" (TOB 98:2). Each of the Seven Sacraments comes "forth from the spousal gracing of the Church by Christ" (TOB 98:4), which was foreshadowed and signified in the primordial sacrament of marriage. Thus Marriage unites the orders of creation and redemption in a unique way.

After the Fall, the primordial sacrament of marriage suffers from sin and needs to be redeemed. The conjugal communion of persons that is natural marriage is now threatened by domination, jealousy, infidelity, lust, etc. (CCC, 1606–1607). However, while the communion of persons is ruptured, it is not destroyed (CCC, 1607). Marriage in the order of nature still bears some reference to God, but finds itself in need of God's grace to assist it in realizing God's original design (CCC, 1608). As was pointed out in our discussion of conjugal love, the love of spouses can be deepened and preserved only by divine love (LF, 7). The good news is that this love is precisely the gift that is guaranteed to spouses in the Sacrament of Marriage, which is an efficacious sign of the "great mystery" of Christ's spousal union with the Church. However, leading up to discussing the Sacrament of Marriage given by Christ to the Church in the New Testament, we need to trace the history of marriage as the primordial sacrament in the pages of the Old Testament. This will allow us to see more clearly the centrality of marriage in God's plan of creation and redemption.

Part III

Marriage from the Garden of Eden to the Wedding Feast of the Lamb

The next two chapters present an overview of marriage as it appears in the pages of Scripture, both Old and New Testaments. These chapters highlight the centrality of marriage in God's plan of salvation. They also show that the covenanted people of the Old Testament grew in their understanding of God's love for them and that the revelation of God's love was linked to his plan for marriage. In the New Testament we see Jesus reaffirming this plan and elevating marriage to a participation in his own redemptive and spousal love.

Chapter 7

Marriage in the Old Testament

INTRODUCTION

Without an understanding of the nature of marriage, covered in the previous chapters, elements of salvation history set forth in biblical texts will remain opaque. From the beginning to the end of the Bible, marriage plays a central role in the unfolding of salvation history. This is because, "God . . . has given married love . . . a special significance in the history of salvation."[1] Scripture begins with the Book of Genesis that recounts the institution of marriage in the Garden of Eden (Gen 2:24–25). It ends with the Book of Revelation that speaks of the "wedding feast of the Lamb" (Rev 19:7, 9), which is the marriage of Christ and the Church (CCC, 1602), and includes a call to everyone to enter into the heavenly wedding feast: "The Spirit and the Bride say, 'Come'" (Rev 22:17). John Paul II pointed out that the mystery of "God's salvific plan for humanity . . . is in some sense the central theme of the whole of revelation, its central reality" (TOB 93:2). He further noted that marriage is *the most ancient revelation* (and 'manifestation') of that plan in the created world" (TOB 93:1), making marriage the "primordial sacrament" that we discussed previously. From the beginning to the end of the Bible, God's plan to draw humanity into his own divine life of love is correlated with marriage.

In the Old Testament, God's love for his people is described as the love of a husband for his bride, and in the New Testament Christ incarnates this spousal love by coming to unite himself forever to his bride, the Church. However, God leads his people progressively into an understanding of his plan for marriage, enabling them over time to see marriage as a sign of his saving love. The ability of God's

---

1. BB, "Order of Blessing within Mass on the Anniversary of Marriage," no. 100.

people to see the nature of marriage was often clouded by sin, and God slowly restored their sight over time. As the *Catechism* states: "Scripture speaks throughout of marriage and its 'mystery,' its institution and the meaning God has given it, its origin and its end, its various realizations throughout the history of salvation, the difficulties arising from sin and its renewal 'in the Lord' in the New Covenant of Christ and the Church" (CCC, 1602). Tracing the presentation of marriage in the pages of Scripture reveals a progressively clearer understanding of the importance of marriage in the order of creation and the order of redemption. The focus of this chapter and the next will be on the state of being married (*matrimonium in facto esse*) instead of on the process of becoming married (*matrimonium in fieri*). Within the pages of Scripture, it is the conjugal communion of husband and wife that is the main focus of the analogy between human marriage and the covenant (*berith* in Hebrew) of God with his people.[2]

When dealing with the presentation of marriage in the many pages of the Old Testament, it is useful and convenient to distinguish different genres of literature. For the purposes of our relatively brief survey of the Old Testament treatment of marriage, we will discuss the historical narratives, the legal texts, the wisdom literature, and the prophetic literature. Old Testament texts can additionally be classified into two main bodies of writing. The first corpus is the preexilic Old Testament literature—the writings of the Old Testament that were produced before and during the exile of the residents of the southern Kingdom of Judah, subsequent to the conquest of Judea by the Babylonians. This body of texts was produced from approximately 1700 to 520 BC. The second corpus of Old Testament literature is the postexilic Old Testament literature—the writings of the Old Testament that were produced after 520 BC, when the Jews returned from the Babylonian exile and built the second Temple in Jerusalem. This chapter will not provide an exhaustive treatment of marriage in the Old Testament, but will merely provide an overview of the developing understanding of marriage among the Old Testament people.

---

2. For information on marriage contracts and marriage ceremonies in the Old and New Testaments see John J. Collins, "Marriage in the Old Testament," in *Marriage in the Catholic Tradition: Scripture, Tradition, and Experience*, ed. Todd A. Salzman, Thomas M. Kelly, and John J. O'Keefe (New York: Crossroad, 2004), 12–15; and Kenneth Stevenson, *Nuptial Blessing: A Study of Christian Marriage Rites* (New York: Oxford University Press, 1983), 3–13.

Marriage in the Old Testament Historical Narratives

In the historical narratives of the Old Testament, especially the narratives dealing with the great patriarchs of Israel—Abraham, Isaac, and Jacob—there is a clear emphasis on procreation as the main goal of marriage. In the ancient world, marriage was viewed primarily as the means to perpetuate a family line. As such, a man desired to sire many children, especially male heirs, and marriage was viewed primarily in light of this end. This drive to perpetuate a family line often resulted in compromising the nature of marriage.[3] In the patriarchal narratives of the Old Testament, we can see the overemphasis that is placed on procreation in the instance that a wife turns out to be barren. In this circumstance, a husband could divorce his wife, he could take a second wife, or he could attempt to sire children through the agency of one of his barren wife's servants, taking her as a concubine.[4] In

---

3. Medieval theologians, like St. Thomas Aquinas, tried to explain the practice of polygamy among the patriarchs of the Old Testament. They argued that polygamy is not opposed to the primary precept of the natural law regarding marriage, which is that marriage is for the begetting of offspring, but that polygamy is only opposed to secondary precepts of the natural law, such as the fidelity of marriage (see ST Suppl., q. 65, a. 1). Furthermore, Thomas and others argued that God had granted the Patriarchs a dispensation from the secondary precepts of the natural law regarding marriage, to allow them to have many wives or to take concubines in order to produce many offspring (see ST Suppl., q. 65, a. 2, 5; SCG III, ch. 125, no. 10).

4. Francis Martin, "Marriage in the Old Testament and Intertestamental Periods," in *Christian Marriage: A Historical Study*, ed. Glenn Olsen (New York: The Crossroad Publishing Company, 2001), 3. This essay by Francis Martin is a wonderful overview of marriage in the Old Testament, and I have relied on it heavily in the process of crafting this chapter, especially Martin's insights into the Old Testament legal texts dealing with marriage. There are other sources that treat this material, including Michael J. Broyde, "The Covenant-Contract Dialectic in Jewish Divorce Law," in *Covenant Marriage in Comparative Perspective*, ed. John Witte Jr. and Eliza Ellison (Grand Rapids, MI: William B. Eerdmans Publishing Company, 2005), 53–69; John J. Collins, "Marriage in the Old Testament," 12–20; Louis M. Epstein, *Marriage Laws in the Bible and the Talmud* (Cambridge, MA: Harvard University Press, 1942); Michael Lawler, "Marriage in the Bible," in *Perspectives on Marriage: A Reader*, ed. Kieran Scott and Michael Warren, 3rd ed., (New York: Oxford University Press, 2007), 7–21; Theodore Mackin, *Divorce and Remarriage*, Marriage in the Catholic Church (New York: Paulist Press, 1984), 20–42; Theodore Mackin, *The Marital Sacrament*, Marriage in the Catholic Church (New York: Paulist Press, 1989), 24–58; Theodore Mackin, *What is Marriage?*, Marriage in the Catholic Church (New York: Paulist Press, 1982), 38–52; David Nowak, "Jewish Marriage: Nature, Covenant, and Contract," in *Covenant Marriage in Comparative Perspective*, ed. John Witte Jr. and Eliza Ellison (Grand Rapids, MI: William B. Eerdmans Publishing Company, 2005), 26–52; and Ronald A. Simkins, "Marriage and Gender in the Old Testament," in *Marriage in the Catholic Tradition*. However, Martin's essay is the one of the clearest treatments of the Old Testament legislation on marriage, and on marriage in the Old Testament in general.

Genesis 16:1–16 we see Abraham availing himself of the third option, taking Sarah's servant Hagar, so that Sarah, who was barren until God intervened, could obtain children by her. In addition, even after Sarah gives birth to Isaac, Abraham eventually takes a second wife, Keturah, who bears him six additional children (Gen 25:1–2). We also see a clear emphasis placed on procreation in marriage in the account of Jacob. We see Jacob taking two sisters, Rachel and Leah, as his wives (Gen 29:15–35), as well as siring children through Rachel's and Leah's handmaids, Bilhah and Zilpah respectively (Gen 30:1–13). It is through these four women that the twelve tribes of Israel will emerge.

However, it is important to observe that even if recourse to a concubine or a second wife was generally acceptable among the patriarchs, such action is presented in the historical narratives as "a lack of faith by the patriarchs and their wives in God's promise or his willingness to answer their prayers. Furthermore, every biblical example we see of multiple women in the household of one man is a disaster. This theological preference for monogamy, by far the most common arrangement in Israel, is manifest in nearly every aspect of the Old Testament tradition."[5]

In the account of Abraham, we can see Abraham expressing doubt that the Lord can fulfill his promise to grant him a son by Sarah (Gen 17:15–22). In the story of Jacob, recourse to a surrogate to beget more children evidences a lack of faith on the part of both Rachel and Leah, whose prayers will eventually be heard by God, granting each of them more children of their own (Gen 30:17–24). Certainly, Abraham's and Jacob's households, in which more than one wife or concubine dwelt, experienced discord, with animosity ensuing almost immediately between Sarah and Hagar (Gen 16:4–6), and rivalry and competition emerging between Rachel and Leah (Gen 29:31—30:2). So at least with respect to their marriages, neither Abraham nor Jacob is presented as a model to emulate. In contrast to these marriages of his father Abraham and his son Jacob, Isaac's marriage to Rebekah seems to have been monogamous and more tranquil (Gen 24:67).

Later in Israel's history, the households of King David and King Solomon provide further instruction regarding marriage, by way of their negative examples. David takes several wives and concubines

---

5. Ibid., 3–4.

(2 Sam 12:8; 19:6). One of his wives is a woman with whom David commits adultery, Bethsheba, whom David marries after successfully plotting to bring about the death of her husband, Uriah (2 Sam 11). As punishment for this sin, the son that David conceived in adultery with Bethsheba dies (2 Sam 12:14–18) and the prophet Nathan pledges that great turmoil ("the sword") will plague David's house (2 Sam 12:10). We then see David's children by his different wives engage in all types of dysfunctional behavior. Amnon, David's oldest son, rapes his half-sister Tamar (2 Sam 13:1–21), which instills a great hatred for Amnon in Tamar's brother Absalom (2 Sam 13:22). As a result of this hatred, Absalom has Amnon murdered and then flees David's house (2 Sam 13:29–38). Treachery and tragedy continue to befall David's household when, after David pardons Absalom (2 Sam 14), Absalom plots to overthrow his father, forcing David to flee (2 Sam 15:1–18). Finally, Absalom is killed in the battle that ensues between his army and David's army (2 Sam 18:9–18) and David weeps in mourning (2 Sam 19:1). Thus, although David's many wives and consorts bore him many children, David's sin of adultery, and his life of polygamy, brought ruin upon his palace.

David's wife Bethsheba did bear a living son to David, Solomon (2 Sam 12:24), who eventually succeeded David as king of Israel (1 Kgs 1). Initially, Solomon was renowned for his wisdom (1 Kgs 3) and his wealth (1 Kgs 10:14–29). However, Solomon also took seven hundred wives and three hundred concubines, many of them from foreign nations, who "turned his heart" away from the Lord to the worship of other gods (1 Kgs 11:1–4). This infidelity of Solomon to God, fostered by his many wives and concubines, eventually led to the downfall of his kingdom (1 Kgs 11:11–43).

Thus, far from condoning polygamy among Israel's patriarchs and kings, the authors of the Old Testament historical narratives exhibit a preference for marriage as an exclusive union between one man and one woman by showing the consequences of deviating from this design. Yet despite this preference, it is true nonetheless, as John Paul II noted, that in the history of Israel, monogamy was compromised, often in the drive to beget children (TOB 35:2).

Apart from the narratives dealing with the patriarchs and kings, there are some positive examples of marriage among other historical books of the Old Testament. "The books of Ruth and Tobit bear moving witness to an elevated sense of marriage and to the fidelity and tenderness of spouses" (CCC, 1611). The Book of Ruth recounts the story of a Moabite woman, Ruth, who converts to the worship of the God of Israel due to the influence of her Israelite mother-in-law Naomi. After her first Israelite husband dies, Ruth eventually marries another Israelite named Boaz. In the marriage of Ruth and Boaz we see depicted a tender and we presume monogamous love (Ru 3–4). It is Ruth who will become the great-grandmother of King David and an ancestor of Jesus (Mt 1:5).

Traditionally numbered among the historical books of the Old Testament, but having many characteristics of the wisdom literature, the Book of Tobit, written around the early second century BC, presents us with the marriage of Tobias and Sarah. Sarah had been married seven times previously, but each of her husbands had been killed on their wedding night by a demon named Asmodeus (Tb 3:8). In response to prayers (Tb 3:2–6; 11–17), God sent the angel Raphael to help Tobias and Sarah drive away Asmodeus (Tb 8:1–3). Then, before consummating their marriage on their wedding night, following the advice of Raphael, Tobias and Sarah pray together:

> When the door was shut and the two were alone, Tobias got up from the bed and said, "Sister, get up, and let us pray that the Lord may have mercy upon us." And Tobias began to pray, "Blessed art thou, O God of our fathers, and blessed be thy holy and glorious name for ever. Let the heavens and all thy creatures bless thee. Thou madest Adam and gavest him Eve his wife as a helper and support. From them the race of mankind has sprung. Thou didst say, 'It is not good that the man should be alone; let us make a helper for him like himself.' And now, O Lord, I am not taking this sister of mine because of lust, but with sincerity. Grant that I may find mercy and may grow old together with her." And she said with him, "Amen." Then they both went to sleep for the night. (Tb 8:4–9)

In this beautiful prayer the couple first acknowledges that God is the origin of marriage, and their prayer implies their intention to follow God's design for marriage. Their prayer also underlines the importance of a married couple invoking God's blessing on their life together. In addition, the prayer of Tobias and Sarah evidences the need for spouses to drive lust out of their hearts, respecting each other's dignity as brother and sister in the Lord (see TOB 114:3). It is also important to note that Tobias faced a particular evil, but that his love for Sarah allowed him to battle this evil with God's help.

Perhaps no other couple has ever had a more pressing reason to pray for God's blessing on their marital union than Tobias and Sarah. However, although Tobias and Sarah faced a particular "test of life-or-death," John Paul II observed of every married couple that, "when they unite as husband and wife, they must find themselves in the situation in which *the powers of good and evil fight against each other and measure each other*" (TOB 115:2). Every couple must struggle with the evil that they find within themselves, including the evil of lust, as well as with the different external evils they will face together in their married life, including suffering and death (TOB 115:5). As John Paul II noted: "The truth and the strength of love show themselves in the ability to place oneself between the forces of good and evil that fight within man and around him, because love is confident in the victory of good and is ready to do everything in order that good may conquer" (TOB 115:2).

John Paul II further pointed out that on their wedding night, when Tobias and Sarah have the right to "speak" the truth of love as husband and wife in the "language of the body," they first give voice to this truth, invoking God in the unison of prayer (TOB 115:6). This is why John Paul II saw in this prayer of Tobias and Sarah the truth of the "language of the body" becoming "the language of the liturgy" (TOB 116:2), a language of praise, thanksgiving, and petition spoken together by the spouses (TOB 116:1). We will have much more to say about how the language of the liturgy is based on the "language of the body" in chapters 15 and 16 that present a systematic treatment of the Sacrament of Marriage, but the foundation of this relationship can be seen here in the Old Testament Book of Tobit.

MARRIAGE IN THE OLD TESTAMENT LEGAL TEXTS

The legal texts of the Old Testament were always understood in relation to the covenant relationship that Israel shared with God, specifying the practical consequences of the covenant in daily living. The Old Testament legal texts, primarily found in Exodus, Leviticus, Numbers, and Deuteronomy, contain significant material pertinent to Israel's developing understanding of marriage. First of all, like the historical books of the Old Testament, "the marriage law of the Old Testament places the procreative end of marriage in the foreground" (TOB 36:2). In the legal thinking of Israel, which was influenced by other legal codes of the ancient Near East, "the primary reason for the institution of marriage . . . was to insure for the man a legitimate heir to continue the family line and possess the family property. The whole logic of the legal system governing marriage derived from this premise."[6] It may be difficult for us to understand the overriding importance of this motive, unless we understand "that people in this culture [of the ancient Near East] achieved immortality in their 'seed'" (see Jgs 9:56; 2 Sam 14:7; Jer 16:1–4; Num 16:31–33).[7] It is true that the ancient world viewed only the male as having an active biological role in generating a new child, with the woman seen as the passive receptacle for the male seed, effectively relegating her to an inferior position in the realm of procreation.[8] Nonetheless, even with their male-centric focus, the legal texts' stress on the primary end of marriage as procreation "contributed to the formation of a social role for the father and to the permanent bonding of husband and wife."[9] In this way the education of children and the permanence of marriage were fostered, although not absolutely required.

The legal texts also dealt with the rights and duties of husbands and wives toward each other.[10] These rights and duties were linked to the primary purpose of marriage as securing a legitimate heir for the husband. The legal duties of the husband toward his wife included: undertaking a common life with her, which involved caring for her physical needs (food, clothing, and shelter); rendering the marital debt (sexual intercourse); and treating his wife with respect (Ex 21:10; Is 4:1). The last duty of showing respect included: not abusing his wife by treating her like a slave or a prostitute, honoring the rights of her children even if the husband took another wife (Dt 21:15–17), and respecting his wife's right to her dowry including

---

6. Ibid., 12.

7. Ibid.

8. Ibid., 12–13.

9. Ibid., 13.

10. The information and quotation in this paragraph are taken from Francis Martin, "Marriage in the Old Testament," 13.

rendering it to her in case of divorce. Regarding a wife's duties to her husband:

> The primary duty of the wife was to give her husband the unilaterally exclusive right to have intercourse with her . . . to provide absolute security regarding the identity of the (male) children who were born to her. . . . Other obligations, such as raising the children, caring for the home, etc., had the force of custom, not law, although failure to meet them might result in divorce.

It should be noted that while the main duty of the wife was to give her husband exclusive rights to her body, these reciprocal rights and duties did not allow a husband to treat his wife merely as a piece of property.

While calling the husband the "lord" (*baal*) of his wife did imply the husband's exclusive conjugal rights, this title did not imply that the husband could dispose of his wife as he pleased.[11] He too had duties to fulfill toward her, and he could not dispense with her like a piece of property by selling her into slavery or granting other men rights to her body.[12] Thus the wording of the tenth commandment (Ex 20:17; Dt 5:21) cannot properly be construed to presume that a husband owns his wife as if she were mere property.[13] Also, the provisions made for widows ensured that a wife was not treated as mere property (Dt 10:18; 27:19; Ex 22:22). One of these provisions, that of levirate marriage (from the Latin term *levir*, meaning brother-in-law), required a man to marry his brother's widow if the brother had died without leaving a male heir (Dt 25:5–10). Along with the concern for maintaining the deceased man's family line, this law also provided for the care of the widow, placing an onus on the brother-in-law.[14] In several instances, "the law given to Moses aims at protecting the wife from arbitrary domination by the husband" (CCC, 1610). However, while the legal code did support the dignity of both husband and wife to some degree, men and women were not completely equal before the law, and "on the whole it judges the woman differently

---

11. Ibid., 13–14.

12. Ibid., 14.

13. Ibid.

14. For more on the practice of levirate marriage see Louis M. Epstein, *Marriage Laws in the Bible and the Talmud*, 77–93.

and treats her with more severity" (TOB 36:3). This can be seen in how the law treats adultery.

As could be expected, the legal texts considered adultery as a violation of the husband's exclusive right to his wife (TOB 35:4). Although in the history of the Old Testament legal punishments for adultery ranged from the death penalty (Dt 22:22; Lev 20:10) to public humiliation (Hos 2:3) and ostracism (see Prv 5:3–14),[15] on the whole the Old Testament law judged women more severely for infidelity because adultery was considered primarily an offense against the husband (TOB 36:2). All of the legislation dealing with adultery shows that the Israelites took the obligation to fidelity in marriage seriously, although more seriously for the wife than for the husband when one takes into account the significant caveat that monogamy, while the preference, was not strictly enforced. On this point John Paul II noted that "the history of the Old Testament is clearly the theater of the systematic defection from monogamy, which must have had a fundamental significance for the understanding of the prohibition, 'You shall not commit adultery'" (TOB 35:2). John Paul pointed out that in the Old Testament:

> By *adultery* one understood *only the possession of another's wife*, but not the possession of other women as wives next to the first one. The whole tradition of the Old Covenant indicates that the effective necessity of monogamy as an essential and indispensable implication *of the commandment "You shall not commit adultery"* never reached the consciousness and ethos of the later generations of the Chosen People. (TOB 35:3)

Therefore, one man taking many wives was seen as permissible, even if not the ideal, as long as this man did not wed a woman who was already another man's wife. Thus John Paul II pointed out that the people of the Old Testament "bypassed" a reading of the sixth commandment that required monogamy, thus distorting God's intention for this commandment (TOB 35:5).

In the legal texts of the Old Testament the practice of polygamy is acknowledged but never formally approved.[16] There are texts which try to dissuade men from practicing polygamy, like Dt 17:17,

---

15. Francis Martin, "Marriage in the Old Testament," 15.

16. Louis M. Epstein, *Marriage Laws in the Bible*, 4; for more on polygamy in the Old Testament see, Epstein, 3–12.

which warns a king not to "multiply wives for himself." Yet enforcing levirate marriage could also result in a polygamous situation. In the legal texts, as in the rest of the Old Testament, there is a preference for monogamous marriage, and monogamy was the practical pattern of behavior for most ordinary Israelites, even though polygamy was never excluded.[17] Nevertheless, John Paul II noted that the explicit commandment given through Moses legislating against adultery did not change the fact "that effective polygamy established itself, and it did so for reasons of concupiscence" (TOB 35:3).

There were also clearly differing rights and expectations for men and women with regard to sexual fidelity and the permanence of the marriage bond. While later traditions will attempt to forbid extramarital sex for men (2 Sam 12; Job 31:1, 9–12; Prv 5:15–23; Sir 9:5–9), a husband could have sexual relations with prostitutes and unmarried women without violating the commandment forbidding adultery.[18] We have already seen in the historical narratives that while a wife was expected to belong exclusively to her husband, a husband could take more than one wife or concubine, and could even have relations with a slave woman (TOB 36:1; see Dt 21:10–14).[19]

Concerning divorce and remarriage in the legal texts of the Old Testament, contrary to common misperception, a husband could not arbitrarily divorce his wife for any reason. There were "situations in which a man *might* divorce his wife. These included, first, instances where there was some fault on the part of the woman: desire to leave the house; [or] lying about her husband's conduct in order to free herself from her obligation to him."[20] There were, however, cases in which a man was required to divorce his wife.[21] Divorce was required in instances of adultery, and the death penalty was imposed until late in Israelite history. Laws forbidding incest invalidated marriages within certain degrees of relationship (Dt 27:20, 22, 23; Lev 18:6–17; 20:11–20). In postexilic Israel, divorce was imposed on marriages

---

17. Ibid., 9.

18. John S. Grabowski, *Sex and Virtue: An Introduction to Sexual Ethics* (Washington, DC: Catholic University of America Press, 2003), 39-40.

19. For more on the practice of taking concubines in the Old Testament see, Louis M. Epstein, *Marriage Laws in the Bible*, 49-62.

20. Francis Martin, "Marriage in the Old Testament," 18.

21. Ibid., 20.

between Israelites and non-Israelites in an attempt to preserve the purity of Israel's faith and promote its fidelity to Yhwh after suffering the period of the exile in Babylonia (see Ezr 10:7–8; also Ezr 9:10; Neh 10:30–31).[22]

Along with specifying situations in which a man might divorce his wife, or situations in which he was required to divorce his wife, the legal code also specified instances in which divorce was not allowed. Most of these instances were designed to protect a woman who had been wronged by her husband. "A man who forced a virgin to have intercourse was required to marry her and could not divorce her (Dt 22:28–29)." Also, "a false accusation regarding non-virginity at [the time of the] marriage also prohibited the man from ever divorcing his wife (Dt 22:19)." In addition, the law "forbade a man to divorce his sick wife, while allowing him to marry another woman."[23]

It is important to note that: "Most divorce legislation . . . seemed to have been designed to protect the woman from neglect, especially in the case of illness or infertility."[24] "In Israel, if a woman were divorced with no fault on her part, her husband was obliged to render to her the *mohar* [the payment normally given to the bride's father by the husband, see Gen 34:12; Ex 22:26; 1 Sam 18:25] he paid when the marriage was agreed upon . . . (Dt 22:29). In addition, the husband was obliged to return the woman's dowry and provide her with a bill of divorce in order to establish the fact that she was free to remarry (Dt 24:1–4)."[25] Also, if a husband brought false charges against his wife in an attempt to divorce her and avoid paying the *mohar*, he had to pay remuneration to his father-in-law and could never divorce his wife.[26] A woman might also invoke the right to divorce her husband for:

(1) failure to consummate the marriage, (2) failure to support the woman, whether because the husband is held captive, has failed to return, has fled the city, or for some other reason . . . ; (3) lack of respect [being treated

---

22. For more on the practice of intermarriage in the Old Testament see Louis M. Epstein, *Marriage Laws in the Bible*, 145–167.

23. Francis Martin, "Marriage in the Old Testament," 19.

24. Ibid., 18.

25. Ibid., 19.

26. Ibid.

like a slave or a prostitute]; and (4) annulment of the matrimonial agreement before consummation (with payment of a fine). [27]

Thus, even though it cannot be claimed that the society of the Old Testament was emancipated, women could not be treated as mere chattel by their husbands. Nonetheless, the legal codes, by allowing and even mandating divorce in certain circumstances, practically denied the indissolubility of marriage. While the legal texts of the Old Testament made rationalizations and concessions for human weakness in the area of divorce and other areas pertaining to marriage, it is also necessary to take into account the wisdom and prophetic literature to see how God's chosen people were growing in their ability to see and understand his plan for marriage.

MARRIAGE IN THE OLD TESTAMENT WISDOM LITERATURE

Concerning the wisdom literature of the Old Testament, Francis Martin points out three themes that emerge pertaining to marriage: (1) the relation between spouses; (2) fidelity to one's spouse; and (3) the rearing of children. [28] First of all, regarding the relation between spouses, these wisdom texts, like the historical narratives, presuppose monogamy in their description of marriage. [29] While this preference for monogamy can be seen in several texts (see Prv 12:4; 18:22; 19:14; 31:10–12; Eccl 9:9), this passage from Proverbs provides a clear example:

> Drink water from your own cistern, flowing water from your own well. Should your springs be scattered abroad, streams of water in the streets? Let them be for yourself alone, and not for strangers with you. Let your fountain be blessed, and rejoice in the wife of your youth, a lovely hind, a graceful doe. Let her affection fill you at all times with delight, be infatuated always with her love. (Prv 5:15–19)

It is true that the wisdom texts view marriage from a man's perspective, with prose that speak of the joys of finding a good wife (see Prv 18:22; 12:4; 31:10–31). For instance, the Book of Sirach states:

---

27. Ibid., 20.

28. Ibid., 6.

29. See Edward Schillebeeckx, *Marriage: Human Reality and Saving Mystery*, 2 vols., trans. N.D. Smith (New York: Sheed and Ward, 1965), 89–90.

Happy is the husband of a good wife; the number of his days will be doubled. A loyal wife rejoices her husband, and he will complete his years in peace. A good wife is a great blessing; she will be granted among the blessings of the man who fears the Lord. Whether rich or poor, his heart is glad, and at all times his face is cheerful. (Sir 26:1–4)

The woman is presented as important because she is the one who orders the home and gives the man his place in society, for, "where there is no wife, a man will wander about and sigh" (see Sir 36:25).[30] There is value placed on a wife's outward beauty, as well as her virtue and character:

A wife's charm delights her husband, and her skill puts fat on his bones. A silent wife is a gift of the Lord, and there is nothing so precious as a disciplined soul. A modest wife adds charm to charm, and no balance can weigh the value of a chaste soul. Like the sun rising in the heights of the Lord, so is the beauty of a good wife in her well-ordered home. Like the shining lamp on the holy lampstand, so is a beautiful face on a stately figure. Like pillars of gold on a base of silver, so are beautiful feet with a steadfast heart. (Sir 26:13–18)

In addition, the wisdom sages wrote about mutual affection between spouses praising "a wife and a husband who live in harmony" (Sir 25:1). It should be noted that none of these descriptions of a relationship between a husband and a wife could pertain if monogamy were not the presumed norm. Thus the wisdom literature attests to the property of unity and the good of fidelity in marriage.

Regarding fidelity to one's spouse, like the legal texts, the wisdom writers viewed adultery as primarily an offense against the husband, thereby maintaining a male perspective in the attention they gave the adulteress.[31] For example, the Book of Proverbs states:

My son, be attentive to my wisdom, incline your ear to my understanding; that you may keep discretion, and your lips may guard knowledge. For the lips of a loose woman drip honey, and her speech is smoother than oil; but in the end she is bitter as wormwood, sharp as a two-edged sword. Her feet go down to death; her steps follow the path to Sheol; she does not take heed to the path of life; her ways wander, and she does not know it. (Prv 5:1–6)

---

30. Francis Martin, "Marriage in the Old Testament," 6.
31. Ibid., 7.

The wisdom writers provide strenuous warnings against adultery, "stressing the shame and corrupted relationships that result" (see Prv 5:1–23; 7:4–27; Sir 23:18–27).[32] In this way, the wisdom literature again attests to the property of unity and the good of fidelity in marriage.

Commenting on the rearing and formation of children, the wisdom writers first make it clear that children are blessings from God and signs of God's favor. The Psalmist states:

> Blessed is every one who fears the LORD, who walks in his ways! You shall eat the fruit of the labor of your hands; you shall be happy, and it shall be well with you. Your wife will be like a fruitful vine within your house; your children will be like olive shoots around your table. Lo, thus shall the man be blessed who fears the LORD. The LORD bless you from Zion! May you see the prosperity of Jerusalem all the days of your life! May you see your children's children! Peace be upon Israel! (Ps 128)

Fathers *and* mothers are exhorted to educate their children, which is unique for that time,[33] when the Book of Proverbs states: "Hear, my son, your father's instruction, and reject not your mother's teaching" (Prv 1:8). Parents are presented with God himself as the model for their parenting: "My son, do not despise the LORD's discipline or be weary of his reproof, for the LORD reproves him whom he loves, as a father the son in whom he delights" (Prv 3:11–12). Love, respect, and tenderness are also encouraged in relations between parents and children.[34] This is evidenced when the Book of Sirach states:

> Listen to me your father, O children; and act accordingly, that you may be kept in safety. For the Lord honored the father above the children, and he confirmed the right of the mother over her sons. Whoever honors his father atones for sins, and whoever glorifies his mother is like one who lays up treasure. (Sir 3:1–4; see also verses 5–16)

Thus the wisdom literature attests to the good of marital fruitfulness and marriage's primary end of the procreation and education of children, as well as the mutual respect and affection that should pervade the home.

---

32. Ibid.
33. Ibid., 8.
34. Ibid.

The writers of the wisdom tradition also reflected on cosmology and especially the origin of the human race. This tradition's key
insights into the human person can be found in Genesis 1–3. These
insights were discussed in chapter three of this book in the process of
outlining important principles of theological anthropology. Some of
the central insights of this tradition that were discussed included: the
uniqueness of the human person made in the image and likeness of
God (Gen 1:27); the human person as an embodied spirit (Gen 2:7);
the equal dignity (Gen 1:27) yet complementary difference of man
and woman (Gen 2:18, 21–23); the fact that man and woman are called
to exist in communion (Gen 2:24); the meaning of human freedom
(Gen 3:1–13); and the effects of sin on the image of God found in
man and woman (Gen 3:16–24). In these texts of Genesis we see God
instituting marriage in the order of creation (Gen 2:24–25) and blessing
the union of the first man and woman, calling them to be fruitful
(Gen 1:28). It is in these texts that we find the model marriage to be
that of one man and one woman, united in "one flesh" (Gen 2:24),
implying a union of their persons and their lives that is faithful and
permanent. These texts in the Book of Genesis will provide the foundation for the prophets to view marriage as a symbol of the covenant
between God and his people. This prototypical view of marriage took
centuries to crystallize in the minds of the Old Testament people,[35]
and once this understanding was articulated it remained, in many
ways, unrealized.

MARRIAGE IN THE OLD TESTAMENT PROPHETS

In the prophetic tradition of the Old Testament we see some of
the most important developments in the Israelites' understanding of
marriage. In the prophetic literature we see the prophets correlating
marriage with Israel's covenant relationship with God. Initially, the
prophets used the human relationship of marriage as a means to express
Israel's relationship with God.[36] However, not only do the prophets

---

35. Remember that Genesis 1:1a–2:4a is the creation narrative structured around the seven
days of creation, and stems from around the fifth century BC, while Gen 2:4b–2:24 is focused
more precisely on the creation of man, and is the older creation narrative, written as early as the
ninth century BC.

36. Schillebeeckx, *Marriage*, 31–32.

view the covenant with God in light of marriage, but in light of Israel's relationship with God, they also begin to view marriage itself as a covenant (TOB 104:2). This correlation between marriage and the covenant therefore provided a cross-fertilization of sorts that resulted simultaneously in a deepened understanding of the covenant as well as a deepened understanding of marriage.[37] As part of this mutual inter-penetration of marriage and covenant, the prophets compare marital infidelity with infidelity to the covenant with God, developing an analogy between adultery and idolatry (TOB 36:5; 37:3). "The image of marital infidelity can all the more readily be understood if it is remembered that Israel's marital infidelity to Yhwh was concretely situated in the worship of the Baals or alien gods, and that this worship was accompanied by all kinds of sexual debauchery in connection with the cult of the fertility gods."[38]

On this score, the prophet Hosea, active around the mid-eighth century BC, is the first to compare God's covenant with Israel to a marriage. In his writing, Hosea presents his own marriage to a prostitute named Gomer as symbolic of Israel's infidelity to God, stating: "When the LORD first spoke through Hosea, the LORD said to Hosea, 'Go, take to yourself a wife of harlotry and have children of harlotry, for the land commits great harlotry by forsaking the LORD'" (Hos 1:2). Thus Hosea saw his marriage as symbolic of the covenant relationship that God had forged with Israel, and of Israel's lack of fidelity to that covenant. He makes this comparison even more clear when he states: "And the LORD said to me, 'Go again, love a woman who is beloved of a paramour and is an adulteress; even as the LORD loves the people of Israel, though they turn to other gods'" (Hos 3:1).

Hosea's emphasis on love as the basis of the relationship between God and his people is important. "Based on his own experience of his marriage to his wife, Hosea was able to understand that Israel's infidelity to Yhwh offended not only against an agreed upon relationship, but more profoundly against the love that was meant to animate that relationship."[39] Although the law would have allowed, and even prescribed, Hosea to break the marriage contract and divorce his adulterous wife, God commands Hosea to go beyond the legalistic

---

37. See ibid., 33–34.

38. Ibid., 43.

39. Francis Martin, "Marriage in the Old Testament," 9.

understanding of marriage to continue to offer Gomer his love. Hosea does this because he understands that God offers his tender, merciful, gracious love (in Hebrew *hesed*) to Israel. It is Israel's failure to respond to God's love, not just the infraction of some type of legal arrangement, which makes Israel's sin so egregious. Israel's failure to respond to God's love, and the consequences of this waywardness, are highlighted when God states through Hosea: "They shall eat, but not be satisfied; they shall play the harlot, but not multiply; because they have forsaken the LORD to cherish harlotry" (Hos 4:10). Yet, even though Israel's infidelity will bring hard times upon the people, the prophet Hosea also stresses God's constant desire to draw Israel into his love.

God's unfailing desire for his beloved is clear when he says to Israel through Hosea:

> And I will make for you a covenant on that day with the beasts of the field, the birds of the air, and the creeping things of the ground; and I will abolish the bow, the sword, and war from the land; and I will make you lie down in safety. And I will betroth you to me forever; I will betroth you to me in righteousness and in justice, in steadfast love, and in mercy. I will betroth you to me in faithfulness; and you shall know the LORD. (Hos 2:18–20)

It should be noted that in the Old Testament the verb "to know" (*yada* in Hebrew) signified the intimacy that a husband and a wife experienced through sexual intercourse, and thus the "knowledge" they gained about each other through this embrace (see Gen 4:1). Thus, Hosea is reminding Israel of the deep intimacy the Lord desires to share with them. Far from forsaking his unfaithful bride, God exhorts her: "Return, O Israel, to the LORD your God, for you have stumbled because of your iniquity" (Hos 14:1).

Thus, Hosea contrasts God's steadfast, faithful, and permanent love for Israel with Israel's infidelity and betrayal, which is likened to adultery. Understanding God's love for Israel, Hosea embraces the prophetic action of loving his unfaithful wife as God loves Israel.[40] God had freely chosen to love Israel (Hos 14:4), and he would not withdraw this love (Heb 11:1–11). Thus we can see an understanding in Hosea that married love, likened to the covenant love of God, should be free, faithful, and forever, as well as called to love even in

---

40. Schillebeeckx, *Marriage*, 40.

the face of infidelity, like Hosea is called to love Gomer. Hosea's influence can be seen in the prophets that came after him, including Jeremiah, Ezekiel, and Isaiah.

In the prophet Jeremiah, from around the turn of the sixth century BC, we find a similar comparison between marriage and God's covenant with his people, highlighting again God's fidelity and Israel's infidelity. Through Jeremiah, God convicts Israel of its infidelity when he says: "Can a maiden forget her ornaments, or a bride her attire? Yet my people have forgotten me days without number" (Jer 2:32). Jeremiah makes the explicit comparison between Israel's lack of faithfulness and adultery when he states: "Surely, as a faithless wife leaves her husband, so have you been faithless to me, O house of Israel, says the LORD" (Jer 3:20). Jeremiah illustrates the consequences of Israel's adultery and its shame when he says:

> Therefore thus says the LORD: Ask among the nations, who has heard the like of this? The virgin Israel has done a very horrible thing. . . . But my people have forgotten me, they burn incense to false gods; they have stumbled in their ways, in the ancient roads, and have gone into bypaths, not the highway, making their land a horror, a thing to be hissed at for ever. Every one who passes by it is horrified and shakes his head. Like the east wind I will scatter them before the enemy. I will show them my back, not my face, in the day of their calamity. (Jer 18:13, 15–18)

And also:

> All your lovers have forgotten you; they care nothing for you; for I have dealt you the blow of an enemy, the punishment of a merciless foe, because your guilt is great, because your sins are flagrant. (Jer 30:14)

Jeremiah presents God as threatening to give Israel a bill of divorce (Jer 3:7–8), but God exhorts Israel to return to his merciful love (Jer 3:12). When a "remnant of Israel" (Jer 31:7) proves to be faithful, Jeremiah presents God as retracting His threat of divorce and promising his everlasting love: "'At that time, says the LORD, I will be the God of all the families of Israel, and they shall be my people.' Thus says the LORD: ' . . . I have loved you with an everlasting love; therefore I have continued my faithfulness to you'" (Jer 31:1–3). Thus Jeremiah, similar to Hosea, contrasts Israel's infidelity/adultery with God's undying love, comparing God's love to that of a faithful spouse.

The prophet Ezekiel, writing in the early sixth century BC during the Babylonian exile, enriches the imagery of God's spousal love for his people when he writes:

> When I passed by you again and looked upon you, behold, you were at the age for love; and I spread my skirt over you, and covered your naked-ness: yea, I plighted my troth to you and entered into a covenant with you, says the Lord God, and you became mine. Then I bathed you with water and washed off your blood from you, and anointed you with oil. I clothed you also with embroidered cloth and shod you with leather, I swathed you in fine linen and covered you with silk. And I decked you with ornaments, and put bracelets on your arms, and a chain on your neck. And I put a ring on your nose, and earrings in your ears, and a beautiful crown upon your head. Thus you were decked with gold and silver; and your raiment was of fine linen, and silk, and embroidered cloth; you ate fine flour and honey and oil. You grew exceedingly beauti-ful, and came to regal estate. And your renown went forth among the nations because of your beauty, for it was perfect through the splendor which I had bestowed upon you, says the Lord God. But you trusted in your beauty, and played the harlot because of your renown, and lavished your harlotries on any passer-by. (Ez 16:8–15)

Ezekiel points out that it is God, in his gratuitous love (*hesed*), who has chosen Israel as his bride and made her beautiful; yet, Israel has responded with ingratitude, infidelity, and betrayal, playing the harlot. God goes on to call Israel an "adulterous wife, who receives strangers instead of her husband!" (Ez 16:32), and he promises to "judge you as women who break wedlock" (Ez 16:38).

Yet Ezekiel makes it clear that God's punishment seeks the conversion of his people, attempting to get them to realize their sin, and to return to him and live in the love he has for them:

> Yea, thus says the Lord God: I will deal with you as you have done, who have despised the oath in breaking the covenant, yet I will remember my covenant with you in the days of your youth, and I will establish with you an everlasting covenant. . . . I will establish my covenant with you, and you shall know that I am the Lord, that you may remember and be confounded, and never open your mouth again because of your shame, when I forgive you all that you have done, says the Lord God. (Ez 16:59–60, 62–63)

Thus regardless of Israel's infidelity, God's covenant love is merciful, forgiving, and undying. God is the ever-faithful spouse, and his love for Israel is presented as the model for married love.

Thus in the prophetic tradition we can clearly see the equation of marriage with a covenant relationship whose essence is a communion of love. John Paul II said of these writings:

> In the revelations of the prophets . . . the God of the covenant, Yhwh, is often represented as Bridegroom, and the love with which he joined himself to Israel can and should be equated with the spousal love of a couple. Because of its idolatry and desertion of God, the Bridegroom, Israel commits a betrayal before him that can be compared to that of a woman in relation to her husband: it commits, in fact, "adultery" (TOB 36:5).

It is out of love that God forges a covenant relationship with Israel, and "for Israel he becomes a Bridegroom and Husband who is most affectionate, attentive, and generous toward his Bride," remaining faithful to her even in the face of her many betrayals (TOB 37:3). Furthermore, the prophets see the bond of God with his people as a "profoundly personal" bond, not just a contract (TOB 104:2). John Paul II highlighted the fact that through the spousal analogy of marriage to the covenant, the prophets go beyond treating adultery as a violation of the exclusive rights that a husband has to his wife. They present adultery as a "sin because it is *the breaking of the personal covenant between the man and the woman*," a violation of their communion of love (TOB 37:4).

In addition, John Paul II noted how in their treatment of adultery, the prophets point to a "prophetism of the body" (TOB 104:1). He pointed out that the whole Old Testament tradition attests to the fact that adultery is a "sin of the body" (TOB 37:5), because "adultery indicates the act by which a man and a woman who are not husband and wife form 'one flesh'" (TOB 37:6). Thus, while the one-flesh union between a husband and a wife is a "truthful sign" of the communion of persons, adulterous intercourse is a lie with the body (TOB 37:6). By portraying the covenant between God and his people as a marriage, and analogizing adultery to idolatry, the prophets bring the body into this spousal analogy (TOB 104:2). There is therefore a "prophetism of the body" which equates with the "language of the body" that we saw in the Book of Tobit and which speaks either truth or falsehood (TOB 104:1). John Paul II explained:

> It is characteristic of the way the prophets express themselves that, presupposing the "language of the body" in the objective sense, they go on at the same time to *its subjective meaning*: that is, they allow *the body itself*, as it were, *to speak*. In the prophetic texts about the covenant based on the analogy of the spousal union of the couple, it is the body itself that "speaks"; it speaks with its masculinity and femininity, it speaks with the mysterious language of the personal gift, it speaks finally—and this happens more often—both in the language of faithfulness, that is, of love, and in the language of conjugal unfaithfulness, that is, of "adultery." (TOB 104:4)

Thus the prophets point to the reality that in the conjugal act husbands and wives "speak" a "language of the body" that is meant to be spoken in truth, and by doing so human spouses reflect the communion of love that God desires with his covenanted people.

This points to the fact that in addition to equating the "language" of adultery with infidelity to God, the spousal analogy that presents marriage as a symbol of God's covenant love for his people also "came to be used in promises of restoration."[41] In the prophet Isaiah "the love of God-Yahweh for Israel, the Chosen People, is expressed as the love of a human bridegroom for the woman chosen to be his wife through the conjugal covenant" (TOB 95:2). Isaiah proclaims to Israel: "For as a young man marries a virgin, so shall your sons marry you, and as the bridegroom rejoices over the bride, so shall your God rejoice over you" (Is 62:5). Thus God takes delight in his people, like a bridegroom delights in his new bride. Furthermore, Isaiah testifies to the restorative love of Israel's divine bridegroom when he proclaims:

> Fear not, for you will not be ashamed; be not confounded, for you will not be put to shame; for you will forget the shame of your youth, and the reproach of your widowhood you will remember no more. For your Maker is your husband, the LORD of hosts is his name; and the Holy One of Israel is your Redeemer, the God of the whole earth he is called. For the LORD has called you like a wife forsaken and grieved in spirit, like a wife of youth when she is cast off, says your God. For a brief moment I forsook you, but with great compassion I will gather you. In overflowing

---

41. Francis Martin, "Marriage in the Old Testament," 31.

wrath for a moment I hid my face from you, but with everlasting love
I will have compassion on you, says the LORD, your Redeemer. . . . For
the mountains may depart and the hills be removed, but my steadfast love
shall not depart from you, and my covenant of peace shall not be
removed, says the LORD, who has compassion on you. (Is 54:4–8, 10)

In this passage God "is explicitly called 'husband' of the Chosen
People," and "the motif of *spousal love and of marriage* is linked with
the motif of the *covenant*" (TOB 95:4). Furthermore, "Isaiah explains
the events that make up the course of Israel's history, by going back to
the mystery hidden, as it were, in the very heart of God" (TOB 95:2).
This mystery is the desire that God has to redeem humanity and invite
us to share in his own life. This redemption takes place by virtue of
God making a gift of himself to his people as a spouse (TOB 95:5–6).
Thus God's offering of the gift of his compassionate and merciful love
to his bride presents the promise of redemption and restoration for her
(TOB 95:3).

It is implied by the spousal analogy that spouses must "speak"
this same language of compassionate and restorative love as they make
a gift of themselves to each other through the "language of the body."
Even though the Song of Songs is unique among all biblical literature
and is not properly part of the prophetic tradition, it is a "work which
promises restoration using the imagery of spousal love."[42] While the
rest of the Old Testament says little about the interpersonal relations
between husband and wife, perhaps presuming them, the Song of
Songs is an extended poem that extols the goodness and the beauty of
romantic love between a man and a woman.[43] In fact, the Song of
Songs is unique in the Bible because it is a love poem that compares
human sexual love, *eros* in its proper sense, to the passionate love God
has for his people (CCC, 1611). "In so doing, the Song of Songs builds
upon the prophetic and wisdom literature's ability to transpose the
human reality of marriage to the level of the relation between God and
his people."[44] In the Song of Songs it is human sexual love and
marriage that "embody God's restorative purpose for his people."[45]

---

42. Ibid., 32.
43. Schillebeeckx, *Marriage*, 30.
44. Francis Martin, "Marriage in the Old Testament," 32.
45. Ibid.

John Paul II explained that in the Song of Songs, "the words, movements and gestures of the spouses, their whole behavior, corresponds to the inner movement of their hearts," so that they experience each other's entire person through the "language of the body" (TOB 108:5–6).[46] "Both the femininity of the bride and the masculinity of the bridegroom speak without words: *the language of the body* is a language without words," a language of love (TOB 109:1). By rereading the language of the body in truth, the spouses encounter the depths of each other's persons (TOB 110:8), without exhausting the depths of each other's personal mystery. They become aware of each other "as a gift" (TOB 111:2), stating: "Behold, you are beautiful, my love, behold, you are beautiful!" (Sg 4:1). They also become aware of "belonging to each other" as they give and receive the gift of their persons in truth and freedom (TOB 110:8). Thus the Song states: "I am my beloved's and my beloved is mine" (Sg 6:3; see also Sg 2:16). As they speak the truth of love through their bodies "the man and the woman together must constitute that sign of the reciprocal gift of self, which *sets the seal on their whole life*" (TOB 111:5; see Sg 8:6). This sign of the reciprocal gift of self is a "visible sign of man and woman's participation in the covenant of grace and love offered by God to man," which offers them the promise of restoration (TOB 108:3). Thus we can see yet again why marriage is the "primordial sacrament" of God's love (TOB 111:4), a love of restoration, a love "strong as death" (Sg 8:6), a love that couples have the responsibility of "speaking" in and through the "language of the body."

One final point of emphasis that should be noted is the later prophetic tradition's clear opposition to divorce. This opposition can be seen strikingly in the prophet Malachi from the mid-fifth century BC. Malachi writes:

> Have we not all one father? Has not one God created us? Why then are we faithless to one another, profaning the covenant of our fathers? Judah has been faithless, and abomination has been committed in Israel and in Jerusalem; for Judah has profaned the sanctuary of the LORD, which he loves, and has married the daughter of a foreign god. May the LORD cut off from the tents of Jacob, for the man who does this, any to witness or answer, or to bring an offering to the LORD of hosts! And this again you

---

46. John Paul II said more about the Song of Songs and what it reveals about the "language of the body" and the relationship between *eros* and *agape* in TOB 108–113.

do. You cover the LORD's altar with tears, with weeping and groaning because he no longer regards the offering or accepts it with favor at your hand. You ask, "Why does he not?" Because the LORD was witness to the covenant between you and the wife of your youth, to whom you have been faithless, though she is your companion and your wife by covenant. Has not the one God made and sustained for us the spirit of life? And what does he desire? Godly offspring. So take heed to yourselves, and let none be faithless to the wife of his youth. For I hate divorce, says the LORD the God of Israel, and covering one's garment with violence, says the LORD of hosts. So take heed to yourselves and do not be faithless. (Mal 2:10–16)

In this passage, Malachi is using the spousal analogy of marriage to God's covenant to teach something specific about marriage. He explicitly calls the marriage of a husband and a wife a covenant (Mal 2:14). Malachi also points to the fact that the primary end of marriage is the procreation *and* education of children when he states that God desires "Godly offspring" (Mal 2:15). Furthermore, faithfulness to the marriage covenant is clearly compared to Israel's faithfulness to its covenant with God, and as part of this comparison Malachi contains the clearest opposition to divorce in the Old Testament: "For I hate divorce, says the LORD the God of Israel" (Mal 2:16). Malachi even states that one of the reasons why God is displeased with Israel is because of its practice of divorce (Mal 2:14). Malachi also teaches that God is involved in each marital union when he says, "The Lord was witness to the covenant between you and the wife of your youth" (Mal 2:14). Thus we can see in this prophetic text a development in the understanding that the covenant of marriage, as a sign of the covenant love of God for his people, should be faithful, fruitful, and indissoluble.

By the time we reach Malachi in the Old Testament, we can see a clear development in the understanding of marriage in its relationship to God's covenant. John Witte Jr. has identified six "major lessons for human marriage" that emerge in the prophetic tradition culminating in Malachi:

First, the covenant metaphor confirms the created form of marriage as a monogamous union between one man and one woman. . . .

Second, the covenant metaphor confirms that God participates in each marriage. . . .

Third, the covenant metaphor confirms the created procreative function of marriage. . . .

Fourth, the covenant metaphor confirms the divine laws governing marriage formation, as set out in both the Mosaic law and in the natural law revealed before Moses. . . .

Fifth, the covenant metaphor elevates these Mosaic laws of marriage, both by adding new provisions and by exemplifying how to live by the spirit of the law. . . .

Sixth, the covenant metaphor makes clear that each individual marital covenant between husband and wife is part and product of a much larger covenantal relationship between God and humanity.[47]

It took centuries for God to teach his people these lessons about human marriage, to clarify their vision of the nature of marriage that had been obscured by sin, and to get them to see marriage in relationship to the mystery of his love. By the end of the Old Testament period, many of these lessons still had to be taken fully to heart and many eyes still had to be fully opened. It is Jesus who will address and bring restoration to the hearts of men and women enabling them to see the truth of the mystery of marriage.

SUMMARY

Peter Elliott pointed out: "Marriage in Israel, according to the Old Testament, presents us with a changing complex of laws, customs and social conventions."[48] These laws, customs, and social conventions embody positive and negative trends. Throughout the Old Testament we see procreation stressed as the primary end of marriage. In the historical narratives we see a preference for monogamous marriages, and thus the good of fidelity and the property of unity, expressed through the negative examples of patriarchs and kings. However, we also see positive examples of marital fidelity and tenderness portrayed in the books of Ruth and Tobit. This latter book even provides us with an analogy between the "language of the body" that is spoken by

---

47. John Witte Jr., *From Sacrament to Contract: Marriage, Religion, and Law in the Western Tradition*, 2nd ed. (Louisville: KY: John Knox Press, 2012), 43–45.

48. Peter J. Elliott, *What God Has Joined: The Sacramentality of Marriage* (New York: Alba House, 1990), 12.

spouses and the "language of the liturgy." Through their prioritization of procreation as the primary purpose of marriage, the legal texts of the Old Testament also foster the stability of marriages for the purpose of rearing children in God's laws. This fosters the good and the property of permanence, as well as enforcing the good of fidelity. While polygamy was not explicitly rejected in the legal texts, and divorce was never forbidden, there was a developing understanding regarding marriage's properties of unity and indissolubility (CCC, 1610). The wisdom literature again stresses the procreation and education of children as the primary end of marriage, but also presupposes monogamous marriage, and thus supports the good of fidelity and the property of unity. The wisdom literature also provides Israel with the prototype of marriage in the creation narratives.

It is the prophets who explicitly begin to present marriage as analogous to God's covenant relationship with Israel. The essence of this covenant is mutual love, which is given and received freely, and has the hallmarks of fidelity, permanence, and fruitfulness. In the prophets, we see the procreation and education of children presented as the primary end of marriage, in their call for the Israelites to raise Godly children. In addition, the secondary end of marriage is present in God's covenant love (*hesed*) for his people which seeks nothing but their good. As God's people experience his love in their covenant relationship, they begin to understand what is required of them in their marriages. Over the centuries, "marriage based on exclusive and definitive love becomes the icon of the relationship between God and his people" (DCE, 11). Contrary to the concessions made for divorce in the legal code of the Old Testament, and in the history of its people, the prophetic literature presupposes the absolute fidelity and permanence of the marriage bond in its comparison to the undying love of God for his people. "Seeing God's covenant with Israel in the image of exclusive and faithful married love, the prophets prepared the Chosen People's conscience for a deepened understanding of the unity and indissolubility of marriage" (CCC, 1611), namely, the two essential properties of marriage. In addition, the prophets present us with a "prophetism of the body" that correlates with the "language of the body" that can be spoken either in falsehood or in truth.

As we look at how marriage was lived out in the Old Testament, we are led to the inexorable conclusion that the history of the Old

Testament from the time of Abraham shows a failure to live up to God's intended design for marriage (TOB 35:2). In the Old Testament the understanding of God's intention for marriage developed over time, primarily in conjunction with Israel's understanding of its covenant relationship with God. It is Jesus who will bring this covenant to its fulfillment. As a result, he will also fully reveal God's original intention for marriage as the "primordial sacrament" of his love, and will enable his disciples to live in accord with this design. Furthermore, Jesus will restore and elevate marriage to the level of a grace-giving sacrament, so that human spouses can participate in his spousal love for the Church. This will enable men and women to realize the vision of marriage presented by the prophets in their comparison of marriage to God's covenant with his people.

Chapter 8

Marriage in the New Testament

INTRODUCTION

In our overview of marriage in the Old Testament we saw God instituting his original plan for marriage as the "primordial sacrament" of his love. However, over the course of history we also saw God's people defecting from this plan. During the time of the later prophetic tradition, in the correlation of marriage with God's covenant love, we saw the prophets providing strong exhortations for the people to return to God's plan for marriage. As we turn to the New Testament, we see Jesus building on these exhortations, calling his followers to see and live the full truth of married love. At the time Jesus walked the earth, the people of God had inconsistently embraced God's design for marriage. Francis Martin has pointed out:

> The period into which Jesus was born was characterized by great variety in culture and religious practice. Most marriages were monogamous, fidelity and affection were esteemed, and children were cared for. Nevertheless, the position of women was generally inferior to that of men, and the availability of divorce, at least in some quarters, made life uncertain for them.[1]

Thus Jesus, building on what was correctly understood about marriage in his time, needed to purify people's vision of marriage and give them the ability to live out the fullness of God's design for it. We see him doing exactly this in the Gospels.

---

1. Francis Martin, "Marriage in the Old Testament and Intertestamental Periods," in *Christian Marriage: A Historical Study*, ed. Glenn Olsen (New York: The Crossroad Publishing Company, 2001), 38.

JESUS REASSERTS GOD'S PLAN FOR MARRIAGE FROM THE "BEGINNING"

Jesus initially showed his concern for marriage when he worked his first miracle at a wedding feast in Cana (Jn 2:1–11). It is here that he turned six large stone jars of water into wine, beginning to manifest his glory (Jn 2:11). The Church has always seen in Christ's presence at this wedding "the confirmation of the goodness of marriage and the proclamation that thenceforth marriage will be an efficacious sign of Christ's presence" (CCC, 1613). Later in his ministry Jesus will even proclaim that the Kingdom of God is like a wedding feast (Mt 22:1–14). At Cana, as the Messiah who came to usher in the reign or Kingdom of God, Jesus' presence was a prophetic action that similarly "proclaimed" the Kingdom of God as a wedding feast (Mt 22:1–14). [2]

As the first miracle that the God-man worked cannot be accidental, could it be that part of the reason Jesus worked the first of his great signs at a wedding feast was to signal that he had come to restore God's original plan for married love, so as to enable marriage to be a clearer sign of God's heavenly Kingdom? If such was Jesus' intention at the wedding in Cana, it is consistent with what Jesus taught about marriage when direct questions were posed to him about it.

Jesus explicitly announced his intention to reestablish God's original design for marriage in his response to a group of Pharisees who question him about the practice of divorce. This dialogue appears in the Gospels of both Matthew and Mark. We will analyze the dialogue as it is recorded in both Gospels, subdividing the dialogue into smaller pieces. The dialogue begins in the following way in Matthew's Gospel:

> And Pharisees came up to him and tested him by asking, "Is it lawful to divorce one's wife for any cause?" He answered, "Have you not read that he who made them from the beginning made them male and female, and said, 'For this reason a man shall leave his father and mother and be joined to his wife, and the two shall become one flesh'? So they are no longer two but one flesh. What therefore God has joined together, let not man put asunder." They said to him, "Why then did Moses command one to give a certificate of divorce, and to put her away?" He said to them,

2. Edward Schillebeeckx, *Marriage: Human Reality and Saving Mystery*, 2 vols., translated by N. D. Smith (New York: Sheed and Ward, 1965), 109.

"For your hardness of heart Moses allowed you to divorce your wives, but from the beginning it was not so." (Mt 19:3–8)

Note, also, the parallel text from Mark:

And Pharisees came up and in order to test him asked, "Is it lawful for a man to divorce his wife?" He answered them, "What did Moses command you?" They said, "Moses allowed a man to write a certificate of divorce, and to put her away." But Jesus said to them, "For your hardness of heart he wrote you this commandment. But from the beginning of creation, 'God made them male and female.' 'For this reason a man shall leave his father and mother and be joined to his wife, and the two shall become one flesh.' So they are no longer two but one flesh. What therefore God has joined together, let not man put asunder." (Mk 10: 2–9)

First of all, John Paul II emphasized how important it is to realize that in his response to the Pharisees' question about divorce, Jesus took the Pharisees back to the "beginning" (TOB 1:2). Jesus quotes both Genesis 1:27: "God made them male and female"; and Genesis 2:24: "Therefore a man leaves his father and his mother and cleaves to his wife, and they become one flesh." By quoting these texts, Jesus is taking the Pharisees, and us, back to the origins of our existence to reaffirm God's original plan for marriage and his original plan for the human person made male and female in God's image and likeness (TOB 1:4). As Jesus' response takes us back to the very "beginning" of humanity, John Paul II began the whole project of his *Theology of the Body* by addressing this dialogue between Jesus and the Pharisees. He called Christ's response to the Pharisees' question about divorce the first of three "words" that Jesus speaks which provide us with a theology of the body (TOB part 1 heading; these three words were discussed in chapter 2). The text of Genesis 1:27 reminds us that only as male *and* female is humanity made in the image and likeness of God. It also reminds us how important gender is in God's design, facilitating the formation of the fundamental "communion of persons" (TOB 9:2) in the one-flesh union referred to in Genesis 2:24. Both of these texts from the book of Genesis cited by Jesus recall the communal dimension of the *imago Dei* (see TOB 9:3) that we discussed in chapter 3. They recall the fact that "the 'definitive' creation of man consists in the creation of the unity of two beings" (TOB 9:1). Thus, by reminding the Pharisees that "God made them male and female," so that they may "become one flesh," Jesus reminds us that the "mystery of the relating of the sexes in marriage is inscribed by the Creator into the very fabric of humanity."[3]

      Secondly, in Jesus' response to the Pharisees' question about divorce, he definitively judges the Old Testament legislation on marriage, exemplified in Deuteronomy 24:1–4, in which Moses allowed for a "certificate of divorce" (Mt 19:7; Mk 10:3). By referring to the origin of this legislation as a "hardness of heart" (Mt 19:8; Mk 10:5), Jesus makes it clear that the bill of divorce was a concession to human weakness and sin. This "hardness of heart" denotes a "disobedience and lack of faith response to God" that was accommodated by a provisional commandment in the old law.[4] Jesus explicitly contrasts this provisional aspect of the Old Testament legal code with God's plan for marriage "in the beginning," reaffirming the perennial value of this plan and noting that there was no such provision for divorce in God's original design for marriage. By judging the Old Testament laws dealing with divorce, Jesus is asserting his own authority as God incarnate, and he is making it clear that with his coming the time for "hard hearts" is over. He then emphasizes the necessity of returning to God's original plan for marriage by stating, "What therefore God has joined together, let not man put asunder" (Mt 19:6; Mk 10:9), making it clear that the reference to the two becoming one in Genesis 2:24 "states the principle of the unity and indissolubility of marriage" (TOB 1:3). He also makes it clear that he is ushering in the renewal of married love.

JESUS ON DIVORCE

It is the Pharisees' question about divorce that prompted Jesus to reassert God's original design for marriage. After rooting his response "in the beginning," Jesus addresses the issue of divorce even more directly. Mark's Gospel states:

> And in the house the disciples asked him again about this matter. And he said to them, "Whoever divorces his wife and marries another, commits

---

3. Francis Martin, "Marriage in the New Testament Period," in *Christian Marriage: A Historical Study*, edited by Glenn Olsen (New York: The Crossroad Publishing Company, 2001), 53.

4. Ibid.

adultery against her; and if she divorces her husband and marries another, she commits adultery." (Mk 10:10–12)

A similar statement of Jesus appears in Luke's Gospel, even though it does not occur in the context of a dialogue with the Pharisees about divorce:

Everyone who divorces his wife and marries another commits adultery, and he who marries a woman divorced from her husband commits adultery. (Lk 16:18)

In Matthew's Gospel we have the same teaching in two places, once in the context of Jesus' discussion with the Pharisees, and another time in the context of Jesus' Sermon on the Mount. In both instances Jesus' teaching on divorce is the same as that contained in the Gospels of Mark and Luke, but with the addition of an exception clause:

And I say to you: whoever divorces his wife, except for unchastity, and marries another, commits adultery. (Mt 19:9)

It was also said, "Whoever divorces his wife, let him give her a certificate of divorce." But I say to you that everyone who divorces his wife, except on the ground of unchastity, makes her an adulteress; and whoever marries a divorced woman commits adultery. (Mt 5:31–32)

At first glance it can appear that there is a discrepancy between Mark and Luke, who present Jesus as opposing divorce without exception, and Matthew, who presents Jesus as opposing divorce except in the one instance of "unchastity," thus providing some type of an out. Much has been written by scholars and biblical exegetes about these exception clauses, and thus about how firm Jesus' condemnation of divorce really is. Thus, a brief articulation of the Catholic Church's position on these passages is warranted here.

The Greek term used in the exception clauses of Matthew 19:9 and Matthew 5:32, translated as "unchastity" above, is the word *porneia*, a word that could be used to refer to any kind of unlawful sexual conduct.[5] This is why various translations of Matthew 19:9 and Matthew 5:32 will render the term *porneia* as "fornication" (see the King James Version) or "sexual immorality" (see the New International

---

5. Raymond E. Brown, Joseph A. Fitzmyer, and Roland E. Murphy, eds., *The New Jerome Biblical Commentary* (Englewood Cliffs, NJ: Prentice Hall, 1990), 643.

Version). With these various renderings, the Eastern Orthodox as well as different Protestant traditions see the exception clauses of Matthew 19:9 and Matthew 5:32 providing for the possibility of divorce and remarriage in the instance that a spouse commits adultery. In the next chapter we will see that many in the early Church also understood *porneia* as referring to adultery. However, the early Church did not understand "divorce" as we do today in terms of the breaking of a marriage bond that allows for the possibility of forging a new marital union. Instead, as will be discussed in the next chapter, divorce in the early Church was understood as separation from one's spouse without the possibility of remarriage.

Furthermore, scholars note that the problem with rendering *porneia* in the Matthean exception clauses as "adultery" is that if Matthew had wanted to say that adultery allowed for divorce and remarriage, he would have used *moicheia*, the technical and more precise term for adultery.[6] Furthermore, in the Jewish milieu of Matthew's day, *porneia* could refer to incestuous unions that were within forbidden degrees of kinship, like those forbidden in Leviticus 18:6–18,[7] but which would have been permitted in the larger pagan Roman culture. If *porneia* is understood in this way, then what Jesus is saying in the exception clauses of Matthew's Gospel is that marriages within certain degrees of consanguinity (i.e., incestuous relationships) are invalid.[8] This is why other Catholic translations of the exception clauses are rendered in the following ways:

I say to you, whoever divorces his wife (unless the marriage is unlawful) and marries another commits adultery. (Mt 19:9) (New American Bible)

Now I say this to you: anyone who divorces his wife—I am not speaking of an illicit marriage—and marries another, is guilty of adultery. (Mt 19:9) (Jerusalem Bible)

Understanding *porneia* as referring to unlawful or illicit relationships makes it clear that when it comes to Jesus' teaching about divorce, there is no discrepancy between Matthew on the one hand

---

6. Ibid.

7. Ibid.

8. For further comments on various readings of *porneia* see *The New Jerome Biblical Commentary*, 643, and also Schillebeeckx, *Marriage*, 147-151.

and Mark and Luke on the other. It should also be noted that understanding the exception clauses of Matthew's Gospel as referring to illicit marriages helps to provide a basis for the Catholic Church's authority to grant annulments. Jesus is presenting us with the situation in which what might look like marriage, or might even be considered marriage by cultural and societal standards, may in fact be illicit/unlawful according to God's law, and therefore not a real marriage.

Regardless of how *porneia* is translated, the magisterium of the Catholic Church has never taught that the exception clauses in Matthew's Gospel refer to a situation in which a faithful spouse would be allowed to divorce an unfaithful spouse and remarry someone else because of the infidelity. First of all, this reading of Jesus' teaching on divorce would depart little from the legal provisions of the Old Testament and would be much less radical. Secondly, this would not be consistent with the spousal analogy present in the prophetic writings of the Old Testament in which God is presented as the model spouse *precisely because* he remains faithful to his bride, Israel, *even when* Israel is guilty of infidelity and therefore "adulterous" behavior. Third, if Jesus truly had offered adultery as an exception to the permanence of marriage, then committing an act of marital infidelity would allow an unfaithful and wayward spouse to get exactly what he or she presumably wants—the opportunity to dissolve the marriage and the ability to try again with someone he or she finds more desirable. Finally, that Jesus clearly forbade the divorce of lawful marriages can be seen in the reaction of his disciples who, upon hearing how Jesus responded to the Pharisees' question about divorce, say, "If such is the case of a man with his wife, it is not expedient to marry" (Mt 10:10). Their response shows that they understood clearly just how radical Jesus' teaching was.

The Catholic tradition has always read Jesus' teaching on divorce in Matthew's Gospel as consistent with the teaching presented in the Gospels of Mark and Luke. Francis Martin described Jesus' denial of divorce as a "revolutionary notion" because Jesus teaches that anyone who attempts to divorce and marry someone else commits adultery. Martin indicates that this notion had "never been encountered in Judaism" because it implies the "mutuality of personal rights" of both spouses, and does not treat adultery primarily "as an offense against a man's right to be sure that his children are truly his."[9] By clearly forbidding divorce Jesus enunciated a teaching that is consistent with the prophets' growing understanding of the permanence of marriage that culminates in the teaching of Malachi in which God says, "I hate divorce" (Mal 2:10–16). Asserting his own authority to interpret the law, Jesus as God incarnate unequivocally states that whoever divorces his or her spouse and marries someone else commits adultery. By going back to "the beginning" in the creation accounts in Genesis and reasserting the indissolubility of marriage, Jesus is renewing God's original intention for the "primordial sacrament" of married love.

JESUS ON ADULTERY

Jesus' intention to restore God's original design for married love can be seen further in his teaching on adultery. In the midst of his Sermon on the Mount, Jesus states: "You have heard that it was said, 'You shall not commit adultery.' But I say to you that every one who looks at a woman lustfully has already committed adultery with her in his heart" (Mt 5:27–28). It is in this text, dealing with the condition of man after the Fall, or "historical man" (TOB 25:1), that John Paul II saw the second of the three "words" of Christ that present us with a theology of the body, and thus a fundamental understanding of what it means to exist as male and female. In this exhortation of the Sermon on the Mount, Jesus rejects the understanding, inscribed in the legal codes of the Old Testament, that adultery is purely an external activity which involved having intercourse with another man's wife. In this way "Jesus brings about a *fundamental revision of the way of understanding and carrying out the moral law of the Old Covenant*" (TOB 24:1). The reality is that the old "law, while *combating sin, at the same time* contained in itself *the 'social structures of sin'*; in fact, it *protected* and legalized them" (TOB 36:1). John Paul II said that Christ "clearly sees the fundamental contradiction contained in the marriage law of the Old Testament inasmuch as it accepted effective polygamy, that is, the institution of concubines in addition to legitimate wives, or the right of cohabitation with a slave woman" (TOB 36:1). Jesus rejects "the casuistry of the books of the Old Testament, which . . . opened

9. Martin, "Marriage in the New Testament Period," 54.

various legal 'loopholes' for adultery" (TOB 24:4), and made various concessions for human sinfulness (TOB 35:1). "Christ wants to correct these distortions" (TOB 35:5). He has come to fulfill the law (Mt 5:17) and therefore also to fulfill the prophecy of Jeremiah through whom God promised to write his law in the hearts of his people (Jer 31:33).

Addressing adultery, Jesus literally takes us to the heart of the matter. While the old law recognized marriage and family as the basis of social life, its shortcoming was that it tried to regulate external behavior without ordering the heart (TOB 36:3). In the Bible the heart is understood as *"the center of man . . . [his] . . . source of will, emotion, thoughts, and affections"* (TOB 25:2, fn. 40). Just as Jesus diagnoses the cause of divorce as a "hardness of heart" (Mt 19:8), he similarly diagnoses the origin of adultery as a disorder of the heart. The "adultery of the heart" Jesus speaks of refers to concupiscence (TOB 26), or disordered desire, which we discussed in chapter 3. The hearts of fallen humanity struggle with concupiscence because original man and woman broke the covenant with God in their hearts (TOB 26:2). Now, Jesus has come to forge an everlasting covenant with humanity that seeks the renewal of the human heart. It is the disordered desire of lust, a disorder of the heart, that causes men and women to "depersonalize" each other, to lose sight of the "spousal meaning of the body" and the person as a gift (TOB 32:3), and tempts us to turn each other into objects of desire and appropriation (TOB 32:4–6). Even husbands and wives, giving into concupiscence in their hearts, can lose sight of the communion of persons they are called to form and instead, turn each other into objects of desire, using each other merely to satisfy a sexual urge (TOB 41:5; 43:1–3). This is confirmed when Jesus says in his Sermon on the Mount that *"every one"* is guilty of "adultery in the heart" when he looks at *"a woman,"* not just when a married man looks at a woman who is not his wife (TOB 43:2). John Paul II said that in our fallen state, "the 'heart' has become a battlefield between love and concupiscence" (TOB 32:3). However, Jesus has come not only to call us to acknowledge this interior struggle, but to help us win this battle. He has come to exhort us to "purity of heart" (TOB 43:5; see Mt 5:8) and to liberate our hearts from concupiscence so that we may find ourselves once more "in the freedom of the gift" (TOB 43:6).

However, as John Paul II pointed out, we must *"want to regain"* the fullness of our humanity that Christ offers us when he speaks to our hearts (TOB 43:7). We must be willing to rely upon the grace of redemption that Christ offers to help us reorder our hearts through the practice of temperance and continence so that we may achieve self-mastery and live in true freedom (TOB 49:1–5). In the Sermon on the Mount, Christ explains "the correct meaning of the commandment, 'You shall not commit adultery,'" by appealing to the hearts of all men and women, married and unmarried, calling all to a purity of heart (TOB 50:1–2). This purity is made possible through the indwelling power of the Holy Spirit whom he sends (TOB 51). Thus, as in his discussion with the Pharisees about divorce, Jesus calls us to realize God's original plan for love between man and woman, not only by forbidding sexual activity with anyone except one's spouse, but also by calling and empowering all of us to overcome lust in our hearts and to reverence each other as gifts. More will be said about the implications of this ethical call to reverence in the chapters dealing with married spirituality and sexual morality.

It should not be overlooked that in the course of reasserting God's original plan for the "primordial sacrament" of marriage in Matthew 19, Jesus also teaches us about the vocation to celibacy. Both Jesus (Mt 19:12) and St. Paul (1 Cor 7:7) present celibacy as a gift that is to be preferred to the vocation of marriage. This is important because understanding the vocation to consecrated celibacy helps us to understand the vocation to marriage and to put it in its proper perspective. We will have more to say about the New Testament teaching on celibacy and the relationship between marriage and celibacy in the final chapter of this book. For now, let us focus precisely on the New Testament teaching on marriage.

MARRIAGE AS A SACRAMENT OF THE NEW COVENANT

Now that we have covered Jesus' explicit teachings regarding marriage, we are poised to discuss the New Testament presentation of marriage as a sacrament of the New Covenant. John Paul II pointed out that "the one and only key for understanding the sacramentality of marriage is the spousal love of Christ for the Church" (TOB 81:4). Therefore, as we look for evidence in the New Testament that marriage is a sacrament of the new covenant, and thus one of the Seven Sacraments of the Catholic Church we must first note what is said about Jesus as spouse in the Gospels. In John's Gospel, John the Baptist refers to Jesus as the bridegroom when he says: "You yourselves bear me witness that I said, I am not the Christ, but I have been sent before him. He who has the bride is the bridegroom; the friend of the bridegroom, who stands and hears him, rejoices greatly at the bridegroom's voice; therefore this joy of mine is now full" (Jn 3:28–29). Jesus himself refers or alludes to himself as the bridegroom in Matthew's Gospel in the following passages:

> Then the disciples of John came to him, saying, "Why do we and the Pharisees fast, but your disciples do not fast?" And Jesus said to them, "Can the wedding guests mourn as long as the bridegroom is with them? The days will come, when the bridegroom is taken away from them, and then they will fast." (Mt 9:14)

> And again Jesus spoke to them in parables, saying, "The kingdom of heaven may be compared to a king who gave a marriage feast for his son." (Mt 22:1–2)

> "Then the kingdom of heaven shall be compared to ten maidens who took their lamps and went to meet the bridegroom." (Mt 25:1)

In addition, the whole New Testament ends with a reference to the heavenly wedding of the New Jerusalem with God who has come to dwell with her, which the Christian tradition has understood as the marriage between Christ and his Church:

> Then I saw a new heaven and a new earth; for the first heaven and the first earth had passed away, and the sea was no more. And I saw the holy city, new Jerusalem, coming down out of heaven from God, prepared as a bride adorned for her husband; and I heard a loud voice from the throne saying, "Behold, the dwelling of God is with men. He will dwell with them, and they shall be his people, and God himself will be with them." (Rev 21:1–3)

All of the above passages from the New Testament provide the foundation for seeing the relationship between Christ and the

Church as a marriage. In this analogy Christ is the bridegroom and the Church is the bride. Christ's bride is thus a universal union of corporate persons, composed of all believers in Christ, wherein Christ weds himself to each individual in the corporate personality of the Church beginning at the individual person's Baptism.

Building on the above references to Jesus as the bridegroom of the Church (that would have been transmitted orally in the tradition of the early Church), the fifth chapter of the Letter to the Ephesians provides us with probably the most important text for understanding marriage as a sacrament. The passage of Ephesians 5:21–33, which addresses Christian marriage, appears in the overall context of the Letter to the Ephesians, which begins "by presenting *the eternal plan of man's salvation in Jesus Christ*" (TOB 88:1; see Eph 1:3, 4–7, 10). The opening of the letter refers to the plan by which God "chose us in him [Christ] before the foundation of the world, that we should be holy and blameless before him" (Eph 1:4). The entirety of the Letter to the Ephesians, including chapter 5, must be read in light of this plan of God to save us in Christ, which Ephesians 1:9 calls the "mystery of his will." The particular section of Ephesians 5 reads as follows:

> Be subject to one another out of reverence for Christ. Wives, be subject to your husbands, as to the Lord. For the husband is the head of the wife as Christ is the head of the church, his body, and is himself its Savior. As the church is subject to Christ, so let wives also be subject in everything to their husbands. Husbands, love your wives, as Christ loved the church and gave himself up for her, that he might sanctify her, having cleansed her by the washing of water with the word, that he might present the church to himself in splendor, without spot or wrinkle or any such thing, that she might be holy and without blemish. Even so husbands should love their wives as their own bodies. He who loves his wife loves himself. For no man ever hates his own flesh, but nourishes and cherishes it, as Christ does the church, because we are members of his body. For this reason a man shall leave his father and mother and be joined to his wife, and the two shall become one flesh. This mystery is a profound one, and I am saying that it refers to Christ and the church; however, let each one of you love his wife as himself, and let the wife see that she respects her husband. (Eph 5:21–33)

Notice that at the outset this passage places the marriage of Christian spouses in relationship to Christ by saying, "Be subject to one another out of reverence for Christ" (Eph 5:21). It is the joint relationship of the spouses to Christ that provides the overall context for understanding Christian marriage as a sacrament of the new covenant. This one verse alone shows that "the reciprocal relations of husband and wife must spring from their common relation with Christ" (TOB 89:1). The behavior of Christian spouses toward each other must therefore be formed by the mystery of Christ (TOB 89:2) and the plan of salvation that is accomplished in him, which was referred to in Ephesians 1:1–9. As John Paul II said: "This is unquestionably a new presentation of the eternal truth about marriage and the family in the light of the new covenant" (LF, 19).

We should also draw attention to the fact that in Ephesians 5:21, spouses are exhorted to be mutually subject to each other. Francis Martin noted that "subordinate", rather than "subject" or "submissive", is a better rendering of the verb in this passage and that this expression is uncommon in pagan or Jewish literature.[10] He stated that "subordination" connotes a readiness to renounce one's own will for the sake of the other, and thus is based in love.[11] He noted further: "It is difficult to understand what kind of relation the New Testament is describing by using this vocabulary, but, from the fact that Ephesians urges mutual subordination, we see that an advance has been made in a biblical understanding of anthropology: it is a question of love."[12] The relationship of mutual subordination/subjection/submission to love becomes clearer when one is reminded that this mutual subjection flows out of the couple's reverence for Christ (TOB 89:2). "Love makes the *husband simultaneously subject* to his wife, and *subject* in this *to the Lord himself*, as the wife is to the husband" (TOB 89:4). Thus, Ephesians 5:21 is highlighting the fact that marriage is "a reciprocal gift [of love], which is also a mutual submission" (TOB 89:4). This mutual submission of wife to husband and husband to wife "is evidently something 'new': it is an innovation of the Gospel" (MD, 24). It is in this mutual submission to each other out of reverence for Christ that a "true *'communion' of persons* is realized" (TOB 89:6) between the married couple.

---

10. Martin, "Marriage in the New Testament Period," 83.
11. Ibid., 84.
12. Ibid.

Following the opening verse of this exhortation to married couples, there is an exhortation directed toward wives (Eph 5:22–24). In this part of the text we immediately see the relationship between husband and wife analogized to the relationship between Christ and the Church. "Husbands and wives thus discover in Christ *the point of reference for their spousal love*" (LF, 19). In this way the spousal analogy that had been applied to the relationship between Yahweh and his people in the Old Testament is being applied to the relationship between Christ and his Church (TOB 87:4; 95:1). Just as the comparison of marriage to the covenant relationship between God and his people in the Old Testament led to a mutual illumination of both marriage and the covenant, likewise the comparison of Christian marriage to the relationship between Christ and the Church offers a mutual illumination of Christian marriage and the manner in which Jesus accomplishes the plan of salvation in the new covenant (TOB 95b:5). According to this spousal analogy Christ is the divine bridegroom and his bride is the "collective subject . . . the People of God" (MD, 25). This spousal union of Christ with the Church is a continuation and perfection of the spousal love God showed for Israel in the Old Testament (TOB 94:6). The author of Ephesians is showing that Jesus reveals the depths of the mystery of God's spousal love to which the prophets referred (TOB 95:2).

In the exhortation directed to wives, wives are asked to relate to their husbands as the Church relates to its "head," who is Christ. First of all, this reference to "headship" implies a relationship of origin, priority, and source, as can be seen in other Pauline texts which emphasize that the man was created first, and out of him the woman was made (1 Cor 11:8–9; 1 Tim 2:13).[13] It also implies a hierarchy in which the man assumes a function of leadership.[14] It would be impossible for us to expect that the understanding of this leading role of the husband in relation to his wife expressed in Ephesians would be free from the social and cultural influences of the day. Examples of this influence can be seen in other Pauline texts where a woman is forbidden to pray with her head uncovered (1 Cor 11:3–16) or to teach or hold authority over men (1 Tim 2:11–15) because of her relation to her

---

13. See Peter J. Elliott, *What God Has Joined: The Sacramentality of Marriage* (New York: Alba House, 1990), 51.

14. Edward Schillebeeckx, *Marriage*, 191–192.

husband as her "head." Still other instances exist in the New Testament in which the wife's subordination to the headship of the husband is presented according to the religious tradition of Israel (Col 3:18; 1 Pt 3:1–6; Tit 2:4–5; 1 Cor 14:33–35; see MD, 24). However, the view of the headship of the husband in the Letter to the Ephesians breaks away from the broader cultural vision of the "head of the family" or *pater familias* according to which the husband exercised an overbearing, almost absolute, authority in the home.[15] Ephesian's vision of headship also departs from traditional Jewish models. It can be seen that the letter presents a new Christian vision of "headship" when it says that the husband is the head of his wife "*as* Christ is the head of the church" (Eph 5:22), effectively commanding the husband to exercise his headship in imitation of Christ. Moreover, Ephesians immediately presents "headship" as having a saving function, implying that the husband as head of his wife should seek to provide for her salvation, as Christ saves the Church.[16]

As we continue to examine the exhortation to wives present in the Letter to the Ephesians, the letter emphasizes the fact that the marriage of Christian spouses must be understood in light of Christ and in light of his relationship with his Church. This *must* be kept in mind when we read the verses that call for the wives to be subordinate to their husbands (Eph 5:22, 24).[17] At times in Christian circles these verses referring to wifely subordination/subjection/submission have been used to support some type of dysfunctional vision of the relationship between spouses wherein the husband functions as the king of his castle and the wife is his servant. John Paul II noted: "The author does not intend to say that the husband is the 'master' of the wife and that the interpersonal covenant proper to marriage is a contract of domination by the husband over the wife" (TOB 89:3). This would be a complete and utter distortion of the meaning of the text, which makes it clear that the model of subordination/subjection/submission of wife to husband is to be found in the relationship of the Church to

---

15. Ibid., 189.

16. Ibid., 136.

17. Paul had issued a similar exhortation for wives to be subordinate to their husbands in his letter to the Colossians 3:18–19. An additional instruction regarding this subordination can be found in the First Letter of Peter. In this letter, wives are exhorted to be subordinate to their husbands, even if their husbands are not Christian, so their husbands might be won over to Christ through their reverence and their inner beauty (1 Pet 3:1–7).

Christ—and Christ said explicitly that he did not come to be served, but to serve (Mt 20:28; Mk 10:45). Regarding the exhortation of the wife to be subordinate to her husband, Francis Martin stated:

> We have here a Christian adaptation of an existing, specific vocabulary to describe a new reality. The term *hypotassesthai* [to be subordinate] is in the middle voice, addressing the woman as a free person exhorted to conform freely to the will of God in relation to her husband. Thus, while the term indicates a willingness to "give way" to another, the avoidance of the usual obedience vocabulary in regard to the wife (though it is used of children and slaves) shows that something new is being suggested within a culture that could not envisage actual reciprocity between man and wife. [18]

So, far from commanding the wife to be passively submissive to her husband, the Letter to the Ephesians is exhorting her to renounce her will out of love for her husband, seeking his good in the mystery of Christ. Thus even though the ideas of headship and subordination may be "rooted in the customs and religious traditions of the time, [we must remember that this manner of speaking] is to be understood and carried out in a new way: as a *'mutual subjection out of reverence for Christ'* (cf. Eph 5:21)" (MD, 24).

After addressing wives, the Letter to the Ephesians turns to addressing husbands, who receive a longer exhortation than wives (Eph 5:25–31). Husbands are immediately exhorted to love their wives (Eph 5:25). What is more, the love husbands are commanded to offer is *agape*, loving as God loves. This makes clear the type of "headship" the husband must exercise, and it clarifies that the mutual subordination of spouses is grounded in love. As John Paul II noted: "Love excludes every kind of submission by which the wife would become a servant or slave of the husband, an object of one-sided submission" (TOB 89:4). The fact that the language of "subordination" is applied more directly to the wife and "love" is applied more directly to the husband may show some cultural residue still present in the letter to the Ephesians. However, "it may be that within the exercise of mutual self-subordination the mystery of this relationship still contains aspects that are hidden from our highly individualistic and rights-oriented thinking." [19] Whatever the case, the Letter to the

---

18. Martin, "Marriage in the New Testament Period," 84.
19. Ibid., 91.

Ephesians is presenting a new paradigm for spousal relations. This becomes clear when one realizes that the love (*agape*) that the husband is commanded to offer his wife has as its prototype the love that Christ offers to the Church by giving his life for her (Eph 5:25), a love that no man can offer without being empowered to do so by God's grace.

In language that is reminiscent of the prophet Ezekiel (Ez 16:8–14), the letter to the Ephesians shows Christ, through his self-oblation of love, sanctifying his bride (Eph 5:26), making her beautiful with his love (Eph 5:27), and thus serving as her Savior (Eph 5:23). Analogously, "love binds the bridegroom (husband) to be concerned for the good of the bride (wife); it commits him to desire her beauty and at the same time to sense this beauty and care for it" (TOB 92:4). Likewise, a husband is exhorted to love his wife with an outpouring of self, through which he seeks his wife's sanctification (TOB 91:6). He should seek to make her beautiful with his love and serve her good in such a way that he facilitates her salvation. John Paul II provided an interesting insight here when he stated: "*The husband* is above all *the one who loves* and the wife, by contrast, is the *one who is loved*. One might even venture the idea that the wife's 'submission' to the husband, understood in the context of the whole of Ephesians 5:22–23, means above all 'the experience of love'" (TOB 92:6). Thus once again it becomes clear that the headship and the submission/subordination/subjection about which Ephesians speaks must be viewed in the context of love. It also becomes abundantly clear that the couple cannot realize this type of *agape* love in their marriage unless Christ himself is somehow operative in their union.

The next four verses (Eph 25:28–31), continue to address husbands. Just as the prophetic literature of the Old Testament incorporated the body into the spousal analogy of God's love for his people, these verses draw attention to the body in the analogy of spousal love to Christ's love for his Church. The body had already peripherally entered into the spousal analogy earlier in the passage with the head-body analogy of Christ/husband/head–Church/wife/body. Now, the emphasis on the body becomes more pronounced when husbands are called to love their wives as they love their own bodies (Eph 5:28), showing the intimacy and the unity that should exist between spouses. By exhorting a husband to love his wife as he loves his own body, Ephesians shows that "love makes the 'I' of the other person one's own 'I'" (TOB 92:6). Since husbands and wives hand themselves over to each other through their bodies, their bodies now belong to each other, and they have the moral responsibility of caring for each other's bodies in love (TOB 92:6). A husband is exhorted to nourish and cherish his wife as he does his own body, and he is commanded to do this in the manner in which Christ nourishes and cherishes his body, the Church (Eph 5:29–30), presenting us with Eucharistic allusions (TOB 92:8). The head-body and husband-wife analogies used in Ephesians 5 come together to show that Christ and the Church, and husbands and wives, join to form an "organic union" in which the spouses remain distinct, yet are inseparably united in one flesh (TOB 91:2) and *become in some sense a single subject*" (TOB 91:3).

It is at this point, after presenting the analogy between marriage and Christ's union with his Church, that the author of Ephesians cites "the fundamental text on marriage in the whole Bible, Genesis 2:24" (TOB 93:1): "For this reason a man shall leave his father and mother and be joined to his wife, and the two shall become one flesh" (Eph 5:31). By citing Genesis 2:24, the author of Ephesians links Christian marriage to God's original plan for marriage and emphasizes the unity that exists between husband and wife and between Christ and the Church. He also places undeniable emphasis on the body. On this score, John Paul II called Ephesians 5:21–33 the "crowning" (TOB 87:2) of the other three words Jesus had spoken regarding a theology of the body when he addressed original man (Mt 19:4; Mk 10:6), historical man (Mt 5:28), and resurrected man (Mt 22:30; Mk 12:25; Lk 20:35–36; this last word will be addressed in the final chapter). John Paul noted that the words of Ephesians 5:21–33 "are centered on the body, both in its *metaphorical meaning*, that is, on the body of Christ which is the Church, and *in its concrete meaning*, that is, on the human body in its perennial masculinity and femininity, in its perennial destiny for union in marriage" (TOB 87:3). Thus, in this passage of the Letter to the Ephesians, the body itself is presented as a "sacrament, which is 'a visible sign of an invisible reality,' namely, of the spiritual, transcendent, and divine reality" (TOB 87:5) of Christ's union with the Church.

It is at this point that the passage of Ephesians which is addressed to Christian spouses culminates in its penultimate verse, stating: "This mystery is a profound one, and I am saying that it refers to Christ and the church" (Eph 5:32). What the author says here is profoundly rich and deep. First of all, having just cited Genesis 2:24, which refers to the man and the woman becoming one flesh, the author applies this one-flesh reality to the relationship of Christ and his Church. The Letter to the Ephesians is therefore intertwining the mystery of Christ's union with the Church with marriage between a man and a woman, instituted by God in the beginning as the "primordial sacrament" of his love. These two realities of Christ/Church and husband/wife are so closely associated with each other that John Paul II wrote:

> The Church cannot therefore be understood as the mystical body of Christ, as the sign of man's covenant with God in Christ, or as the universal sacrament of salvation, unless we keep in mind the "great mystery" involved in the creation of man as male and female and the vocation of both to conjugal love, to fatherhood and motherhood. The "great mystery," which is the Church and humanity in Christ, does not exist apart from the "great mystery" expressed in the "one flesh" (cf. Gen 2:24; Eph 5:3–32), this is, in the reality of marriage and the family. (LF, 19)

In this comment, John Paul identified two referents for the "great mystery," both of which mutually interpenetrate each other. Primarily, the author of the Letter to the Ephesians is pointing out that the union of Christ with the Church is a profound or "great mystery" (*mega mysterion* in Greek; *magnum sacramentum* in Latin), as Christ came to give himself to the Church through the flesh so that he might be one with her. In the Letter to the Ephesians, Christ's love for the Church is presented as *the* great mystery or sacrament, which is *the* spousal love, and his relationship to the Church is presented as *the* marriage. The rite of marriage acknowledges this when it states: "O God, who consecrated the bond of Marriage / by so great a mystery / that in the wedding covenant you foreshadow / the Sacrament of Christ and his Church / . . . "[20] Thus marriage is a sign of the greatest manifestation of God's love, which is Christ's offering of himself for the Church. By comparing the original one-flesh union of the original husband and wife (Gen 2:24) to Christ's union with the Church, the author of the Letter to the Ephesians presents the "primordial sacrament" of the marriage of the original man and woman as a sign not

---

20. RM, "Collect B."

only of God's love, but of the union of Jesus as the New Adam with the Church as the New Eve.[21] The spousal love, according to which the Son of God becomes incarnate and offers himself for the restoration and the salvation of his beloved, is the union which all marriages foreshadowed. This is also the fulfillment of the spousal love that God offered his people in the Old Testament. "The marriage imagery applied to Yhwh and Israel has now taken on a human form in Christ and the Church."[22] This mystery of Christ's union with the Church is great because it fully reveals the mystery "'hidden' for eternity in God," namely his desire to draw us into his own life of love (TOB 90:1).

However, as marriage was intended by God to be the "primordial sacrament" of his love for man that foreshadowed Christ's spousal self-offering to the Church, the "great mystery" also refers to the marriage between a husband and a wife. Similar to the spousal analogy applied by the prophets, according to whom marriage and God's covenant with his people shed light on each other, the Letter to the Ephesians presents us with a mutual illumination of two realities. John Paul II made this clear when he wrote:

> The *image of spousal love*, together with the figure of the divine Bridegroom—a very clear image in the texts of the Prophets—finds crowning confirmation in the Letter to the Ephesians (5:23–32). . . . In St. Paul's text the analogy of the spousal relationship moves simultaneously in two directions which make up the whole of the "great mystery" ("*sacramentum magnum*"). The covenant proper to spouses "explains" the spousal character of the union of Christ with the Church, and in its turn this union, as a "great sacrament," determines the sacramentality of marriage as a holy covenant between the two spouses, man and woman. (MD, 23)

Thus not only does marriage help to illuminate the mystery of salvation that is accomplished in Christ's self-offering for his Church, but the mystery of Christ's relationship with his Church illuminates marriage (TOB 90:2; 95b:5). John Paul II elaborated on this point when he stated:

> While the analogy used in Ephesians clarifies the mystery of the relationship between Christ and the Church, at the same time *it reveals the essential truth about marriage*, namely, that marriage corresponds to

---

21. Martin, "Marriage in the New Testament Period," 89–90.
22. Ibid., 92.

the vocation of Christians only when it mirrors the love that Christ, the Bridegroom, gives to the Church, his Bride, and which the Church . . . seeks to give back to Christ in return. This is redeeming, saving love, the love with which man has been loved by God from eternity in Christ [see Ephesians 1:4]. (TOB 90:2)

By saying, "This mystery [of the one-flesh union of husband and wife referred to in the previous verse] is a profound one, and I am saying that it refers to Christ and the church" (Eph 5:32), the author of the Letter to the Ephesians is identifying Christian marriage itself as a mystery because it now has reference to, and is drawn into, the relationship of Christ with his Church. It is clear in Ephesians 5 that "Christians should understand the reciprocal relationship between spouses, husbands and wives, according to the image of the relationship between Christ and the Church" (TOB 90:1). Throughout this whole passage of Ephesians that is addressed to Christian spouses, it is evident that the marriages of Christians are set in a special relationship to Christ and that they are supposed to be *living signs* of Christ's love for his Church. This is, in fact, the whole basis of the exhortations that the author of Ephesians issues to Christian husbands and wives. Furthermore, "to be able to recommend such an obligation [to spouses], one must admit that the very essence of marriage contains *a particle of the same mystery* [of the relationship between Christ and the Church]. Otherwise, this whole analogy would hang in a void" (TOB 90:3).

More than just exhorting Christian spouses to look to Christ's love for his Church as a model for them to emulate, this passage of Ephesians presents Christ's relationship with his Church "as a reality from which . . . [spouses] . . . can draw life and empowerment."[23] They can do this because they have been baptized into Christ and are members of his body (Eph 5:30). Thus, Christian spouses are supposed to be signs—sacraments—of Christ's relationship with his Church, and as baptized members of Christ, he empowers them by giving them the grace they need to be this sign. Participating in the "great mystery" of Christ's love for his Church in the Sacrament of Marriage, "the love of the husband for his wife and his willingness to lay down his life for her makes the action of Christ present to her, just as her response to him makes their marriage a realization of the

---

23. Ibid., 90.

Church."[24] Thus Christian "marriage . . . is itself a realization on another level of this mystery of love," "by which Christ created his Bride . . . sustains her and builds her up."[25] Being one in Christ and sharing in the "great mystery" of his relationship to his Church, Christian spouses build up the Body of Christ and its unity in their own marriages.[26] The Letter to the Ephesians, therefore, effectively brings the visible sign of Christ and the Church and the visible sign of Christian marriage together, "making of them *the single great sign . . . a great sacrament ('sacramentum magnum')*" (TOB 95b:7).

With its reference to the "great mystery" Ephesians 5:32 presents us with the foundation for understanding the sacramentality of marriage (TOB 93:4). The *Catechism of the Catholic Church* defines the Seven Sacraments of the New Covenant as "efficacious signs of grace, instituted by Christ and entrusted to the Church, by which divine life is dispensed to us" (CCC 131). Thus a sacrament of the New Covenant is not just any sign, but a sign that effects, or brings into being, the reality of grace that it signifies (TOB 93:5). Each of the Seven Sacraments of the Catholic Church is a visible sign of the mystery of salvation that makes that mystery present and becomes "a means for accomplishing [that mystery] in man" (TOB 93:5). We need to remember that the mystery of salvation is that "mystery hidden from eternity in God, about which Ephesians speaks immediately at the beginning (see Eph 1:9)" (TOB 93:5). Ephesians presents us with the reality that this mystery is made fully manifest in Christ's spousal union with his Church, of which Christian marriage is a visible and effective sign (TOB 95b:7), empowering couples to love with spousal *agape*. Walter Kasper briefly explained the basis for understanding marriage as a sacrament that is found in the Letter to the Ephesians when he noted that in the Pauline writings "*mysterion* always points to God's eternal plan of salvation and his saving will that became a historical reality in Jesus Christ and a present reality in the Church. It is within this all-embracing reality of salvation that marriage is included."[27] The author of Ephesians does indeed include marriage in

---

24. Ibid.

25. Ibid., 91.

26. Ibid.

27. Walter Kasper, *Theology of Christian Marriage*, translated by David Smith (New York: Seabury Press, 1980), 30.

God's plan of salvation. He presents the love of Christian spouses as an effective sign of the redemptive spousal love of Christ, by which he gives himself up for the Church and accomplishes the very mystery of salvation hidden in God for all eternity (TOB 95b:1).

If one is to ask when exactly Jesus instituted marriage as one of the Seven Sacraments of the Church, "which express and confer divine grace on the person who receives" them (TOB 98:7), the first answer is that "Christ by his actions [as the Bridegroom] is already rendering Marriage sacramental."[28] As Walter Kasper noted: "The sacramental nature of marriage cannot be proved by using individual words of institution. It is more important to show that marriage is sacramental because it is fundamentally related to the saving work of Jesus Christ."[29] Therefore, referring to himself as the bridegroom who comes to save us, Christ already reveals that he is endowing marriage with a higher significance. However, it is possible to say that Christ institutes the Sacrament of Marriage more precisely in his conversation with the Pharisees (Mt 19; Mk 10). It is in this conversation that Jesus makes clear his intention to renew married love as part of his work of redemption. It is here that he proclaims marriage to be indissoluble and "thereby opens marriage to the salvific action of God . . . to build the unity of man and woman according to the Creator's eternal plan" (TOB 100:2).

Not only does Ephesians 5 present us with the foundation for understanding marriage as a sacrament but it also provides the basis for understanding the origin of all of the sacraments of the New Covenant (TOB 93:4). Ephesians shows that from the institution of marriage in the beginning as a "primordial sacrament" of God's love, there is a gradual unfolding of the mystery of salvation that culminates in Christ's spousal union with his Church (TOB 93:2–3), which John Paul II called "the sacrament of redemption" (TOB 97:2). By comparing "the indissoluble relationship of Christ and the Church to the relationship between husband and wife" and by referring to "the beginning," Ephesians summarizes all of salvation history, and presents marriage as *"the foundation of the whole sacramental order"* (TOB 95b:7).

---

28. Peter J. Elliott, *What God has Joined*, 19.
29. Walter Kasper, *Theology of Christian Marriage*, 28.

John Paul II elaborated on this reality, which is often given little attention, when he stated:

> The Mystery hidden from all eternity in God—a mystery that in the beginning in the sacrament of creation became *a visible reality through the union* of the first man and the first woman in the perspective of marriage—becomes in the sacrament of redemption *a visible reality in the indissoluble union of Christ with the Church*, which the author of Ephesians presents as the spousal union of the two, husband and wife. (TOB 97:4)

Thus, as was mentioned in chapter 6, natural marriage is the "primordial sacrament" of God's love offered in the beginning of creation, and Christian marriage is the effective sacrament of God's offering of redemptive love in Christ. This means that throughout salvation history, even after sin, "marriage has remained the platform for the realization of God's eternal plans" (TOB 97:1). From the beginning of creation the love of a husband and a wife was intended to be "an image of the absolute and unfailing love with which God loves man" (CCC, 1604). In the fullness of time (Gal 4:4), God gave "a total and irrevocable gift of self . . . to man in Christ" and by this gift accomplished salvation (TOB 95b:2). Marriage therefore "reaches its definitive fullness in the gift of love which the Word of God makes to humanity in assuming a human nature, and in the sacrifice which Jesus Christ makes of himself on the Cross for his bride, the Church" (FC, 13). Thus, "The author of Ephesians proclaims that this primordial sacrament is realized in a new way in the 'sacrament' of Christ and the Church" (TOB 99:2).

Christ's spousal gift of self to the Church is the source of not only the Sacrament of Marriage, but of all the sacraments of the New Covenant. Christ gives the fruits of redemption and his very self to the Church, his bride, in an act of spousal donation, "according to the likeness of the spousal relationship between husband and wife" (TOB 94:5). It is from this spousal giving of self, this "great sacrament" of Christ's union with the Church, that all of the graces of the sacraments flow (TOB 99:1). The *Catechism of the Catholic Church* elaborates on this spousal paradigm when it states:

> The entire Christian life bears the mark of the spousal love of Christ and the Church. Already Baptism, the entry into the People of God, is a nuptial mystery; it is so to speak the nuptial bath which precedes the wedding

feast, the Eucharist. Christian marriage in its turn becomes an efficacious sign, the sacrament of the covenant of Christ and the Church. (CCC, 1617)

Marriage, therefore, is the basis upon which we can understand the whole sacramental economy that Christ brings into being through the Church. All of the grace that he offers comes as a result of his spousal offering of self on the Cross, as the bridegroom who seeks to make his bride holy and beautiful so as to save her—this is truly a "great mystery"!

The "Pauline Privilege" and the Sacrament of Marriage

Exhorted and empowered to be a sacrament of Christ's love for the Church, and thereby to build up the unity of the Church, we need to turn to what St. Paul has to say about Christian marriages in the seventh chapter of his First Letter to the Corinthians. Paul states:

> To the married I give charge, not I but the Lord, that the wife should not separate from her husband (but if she does, let her remain single or else be reconciled to her husband)—and that the husband should not divorce his wife. (1 Cor 7:10–11)

Paul's teaching, which he credits to Jesus, is clear and simple: for Christians there is no such thing as divorce that would allow for remarriage. Even if a couple is estranged from each other and cannot live together, this does not afford them the opportunity to find a new spouse. They are married "in the Lord" (1 Cor 7:39), and in light of Ephesians 5, for them to try to divorce would mean falsifying the living sign of Christ's love for his Church that they are called to be.

Paul continues with his instructions about divorce in 1 Corinthians 7, addressing the situation in which a non-Christian couple is already married, and one spouse converts to Christianity while the other does not. Paul states:

> To the rest I say, not the Lord, that if any brother has a wife who is an unbeliever, and she consents to live with him, he should not divorce her. If any woman has a husband who is an unbeliever, and he consents to live with her, she should not divorce him. For the unbelieving husband is consecrated through his wife, and the unbelieving wife is consecrated

through her husband. Otherwise, your children would be unclean, but as it is they are holy. (1 Cor 7: 12–14)

Here we see Paul admittedly presenting pastoral advice of his own, not the Lord's. He is applying Jesus' teaching about the non-admissibility of divorce to a particular situation. Doing so, Paul presents the newly converted Christian spouse as a type of evangelizer and sanctifier in the home, consecrating the non-Christian spouse and their children through his or her love. The difference in the spouses' faith does not give the newly Christian spouse the right to divorce the non-Christian spouse, as long as the non-Christian spouse is willing to continue to live with the Christian spouse in peace.

However, in 1 Corinthians 7, Paul also addresses the situation in which a non-Christian spouse is unwilling to live in peace with a spouse who converts to Christianity. He says:

But if the unbelieving partner desires to separate, let it be so; in such a case the brother or sister is not bound. For God has called us to peace. Wife, how do you know whether you will save your husband? Husband, how do you know whether you will save your wife? (Cor 7: 15–16)

In this final case, we see Paul remaining consistent in applying his rule that the impetus for a divorce must not start with the newly converted Christian spouse. The implication is that the Christian spouse has the responsibility of always working for unity and peace in the home, consecrating his household to God. Yet, Paul points out that it could be the case that the non-Christian spouse may be unwilling to live in peace with the newly converted Christian spouse, and may take the initiative to divorce the Christian spouse. In this case, which is called the "Pauline Privilege" in Christian tradition and in the *Code of Canon Law* (see CIC 1143–1147), Paul says that the Christian spouse is not bound to the marriage. While it is implied that the Christian spouse is obligated to do everything possible to live in peace and harmony with the non-Christian spouse, the non-Christian, not participating in the life of Christ through Baptism, may decide not to tolerate the Christian spouse's new-found commitment of faith.

This pastoral instruction of St. Paul is important because it points to the fact that there is something unique about Christian marriage. In light of the Letter to the Ephesians' presentation of

Christian marriage as a participation in the "great mystery" of Christ's love for the Church, Paul's counsel highlights the fact that Christian marriages, in which both spouses have been incorporated into Christ's Mystical Body (see 1 Cor 12:12–31) through Baptism, are absolutely indissoluble. Paul is not denying that all marriages are covenants, or that they should be permanent, as he indicates by forbidding a Christian spouse to divorce a non-Christian spouse. As we discussed in chapters 4 and 5, because spouses have handed themselves over to each other, a new reality has come into being and no true marriage, even among nonbelievers, can be dissolved based upon the arbitrary whim of the spouses.[30] However, relying upon merely human resolve, spouses and society may find reasons to compromise the permanence of marriage. By articulating his provision, St. Paul is clearly prioritizing the Christian spouse's salvation and relationship with Christ above everything else in a situation where the non-Christian spouse is hostile to their spouse's newly found faith in Jesus. Paul is, in fact, subordinating all human relationships to a person's relationship with Christ. However, Paul is also implying that marriage between Christians has taken on a new quality precisely because their spousal union has been subordinated and incorporated into Christ. In its connection with Christ's indissoluble union with the Church, Christian marriage itself is made absolutely indissoluble, depending no longer on mere human resolve. Thus, because of the uniqueness of Christian marriage that is being attested to by Pauline instruction, Edward Schillebeeckx stated that he believed "the strongest biblical basis for the sacramental aspect of marriage is to be found in 1 Corinthians 7:15."[31] It is only Christian spouses who fully participate in Christ's love for his Church, and

---

30. Dietrich von Hildebrand, *Marriage: The Mystery of Faithful Love* (Manchester, NH: Sophia Institute Press, 1991), 56. On the indissolubility of natural marriage vs. Christian marriage von Hildebrand noted: "If we were to conceive the world merely as a mechanism not ruled by an almighty and infinitely good God, a world in which our being ceases completely with death, then an objectivity which is beyond the arbitrary decision of the spouses would be nonsense.

"Once the existence of God is admitted, the marriage bond is immediately placed beyond the arbitrary decision of the consorts, even if they do not refer themselves subjectively to God.

"Therefore, no real marriage (even among pagans) can be dissolved according to the whim of the partners. But that its indissolubility is not absolute is proved by the Pauline privilege. Only sacramental marriage as an image of the union of Christ and the Church possesses that full validity and reality which make it absolutely indissoluble."

31. Schillebeeckx, *Marriage: Human Reality and Saving Mystery*, 159.

because of this participation in the "great mystery" Christian marriages attain the absolute permanence for which all true lovers long.

SUMMARY

In the New Testament we see Jesus building on the foundational understanding of marriage that was presented in the Old Testament, including building on the exhortations of the prophets to live marriage in a way that reflects God's covenant love with his people. Jesus makes it clear that he intends to renew God's original plan for marriage as a "primordial sacrament" of God's love (Mt 19:3–8; Mk 10:2–9), and he shows the implications of this intention in what he says about divorce (Mt 5:31–32, 19:9; Mk 10:10–12; Lk 16:18) and adultery (Mt 5:27–28). In the process of reasserting the plan for marriage from the "beginning," he also presents his followers with the possibility of living a life of celibacy (Mt 19:10–12), thus allowing us to place marriage in its proper perspective in relation to the Kingdom of Heaven (Mt 22:23–30). Finally, Jesus provides the basis for seeing in marriage a sacrament of the New Covenant when he presents himself as the bridegroom (Mt 9:14; Mt 22:1–2; Mt 25:1). The Pauline letters elaborate on marriage in several places (1 Cor 7, 14:33–35; Col 3:18; Tit 2:4–5), but it is in the letter to the Ephesians (5:21–33) that "the author has opened up the full implications of the wedding between the Word and humanity."[32] This has laid the theological foundation for understanding marriage as a sacrament of the New Covenant, an integral part of the "great mystery" of Christ's union with his Church. Throughout the centuries theologians and the teaching authority of the Church will seek to explore the depths of the "great mystery" to articulate more clearly the gift that Christ gives to the Church in the Sacrament of Marriage. Part 4 of this book will provide an overview of this clearer vision of, growing appreciation for, and deeper understanding of Christian marriage that has emerged over the past two thousand years.

---

32. Martin, "Marriage in the New Testament Period," 92.

Part IV

The Development of the Theology of Marriage: A Brief Survey

The fourth part of this book will trace the development of the Church's corporate understanding of marriage from the time of the post-Apostolic period up through the twentieth century. From the earliest days of the Church, Christian marriage was seen as something holy, intimately related to Christ's love for the Church as expressed in the Letter to the Ephesians. Over the centuries, the Holy Spirit guided the Church into a deeper understanding of marriage as one of the Seven Sacraments that were instituted by Christ to confer grace. A developing understanding of marriage took time and included the need to overcome erroneous theological opinions pertaining to marriage and the marital act. This historical survey concludes with the insights of John Paul II who, in response to modern tendencies that challenged the dignity of the human person and the dignity of sexual love, articulated and developed a theology of human sexuality that made it possible to articulate a beautiful theology of marriage.

Chapter 9

The Patristic Period: From St. Ignatius of Antioch to St. John Chrysostom

INTRODUCTION

Throughout the Old and New Testament periods God led his people, especially through the prophets, into a deeper understanding of his plan for marriage so that they began to see marriage more clearly as a sign of his love for them. In an analogous way, after his Ascension into heaven, Jesus sent the Holy Spirit to continue to lead the members of the Church into a more complete understanding and vision of the mystery of marriage, as part of the process of leading the faithful into the fullness of truth (Jn 14:16–17, 26; 16:12–14). Although the time of public revelation has ended and revelation itself "is already complete, it has not been made completely explicit; it remains for Christian faith gradually to grasp its full significance over the course of the centuries" (CCC, 66). The Holy Spirit lead the Church deeper into the revealed truth about marriage as a sacrament of divine love, and he did so progressively and over time, guiding the members of the Mystical Body into an ever deeper appreciation of the gift of sacramental Marriage that Christ has given to his bride.

  The focus of this chapter and chapters 10 through 14 will be on the teachings that the Catholic Church, guided by the Holy Spirit, declared in order to clarify the mystery of marriage, as well as on significant contributions to the theology of marriage that have been articulated by Church theologians. Special attention will be given to the developing articulation and understanding of marriage as one of the Seven Sacraments of the New Covenant instituted by Christ and entrusted to the Church. Although these chapters will address the development of attitudes toward sexual intercourse in marriage, the primary focus will be on the developing sacramental theology of marriage.[1] Focusing precisely on developing theological articulations, these chapters will not focus on social or legal customs surrounding marriage, nor will they focus on the sociological reality of how Christian married couples lived their lives and how these lives coincided with the Church's teachings.[2] Part 4 will not focus on the developing customs surrounding the celebration of marriage or the development of the rite of marriage in the Church.[3] As it will not be possible to mention every theologian who has commented on marriage throughout the ages, these chapters will focus mainly on those prominent thinkers who made significant contributions to the overarching development of the theology of marriage, as this development was validated by the magisterium of the Church.[4] In addition, since

1. For the development of attitudes towards and teachings on sexual intercourse see: Peter Brown, *The Body and Society: Men, Women, and Sexual Renunciation in Early Christianity* (New York: Columbia University Press, 1988); Vern L. Bullough and James A. Brundage, *Sexual Practices in the Medieval Church* (Buffalo, NY: Prometheus Books, 1982); Joseph E. Kerns, *The Theology of Marriage: The Historical Development of Christian Attitudes Toward Sex and Sanctity in Marriage* (New York: Sheed and Ward, 1964).

2. For studies dealing with the cultural, social, and legal aspects of marriage see: Christopher N. L., Brooke, *The Medieval Idea of Marriage* (Oxford: Oxford University Press, 1989); James A. Brundage, *Law, Sex, and Society in Medieval Europe* (Chicago: University of Chicago Press, 1987); Philip Lyndon Reynolds, *Marriage in the Western Church: The Christianization of Marriage During the Patristic and Early Medieval Periods*, Supplements to *Vigiliae Christianae*, Vol. 24 (New York: E.J. Brill, 1994). Reynolds' book also provides useful information regarding the development of rites of marriage and the development of the theology of matrimony; Philip L. Reynolds and John Witte, eds. *To Have and to Hold: Marrying and its Documentation in Western Christianity, 400–1600* (New York: Cambridge University Press, 2007). This book also provides useful information regarding the development of marriage rites; John Witte, Jr., *From Sacrament to Contract: Marriage, Religion, and Law in the Western Tradition*, 2nd edition (Louisville, KY: Westminster John Knox Press, 2012). Witte's book also provides useful information regarding the development of the theology of marriage.

3. For the development of the rite of marriage see: Maxwell E. Johnson, ed. *Sacraments and Worship: The Sources of Christian Theology* (Louisville, KY: Westminster John Knox Press, 2012), which is a collection of primary texts; Kenneth Stevenson, *Nuptial Blessing: A Study of Christian Marriage Rites* (New York: Oxford University Press, 1983).

4. For a more detailed study of the development of the theology of marriage see: Seamus Heaney, *The Development of the Sacramentality of Marriage from Anselm of Laon to Thomas Aquinas* (Washington, D.C.: Catholic University of America Press, 1963); George Hayward Joyce, *Christian Marriage: An Historical and Doctrinal Study* (New York: Sheed and Ward, 1933); Theodore Mackin, *What Is Marriage?* Marriage in the Catholic Church (New York: Paulist Press,

chapters 9 through 14 will cover the trajectory of the development of the theology of marriage in a summary fashion, they will not provide an exhaustive treatment or analysis of any one Christian thinker, but will merely point out the significant contributions of representative thinkers.

As we proceed through Church history it is important to distinguish between official teachings of the Church that receive approbation from the office of the papacy on the one hand, and widely held but unofficial teachings on the other hand, even if these unofficial teachings are propounded by major theologians in the Church's history. While Jesus assures us that the official teachings of the Church that are taught in union with the Successor of Peter will not lead us into error (see Mt 16:18; CCC, 888–892), it is possible for the most brilliant of theologians to present teachings on faith and morals that are erroneous. In this historical survey we will see some misguided and even erroneous teachings on marriage which were widely held, and that will take centuries to correct and root out of the life of the Church.

Many readers may find it surprising that the Catholic Church did not officially define marriage as one of the Seven Sacraments until the twelfth century. Regarding this "late" definition, it should first be noted, with Walter Kasper, that "the fact that marriage was not until that time explicitly regarded as a sacrament did not mean that it was on the contrary seen, until about the twelfth century, simply as a secular reality and only later sacralized."[5] From the earliest days of the Church, Christian couples have lived their married lives in the context

---

1982) and *Divorce and Remarriage*, Marriage in the Catholic Church (New York: Paulist Press, 1985), and *The Marital Sacrament*, Marriage in the Catholic Church (New York: Paulist Press, 1989). Mackin's works provide much useful detail, but they are not always reliable. Mackin tends to view natural marriage as more of a social construct than a created reality possessing objective characteristics, and he views sacramental marriage as more of an ecclesial creation than a revealed reality. His disagreement with Catholic teachings, like the indissolubility of marriage and certain aspects of sexual morality, influence his interpretation of historical data; Glenn W. Olsen, editor, *Christian Marriage: A Historical Study* (New York: The Crossroad Publishing Company, 2001). The essays in Olsen's book also provide useful information regarding developing attitudes towards sexual intercourse, cultural, social, and legal aspects of marriage, as well as the development of the celebration of marriage; Edward Schillebeeckx, *Marriage: Human Reality and Saving Mystery*, 2 vols., translated by N.D. Smith (New York: Sheed and Ward, 1965). Schillebeeckx's book is also useful for tracing the development of marriage rites. The reader should be aware that in his theological treatment of marriage, Schillibeeckx presents a distinction between marriage as a secular reality (instead of a created reality) and marriage as a sacrament.

5. Walter Kasper, *Theology of Christian Marriage* (New York: Seabury Press, 1980), 32.

of their baptismal commitment, as the fifth chapter of the Letter to the Ephesians exhorted them to do. The reality is that it took time for theologians to understand the mystery of Christ's nuptial relationship with the Church in order to "'realize' what was revealed and lived for so long" regarding marriage.[6] In other words, it took time for the Church to understand marriage lived "in the Lord" (1 Cor 7:39) as a formal sacrament instituted by Christ.

One reason marriage was not defined as one of the Seven Sacraments until the twelfth century is the fact that the actual number of sacraments was not defined until that time. As has already been pointed out, the word "sacrament" has its origins in the Greek word *mysterion*.[7] In the Pauline letters, *mysterion* is used to refer to the mystery hidden from eternity in God to bring about the salvation of humanity, a mystery which is made manifest and accomplished in Christ (see Rom 16:25–26). In fact, the later Pauline letters identify the *mysterion* with Jesus Christ himself. In the Patristic period *mysterion* was used by the Fathers of the Church to refer to all of the historical events that manifested God's will to save man, events which culminated in the life, Death, Resurrection, and Ascension of Jesus Christ. It is in the third century that the word *mysterion* is translated into Latin as *sacramentum*. Originally, *sacramentum* referred to a military oath taken by Roman soldiers by which they were initiated into a new form of life that entailed an unreserved commitment and faithful service unto death. It is easy to see how this Roman understanding of *sacramentum* could be transposed onto the relationship between Christ and members of the Church. Since all of the previously delineated elements of *sacramentum* (hidden mystery, historically salvific event, sacred oath) are present in the ritual actions of the Church by which one is incorporated into the life of Christ, by the third century *sacramentum* was used not only to refer to the mystery of God's salvific plan in Christ (see Eph 5:32), but also to the realization of this plan through the sacraments of the Church. So, initially "sacrament" had a broad meaning pertaining to any sacred sign, and over time it was used to refer to specific signs

---

6. T. Norris, "Why Marriage is One of the Seven Sacraments," *Irish Theological Quarterly* 5.1 (1985): 50.

7. John Paul II provides an excellent discussion of the semantic history of the word "sacrament" in an extended footnote of his *Theology of the Body* (TOB 93, fn. 88). The information in this paragraph is largely taken from that footnote.

instituted by Christ that confer grace and bind the believer to Jesus. However, apart from the semantic development of the word "sacrament," it is true that "[f]rom her beginning, the Church has lived in virtue of the power of the seven sacraments instituted by Christ. This is so even if the doctrine of her sacraments had not yet been elaborated as we know them today."[8]

In addition to the development of a more precise use of the word "sacrament," the "delay" in defining marriage as one of the Seven Sacraments instituted by Christ also had to do with the unique nature of the Sacrament of Marriage itself. In short, it took time to discern the outward sign of the Sacrament of Marriage as well as the particular grace that it confers. This discernment was necessary because among all of the Seven Sacraments, Marriage is unique in that all of its essential elements were present from "the beginning." Unlike the other sacraments, Marriage does not involve anything "new" with regard to its outward sign. Whereas Jesus gave the Apostles the Trinitarian formula ("Go therefore and make disciples of all nations, baptizing them in the name of the Father and of the Son and of the Holy Spirit," Mt 28:19) to use as part of the outward sign of Baptism, and whereas he instituted the Sacrament of the Eucharist through an outward sign that consecrates bread and wine so as to transform them into his Body and Blood ("Take, eat; this is my body. . . . Drink of it, all of you; for this is my blood of the covenant," Mt 26:26–28), Jesus provides nothing new for the outward sign of the Sacrament of Marriage. Just like "in the beginning," Christian spouses mutually hand themselves over to each other by consenting to a life of conjugal communion. It took time for the Church, guided by the Holy Spirit whom Jesus sent to lead her into all truth (Jn 16:13), to discern and explain how Christ could have instituted marriage as one of the Seven Sacraments without providing a new aspect of its outward sign. It also took time to discern what particular grace the Sacrament of Marriage confers. It is fair to note that one of the reasons theologians were reluctant to posit that marriage is a sacrament that can confer grace is because married life entails sexual union, which in a fallen world is subject to the disordered desires of concupiscence. Although the process

---

8. Ramón García de Haro, *Marriage and the Family in the Documents of the Magisterium: A Course in the Theology of Marriage*, 2nd edition, translated by William E. May (San Francisco: Ignatius Press, 1993), 65.

of discerning the Sacrament of Marriage was gradual, it is nonetheless true, as one scholar has noted, that "the sense of the distinctiveness of Christian marriage was present long before marriage became regarded as one of the seven sacraments."[9] It is the understanding of this distinct reality that will develop over time.

The Early Church Fathers on Marriage

The early Church Fathers, the great Christian teachers and writers of the first five to six centuries of Christianity, provide an invaluable witness to the Tradition of the Church as it is embodied in the Church's living, teaching, and worshiping. Their goal was to pass on the faith that had been inherited from the Apostles, explaining and defending this faith in the face of challenges that came both from non-Christians and from heresies that emerged inside the Church. The Fathers of the Church gave birth to Christian theology, not as an academic discipline, but as a pastorally and evangelically oriented endeavor to strengthen the faith of Christians and to propose the love of Jesus Christ to nonbelievers. As part of their endeavor to explain the mysteries of Christianity, the Fathers wrote and taught about Christian marriage. Although not everything that the Church Fathers taught or wrote about marriage was ultimately deemed to be correct by the magisterium of the Church, the writings of the Fathers give us some insight into how marriage was lived by Christians in the early centuries and the Fathers' reflections on marriage laid the foundation upon which later theologians would build.

Second-Century Christianity

St. Ignatius of Antioch (d. ca. 110)

The earliest reference to Christian marriage in postbiblical Christian literature occurred at the beginning of the second century of Christianity, around 110 AD, in the writings of St. Ignatius of Antioch. In a letter he wrote to Bishop Polycarp of Smyrna, on Ignatius' way to his martyrdom in Rome, Ignatius stated: "It is right for men and women who marry to be united with the bishop's

---

9. Philip Lyndon Reynolds, *Marriage in the Western Church*, xv.

approval. In that way their marriage will follow God's will and not the promptings of lust. Let everything be done so as to advance God's honor."[10] Although it would take centuries for a Christian rite of marriage to develop, this reference from Ignatius provides evidence that Christians entered into marriage in a manner that reflected their Christian commitment. It also shows that "[f]rom the very outset . . . the church surrounded the civil and family marriages of her faithful with pastoral care."[11] Also, Ignatius of Antioch provides us with evidence to show that the lack of a Christian rite of marriage in the first several centuries did not mean that Christians ignored the religious significance of marriage. Instead, Christians entered into marriage according to their own local customs, often receiving the blessing of a priest or bishop in their home or at their wedding feast, and then they lived this commitment within the context of their Christian life in the Church.[12] We see Ignatius emphasizing marriage as part of Christian spouses' baptismal commitments when he repeated St. Paul's exhortation to husbands "to love their wives as the Lord loves the Church."[13]

Shepherd of Hermas

Also in the first half of the second century we have a reference to Christian marriage in the anonymous document called the *Shepherd of Hermas*. The author of the *Shepherd* addressed the issue of divorce and the issue of remarriage after the death of a spouse. In the *Shepherd* we see the typical Patristic reading of *porneia* which "was universally understood from the early patristic period to denote adultery (an interpretation that has few adherents among modern commentators)."[14] Although they are not cited explicitly, this is the first written evidence that shows how the "exception clauses" of Matthew's Gospel were applied – namely, that "divorce" in the case of *porneia* was not seen to

---

10. Ignatius of Antioch, *Letter to Polycarp* (*Ad Polycarpum*), in *Early Christian Fathers*, translated and edited by Cyril C. Richardson (New York: Collier Books, 1970), 5.2.

11. Edward Schillebeeckx, *Marriage: Human Reality and Saving Mystery*, 245.

12. For a brief overview of the development of a Christian rite of marriage see Joseph M. Champlain, "Marriage, Liturgy of," in *New Dictionary of Sacramental Worship*, ed. Peter E. Fink (Collegeville, MN: Liturgical Press, 1990), 796.

13. Ignatius of Antioch, *Letter to Polycarp*, 5.

14. Philip Lyndon Reynolds, *Marriage in the Western Church*, xxiv.

grant the permission to contract a new marriage. If a spouse is guilty of adultery, the innocent spouse is commanded to "divorce" the adulterous spouse, but is forbidden to remarry.[15] The *Shepherd* even encouraged reconciliation between spouses who had "divorced" as a result of adultery.[16] Here we see the typical understanding of "divorce" in the case of adultery, understood not in the modern sense of a divorce that would allow a spouse to contract another marriage, but as the separation of two spouses who continue to remain married to each other.[17] The *Shepherd* stated that second marriages following the death of a spouse are allowed, but asserted that the widow or widower who remains single "gains . . . more extraordinary honor and great glory with the Lord."[18] This is also a common position among the early Church Fathers.

St. Justin Martyr (100–ca. 165) and Athenagoras of Athens (ca. 133–190)

In presenting his rational arguments for the veracity of Christianity to larger Greco-Roman culture, the second-century apologist St. Justin Martyr contrasted the sexual promiscuity of the Romans with the behavior of Christians whom he said only marry for the sake of bringing up children. He said that "we [Christians] do not marry except in order to bring up children, or else, renouncing marriage, we live in perfect continence."[19] Athenagoras, another Christian apologist, echoed the thought of Justin, stating: "According to our laws, each of us thinks of the woman he has married as his wife only for the purpose of bearing children. For as the farmer casts his seed on the soil and

---

15. *Shepherd of Hermas*, in David G. Hunter, editor and translator, *Marriage in the Early Church*, Sources of Early Christian Thought, ed. William G. Rusch (Minneapolis: Fortress Press, 1992), 4.29.1.

16. Ibid.

17. Edward Schillebeeckx commented: "Remarriage was not permitted in the apostolic church, no matter what reasons were given for the separation. . . . No other line has in fact ever been followed in ecclesiastical legal practice. There have been very few dissentient opinions" (*Marriage*, 146). These few dissenting opinions include some evidence, which will be noted in this chapter, that in the Eastern Church remarriage after adultery was occasionally permitted. While Philip Reynolds argues that in the West the exclusion of remarriage after divorce in the case of adultery only became normative in the fourth century, and that prior to this time remarriage was allowed, his argument is self-admittedly one that lacks evidence in Christian literature (*Marriage in the Western Church*, 176–77).

18. *Shepherd of Hermas*, 4.32.4.

19. Justin Martyr, *First Apology*, in *Early Christian Fathers*, translated and edited by Cyril C. Richardson (New York: Collier Books, 1970), 29; written ca. 155 AD.

awaits the harvest without sowing over it, so we limit the pleasure of intercourse to bearing children." [20] This teaching of Justin and Athenagoras that sexual intercourse between spouses should ideally be limited to the express purpose of having children is reiterated throughout the Patristic period. Clearly this teaching highlights the primary end of marriage as being the procreation and education of children, and it rightly opposes engaging in sexual activity for a hedonistic pursuit of pleasure. However, it is fair to point out that behind this position first articulated by Justin and Athenagoras lies the Church Fathers' acute concern regarding the need to master the unruliness of fallen sexual desire. Hints of this concern can also be seen in Ignatius of Antioch's *Letter to Polycarp* when he said that those who marry should "follow God's will and not the promptings of lust."[21]

This concern means that even though the early Church Fathers defended the goodness of marriage, there was also a certain tension in their thought regarding marriage throughout the Patristic period. The Fathers defended marriage as a good creation of a good God, and as having been blessed by Christ and elevated to a sign of Christ's union with the Church in some way. Yet, there was a tension in the Fathers' thought regarding the carnality of marriage, and the fact that sexual intercourse with its attendant concupiscible desire is central to married life.[22] Thus, on the whole, the Fathers viewed sexual intercourse, which is scarred by lust, with a certain amount of suspicion, and saw the pursuit of a child as that which excused the marital act.[23] It will take centuries for this suspicion to be overcome.

In addition to expressing the position that sexual intercourse should take place only for the explicit purpose of having children, Athenagoras added his opposition to divorce and remarriage. He stated: "We hold that a man should either remain as he is born or else marry only once. For a second marriage is a veiled adultery. The Scripture says, 'Whoever puts away his wife and marries another, commits adultery [Mt 19:9; Mk 10:11].' Thus a man is forbidden both

20. Athenagoras, *Plea*, in *Early Christian Fathers*, translated and edited by Cyril C. Richardson (New York: Collier Books, 1970), 33; written ca. 176 AD.

21. Ignatius of Antioch, *Letter to Polycarp*, 5.

22. Philip Lyndon Reynolds, *Marriage in the Western Church*, xix.

23. Joseph Kerns traces this view of sexual intercourse by the theologians of the Patristic and early medieval periods in *The Theology of Marriage: The Historical Development of Christian Attitudes Toward Sex and Sanctity in Marriage*, Chapter 4, "*Libido*," 41–60.

to put her away whose virginity he has ended, and to marry again."[24] However, not only did Athenagoras oppose divorce and remarriage, but he also opposed remarriage after the death of a spouse stating, "He who severs himself from his first wife, even if she is dead, is an adulterer in disguise."[25] The Fathers' position on remarriage after the death of a spouse will vary, but ultimately the consensus will be, in accord with 1 Corinthians 7:39–40, to encourage widows to remain unmarried, but to allow for second marriages.

Third-Century Christianity

Tertullian of Carthage (ca. 160–ca. 222)

Early in the third century, before becoming a champion of the Montanist heresy, Tertullian of Carthage wrote a short treatise *To His Wife* (written between 200 and 206 AD) in which he advised his wife not to remarry after his death, although he admitted that remarriage in such a case was not a sin.[26] In this same treatise Tertullian praised the goodness of Christian marriage when he wrote:

> How shall we ever be able to describe the happiness of that marriage which the Church arranges, the Sacrifice strengthens, upon which the blessing sets a seal, at which angels are present as witnesses, and to which the Father gives His consent? . . . How beautiful, then, the marriage of two Christians, who are one in hope, one in desire, one in the way of life they follow. They are as brother and sister, both servants of the same Master. Nothing divides them, either in flesh or in spirit. They are, in very truth, *two in one flesh*; and where there is but one flesh, there is also but one spirit.[27]

The above praise of Christian marriage may be evidence of some type of early Christian marriage liturgy in its infancy, perhaps even celebrated in conjunction with the Eucharist. Regardless, it is obvious

---

24. Athenagoras, *Plea*, 33.

25. Ibid.

26. Tertullian, *To His Wife*, in *Tertullian: Treatises on Marriage and Remarriage*, trans. William P. Le Saint, ACW, vol. 13(1951), I.1. Tertullian's positions became more severe as he moved closer to embracing the rigorist morality of Montanism, a schismatic movement which he embraced definitively around 211–212 A.D. In *An Exhortation to Chastity* (ca. 204–212) he showed stronger opposition to second marriage after the death of a spouse, and in a treatise *On Monogamy* (ca. 217) he firmly condemned such marriages.

27. Tertullian, *To His Wife*, II.8.

that Tertullian was highlighting a clear difference between Christian marriage and the marriage of pagans. As a result of this difference he strongly discouraged Christians from marrying non-Christians.[28]

St. Clement of Alexandria (ca. 150–ca. 215)

Several early Church Fathers defended the goodness of marriage in response to the errors of Gnostics, who condemned marriage as part of a dualistic vision of reality according to which spiritual realities are good and material realities are evil. Thus, for the Gnostic it would be abhorrent to marry and procreate, thereby trapping good spiritual souls in corrupt physical bodies. St. Irenaeus of Lyons (ca. 130–ca. 202), in the late second century, was one of the first to refute the Gnostic condemnation of marriage by reaffirming marriage as a good creation of God.[29] Also responding to the Gnostic condemnation of marriage in the early third century, St. Clement of Alexandria upheld marriage as a good creation of God[30] and as holy.[31] Citing Aristotle and the Book of Genesis, Clement stated, "'Nature has made us equipped for marriage,' [*Politics*, 7.1134] as is clear from the organization of the male and female bodies, and they continually blare at us, 'Be fruitful and multiply' [Gen 1:28]."[32] Clement stressed that the primary end of marriage is procreation,[33] and he interpreted Jesus' comments on overcoming adultery in the heart (Mt 5:27–28) as meaning that husbands should "have responsible sexual relations with their marriage partners, solely for the production of children."[34] He exhorted husbands to rely upon God's grace and control their sexual desire for their wives so as to restrict sexual intercourse for the purpose of having children.[35] Stressing the need for sexual self-restraint, Clement "enjoins husbands not to treat their wives as sex-objects, making their goal the violation of their bodies, but directing their marriage to support

---

28. Ibid.

29. Irenaeus, *Against Heresies*, ANF, vol. 1, I.28.1.

30. Clement of Alexandria, *Stromateis*, in *Clement of Alexandria: Stromateis Books One to Three*, trans. John Ferguson, FOC, vol. 85, (1991), III.6.45.

31. Ibid., III.12.84.2.

32. Ibid., II.23.139.3.

33. Ibid., II.23.137.1.

34. Ibid., III.11.71.4.

35. Ibid., III.7.57–58.

throughout life and to self-control at the highest level."[36] In this way, marriage will "be kept pure, like a sacred object to be preserved from all stain."[37] Clement also made it clear that Christ has forbidden remarriage after "divorce", which is to be understood as separation.[38] Clement referred to a blessing imparted upon marriage by Jesus in his commentary on the wedding at Cana in John's Gospel:

> He Himself, invited along with the disciples, comes not so much to dine as to perform a miracle and also to sanctify the source of man's bodily generation. For it was fitting that He who was to renew the very nature of man and recall the whole of it to a better state, should not only impart a blessing on those who had already been brought to birth but also prepare grace for those to be born later and make their birth holy.[39]

Thus Clement testified not only to the goodness of the married state, but also to a blessing from Christ that helps to make marriage holy and to sanctify the generation of children.

Origen of Alexandria (ca.185–254)

In the mid-third century, Origen of Alexandria, like Clement, told couples that in order to avoid lustful behavior they should restrict their use of sexual intercourse to the purpose of having children.[40] Following St. Paul (1 Cor 7:7), Origen also attested to the gift of marriage for those who are joined together by God.[41] Although Origen opposed divorce,[42] he provided us with evidence of bishops who permitted a man or a woman, who was separated from an adulterous spouse, to remarry while the first spouse was still alive.[43] However, Origen was aware that this practice was contrary to Scripture, and he viewed it as an accommodation to human weakness to avoid potentially worse

---

36. Ibid., II.23.143.1.

37. Ibid., II.23.145.1.

38. Ibid., II.23.145.3.

39. Clement of Alexandria, *On John*, II.11, quoted in Mackin, *The Marital Sacrament: Marriage in the Catholic Church* (New York: Paulist Press, 1989), 175–176.

40. Origen, *Genesis Homily III*, in *Origen: Homilies on Genesis and Exodus*, trans. Ronald E. Heine, FOC, vol. 71 (1982), 6.

41. Origen, *Commentary on the Gospel of Matthew*, ANF, vol. 9, XIV.16.

42. Ibid.

43. Ibid., XIV.23.

occurrences.[44] In contrast to this practice in the East to which Origen testified, in the Western Church the canons of the Spanish Synod of Elvira (ca. 300–303; DS, 117) at the beginning of the fourth century provide us with evidence that second marriages after separation due to adultery were strictly forbidden.

Fourth-Century Christianity

St. Basil (the Great) of Caesarea (329–379)

In the fourth century, St. Basil of Caesarea, like Origen, provided evidence that in some instances Christians did procure second marriages after divorce. Basil wrote of the situation of a man who remarries after divorcing his wife stating:

> He who leaves the wife lawfully joined to him and unites himself with another, according to the sentence of the Lord lies under the charge of adultery. And it has been ruled by our Fathers that such should weep for one year, should be hearers for a period of two years, should be prostrates for a period of three years, and in the seventh year stand with the faithful. And then they will be considered worthy of Holy Communion if they do penance with tears.[45]

It should be noted that in the above passage Basil was not questioning the wrongfulness of a second marriage while one's first spouse is still living, but instead he was noting the necessity of protracted penance before readmittance into the ecclesial community. It is worth pointing out that St. Basil could have been assuming that the penitent in question would also separate from his second wife.

In another letter Basil questioned whether a man or a woman whose spouse had been deserted by a previous spouse should be considered guilty of adultery, and he counseled pardon after penance for people in these situations.[46] Again, Basil was not questioning the wrongfulness of these second marriages that occurred after abandonment, but instead was counseling a penance other than that imposed

---

44. Ibid.

45. Basil the Great, *Letter 217*, in *Saint Basil: Letters Volume II (186–368)*, trans. Sister Agnes Clare Way, FOC, vol. 28 (1955), 77; written in 375.

46. Basil the Great, *Letter 188*, in *Saint Basil: Letters Volume II (186–368)*, trans. Sister Agnes Clare Way, FOC, vol. 28 (1955), 9; written in 374.

on adulterers, which he made clear would be imposed on the abandoning spouses.[47]

Walter Kasper points to the fact that this evidence from Basil, as well as from Origen, regarding the existence of remarriage after divorce is at the root of the Eastern Orthodox Church's practice of permitting divorce. Kasper notes that the Orthodox do not see the practice of divorce as violating the principle of indissolubility as such, but as providing "the Christian who is ready to do penance, on the basis of God's mercy, with a new possibility of a human and Christian life within the Church in certain difficult situations. This is why the liturgy in the Eastern Church for a second marriage is dominated by the theme of penance."[48] More will be said in chapter eleven about the differing practice of the Orthodox Church regarding divorce. For now, it is important to note that Basil was presenting pastoral solutions to what he viewed as complicated situations, while not condoning divorce and remarriage.

St. Gregory of Nazianzen (329–ca. 389)

St. Gregory of Nazianzen, close friend of Basil the Great, "anticipates the later theology of the sacrament"[49] of marriage when he stated:

> The two, He says, shall be one Flesh; so let the one flesh have equal honor. And Paul legislates for chastity by His [Christ's] example. How, and in what way? "This Sacrament is great," he says, "but I speak concerning Christ and the Church." It is well for the wife to reverence Christ through her husband: and it is well for the husband not to dishonor the Church through his wife. Let the wife, he says, see that she reverence her husband, for so she does Christ; but also he bids the husband cherish his wife, for so does Christ with the Church.[50]

47. Ibid.

48. Walter Kasper, *Theology of Christian Marriage*, 56–57. For Orthodox writers who point to St. Basil as Patristic support for the possibility of successive marriages after divorce see John Meyendorff, *Marriage: An Orthodox Perspective*, 2nd expanded ed. (Crestwood, NY: St. Vladimir's Seminary Press, 1975), 49. Meyendorff explains the penitential nature of the celebration of second marriages on pages 48–52, and the Orthodox approach to divorce on pages 60–65. See also Paul Evdokimov, *The Sacrament of Love: The Nuptial Mystery in the Light of the Orthodox Tradition*, trans. Anthony P. Gythiel and Victoria Steadman (Crestwood, NY: St. Vladimir's Seminary Press, 1985), 184.

49. Theodore Mackin, *The Marital Sacrament*, 166.

50. Gregory of Nazianzen, *Oration XXXVII*, NPNF, Second Series, vol. 7, 6.

Here Nazianzen clearly exhorted married couples to reflect the love between Christ and the Church, and he saw the Christian married couple as a sign of Christ's relationship with the Church. Following Jesus' teaching, Nazianzen also opposed divorce, but allowed for separation from an adulterous spouse.[51] Regarding the conjugal embrace, Nazianzen stated:

> It is good to marry; I too admit it, for marriage is honorable in all, and the bed undefiled. It is good for the temperate, not for those who are insatiable, and who desire to give more than due honour to the flesh. When marriage is only marriage and conjunction and the desire for a succession of children, marriage is honourable, for it brings into the world more to please God. But when it kindles matter, and surrounds us with thorns, and as it were discovers the way of vice, then I too say, it is not good to marry.[52]

In this passage Nazianzen attested to the goodness of marriage, but like other Fathers, saw marital intercourse as truly honorable only when utilized for the purpose of having children. Anything beyond this is giving the flesh more than it is due.

St. Gregory of Nyssa (335–394)

Gregory of Nazianzen's position is another example of what one might call a "suspicious" view of marital intercourse on the part of the Church Fathers. Partly because of this suspicion, the Fathers showed a decided preference for the "higher" call of consecrated celibacy or virginity, and there was a "continuing tension between marriage, viewed as legitimate, and celibacy, viewed as more perfect."[53] St. Gregory of Nyssa, Basil the Great's brother, showed a marked preference for celibacy and a less than glowing assessment of marriage in *On Virginity*. Even though Gregory was married, he lamented not being able to experience the blessings of a life of celibacy when he stated:

> Happy they who have still the power of choosing the better way, and have not debarred themselves from it by engagements of the secular life, as we have, whom a gulf now divides from glorious virginity: no one can climb

---

51. Ibid., XXXVII.7.

52. Ibid., XXXVII.9.

53. Glenn W. Olsen, "Progeny, Faithfulness, Sacred Bond: Marriage in the Age of Augustine," in *Christian Marriage: A Historical Study*, ed. Glenn W. Olsen (New York: Crossroad Publishing Company, 2001), 104.

up to that who has once planted his foot upon the secular life. We are but spectators of others' blessings and witnesses to the happiness of another class. . . . The more exactly we understand the riches of virginity, the more we must bewail the other life; for we realize by this contrast with better things, how poor it is.[54]

Nyssa saw even the happiest marriages as always subject to the pain of loss, the shadow of death, and anxiety for one's family.[55] Whereas marriage can be a source of vice and error, virginity allows one to progress in virtue undistracted by concerns of the world.[56] Nyssa recognized virginity as an eschatological sign when he stated, "In fact, the Life of Virginity seems to be an actual representation of the blessedness in the world to come, showing as it does in itself so many signs of the presence of those expected blessings which are reserved for us there."[57]

Not only did Nyssa see that everyone is called to a state of eschatological virginity, he also proposed that human gender and marriage were provisions or compensations created by God, who foresaw that humanity would sin. According to Nyssa, God instituted marriage "as the compensation for having to die."[58] Nyssa explained:

Perceiving beforehand by His power of foreknowledge what, in a state of independence and freedom, is the tendency of the motion of man's will, as He saw, I say, what would be, He devised for His image the distinction of male and female, which has no reference to the Divine Archetype, but, as we have said, is an approximation to the less rational nature.[59]

Thus, in Nyssa's thought gender is not constitutive of the human person, but is simply a provision implemented by God so that the human race could perpetuate itself after the Fall. Nyssa maintained that "marriage did not exist in Paradise"[60] and that without the advent of sin, humanity would have had angelic or spiritual bodies lacking in sexual differentiation and would have procreated in an angelic

---

54. Gregory of Nyssa, *On Virginity*, NPNF, Second Series, vol. 5, III.
55. Ibid.
56. Ibid., IV.
57. Ibid., XIII.
58. Ibid., XII.
59. Gregory of Nyssa, *On the Making of Man*, NPNF, Second Series, vol. 5, XVI.14.
60. Ibid., XVII.1.

manner.[61] Nyssa admitted that his position regarding gender and marriage being concessions to sin was his own speculation,[62] yet among the early Church Fathers he was not alone in seeing marriage as being necessitated by the Fall.

St. Ambrose of Milan (339–397)

In the late fourth century, St. Ambrose of Milan reiterated the position that sexual intercourse should be reserved for the purpose of conceiving children.[63] Ambrose also evidenced his preference for virginity and a less than resounding endorsement of marriage in his work *Concerning Virginity* in which he stated, "I do not then discourage marriage, but recapitulate the advantages of holy virginity."[64] He explained, "The one sins not if she marries, the other, if she marries not, it is for eternity. In the former is the remedy for weakness, in the latter the glory of chastity. The former is not reproved, the latter is praised."[65] Even though Ambrose's praise was reserved for virginity, he did refer to Christian marriages being "sanctified by Christ."[66] He noted the uniqueness of Christian marriage when he wrote:

> He [Jesus] had also said that not a jot of the Law can be dropped. Then He adds: *"Whoever leaves his wife and takes another, is guilty of adultery."* This is where the great mystery is: concerning Christ and the Church no one can doubt that God has united them, seeing that Jesus Himself says: *"No one comes to me unless the Father who has sent me draws him"* (Jn 6:44). In truth, none but God could tie a nuptial knot such as this; and that is why Solomon, speaking mystically, says: *"It is God who prepares for man his spouse"* (Prv 19:14). The bridegroom is Christ; the Bride is the Church: bride through love, virgin through chastity.[67]

---

61. Ibid., XVII.2.

62. Ibid., XVI.15; XVII.2.

63. Ambrose, *Commentary of Saint Ambrose on the Gospel according to Saint Luke*, trans. Íde M. Ní Riain (Dublin: Halycon Press, 2001), I.43–45.

64. Ambrose, *Concerning Virginity*, NPNF, Second Series, vol. 10, I.7.35.

65. Ibid., I.6.24.

66. Ambrose of Milan, *Letter 42 To Siricius, Bishop of Rome*, in *Saint Ambrose: Letters*, trans. Sister Mary Melchior Beyenka, FOC, vol. 26 (1954), 3.

67. Ambrose of Milan, *Commentary of Saint Ambrose on the Gospel according to Saint Luke*, VIII.9

In this passage Ambrose saw Christian marriage as a sign of Christ's nuptial union with his virgin bride, the Church. Ambrose also reflected on the virginal marriage of Mary and Joseph, noting that it is "not the deflowering of virginity but the nuptial compact which makes a marriage."[68] This is one of the first reflections on whether consent or consummation constitutes a marriage, a consideration which will continue throughout the Middle Ages.

Additionally, Ambrose provided us with evidence that by the fourth century the Fathers of the early Church saw Christian marriage as subject to divine law (*lex divina*) instead of human law (*lex humana*).[69] As such they understood that the Church, and not the civil authority, has jurisdiction over Christian marriage.[70] Ambrose even made it clear that some marriages which are deemed valid by civil law, such as second marriages after a divorce, may in fact be invalid according to God's law and the judgment of the Church.[71]

Fifth-Century Christianity

St. Jerome (347–420)

The writings of St. Jerome clearly evidence the Patristic tension of affirming marriage while being suspicious of the marital embrace. Jerome stated clearly that if spouses engage in sexual intercourse for a reason other than to purposely conceive a child then they are guilty of lust.[72] However, Jerome's ambivalent assessment of marriage continued in his response to a Roman monk named Jovinian who was teaching that there is no difference in merit between the married state and the state of consecrated virginity. Jerome responded to this error by stating that he does not "disparage marriage"[73] and that "while we honor marriage we prefer virginity which is the offspring of marriage."[74] However, he said to married couples, "Since your outer man is

---

68. Ambrose, *Concerning Virginity*, II.6.41.

69. Philip Lyndon Reynolds, *Marriage in the Western Church*, 121.

70. Ibid., 142.

71. See Ambrose, *Commentary of Saint Ambrose on the Gospel according to Saint Luke*, VIII.5.

72. Jerome, *Commentary on Galatians*, trans. Andrew Cain, FOC, vol. 121 (2010), III.5.19–21.

73. Jerome, *Against Jovinian*, NPNF, Second Series, vol. 6, I.3.

74. Ibid.

corrupt, and you have ceased to possess the blessing of incorruption characterized by virgins, at least imitate the incorruption of the spirit by subsequent abstinence, and what you cannot show in the body exhibit in the mind. For these are the riches, and these are the ornaments of your union, which Christ seeks."[75] With this statement, Jerome seemed to imply that marital intercourse entails some sort of corruption. He went on to undermine marriage as an unqualified good when he commented on St. Paul's statement that "it is better to marry than to burn" (1 Cor 7:9; we will say more about this passage from St. Paul in the final chapter of this book dealing with the relationship between marriage and consecrated celibacy). Jerome explained:

> The reason why it is better to marry is that it is worse to burn. Let burning lust be absent, and he will not say it is better to marry. The word *better* always implies a comparison with something worse, not a thing absolutely good and incapable of comparison. . . . When you come to marriage, you do not say it is good to marry, because you cannot then add "*than to burn*"; but you say, "It is better to marry than to burn." If marriage in itself be good, do not compare it with fire, but simply say, "It is good to marry." I suspect the goodness of that thing which is forced into the position of being only the lesser of two evils. What I want is not a smaller evil, but a thing absolutely good.[76]

To maintain that marriage is not absolutely good, and even a "lesser evil" is certainly a damaging defense of marriage. The best that Jerome said of marriage was: "The difference, then, between marriage and virginity is as great as that between not sinning and doing well; nay rather, to speak less harshly, as great as between good and better."[77] Given this rather unenthusiastic evaluation of marriage, which veered toward begrudging tolerance, it is not surprising that Jerome shared Gregory of Nyssa's opinion that marriage had no place in paradise. Jerome asserted, "And as regards Adam and Eve we must maintain that before the fall they were virgins in Paradise: but after they sinned, and were cast out of Paradise, they were immediately married."[78] Thus Jerome stands out as the supreme, and rather unsuccessful, example of

---

75. Ibid., I.7.
76. Ibid, I.9.
77. Ibid., I.13.
78. Ibid., I.16.

the Patristic attempt to deal with the tension of affirming marriage in the presence of unruly sexual desire.

St. John Chrysostom (347–407)

The most prominent Eastern Church Father to contribute to the theology of marriage was St. John Chrysostom. Chrysostom affirmed the goodness of marriage as "a bond ordained by God."[79] He likewise affirmed the primary and secondary ends of marriage when he said, "You are marrying your wife for the procreation of children and for moderation of life."[80] In one sermon Chrysostom even emphasized the mutual support of spouses above the end of procreation when he stated:

> Marriage was not instituted for wantonness or fornication, but for chastity. Listen to what Paul says: "Because of the temptation to immorality, each man should have his own wife and each woman her own husband [1 Cor 7:2]. These are the two purposes for which marriage was instituted: to make us chaste, and to make us parents. Of these two, the reason of chastity takes precedence. When desire began, then marriage also began. It set a limit to desire by teaching us to keep to one wife. Marriage does not always lead to child-bearing, although there is the word of God which says, "Be fruitful and multiply, and fill the earth" [Gen 1:28]. We have as witnesses all those who are married but childless. So the purpose of chastity takes precedence, especially now, when the whole world is filled with our kind.[81]

In the above passage, by stressing that marriage is for the purpose of making us chaste, St. John appeared to stress marriage as a cure for concupiscence. His statement, "When desire began, then marriage also began," could imply that Chrysostom saw marriage as being instituted by God only after the Fall. Chrysostom explicitly affirmed this position in another work,[82] thereby agreeing with Gregory of Nyssa's opinion that marriage and sexual intercourse are concessions

---

79. John Chrysostom, "Homily 12: On Colossians 4:18," in *St. John Chrysostom on Marriage and Family Life*, trans. Catherine P. Roth and David Anderson (Crestwood, NY: St. Vladimir's Seminary Press, 2000), 74.

80. Ibid.

81. John Chrysostom, "Sermon on Marriage," in *St. John Chrysostom on Marriage and Family Life*, 85.

82. John Chrysostom, "On Virginity," in *John Chrysostom: On Virginity; Against Remarriage*, trans. Sally Rieger Shore, Studies in Women and Religion, vol. 9 (New York: Edwin Mellon Press, 1983), 17.

for the Fall. In another of his homilies on 1 Corinthians 7, St. John also showed some slight ambivalence toward sexual intercourse when he said, "Sex is not evil, but it is a hindrance to someone who desires to devote all her strength to a life of prayer."[83] However, even though John Chrysostom did not give marriage or sexual intercourse a place in paradise, and even though one can detect in him a slight ambivalence toward the marital embrace, St. John clearly maintained the beauty and the goodness of marriage, delivering beautiful homilies on married life and love.

The golden-mouthed bishop pointed out the uniqueness of marriage by stating, "There is no relationship between human beings so close as that of husband and wife, if they are united as they ought to be."[84] He also extolled the beauty of married love perhaps more than any other Church Father saying, "The love of husband and wife is the force that welds society together."[85] Chrysostom ultimately argued for the goodness of marriage by explaining its relationship to Christ and the Church. He said:

> How foolish are those who belittle marriage! If marriage were something to be condemned, Paul would never call Christ a bridegroom and the Church a bride, and then say this is an illustration of a man leaving his father and his mother, and again refer to Christ and the Church.[86]

Thus St. John Chrysostom saw Christian marriage as having reference to the relationship between Christ and the Church, a relationship that gives a new dignity to marriage. Chrysostom certainly pointed to the sacramentality of marriage when he said, "If you have no respect for marriage, at least respect what it symbolizes: 'This is a great mystery, and I take it to mean Christ and the Church' [Eph 5:32]. . . . How is marriage a mystery? The two have become one. This is not an empty symbol. They have not become the image of anything on earth, but of God Himself."[87] Thus for Chrysostom marriage is not only a sign of the union of Christ with the Church,

---

83. John Chrysostom, "Homily 19: On 1 Corinthians 7," in *St. John Chrysostom on Marriage and Family Life*, 41.

84. John Chrysostom, "Homily 20: On Ephesians 5:22–33," in *St. John Chrysostom on Marriage and Family Life*, 43.

85. Ibid., 44.

86. Ibid., 55.

87. John Chrysostom, "Homily 12: On Colossians 4:18," 75.

but it is also an earthly symbol of a divine reality. St. John said that as the two spouses become one, we "see the mystery of love!"[88] He further supports the sacramentality of marriage in the New Covenant when he said, "Marriage is an image of the presence of Christ,"[89] and he encouraged Christian married couples to take heed of this sacramental reality, saying, "Beseech Christ to be present at the wedding. He is not ashamed to come, for marriage is an image of His presence in the Church."[90]

Following St. Paul, Chrysostom saw that the relationship of Christian marriage to the union of Christ with the Church has implications for the lives of Christian spouses. He emphatically exhorted Christian spouses to be living signs of Christ's love for the Church when he said:

> Do you want your wife to be obedient to you, as the Church is to Christ? Then be responsible for the same providential care of her, as Christ is for the Church. And even if it becomes necessary for you to give your life for her, yes, and even to endure and undergo suffering of any kind, do not refuse. . . . In the same way, then, as He honored her by putting at His feet one who turned her back on Him, who hated, rejected, and disdained Him, as He accomplished this not with threats, or violence, or terror, or anything else like that, but through His untiring love; so also you should behave toward your wife. Even if you see her belittling you, or despising and mocking you, still you will be able to subject her to yourself, through affliction, kindness, and your great regard for her. There is no influence more powerful than the bond of love, especially for husband and wife.[91]

Chrysostom continued to exhort husbands and wives to love each other saying:

> The principal duty of love is assigned to the husband. . . . Your obligation is to love her; do your duty! Even when we don't receive our due from others, we must always do our duty. . . . A wife should respect her husband even when he shows her no love, and a husband should love his wife even when she shows him no respect.[92]

---

88. Ibid.

89. Ibid., 77.

90. Ibid., 79.

91. John Chrysostom, *Homily 20*, 46–47.

92. Ibid., 54.

Certainly with the above words, the golden-mouthed bishop helped to explain the dynamic of subordination and the reality of headship that are referred to in Ephesians 5. With these words he also helped to address modern excuses for divorce based on "loveless" marriages. St. John even seemed to posit a special grace at work in Christian marriage to assist couples to love each other "no matter what" when he said, "Christ himself will come to your wedding. . . . If you ask Him, He will work for you an even greater miracle than He worked in Cana: that is, He will transform the water of your unstable passions into the wine of spiritual unity." [93] In this way, St. John saw a grace at work in Christian marriage that is healing, transformative, and empowering.

St. John Chrysostom also supported the dignity of married love by pointing out that the Christian household, based upon the love of husband and wife, "is a little Church." [94] He did maintain the superiority of virginity over marriage but, unlike Jerome, he did so while simultaneously maintaining the complementarity of the married and the virgin states. He said: "Whoever denigrates marriage also diminishes the glory of virginity. Whoever praises it makes virginity more admirable and resplendent. What appears good only in comparison with evil would not be truly good. The most excellent good is something even better than what is admitted to be good." [95] Thus even though Chrysostom did not affirm marriage as part of God's plan before the Fall, he did succeed in elaborating the gift and beauty of married love in a manner that surpassed other early Church Fathers.

Even though St. John Chrysostom's preaching on married life is the most beautiful among the Fathers, beyond any other Church Father, it is St. Augustine of Hippo whose teachings on marriage laid a foundation that would be influential for centuries to come. We will devote a separate chapter to Augustine's insights because of the importance of his teachings on marriage in the history of the Church. It is to this chapter that we will now turn.

---

93. John Chrysostom, *Homily 12*, 78.
94. John Chrysostom, *Homily 20*, 57.
95. John Chrysostom, *On Virginity*, 10.1; quoted in CCC, 1620, and FC, 16.

Chapter 10

The Patristic Period: St. Augustine of Hippo

INTRODUCTION

St. Augustine of Hippo (354–430) was the most prolific writer of all the early Church Fathers. Augustine addressed topics that no other Church Father explored, and of the topics that he addressed in common with other Church Fathers he often wrote on them in greater length, thereby providing deeper insights. Augustine laid the foundations for further reflections in many areas of theology, and it is certain that he made more important contributions to the theology of marriage and the understanding of marriage as a sacrament than any other Church Father. His impact on the theology of marriage was felt for centuries after his death, and although some of his insights represent teachings that needed to be corrected, many of his insights have been judged by the magisterium of the Catholic Church to be perennially important. For this reason I will devote this chapter to discussing Augustine's contributions to the theology of marriage.[1]

---

1. Portions of the following articles have been adapted for use in this chapter: Perry J. Cahall, "Saint Augustine on Conjugal Love and Divine Love," *The Thomist* 68 (2004): 343–73; "Saint Augustine on Marriage and the Trinity," *Josephinum Journal of Theology* 11.1 (Winter/Spring 2004): 82–97; "The Trinitarian Structure of St. Augustine's Good of Marriage," *Augustinian Studies* 34:2 (2003): 223–232.

BACKGROUND TO AUGUSTINE'S THEOLOGY OF MARRIAGE

When surveying Augustine's thought on marriage it should be noted that his thought on this subject, as on most subjects, developed throughout his lifetime. Augustine addressed the topic of Christian marriage in several of his works and he devoted three different treatises specifically to marriage or aspects of marriage.[2] Augustine modified and expanded his thought on marriage largely in response to challenges to marriage that were proposed by different heretical groups. In each of these controversies and throughout his life as a Christian Augustine upheld the goodness of marriage. Early in his life as a Christian, Augustine addressed the Manichean view of marriage; the Manichees believed that sexual intercourse and procreation were intrinsically evil. In contrast, Augustine defended the goodness of the married state and the fact that marriage was instituted by God at the beginning of creation.[3] Shortly after the year 400, Augustine addressed the errors of Jovinianism; the Roman monk Jovinian asserted that there is no difference in merit between the married state and the state of consecrated virginity. Instead, Augustine sought to extol virginity as the higher calling without denigrating the goodness of marriage. [4] Augustine also undertook this endeavor as a corrective to some Christians, like St. Jerome, who in responding to Jovinian had nearly succeeded in condemning marriage.[5] Finally, at the end of his life Augustine entered theological battles with the Pelagians. Augustine's Pelagian opponents, and especially the Pelagian bishop Julian of Eclanum, maintained that carnal concupiscence is a normal part of

---

2. These treatises are: *On the Good of Marriage* (*De bono coniugali*) written in 401, *On Adulterous Marriage* (*De adulterinis coniugiis*) written in 419/420, and *On Marriage and Concupiscence* (*De nuptiis et concupiscentia*) written in 419/420.

3. For Augustine against the Manichees see: *On the Morals of the Church and on the Morals of the Manichees* (*De moribus ecclesiae et de moribus Manichaeorum*) written 387–389; *On Genesis Against the Manichees* (*De Genesi contra Manichaeos*) written 388–389; *On the Literal Meaning of Genesis, an Unfinished Work* (*De Genesi ad letteram liber imperfectus*) written 393–394; *Against Faustus the Manichee* (*Contra Faustum Manicaeum*) written 397–399; *On Continence* (*De continentia*) written in 395/396, although some scholars are now proposing that this work was actually addressed to the Pelagians and date it 418–420.

4. For Augustine against Jovinian see *On the Good of Marriage* written in 401 and *On Holy Virginity* (*De sancta virginitate*) written in 401, which should be read as companion pieces.

5. David Hunter, "*Bono conjugali, De,*" in *Augustine through the Ages: An Encyclopedia*, ed. Allan D. Fitzgerald (Grand Rapids, MI: Eerdmans, 1999), 110.

human existence, and he accused Augustine of having reverted to
Manicheism for believing otherwise. Responding to Julian, Augustine
maintained that carnal concupiscence is a disorder engendered in
humanity since the Fall, and that it must be curbed in humanity's
present state with the help of God's grace through the virtues of
continence and chastity.[6] As with all of Augustine's polemical writings, the subject matter of these debates was circumscribed by his
opponents' errors, and there were specific issues of concern that
Augustine limited himself to addressing. In his responses to the
Manichees and the Pelagians, Augustine was responding to two
extremes that confronted him at opposite ends of his Christian life:
one a radical denial of the goodness of the material world, and the
other an unrealistic denial of the effects of sin on the world. Augustine's
response to Jovinian allowed him the opportunity to produce a more
wide-ranging treatise on marriage. However, this treatment of
marriage occurred fourteen years after Augustine's Baptism and five
years after his episcopal consecration. During the remaining twenty-
nine years of his life, he never attempted to write another comparably
comprehensive treatment of Christian marriage.[7]

In highlighting some aspects of the evolution of Augustine's
thought on marriage it must be noted that the first words Augustine
wrote about marriage in his *Soliloquies*, shortly after his conversion,
were nearly disparaging, at least with regard to whether Augustine
saw marriage as an option for himself.[8] However, as his life progressed
Augustine became an ardent defender of the goodness of marriage.
He eventually came to the point where he opposed the widespread
opinion of his day and assigned marriage, sexual differentiation, and

6. For Augustine against the Pelagians see: *On the Grace of Christ, and on Original Sin*
(*De gratia Christi et peccato originali*) written in 418; *On Marriage and Concupiscence* written in
419–421; *Answer to the Two Letters of the Pelagians* (*Contra duas epistolas Pelagianorum*) written
in 421; *Answer to Julian* (*Contra Julianum*) written in 421; *Unfinished Work in Answer to Julian*
(*Contra Julianum opus imperfectum*) written in 428–430.

7. Other works in which Augustine addressed marriage, that have not already been
mentioned, are: *On the Lord's Sermon on the Mount* (*De sermone Domini in monte*, 393–395);
Confessions (*Confessiones*, 395–397); *On the Good of Widowhood* (*De bono viduitatis*, 414); *The
Literal Meaning of Genesis* (*De Genesi ad litteram*, 401–415); *City of God* (*De civitate Dei*, 413–426;
especially Books XI and XIV).

8. Augustine, *The Soliloquies*, trans. Thomas F. Gilligan, FOC, vol. 1 (1948), I.10.17.

the conjugal embrace prominent places in paradise before the Fall.[9] In fact, Augustine was one of only two early Church Fathers (the other being Pseudo-Ambrose, or Ambrosiaster) who maintained that Adam and Eve were married in paradise and would have had sexual intercourse even if they had not sinned,[10] although in paradise the conjugal act would have been free of carnal concupiscence.[11] In contrast to the position held by Gregory of Nyssa, Jerome, John Chrysostom, and other early Church Fathers, Augustine affirmed sexuality and marriage as being part of God's original plan for humanity.[12] Thus Augustine was able to see in marriage from "the beginning" a figure or sign of the great mystery of Christ's nuptial union with the Church,[13] a union which in turn will impact Christian marriages.

AUGUSTINE, MARRIAGE, AND LOVE

Not only did Augustine affirm that marriage was instituted by God at the beginning of the creation of humanity,[14] but he also saw that the

---

9. In *The Literal Meaning of Genesis*, trans. John Hammond Taylor, ACW, vols. 41–42 (1982), III.21.33; IX.3.5-7. In this work Augustine stated for the first time that Adam and Eve would have had sexual intercourse even had they not sinned. Although he had already affirmed that Adam and Eve were married in paradise when writing *The Good of Marriage* in 401, he had not yet arrived at the conclusion that the first couple would have had marital relations before they sinned.

10. Carol Harrison, "Marriage and Monasticism in St. Augustine: The Bond of Friendship," *Studia Patristica* 33 (1997): 96. This fact is also noted by Philip Lyndon Reynolds, *Marriage in the Western Church: The Christianization of Marriage during the Patristic and Early Medieval Periods*, 242–43.

11. See *Concerning the City of God against the Pagans*, trans. Henry Bettenson (London: Penguin Books, 1987), XIV.23; *On the Grace of Christ, and on Original Sin*, trans. Peter Holmes and Robert Ernest Wallis, NPNF, Series 1, vol. 5, II.35.40; *The Literal Meaning of Genesis*, IX.3–4, 10; *Marriage and Desire*, trans. Roland J. Teske, WSA, part 1, vol. 24 (1998), II.7.17; II.22.37; II.31.53; II.32.54; *Unfinished Work in Answer to Julian*, trans. Roland J. Teske, WSA, part 1, vol. 25 (1999), V.16.

12. Lawrence J. Welch highlights the importance of Augustine's affirmation that sexuality, marriage, and sexual intercourse would have been part of humanity's existence in paradise in "Chapter 10: The Augustinian Foundations of Nuptial Theology of the Body: 'He Who Created Both Sexes Will Restore Both,'" in *The Presence of Christ in the Church: Explorations in Theology* (Ave Maria, FL: Sapientia Press, 2012), 147–168. Welch points out how this affirmation emphasizes the central importance of marriage and sexuality in Christian revelation.

13. Augustine, *Marriage and Desire*, II.32.54.

14. Augustine, *The Good of Marriage*, trans. Charles T. Wilcox, FOC, vol. 27 (1955), 1.1; *City of God*, XIV.22; *Tractates on the Gospel according to John*, trans. John Gibb and James Innes, NPNF, First Series, vol. 7, X.2; *Answer to the Two Letters of the Pelagians*, trans. Roland J. Teske, WSA, part 1, vol. 24 (1998), I.5.9.

essence of this primordial relationship of man and woman is friend-ship based in love.[15] At the beginning of *The Good of Marriage* Augustine places his discussion of marriage in the context of the love of real friends. He begins this treatise by stating:

> Since every man is a part of the human race, and human nature is some-thing social and possesses the capacity for friendship as a great and natu-ral good, for this reason God wished to create all men from one, so that they might be held together in their society, not only by the similarity of race, but also by the bond of blood relationship. And so it is that the first natural tie of human society is man and wife. Even these God did not create separately and join them as if strangers, but He made the one from the other indicating also the power of union in the side from where she was drawn and formed. They are joined to each other side by side that walk together and observe together where they are walking. A consequence is the union of society in children who are the only worthy fruit, not of the joining of male and female, but of sexual intercourse. For there could have been in both sexes, even without intercourse, a kind of friendly and genuine union of the one ruling and the other obeying.[16]

This quote provides the context within which everything else Augustine said in *The Good of Marriage* can be understood. Later in the same work, Augustine explained that marriage is good not only "because of the procreation of children, but also because of the natural companionship between the two sexes."[17] He noted that in a good marriage there is an "order of charity" which "flourishes between husband and wife," even in spouses who are too old to bear children or who have been deprived of children.[18] Years later (around 418–419), in *City of God*, Augustine categorized the first marriage in paradise as "a faithful partnership based on love and mutual respect."[19] He also stated that the degree of intimacy and the strength of the bond between the first couple were evidenced by the fact that Eve was created from

---

15. Émile Schmitt, *Le mariage chrétien dans l'oeuvre de Saint Augustin. Une théologie baptismale de la vie conjugale* (Paris: Études Augustiniennes, 1983), 280–281, provides a list of expressions Augustine used to characterize the reciprocal love that exists between spouses.

16. Augustine, *The Good of Marriage*, 1.1.

17. Ibid., 3.3.

18. Ibid.

19. Augustine, *City of God*, XIV.26; see also XII.22; XIX.2.14.

Adam's rib.[20] Augustine explained that the beginning of friendship in the human race is marriage,[21] and he pointed out that it is spouses' "friendship that lays down the first strands of life."[22] This friendship that began in the marriage of the first couple will be perfected in the Heavenly City where there will be "a perfectly ordered and perfectly harmonious fellowship in the enjoyment of God, and a mutual fellowship in God."[23] Thus Augustine saw primordial marriage and ideally all marriages as being characterized by a mutuality of husband and wife based in love.

Augustine and the Good of Marriage

One of Augustine's perennial contributions to a theology of marriage is his articulation of the three goods (*bona*) of marriage. St. Augustine delineated three goods of marriage for the first time around 401 in his work *The Good of Marriage*, and they are: offspring (*proles*), faithfulness (*fides*), and sacrament (*sacramentum*).[24] He arrived at this division of goods according to Scripture, having seen the good of offspring presented in 1 Timothy 5:14[25] and Genesis 1:28;[26] the good of faithfulness presented in 1 Corinthians 7:4[27] and Genesis 2:24;[28] and the good of the sacrament of marriage presented in 1 Corinthians 7:10,[29]

---

20. Augustine, *The Literal Meaning of Genesis*, IX.13.23; *City of God*, XII.28.

21. Augustine, *Sermon* 299D, trans. Edmund Hill, WSA, part 3, vol. 8 (1994), 1. Delivered on July 17 sometime before 413.

22. Augustine, *Sermon* 9, trans. Edmund Hill, WSA, part 3, Vol. 1 (1990), 7. Hill dates this sermon to around 420.

23. Augustine, *City of God*, XIX.13.

24. Émile Schmitt, *Le mariage chrétien dans l'oeuvre de Saint Augustin. Une théologie baptismale de la vie conjugale*, 232–233, provides a chronological listing of Augustine's works in which he refers to the three goods of marriage: *The Good of Marriage*, III.3–VII.7; XXIV.32; *Holy Virginity*, XII.12; *The Literal Meaning of Genesis*, IX.7.12; *On the Good of Widowhood*, IV.5; *On the Grace of Christ, and on Original Sin*, II.34.39; 37.42; *Marriage and Desire*, I.10.11; 11.13; 17.19; 21.23; *Against Julian*, II.7.20; III.16.30; 25.57; V.12.46.

25. Augustine, *The Good of Marriage*, 24.25; *On the Grace of Christ, and on Original Sin*, II.34.39.

26. Augustine, *Marriage and Desire*, I.21.23.

27. Augustine, *The Good of Marriage*, 24.25; *On the Grace of Christ, and on Original Sin*, II.34.39.

28. Augustine, *Marriage and Desire*, I.21.23.

29. Augustine, *The Good of Marriage*, 24.25.

Matthew 19:6,[30] and Ephesians 5:32.[31] In one of his clearest articulations of the three goods of marriage Augustine stated:

> Now this good is threefold: fidelity, offspring, and sacrament. *Fidelity* means that there must be no relations with any other person outside the marriage bond. *Offspring* means that children are to be lovingly received, brought up with tender care, and given a religious education. *Sacrament* means that the marriage bond is not to be broken, and that if one partner in a marriage should be abandoned by the other, neither may enter a new marriage even for the sake of having children.[32]

In Augustine's writings on the goods of marriage, and especially where he refers to the goods as "threefold" (*tripertitum*), it is possible to see the three goods of marriage as three inseparable aspects of marriage all pertaining to the essence of marriage, which is love. In Augustine's thought, married love possesses a trinitarian structure based upon the three goods of marriage that Augustine delineates. The link between love and the *sacramentum* of marriage is apparent because Augustine, following St. Paul, related the indissoluble bond effected by the *sacramentum* of Christian marriage to the indissoluble love that Christ has for the Church.[33] Yet, Augustine also placed the other two goods in the context of the loving friendship by which he characterizes marriage. In *The Good of Marriage* Augustine saw the good of procreation (*proles*) as occurring within the context of the good of friendship.[34] In one of his aforementioned sermons, Augustine stated that the good of children flows from the friendship of spouses. He wrote, "It's your parents you see when you first open your eyes, and it is their friendship that lays down the first strands of this life."[35] Finally, the good of fidelity (*fides*) shows the exclusive and supportive nature of the love between spouses.[36] Augustine also implied that the three goods of marriage are intertwined in the inseparable structure of marital love when he stated that a marriage that possesses all three

---

30. Augustine, *On the Grace of Christ, and on Original Sin*, II.34.39.
31. Augustine, *Marriage and Desire*, I.21.23.
32. Augustine, *The Literal Meaning of Genesis*, IX.7.12.
33. Augustine, *Marriage and Desire*, I.10.11.
34. Augustine, *The Good of Marriage*, 9.9.
35. Augustine, *Sermon 9*, 7.
36. Augustine, *The Good of Marriage*, 4.4.

goods possesses the same structure as the marriage instituted by God in the beginning.[37]

This is not to say that Augustine meant that spouses who are biologically incapable of having children were less married than those with progeny. Infertile couples can still have spiritual children and thus participate in the procreative good of marriage. This is implied in Augustine's thinking when he spoke of St. Paul begetting children in the Gospel,[38] and when he explained how virgins can be true mothers, stating: "Both married women of the faith and virgins consecrated to God, by holy lives and by charity 'from a pure heart and a good conscience and faith unfeigned,' [1 Tim 1:5] are spiritually the mothers of Christ because they do the will of His Father."[39]

It should be noted, however, that Augustine saw that spouses cannot be spiritual parents living holy lives of love with pure hearts, clear consciences, and unfeigned faith if they purposefully render any act of marital intercourse barren. This would intentionally oppose one inseparable aspect of the triune good of marriage. This is implied when Augustine stated that spouses who seek sexual pleasure while preventing procreation by either evil intention or evil act are not truly husband and wife.[40] Thus in his presentation of the three goods of marriage Augustine insinuated that in order to be the institution of loving friendship that God made, marriage must incorporate all three goods.

Augustine viewed the marriage of Mary and Joseph as the model Christian marriage,[41] possessing the fullness of the triune good of marriage (offspring, fidelity, and sacrament or permanent bond),[42] and therefore the fullness of conjugal love.[43] Regarding Mary and Joseph, Augustine stated:

> Heaven forbid that in the case of those who have decided by mutual consent permanently to abstain from the use of carnal concupiscence the marital bond between them is broken. In fact, it will be stronger to the

37. Augustine, *Marriage and Desire*, II.32.54.

38. Augustine, *Confessions*, trans. Henry Chadwick, Oxford World's Classics (New York: Oxford University Press, 1991), XIII.xxii.32.

39. Augustine, *Holy Virginity*, trans. J. McQuade, FOC, vol. 27 (1955), 6.6.

40. Augustine, *Marriage and Desire*, I.15.17.

41. Ibid., I.11.12.

42. Ibid., I.11.13.

43. Augustine, *Sermon* 51, trans. Edmund Hill, WSA, part 3, vol. 3 (1991), 21.

extent that they have entered more deeply into those agreements with each other, which have to be observed in greater love and harmony, not by pleasureful embraces of their bodies, but by willing affections of their hearts. After all, the angel did not speak to Joseph words that were false, when he said, *Do not be afraid to take Mary as your wife* (Mt 1:20). She is called "wife" because of the first pledge of their engagement, though Joseph had not known and would not know her through intercourse.[44]

By affirming the true marital status of the virginal union of Mary and Joseph, Augustine, like Ambrose, affirmed that it is consent, and not consummation, that makes a marriage—an issue which will receive further treatment in the medieval period.

AUGUSTINE AND THE MARITAL ACT

In his writings on marriage and the goods of marriage Augustine clearly affirmed the primary end of marriage—the procreation and education of children. This is clear when he stated that "the procreation of children is itself the primary, natural, legitimate purpose of marriage."[45] Stressing procreation as the primary purpose of marriage and of sexual intercourse,[46] Augustine did not see how a couple can be acting according to reason, without committing "venial sin," if they engage in sexual intercourse without an explicit intention to procreate.[47] He did, however, distinguish between a couple who willfully opposes life by engaging in an act of sexual intercourse with an evil device or intention (i.e., contraceptive intercourse), and a couple who may not directly intend that their act of intercourse result in a child but nonetheless does not directly oppose the child coming to be.[48] This second case would include couples who engage in sexual intercourse even if circumstances beyond their control (i.e., intercourse during pregnancy, postmenopausal intercourse, or intercourse during infertile days of a woman's menstrual cycle) make it impossible for their act of sexual

---

44. Augustine, *Marriage and Desire*, I.11.12.

45. Augustine, *Adulterous Marriage*, trans. C.T. Huegelmeyr, FOC, vol. 27 (1955), II.12.

46. See Augustine, *The Good of Marriage*, 1.1: "children who are the only worthy fruit, not of the joining of male and female, but of sexual intercourse."

47. See *The Good of Marriage*, 6.6; *Marriage and Desire*, I.14.16; *Answer to Julian*, trans. Roland J. Teske, WSA, part 1, vol. 24 (1998), IV.3.33; V.16.63.

48. See Augustine, *Marriage and Desire*, I.15.17.

intercourse to result in the conception of a child. He qualified the couple in the first case as being guilty of serious sin while the couple in the second case as being guilty of "venial sin."

However, while Augustine maintained that it is a venial sin to engage in sexual intercourse with one's spouse beyond the necessity of begetting children,[49] he also condemned the adoption of celibacy by one spouse without the consent of the other.[50] In addition, he stated that a spouse who renders the conjugal debt when it is demanded by the other spouse, even if children are not sought, performs an act of charity, mercy, and even continence in the faithful support of his or her spouse.[51] Thus, David Hunter argues that at least in this "very limited instance" Augustine was proposing sexual intercourse as an act of love.[52] Moreover, even the spouse who demands sexual intercourse beyond that necessary for procreation is guilty of a sin that is a "daily sin," that is so slight that it can be remitted by daily recitation of the Lord's Prayer.[53]

Even though Augustine was incorrect for requiring an explicit intention to procreate for the *ideal* use of sexual intercourse, and even though he may be faulted for not commenting more explicitly on how the conjugal act can serve conjugal love (outside of the limited instance noted by Hunter above), he did explicitly acknowledge the service that sexual intercourse renders to marital fidelity. Thus Augustine saw that spouses can engage in sexual intercourse in such a way so as to support and serve the faithful dimension of their friendship and love. Although he believed that the ideal use of marital intercourse was that which was engaged in with the explicit intention of procreating, Augustine acknowledged that even marital intercourse pursued out of incontinence, which for him was intercourse engaged in without directly intending to conceive a child, could support the bond of fidelity as long as procreation was not purposefully eliminated from that act by any evil devise or intention.[54]

---

49. Augustine, *Sermon 354A*, trans. Edmund Hill, WSA, Part III, vol. 11 (1997), 8–9.

50. Augustine, *Sermon 354A*, 3, 5.

51. David Hunter, "Augustine, Sermon 354A: Its Place in His Thought on Marriage and Sexuality," *Augustinian Studies* 33.1 (2002): 47–49; see Augustine, *Sermon 354A*, 13.

52. Hunter, "Augustine, Sermon 354A: Its Place in His Thought on Marriage and Sexuality," 49.

53. Ibid., 46; see Augustine, *Sermon 354A*, 12.

54. Augustine, *Marriage and Desire*, I.15.17.

It is true that Augustine did not sufficiently elaborate upon the interpersonal relations between spouses, nor did he attempt to explain how the conjugal act might express, intensify, or increase the interpersonal union between spouses. However, by condemning the unilateral adoption of celibacy by one spouse and by saying that a spouse performs an act of charity when rendering the conjugal debt to faithfully support the other spouse, even when children are not explicitly sought, Augustine also affirmed the secondary end of marriage—the good of the spouses. As part of this good, Augustine presented marriage as providing a remedy for concupiscence. He understood that the three goods of marriage can help spouses to overcome the effects of disordered carnal concupiscence. He presented the three goods of marriage as "the rule of marriage: by it fertility of nature is made honorable and the disorder of concupiscence is regulated."[55] Especially in Christian marriage, carnal concupiscence is confined to a permanent union (the *sacramentum*) and can be directed toward serving the goods of procreation (*proles*) and fidelity (*fides*),[56] according to the virtue of conjugal chastity.[57]

This is what Augustine meant when he stated that marriage makes good use of the evil of carnal concupiscence,[58] or that marriage is a cure or remedy for the vice of incontinence.[59] Augustine saw Christian marriage as a healing institution not primarily because it provides a legitimate outlet for sexual concupiscence, but because it offers motivation for its control,[60] and empowers the couple in this effort. Benedict Ashley has explained quite succinctly that when Augustine spoke of controlling concupiscence as one of the benefits of marriage, "this must be understood not merely in a negative sense, that the married need not seek sexual satisfaction outside of marriage,

55. Augustine, *The Literal Meaning of Genesis*, IX.7.12.

56. Augustine, *The Good of Marriage*, 3.3; 4.4.

57. Augustine, *Marriage and Desire*, I.3.3–4; *Letter 6**, trans. Robert B. Eno, FOC, vol. 81 (1989), 5, 8; *Unfinished Work in Answer to Julian*, I.68.

58. Augustine, *The Good of Marriage*, 3.3; *On the Grace of Christ, and on Original Sin*, II.37.42; *Continence*, trans. M. F. McDonald, FOC, vol. 16 (1952), 12.27; *Letter 6**, 7; *Marriage and Desire*, II.21.36; *Answer to Julian*, III.20.41; 21.49; 25.57; V.12.46; 16.63; *Unfinished Work in Answer to Julian*, I.68; *Retractations*, trans. M. I. Bogan, FOC, vol. 60 (1968), II.79.

59. Augustine, *Adulterous Marriage*, II.12.12.

60. John R. Connery, "The Role of Love in Christian Marriage: A Historical Overview," *Communio* 11 (1984): 245.

but in the positive sense that the Sacrament enables the married couple to acquire the virtue of chastity as the holy and humanly fulfilling use of God's gift of sexuality."[61]

Nonetheless, it should be noted that even though Augustine saw marriage as pardoning and providing a remedy for sexual concupiscence, he did maintain that it is the disorder of concupiscence present in sexual intercourse that serves as the vehicle for the transmission of original sin.[62] Thus, while marriage and sexual intercourse are good in themselves, sexual concupiscence is a disorder engendered by original sin which perpetuates the hereditary transmission of sin. When engaging in the marital act, this is a disorder that spouses cannot escape, a reality which lead Augustine and other Church Fathers to view sexual intercourse with suspicion, or at least a certain amount of ambivalence.

Augustine and Sacramental Theology

After outlining how Augustine saw the primary and secondary ends of marriage relating to the triune structure of marital love, it is important to say more about Augustine's contributions to articulating the *sacramentum* that is present in marriage.[63] As Peter Elliott has noted and as we have seen in the previous chapter, "The evidence for a sacramental understanding of Marriage up to, or apart from, Saint Augustine is admittedly fragmentary and imprecise."[64] The evidence in the previous chapter shows that early Christians saw a difference between their marriages and the marriages of non-Christians, precisely because they viewed their marriages in light of the relationship between Christ and his Church. However, Augustine significantly developed what it means to understand Christian marriage as a sign of Christ's union with the Church.

---

61. Benedict M. Ashley, *Living the Truth in Love: A Biblical Introduction to Moral Theology* (New York: Alba House, 1996), 245.

62. See Augustine, *Marriage and Desire*, I.1.1; I.13.12; I.19.21; I.22.24; I.35.40; II.12.25.

63. A good overview of Augustine's understanding of "sacrament" is provided by Emmanuel J. Cutrone, "Sacraments," in *Augustine through the Ages: An Encyclopedia* (Grand Rapids: Eerdmans, 1999), 741–47.

64. Peter J. Elliott, *What God Has Joined:The Sacramentality of Marriage* (New York: Alba House, 1990), 77.

When dealing with Augustine's treatment of marriage as a sacrament, it must be noted that Augustine uses *sacramentum* in more than one sense. [65] Resonating with the larger cultural use of the term, Augustine used *sacramentum* to refer to a binding oath. [66] He also applied *sacramentum* "to the religious rites of both the Old and the New Testaments, to the biblical symbols and figures, and also to the revealed Christian religion. All of these 'sacraments,' according to St. Augustine, belong to the great sacrament, namely, the mystery of Christ and the Church" (TOB 93:5, fn. 88). In this sense, Augustine was using *sacramentum* to refer to visible signs that represent invisible divine realities. [67] In a more specific sense, Augustine used *sacramentum* to refer to sacred signs that have a likeness to what they signify and also confer what they signify. [68] He even made a distinction between the outward sign of the sacrament (what would become known as the *sacramentem tantum*, or the sign itself), composed of both words and material things, [69] and the invisible reality that is signified (what would become known as the *res tantum*, or the reality itself). [70] Medieval scholars will further refine the sense of "sacrament" understood as a sacred sign that effects an invisible reality of grace.

Additionally, Augustine laid the groundwork for reflections on sacramental causality, in other words, what causes the sacraments to be effective of grace. In his refutation of the Donatists, who taught that the effectiveness of the Sacrament of Baptism depended on the holiness of the minister of the sacrament, Augustine maintained that it is Christ who makes the sacraments effective. [71] Thus Christ offers his grace by virtue of the sacramental action itself, and not by virtue

---

65. Much of the information in this paragraph is taken from TOB 93:5, footnote 88.

66. See Augustine, *On Baptism, Against the Donatists*, trans. J.R. King, NPNF, First Series, vol. 4, I.4.5.

67. See Augustine, *Letter CXXXVIII*, trans. J.G. Cunningham, NPNF, First Series, vol. 1, 7.

68. See Augustine, *Letter XCVIII*, trans. J.G. Cunningham, NPNF, First Series, vol. 1, 9; and *Tractates on the First Epistle of John*, trans. John W. Rettig, FOC, vol. 92 (1995), VI.11.2.

69. See Augustine, *Tractates on the Gospel According to St. John*, XV.4. In this passage Augustine distinguishes between the water used in the Sacrament of Baptism and the words used in the Sacrament of Baptism, maintaining the necessity of each.

70. In *Letter XCVIII.2*, Augustine distinguishes between water as the outward form of the Sacrament of Baptism and the inner power of grace that is bestowed. In *On Baptism, Against the Donatists*, III.10.15, Augustine distinguishes between the outward signs of the water that is used, the words that are spoken in Baptism, and the divine reality of the sacrament.

71. See Augustine, *On Baptism, Against the Donatists*, IV.11.18; 16.24.

of the worthiness of the person administering the sacrament. Augustine also made it clear that although Christ makes grace available through the sacramental action itself, the effect of this grace on the recipient of the sacraments depends on how well-disposed the recipient is to receive that grace.[72] He even identified that the grace of certain sacraments that are received in an unfit state, and thus with no effect on their recipient, can revive and have an effect on the recipient after repentance takes place.[73] Medieval theologians will further refine an understanding of sacramental causality.

Augustine and the Sacrament of Marriage

In Augustine's treatment of marriage he used *sacramentum* in both general and more specific senses. For Augustine, marriage as it was instituted in the order of creation possessed the good of the *sacramentum*, understood as the permanence of a binding oath.[74] In this sense (of a binding oath), Augustine was using *sacramentum* as it was understood in the Roman culture and he was positing this *sacramentum* as one of the three goods that are present in every marriage. However, Augustine also spoke of a *sacramentum* unique to Christian marriage when he stated:

> The good, therefore, of marriage among all nations and all men is in the cause of generation and in the fidelity of chastity; in the case of the people of God, however, the good is also in the sanctity of the sacrament. Because of this sanctity it is wrong for a woman, leaving with a divorce, to marry another man while her husband still lives, even if she does this for the sake of having children.[75]

This quote is an example of Augustine presenting the goods of children and fidelity as belonging to all marriages, while presenting Christian marriages as possessing the sanctity of a sacrament that makes these unions truly indissoluble; indissoluble in a way that is more perfect than the binding oath of non-Christian marriages.

---

72. See *On Baptism, Against the Donatists*, I.12.18–20.
73. See ibid.
74. Augustine, *The Literal Meaning of Genesis*, IX.7.12.
75. Augustine, *The Good of Marriage*, 24.32.

Augustine focused on this absolutely indissoluble bond when commenting on the sacrament in Christian marriage. He compared the indelible bond of Christian marriage to the Sacrament of Orders which remains in the clergy for life,[76] and he also compared the sacrament in Christian marriage to the lifelong effect of Baptism which indelibly marks a person as belonging to Christ.[77] In Christian married couples he referred to a "marital something" (*quiddam coniugale*) that remains as a lifelong covenantal bond between the couple.[78] For Christians this bond is absolutely indissoluble because Christian marriage is an effective sign of Christ's undying love for the Church.[79] Allowing the Christian Sacrament of Marriage to speak for itself, Augustine stated:

> The sacrament of marriage will also reply: Before the sin it was said of me in paradise, *A man will leave father and his mother, and will cling to his wife, and they will be two in one flesh* (Gen 2:24), and the apostle calls this a great sacrament in Christ and of the Church. That which is something great, then, in Christ and the Church is quite small in each individual husband and wife, but it is still a sacrament of an inseparable union.[80]

Thus, in its most specific sense, for Augustine the sacrament in Christian marriage is a sign of Christ's union with the Church that effects the indissolubility of the couple's union.[81] Augustine identified the indissoluble bond as the reality that is effected by the Christian sacrament in marriage when he stated: "Beyond any doubt the reality signified by this sacrament (*res sacramenti*) is that the man and the woman united in marriage persevere inseparably in that union as long as they live, and it is not permitted that one be separated from the other except on account of fornication."[82]

Although Augustine advanced theological reflection on the Sacrament of Marriage more than any other Church Father, his thought in this area is not without shortcomings. While Augustine

---

76. Ibid.
77. Augustine, *Marriage and Desire*, I.10.11.
78. Ibid., I.11.12.
79. Augustine, *The Good of Marriage*, 44.32.
80. Augustine, *Marriage and Desire*, I.21.23.
81. Ibid., I.10.11.
82. Ibid.

constantly reiterated the goodness of the married state and defended the possibility of spouses growing in holiness, he did seem to view living in the married state as an indulgence in the age of grace. Augustine stated on several occasions that he believed the "time for embracing" [Ecclesiastes 3:5] was over,[83] and that those who married were permitted to do so because they lacked the gift of continence. While acknowledging that the Sacrament of Marriage is to symbolize the union of Christ and the Church, and acknowledging that married people have a place in the Body of Christ, Augustine did not seem to have sufficiently worked out in his mind the proper role of those existing in the married state under the reign of grace. Nonetheless, Augustine did see the love of spouses reflecting and participating in the indissoluble love of Christ for his Church. Thus a recent scholar has pointed out that Augustine "never draws the explicit conclusion that matrimony is a grace-giving sacrament of the New Law, as subsequently has become defined Catholic doctrine, but everything he says on this point has sacramental connotations, and makes such a conclusion almost inevitable."[84] Later theologians in the Church's history will draw out this inevitable conclusion, which will eventually be defined as a doctrine by the Church's magisterium. It is to these later theologians that we must now turn.

---

83. Augustine, *The Good of Marriage*, 9.9; *Marriage and Desire*, II.12.12; *The Literal Meaning of Genesis*, IX.7.12.

84. Augustine Regan, "The Perennial Value of Augustine's Theology of the Goods of Marriage," *Studia Moralia* 21 (1983): 358.

Chapter 11

"After St. Augustine": The Medieval Period through Aquinas

INTRODUCTION TO THE MEDIEVAL THEOLOGY OF MARRIAGE

For about two-thirds of a millennium after St. Augustine's death, his thought continued to shape the Western Church's approach to marriage. Peter Elliott stated: "The period of almost seven hundred years, from the early Fifth to the Twelfth Century, may justly be described as 'After Saint Augustine' in terms of the sacramentality of Marriage."[1] Similarly, after St. John Chrysostom, the theology of marriage in the Eastern Church remained underdeveloped even into the twentieth century.[2] Part of the reason for this lack of development in the West and in the East is due to societal and cultural factors, respectively. Beginning in the fifth century the Western Church was forced to address the invasion of the barbarian tribal peoples into Western Europe, which contributed to the subsequent decline and fall of the Western Empire itself. In the East, the seventh century brought the rise of Islam. Dealing with their respective socio-cultural problems, communication between the East and West became strained and tenuous at best, and theological development slowed considerably.

---

1. Peter J. Elliott, *What God Has Joined: The Sacramentality of Marriage* (New York: Alba House, 1990), 84.

2. Catharine P. Roth, "Introduction," in *St. John Chrysostom: On Marriage and Family Life* (Crestwood, NY: St. Vladimir's Seminary Press, 2000), 11.

After the fall of the Roman Empire in the West at the end of the fifth century, an emperor remained on the throne in the East for almost another millennium. These emperors sought to rule not only the temporal order, but also the ecclesial order, a phenomenon referred to as caesaropapism. It is largely due to the influence of the Eastern emperors that the Eastern Church began to permit remarriage after divorce.[3] Until around the sixth century the Eastern Church's view of the indissolubility of marriage had largely coincided with that of the West. Peter Elliott noted that "a clear history may be set out describing the stages whereby the hierarchy in the East capitulated over divorce and remarriage to the Byzantine Emperors."[4] The reign of Byzantine Emperor Leo VI, 886–912, seems to have been influential in this regard. Orthodox scholar John Meyendorff pointed out how during his reign, Leo put the Church, and not the civil arm, in charge of all marriages. Meyendorff noted:

> After Leo VI the Church had to determine the legal status of all marriages, even those which contradicted Christian norms. Of course the new situation, in principle, gave the Church an upper hand over the morals of all citizens; but in practice, since these citizens were not all saints, the Church was obliged not only to bless marriages which it did not approve, but even to "dissolve" them (i.e., give "divorces"). The distinction between the "secular" and the "sacred," between fallen human society and the Kingdom of God, between marriage as contract and marriage as sacrament, was partially obliterated.
>
> The Church had to pay a high price for the new social responsibility which it had received. . . . As soon as the sacrament of marriage—received in the Church—became obligatory, compromises of all sorts became unavoidable.[5]

Thus the entanglement of Church and Empire seemed to have played a decisive role in the practice of divorce and remarriage in the Orthodox Church.

---

3. For a discussion of the Eastern emperors' influence on marriage see George Howard Joyce, *Christian Marriage: An Historical and Doctrinal Study* (New York: Sheed and Ward, 1933), 362–376.

4. Peter J. Elliott, *What God Has Joined*, 206.

5. John Meyendorff, *Marriage: An Orthodox Perspective*, 2nd expanded ed, (Crestwood, NY: St. Vladimir's Seminary Press, 1975), 29.

As was noted earlier, the Orthodox Church allows for remarriage, but the ceremony surrounding a second or subsequent marriage (whether the previous spouse is still living or dead) has a marked penitential tone.[6] It is also true that the Orthodox provide theological justifications for allowing divorce and remarriage, explaining that remarriage can take place when the love of the spouses has in some way "died."[7] While some of these reasons would be grounds for declaring a marriage null in the Catholic Church (such as the inability to consummate), other grounds on which a divorce can be granted in the Orthodox Church (like implacable hatred, involving a total breakdown in personal relations) result in making the durability of the Sacrament of Marriage depend upon the vacillating wills of the spouses.[8] It does seem, however, that some Orthodox theologians are open to ecumenical dialogue regarding the practice of divorce and remarriage.[9]

Perhaps it is the same entanglement between Church and State of the ninth century that led to the Orthodox position that the priest is the minister of the Sacrament of Marriage, instead of the married couple themselves. At the same time Emperor Leo VI required the Church in the East to validate all marriages, the priest's blessing also "received a juridical value."[10] The new law (*novella* 89) that Leo issued in 895 stated: "Matrimony draws its strength from the blessing [given] by the priest, so that if anyone is married without it, this marriage is null."[11] It is true that the Orthodox see mutual consent of the spouses as a condition that is required for the valid celebration of the Sacrament of Marriage. However, they do not see consent as the content of marriage, which is found instead in the nuptial blessing given by the

6. See John Meyendorff, *Marriage: An Orthodox Perspective*, 51.

7. See Paul Evdokimov, *The Sacrament of Love: The Nuptial Mystery in the Light of the Orthodox Tradition*, trans. Anthony P. Gythiel and Victoria Steadman (Crestwood, NY: St. Vladimir's Seminary Press, 1985), 184.

8. For a good, brief treatment of the Orthodox theology and practice of divorce and remarriage see, Kallistos Ware, "The Sacrament of Love: The Orthodox Understanding of Marriage and Its Breakdown," *Downside Review* 109 (1991): 79–93.

9. See, for example, Theodore G. Stylianopoulos, "Toward a Theology of Marriage in the Orthodox Church," in *Intermarriage: Orthodox Perspectives*, ed. Anton C. Vrame (Brookline, MA: Holy Cross Orthodox Press, 1997), 29–31. This article was previously published in *Greek Orthodox Theological Review* 22.3 (1977): 249–283.

10. Paul Evdokimov, *The Sacrament of Love*, 129.

11. Quoted in Paul Evdokimov, *The Sacrament of Love*, 129.

priest.[12] The entanglement between throne and altar seems to have been decisive in solidifying this position. However, there seems to be room for ecumenical dialogue on this issue as well, as some recent Orthodox theologians point out that the mutual consent of the couple has often been undervalued and needs to be reemphasized in the Orthodox tradition.[13]

In the Western Church, the popes were more successful at defending the indissolubility of marriage against various barbarian tribal chieftains and kings who replaced the temporal leadership of the Western Roman Emperor. During the Patristic period there were very few magisterial teachings regarding marriage. However, a letter sent from Pope Leo the Great to Bishop Nicetas of Aquileia in 458 evidenced a defense of the indissoluble nature of Christian marriage. In this letter Pope Leo addressed the situation of women who were presumed to be widows and remarried, believing that their husbands had been killed in battle, but whose husbands later returned. Citing the indissoluble nature of marriage referenced in Matthew 19:6, Leo judged that "the bonds of the legitimate [first] marriages must be reestablished" (DS, 311). This is just one piece of early evidence that showed the Church in the West defending the indissolubility of marriage in the face of challenges.

One of the questions that became more acute in the West after Augustine was, "What makes a marriage?" This was a legitimate question because as Edward Schillebeeckx noted, "Although Christ had said that marriage was indissoluble, he had not said in what the anthropological reality of marriage precisely consisted."[14] While the laws of the Roman Empire maintained that it is the exchange of consent that makes a marriage (although the consent in question was mainly that of the spouses' families), many of the Germanic peoples who migrated into the Roman Empire from northern Europe emphasized the importance of consummation as that which makes a marriage. In the Middle Ages, theological arguments were crafted to rectify these positions with each other. Very few scholars argued that

---

12. John Meyendorff, *Marriage: An Orthodox Perspective*, 39.

13. See Theodore G. Stylianopoulos, "Toward a Theology of Marriage in the Orthodox Church," 25–27.

14. Edward Schillebeeckx, *Marriage: Human Reality and Saving Mystery*, 2 vols., trans. by N.D. Smith (New York: Sheed and Ward, 1965), 287.

consummation alone made a marriage, since this would mean that any sexual intercourse would effect a marriage bond. It would also mean that Mary and Joseph, who were always at the center of this debate, were not truly married.[15] However, theologians and canonists tried to explain the roles that consent and consummation play in bringing a marriage into being. Hincmar of Rheims (806–882) was instrumental in this debate, maintaining that while marriage did not exist without consent, it is consummation that makes the marital bond truly indissoluble.[16] In the eleventh and twelfth centuries, canonists in the school of Bologna argued in favor of consummation, while theologians in the school of Paris argued in favor of consent.

One of the biggest contributors to this debate was the medieval canonist Gratian, who in his collection and commentary on canon law, the *Decretum* (ca. 1140), maintained that while marriage begins with consent it is ratified or completed by consummation, which makes the marital bond indissoluble. However, Gratian placed such emphasis on consummation that he said it is necessary for the Sacrament of Marriage to exist.[17] Although scholars took differing positions on the matter, the teaching authority of the Church upheld consent of the couple as that which is essential for marriage.[18] Already in 866, in a letter to the Bulgarians, Pope Nicholas I affirmed that it is consent that makes a marriage (DS, 643). By the latter part of the twelfth century Pope Alexander III (1159–1181), setting aside his previously held personal position, ruled in favor of consent explaining that it is

---

15. For the importance of the marriage of Mary and Joseph to the medieval debate over consummation versus consent see Penny S. Gold, "The Marriage of Mary and Joseph in the Twelfth-Century Ideology of Marriage," in *Sexual Practices & the Medieval Church*, ed. Vern L. Bullough and James Brundage (Buffalo, NY: Prometheus Books, 1982), 102–117.

16. See Glenn W. Olsen, "Marriage in Barbarian Kingdom and Christian Court: Fifth through Eleventh Centuries," in *Christian Marriage: A Historical Study*, ed. Glenn Olsen (New York: The Crossroad Publishing Company, 2001), 161–162; Edward Schillebeeckx, *Marriage*, 270–271.

17. Teresa Olsen Pierre, "Marriage, Body, and Sacrament in the Age of Hugh of St. Victor," in *Christian Marriage: A Historical Study*, ed. Glenn Olsen (New York: The Crossroad Publishing Company, 2001), 220; for further comments on Gratian see Theodore Mackin, *What Is Marriage?*, Marriage in the Catholic Church (New York: Paulist Press, 1982), 158–164.

18. It should be noted that one of the discussions regarding consent was whether consent involved just the couple or the consent of their families. Although arguments were made on both sides, by the twelfth century the prevailing theological opinion was that the consent essential to the marriage was that of the marrying couple, thus effectively liberating bridegroom and bride from family control. On this point see Teresa Olsen Pierre, "Marriage, Body, and Sacrament in the Age of Hugh of St. Victor," 158–159, and Edward Schillebeeckx, *Marriage*, 299–300.

consent that makes a marriage, but consummation that makes it absolutely indissoluble (DS, 754–756). He also explained that an unconsummated marriage can be dissolved if one of the spouses wants to
enter religious life (DS, 754–755). In a Letter to the Archbishop of Arles
in 1198, Pope Leo III reiterated that it is consent that makes a marriage (DS, 766), and by 1216 the Church had codified in canon law
that the consent of the couple is all that is required for a valid marriage.[19]

In addition, the Catholic Church responded to questions
regarding consent versus consummation by influencing the customs
according to which marriages were contracted. Lacking the oversight
of Roman civil law after the collapse of the empire, the Church was
forced to develop more formalized means for celebrating and monitor-
ing the marriages of its own people. The Church exerted this influence through its liturgy and its own ecclesial laws. Throughout the
Patristic and early medieval periods marriages were largely entered into
at home, with a blessing conferred on the couple by a priest or bishop.
By the end of the first millennium of Christianity, jurisdictional oversight of marriages had been transferred into the hands of the
Church.[20] During the eleventh and twelfth centuries Church authorities
began to insist that marriages take place in a parish church.[21] Church
authorities did this not to take control of marriages, but to ensure
publicly the valid exchange of marital consent.[22]

Once it became clear that consent is that which makes a marriage, consent began to be treated by canonists and theologians as a
contractual agreement. Throughout the medieval period in the West
there emerged a juridical and legalistic approach to marriage, according
to which the exchange of consent between spouses was viewed as a
contract that imposed rights and obligations on the spouses. By the end
of the twelfth century this contractual view of marriage was firmly in

---

19. Teresa Olsen Pierre, "Marriage, Body, and Sacrament in the Age of Hugh of
St. Victor," 216.

20. Edward Schillebeeckx, *Marriage*, 272–279.

21. See Teresa Olsen Pierre, "Marriage, Body, and Sacrament in the Age of Hugh of
St. Victor," 222.

22. Edward Schillebeeckx, *Marriage*, 314–319.

place in both civil and canon law.[23] This primary view of marriage as a "contract" would endure beyond the Middle Ages as well.[24]

After the definitive fall of the Western Roman Empire in 476 AD, the Church was preoccupied with trying to rebuild society, and significant theological development was delayed. The monks assumed the task of Christianizing the barbarians, and monastic theology, with its emphasis on penance and asceticism, became dominant in the early Middle Ages. Without denigrating the human family, the monks stressed "the biblical idea that the new and true family is the spiritual family of those who do the will of God."[25] Historian Glenn Olsen noted that there resulted an "absorption with the virgin ideal [that] continued to deflect attention from consideration of marriage's special situation and needs."[26] "The assumption was that a good married life was simply a diluted imitation of monastic perfection."[27] A focus on consecrated virginity or celibacy as the more perfect life even led to the encouragement of virginal marriages, or the mutual agreement of spouses to forego the rights of marriage and enter into consecrated religious life.[28]

The opinion of the early Church Fathers that sexual intercourse was at least venially sinful unless a child was explicitly sought persisted throughout the medieval period.[29] "That the marital act is meritorious and holy for spouses in a state of grace, a view that strikes us now as obvious, was routinely denied in the Middle Ages."[30] Throughout the early Middle Ages theologians and canon lawyers employed what one might call a "negative" approach to marriage,

23. Theodore Mackin, *The Marital Sacrament*, Marriage in the Catholic Church (New York: Paulist Press, 1989), 327.

24. Edward Schillebeeckx, *Marriage*, 301–302.

25. Glenn W. Olsen, "Marriage in Barbarian Kingdom and Christian Court: Fifth through Eleventh Centuries," 146.

26. Ibid., 146.

27. Ibid., 147.

28. See Dyan Elliott, *Spiritual Marriage: Sexual Abstinence in Medieval Wedlock* (Princeton, NJ: Princeton University Press, 1993).

29. Joseph Kerns, *The Theology of Marriage: The Historical Development of Christian Attitudes Toward Sex and Sanctity in Marriage* (New York: Sheed and Ward, 1964), 45. On pages 41–83, Kerns provides citations of many medieval authors to illustrate their attitudes toward sexual intercourse in marriage.

30. Peter Kwasniewski, "St. Thomas on the Grandeur and Limitations of Marriage," *Nova et Vetera*, English Edition 10.2 (2012): 420.

focusing on marriage as a remedy for the disordered desires of sexual concupiscence.[31] With Augustine's thought as the main foundation, "various factors combined to emphasize the stricter elements of his thought on Marriage and sexuality."[32] This negative and strict approach was evidenced by certain customs and attitudes. "Women were viewed as unclean after childbirth until churched. Men were given severe penances for nocturnal emissions. Intercourse itself was commonly viewed as polluting."[33] That the conjugal act was seen as polluting had to do with the fact that sexual intercourse was viewed as involving the unruliness of sexual concupiscence. From this view there arose a custom among churchmen of counseling "abstinence from sexual relations on holy days, in sacred places, and during a wife's menses."[34] This continuing suspicion surrounding sensual desire meant that medieval theologians, like the early Church Fathers, had difficulty in acknowledging that the Sacrament of Marriage could confer a grace that was anything more than remediation for concupiscence. As one scholar noted regarding theologians of the twelfth and thirteenth centuries, "The tendency to inordinate expression on the part of concupiscence, and the intimate relationship between concupiscence and the exercise of the marital act creates many difficulties when it comes to recognizing marriage as a cause of grace."[35] This suspicion surrounding sexual desire also meant that many medieval authors presented a rather negative assessment of marriage itself, seeing it as a concession to sin or an indulgence for those who were unable to live a more perfect monastic existence.[36] Medieval theologians pointed to the three goods of marriage, delineated by Augustine, as merely aspects of marriage that excused the act of sexual intercourse.[37] As one recent scholar noted

---

31. Walter Kasper, *Theology of Christian Marriage*, (New York: Seabury Press), 36.

32. Peter J. Elliott, *What God Has Joined*, 84.

33. Glenn W. Olsen, "Marriage in Barbarian Kingdom and Christian Court: Fifth through Eleventh Centuries," 147.

34. Elizabeth M. Makowski, "The Conjugal Debt and Medieval Canon Law," in *Equality in God's Image: Women in the Middle Ages*, ed. Julia Bolton Holloway, Constance S. Wright, and Joan Bechtold (New York: Peter Lang, 1990), 136. This essay was originally published in *The Journal of Medieval History* 3 (1977): 99–114.

35. Seamus Heaney, *The Development of the Sacramentality of Marriage from Anselm of Laon to Thomas Aquinas* (Washington, D.C.: Catholic University of America Press, 1963), 72.

36. See Glenn W. Olsen, "Marriage in Barbarian Kingdom and Christian Court: Fifth through Eleventh Centuries," 150–158.

37. Seamus Heaney, *The Development of the Sacramentality of Marriage*, 72–73.

regarding the medieval treatment of marriage, "It should not embarrass Catholic theologians to admit that the medieval period, notwithstanding its incomparable achievements, bequeathed to succeeding ages certain erroneous habits of thought and omission that have taken centuries to redress."[38]

Sacramental Theology of Marriage in the Twelfth and Thirteenth Centuries

Theologians in the medieval period refined the understanding of "sacrament" bequeathed to them by St. Augustine. In the seventh century St. Isidore of Seville emphasized "the mysterious nature of a sacrament, which, under the veil of material appearances, conceals the action of the Holy Spirit in man's soul" (TOB 93:5, fn. 88). However, in the twelfth century, especially between 1120 and 1160, theologians focused on refining the definition of "sacrament."[39] It was the twelfth century that witnessed a development of sacramental theology in general, and the theology of the Sacrament of Marriage in particular. The scholastic theologians of the twelfth and thirteenth centuries formulated a more systematic definition of the sacraments. By the end of the twelfth century, "'sacrament' was understood exclusively in the sense of the seven sources of grace, and theological studies focused on delving into the essence and the action of the seven sacraments, thereby working out in a systematic way the main lines contained in the Scholastic tradition" (TOB 93:5, fn. 88).

As part of this systematic treatment of the Seven Sacraments, theologians of the twelfth century started to analyze the reality of the sacraments, and as a result they distinguished a threefold reality present in every sacrament. The first element of every sacrament that they identified is the visible or external sign, the *sacramentum tantum* ("the sign itself"). Theologians of the twelfth and thirteenth centuries, beginning with Stephen Langton (ca. 1150–1228) and William of Auxerre (d. 1231), further identified two aspects of the outward sign

---

38. Peter Kwasniewski, "St. Thomas on the Grandeur and Limitations of Marriage," 420, fn. 29.

39. Edward Schillebeeckx, *Marriage*, 328.

of the sacraments, the matter and the form. [40] While the matter is the actual sensible object(s) that are used in the sacraments, the form is the words or prayers that accompany the use of these sensible objects. The second reality present in every sacrament is an abiding reality brought into being by the sacrament, the *res et sacramentum* ("the reality and the sign"). For three of the sacraments—Baptism, Confirmation, and Holy Orders—this abiding reality is referred to as a "character," described as an indelible mark or seal on the soul (CCC, 1121). This reality had its origins in Scripture (2 Cor 1:22; Eph 1:13; 4:30), received a more developed articulation by St. Augustine in his disputes with the Donatists, [41] and was affirmed by Innocent III in 1201 (DS, 781) and eventually by the Council of Trent in 1547 (DS, 1609). The abiding reality that is brought into being (*res et sacramentum*) by each of the sacraments is also a further sign of the grace, or the *res tantum* ("the reality itself") that is imparted by the sacrament. These three realities (*sacramentum tantum*, *res et sacramentum*, *res tantum*) that medieval theologians recognized in the sacraments are further refinements of the distinct realities that Augustine identified: the sign (*sacramentum*) of the sacraments, including words and material elements; and the reality (*res sacramenti*). [42] This terminology gained acceptance through the popularity of Peter Lombard's *Sentences* (ca. 1150), and by 1202, Pope Innocent III used these terms pertaining to the threefold reality of a sacrament in a letter to the Archbishop of Lyons concerning the Eucharist (DS, 783). [43]

The theologians of the high Middle Ages also discussed sacramental causality, in other words, what causes the sacraments to be effective. Already in his refutation of the Donatists, Augustine made it clear that sacraments confer grace not because of the holiness of the minister but because of the sacramental action itself. Medieval theologians systematized Augustine's thought to make it clear that the sacraments produce grace *ex opere operato* ("out of the work that is performed"), not *ex opere operantis* ("out of the work of the one who is

---

40. Bernard Leeming, *Principles of Sacramental Theology* (Westminister, MD: Newman Press, 1956), 404.

41. See Augustine, *On Baptism, Against the Donatists*, trans. J.R. King, NPNF, First Series, vol. 4, VI.1.1.

42. Seamus Heaney, *The Development of the Sacramentality of Marriage*, 138.

43. Bernard Leeming, *Principles of Sacramental Theology*, 255–256.

working"). These phrases that explain sacramental causality were first found in the writings of Peter of Poitiers (ca. 1130–1205)[44] and they entered into common usage in the thirteenth century, eventually being formally adopted by the Catholic Church at the Council of Trent (DS, 1608).

Eventually all of the preceding terms were applied to the Sacrament of Marriage. What follows is a survey of some of the theologians who contributed to the development of the theology of marriage in the twelfth and thirteenth centuries. While there are other theologians who wrote on marriage during this period, the following theologians represent some of the more significant contributors.[45]

Hugh of St. Victor (1096–1141)

At the end of the eleventh and beginning of the twelfth centuries, Anselm of Laon (d. 1117) made some important contributions to the sacramental theology of marriage. He maintained that all marriages are signs of the relationship between God and man, but that only baptized couples receive grace (*res sacramenti*) that allows them to participate in Christ's union with the Church, making their unions indissoluble and helping them to overcome sexual concupiscence.[46] He also began to distinguish between the sign of marriage, which he stated was sexual consummation; the reality signified, which he said was the indissoluble union between Christ and the Church; and the effect of the sign, which he said was a participation in Christ's union with the Church.[47]

However, it was Hugh of Saint Victor who was one of the first scholars since Augustine to provide a systematic treatment of marriage. In fact, Hugh was the first Western theologian since Augustine to write a treatise on marriage, although he relied heavily on Augustine in his own formulations.[48] Hugh used a broader understanding of

---

44. Ibid., 7.

45. For other contributors to a theology of marriage in the twelfth and thirteenth centuries, see Seamus Heaney, *The Development of the Sacramentality of Marriage*.

46. For a summary of the contributions of Anselm of Laon see Theodore Mackin, *The Marital Sacrament*, Marriage in the Catholic Church (New York: Paulist Press, 1989), 302–303.

47. See Teresa Olsen Pierre, "Marriage, Body, and Sacrament in the Age of Hugh of St. Victor," 218.

48. Edward Schillebeeckx, *Marriage*, 320.

"sacrament" as "a sign of a sacred thing" that would include many ceremonies and rituals that we would today classify as sacramentals. [49] According to this broad understanding, he saw all marriages from "the beginning" as sacraments, but he made the distinction that at the beginning of creation marriage was instituted as an office for the purpose of procreation, and that after sin marriage was instituted as a remedy for vice. [50] In a broad sense he maintained that all marriages, even marriages between non-Christians, are sacraments of Christ's union with the Church. [51] However, Hugh also spoke of a sacrament as "a corporeal or material element set before the senses without, representing by similitude and signifying by institution and containing by sanctification some invisible and spiritual grace." [52] He maintained that the marriages of baptized Christians are sacraments in this sense of a sacred sign that contains sanctification. [53]

Hugh defined marriage as "an agreement between male and female that preserves their individual association in life," adding that this agreement must be "legitimate" as judged by the Church. [54] He maintained that there are actually two sacraments in marriage. First, through consent marriage is a sacrament of the union of love between God and the soul. [55] Second, through sexual intercourse marriage is a sacrament of the incarnate union between Christ and the Church. [56] He even distinguished two aspects of marital consent—one aspect that consents to the marital association of life, and another that consents to sexual intercourse. [57] According to Hugh, it is the consent to association of life that makes the marriage. [58] Hugh's distinction of two sacraments in marriage, and two consents, makes it possible for him to affirm virginal marriages, like that of Mary and Joseph, as true marriages. [59]

---

49. See Hugh of St. Victor, *Hugh of Saint Victor on the Sacraments of the Christian Faith (De Sacramentis)*, trans. Roy J. Deferrari (Eugene, OR: Wipf and Stock Publishers, 2007), I.9.2.

50. Ibid., II.11.3.

51. Ibid., II.11.8, 13.

52. Ibid., I.9.2.

53. Ibid., II.11.8, 13.

54. Ibid., II.11.4.

55. Ibid., I.8.13.

56. Ibid., I.8.13.

57. Ibid., II.11.4.

58. Ibid., II.11.5.

59. Ibid., II.11.5.

Hugh's hesitance to affirm the goodness of sexual intercourse in marriage can be seen when he stated that an unconsummated marriage is truer and holier than a consummated marriage because the spiritual union of an unconsummated marriage finds "nothing in it at which chastity may blush."[60] He also stated "the fact that after sin the bond of flesh is admitted in marriage is rather a matter of indulgence and compassion,"[61] and he spoke of the three goods of marriage as blessings that marriage places over the concupiscence of the flesh to make it no more than a venial sin.[62] Like Augustine, he saw the ideal use of sexual intercourse as that which is undertaken with the explicit purpose of procreating.[63]

Hugh of St. Victor furthered the theology of marriage by recognizing "that marriage must have something in common with the other great sacraments in the Church," and with his emphasis on marriage as an association of life he also succeeded in placing some "focus on the affective nature of the bond."[64] However, Hugh did not see the sacrament of Christian marriage as conferring grace upon the spouses, but instead as in some way containing grace like a "vessel,"[65] providing an opportunity for grace for those who receive the sacrament worthily.[66] Hugh did not elaborate on the manner in which this grace is received.

Peter Abelard (1079–1142)

A contemporary of Hugh of Saint Victor, Peter Abelard also made contributions to sacramental theology and the theology of marriage. One scholar noted that Abelard's "personal contribution to the theology of marriage is more important for the attitude of mind it sought to create, than for his actual treatment of the subject."[67] Part of this

---

60. Ibid., II.11.3.

61. Ibid., II.11.3.

62. Ibid., II.11.7.

63. Ibid., II.11.9.

64. Teresa Olsen Pierre, "Marriage, Body, and Sacrament in the Age of Hugh of St. Victor," 223.

65. Hugh of St. Victor, *Hugh of Saint Victor on the Sacraments of the Christian Faith (De Sacramentis)*, I.9.4.

66. Ibid., II.11.11, 13.

67. Seamus Heaney, *The Development of the Sacramentality of Marriage*, 82.

attitude of mind included Abelard's enumeration of five sacraments, in which he included Baptism, Confirmation, the Eucharist, Extreme Unction, and Matrimony.[68] Whereas other theologians, like Hugh of Saint Victor, maintained that sexual union is the sign of Christ's union with the Church, Abelard maintained that spousal consent provided this signification.[69] Although he included marriage in his list of sacraments, Abelard did not see marriage as a means of grace, but instead as a remedy for concupiscence and a safeguard against sin for those who could not embrace celibacy.[70] However, in speaking about marriage as a "remedy," Abelard was insistent that sexual intercourse and its attendant pleasure are goods coming from God.[71] This position might be expected from a writer whose affair with his student Heloise has become legendary. Nonetheless, when Abelard spoke of marriage as a "remedy," he did not mean that marital intercourse or the concupiscence which inevitably accompanies it need to be excused, but merely that marriage "presents an occasion for the legitimate exercise of sexual activity" which would otherwise be immoral outside the context of marriage.[72] Thus, when Abelard referred to marriage as a "remedy" he simply meant that marriage provided the context within which sexual intercourse can be engaged in legitimately. By "seeking to establish the intrinsic morality of the sexual act,"[73] Abelard was instrumental in destroying "the cloud of suspicion that surrounded the morality of marriage, and so indirectly ensured the progress of the theology of marriage as a whole."[74]

Peter Lombard (1095–1160)

Some of the great developments in sacramental theology and the theology of marriage can be attributed to Peter Lombard. Lombard's *Book of Sentences* became the standard textbook of theology in the

---

68. Peter J. Elliott, *What God Has Joined*, 88.

69. Edward Schillebeeckx, *Marriage*, 319.

70. George Howard Joyce, *Christian Marriage: An Historical and Doctrinal Study* (New York: Sheed and Ward, 1933), 168.

71. Peter Abelard, *Ethics*, trans. D. E. Luscombe (Oxford: The Clarendon Press, 1971), 18–23.

72. Seamus Heaney, *The Development of the Sacramentality of Marriage*, 86.

73. Ibid., 86.

74. Ibid., 87.

thirteenth century, upon which every major theologian of the period wrote a commentary. Although Lombard relied heavily on Augustine in his treatment of marriage, he advanced Augustine's thought in several areas. In the *Sentences* Lombard defined a sacrament as a sign that both symbolizes the invisible gift of grace and causes what it symbolizes, for the purpose of sanctifying.[75] He further specified that sacraments consist of words and things,[76] and he identifies seven sacraments, an enumeration which is not original to him but which he made explicit,[77] including marriage as one of the sacraments.[78] Lombard defined marriage as "the marital joining of husband and wife of lawful standing, maintaining an undivided manner of life."[79] He pointed out that marriage was instituted by the Lord before sin to serve the function of procreation, but that after sin it exists also as a remedy for concupiscence.[80] Thus Lombard specified procreation and the avoidance of fornication respectively as the primary and secondary ends of marriage.[81] He also specified that while separation of spouses may be allowed for reasons of fornication or by mutual consent to take religious vows, the marriage bond itself is indissoluble.[82]

Although Lombard insisted that as a sacrament marriage is sacred,[83] he classified marriage as a lesser good, since marriage exists as a remedy.[84] Lombard commented on the three goods of marriage and how each good contributes to "excusing" sexual intercourse for married couples.[85] He indicated that marriage renders a venial sin intercourse that is undertaken for purposes beyond that of procreating,[86] maintaining that only intercourse "in which the three goods are

[75]. Peter Lombard, *The Sentences—Book 4: On the Doctrine of Signs*, trans. Giulio Silano, Mediaeval Sources in Translation 48 (Toronto: Pontifical Institute of Mediaeval Studies, 2010), IV, d. 1, c. 4, n. 2.

76. Ibid., IV, d. 1, c. 5, n. 6.

77. Edward Schillebeeckx, *Marriage*, 328.

78. Lombard, *Sentences*, IV, d. 2, c. 1.

79. Ibid., IV, d. 27, c. 2.

80. Ibid., IV, d. 26, c.1–3.

81. Ibid., IV, d. 30, c. 3, n. 2.

82. Ibid., IV, d. 31, c. 2, n. 1.

83. Ibid., IV, d. 26, c. 5.

84. Ibid., IV, d. 26, c. 4.

85. Ibid., IV, d. 31, c. 1, c. 5–7.

86. Ibid., IV, d. 26, c.4; d. 31, c. 1, c. 5–7.

present is preserved from sin."[87] Peter Lombard was inconsistent regarding his own definition of a sacrament as a sign that causes grace, since he did not see marriage as providing a grace beyond the remediation of concupiscence. Regarding the sacraments he explained, "some offer a remedy against sin and confer helping grace, like baptism; others are only a remedy, like marriage; others fortify us with grace and virtue, like the Eucharist and orders."[88] Thus it would seem that Peter Lombard's suspicion of sexual concupiscence caused him to view marriage as only a lesser good that provides a remedy.

Unlike Hugh of St. Victor, Peter Lombard posited a single sacrament in Christian marriage, but one that reflects two aspects of Christ's union with the Church, spiritual and incarnate.[89] Lombard explained that "the consent of the partners signifies the spiritual joining of Christ and the Church, which happens through charity; but the intermingling of the sexes signifies that union which happens through the conformity of nature."[90] Lombard's distinction between the spiritual signification of unconsummated marriage versus the incarnate signification of consummated marriage will become standard throughout the rest of the Middle Ages. When commenting on the role of consent, Lombard made it clear that it is freely given consent expressed outwardly in words or other signs that makes a marriage.[91] Otherwise Mary and Joseph would not have been married, and this would be "impious" since their "marriage was so much the more holy and complete the more it was free of carnal work."[92] Lombard maintained that Mary and Joseph and all spouses consent to the formation of a conjugal partnership in making a marriage, not sexual intercourse or cohabitation.[93] Lombard praised as holier married couples who "profess continence with a common vow."[94] Nonetheless, while unconsummated marriages are signs of the union of Christ and the Church in love, consummated marriage "bears an express and full configuration

---

87. Ibid., IV, d. 31, c. 8, n. 1.
88. Ibid., IV, d. 2, c. 1, n. 1.
89. Ibid., IV, d. 26, c. 6, n. 1.
90. Ibid., IV, d. 26, c. 6, n. 1.
91. Ibid., IV, d. 27, c. 3–4; d. 29, c. 1.
92. Ibid., IV, d. 26, c. 6, n. 3.
93. Ibid., IV, d. 28, c. 3, n. 2; c. 4; d. 30, c. 1.
94. Ibid., IV, d. 30, c. 2, n. 3.

of the joining of Christ and the Church . . . in the conformity of nature,"[95] perfecting marriage as a sign of the union of Christ and the Church.[96] Thus Peter Lombard provides a more consistent treatment of how consent and consummation relate to the one Sacrament of Marriage. He also spent a great deal of time discussing situations that might provide impediments to the exchange of valid consent.[97]

Three other theologians made notable contributions to the theology of marriage, building and commenting on the insights of Peter Lombard. The English Franciscan Alexander of Hales (1185–1245) maintained that consummated Christian marriages are signs of the union of Christ with the Church, and also of God with human nature, and as such they are indissoluble. He held that unconsummated marriages are signs of the union of the faithful soul with Christ in love. Alexander defined the sign (*sacramentum tantum*) of marriage as the external (verbal) expression of consent and he maintained that the spouses are the ministers of the Sacrament of Marriage. He also noted that Marriage must confer grace as one of the Seven Sacraments of the Church. However, Alexander maintained that this grace serves the purpose of reducing sexual intercourse to no more than a venial sin, and he stated that this grace was conferred only if the couple was committed to bringing up children for God's honor in accord with marital chastity. In other words, the grace is conferred by virtue of the merits of those who are conferring the sacrament (*ex opere operantis*).[98] In contrast to Alexander of Hales, William of Auxerre (d. 1231) maintained that the Sacrament of Marriage does not confer grace, but instead keeps married couples from falling into sin. He also maintained that the object of the consent of a marrying couple is not just consent to sexual intercourse or to cohabitation, but to everything that is entailed in conjugal union.[99] William of Auvergne (ca. 1180/90–1249)

---

95. Ibid., IV, d. 26, c. 6, n. 4.

96. Ibid., IV, d. 30, c. 2, n. 5.

97. See Ibid., d. 34–42.

98. For a summary of the contributions of Alexander of Hales see Seamus Heaney, *The Development of the Sacramentality of Marriage*, 49–56, 115–120; Theodore Mackin, *The Marital Sacrament*, 306–307; and Edward Schillebeeckx, *Marriage*, 334–335.

99. For a summary of the contributions of William of Auxerre see Seamus Heaney, *The Development of the Sacramentality of Marriage*, 41–42, 110–111; Theodore Mackin, *What Is Marriage? Marriage in the Catholic Church* (New York: Paulist Press, 1982), 189; and Edward Schillebeeckx, *Marriage*, 334.

tried to describe more precisely what the society of marriage entails, delineating five parts of marital communion: communion in religion; communion of bodies for the purpose of procreation; communion of temporal goods; communion of physical presence to provide service to each other; and communion of offspring in the family. He also maintained that the Sacrament of Marriage did confer grace on the couple, but that it was the priest's blessing, or nuptial blessing, which did so.[100]

St. Bonaventure (1221–1274)

Saint Bonaventure relied on the definitions of both Hugh of St. Victor[101] and Peter Lombard[102] in his understanding of sacraments as "sensible signs divinely instituted as remedies"[103] that "confer grace."[104] Also following Peter Lombard, Bonaventure defined marriage as "a legitimate union of male and female, maintaining a single [i.e., undivided] sharing of life."[105] Bonaventure stated that this marital union existed before the Fall as a duty to produce offspring, but since the Fall it also exists "as a remedy against the disease of concupiscence."[106] Bonaventure maintained a view of sexual concupiscence consistent with that of Augustine stating, "in the very act of procreation [after the Fall] there is something of sin, namely concupiscence, which passes on the disease [of original sin]."[107] Bonaventure included matrimony as one of the seven sacraments of the new law,[108] and like the other sacraments, he stated that marriage was instituted by God to provide healing.[109] In particular, marriage was instituted to provide healing for sexual concupiscence. Furthermore, Bonaventure explained that the Sacrament of Marriage provides a remedy against concupiscence, to both temper

100. For a summary of the contributions of William of Auvergne see Seamus Heaney, *The Development of the Sacramentality of Marriage*, 42–43, 111–114; Theodore Mackin, *What Is Marriage?*; and Edward Schillebeeckx, *Marriage*, 334.

101. Bonaventure, *Breviloquium*, *Works of St. Bonaventure*, vol. 9, trans. Dominic V. Monti (Saint Bonaventure, NY: Franciscan Institute Publications, 2005), VI.1.3.

102. Ibid.
103. Ibid.
104. Ibid., VI.1.4.
105. Ibid., VI.13.1.
106. Ibid., VI.13.1.
107. Ibid., VI.13.2.
108. Ibid., VI.3.1.
109. Ibid., VI.3.2.

and excuse it,[110] restores health by preserving temperance, "which is threatened mainly by the weakness of the flesh but is saved through honest marriage,"[111] and maintains health by replenishing "the multitude of humanity in their natural existence."[112] While presenting Marriage as a sacrament that provides healing, Bonaventure also stated that Marriage "was the first to be instituted, before all others. But because it is linked with the disease of concupiscence and is the sacrament with the least sanctifying power—even though in its signification it is *a great sacrament* [Eph 5:32]—Marriage is listed as the last and lowest of the spiritual remedies."[113] Thus for Bonaventure the grace provided to spouses through the Sacrament of Marriage is purely remedial, providing a remedy for concupiscence,[114] and he evaluated marriage as the least of all the sacraments.

Following both Hugh of St. Victor and Peter Lombard, Bonaventure asserted that marriage was a sacrament both before and after the Fall, explaining that in the beginning marriage "was a symbol of the union of God and the soul; now, however, it signifies the union of Christ with the Church and of the two natures in a unity of person."[115] Bonaventure maintained that Christ instituted the Sacrament of Marriage by confirming, approving, and bringing to perfection what was already present in nature.[116] Bonaventure seemed to maintain that the priest is the primary minister of the Sacrament of Marriage. Concerning the administration of the sacraments he stated: "Although Baptism and Matrimony normally pertain to priests, a person without priestly orders, particularly in case of necessity, may in fact administer them."[117] However, Bonaventure maintained that it is the consent of the spouses that brings a marriage into being and ratifies it, "a consent outwardly expressed in some sensible sign and consummated by sexual intercourse."[118] Bonaventure maintained that

110. Ibid., VI.3.2.
111. Ibid., VI.3.3.
112. Ibid., VI.3.4.
113. Ibid., VI.3.4; also VI.3.1.
114. Ibid., VI.13.2.
115. Ibid., VI.13.1, 2.
116. Ibid., VI.4.1, 4.
117. Ibid., VI.5.1.
118. Ibid., VI.13.1; also VI.13.3.

consummation in which the spouses become one flesh is part of the full reality of marriage, completing their union and fully signifying Christ's union with the Church.[119] Bonaventure also referenced the three goods of marriage as "three benefits" attached to the sacrament,[120] and he taught that as with the other sacraments, the Church "has received a special commission to regulate the sacrament of Matrimony;" but he says not even the Church can annul a marriage that has been entered into legitimately.[121]

St. Albert the Great (1193–1280)

Much of Albert the Great's teaching on marriage was maintained by his student Thomas Aquinas,[122] so a few brief comments will suffice. Like others before him, Albert maintained a spiritual and a carnal signification in marriage. He stated that an unconsummated marriage is a sign of Christ's love for the Church, while a consummated marriage is an image of Christ's union with the Church in his human nature, as well as an image of the union of two natures in Christ.[123] Albert explained that the Sacrament of Marriage does not effect what it signifies, as the other sacraments do, because along with being a sacrament, marriage is also an office of nature.[124] He maintained that the sign (*sacramentum tantum*) of the Sacrament of Marriage is composed of a form, which is the external expression of the couple's consent, and matter, which is the spouses themselves and their will to have sexual intercourse.[125] Albert held the position that instead of just providing a remedy for concupiscence, it is highly probable that the Sacrament of Marriage confers grace.[126] In this sense, Albert was the first theologian "who considers the *res tantum* of marriage to be grace, taken in the strict sense of a positive and interior effect."[127] He also stated that this grace is conferred through the act of the exchange of consent

---

119. Ibid., VI.13.3.
120. Ibid., VI.13.1, 4.
121. Ibid., VI.13.5.
122. Seamus Heaney, *The Development of the Sacramentality of Marriage*, 125.
123. Theodore Mackin, *The Marital Sacrament*, 361.
124. Seamus Heaney, *The Development of the Sacramentality of Marriage*, 63.
125. Ibid., 61.
126. Edward Schillebeeckx, *Marriage*, 336–337.
127. Seamus Heaney, *The Development of the Sacramentality of Marriage*, 187.

(*ex opere operato*), and not by virtue of the worthiness or devotedness of the spouses (*ex opere operantis*).[128] St. Thomas Aquinas incorporated these insights of St. Albert into his own comments on marriage.

St. Thomas Aquinas (1225–1274)

In the development of sacramental theology, St. Thomas Aquinas' definition of "sacrament" held a place of particular importance (TOB 93:5, fn. 88). Thomas stated that "a sacrament properly so called is that which is the sign of some sacred thing pertaining to man; so that properly speaking a sacrament . . . is defined as being the *sign of a holy thing so far as it makes men holy*."[129] He specified that sacraments are "sensible things,"[130] "determined by divine institution,"[131] comprised of words (form) and sensible objects (matter),[132] which cause grace,[133] for the purposes of remedying sin and perfecting our souls to offer worship to God.[134] Thomas held that along with bestowing or increasing sanctifying grace, each sacrament provides a particular sacramental grace to achieve the purpose of that particular sacrament.[135] Thomas also discussed the threefold reality that is present in a sacrament, the *sacramentum tantum*, the *res et sacramentum*, and the *res tantum*.[136] According to Thomas, matrimony is a sacrament with all of the preceding characteristics.[137]

Rather than contributing anything particularly original to the theology of marriage, Thomas Aquinas mainly analyzed and synthesized the reflections that preceded him.[138] Before addressing marriage in the sacramental questions of his *Summa Theologica* Aquinas died, but his thought on marriage can be found in one of his earliest works,

---

128. Ibid., 71, 125.
129. ST III, q. 60, a. 2 (italics in the translation).
130. ST III, q. 60, a. 4.
131. ST III, q. 60, a. 5.
132. ST III, q. 60, a. 7.
133. ST III, q. 62, a. 1.
134. ST III, q. 63, a. 1.
135. See ST III, q. 62, a. 2. See also Bernard Leeming, *Principles of Sacramental Theology* (Westminster, MD: Newman Press, 1956), 107–112.
136. ST III, q. 63, a. 6, ad 3.
137. ST III, q. 42, a. 1.
138. Peter Kwasniewski, "St. Thomas on the Grandeur and Limitations of Marriage," 416.

Commentary on the Sentences of Peter Lombard. The passages on marriage from this early work are included in the *Supplement* that was appended to the *Summa* by other Dominican friars after Thomas' death. Thomas also addressed marriage in one of his other major works, the *Summa Contra Gentiles*, which was written as a defense of the Christian faith against Islam.

Thomas explained that the essence of marriage is the union between husband and wife.[139] He described this union elsewhere when he stated that the "form" of marriage, or that which makes marriage what it is (which is distinct from the "form" of the sacrament), "consists in a certain inseparable union of souls, by which husband and wife are pledged by a bond of mutual affection that cannot be sundered."[140] St. Thomas affirmed the existence of the three goods of marriage that had been delineated by Augustine,[141] and he maintained that in order for a marriage to be valid the couple must consent to these three goods.[142] He maintained that the procreation and education of children is the principal end of marriage, while the secondary end is "the mutual services which married persons render one another in household matters."[143]

Thomas maintained that while marriage is an office according to nature for the purpose of procreation, it was instituted as a sacrament of the New Law by Christ as a remedy for sin.[144] He explained that while procreation is the primary good and end of marriage according to nature, the good of the sacrament is more excellent because it pertains to grace.[145] Thomas maintained that the sign (*sacramentum tantum*) of the Sacrament of Marriage is consent.[146] He stated that the form of the sign is the external expression of the consent of the spouses, "and not the priest's blessing, which is a sacramental."[147] He also explained that the matter of the sacrament is the "sensible acts" of

---

139. ST Suppl., q. 44, a. 3.
140. ST III, q. 29, a. 2.
141. SCG IV, ch. 78, no. 6; ST, Suppl., q. 49, a. 2.
142. ST Suppl., q. 49, a. 3.
143. ST Suppl., q. 41, a. 1.
144. ST Suppl., q. 42, a. 2.
145. ST Suppl., q. 49, a. 3.
146. ST Suppl., q. 44, a. 1, ad 2.
147. ST Suppl. q.42, a. 1, ad 1; see also q. 46, a. 5, ad 2.

marriage.[148] However, Thomas also stated that the persons themselves, who are lawfully able to contract marriage, are the matter of
the sacrament.[149] Taking these two comments about the matter of the
sacrament together, we can say that Thomas identified the matter of
the sacrament of marriage as the content of the externally expressed
consent, in other words, the mutual handing over of the spouses one
to the other. Thus for Thomas the externally expressed consent
"contains" both the form (the words spoken) and the matter (what is
promised by the words) of the sign of the sacrament of marriage.

St. Thomas held that consummation is not essential to the sign
of marriage, and thus not essential for effecting the bond, which is the
res et sacramentum of marriage;[150] nor is it essential to the grace of the
sacrament (*res tantum*).[151] Instead, it is consent that is the essential
sign of Christ's will to unite himself to the Church.[152] Regarding the
relationship of sexual union to consent and to the sign of the sacrament
of marriage, Thomas wrote:

> Marriage is not essentially carnal union itself, but a certain joining together
> of husband and wife ordained to carnal intercourse . . . in so far as they
> each receive power over the other in reference to carnal intercourse, which
> joining together is called the nuptial bond. Hence . . . to consent to
> marry is to consent to carnal intercourse implicitly and not explicitly.[153]

Thus, for St. Thomas freely given consent, and not intercourse,
makes the marriage.[154] He explained that the virginal marriage of
Mary and Joseph was a true marriage "because both consented to the
nuptial bond, but not expressly to the bond of the flesh, save on the
condition that it was pleasing to God."[155] This means that by exchanging consent a couple have handed themselves over to each other, and
thus have become married. However, as in the case of Mary and

---

148. ST Suppl. q. 42, a. 1, ad 2.

149. ST Suppl., q. 45, a. 5.

150. ST Suppl., q. 42, a. 1, ad 5; q. 44, a. 1, ad 2.

151. ST Suppl., q. 42, a. 1, ad 5.

152. ST Suppl., q. 45, a. 1, ad 2.

153. ST Suppl., q. 48, a. 1.

154. ST Suppl., q. 42, a. 4; q. 45, a. 1; q. 47, a. 3, ad 1; on the freedom of consent see q. 45,
a. 2, ad 3; q. 47, a. 3.

155. ST III, q. 29, a. 2.

Joseph, for a higher reason a couple could mutually agree to forgo the right that each has to sexual intercourse.

It should also be noted that while Thomas, as well as Albert the Great, referred to marital consent as a "contract"[156] he did not do so without qualification. He referred to marriage as "a kind of contract" (*ad modem*), pointing to the fact that marriage can only be considered a contract by way of analogy.[157] He provided hints of a more relational view of marriage in his description of the essence of marriage as an "inseparable union of souls, by which husband and wife are pledged by a bond of mutual affection."[158] Thomas also evidenced a relational view of marriage when in the context of arguing for the indissolubility of marriage he stated: "Furthermore, the greater the friendship is, the more solid and long-lasting will it be. Now, there seems to be the greatest friendship between husband and wife, for they are united not only in the act of fleshly union, which produces a certain gentle association even among beasts, but also in the partnership of the whole range of domestic activity."[159] Thomas also asserted that "the joining of husband and wife by matrimony is the greatest of all joinings, since it is a joining of soul and body, wherefore it is called a *conjugal* union."[160] Thus Thomas's view of marriage cannot be accused of being exclusively and narrowly legalistic.

Like some of his predecessors, St. Thomas saw two different significations in the one sacrament of marriage. Through consent, but "before consummation marriage signifies the union of Christ with the soul by grace, which is [capable of being] dissolved . . . by mortal sin."[161] Through sexual union marriage "signifies the union of Christ with the Church, as regards the assumption of human nature into the unity of person, which union is altogether indissoluble."[162] Hence an unconsummated marriage could be dissolved for some higher spiritual

---

156. ST Suppl., q. 45, a. 2.

157. See Theodore Mackin, *The Marital Sacrament*, 326, fn. 97; and Edward Schillebeeckx, *Marriage*, 302.

158. ST III, q. 29, a. 2.

159. SCG III, ch. 123, no. 6.

160. ST Suppl., q. 44, a. 2, ad 3.

161. ST Suppl., q. 61, a. 2, ad 1.

162. ST Suppl., q. 61, a. 2, ad 1.

reason, like entering religious life, but a consummated marriage can be dissolved only by death.

Thomas, like Peter Lombard before him, maintained that all the sacraments derive their efficacy from the Passion of Christ. Thomas stressed that it is through his Passion that Christ merits the forgiveness of sins for all of humanity by way of satisfaction.[163] He noted that we unite ourselves to Christ's Passion through the sacraments that are born on the Cross when water and blood, which are signs of Baptism and Eucharist, flow from the side of the crucified Jesus.[164] Thomas also maintained that each of the sacraments has a threefold signification that is linked to Christ's Passion and that pertains to the past, present, and future.[165] First, Thomas stated that the sacraments serve as signs of Christ's Passion, which occurred in the past and which is the cause of our sanctification. Second, he maintained that the sacraments are signs of the grace that is effected in the present because of Christ's Passion. Third, he asserted that the sacraments are signs of the ultimate end of our sanctification, eternal life, which is opened up to us by Christ's Passion. Thomas endeavored to explain how marriage can be linked to and derive its efficacy from Christ's Passion when marriage involves pleasure rather than pain. He solved this problem by noting, "Although matrimony is not conformed to Christ's Passion as regards pain, it is as regards charity, whereby he suffered for the Church who was to be united to him as his spouse."[166] Thus Thomas saw that the Sacrament of Marriage is linked to and signifies the Passion because the Passion is the ultimate sign of Christ's love for his bride.

Thomas also explained that while marriage signifies the union of Christ and the Church, it does not effect this union.[167] Instead, the reality that is signified and contained by the Sacrament of Matrimony is the indissoluble bond between husband and wife.[168] He maintained that the bond between husband and wife is the abiding reality (*res et sacramentum*) brought into being through the sacrament. He analogized

---

163. ST III, q. 62, a. 5.
164. Ibid.; see also ST I, q. 92, a. 3.
165. ST III, q. 60, a. 3.
166. ST Suppl., q. 42, a. 1, ad 3.
167. ST Suppl., q. 42, a. 1, ad 4.
168. ST Suppl., q. 42, a. 1, ad 5.

this bond to the indelible character imparted by the Sacraments of Baptism, Confirmation, and Holy Orders.[169] It is the marital bond that is a further sign of the grace (*res tantum*) that is given to married couples to enable them to live out what their marriage signifies,[170] namely Christ's union with the Church. Thomas was very clear that the Sacrament of Marriage confers grace upon the spouses when he stated, "Because the sacraments effect that of which they are made signs, one must believe that in this sacrament a grace is conferred on those marrying, and that by this grace they are included in the union of Christ and the Church."[171] Thomas maintained that the Sacrament of Marriage must offer a grace beyond the ability to restrain concupiscence, since natural marriage itself helps to provide this restraint.[172] Thus for Thomas the Sacrament of Marriage bestows a grace that not only helps spouses to avoid sin, but also helps spouses to grow in holiness. Thomas' position, that Marriage causes grace like the other sacraments, became the dominant theological opinion by the last quarter of the thirteenth century.[173]

It should be noted that even though St. Thomas agreed with Peter Lombard in listing Marriage as last among the sacraments "because it has the least amount of spirituality,"[174] he did show signs of overcoming the suspicion of sexual intercourse in marriage that had endured since the Patristic period. Thomas clearly condemned the idea that all sexual intercourse is sinful.[175] He also distinguished between sexual concupiscence and sin itself. He stated that married couples are not guilty of sin because their "lower powers and . . . members do not obey reason," since this sexual "concupiscence that always accompanies the marriage act" is a condition that resulted from original sin but is not sin itself.[176] He stated elsewhere that "the rebellion of concupiscence against reason" is not sin.[177] Thomas, unlike Augustine, mentioned

---

169. ST Suppl., q. 49, a. 3, ad 5.

170. ST Suppl., q. 42, a. 3, ad 2.

171. SCG IV, ch. 78, no. 4.

172. ST Suppl., q. 42, a. 3.

173. George Howard Joyce, *Christian Marriage*, 174.

174. ST III, q. 65, a. 2, ad 1.

175. SCG III, ch. 126, no. 1; ST, Suppl., q. 41, a. 3.

176. ST Suppl., q. 41, a. 3, ad 3.

177. ST Suppl., q. 49, a. 4, ad 2.

that even though the intensity of the pleasure of the marriage act prevents it from being directed by reason at every moment, this does not prevent couples from engaging in sexual intercourse "according to reason."[178] He also clearly distinguished between sexual pleasure itself, which is good, and a disordered desire for sexual pleasure, or lust.[179] Thomas even maintained, following the teachings of his master Albert the Great,[180] that Adam and Eve would have experienced greater pleasure in sexual intercourse before sin, but that this pleasure would have been experienced in obedience to reason and will.[181]

Aquinas did maintain that there are only two ways for spouses to engage in sexual intercourse without any fault, "in order to have offspring, and in order to pay the debt: otherwise it is always at least a venial sin."[182] He stated that if spouses engage in the marital act out of lust and only for pleasure, they are guilty of only venial sin as long as they do not exclude the three goods of marriage.[183] Thomas stated that spouses are guilty of mortal sin if they engage in intercourse while excluding the goods of marriage, which means that they are purely using or instrumentalizing each other and would in reality be willing to have intercourse with someone else.[184] What is perhaps more important is that Thomas indicated that if performed in a state of grace out of justice or charity, sexual intercourse between spouses is meritorious.[185] In addition, Thomas maintained that the grace particular to the Sacrament of Marriage is "the grace which enables us to do those works which are required in matrimony,"[186] a grace to perform bodily actions,[187] which includes the marital act. In his discussion of how the three goods of marriage "excuse" sexual intercourse, Thomas explained that while children and fidelity bestow virtue on sexual union, the Sacrament of Marriage makes sexual intercourse "not only

---

178. ST II-II, q. 153, a. 2, ad 2; Suppl., q. 41, a. 3, ad 6; q. 49, a. 4, ad 3.

179. ST II-II, q. 153, a. 2, ad 2.

180. Albert the Great, *Commentary on the Sentences*, IV, d. 26, a. 7, quoted in Kerns, *The Theology of Marriage*, 74.

181. ST I, q. 98, a. 2, ad 3.

182. ST Suppl., q. 49, a. 5.

183. ST Suppl., q. 41, a. 4; q. 49, a. 6.

184. Ibid.

185. ST Suppl., q. 41, a. 4, including ad 1.

186. ST Suppl., q. 42, a. 3.

187. ST Suppl., q. 49, a. 3, ad 5.

good, but also holy."[188] Elsewhere Thomas stated that the grace of the Sacrament of Marriage helps spouses so that "in fleshly and earthly things they may purpose not to be disunited from Christ and the Church."[189] For Thomas the Sacrament of Marriage provides a "remedy for concupiscence"[190] not merely by providing a legitimate outlet for sexual intercourse, nor by excusing intercourse which is sought beyond the purpose of having children, but by providing the grace to overcome concupiscence in married life,[191] and to make the couple holy. Thus, by the time we reach St. Thomas Aquinas marriage is seen fully as a sacrament of the New Covenant, signifying and effecting grace.

Magisterial Statements on Marriage from the Twelfth Century up to the Reformation

Along with reviewing the contributions of medieval theologians to the development of a theology of marriage, it is also important to note official teachings offered by the magisterium of the Church as it is ultimately these teachings that definitively guide and determine the direction of theological development. In 1139, the Second Lateran Council proclaimed that Marriage is one of the sacraments (DS, 718). We have already mentioned that in the latter part of the twelfth century Pope Alexander III (1159–1181) taught that consent makes a marriage, but it is consummation that makes the marriage bond absolutely indissoluble (DS, 754–756). In 1184, at the Synod of Verona, Pope Lucius III, against the Manichean tendencies of the Cathars, again listed Marriage as one of the sacraments (DS, 761).

Pope Innocent III issued several statements pertaining to marriage. As noted earlier, in 1198 he affirmed that consent makes a marriage (DS, 766). In a letter to the bishop of Ferrara in 1199, he reaffirmed the indissolubility of Christian marriage, refusing to allow a spouse to seek a second marriage when his or her first spouse apostatized (DS, 769). In 1200, in a letter to the bishop of Modena, Innocent once again affirmed that consent creates a marriage. In a letter to the bishop of Tiberius written in 1201, Innocent addressed the issue of

---

188. ST Suppl., q. 49, a. 4.
189. SCG IV, ch. 78, no. 4.
190. ST III, q. 65, a. 1.
191. ST Suppl., q. 42, a. 3, including ad 4.

polygamy that had arisen in the missions, reasserting the monogamous nature of marriage (DS, 777–779). In 1206, in a letter to the archbishop of Lund, Innocent reiterated the teaching of Alexander III that an unconsummated marriage may be dissolved if one of the spouses chooses to enter religious life (DS, 786). Finally, in 1208, Pope Innocent III proclaimed the goodness and the indissolubility of marriage against the Manichean tendencies of the Waldensians (DS, 794), once again including Marriage as one of the Seven Sacraments (DS, 793, 794). At the Fourth Ecumenical Lateran Council in 1215, called by Pope Innocent III, the Church reasserted the goodness of the married state against the Albigensians, Cathars, and Waldensians, all groups with Manichean tendencies.

In the first third of the thirteenth century, Pope Gregory IX issued a decree which made it clear that to enter into a marriage validly there can be no conditions placed on one's consent (DS, 827). In 1274 at the Second Ecumenical Council of Lyons Marriage was solemnly declared to be one of the Seven Sacraments (DS, 860). In a decree written against the Spiritual Franciscans in 1318, John XXII reaffirmed the sacramentality of marriage (DS, 916). In 1341, Pope Benedict XII, responding to errors of the Armenians, condemned the idea "that the marriage act and even matrimony itself is a sin" (DS, 1012). In 1439 the Council of Florence, along with making the three goods of marriage an official teaching of the Church (DS, 1327), again reaffirmed that Marriage is one of the Seven Sacraments, taught that consent is the efficient cause of marriage, and reasserted the indissolubility of the marriage bond (DS, 1327). Finally, in 1537, Pope Paul III reasserted the monogamous nature of marriage, directing Franciscan missionaries in the West Indies to rectify polygamous situations by having a man exchange valid consent with his first wife (DS, 1497). These teachings formed the body of the Catholic Church's doctrine on marriage up to the time of the Protestant Reformation, serving as guides to direct authentic theological development.

At this point in our historical survey of the development of the theology of marriage, it is important to clarify that authentic theological development is not the sum total of contributions made by individual theologians to a particular topic. Although individual thinkers within the Church may offer important insights into divine mysteries (see CCC, 94), and although the Holy Spirit guides the whole body of the faithful into a deeper understanding of revealed truth,[192] the task of discerning authentic insights into the faith from distortion of the faith has been entrusted by Jesus to the teaching office of the Church, the magisterium, composed of the bishops in communion with the successor of Peter (CCC, 85). No individual theologian, no matter how brilliant or saintly, will always be correct in every insight that he or she proposes. Although individual insights may be instrumental and even crucial in helping the People of God to grow in its appropriation of the truth that leads to salvation, the Holy Spirit guides the teaching office of the Church in a special way to make sure that the teachings it proposes for belief are authentic developments in the understanding of the faith and not distortions (see CCC, 890). The magisterium can glean insights from brilliant minds like St. Augustine or St. Thomas Aquinas, but it is ultimately the divine mind of the Holy Spirit that guides and directs the development of the Church's doctrine. Authentic doctrinal development is not the result of one theologian, or group of theologians, paving their own religious path in a journey toward God, no matter how many people may follow them or how much consensus they may garner. Instead, authentic development always occurs within the context of the Church that is guided by the Holy Spirit and the teaching office that is empowered by that Spirit. The guidance that the Holy Spirit provides to the faithful through the teaching authority of the Church is a gift that allows us to grow in our knowledge of the truth that liberates, and it provides direction for theological exploration into the truth. Only the Holy Spirit can guide the Church into a clear vision of the truth, clarifying this vision throughout the ages. To propose teachings that depart from this Spirit-guided vision and context is to depart from the saving truth that comes to us from Christ through the Apostles and their successors, ultimately subjecting this truth to mere human vision, judgment, and innovation.

---

192. The gift of the Holy Spirit by which he guides the entire body of the faithful into a deeper knowledge and appropriation of the truth is referred to as the "sense of the faith" (*sensus fidei*) (see CCC, 91–93).

Chapter 12

The Reformation through the Nineteenth Century

Reformation Theologians

In the turbulent times that led up to the Protestant Reformation, a Catholic priest named Martin Luther sought to find a way to address corruption and scandal in the Catholic Church of his day. Ultimately Luther's solution to the problems he saw in the life of the Catholic Church was to reject the institutional Church as a necessary means of salvation. Luther proclaimed that we are justified by faith, understood as trust in the saving power of Christ, alone (*sola fide*). In the place of the guidance of the Church, Luther proposed that the Bible alone (*sola scriptura*) is all that Christian believers need to guide them in an understanding of the faith. The rejection of the institutional Church meant that Luther and the other Protestant Reformers rejected much of the sacramental life of the Church. As the Reformers rejected the institutional Church and its hierarchy, maintaining instead that the church founded by Christ is primarily invisible, they did not view the Church as a sacrament of Christ's continued presence in the world. They also presented the sacraments themselves as creations of the Catholic Church, with the exception of Baptism and Eucharist. In addition, because the Reformers held that justification did not involve the renewal of the inner man but only a remission of sins, they taught that one did not need the grace of the sacraments to grow in holiness. For the Protestant Reformers, the sacraments served merely as signs to awaken and nourish subjective faith.[1] These positions clearly posed a challenge to the Catholic Church's belief in the Sacrament of Marriage.

Martin Luther (1483–1546)

In his *Babylonian Captivity of the Church*, Martin Luther denied the existence of the Sacrament of Marriage. Employing his hermeneutic of "Scripture alone," he pointed out that the Gospels do not show Christ instituting the Sacrament of Marriage in the same way that they show him instituting Baptism and Eucharist. Luther stated his position as follows:

> We have said that in every sacrament there is a word of divine promise, to be believed by whoever receives the sign, and that the sign alone cannot be the sacrament. Nowhere do we read that the man who marries a wife receives any grace of God. There is not even a divinely instituted sign in marriage, nor do we read anywhere that marriage was instituted by God to be a sign of anything.[2]

Since Christ did not institute a new sign associated with marriage, Luther maintained that there is no difference between Christian marriage and marriage that has existed since the beginning of creation. He wrote:

> Furthermore, since marriage has existed from the beginning of the world and is still found among unbelievers, there is no reason why it should be called a sacrament of the New Law and of the church alone. The marriages of the ancients were no less sacred than are ours, nor are those of unbelievers less true marriages than those of believers, and yet they are not regarded as sacraments.[3]

Luther also made use of Erasmus of Rotterdam's (1469–1536) scholarship, which pointed out that the word *mysterion* used in the

---

1. For more on the general Reformation approach to the sacraments, see George Hayward Joyce, *Christian Marriage: An Historical and Doctrinal Study* (New York: Sheed and Ward, 1933), 177. See also Martin Luther, *Babylonian Captivity of the Church*, trans. A. T. W. Steinhäuser, rev. Frederick C. Ahrens and Abdel Ross Wentz, in *Luther's Works*, vol. 36, ed. Abdel Ross Wentz (Philadelphia: Fortress Press, 1959), 64–66.

2. Martin Luther, *The Babylonian Captivity*, 92.

3. Ibid.

Letter to the Ephesians does not mean "sacrament" in the same sense as some of the medieval theologians meant. Luther explained:

> Nowhere in all of the Holy Scriptures is this word *sacramentum* employed in the sense in which we use the term; it has an entirely different meaning. For wherever it occurs it denotes not the sign of a sacred thing, but the sacred, secret, hidden thing itself. . . . For where we have [in the Vulgate] the word *sacramentum* the Greek original has *mysterion*, which the translator sometimes translates and sometimes retains in its Greek form. Thus our verse in the Greek reads: "The two shall become one. This is a great mystery." This explains how they came to understand a sacrament of the New Law here, a thing they would never have done if they had read *mysterium*, as it is in the Greek.[4]

Luther went on to explain that the "mystery" referred to by St. Paul in Ephesians 5:31–32 is not marriage, but Christ and the Church, stating:

> Christ and the church are, therefore, a mystery, that is, a great and secret thing which can and ought to be represented in terms of marriage as a kind of outward allegory. But marriage ought not for that reason to be called a sacrament.[5]

Luther then polemically concluded:

> Granted that marriage is a figure of Christ and the church; yet it is not a divinely instituted sacrament, but invented by men in the church who are carried away by their ignorance of both the word and the thing.[6]

Luther reasoned that if Christ did not institute any new sign for the Sacrament of Marriage, then marriage is a natural institution that falls under the jurisdiction of the state and not the Church. As a result, he denied the authority of the Catholic Church to adjudicate impediments to marriage,[7] and he wrote that "ministers interfere not in matrimonial questions . . . because these affairs concern not the Church but are temporal things, pertaining to temporal magistrates. . . . Therefore we must leave them to the lawyers and

---

4. Ibid., 93.
5. Ibid., 95.
6. Ibid., 95–96.
7. Ibid., 96–106.

magistrates."[8] In essence, Luther saw marriage as part of the order of creation, but not the order of redemption.[9] As Luther denied that marriage conferred grace, he viewed it as merely a necessary remedy for concupiscence, understood as a means of legitimately satisfying sexual desire.[10] He also viewed marriage as dissoluble on several grounds: first, because bodily deficiencies prevent the consummation of a marriage; second, because of adultery; and lastly, because one spouse refuses to render the conjugal debt or to cohabitate.[11]

John Calvin (1509–1564)

John Calvin's views on marriage were similar to Martin Luther's. He put much emphasis on the Vulgate "mis-translation" of *mysterion* as *sacramentum*, employed by Catholic theologians in their reading of Ephesians 5:32.[12] Against a Catholic reading, Calvin maintained that when St. Paul spoke of the "great mystery," "he is not speaking of the connection between husband and wife, but of the spiritual marriage of Christ and the Church."[13] Calvin explained that Paul presented us with the example of the spiritual marriage of Christ and the Church "to show husbands how they ought to love their wives."[14] In addition, Calvin only recognized sacraments that were explicitly instituted by Christ with a specific ceremonial celebration, namely Baptism and Eucharist. For him there could be no other sacraments. Calvin wrote, "For in a sacrament, the thing required is not only that it be a work of God, but that it be an external ceremony appointed by God to confirm a promise."[15] Like Luther, Calvin saw marriage as a secular reality subject to the governance of the state, likening marriage to

---

8. Martin Luther, *The Table Talk of Martin Luther*, trans. William Hazlitt (London: G. Bell and Sons, 1902), DCCXLVIII.

9. Walter Kasper, *Theology of Christian Marriage* (New York: Seabury Press, 1980), 33.

10. See Theodore Mackin, *The Marital Sacrament, Marriage in the Catholic Church*, vol. 3 (New York: Paulist Press, 1989), 416.

11. See Martin Luther, "The Estate of Marriage," trans. Walter I. Brandt, in *The Christian in Society II*, Luther's Works, vol. 45, ed. Walter I. Brandt (Philadelphia: Fortress Press, 1962), 30–35.

12. John Calvin, *Institutes of Christian Religion*, trans. Henry Beveridge (Grand Rapids, MI: William B. Eerdmans Publishing Company, 1979), IV.19.36.

13. Ibid., IV.19.35.

14. Ibid., IV.19.35.

15. Ibid., IV.19.34.

"agriculture, architecture, shoemaking, and shaving,"[16] and he accused the Catholic Church of converting marriage into a sacrament so the Church could appropriate to itself authority over marriage.[17]

Regarding the views of Luther and Calvin, it should be pointed out that once marriage is denied its sacred and transcendent meaning, and is viewed as merely a secular reality falling under the purview of the state instead of the Church, it is only a matter of time before the nature of marriage itself will be compromised. Deprived of its divine perspective, marriage will cease to be seen as a social institution intimately linked to the life of the Church and her relationship with Christ, and to the love of the Creator. Instead it will be seen primarily as a means of attaining personal fulfillment and satisfaction. The reality is that "if marriage is not a rite of the Church, not an objective institution of Christ, then its substance and validity result largely from the spouses' experience of fulfillment."[18] Once marriage is viewed through this subjective lens, secular authorities will inevitably find reasons to compromise the permanence of marriage, as well as its primary end of procreation, and perhaps even the good of fidelity. It should also be noted that because marriage is the fundamental building block of society, the Protestant decision to desacralize and secularize marriage was a step that contributed to the overall secularization of society.[19]

One recent scholar has pointed out a deep irony involved in the Protestant desacralization of marriage, explaining:

> When marriage ceases to be regarded as a sacrament . . . and the focus shifts to the personal fulfillment of the spouses rather than the procreation and education of children, then marriage comes under a tremendous burden of expectation. Ironically, for some imaginative souls, non-sacramental marriage assumes the status of a virtual religion—or at least a source of nearly religious bliss and satisfaction. It is the disappointment of such expectations, along with the removal of religious sanctions from what is becoming a secular institution that builds the growing pressure during the modern era for legal divorce."[20]

---

16. Ibid., IV.19.34.

17. Ibid., IV.19.37.

18. R.V. Young, "The Reformations of the Sixteenth and Seventeenth Centuries," in *Christian Marriage: A Historical Study*, ed. Glenn W. Olsen (New York: The Crossroad Publishing Company, 2001), 272.

19. Ibid., 271.

20. Ibid.

The same author notes: "It would seem, then, that Protestantism enhanced marriage as a means of personal companionship and individual earthly happiness, but, in desacramentalizing it, lowered its resistance to the pressures of the secular world."[21] The irony is that when marriage is no longer placed in its sacramental context, and thereby not seen in its proper perspective, married love will be turned into a god and will be found wanting, unable to quench the human longing for a love that satisfies. In reality, it is only the Sacrament of Marriage, which the Protestant reformers denied, that can offer human spouses the means to realize what they so desperately seek—a love that never dies because it truly participates in the love of Christ.

The Council of Trent (1545–1563)

The Catholic Church convoked the Council of Trent with the goal of responding to the challenges of the Protestant reformers, which by the time the council convened included responding to the English Reformation, precipitated by Henry VIII's desire to divorce Catherine of Aragon. In its response to the desacralizing tendencies of the Protestant view of marriage, Trent stressed marriage's sacramental and public aspects. In its decree on marriage, Trent began by proclaiming that all marriages are by nature indissoluble and faithful (DS, 1797–1798). The Council then reaffirmed marriage as one of the Seven Sacraments (DS, 1800), and taught that the grace conferred by the Sacrament of Marriage perfects the natural love of the spouses and strengthens the indissoluble union of the couple (DS, 1799).

The decree on marriage then enumerated twelve canons, condemning erroneous teachings pertaining to marriage. The Canon 1 condemns anyone who denies that the Sacrament of Marriage was instituted by Christ and that it confers grace (DS, 1801). Canon 2 forbids bigamy or polygamy, as they contravene divine law (DS, 1802). Canons 3 and 4 assert the right of the Church to judge conditions that would pose impediments to marriage, or circumstances that would make a marriage null and void (DS, 1803–1804). Canon 5 defends the permanence of the marriage bond, even in the cases of heresy, "irksome

---

21. Ibid., 274.

cohabitation," or desertion (DS, 1805). Canon 6 defends the position that an unconsummated marriage may be dissolved by the profession of religious vows by one of the spouses (DS, 1806). Canon 7 defends the Western Church's teaching that the marriage bond is not dissolved by adultery (DS, 1807). However, the eighth canon makes it clear that in certain circumstances "separation may take place between husband and wife with regard to bed and board or cohabitation for a definite period or even indefinitely" (DS, 1808). Canon 9 is crafted in such a way to defend the Western Church's discipline of forbidding marriage to already ordained clerics, but without condemning the practice of Eastern churches who allowed married men to be ordained (DS, 1809). The tenth canon reasserts the age-old and scriptural teaching, denied by the Protestant reformers, that consecrated virginity or celibacy is a higher state than marriage (DS, 1810). Canon 11 defends the right of the Church to prohibit the celebration of marriage during certain times of the year (e.g., Lent) and denies the accusation that this practice "is a tyrannical superstition derived from pagan superstition" (DS, 1811). Canon 11 also defends the blessing and other ceremonies used by the Church in celebrating marriage (DS, 1811). The twelfth, and last, canon attached to Trent's decree on marriage asserts the right of Church courts to hear matrimonial cases (DS, 1812). While this final canon defends the right of the Church to judge issues dealing with marriage, it does not preclude the right of the state to deal with certain civil aspects of marriage.

The Council of Trent also needed to deal with the problem of clandestine marriages. While the requirement of mutual consent succeeded in upholding the dignity and freedom of men and women to contract a marriage, it also meant that marriages could be entered into secretly. This proved to be a danger especially for women, as a man could secretly exchange consent with his bride, consummate the union, and lacking any witnesses could later deny that he had ever really married. Or, conversely, a man could attempt to exit a marriage by claiming that he had previously entered into a secret marriage with another woman. Both of these problems were discussed in the twelfth century by Hugh of St. Victor.[22] In an attempt to deal with these injustices the Council of Trent established the proper canonical (legal)

---

22. In Hugh of St. Victor, *Hugh of Saint Victor on the Sacraments of the Christian Faith (De Sacramentis)*, trans. Roy J. Deferrari (Eugene, OR: Wipf and Stock Publishers, 2007), I.9.2, II.11.6.

form of marriage in its disciplinary decree, *Tametsi*. While it declared past clandestine marriages to be valid and true, it prohibited further clandestine marriages (DS, 1813). The Council decreed that prior to a Christian marriage the wedding banns should be announced publicly (DS, 1814), and it further clarified that a marriage would not be valid unless it was contracted in the presence of a priest and at least two witnesses (DS, 1815–1816). With Trent's two decrees dealing with marriage, one doctrinal and one disciplinary, the Catholic Church secured its oversight of the celebration of the Sacrament of Marriage, as well as its right to determine impediments to contracting a valid marriage.

At the Council of Trent the Catholic Church asserted that because the Sacrament of Marriage is a sacred reality instituted by Christ and entrusted to the Church, the Church has the authority to legislate the manner in which marriages are celebrated. It also has the authority to identify impediments to marriage according to divine, natural, or ecclesial law. Many people, non-Catholic and Catholic, have a difficult time understanding how the Catholic Church can claim this authority. Ultimately this difficulty can only be resolved by accepting the Catholic belief that the Catholic Church is the Church founded by Christ, and that the bishops in union with the pope, who collectively compose the Magisterium, are successors to Peter and the Apostles; these offices lead the Church under the infallible guidance of the Holy Spirit (see CCC, 77; 880–892). However, even without this assent of faith, all people should be able to realize that because of the social nature of marriage (pointed out in chapter 5), all societies have in some way attempted to regulate how marriages are contracted. In fact, precisely because of the social ramifications of marriage, societies have a right to regulate how marriages are contracted, as long as these regulations do not contravene the dignity of the spouses or natural law. As Christian marriage is a sacrament entrusted by Christ to the society of the Church, the Church has a vested interest, and the right, to determine the way in which its citizens will enter into the holy state of marriage. The Church's canonical rules and regulations surrounding marriage are not meant to make people's lives difficult, but instead they are intended to safeguard the good of the spouses and the sanctity of the Sacrament of Marriage. This is the rationale behind the disciplinary decree on marriage issued at the Council of Trent. By requiring a proper canonical form for the validity of Christian marriage, Trent helped to put an end to the abuses surrounding clandestine marriages and it emphasized the dignity and holiness of marriage.

However, it is fair to point out that the Council of Trent focused primarily on the regulation of marriages with a legalistic or juridical focus. This approach is also evidenced in *The Roman Catechism* of 1566 commissioned by the Council of Trent. A predisposition toward legalism can be seen in *The Roman Catechism* definition of marriage as "the conjugal union of man and woman, in which the two persons lawfully contract to live together until death."[23] It explains that "the only element [of the definition of marriage] which is proper to the very essence of marriage is the mutual contract or bond expressed by the word 'union.'"[24] It further states, "The essence of matrimony, therefore, is the mutual bond,"[25] which is formed by outwardly expressed consent;[26] but it describes the consent in legal language stating, "Marriage is not a mere giving; it is a mutual contract."[27] Regarding marriage as a contract, the Tridentine catechism states quite plainly, "The pastor will thus teach the faithful that the essence of marriage consists in the contract itself and in its consequent obligations."[28] The catechism is clear that consent makes a marriage, explaining that even if the obligations of the marital contract are not actually fulfilled, including consummation, the marriage has come into being.[29] "The consent which constitutes marriage" is further described in legal terms as "a mutual giving here and now of an exclusive right: the man giving to the woman the right to his body, and the woman giving to the man the right to hers."[30] *The Roman Catechism* states "once that consent is mutually given and received, the husband and wife are united by a

---

23. *The Roman Catechism*, trans. Robert I. Bradley and Eugene Kevane (Boston, MA: St. Paul Editions, 1985), II.7.3.

24. Ibid.

25. Ibid., II.7.4.

26. Ibid.

27. Ibid., II.7.5.

28. Ibid., II.7.8.

29. Ibid., II.7.8. On this point, *The Roman Catechism* cites the fact that Adam and Eve were married before consummating their union, and it also cites the teaching of the Church Fathers, mentioning St. Ambrose by name.

30. Ibid., II.7.6.

bond which cannot be dissolved."[31] It explains the indissolubility of marriage in contractual terms as well, stating, "Once the actual contract is made, the marriage bond cannot be broken or changed, regardless of how much either or both of the parties may later regret it."[32] Thus the approach to marriage in the catechism of the Council of Trent is clearly legalistic and juridical, explaining marriage primarily as a contract that imposes mutual rights and obligations.

The Roman Catechism explains that marriage is both a natural institution and a sacrament. As a natural institution marriage was created by God[33] to be an indissoluble union.[34] The catechism evidences a broader, less legalistic, view of marriage when it explains the reasons for this natural institution. It begins by stating, "The first reason is the instinctive mutual attraction of the two sexes to form a stable companionship of the two persons, as a basis for mutual happiness and help amid the trials of life extending even to sickness and old age."[35] It states that the second reason for marriage "is another instinctive desire: to have offspring."[36] A third reason for the natural institution of marriage is found in the need for humanity to deal with the effects of the Fall. The catechism explains, "After his loss of that innocence in which he had been created, man's sexual appetite became rebellious against reason."[37] In this situation marriage serves as "an escape from sinful lust,"[38] (i.e., the remedy for concupiscence) based in the writings of St. Paul and articulated in different ways by almost every Church Father and medieval theologian.

After treating marriage as a natural institution, *The Roman Catechism* explains marriage as a sacrament. The catechism explains that Christ elevated marriage "to the supernatural dignity of a sacrament."[39] Beyond just ensuring "the propagation of the human race," the purpose of sacramental marriage "is to procreate and

---

31. Ibid., II.7.6.
32. Ibid., II.7.6.
33. Ibid., II.7.10.
34. Ibid., II.7.11.
35. Ibid., II.7.13.
36. Ibid.
37. Ibid., II.7.14.
38. Ibid.
39. Ibid., II.7.15; see also II.7.1.

educate a holy people in the faith and worship of the one true God and of Christ our Savior."[40] The catechism points to Ephesians 5:28–32 and its reference to the "great mystery" as a key scriptural text for understanding marriage as a sacrament. It states, "The divinely instituted conjugal union of husband and wife is a sacrament because it is the sacred sign of the most holy union of Christ and his Church."[41] The catechism then states:

> When he in fact wishes to exemplify that closest of all bonds which subsists in boundless love between himself and his Church, Christ describes this divine mystery by comparing it with the holy union of husband and wife (see Mt 22:2; 25:20; Rev 19:7). This example is most appropriate because there is no other human relationship as binding as that of marriage, and because the two persons bound are united in the most intimate and enduring love. That is why the Sacred Scriptures put before us the union of Christ with his Church in terms of marriage.[42]

The above statement exhibits a vision of marriage that goes beyond legalistic and juridical categories, presenting marriage as a loving union of persons. *The Roman Catechism* continues in this vein stating, "The definition of a sacrament as that reality which both signifies and confers grace is completely verified in Matrimony. . . . The faithful should therefore be taught that by the grace of this sacrament the husband and wife are united in a bond of mutual love, and that they are enabled to repose in each other's affection, unhindered by any other illicit love."[43] The catechism then explains how Christian marriage, empowered by this grace "should far excel in nobility and perfection the marriages of all other peoples."[44] It is statements like these that warrant Walter Cardinal Kasper seeing in Trent's catechism, "evidence of a wider and more all-embracing view of marriage,"[45] even if this view remains underdeveloped in the catechism itself.

The Roman Catechism also discusses the three goods of marriage, which it calls "the three great blessings."[46] Speaking of these

---

40. Ibid., II.7.15.
41. Ibid., II.7.16.
42. Ibid., II.7.15.
43. Ibid., II.7.17.
44. Ibid., II.7.22; see also II.7.18–21.
45. Walter Kasper, *Theology of Christian Marriage*, 13.
46. *The Roman Catechism*, II.7.23.

blessings in the context of Christian marriage, the catechism reminds spouses that the blessing of progeny includes rearing children in the faith.[47] The blessing of fidelity is explained as the faithfulness "by which the husband and the wife pledge to each other the reciprocal dominion of their bodies, and promise never to violate that pledge."[48] Yet the catechism goes on to explain faithfulness in more relational language stating, "This marital fidelity demands of both husband and wife a totally exclusive and pure love," a love patterned on the love between Christ and the Church which seeks "not its own satisfaction, but only the happiness and good of its beloved spouse."[49] The catechism explains that the third blessing of marriage, sacramentality, "consists essentially in the indissolubility of the marriage bond" precisely because marriage "is the sign of Christ's union with his Church," a union which is inseparable.[50] Echoing a teaching that finds its origin in St. Augustine, *The Roman Catechism* says of the three blessings, "it is these blessings which make sexual intercourse —totally illicit outside of marriage—most honorable in marriage."[51]

As *The Roman Catechism* ends its treatment of marriage, it specifically addresses the marital act, stressing two points of instruction. "The first is that marriage should not be used out of the sole motive of sensual pleasure. Rather, the motive should reflect—and remain within—the purposes of marriage as instituted by God [mutual help, progeny, struggling against concupiscence]."[52] The second point of instruction asserts "the value of occasional abstinence from the marital act, precisely as an occasion for greater prayer."[53] The catechism even states that married couples should be taught "the pious traditions of our fathers," according to which spouses abstain from intercourse "for three days prior to their receiving of Holy Communion, and also for the duration of the Lenten fast."[54] The part of the catechism that deals with the sixth commandment, "Thou shall not commit adultery"

---

47. Ibid., II.7.23.
48. Ibid., II.7.24.
49. Ibid., II.7.24.
50. Ibid., II.7.25.
51. Ibid., II.7.23.
52. Ibid., II.7.33.
53. Ibid., II.7.34.
54. Ibid., II.7.34.

(Ex 20:14), does not provide much more perspective on the marital act. In fact, the catechism counsels pastors to address this commandment "with fewer words rather than more," because a "detailed explanation of how one can transgress against this commandment can actually be conducive to such transgression, by stimulating—even unwittingly—the very passions which this commandment would restrain."[55] As a result, the catechism's commentary on the sixth commandment is limited to explaining the scope of the commandment as covering all sins of impurity,[56] the seriousness of these sins,[57] and ways of practicing purity and avoiding sin.[58] It is fair to see in this rather anemic treatment of marital intercourse an ambivalent attitude toward sexual relations that had endured throughout the Patristic and medieval periods.

The Roman Catechism also shows a lack of integration in its treatment of the married state and the vocation to consecrated celibacy or virginity when it states, "The state of virginity is commended in the Sacred Scriptures as actually superior to marriage, as being a state of greater perfection and holiness."[59] While this is technically accurate, it could be misread to imply that those who embrace celibacy instead of marriage are de facto holier and more perfect. It is also worth pointing out that the whole section of The Roman Catechism treating marriage opens with these lines:

> Since the pastor should seek for his people the very perfection of the Christian life, it seems he should say to them what St. Paul said to his Corinthians: "I wish that all were as I myself am" (1 Cor 7:7). That is to say, that all the faithful could live the life of perfect continence. No state of life can be more blessed than that in which the soul is freed from worldly cares and sheltered from bodily passions, and so can give itself exclusively to the knowledge and love of the things of heaven.[60]

While there is nothing inappropriate in praising celibacy or virginity as the higher calling, prefacing a treatment of marriage with the above statements is a less than resounding endorsement of the

---

55. Ibid., III.6.1.
56. Ibid., III.6.3–5.
57. Ibid., III.6.7–9.
58. Ibid., III.6.10–13.
59. Ibid., II.7.12.
60. Ibid., II.7.1.

beauty and dignity of married life. Additionally, while there are hints of a broader and more all-encompassing vision of marriage in *The Roman Catechism*, the predominant legalistic tone which treats marriage as a contract with attendant rights and obligations offers precious little inspiration and edification to those who embrace the married state. This rather narrow lens of *The Roman Catechism* coming from the Council of Trent was the predominant lens through which marriage was viewed for several hundred years, up to the mid-twentieth century.

Along with its rather restricted view of marriage, there were certain issues regarding marriage that Trent did not address. While the Council was unfolding, the Dominican priest Melchior Cano (1509–1560) composed a work in which he maintained that the marital contract could be separated from the Sacrament of Marriage. He claimed that the matter of the Sacrament of Marriage is the contractual consent of the spouses while the form is the blessing of the priest, who is the real minister of the sacrament.[61] Remaining focused on responding to Protestant challenges, the participants in the Council of Trent chose not to deal with internal ecclesial disputes and thus left open questions regarding the form and matter of the Sacrament of Marriage, its minister, and whether the contractual nature of marital consent can in some way be separated from the Sacrament of Marriage.[62] These are questions that were addressed in the centuries that followed, and to which we will now turn our attention.

THEOLOGY OF MARRIAGE FROM THE SIXTEENTH THROUGH THE NINETEENTH CENTURY

Due to the Protestant denial of the Catholic Church's authority pertaining to marriage, in Protestant countries marriage fell under the jurisdiction of the state, even though there was still no such thing as a purely "civil" marriage.[63] While the Protestant Reformers denied the Catholic Church's jurisdiction over marriage, the extreme rationalists of the Enlightenment in the seventeenth and eighteenth centuries

61. Edward Schillebeeckx, *Marriage: Human Reality and Saving Mystery*, 2 vols., trans. N.D. Smith (New York: Sheed and Ward, 1965), 372–373.

62. See Peter J. Elliott, *What God Has Joined: The Sacramentality of Marriage* (Staten Island, NY: Alba House, 1990), 103; Theodore Mackin, *The Marital Sacrament*, 443–444.

63. Edward Schillebeeckx, *Marriage*, 373.

denied that marriage had any religious aspects.[64] They argued that because marriage is an institution of nature, the state should have the right to determine the conditions under which the contract of marriage could be deemed valid.[65] This argument was fueled by the Protestant position that marriage is a secular reality subject to the authority of the state. In the seventeenth and eighteenth centuries the Catholic Church dealt with monarchs, as in France and Austria, who asserted the right to regulate marriage as a civil contract while leaving to the Church only the right to bless marital unions.[66] After the French Revolution and the rise of secular states and Nationalism, with the accompanying rise of properly civil marriage, the Church had to assert her rights regarding the marital contract in the face of civil regulations dealing with marriage.[67] Within the Church, from the seventeenth through the nineteenth centuries, marriage was commented on from a juridical perspective, thus focusing on marriage as a contract in which the spouses exchange the right to sexual intercourse.[68] In fact, by the beginning of the twentieth century this was the dominant model for discussing marriage in the Church.[69]

St. Robert Bellarmine (1542–1621)

Following the Protestant Reformation and the Council of Trent, Catholic theologians articulated only isolated developments in the understanding of the sacramentality of marriage. In fact, there was precious little development in the theology of marriage until the twentieth century. One of the theologians who did contribute to this development soon after Trent is St. Robert Bellarmine. Bellarmine developed St. Thomas Aquinas' understanding of the grace (*res tantum*) of marriage by making it clear that the state of Christian marriage

---

64. Theodore Mackin, *The Marital Sacrament*, 509.

65. John Haas, "The Contemporary World," in *Christian Marriage: A Historical Study*, ed. Glenn W. Olsen (New York: The Crossroad Publishing Company, 2001), 338–339.

66. Ibid., 374–375; Peter J. Elliott, *What God Has Joined*, 107–108; George Hayward Joyce, *Christian Marriage*, 243–260.

67. Edward Schillebeeckx, *Marriage*, 376–377; Peter J. Elliott, *What God Has Joined*, 108; George Hayward Joyce, *Christian Marriage*, 260–268.

68. Theodore Mackin, *What is Marriage?*, Marriage in the Catholic Church (New York: Paulist Press, 1982), 201–202.

69. Ibid., 205–206.

is a permanent sacrament, continuously making grace present.[70] In contrast to the opinions of Melchior Cano, Bellarmine maintained that the contract of marriage which is brought into being by the mutual consent of the spouses is inseparable from the Sacrament of Marriage.[71] He maintained that it is the spouses who are the ministers of the Sacrament of Marriage, and that it is not possible for Christian spouses to validly contract a marriage without that marriage also being a sacrament.[72] Bellarmine explained that Christ raised the natural contract of marriage, entered into through mutual consent, to the supernatural order.[73] Thus the Church has the right to establish conditions for Christian couples to contract marriage validly.[74] Bellarmine gave attention not only to marriage as a contract (*in fieri*) but also as a lived communion (*in facto esse*).[75] In this way he saw not only the consent of marriage, but also the very lives of Christian married couples as a sign of the union of Christ with the Church.[76]

Bl. Pope Pius IX (1846–1878)

Pope Pius IX responded to some of the extreme secular challenges to marriage and the Church's authority over marriage in his *Syllabus of Errors*. Pius condemned those who assert that Christ did not raise matrimony to the level of a sacrament (DS, 2965). He denied the assertion that the Sacrament of Marriage is appended to and separable from the marriage contract, and that the sacrament "consists merely in the nuptial blessing" (DS, 2966). Similarly, he condemned the idea that Christians can enter into a purely civil marriage contract without their marriage simultaneously being a sacrament (DS, 2973), an issue which will be further explained in chapter 15. Pius condemned those who hold that marriage is dissoluble (DS, 2967), and he refuted those who deny the power of the Church to establish impediments to marriage (DS, 2968, 2969, 2970). Finally, he condemned those who

---

70. Peter J. Elliott, *What God Has Joined*, 105.

71. Ibid., 105–106.

72. Theodore Mackin, *The Marital Sacrament*, 441–442. For a further summary of Bellarmine's thought on marriage see *The Marital Sacrament*, 436–442.

73. Peter J. Elliott, *What God Has Joined*, 107.

74. Edward Schillebeeckx, *Marriage*, 370–371.

75. Peter J. Elliott, *What God Has Joined*, 106.

76. Ibid.

maintain that marriage cases should be adjudicated in civil courts (DS, 2974).

Pope Leo XIII (1878–1903)

At the end of the nineteenth century Pope Leo XIII issued his encyclical *Arcanum Divinae Sapientiae* (1880) to respond to the growing challenge of secular marriage and divorce. He was intent on refuting the idea that marriage is a purely secular reality subject to the sole jurisdiction of the state. He made it clear that the Sacrament of Marriage is inseparable from the contract of marriage stating, "in Christian marriage the contract is inseparable from the sacrament and . . . for this reason, the contract cannot be true and legitimate without being a sacrament as well" (DS, 3145). This means that there is no secular aspect of marriage between two Christians, nor is the sacrament "a certain added ornament, or outward endowment, which can be separated and torn away from the contract at the caprice of man" (DS, 3146). Due to the inseparability of the sacrament from the contract, Leo reaffirmed that the Church has authority over Christian marriages (DS, 3144).

Matthias Scheeben (1835–1888)

In the nineteenth century the German priest Matthias Scheeben contributed to a deepening understanding of the Sacrament of Marriage. Instead of focusing on marriage from a legalistic or juridical perspective, Scheeben stressed the mystical and sacramental nature of Christian marriage.[77] He lamented, "With regard to the sacramentality of matrimony, many theologians have paid no attention to the new, proper, mystical character that exalts sacramental marriage and that is the basis for its fruitfulness in the production of grace."[78] Counter to any reductionistic treatments of marriage, Scheeben insisted that "nowhere does the mystical life of the Church penetrate more deeply into natural life than in matrimony."[79] Scheeben treated Christian marriage in an ecclesial context, stressing that the Sacrament

---

77. John Haas, "The Contemporary World," 354.

78. Matthias Joseph Scheeben, *The Mysteries of Christianity*, trans. Cyril Vollert (St. Louis: B. Herder Book Co., 1946), 593.

79. Ibid., 610.

of Marriage "must assign a definite, high position in the mystical body of Christ to the united pair, and a special vital force must flow to them from the head."[80] He stated "that an objective consecration is imparted by God to the contracting parties to equip them for His service."[81] Due to this consecration and because of the ecclesial role of Christian spouses, Scheeben maintained that Christian marriages are superior to the marriage between Adam and Eve in paradise.[82] He stressed that at the heart of the mystery of Christian marriage is the fact that two baptized spouses exist as members of the Mystical Body.[83] Their organic relation to the Mystical Body is the reason why Christian spouses cannot contract a marriage without it being a sacrament.[84] The organic connection of Christian spouses to the Mystical Body also means that their marital union partakes of the spousal union between Christ and the Church, a mystery which is "active and operative" in their own marriage.[85] Scheeben's insights into the mystical and sacramental nature of Christian marriage became influential during the twentieth century, especially in the pontificates of Pius XI and Pius XII.[86] It is to this century that we will now turn; a century which witnessed more magisterial pronouncements on marriage than any previous century.

---

80. Ibid., 593.
81. Ibid., 598.
82. Ibid., 599.
83. Ibid., 603.
84. Ibid., 599–600.
85. Ibid., 601–602.
86. John Haas, "The Contemporary World," 354.

Chapter 13

The 1917 *Code of Canon Law* through the Papacy of Paul VI

INTRODUCTION

The twentieth century was a century of worldwide societal and cultural transformation. Church historian James Hitchcock has stated, "Beginning before 1800 and extending over the next two centuries, there occurred, simultaneously, the greatest revolutions in the history of the world—political, social, economic, intellectual, and scientific."[1] The intellectual and scientific shifts of the seventeenth- and eighteenth-century Enlightenment, the political changes evidenced in nineteenth-century Nationalism, and the social and economic changes of the Industrial Age of the eighteenth and nineteenth centuries all served as a backdrop to the twentieth century. In the wake of these changes and experiencing the desolation of the two worldwide conflicts, the twentieth century saw a progressive secularization of culture on a worldwide scale. Part of the reason ecclesiastical documents in the twentieth century focused predominantly on marriage as a "contract" is because in the face of an increasingly secular society, the Church had to reassert its authority over Christian marriage as both a sacrament and a contract. The periods after both World Wars also saw a lowering of moral standards, including a laxity in the area of sexual morality. In addition, the Church was forced to address a plethora of moral problems in the area of sexual ethics, due to rapid advances in the human sciences and the explosion of technology in

---

1. James Hitchcock, *History of the Catholic Church: From the Apostolic Age to the Third Millennium* (San Francisco: Ignatius Press, 2012), 342.

the twentieth century. By the end of the twentieth century, it is fair to say that modern Western society was faced with a crisis of the human person, in which the basic understanding of human nature was being questioned. This obviously led to a corollary crisis in understanding the nature of marriage. These challenges to the sanctity and nature of marriage and the human person that emerged in the twentieth century prompted more magisterial pronouncements on marriage than in any other century. In responding to these crises the Church gradually adopted a new mode of expressing its teachings on marriage.

The 1917 *Code of Canon Law*

Most people are surprised to learn that the Catholic Church did not produce a single, unified code of canon law until 1917. Before that date the Church utilized ecclesial laws to organize her daily life, but until 1917 these canons existed in a corpus that was continuously amended and that was not collated into a single coherent resource. Pope Pius X ordered the crafting of a coherent code of canon law, and he appointed Cardinal Pietro Gasparri to serve as the principal architect of the code, overseeing and directing its production. The work of compiling the code began in 1904 and the code was finally promulgated by Pope Benedict XV in 1917. In its treatment of marriage, the 1917 code focused on marriage as a contract,[2] a juridical emphasis which was not surprising in a legal code, but which had become more pronounced over the previous several centuries. The code also made it clear that "among the baptized there can be no valid contract of marriage without its also being a sacrament."[3] The 1917 code was the first official Church document to refer explicitly to the "primary" and "secondary" ends of marriage,[4] stating: "The primary end of marriage is the procreation and education of children; the secondary [end] is mutual support and remedy for concupiscence."[5] Marriage's essential properties of unity and indissolubility were also

---

2. *The 1917 or Pio-Benedictine Code of Canon Law in English Translation* (San Francisco: Ignatius Press, 2001), c. 1012 §1.

3. Ibid., 1012 §2.

4. Theodore Mackin, *What is Marriage? Marriage in the Catholic Church* (New York: Paulist Press, 1982), 213.

5. *The 1917 Code of Cannon Law*, 1013 §1.

affirmed, which the code stated "obtain special firmness by reason of the sacrament."[6] In affirming that consent makes a marriage, the code rather narrowly defined the object of consent as "an act of the will by which each party gives and accepts perpetual and exclusive rights to the body, for those actions that are of themselves suitable for the generation of children."[7] Although the 1917 code defined marriage primarily in terms of its ends, the code supplemented the definition of marriage when it stated: "In order that matrimonial consent be considered [valid], it is necessary that the contractants at least not be ignorant that marriage is a permanent society between a man and woman for the procreation of children."[8] The reference to marriage as "a permanent society between a man and woman" was probably the broadest statement in the code addressing the essence of marriage.

POPE PIUS XI (1922–1939)

In the aftermath of World War I there arose the more libertine environment of the 1920s. In 1930, at its Lambeth Conference, the Anglican Church became the first Christian communion to approve the use of contraception, but only for married couples. In response, Pope Pius XI issued his encyclical *Casti Connubii* in which he reasserted the Catholic Church's teaching on the immorality of contraception (CC, 56), as well as the immorality of abortion (CC, 63–64), sterilization and eugenics (CC, 68–72), adultery (CC, 73), and divorce (CC, 85–93); these are issues that will be addressed in chapters 19 and 20 of this book. However, lest *Casti Connubii* be seen as a mere list of condemnations, Peter Elliott called this encyclical "the most significant moment since Trent in the Church's developing awareness of the sacramentality of Marriage."[9] *Casti Connubii* was cited in chapter 5 in our discussion of the nature of marriage, a nature which Pope Pius XI stressed comes from God (CC, 5–9). In his encyclical, Pius clarified that he wished to treat the topic of marriage in more detail than did his predecessor, Leo XIII (CC, 4). Pius also situated his encyclical in

---

6. Ibid., 1013 §2.

7. Ibid., 1081 §2.

8. Ibid., 1082 §1.

9. Peter J. Elliott, *What God Has Joined: The Sacramentality of Marriage* (Staten Island, NY: Alba House, 1990), 111.

the Church's larger theological tradition regarding marriage by citing Augustine ten times. Pope Pius commented on the three goods of marriage that had been articulated by Augustine—offspring, fidelity, sacrament—referring to them as "blessings" (CC, 10–43), and he reaffirmed procreation and the education of children as the primary end of marriage (CC, 17). While Pius referred to marriage as a "contract" (CC, 7), and stressed the primary end of marriage, he also presented a broader understanding of marriage when he wrote:

> This mutual inward molding of husband and wife, this determined effort to perfect each other, can in a very real sense, as the Roman Catechism teaches, be said to be the chief reason and purpose of matrimony, provided matrimony be looked at not in the restricted sense as instituted for the proper conception and education of the child, but more widely as the blending of life as a whole and the mutual interchange and sharing thereof. (CC, 24)

Thus Pius expanded on the hints of a broader view of marriage that were present in *The Roman Catechism* of the Council of Trent, which was discussed in the previous chapter. Subsequent to *Casti Connubii*, many struggled to harmonize Pius XI's reference to the chief purpose of marriage as a mutually shared life with the traditional teaching of the primary and secondary ends of marriage. However, by making the statement about marriage as "mutual inward molding" Pius XI was not contradicting the traditional teaching on the primary and secondary ends of marriage. Instead, he affirmed that the *essence* of marriage includes, but is more than, the begetting of children. His reference to a wider view of marriage "as the blending of life as a whole and the mutual interchange and sharing thereof" is consistent with viewing the essence of marriage as a communion of conjugal love that was discussed in chapter 5. This is supported by the fact that Pius XI made the above statement in the context of discussing "the love of husband and wife which pervades all the duties of married life and holds pride of place in Christian marriage" (CC, 23). With this emphasis on love, Pius XI paved the way for later emphasis on conjugal love as a vital principle of marriage.[10] Evidencing the influence of Matthias Scheeben, Pius also

---

10. Ramón García de Haro, *Marriage and the Family in the Documents of the Magisterium: A Course in the Theology of Marriage*, 2nd ed., trans. William E. May (San Francisco: Ignatius Press, 1993), 143.

stressed that the grace of the Sacrament of Marriage is continuously available to Christian spouses throughout their married lives (CC, 40–41), referring to a consecration that the Sacrament of Marriage offers (CC, 41).

Dietrich von Hildebrand (1889–1977)

After Pius XI presented a broader vision of marriage in *Casti Connubii*, some Catholic thinkers attempted to provide a corrective to what they saw as a narrow view of marriage that had reduced it to a juridical reality. In addition, faced with more complex societal changes in the twentieth century, Catholic thinkers, also following the lead of Pius XI, began to stress marriage "as a permanent, lived sacrament."[11] One of the most influential Catholic thinkers who wrote on marriage during this time was Dietrich von Hildebrand. We have already reviewed some of his insights into marriage and conjugal love in chapters 4 and 5 of this book. Von Hildebrand wrote his short book, *Marriage: The Mystery of Faithful Love*, first published in German in 1929, as a result of his concern that the narrowly juridical presentation of marriage that dominated the Church of his day was neglecting the relational aspects of marriage and the role of love in the lives of spouses. Von Hildebrand's reaction to this overly juridical environment can be seen when he wrote: "The expression *marriage-contract* is not a happy choice of words since marriage differs essentially from any other real contract."[12] He also stated, "In stressing the primary *end* of marriage—procreation—certain theological treatises have overlooked the primary *meaning* of marriage, which is love."[13] Concerned with the attempt to define marriage solely in terms of its primary and secondary ends, von Hildebrand argued that the essence of marriage is a communion of love,[14] which exists for its own sake regardless of any result it produces.[15] Without denying that the procreation and education of children is the primary end of marriage, von Hildebrand argued that

---

11. Peter J. Elliiott, *What God Has Joined*, 110.

12. Dietrich von Hildebrand, *Marriage: The Mystery of Faithful Love* (Manchester, NH: Sophia Institute Press, 1991), 23.

13. Ibid., xxvi.

14. Ibid., xxv, 25.

15. Ibid., 29.

love is the primary "meaning" of marriage.[16] In writing on the centrality of love in marriage von Hildebrand was responding to what he called "anti-personalism" prevalent in his day,[17] and he followed the lead of Pius XI who in *Casti Connubii* referred to conjugal love as "the ultimate meaning of marriage."[18] Von Hildebrand also stressed that the grace offered to spouses in the Sacrament of Marriage transfigures their love for each other in their joint consecration to Jesus Christ.[19] He and other authors, following the implications of Pius XI, ushered in a more personalist approach to marriage in the first half of the twentieth century.[20] In general, personalism sees the human person as the locus of philosophical and theological reflection, stressing that the person is not an isolated individual, but a being who exists in relation to others. The influence of von Hildebrand's more personalist treatment of marriage in particular can be seen in the writings of the Second Vatican Council, Pope Paul VI, and Pope John Paul II.[21]

Pope Pius XII (1939–1958)

The post–World War II era saw a growing secular mentality in which marriage came to be seen as merely a civil contract with no particular durability. This era also saw a continued lowering of sexual morals and eventually the advent of the "sexual revolution" in some regions in the 1960s. In this environment, Pope Pius XII made contributions to the Church's teaching on marriage. Although he encouraged Dietrich von Hildebrand's work in which von Hildebrand focused on love as the meaning of marriage,[22] in a Decree of the Holy Office in 1944, Pius XII also affirmed the primary and secondary ends of marriage against those who did not acknowledge the procreation and education of children as the primary end (DS, 3838). Presumably, one of these people was Heribert Doms, a German priest whose book *The Meaning of Marriage*

---

16. Ibid., 7.

17. Ibid., xxv.

18. Ibid., xxvi.

19. Ibid., 41–50.

20. Theodore Mackin, *What is Marriage?*, 225–229.

21. John Haas, "The Contemporary World," in *Christian Marriage: A Historical Study*, ed. Glenn W. Olsen (New York: The Crossroad Publishing Company, 2001), 341.

22. Alice von Hildebrand, "Introduction," in *Marriage: The Mystery of Faithful Love* (Manchester, NH: Sophia Institute Press, 1991), xv.

was withdrawn from publication by the Holy Office in the early 1940s. Unlike von Hildebrand's work, Doms' book failed to maintain the primary end of marriage as procreation, stressing instead the immediate purpose of marriage as forming a union of persons.[23] However, evidencing at least some attention to the personalist dimension of marriage, in an allocution to Italian midwives in 1951, Pius XII stressed that the conjugal act "is a personal act" which is "to be the expression of a reciprocal gift" (ND, 2210). In the same allocution Pius addressed sexual pleasure in light of the ends of marriage. He stated that married couples "by seeking and enjoying this pleasure, do no wrong. They accept what the Creator has destined for them" (ND, 2211). Yet Pius made it clear that pursuing pleasure in sexual intercourse must be done "in the service of, and in accordance with the ends of marriage itself" (ND, 2212). This statement by Pius XII was important because it helped to remove any lingering suspicion regarding marital intercourse and its attendant pleasure. It also clarified that in enjoying the marital embrace Christian spouses cannot act in a hedonistic fashion, but must act in a way that reverences and prioritizes the ends of procreation and the good of each other.

The Second Vatican Council (1962–1965)

The Second Vatican Council contributed to a renewed understanding of marriage, which it accomplished first of all in a renewed approach to the sacraments in general. Pope John Paul II noted that only in the twentieth century was attention given to aspects of the sacraments that had been neglected in the course of the previous centuries—namely the "ecclesial dimension" of a sacrament, as well as the view of a sacrament as a "personal encounter with Christ" (TOB 93:5, fn. 88). He maintained that the Second Vatican Council helped to bring attention to these aspects of the sacraments in its *Constitution on the Liturgy* (*Sacrosanctum Concilium*) as well as in its *Dogmatic Constitution on the Church* (*Lumen Gentium*). John Paul II noted that the Council highlighted the biblical meaning of "sacrament" as the "mystery" of God's

---

23. Theodore Mackin, *What is Marriage?*, 231–235; for a good comparison of the views of von Hildebrand and Doms see Mary Shivanandan, *Crossing the Threshold of Love: A New Vision of Marriage in Light of John Paul II's Anthropology* (Washington, DC: The Catholic University of America Press, 1999), 199–202.

plan of salvation that is accomplished in Christ. Thus the Church is called "the universal sacrament of salvation" (LG, 48), as well as "a sign and instrument . . . of communion with God and of unity of the entire human race" (LG, 1). By contextualizing the understanding of all of the sacraments in terms of the relationship of Christ and the Church, Cardinal Marc Ouellet has noted that in the texts of the Second Vatican Council, "the seven sacraments appear more clearly as concretizations and actualizations of the relationship between Christ and the Church."[24] Since the relationship of Christ and the Church is nuptial, the Council invited us to understand "the sacraments not only as salvific gestures made by Christ to individuals, but also as the gift of Christ the Bridegroom to his Church."[25] In this way the Council also set the stage for a new appreciation of the Sacrament of Marriage. As a result of the Council's approach to the sacraments, the *Catechism of the Catholic Church*, a fruit of the Second Vatican Council, states, "The entire Christian life bears the mark of the spousal love of Christ and the Church" (CCC, 1617).

When the Second Vatican Council addressed marriage in particular, it did so in what one might call a "new mode." One of the most basic points stressed in the Council's *Dogmatic Constitution on the Church (Lumen Gentium)* and in its *Pastoral Constitution on the Church in the Modern World (Gaudium et Spes)* is that marriage is a vocation to holiness (LG, 41; GS, 48). The Council made it clear that couples attain this holiness through the fulfillment of the daily duties and obligations of their married life, not in spite of them. The Council even revived from St. John Chrysostom the Patristic phrase "domestic church" in reference to the Christian family, noting the centrality of the family in the life of the Church (LG, 11). This affirmation of marriage and family life as a path to holiness was an important articulation of the Council, since many prior to Vatican II saw holiness as attainable by only a few, namely those in consecrated religious life.[26] Thus the

---

24. Marc Ouellet, *Divine Likeness: Toward a Trinitarian Anthropology of the Family*, trans. Philip Milligan and Linda M. Cicone (Grand Rapids, MI: William B. Eeerdmans Publishing Co., 2006), 212.

25. Ibid., 212.

26. Ramón García de Haro, *Marriage and the Family*, 219. For further insight into the popular perception of the role of laity in the Church and the state of lay spirituality prior to the Second Vatican Council, see Yves Congar, *Lay People in the Church: A Study for a Theology of Laity*,

Council dispelled any misperceptions that somehow the married state is inherently flawed and therefore a barrier to growing in holiness.

We have already seen in chapter 5 that *Gaudium et Spes* concisely defines marriage as an "intimate partnership of life and love" (GS, 48). It states that this partnership "is rooted in the contract (*foedere*) of the partners, that is, in their irrevocable personal consent . . . by which the partners mutually surrender themselves to each other" (GS, 48). "Covenant" would be a better translation of the Latin word *foedere*, translated above as "contract" (*contractus* in Latin). The conciliar texts consistently describe marriage with the more biblical language of "covenant."[27] The Council Fathers chose to emphasize the mutual handing over of persons that occurs in the exchange of consent, rather than to focus more narrowly on the exchange of rights and obligations. This is not to imply, however, that there was some type of radical break between the Second Vatican Council's treatment of marriage as a covenant versus the preconciliar focus on marriage as a contract.[28] As already pointed out in chapter 5, to call marriage a "covenant" implies contractual elements of the relationship, yet "covenant" is a word with implications beyond the merely contractual.

Similarly, as was already mentioned in chapter 5, *Gaudium et Spes* does not refer to a ranking of the ends of marriage in terms of primary and secondary, but instead mentions "various values and purposes" (GS, 48). Yet, as the text goes on to discuss these various benefits and ends, the realities of the primary and secondary ends of marriage are present when *Gaudium et Spes* states, "By its very nature the institution of marriage and married love are ordered to the procreation and education of the offspring and it is in them that it finds its crowning glory" (GS, 48). It then immediately states that "the man and woman . . . help and serve each other by their marriage partnership" (GS, 48). These two sentences are clearly references to the primary and secondary ends of marriage, without using the technical philosophical terminology. The text then mentions the three goods of marriage without explicitly using the language of "goods" when it states, "The intimate union of marriage, as a mutual giving of two persons,

---

trans. Donald Attwater, 2nd rev. ed. (Westminster, MD: Newman Press, 1965), especially the introduction and first two chapters.

27. Peter J. Elliott, *What God Has Joined*, 176–180.

28. John Haas, "The Contemporary World," 340.

and the good of the *children* demand total *fidelity* from the spouses and require an *unbreakable unity* between them" (GS, 48; emphasis added).

Thus in an attempt "to present certain key points of the church's teaching [on marriage] in a clearer light" (GS, 47), the Council Fathers deliberately used language that is less technical and that presents a broader and deeper vision of marriage. This is consistent with the Council's overall goal of presenting the truths of the Catholic faith to the modern world "in a language accessible to all men."[29] However, in this process of presenting the Church's teaching on marriage in a new mode, the Council "incorporates the personalist developments in Catholic thought [that led up to the Council] even while it does not forsake any of the essential insights of the more ancient tradition."[30]

When it turned to treating the Sacrament of Marriage in particular, the Second Vatican Council made it clear that Christ "encounters Christian spouses through the sacrament of marriage" and "abides with them" (GS, 48). *Gaudium et Spes* explains that in the Sacrament of Marriage "married love is caught up into divine love" (GS, 48). The Council Fathers taught that Christ empowers the couples not only to accomplish the duties of married life, but also to lead each other to God (GS, 48). The Council even speaks of Christian married couples being "consecrated" by the Sacrament of Marriage as they grow in "mutual sanctification" (GS, 48). This is certainly a much loftier vision of the grace offered by the Sacrament of Marriage than was present in any previous conciliar texts or magisterial documents.

Vatican II also gave attention to married love, stressing that true married love "embraces the good of the whole person" (GS, 49). *Gaudium et Spes* states that married love "leads the partners to a free and mutual giving of self, experienced in tenderness and action." Citing *Casti Connubii* by Pius XI, *Gaudium et Spes* explains that this love should permeate the whole lives of the couple (GS, 49). The Council then gave attention to marital intercourse as a way of expressing married love (GS, 49). It called the marital act "noble and honorable" and stated that "the truly human performance of these acts fosters the self-giving they signify and enriches spouses in joy and gratitude"

---

29. Pope Paul VI, "Pope Paul VI to the Council Fathers," December 8, 1965, in *The Documents of Vatican II*, ed. Walter M. Abbott (New York: Herder and Herder, 1966), 729.

30. John Haas, "The Contemporary World," 345.

(GS, 49). *Gaudium et Spes* explains the harmony that should exist between conjugal love and procreation, reiterating that "children are the supreme gift of marriage" who "greatly contribute to the well-being of the parents themselves" (GS, 50). *Gaudium et Spes* asserts, "When it is a question of harmonizing married love with the responsible transmission of life . . . objective criteria must be used, criteria drawn from the nature of the human person and human action, criteria which respect the total meaning of mutual self-giving and human procreation in the context of true love" (GS, 51). The document also forbids the faithful from using methods of birth regulation that are "disapproved of by the teaching authority of the Church in its interpretation of divine law" (GS, 51), but the Council deferred any more specific teaching to the pope. Paul VI later issued further teaching in his encyclical *Humanae Vitae*, but *Gaudium et Spes* is important because it treats the marital act in the context of married love with an emphasis on the good of the person and mutual self-giving.

Pope Paul VI (1963–1978)

Perhaps one of the most well-known Church documents of the modern era is the encyclical letter *Humanae Vitae* (Of Human Life) issued by Pope Paul VI in 1968. In this document Paul VI provided more specificity to the teaching of the Second Vatican Council regarding the regulation of births. Paul VI reiterated the Church's teaching, unchanged throughout the ages,[31] that all forms of contraceptive behavior are intrinsically immoral (HV, 14). This teaching is understood by few people, including Catholics, in a world that has become thoroughly contraceptive in its approach to regulating births. Chapter 20 of this book devoted to responsible parenthood will highlight the importance of this teaching for a proper understanding of marriage. It is important to note that Paul VI rearticulated this teaching to the world in language that focuses on the meaning of conjugal love and marriage as a personal communion. Thus Paul VI provided an explanation for the immorality of contraception that went beyond Pius XI's explanation in *Casti Connubii*, in which Pius stated

---

31. For a history of the Catholic Church's teaching on contraception, see John T. Noonan Jr., *Contraception: A History of Its Treatment by the Catholic Theologians and Canonists* (New York: Mentor-Omega Books, 1965).

that contraception frustrates the natural purpose of the marital act (CC, 53–54). In *Humanae Vitae*, Paul VI stated that marriage "is in reality the wise and provident institution of God the Creator, whose purpose was to effect in man His loving design." In addition, he stated that, "husband and wife, through that mutual gift of themselves, which is specific and exclusive to them alone, develop that union of two persons in which they perfect one another" (HV, 8). He continued to describe conjugal love as a "fully human" love that is by its nature permanent, faithful, and fruitful, and he stated, "Whoever really loves his partner loves not only for what he receives, but loves that partner for the partner's own sake, content to be able to enrich the other with the gift of himself" (HV, 9). Paul VI clarified that maintaining the inseparability of the unitive and procreative meanings of the conjugal act is not just about maintaining the integrity of a biological function, but is about preserving the fullness of "true mutual love" between a couple (HV, 12). Thus Paul VI presented a highly personalist vision of marriage as a communion of persons in which spouses exist as mutual gifts for each other in conjugal love. John Paul II further elaborated on this vision of marriage during his papacy, leaving a valuable legacy to the Church and the world.

Chapter 14

The Legacy of Pope St. John Paul II

POPE ST. JOHN PAUL II (1978–2005)

Against the backdrop of this historical survey in part 4, it is now possible to highlight John Paul II's contributions to the theology of marriage. Pope John Paul II wrote more extensively on the topic of marriage than any other pope in the history of the Catholic Church. With his writings we witness the most significant development in the Catholic Church's theology of marriage since St. Augustine. One of the most obvious aspects of John Paul's writings on marriage is his innately "positive approach to the body and sexuality."[1] In language that is both profound and beautiful, John Paul defended the truth of the human body, including its sexual differentiation, and the truth of married love that is expressed through the body. With his background in phenomenology and his focus on personalism John Paul addressed marriage in a way unlike any pope before him.[2] He did so in a conscious effort to respond to the fallout of the sexual revolution and what he perceived as a crisis of the human person.[3] Yet John Paul was

---

1. Mary Shivanandan, *Crossing the Threshold of Love: A New Vision of Marriage* (Edinburgh: T&T Clark, 1999), 139.

2. For an overview of the academic and intellectual background of John Paul II, see Mary Shivanandan, *Crossing the Threshold of Love*, especially chapters 1–3. See also Michael Waldstein, "Introduction," in *Man and Woman He Created Them: A Theology of the Body* (Boston: Pauline Books and Media, 2006), 23–94; and Rocco Buttiglione, *Karol Wojtyla: The Thought of the Man Who Became John Paul II*, trans. Paolo Guietti and Francesca Murphy (Grand Rapids, MI: Eerdmans, 1997).

3. See George Weigel, *Witness to Hope: The Biography of Pope John Paul II* (New York: HarperCollins Publishers, 1999), 334–335.

not naive. He understood clearly the effects of concupiscence on fallen humanity, devoting the entire second chapter of his *Theology of the Body* to the human struggle with concupiscence. In that chapter, which includes more general audiences than any other chapter, John Paul stated very clearly that we cannot "return to the state of original innocence, because humanity has left it irrevocably behind" (TOB 49:4). He evidenced profound realism by discussing "concupiscence of the flesh as a permanent element" of existence in a fallen world (TOB 43:3). John Paul II understood that "the 'heart' has become a battlefield between love and concupiscence" (TOB 32:3). However, he also maintained that if men and women open themselves up to the grace of redemption and "life according to the Spirit," they can be "freed by redemption from the bonds of concupiscence" (TOB 58:5), exercise self-mastery, grow in purity of heart (TOB 58:7), and exist as a communion of persons (TOB 55:6). Thus John Paul announced to the world a hopeful realism.

Probably the most fundamental insight of John Paul II into a theology of marriage is how central a correct understanding of the human person is to a correct understanding of marriage, and, vice versa, how central a correct understanding of marriage is to a correct understanding of the human person. As was discussed in chapters 2 and 3 of this book, John Paul pointed out that every human person, made in the image of the Triune God of love, is called to exist in a communion of persons through a nuptial gift of self, thus realizing the "spousal meaning of the body" which is "the fundamental component of human existence in the world" (TOB 15:5). John Paul therefore developed our understanding of what it means to be made in the image and likeness of God by highlighting the communal nature of the human person who is made in the image of the Tri-Personal God (TOB 9:3; MD, 7). In this way he incorporated the gendered human body into an understanding of what it means for the human person to be made in the "image of God." As part of this development, John Paul drew attention to marriage as the first and most fundamental communion of persons that serves as the basis for all other communion (FC, 19). John Paul even maintained that in God's design, the self-giving love of husband and wife is supposed to be an image of God's own life of self-giving love (TOB 19:4). This certainly makes it clear that understanding marriage is not a peripheral issue to the discipline of theology or to human existence.

It should be noted that several modern Orthodox theologians have stressed the communal dimension of the "image of God" and the fact that marriage is a fundamental aspect of this image. Paul Evdokimov stated: "It is therefore nuptial man who is in the image of the triune God, and the dogma of the Trinity is his divine archetype, the icon of the nuptial community." [4] Similarly, Alkiviadis C. Calivas has stated: "The nuptial community is understood to be patterned after the divine life of the Holy Trinity."[5] In language which sounds very much like John Paul II's *Theology of the Body*, Bishop Kallistos Ware wrote:

> Formed as an icon of the Trinitarian God, the human person is made for mutual love; and that means, first and foremost, the love between man and woman. . . . The image of God is given, not to the man alone or to the woman alone, but to the two of them together. It comes to its fulfillment only in the "between" that unites them to each other. Personhood is a mutual gift; there is no true human unless there are at least two humans in communion with each other. To say 'I am made in God's image' is to affirm: "I need you in order to be myself." The divine image is in this way a "relational" image, manifested not in isolation but in community—and, above all, in the primordial bond between husband and wife that is the foundation of all other forms of social life.[6]

Hopefully these mutually shared insights will provide fruitful ground for ecumenical dialogue on the Sacrament of Marriage as it is understood in both the Catholic and the Orthodox traditions.

Along with his insights into the communal nature of the *imago Dei*, John Paul also developed the Church's understanding of the language of conjugal love in terms of the concept of "gift."[7] Building on *Gaudium et spes*, 24, which states that "man can fully

---

4. Paul Evdokimov, *The Sacrament of Love: The Nuptial Mystery in the Light of the Orthodox Tradition*, trans. Anthony P. Gythiel and Victoria Steadman (Crestwood, NY: St. Vladimir's Seminary Press, 1985), 117.

5. Alkiviadis C. Calivas, "Marriage: The Sacrament of Love and Communion," in *InterMarriage: Orthodox Perspectives*, ed. Anton C. Vrame (Brookline, MA: Holy Cross Orthodox Press, 1997), 53.

6. Kallistos Ware, "The Sacrament of Love: The Orthodox Understanding of Marriage and Its Breakdown," *Downside Review* 109 (1991): 79.

7. Marc Ouellet, *Divine Likeness*, 228.

discover his true self only in a sincere giving of himself," John Paul II never tired of proclaiming the person-as-gift. Applying this to married life, John Paul stated that spouses must strive to exist as gift for each other. He even grounded the understanding of the primary and secondary ends of marriage in the understanding of the person-as-gift. John Paul II supported the traditional hierarchy of the ends of marriage when he stated:

> This communion [of original man and woman] had been intended to make man and woman mutually happy through the search of a simple and pure union in humanity, through a reciprocal offering of themselves, that is, through the experience of the gift of the person expressed with soul and body, with masculinity and femininity—"flesh of my flesh" (Gen 2:23)—and finally through the subordination of such a union to the blessing of fruitfulness with "procreation." (TOB 30:3)

In the above quote John Paul clearly stated that even in the beginning the union of the spouses, which is the secondary end of marriage and of sexual intercourse, would have been subordinate to procreation, which is the primary end. However, John Paul also made it clear that both the primary and secondary ends of marriage and marital intercourse are accomplished through the mutual self-gift of husband and wife. Elsewhere, John Paul explained the relationship of the ends of marriage to the gift-love of spouses when he stated, "According to the traditional language, love, as a superior 'power,' coordinates the acts of the persons, of the husband and wife, *in the area of the ends of marriage*" (TOB 127:3). John Paul explained that this love, which the couple receives from God in the Sacrament of Marriage, allows them to reverence the inseparability of the two ends (TOB 127:3). Thus, contextualized in love, John Paul stated that "the traditional teaching on the ends of marriage (and on their hierarchy) is confirmed and at the same time deepened from the point of view of the interior life of the spouses, of conjugal and familial spirituality" (TOB 127:3). In short, procreation as the most uniquely distinctive characteristic of the marital relationship (thus the primary end) and the good of the union of the spouses (the secondary end) are both presented by John Paul II as inseparable aspects of the love of total self-gift to which the spouses are called.

Building on the texts of the Second Vatican Council which spoke of the sacraments as having their origin in the relationship between Christ and the Church, John Paul presented marriage as the "primordial sacrament" (TOB 96). We have already mentioned in chapter 6 how John Paul II explained marriage as the primordial sign of God's love in the world, making visible the mystery hidden from eternity in God—the plan to invite mankind into Trinitarian Love (TOB 90:1). The primordial sacrament also foreshadowed the "great mystery" of the spousal union between Christ and his Church. Additionally, we saw in chapter 8 how John Paul explained that the whole sacramental order finds its prototype in marriage, issuing forth from Christ's act of spousal self-donation to the Church (TOB 95b, 98). John Paul explained how Ephesians 5 presents us with the foundation for understanding marriage both as a sacrament and the origin of all of the sacraments of the New Covenant (TOB 93:4). Ephesians shows that from the institution of marriage in the beginning as a "primordial sacrament" of God's love, there was a gradual unfolding of the mystery of salvation that culminates in Christ's spousal union with his Church (TOB 93:2–3). By comparing "the indissoluble relationship of Christ and the Church to the relationship between husband and wife," and by referring to "the beginning," Ephesians summarizes all of salvation history and presents marriage as *the foundation of the whole sacramental order*" (TOB 95b:7). All of the graces of the sacraments flow from the spousal giving of self, the "great sacrament" of Christ's union with the Church (TOB 99:1). Thus John Paul stated that "marriage has remained the platform for the realization of God's eternal plans" (TOB 97:1). All of these insights into marriage as the "primordial sacrament" certainly provide a deepened appreciation for marriage and its importance to the entire sacramental order.

As was pointed out in chapter 5 and chapter 8, John Paul II also deepened our understanding of how the Sacrament of Marriage has its origins in the great mystery of Christ and the Church. John Paul commented at length on the great "spousal analogy" present in the Letter to the Ephesians, according to which Christ is presented as the bridegroom who gives himself in love to sanctify his bride, the Church. He deepened the insight of St. Thomas Aquinas, who saw that the Sacrament of Marriage has its origin in Christ's Passion not by way of suffering but by way of love. John Paul clarified that the

Passion of Christ is in fact a nuptial giving of self, and he affirmed that the Sacrament of Marriage is a sign of this nuptial giving when he stated, "Spouses are therefore the permanent reminder to the Church of what happened on the Cross" (FC, 13). John Paul showed how the Sacrament of Marriage is inseparable from the nuptial relationship of Christ and the Church when he stated, "The 'great mystery,' which is the Church and humanity in Christ, does not exist apart from the 'great mystery' expressed in the 'one flesh' (cf. Gen 2:24; Eph 5:3–32), that is, in the reality of marriage and the family" (LF, 19).

By grounding the Sacrament of Marriage in the spousal analogy of Christ's relationship with the Church, John Paul also helped to show that the sacramentality of Christian marriage does not depend solely on reading the phrase *mega mysterion* ("great mystery") of Ephesians 5:32 as if it were a proof text for the Sacrament of Marriage. Certainly other Catholic theologians prior to John Paul II have made this point. However, John Paul's explanation of the scriptural warrant for sacramental marriage was especially lucid. John Paul consistently spoke of the "great mystery" that is presented in Ephesians 5. He explained how the author of Ephesians, while primarily referencing this mystery as God's plan of salvation that is accomplished in the loving union of Christ and the Church, also asserts that this mystery is signified in Christian marriage (TOB 95b:7; LF, 19). Additionally, John Paul highlighted the fact that in Ephesians 5, Christ's relationship to the Church is presented to Christian spouses as *"the point of reference for their spousal love"* (LF, 19). John Paul explained, "To be able to recommend such an obligation [to spouses], one must admit that the very essence of marriage contains *a particle of the same mystery* [of the relationship between Christ and the Church]. Otherwise, this whole analogy would hang in a void" (TOB 90:3). In other words, John Paul showed that the logic of the exhortation to husbands and wives present in Ephesians 5 demands that Christian marriage be an effective sign of Christ's union with the Church, in order for the exhortation to make sense.

John Paul II also provided some insight into Christ's institution of the Sacrament of Marriage. While it is true that the Church has never officially defined the exact moment when Christ instituted marriage as a sacrament,[8] as was mentioned in chapter 8, John Paul supported the position that Christ instituted the grace-giving Sacrament of Marriage during his conversation with the Pharisees regarding divorce. In this conversation Jesus made clear his intention to renew married love as part of his work of redemption, proclaiming marriage to be absolutely indissoluble. Commenting on this interchange between Jesus and the Pharisees, John Paul stated:

> When Christ, in the presence of his interlocutors in Matthew and Mark (see Mt 19; Mk 10) *confirms marriage as a sacrament instituted by the Creator "at the beginning"*—when he accordingly requires its indissolubility—he thereby *opens* marriage to the salvific action of God, *to the powers flowing "from the redemption of the body,"* which help to overcome the consequences of sin and to build the unity of man and woman according to the Creator's eternal plan. (TOB 100:2)

Thus John Paul seemed to say that when Jesus affirmed the primordial sacrament of marriage and stated his intention to make it possible for men and women to accomplish God's original plan for marriage, he simultaneously opened up marriage to the power of the redemption that he brought, thus elevating marriage and incorporating it into his saving love as one of the seven sacraments of the Church.

John Paul also contributed to the development of our understanding of the sign (*sacramentum tantum*) of the sacrament of marriage, the abiding reality (*res et sacramentum*) brought into being by the sacrament, and the grace (*res tantum*) that is effected by the sacrament. Some of John Paul II's most profound insights referred to the sign (*sacramentun tantum*) of the Sacrament of Marriage. First, he explained that marriage comes into being through the mutual exchange of consent (TOB 103:2). However, when a husband and wife contract a marriage by their words of consent, that marriage is not yet "constituted in its full reality" (TOB 103:2).[9] John Paul explained that the words of consent—"I, N., take you, N., to be my [husband/wife]. / I promise to be faithful to you, in good times and in bad, / in sickness and in health, / to love you and to honor you / all the days of my life." (OCM,

---

8. Ramón García de Haro, *Marriage and the Family*, 67.

9. John Paul pointed out that the canonical distinction between a marriage that is "ratified" through the valid exchange of consent and marriage that is ratified and consummated through sexual intercourse (CIC, c. 1061 §1) means that marriage has not been fully constituted without sexual intercourse.

62)—"can only be fulfilled by the *copula conjugale* (conjugal intercourse)" (TOB 103:2), in which the two really do "take" each other and become one flesh according to God's institution of marriage in the beginning (Gen 2:24). Therefore, John Paul stated that the externally expressed consent "is *a sacramental sign in virtue of its content*" (TOB 103:2). He explained, "*from the words* with which the man and the woman express their readiness to become 'one flesh' according to the eternal truth established in the mystery of creation, we pass *to the reality* that corresponds to these words. Both the one and the other element are important *with regard to the structure of the sacramental sign*" (TOB 103:3). Thus the words of consent serve as the "form" of the sign of the Sacrament of Marriage *because* the content of those words expresses the intention of the couple to mutually hand themselves over to each other and become one flesh according to God's design for marriage. Expressing these words brings the marriage into being, though not in its full reality, because by exchanging these words the couple manifests their intention to realize the content of the expression.

However, John Paul explained more about the sign (*sacramentum tantum*) of Marriage. He stated, "The sign of the sacrament of Marriage is constituted by the words of the new spouses inasmuch as the 'reality' that they themselves constitute corresponds to them. *Both of them, as man and woman*, being ministers of the sacrament at the moment of contracting marriage, at the same time *constitute the full and real visible sign* of the sacrament itself" (TOB 103:4). In other words, John Paul asserted that while the words of consent are the "form" of the sacrament of marriage, the man and the woman themselves are the "matter" of the sacrament. John Paul made explicit what was hinted at previously by Albert the Great and Thomas Aquinas, and what was implied when other theologians referred to the content of the words of consent as the "matter" of the Sacrament of Marriage. John Paul clarified that the "matter" is nothing other than a man and a woman who are able to mutually hand themselves over to each other to become one flesh. He explained this further when he said of the spouses: "The words spoken by them would not of themselves constitute the sacramental sign if the human subjectivity of the engaged man and woman and at the same time the consciousness of the body linked with the masculinity and the femininity of the bride and the bridegroom did not correspond to them" (TOB 103:4). In other words, without a man and a woman we do not have the proper matter of the sacrament, because the human subjectivity of the spouses could not conform to the spoken words. Thus, following John Paul II's thought, it is appropriate to say that while the "form" of the Sacrament of Marriage is the words of consent, the "matter" of the sacrament is a man and a woman who are able to validly hand themselves over to each other in order to become one flesh. This way of expressing the "matter" of the sacrament of marriage is less cumbersome than referring to the "matter" as the "content of the consent." It is also language that is more direct and clear, making explicit what was for centuries implicit and understood, for example, in the thought of St. Thomas Aquinas. This more direct and clear language is necessary in an age that is questioning the nature of marriage as a union between a man and a woman.

However, John Paul II offered an even more concise way of speaking about the sign (*sacramentum tantum*) of the Sacrament of Marriage. John Paul II stated that the essential sign of the Sacrament of Marriage is "the 'language of the body' reread in truth" (TOB 104:8). We discussed in chapter 4 and chapter 7 that the "language of the body" is a language of self-gift "spoken" in sexual intercourse; this is consistent with the "spousal meaning of the body," which reveals to us that we are meant to be self-giving gifts. By saying that the "language of the body" is the sign of the Sacrament of Marriage, John Paul meant that the words of consent presuppose and express verbally the "language of the body" that man and wife will "speak" to each other when they consummate their union. Thus the words of consent express that it is through their masculinity and femininity that the man and the woman "become a reciprocal gift for each other" (TOB 103:5). In fact, John Paul II explained that the words of consent constitute the sign of the Sacrament of Marriage precisely because the words, "I . . . take you . . . as my wife / as my husband," express "the essential *'truth'* of the language of the body" (TOB 105:1). Thus John Paul stated, "The man and the woman, who are to become one flesh by marriage, express in this sign the reciprocal gift of masculinity and femininity as the foundation of the conjugal union of persons" (TOB 103:4). In this way, by the words of consent the couple reread "the perennial 'language of the body,' [and] form . . . the visible and efficacious sign of the covenant with God in Christ" (TOB 103:6). John Paul also noted that as they express their consent, which is based on the "language of the body," the husband and wife "are called to form their lives and their living together as a 'communion of persons' on the basis of this language" (TOB 106:2). In this way, John Paul's concept of the "language of the body" is also incredibly helpful for approaching sexual morality, which we will address in a later chapter.

By explaining the sign of the Sacrament of Marriage in terms of the "language of the body," John Paul also related the "language of the body" to the liturgical celebration of Marriage. We have already mentioned in chapter 7 how John Paul II saw in the prayer of Tobias and Sarah the truth of the "language of the body" becoming "the language of the liturgy" (TOB 116:2), a language of praise, thanksgiving, and petition spoken together by the spouses (TOB 116:1). John Paul explained that the prayer of Tobias and Sarah (TOB 8:4–9) "becomes in some way the deeper model of the liturgy" because before the couple "speaks" the truth of the "language of the body" as husband and wife, they first give voice to this truth in the unison of prayer (TOB 115:6). John Paul explained that "Tobias and Sarah speak the language of the ministers of the sacrament" (TOB 116:4), because: "In that moment, in which, since they just married each other, they should be 'one flesh' as husband and wife, they commit themselves together to rereading the *'language of the body'* proper to their state in its divine source. In this way, the 'language of the body' becomes the language of the liturgy" (TOB 116:2). However, John Paul maintained that the language of the liturgy also becomes the "language of the body" (TOB 117). By this he means that the "language of the body" that spouses "speak" to each other in the marital act must be a language expressing a love for the other that makes "the other 'I' in a certain sense one's own 'I'" (TOB 117:4). This is according to the model "I take you as my wife / as my husband. . . . I promise to be true to you. . . . I will love you and honor you all the days of my life" (TOB 117:3). The language of the liturgy that "assigns love, faithfulness, and conjugal integrity to both man and woman" (TOB 117b:2) must be continually "spoken" in the "language of the body."

Regarding the abiding reality brought into being by the Sacrament of Marriage, John Paul stated that "the first and immediate effect of marriage (*res et sacramentum*) is not supernatural grace itself, but the Christian conjugal bond, a typically Christian communion of two persons because it represents the mystery of Christ's incarnation and the mystery of His covenant" (FC, 13). Thus, John Paul II clarified that this bond is not primarily a juridical abstraction, but a personal and ecclesial reality, uniting the lives of the couple, sealing their union with the Holy Spirit, and taking their union up into the indissoluble bond that exists between Christ and the Church.[10] John Paul said of spouses, "The sign they bring into being with the words of the conjugal consent is not merely an immediate and fleeting sign, but a sign that looks toward the future and produces a lasting effect, namely, the conjugal bond, one and indissoluble" (TOB 105:6). This means that Christian married couples remain a living sign of Christ's nuptial relationship with the Church throughout their entire life together. John Paul made this clear when he stated, "As spouses, the man and the woman bear this sign throughout the whole of their lives, and they remain this sign until death" (TOB 103:7).

Regarding the grace (*res tantum*) of the Sacrament of Marriage, John Paul II made it clear that the Sacrament of Marriage allows couples to "participate in the salvific love of Christ" (TOB 102:2). He stressed that Christian marriage empowers married couples to love as Christ loves, even in and through the "language of the body."[11] Noting the pervasive empowerment that Christian spouses receive through the grace of the Sacrament of Marriage, John Paul stated, "The sacraments infuse holiness into the terrain of man's humanity: they penetrate soul and body, the femininity and masculinity of the personal subject, with the power of holiness" (TOB 117b:2). John Paul stressed the fact that through the Sacrament of Marriage Christian spouses can experience in a particular way the "redemption of the body" (Rom 8:23) that St. Paul discussed (TOB 99:4–5). The Sacrament of Marriage allows a "man and woman to shape their whole life together by drawing strength from the mystery of the 'redemption of the body'" (TOB 101:4). In this way they are empowered to live life "according to the Spirit" (Rom 8:4–5; Gal 5:25), which involves being given the grace to practice chastity and "*master the concupiscence of the flesh*" (TOB 101:4). This gift that the spouses receive and which is operative throughout their married life (FC, 56) allows them to discover the true freedom of being a gift through the

---

10. Marc Ouellet, *Divine Likeness*, 214.

11. See ibid.

spousal meaning of the body (TOB 101:5). John Paul II explained that this is the proper understanding of marriage as a "cure for concupiscence" (TOB 101:3). Due to this particular grace received in the Sacrament of Marriage, John Paul II stated that "conjugal life in some sense becomes liturgy" (TOB 117b:6), which is "the participation of the People of God in 'the work of God' (cf. Jn 17:4)" (CCC, 1069). Certainly the idea that conjugal life itself, including the conjugal act, can in some way form part of the praise, thanksgiving, and petition that a married couple offers to God was a significant development in the theology of marriage.[12]

THE 1983 *CODE OF CANON LAW*

In the wake of the Second Vatican Council, and promulgated by John Paul II, the 1983 *Code of Canon Law* evidenced an attempt to translate into juridical terms the broader understanding of marriage resulting from *Gaudium et Spes*, 48–52. The definition of marriage in the 1983 code, part of which we already viewed in chapter 5, is as follows:

> The matrimonial covenant, by which a man and a woman establish between themselves a partnership of the whole of life and which is ordered by its nature to the good of the spouses and the procreation and education of offspring, has been raised by Christ the Lord to the dignity of a sacrament between the baptized. (CIC, c. 1055 §1; CCC, 1601)

Although the 1983 code still refers to marriage as a "contract" entered into by spouses (CIC, c. 1058), the terms "contract" and "covenant" are used interchangeably.[13] This equation of "contract" and "covenant" represents "a move to a higher viewpoint" according to

---

12. Two theologians have sought to further develop some of the insights of John Paul II. Cardinal Angelo Scola has endeavored to show the centrality of the nuptial mystery—understood as sexual difference, love as gift, and fruitfulness—to all forms of love and to reality itself (Angelo Scola, *The Nuptial Mystery*, trans. Michelle K. Borras [Grand Rapids, MI: Eerdmans, 2005]). Cardinal Marc Ouellet has taken the Trinitarian anthropology of John Paul II and applied it to a Christian understanding of the family (Marc Ouellet, *Divine Likeness*). Both of these theologians, and others, have begun to develop a theology of marriage "in terms of 'gift,' bringing into relief not only the anthropological gift of persons, namely human love, but the 'theological' gift of the sacrament that assumes the conjugal covenant within the nuptial mystery of Christ and the Church" (Marc Ouellet, *Divine Likeness*, 151; see also 175–176).

13. John P. Beal, "Title VII Marriage [cc. 1055–1165]," in *New Commentary on the Code of Canon Law*, ed. John P. Beal, James A. Coriden, and Thomas J. Green (New York: Paulist Press, 2000), 1241.

which all of the contractual elements of marriage are maintained, yet the sacred nature of marriage, the mutual personal commitment of the spouses, and the personal aspects of marriage are emphasized by viewing the contract as a covenant.[14] Also, instead of focusing on marital consent as a contractual exchange of mutual rights to each others' bodies, as did the 1917 code, the new code stated that spouses "mutually give and accept each other" in the covenant that they forge (CIC, c.1057 §2). In addition, as was pointed out in chapter 5, lacking from the new code is any reference to the primary and secondary ends of marriage. Nonetheless, even though the 1983 code dropped the philosophically technical language of "ends," the definition of marriage above still refers to the reality that marriage is ordered toward the procreation and education of children and the good of the spouses. However, Peter Elliott has rightly noted that the "personalist emphasis of the [Second Vatican] Council and in the Magisterium of John Paul II has entered the new *Code of Canon Law*."[15]

CATECHISM OF THE CATHOLIC CHURCH

The *Catechism of the Catholic Church*, promulgated by John Paul II and first published in 1993, is one of the fruits of the Second Vatican Council. The new *Catechism*'s treatment of marriage is much more extensive than the treatment provided in *The Roman Catechism* published after the Council of Trent. The first sections of the *Catechism of the Catholic Church* that are pertinent to marriage are the paragraphs dealing with the creation of man (CCC, 355–384). Among the citations in this section are several references to *Gaudium et Spes*, which is cited in the course of addressing the human person made in the image of God (CCC, 356–361), body and soul (CCC, 362–368), male and female (CCC, 369–373).

The section of the *Catechism* dealing with the Sacrament of Marriage (CCC, 1601–1666) begins by addressing marriage in God's original plan of creation (CCC, 1602–1605), the effects of original sin on marriage (CCC, 1606–1608), marriage under the law of the Old Testament (CCC, 1609–1611), and marriage as it is raised to a

---

14. Ibid., 1241–1242.
15. Peter J. Elliott, *What God Has Joined*, 179.

sacrament by Jesus (CCC, 1612–1617). After addressing the relationship between marriage and virginity for the sake of the Kingdom (CCC, 1618–1620), the section dealing with the Sacrament of Marriage discusses the celebration of Christian marriage (CCC, 1621–1624) and matrimonial consent (CCC, 1625–1637). Next, the *Catechism* discusses the effects of the Sacrament of Marriage (CCC, 1638–1642) including the marriage bond (*res et sacramentum*) and the grace of the sacrament (*res tantum*). The *Catechism* then devotes several paragraphs to discussing conjugal love (CCC, 1643–1654), including its qualities of indissolubility (CCC, 1644–1645), fidelity (CCC, 1646–1651), and fruitfulness (CCC, 1652–654). The treatment of the Sacrament of Marriage ends with a section on the family as domestic church (CCC, 1655–1658). Cited in the *Catechism*'s treatment of the Sacrament of Marriage are the 1983 *Code of Canon Law*, documents from the Second Vatican Council, and *Familiaris Consortio* by John Paul II.

The last section of the *Catechism of the Catholic Church* that is directly pertinent to marriage is the section addressing the Sixth Commandment (CCC, 2331–2400), "You shall not commit adultery" (Ex 20:14; Dt 5:18). Among the sources cited in this section are *Gaudium et Spes* and writings of John Paul II including *Familiaris Consortio* and *Mulieris Dignitatem*. The treatment of the Sixth Commandment opens with an explanation of the importance of sexuality/gender in our understanding of the human person (CCC, 2331–2336). It then discusses the importance of chastity in maintaining the integrity of the person and enabling the person to make a gift of self (CCC, 2337–2347). After discussing forms of chastity (CCC, 2348–2350), offenses against chastity (CCC, 2351–2356), and homosexuality (CCC, 2357–2359), the *Catechism* again discusses the love of husbands and wives (CCC, 2360–2363), highlighting the qualities of fidelity (CCC, 2364–2365) and fecundity (CCC, 2366–2372). The section stresses the notion of children as gifts (CCC, 2373–2379), and it ends with a discussion of offenses against the dignity of marriage (CCC, 2380–2391).

Hopefully, the beautiful insights contained in these sections of the *Catechism*, which synthesize Catholic teaching on marriage, can be seen in how the *Catechism* has been employed in this book. In its teachings pertaining to marriage, the *Catechism* bears the clear mark of not only the Second Vatican Council, but also of John Paul II himself, providing a nourishing and inspiring vision of Christian marriage for which we should all be grateful.

SUMMARY OF PART IV: THE DEVELOPMENT OF THE THEOLOGY OF MARRIAGE

At the end of these chapters dealing with the historical development of the theology of marriage, it is important to note that the Church's growing awareness and clearer articulation of marriage as a sacrament instituted by Christ finds its norm in Scripture.[16] Relying upon this norm, the Church has grown in her understanding of the mystery of marriage over time. The same Spirit who inspired the holy Scriptures and who continues to inspire the Church throughout time to lead her into the fullness of truth regarding all of the mysteries bequeathed to her by Christ (Jn 16:13), also guides this growing understanding and clearer vision of Christian marriage. This growing understanding was not infused into the life of the Church all at once. Instead, the articulation of the understanding of marriage followed the gradual experience of the reality of marriage. The developing articulation was also culturally contingent, influenced and in some ways limited by the mindset of a given age. In this way the Holy Spirit lead the People of God into the truth progressively. This is not to say that the reality of marriage itself has changed over time, only that the Church's understanding of marriage has developed and matured, under the guidance of the Holy Spirit. Defining marriage as a sacrament was gradual because it took time to discern its outward sign and the particular grace that it gives. Theologians were also reluctant to posit marriage as a sacrament because it involves sexual intercourse which is subject to the vicissitudes of sexual concupiscence. Thus, as with most Church doctrines, the Church's teaching on marriage developed in response to particular challenges.

While the previous five chapters have outlined the development of an articulated theology of marriage in the life of the Church, what cannot be traced as accurately are the insights of countless spouses who have lived the vocation of Christian marriage, as well as the

---

16. Edward Schillebeeckx, *Marriage*, 393.

insights of pastors who ministered to these couples. Over the past two millennia these members of the Mystical Body, participating in the Spirit-guided sense of the faithful (CCC, 91–93), could have developed a vision of faith that gave them an intuition into the great mystery of Christian marriage that predated any formal theological articulations. From the beginning of the Church, Christian spouses saw their marriages as distinct from non-Christian marriages. They viewed their marriages as holy because they were called to live out their married lives "in the Lord" (1 Cor 7:39) in the context of their baptismal commitment. This sense grew over time, although not without errors and detours, and it is out of this sense of the Christian vocation of marriage that formal articulations of the theology of marriage flowed.

The earliest evidence from the second century (Ignatius of Antioch) showed that Christians understood the religious significance of their marriages and that the Church provided married couples with pastoral care. There is also evidence from the second century (*Epistle of Barnabas*) that Christians understood their marriages to be indissoluble. In the early Church, marriage was consistently presented as a good creation of a good God and as a sign of Christ's union with the Church, but there was a tension regarding the central place of sexual intercourse in marriage with its attendant carnal concupiscence. Most early Church Fathers stressed the necessity of pursuing procreation as the primary purpose of marriage in order to excuse the concupiscence of sexual intercourse, maintaining that sexual intercourse was venially sinful unless the married couple explicitly intended to procreate a child. In the early Church there was also a greater emphasis on consecrated virginity or celibacy than on marriage. However, the early Church Fathers often defended marriage in response to particular challenges such as Gnosticism, Manicheism, or Pelagianism, and as a result some Patristic writers, such as Gregory Nazianzen, John Chrysostom, and especially Augustine, anticipated the later development of the sacramental theology of marriage.

St. Augustine's thought dominated the Western Church's theology of marriage for nearly seven hundred years, into the high Middle Ages. During this period there was still a preoccupation with the virginal ideal and as a result, not much attention was paid to articulating a theology of marriage. One of the debates within the medieval period was whether consent or consummation "makes" a marriage. Once it was confirmed that consent is the efficient cause of marriage, marriage tended to be treated as a legal contractual agreement that imposes rights and obligations upon the contractants. This mode of approaching marriage was predominant in the life of the Church into the twentieth century.

In the twelfth and thirteenth centuries, some major developments in the theology of marriage took place as sacramental theology in general was advancing. During that time, marriage was eventually universally accepted as one of the Seven Sacraments conferring grace. However, it took time for theologians to see in the Sacrament of Marriage any more than a remedial grace that provided a cure for concupiscence. Marriage also appeared last in the list of the sacraments because it was seen primarily as dealing with the carnal reality of sexual concupiscence.

In the late thirteenth century St. Thomas Aquinas showed hints of providing a more relational view of marriage in his analysis and synthesis of the views that preceded him. He maintained that marriage is a sacrament in the fullest sense of the word, and he held that the Sacrament of Marriage must give a grace beyond that of providing a remedy for concupiscence because natural marriage helps to provide this remedy. St. Thomas stated that the grace of the Sacrament of Marriage aids couples' growth in sanctity, making even the marital act holy. Consistent with tradition that preceded him, Thomas did maintain that sexual intercourse involves venial sin unless procreation is explicitly sought or unless one is rendering the conjugal debt. However, he clarified that couples can engage in sexual intercourse according to reason even though sexual pleasure cannot be controlled by reason.

The next major teachings of the Church on marriage came at the Council of Trent in response to the desacralizing and subjectivizing tendencies of the Protestant Reformers. Trent reaffirmed marriage as a sacrament. In the process of stressing the sacred and public nature of marriage, the council outlined the main Catholic teachings on marriage and curbed the abuses of clandestine marriages. Although there were hints of a broader, more relational treatment of marriage at the Council of Trent, especially in *The Roman Catechism*, Trent also focused on marriage as a contract that imposed mutual rights and obligations, thus heightening the juridical treatment of marriage. Except for a few isolated developments in the theology of marriage, it was the Tridentine doctrine on marriage that dominated the presentation of marriage in the Church until the mid-twentieth century.

The modern period saw the Catholic Church confronting the rise of secular states and their increasing claims to have the right to regulate marriage as a contract apart from the sacrament. In response to these claims, the Church reasserted the religious nature of Christian marriages and her right to oversee them because of the inseparability of the contract and the sacrament. As a result of this ongoing conflict the focus on marriage as a contract and the attendant juridical language continued.

In the sixteenth century Cardinal Bellarmine maintained that marriage is a sacrament of continual grace, and in the late nineteenth century Matthias Scheeben developed the sacramental and mystical nature of marriage, stressing the ecclesial context of Christian marriage. It was the 1930 encyclical *Casti Connubii* issued by Pius XI that represented the most important Church teaching on marriage since the Council of Trent. In this encyclical Pius stressed that the chief purpose of marriage is the blending and mutual interchange of life as a whole, giving a central place to love in his teaching on marriage. Following the lead of Pius XI, other Catholic thinkers, notably Dietrich von Hildebrand, developed a more personalist view of marriage elaborating on the role of conjugal love in the life of spouses. In the mid-twentieth century Pius XII removed suspicion attached to sexual pleasure, clarifying that married couples do nothing wrong in seeking this pleasure as long as they do so with respect to the ends of marriage.

Surveying the contours of the development of the theology of marriage, John Haas has noted:

> Other ages grappled with what it meant for marriage to be a sacrament, what actually brought it into being, consent or consummation, the relationship between the contract and the sacrament, who were the proper ministers of the sacrament, what were property rights within marriage, and so forth. It was left to the twentieth century, however, to grapple with the most fundamental question of what marriage itself is. [17]

---

17. John Haas, "The Contemporary World," 337.

The Second Vatican Council began to grapple with this funda-mental question in its treatment of marriage. The Council Fathers departed from a more juridical presentation of marriage in their description of marriage as an "intimate partnership of life and love" (GS, 48). Instead of focusing on marriage as a "contract" with atten-dant rights and obligations, the Second Vatican Council used the biblical language of "covenant" to describe marriage, and it treated consent as a mutual exchange of persons. The Council presented a broader and deeper vision of marriage including a treatment of married love, the understanding of marriage as a vocation to holiness, and a loftier vision of the grace offered in the Sacrament of Marriage. Subsequent to the Second Vatican Council, Pope Paul VI reaffirmed the Catholic Church's teaching on contraception in personalist terms, stressing both the meaning of conjugal love and marriage as a personal communion.

The writings of Pope John Paul II represented the most signifi-cant development in the theology of marriage since St. Augustine. No other pope has written as much, in such beautiful and positive language, on the topic of marriage. John Paul clarified that the theology of marriage is not a peripheral issue to theology, showing that an under-standing of marriage is central to an understanding of the human person and the human person's relationship to God. He developed an understanding of conjugal love in terms of the language of "gift." He developed an understanding of marriage as the "primordial sacrament," which certainly provides a corrective to the medieval view of marriage as the least of the sacraments. Calling marriage the "primordial sacrament" does not compromise the Catholic understanding of the Eucharist as the sacrament of sacraments, which is "the source and summit of the Christian life" (LG, 11) and the "sum and summary of our faith" (CCC, 1327). Instead, by calling marriage the "primordial sacrament," John Paul meant that marriage is the first sign of God's love, and that marriage is the prototype and foundation for the whole sacramental order, as all of the sacraments flow from Christ's nuptial gift of self to the Church. John Paul also explained how marriage relates to the "great mystery" of God's desire to save humanity that is made manifest in Christ. Additionally, John Paul contributed to an understanding of the threefold reality of the sacrament of marriage by explaining the sign (*sacramentum tantum*) of the sacrament in terms of the "language of the body"; stressing that the abiding reality (*res et sacramentum*) of the sacrament is not a juridical abstraction; and by making it clear that the grace (*res tantum*) of the sacrament enables spouses to love as Christ loves in all aspects of their marriage. John Paul's insights clearly impacted the 1983 *Code of Canon Law* as well as the beautiful synthesis of the *Catechism of the Catholic Church*. Regarding the scope of the development of the theology of marriage in the history of the Church up to the twentieth century, Angelo Scola has stated:

> From the patristic age to the beginning of the twentieth century, Christian reflection on marriage and the family was focused on decisive questions proper to a theology of marriage. Anthropological reflection, such as that on man as person, was in fact a presupposition taken for granted . . . while a specific consideration of the family remained substantially marginalized, limited to the theme of children as one of the *ends* and *goods* of marriage.[18]

It was John Paul II who helped to accomplish a much needed integration and who helped us to see more clearly the mystery of marriage and how marriage relates to the mystery of God's plan of salvation accomplished in Christ.

---

18. Angelo Scola, *The Nuptial Mystery*, 197.

Part V

The Sacrament of Marriage: A Systematic Presentation

We have covered the essential nature of marriage in part 2, marriage in the Bible in part 3, and the history of the development of the theology of marriage in part 4. Drawing on these previous chapters, the next two chapters present a systematic theology of the Sacrament of Marriage, continuing to integrate the thought of John Paul II throughout. We will begin by providing an overview of some foundational principles of sacramental theology and by covering some of the fundamental elements of a sacramental theology of marriage. Then, we will discuss seeing the mystery of the Sacrament of Marriage in its fullness.

Chapter 15

The Systematic Foundation of the Sacrament of Marriage

THE SACRAMENTAL PRINCIPLE

Let us recall the sacramental principle of reality discussed in the first chapter of this book. According to this principle, visible material reality is a sign that points to the invisible, immaterial God who created it. Thus the whole universe is a sign of something beyond itself because God intends to speak to us through created realities (CCC, 1147). The Catholic Church goes even further to maintain that material realities can be not only signs of the spiritual and the divine, but that God uses these realities in the Seven Sacraments as vehicles of his grace to make present the spiritual realities that they signify (CCC, 1131). If some people think it strange that material objects and actions can be vehicles for us to receive grace, then they are forgetting who we are. Remember from chapter 3 that Christian anthropology holds that the human person is an intimate union of body and soul. We are not souls trapped in bodies. We are embodied spirits who are destined to exist in God's presence for all eternity, body and soul. As we are embodied spirits, we need physical creation in order to be human. To attempt to offer worship to God in a way that ignores physical reality is an attempt to offer worship that is quite literally inhuman. God knows our need to perceive and express "spiritual realities through physical signs and symbols" (CCC, 1146), and he communicates his grace to us in a manner that is appropriate to our embodied existence through the sacraments. Thus the sacraments are connected to our bodily condition, and the union of the material and the spiritual in the sacraments is mysterious in the same way that the union of our bodies and souls is mysterious—but God made both of these realities and he can conjoin them in perfect harmony.

The mystery of the Incarnation, the central sacrament in all of history, shows undeniably that God uses matter to convey his gifts to us. The event of God becoming man radically demonstrates the value of material creation in revealing and communicating the divine. "Christ's humanity may be said to be *the* sacrament of the God who saves us."[1] The divine and human mystery of the God-man Jesus Christ is continued in the visible and spiritual reality of the Church (LG, 1) and in the Seven Sacraments that Christ himself gives to the Catholic Church.[2] Through the sacraments, which are "ecclesial acts of worship" of Christ's Mystical Body,[3] Jesus makes it possible for us to offer worship that is truly human.[4]

THE DISTINCTIVENESS OF THE SEVEN SACRAMENTS

The Seven Sacraments of the Catholic Church were given to her by Christ as signs that really effect, or bring into being, what they signify (CCC, 1127). They are, in short, visible signs instituted by Christ that give grace. However, the sacraments are not magic. The goal of magic is to manipulate spiritual powers through the use of material objects or actions. The sacraments are the opposite of magic since they are visible signs and actions given by Christ to convey his love. The Church has no power to change or manipulate the sacramental signs that Christ

---

1. Colman O'Neill, *Meeting Christ in the Sacraments*, rev. ed. (New York: Alba House, 1991), 77 (emphasis added). O'Neill's book is a wonderful treatment of sacramental theology from a Thomistic perspective. For further comments on Christ's humanity as *the* sacrament, see Edward Schillebeeckx, *Christ the Sacrament of the Encounter with God* (New York: Sheed and Ward, 1963), especially pp. 13–20. I have already cited Fr. Schillebeeckx's two-volume biblical and historical work on marriage, noting a problem with his presentation of natural marriage as a secular instead of a created reality. His book *Christ the Sacrament of the Encounter with God* is generally considered to be one of the most important books written on the sacraments in the twentieth century. Although Fr. Schillebeeckx's writings on Christology and ecclesiology were judged to be problematic by the Catholic Church beginning in the late 1970s, *Christ the Sacrament of the Encounter with God* evidences none of Schillebeeck's later writings.

2. For further comments on the Church as sacrament of Christ, see Colman O'Neill, *Meeting Christ*, 77–90, and Edward Schillebeeckx, *Christ the Sacrament*, 47–89.

3. Edward Schillebeeckx, *Christ the Sacrament*, 66.

4. For further comments on the sacraments as necessary for us to offer truly human worship, see Colman O'Neill, *Meeting Christ*, 36–38, and Edward Schillebeeckx, *Christ the Sacrament*, 40–45.

gave to her, and the Church cannot manipulate God with these signs. In the signs of the sacraments, "Christ himself is at work" (CCC, 1127).

Each of the sacraments coincides with a specific point of development in faith, and "each sacrament confers its power to justify or its power to redeem in view of the particular human need Christ intends it to meet."[5] This means that one sacrament cannot be substituted for another because they each offer a particular gift of God's love (CCC, 2003). While each sacrament bestows or increases the abiding presence of God's love in the soul, a grace we call "sanctifying" grace, each sacrament also provides specific inner movements of God's love that assist us in accomplishing the purpose of each of the sacraments, graces we call "actual" graces (CCC, 2000). All of the sacraments give sanctifying grace. Baptism initiates the reception of this grace. Confession restores sanctifying grace when it is lost, or increases it if the sins confessed are not mortal. All of the other sacraments increase sanctifying grace in the soul. The particular grace that each of the sacraments provides is closely associated with the sign of the sacrament (e.g., the washing of Baptism signifies the cleansing of sin, both original and personal). Thus the "vehicle" through which the grace is received shows its effects and how "Christ becomes actively present in each of the seven sacraments."[6]

The sacraments can be classified as: Sacraments of Initiation, which include Baptism, Confirmation, and Eucharist; Sacraments of Healing, which include Confession and Anointing of the Sick; and Sacraments at the Service of Communion, which include Holy Orders and Marriage. While the Sacraments of Initiation "ground the common vocation of Christ's disciples" (CCC, 1533), and the Sacraments of Healing provide both spiritual and sometimes physical healing (CCC, 1421), the Sacraments at the Service of Communion "are directed towards the salvation of others" (CCC, 1534). Orders and Marriage contribute to the personal salvation of the recipient, but through service to others (CCC, 1534). Orders "is not so much for the benefit of the ordained man himself as for that of the wider Church."[7] Likewise, the Sacrament of Marriage provides for the personal

---

5. Paul Gondreau, "The Redemption and Divinization of Human Sexuality through the Sacrament of Marriage: A Thomistic Approach," *Nova et Vetera*, English ed., 10.2 (2012): 398.

6. Edward Schillebeeckx, *Christ the Sacrament*, 79.

7. Aidan Nichols, *Holy Order: Apostolic Priesthood from the New Testament to the Second Vatican Council*, Oscott 5 (Dublin: Veritas Publications, 1990), 76.

salvation of each of the spouses only to the extent that they serve each other's growth in holiness and to the extent that they serve the wider Church, especially by being willing to "accept children lovingly from God / and to bring them up / according to the law of Christ and his Church" (OCM, 60). Both Holy Orders and Marriage confer a particular consecration within the one consecration to Christ (CCC, 1535) for service to the Church.

Although the sacraments guarantee grace that flows from Christ's Passion, we receive this grace according to our dispositions (CCC, 1128). This is another truth which shows that the sacraments are not magic. God respects the integrity of his creation and his grace will never compromise our nature. This means that if a person does not want the grace of the sacrament and is positively opposed to it, there is no effect of grace at all on that individual.[8] It also means that if a person receives a sacrament in the state of unrepentant mortal sin, which is a serious sin that casts out and refuses God's love (CCC, 1855), the grace of the sacrament will not be effective for that person, at least not at that time. God will not impose his love, his grace, on someone who does not want it. In addition, because each of the sacraments is truly a personal encounter with Christ, none of the sacraments offers a one-size-fits-all grace. Even within the context of the particular offering of his love that is specific to each of the sacraments, Jesus meets each individual and his or her needs in all of his or her particularity.[9] All of these points show that the grace that is received in each sacrament differs not only according to the particular mode through which it is received, but also according to the disposition of the one who receives it.

MARRIAGE AS THE PRIMORDIAL SACRAMENT

While the Eucharist is the "Sacrament of sacraments" (CCC, 1211) in the life of the Catholic Church, marriage holds a fundamental place

---

8. In the case of an adult who is capable of preparing to receive a sacrament, the sacrament will not be effectual without the willingness of the recipient to receive it. However, for the Sacraments of Baptism and the Anointing of the Sick, there need not be a prerequisite willingness to receive the sacrament because the recipients may not be capable of performing such human preparation. This highlights the gratuity and initiative of Christ's invitation to a life of love with him.

9. Edward Schillebeeckx, *Christ the Sacrament*, 80–81.

in the whole sacramental order, uniting the orders of creation and redemption. We have already discussed marriage as the "primordial sacrament" in earlier chapters. We have seen that from the very beginning God instituted marriage in the created order to be a sign or "primordial sacrament" of his love. We have seen that in the beginning, God made everything good, and He fashioned the human person as the centerpiece of that creation. God made the human person in his image, male and female, and called man and woman in their masculinity and femininity to form a communion of persons that was to be a reflection of the divine communion of Persons (TOB 9:3; 19:4; MD, 7). God offered his love to humanity, accepting man with his definitive "yes" of covenantal love.[10] We then had to freely utter our "yes" in return. It is the reciprocal giving and receiving of husband and wife, and the mutual "yes" that they exchange which from the beginning was intended to be a sign of God's steadfast love for humanity, a sign of his desire to draw humanity into his own Trinitarian life of love (see TOB 95b:4). Thus John Paul II stated, "This relationship [of marriage] is a revelation and a realization in time of the mystery of salvation, of the election of love 'hidden' from eternity in God" (TOB 90:1).

The history of the Old Testament showed God's people often failing to respond to God's love, and it showed human married couples often failing to reflect the covenantal love between God and his people. However, even when the "primordial sacrament" of marriage experienced "dis-order" and lost its efficacy after the Fall, it still remained a sign of the great mystery of God's love for man (TOB 97:1). This foreshadowed *the* marriage between Christ and the Church which would make this love fully manifest in the sacrament of redemption (TOB 97:2). Thus one of the nuptial blessings in the rite of marriage states:

> O God, who consecrated the bond of Marriage
> by so great a mystery
> that in the wedding covenant you foreshadowed
> the Sacrament of Christ and his Church.
> (RM, "Nuptial Blessing A")

Moving from the first or prime-order, to dis-order, marriage was re-ordered when it found its ultimate expression in Christ's spousal

---

10. Walter Kasper, *Theology of Christian Marriage* (New York: Seabury Press, 1980), 34.

love for his bride, the Church. The Second Person of the Blessed
Trinity became incarnate as a man and uttered the perfect "yes" to
God the Father, forging the New Covenant. He also gave himself to
humanity through a spousal gift of self, forging *the* marriage and *the*
greatest sign of God's "yes" to and love for man. Thus another nuptial
blessing in the rite of marriage states:

> O God, who, to reveal the great design you formed in your love,
> willed that the love of spouses for each other
> should foreshadow the covenant you graciously made with
>   your people,
> so that, by fulfillment of the sacramental sign,
> the mystical marriage of Christ with his Church
> might become manifest
> in the union of husband and wife among your faithful;
> (RM, "Nuptial Blessing B")

To call marriage the "primordial sacrament" also means that
marriage provides the basic model of the whole plan of salvation
(TOB 98:2). It is according to this model of a nuptial gift of self that
Christ creates the Church as his bride and offered her the grace of
redemption. Thus *"the sacramentality of the Church remains in a particular
relationship with marriage,* the most ancient sacrament" (TOB 93:7). It
is from the side of Christ, the new Adam, that the Church, the new
Eve, was born. "For it was from the side of Christ as he slept the sleep
of death upon the cross that there came forth 'the wondrous sacrament
of the whole Church'" (SC, 5). Thus marriage serves as *"the foundation
of the whole sacramental order"* (TOB 95b:7) and the "prototype" of all the
sacraments which flow from Christ's act of nuptial giving (TOB 98:2).

THE INSTITUTION OF THE SACRAMENT

Flowing from his nuptial self-oblation Christ established seven ways
for the use of material realities to bring grace to his people. Each
of these Seven Sacraments has foundation in Scripture: Baptism
(Jn 3:5; Mt 28:19), Confirmation (Acts 8:14–17), Eucharist (Mt
26:26–28; Mk 14:22–24; Lk 22:14–20; 1 Cor 11:23–30; 10:16–17;
Jn 6:22–71), Reconciliation and Confession (Jn 20:19–23), Anointing

of the Sick (James 5:13–15), Holy Orders (1 Tim 3:1–3; 4:14–16; 2 Tim 1:6–7; Tit 1:5; Acts 6:1–6; 11:30; 14:23; Rom 15:15–16), and Marriage (Mt 19:3–9; Eph 5:21–33). However, when we say that Christ instituted the sacraments (CCC, 1114, 1210) we do not mean that he established the explicit rites (ceremonies) in all of their particulars.[11] We mean that he willed holiness to be conferred in certain ways with certain signs, determining, either explicitly or implicitly, that these signs should have a particular meaning.[12] Christ took the first step in instituting the sacraments by establishing the Church as his Mystical Body in order to bring people to holiness and to be his continuing presence in the world. Thus, in order to understand the Seven Sacraments of the Catholic Church, it is first necessary to understand the Church as "the sacrament of Christ's action at work in her through the mission of the Holy Spirit" (CCC, 1118). Christ's institution of the Church as the "instrument . . . of communion with God and of the unity of the entire human race" (LG, 1) shows his desire for the Church to provide the precise means by which holiness is conferred. Christ gave the Apostles, as the visible authority figures in the Church, the power to administer holiness in his name to sanctify the People of God, and he delegated authority to the Church to decide many of the particulars of how this power would be exercised and administered (Mt 16:19). However, the Church was led by the Holy Spirit to recognize that there are only seven facets of the Christian life which Christ himself willed to sanctify through words and actions. The Church decided the precise means (rites) by which the holiness of the sacraments would be conferred. However, the Church has no power to alter the "substance" of the sacraments, which consists of whatever Christ willed to be part of the sacramental sign[13] that conveys his intended meaning.

As discussed in chapters 9, 10, and 11, the number of sacraments instituted by Christ was unclear in the early and medieval Church. It took time for the Church to discern the Seven Sacraments

---

11. For a good discussion of what it means to say that Christ instituted the sacraments, see Bernard Leeming, *Principles of Sacramental Theology* (Westminster, MD: Newman Press, 1956), 408–431. Leeming's book has become a standard reference in sacramental theology. See also Edward Schillebeeckx, *Christ the Sacrament*, 118–132.

12. Bernard Leeming, *Principles of Sacramental Theology*, 417–418; Edward Schillebeeckx, *Christ the Sacrament*, 126–127.

13. Pius XII, Apostolic Constitution *Sacramentum Ordinis*, Nov. 30, 1947 (DS, 3857).

(CCC, 1117) from all of the words and works that Christ performed. Part of this discernment meant distinguishing sacraments from other liturgical celebrations like sacramentals. We saw in chapter 11 how the medieval scholastics refined the definition of a sacrament from being just a sign of a sacred reality to one that effects what it signifies and provides sanctification. The more general definition of a sacrament as a sacred sign would include what we now call "sacramentals," which are sacred signs performed with a prayer that do not confer grace, but prepare us to receive and cooperate with grace (CCC, 1667–1670).[14] Almost any proper use of material things can be "directed toward the sanctification of men and the praise of God" (CCC, 1670; SC, 61), as is evidenced by St. Paul's statement, "So, whether you eat or drink, or whatever you do, do all to the glory of God" (1 Cor 10:31). However, once the Church's definition of a sacrament became more precise, many sacred signs that were once considered sacraments came to be understood as sacramentals or non-sacramental liturgical celebrations.

In addition, we discussed in chapter 9 the reasons the Church took time to define marriage as one of the sacraments. A major barrier was overcome to recognizing marriage as a sacrament when the scholastic theologians of the high middle ages determined that Christ did not institute the sacraments by providing a new sign, but that he could elevate an already existing reality to the level of a sacrament. Thus the definition of marriage contained in the *Code of Canon Law* and the *Catechism of the Catholic Church* states:

> The matrimonial covenant, by which a man and a woman establish between themselves a partnership of the whole of life and which is ordered by its nature to the good of the spouses and the procreation and education of offspring, has been raised by Christ the Lord to the dignity of a sacrament between the baptized. (CIC, c. 1055 §1; CCC 1601)

The uniqueness of marriage is that Christ "did not institute a completely new liturgical ceremony or give new significance to an

---

14. Examples of sacramentals include blessings of persons, meals, objects, places, the Sign of the Cross, all of the "smells and bells" of Catholic liturgical life (incense, holy water, bells, etc.), the veneration of relics, pilgrimages, processions, stations of the Cross, rosaries, sacred images (icons, statues, stained glass windows, crucifixes, medals), hymns, church buildings, and a myriad of other devotions (CCC, 1671–1676). In addition, there are some sacramental actions that have been formalized into their own rites, such as exorcisms (CCC, 1673), and there are other liturgical celebrations that are neither sacraments nor sacramental, such as funerals (CCC, 1684).

existing ritual; he adopted a natural human institution as a sacrament of his Church."[15] Marriage is the only sacrament that was present (in matter and form) at the beginning of creation (FC, 68). The Sacrament of "Marriage is one specific incarnational way in which the saving work of Christ enters peoples' lives,"[16] but "because it uses the most natural of human passions and strivings, the sacrament of holy matrimony perhaps best illustrates . . . [how God uses] . . . human realities as instruments for our salvation."[17] The Sacrament of Marriage shows that nothing in human life is too ordinary for God to use to encounter the human person. In fact, the uniqueness of the Sacrament of Marriage is seen when one realizes that it is the entirety of the day-to-day life of the married couple that is sacramental.[18] God comes to meet the married couple where they are, in the thick of the world, and he empowers them to form a communion of persons so that they may enter into communion with him.

As already mentioned, Jesus' words in Matthew 19:3–9 show that he came to restore the original meaning of marriage and married love (TOB 100:1–2). As Christ came to renew and perfect the covenant between God and humanity, he also came to restore marriage as the sign of this covenant,[19] because marriage was meant from the beginning to be a great sign (*sacramentum magnum*, Eph 5:32) of God's covenantal love (TOB 95b:7). However, Christ not only restored marriage to the beginning, but he "*opens* marriage to the salvific action of God" (TOB 100:2) and thereby elevates natural marriage to an efficacious sign and a means of receiving grace. Thus Christ transformed the earthly, created reality of marriage into a mystery of salvation. In this way the Sacrament of Marriage shows the organic unity between creation and redemption. As *Gaudium et Spes* states,

---

15. Colman O'Neill, *Meeting Christ*, 235.

16. Peter J. Elliott, *What God Has Joined: The Sacramentality of Marriage* (New York: Alba House, 1990), xvii. Until it went out of print, Elliott's book was probably the best sacramental theology of marriage available. While I have already cited Elliott's work throughout this book, I will draw particularly on his insights for part 5. While Elliott did reference the general audiences of Pope John Paul II that would later be collected and referred to as the *Theology of the Body*, Elliott did not have the critical edition of the audiences that is now available. He also did not have at his disposal the *Catechism of the Catholic Church* or other magisterial documents pertaining to marriage that have been issued since 1990.

17. Colman O'Neill, *Meeting Christ*, xiv–xv.

18. Ibid., 236.

19. Ibid., 242.

natural "married love is caught up into divine love" (GS, 48). Thus in the Sacrament of Marriage, as in the other sacraments, the human and the divine are truly one, just as they are in the Church and in Christ.[20] In the Sacrament of Marriage, natural marriage is transformed from within so that it is changed from something holy to something holy-making.[21] In this way natural marriage finds its fulfillment in sacramental marriage.[22]

When St. Paul compared the union of a Christian husband and wife to that of Christ and the Church (Eph 5:21–32), bringing them together in the "great sacrament," he made it clear that Christ's marriage to the Church is *the* redeemed marriage. He also clarified that baptized spouses participate in Christ's spousal love that he shares with his bride (TOB 90:3). Thus the spousal union of Christ with the Church, which is the fulfillment of the mystery of salvation, is "the basis of the understanding of marriage in its very essence" and the foundation of the sacramentality of marriage (TOB 90:4). Jesus instituted the Sacrament of Marriage so that the mystery of his spousal relationship to the Church may illuminate and empower married love (TOB 90:2). Through this sacrament Christ offers "special gifts of grace and divine love" to the couple in order that their love for each other might be "restored, perfected, and elevated" (GS, 49).

THE ADMINISTRATION OF THE SACRAMENT

In each of the sacraments, the ministers of the sacraments give themselves to be used by Christ, allowing Christ to act through them with his power. Thus, because the sacraments are "*human actions where God acts,*"[23] the sacraments effect what they signify "by the very fact of the action being performed" (*ex opere operato*) (CCC, 1128). They do not depend on the personal holiness of the minister or even the minister's maturity of faith (*ex opere operantis*). This principle of sacramental causality holds true for the Sacrament of Matrimony as well.

---

20. Peter J. Elliott, *What God Has Joined*, xxii.

21. Dietrich von Hildebrand, *Marriage: The Mystery of Faithful Love* (Manchester, NH: Sophia Institute Press, 1991), 53.

22. Angelo Scola, *The Nuptial Mystery* (Grand Rapids, MI: William B. Eerdmans Publishing Co., 2005), 264.

23. Peter J. Elliott, *What God Has Joined*, xxxi.

The Sacrament of Marriage is administered by the man and the woman getting married[24] who are both baptized (CCC, 1625). Thus *Order of Celebrating Matrimony* states:

> Through a special Sacrament, / he enriches and strengthens / those he has already consecrated by Holy Baptism, / that they may be faithful to each other for ever / and assume all the responsibilities of married life. (OCM, 59)

It is the Baptism of the spouses that "is the criterion for the essential distinction between sacramental and non-sacramental Marriage."[25] This means that any two validly baptized spouses,[26] who exchange valid consent, enter into a sacramental marriage (CIC, c. 1055 § 2), and not just a natural marriage, whether they are baptized in the Catholic Church or in some other ecclesial community. Baptism enables spouses to administer the Sacrament of Marriage to each other because by virtue of their Baptisms, Christian spouses have been re-created in Christ and have been organically inserted into his Mystical Body the Church (CCC, 1265; 1267). Baptism is "being-in-Christ," and it is the necessary condition for the spouse's love to be taken up into Christ's marital bond with the Church and to become an effective sign of this bond. As the spouses have been incorporated into Christ through Baptism, when they contract their Marriage they are placed within the new and eternal spousal covenant between Christ and his Church. Thus in Familiaris Consortio John Paul II stated: "By means of baptism, man and woman are definitively placed

---

24. The *Catechism of the Catholic Church* states: "According to the Latin tradition, the spouses as ministers of Christ's grace mutually confer upon each other the sacrament of Matrimony by expressing their consent before the Church. In the traditions of the Eastern Churches, the priests (bishops or presbyters) are witnesses to the mutual consent given by the spouses, but for validity of the sacrament their blessing is also necessary" (CCC, 1623). In this passage the *Catechism* seems to be pointing to a way that the Eastern and Western views of the minister(s) of the Sacrament of Matrimony can be seen as complementary. According to each view the mutual consent of the spouses is essential, as is the presence of an ordained minister of the Church. Marc Ouellet has called for a deepened understanding of the ordained minister's role in the celebration of the Sacrament of Matrimony, one that would "provide a better framework for the ministeriality of the spouses" (*Divine Likeness: Toward a Trinitarian Anthropology of the Family*, trans. Philip Milligan and Linda M. Cicone [Grand Rapids, MI: William B. Eerdmans Publishing Company], 219).

25. Peter J. Elliott, *What God Has Joined*, xvi.

26. Baptism "is validly conferred only by a washing of true water together with the proper form of words" (CIC, c. 849), "with the right intention" (CIC, c. 861 §2), which means intending to do what the Catholic Church does when it baptizes (CCC, 1256).

within the new and eternal covenant, in the spousal covenant of Christ with the Church. And it is because of this indestructible insertion that the intimate community of conjugal life and love . . . is elevated and assumed into the spousal charity of Christ, sustained and enriched by His redeeming power" (FC, 13).

However, we must remember that as members of Christ's Body through Baptism it is Christ who gives the spouses to each other and empowers them to live out their call. Thus, Jesus is the source of the Sacrament of Marriage, as he is the source of all of the sacraments. All of the sacraments are "*human actions where God acts*,"[27] and in the Sacrament of Marriage it is Jesus who acts in the spouses' consent to confer grace. Thus marriage, like all of the sacraments, takes place *ex opere operato*. Neither the level of personal holiness, nor the level of personal maturity in the faith of the couple constitutes the Sacrament of Marriage because the sacrament occurs *ex opere operato* (FC, 68). John Paul II explained, "It must not be forgotten that these engaged couples, by virtue of their Baptism, are already really sharers in Christ's marriage Covenant with the Church, and that, by their right intention, they have accepted God's plan regarding marriage and therefore at least implicitly consent to what the Church intends to do when she celebrates marriage" (FC, 68). Thus marriage is a sacrament due to the Baptism of the spouses, and the couple's act of getting married bespeaks implicit faith.[28] Yet, as the quote from John Paul II makes clear, for the Sacrament of Marriage to occur the couple must intend to do what the Church does when it celebrates the sacrament. That the minister must intend to do what the Church does for a sacrament to be valid is true of all the sacraments.[29] For Marriage this means that the couple must intend to commit to a permanent union that is faithful and open to children (CIC, 1096 § 1), in accordance with God's plan for marriage (FC, 68). In other words, as was discussed in chapter 4 when we covered the nature of conjugal love, the couple must really desire *marriage*.

I have often explained the necessary intention that is required of Christian couples to administer the Sacrament of Marriage with

---

27. Peter J. Elliott, *What God Has Joined*, xxxi.

28. See ibid., 192–195.

29. For a good, brief discussion of the intention required of the minister for a valid sacrament, see O'Neill, *Meeting Christ*, 102–10, and Schillebeeckx, *Christ the Sacrament*, 100–106.

a simple, and somewhat silly, analogy to a street corner hot dog stand. If I approach a hot dog vendor on the corner of a busy downtown city block to place an order, the vendor assumes that I want a hot dog, because that is the only item he sells. If instead of ordering a hot dog I order a hamburger, the vendor will tell me (hopefully politely) that I am in the wrong place and that he cannot accommodate my order. Similarly, if a baptized couple approaches the Church for marriage, the Church assumes that they desire what the Church understands as marriage.[30] If however, the couple "reject explicitly and formally what the Church intends to do when the marriage of baptized persons is celebrated, the pastor of souls cannot admit them to the celebration of marriage" (FC, 68). In this instance "it is not the Church that is placing an obstacle in the way of the celebration that they are asking for, but themselves" (FC, 68). In essence, the couple has approached the Church and asked for a "hamburger" when she has only "hot dogs."

As two baptized spouses exchange consent to forge a marital covenant, intending to do what the Church does, Christ allows them to participate in his spousal union with the Church. Thus the mutual consent of the spouses is an entrance into Christ's "yes." This is truly good news, because every marriage yearns to express what Christ, who is truly God and truly man, realizes in his Person. In the new and eternal covenant between God and man, Jesus utters his perfect "yes" to the Father on behalf of humanity, and he utters his perfect "yes" to his bride, the Church. Through the Sacrament of Marriage Christ empowers couples to participate in his perfect "yes" to the Father, and to be effective signs of his "yes" to the Church in their relationship with each other. In allowing Christian spouses to participate in his perfect "yes," Christ has added nothing new, in human words or actions, to the created reality of marriage. Instead Christ acts in and through the human words of consent, and by administering this sacrament to each other the spouses become participants in the mystery of salvation as husband and wife.

---

30. Thus the *Code of Canon Law* states: "The internal consent of the mind is presumed to conform to the words or signs used in celebrating the marriage" (CIC, c. 1101 § 1).

Chapter 16

Seeing the Fullness of the "Great Mystery"

THE THREEFOLD REALITY OF THE SACRAMENT

We have already discussed the threefold reality of the sacraments in chapter 11. First, each sacrament has a visible sign (*sacramentum tantum*) composed of words (form) and objects (matter). Through this sign, each sacrament brings into being an abiding reality (*res et sacramentum*) that is a further symbol of the grace that is conferred by the sacrament. This is a reality that is midway between the visible rite and the sacramental grace. It has in common with the visible rite that it is an efficacious sign of grace. Yet, like grace, it is an invisible spiritual reality brought into being and signified by the rite. For Baptism, Confirmation, and Orders this abiding reality brought into being by the sacrament is an indelible "character" or mark imprinted on the soul that builds up the structure of the visible Church (CCC, 1272, 1304, 1582). These characters allow us to participate in Christ's priesthood, in order to offer worship to God by either receiving (Baptism and Confirmation) or dispensing (Ordination) divine gifts pertaining to the worship of God.[1] Finally, each sacrament bestows grace (*res tantum*) through Christ's action in the sacrament.

The Sign of the Sacrament

Through words and objects each sacrament nourishes, strengthens, and expresses faith (CCC, 1123). "The sacraments are perceptible signs (words and actions) accessible to our human nature" (CCC, 1084). For

---

1. ST III, Q. 63, a. 1-3.

the Sacrament of Marriage, the outward sign (*sacramentum tantum*) must signify the relationship of complete mutual self-donation of Christ and the Church. We have already discussed in part 4, dealing with the development of the theology of marriage, that the sign of marriage is the outwardly expressed consent of the couple. The form of the sign is the words of consent ("I take you . . . ") which express the mutual giving and receiving of the spouses' persons.[2] More formally the consent is "an act of the will by which a man and a woman mutually give and accept each other through an irrevocable covenant in order to establish marriage" (CIC, c.1057 § 2). The Sacrament of Marriage is administered by a baptized man and woman through this exchange of mutual consent (TOB 103:2), by which they swear a covenantal oath to each other. Thus it is the exchange of consent that makes the marriage (CCC, 1626; CIC, c. 1057 § 1), and it is the exchange of consent that is the efficacious sign of the Sacrament of Marriage.

It should be noted that because the couple's Baptism has organically incorporated them into the Mystical Body of Christ, their exchange of consent is an ecclesial act. This is why the Sacrament of Marriage is celebrated "in the presence of the Church" (OCM, 59). We pointed out in chapters 4 and 5 that marriage is not a private but a social institution. For a baptized couple, their consent is never a private act just between the two of them, or even between the two of them and God.[3] As members of the Body of Christ their exchange of consent has ramifications for the whole Church. The baptismal character of the Christian spouses and the fact that two members of Christ's Body are united to each other makes their marriage an ecclesial act. Their marital covenant has been inserted into the covenant between Christ and his Church. "This public and ecclesial aspect of marriage means that it is most important for the couple to enter into marriage in the presence and with the active participation of the Christian community gathered together within the framework of the liturgy."[4] As their exchange of consent affects the whole Church, they are required to exchange their consent publicly in the presence of at least two witnesses in addition to a priest or a deacon, who serves as the official representative of the Church (CIC, c. 1108 §1). As the Church's official

---

2. Peter J. Elliott, *What God Has Joined*, 121.

3. Ibid., 133.

4. Walter Kasper, *Theology of Christian Marriage*, 39.

representative, the ordained minister "receives the consent of the spouses in the name of the Church and gives the blessing of the Church" (CCC, 1630). Also, because of the ecclesial nature of consent, a Catholic is required to follow the proper celebration of the sacrament, or liturgical "form," prescribed by the Church (CCC, 1631; CIC, c. 1119).[5] A Catholic marrying another baptized individual is required to get married in a parish church (CIC, c. 1118 §1), unless given permission from the local bishop to celebrate the wedding in another suitable place (CIC, c. 1118 §2). In this way the Church safeguards the validity of the couple's consent to marriage, the dignity of each of the spouses, and the sanctity of marriage. As Matthias Scheeben explained regarding the celebration of sacramental marriage, "In order that its dignity may be safeguarded, it must be administered in a sacred place and with the cooperation of the priesthood of the Church, so that its inner sanctity and relationship to Christ and the Church may be outwardly manifested."[6]

When the Christian couple exchanges covenantal consent, their consent must possess certain hallmarks, as was explained in part 2 in our discussion of the nature of conjugal love and the nature of marriage. First of all, their consent must be given "freely and whole-heartedly" (OCM, 60). There is no such thing as a valid "shot gun" wedding in which one spouse is forced to marry the other. The gift of self that one spouse gives to the other must be a free gift; free from duress, constraint, coercion, or grave external fear (CCC, 1625, 1628; CIC, c. 1103). The couple must also be free of any circumstance that would impede them from getting married according to natural or ecclesiastical law (CCC, 1625; more on this below). Additionally, the consent that the couple exchanges must evidence the commitment to permanently bind themselves to each other, "all the days of my life" (OCM, 62). Marriage is not a relationship of convenience, nor a commitment to live for someone else until someone better comes along. In addition, the couple's consent must be marked by a pledge of fidelity "to love and honor each other" (OCM, 60). There is no such thing as an "open" or a "trial" marriage. Conjugal love by its nature

---

5. The liturgical or ecclesiastical "form" of the celebration of the wedding liturgy is distinct from the "form" or words that are part of the essential outward sign of the sacrament.

6. Matthias Scheeben, *The Mysteries of Christianity*, trans. Cyril Vollert (St. Louis, MO: B. Herder Book Co., 1946), 609.

seeks to exist exclusively for one's spouse. Finally, the consent of the couple must be marked by an openness to "accept children lovingly from God, / and to bring them up / according to the law of Christ and his Church" (OCM, 60). Consenting to become one flesh means consenting to be fruitful and consenting to the mission of procreating and educating children, which is the primary natural end of marriage. Thus when the Christian couple exchanges consent they are expressing an obedience and a surrender to the truth of marriage, choosing everything that Christ offers them in the sacrament.[7] As was noted in chapter 6, the couple's willingness to surrender to the truth of marriage is evidenced in their positive responses to the questions in *The Order of Celebrating Matrimony* (OCM, 60).

If the outwardly expressed consent is the form of the sign of the Sacrament of Marriage, the matter of the sacrament is the content of the consent, or more precisely the mutual self-donation of a man and a woman to each other. This is why St. Thomas stated that the matter of the Sacrament of Marriage is the persons themselves,[8] and the "sensible acts" of marriage.[9] The mutual consent of the spouses has both a juridical or legal meaning and a covenantal or personalist meaning which make up the matter of the sacrament. Under the juridical meaning we can speak of the marital rights of each spouse and the obligations that each accepts (CIC, c. 1135). Under the personalist and covenantal meaning we speak of "mutual surrender" of persons and of hearts. Thus the matter of the Sacrament of Marriage is not just a juridical exchange. The content of the consent exchanged by the couple is fulfilled in the two becoming one flesh—the consummation of their union. Juridically, consent gives the spouses the right to each others' bodies, but in more personal terms consummation completes the union of two persons by fulfilling their total mutual self-donation, thereby sealing their covenant.[10] Consummating the marriage vows constitutes marriage "in its full reality" (TOB 103:2), meaning that the words of consent are fulfilled through conjugal intercourse when the

7. Peter J. Elliott, *What God Has Joined*, 129.

8. ST Suppl., q. 45, a. 5.

9. Ibid., q. 42, a. 1, ad 2.

10. For a discussion of how sexual intercourse seals and makes indissoluble the marital covenant in a way similar to how the gestures and rituals of the liturgy seal and enact the covenant between God and his people, see John S. Grabowski, *Sex and Virtue: An Introduction to Sexual Ethics* (Washington, DC: Catholic University of America Press, 2003), 45–46.

two become one flesh (CCC, 1627). In terms of the signification of marriage before and after consummation, St. Thomas (in agreement with others who preceded him) explained that before consummation, marriage signifies the union of Christ with the soul by grace, a union which can be dissolved by mortal sin. He asserted that after consummation marriage signifies the union of Christ with the Church through the Incarnation, a union which is indissoluble.[11] Thus after consummation, the consent of the couple is indissoluble because they have in fact handed themselves over to each other to become one, body and soul. No human power can dissolve a marriage that is ratified through the outward expression of consent and consummation (CIC, c. 1141).

To say that the matter of the Sacrament of Marriage is the mutual self-donation of a man and a woman to each other means that the body and the complementarity of gender is an integral part of the sign of matrimony.[12] As a man and a woman give and receive in different yet complementary ways their sexuality is an essential aspect of the matter of the sacrament. Since the body is the expression of the person, this "union of husband and wife in love expresses itself also through the body" (TOB 92:6). The husband and wife belong to each other through the body which is part of the unity of conjugal love. John Paul II noted that the words of Eph 5:21–33, in which marriage is linked to the "great sacrament" of Christ and the Church, "are centered on the body, both in its *metaphorical meaning*, on the body of Christ which is the Church, and *in its concrete meaning*, that is, on the human body in its perennial masculinity and femininity, in its perennial destiny for union in marriage" (TOB 87:3). In the text of Ephesians the body itself is presented as a sacrament, a visible sign of an invisible reality. Thus the bodies of the man and woman getting married become efficacious signs of grace and integral parts of the sign of the Sacrament of Marriage.

John Paul II stated that the essential sign of the Sacrament of Marriage, in both its form and matter, is the "'language of the body' reread in truth" (TOB 104:8). The content of the words exchanged in the wedding vows—"I take you, N., to be my [wife / my husband] . . . " (OCM, 62)—is "a sign of the coming to be of marriage" (TOB

---

11. ST Suppl., q. 61, a. 3, ad 2.
12. Peter J. Elliott, *What God Has Joined*, 126.

103:2). The content of these words of covenantal consent presuppose the "spousal meaning" of the body, the body as gift-sign, and the "language of the body" that is "spoken" in sexual intercourse through which the couple becomes a "communion of persons" (TOB 103:5). This language is authored by God, finds verbal expression in the consent of the spouses, and must be "spoken" authentically by the spouses, both verbally and through their bodies, "as the content and principle of their new life in Christ and the Church" (TOB 105:3).

Thus it is "that the sacramental sign of marriage is built" on the foundation of the "language of the body" which "becomes the *language of the liturgy*" (TOB 117:5). By consummating their union the spouses express the covenantal language of their verbally expressed consent through a "language of the body," which is simultaneously a liturgical language of praise and worship, accepting and expressing God's plan for their love as a sign of his covenantal love that finds its ultimate fulfillment in the union of Christ and the Church. To say that the sign of the Sacrament of Marriage is the "language of the body" reread and spoken in truth means that the couple pledges to hand themselves over to each other in the complementarity of their masculinity and femininity according to God's design for marriage. They utter this pledge verbally in the wedding liturgy, and then "speak" it again in their marriage bed. Thus sexual intercourse is meant to be a physical expression of the wedding vows—a mutual giving and receiving of persons that is free, permanent, faithful, and fruitful. The couple must "speak" this language of complete mutual self-donation, this covenantal language,[13] in truth with the entirety of their persons.

In order to validly administer the Sacrament of Marriage to each other, a prospective married couple must be able to "speak" the "language of the body" in truth with the entirety of their persons. If a couple cannot do this they are impeded from getting married. The Church can declare a marriage null and void (hence the language of "annulment"), meaning that the marriage never existed, based on defects of form or matter (CCC, 1629; CIC, c. 1075 §1, 1095–1107).[14]

---

13. John S. Grabowski comments on the "language of the body" as the language of the covenant in *Sex and Virtue*, 46.

14. We have already discussed in chapter 8 the "exception clauses" found in Mt 5:32 and Mt 19:9 as a way to understand annulments. A good discussion of marriage impediment and annulments can be found in Mark Pilon, *Magnum Mysterium: The Sacrament of Matrimony* (Staten Island, NY: Alba House, 2010), 191–226, 249–258.

A defect of matter would involve a couple who is unable to consummate their union because of permanent impotence (CIC, c. 1084 §1). Therefore, a defect of matter would also include two people of the same gender. In chapter 5 we discussed the necessity of being able to enter into a one-flesh union in order to validly contract a marriage. A defect of form can involve any of a number of potential problems with the consent that is exchanged by a couple. First, potential spouses must have the capacity to exchange consent freely and unconditionally, otherwise there is a defect of form. This means that both potential spouses must be mentally and psychologically capable of understanding the commitment of marriage and what it entails (CIC, c. 1095 1°, 2°, 3°). Free consent also implies that one cannot be in serious error regarding the person one is marrying (CIC, c. 1097 §1) and that there can be no deceit or fraud that would have affected a spouse's consent to the union (CIC, c. 1098). In addition, exchanging free consent means that the consent is unconditional, free from some future condition being placed upon the marriage, such as a prenuptial agreement (CIC, c. 1102 §1). Next, for a couple to exchange consent validly, free of defect, they must consent to do what the Church does in the celebration of the sacrament. "If, however, either or both of the parties by a positive act of the will exclude marriage itself, some essential element of marriage, or some essential property of marriage, the party contracts invalidly" (CIC, c. 1101 §2). To validly exchange consent and administer the Sacrament of Marriage, which is an ecclesial act, baptized Catholics must also follow the proper celebration of the sacrament, or liturgical form, as it is specified by the Church (CIC, c. 1108, 1118, 1119).

To exchange consent that is free from defects, spouses must also not have any other impediments to marriage from divine or Church law (CIC, c. 1059). In addition to what we have already discussed, additional impediments would include the following:

- Age—to ensure that couples have reached a minimum level of maturity to understand the relationship to which they are committing themselves Church law specifies that a man must be at least sixteen and a woman fourteen to contract a valid marriage (CIC, c. 1083 §1), although bishops may modify this in accord with the practices of their particular regions (CIC, c. 1072; c. 1083 §2).

- Previous Bond—a preexisting valid marriage is a divine impediment that prevents someone from marrying another person and thus committing adultery (CIC, c. 1085 §1).
- Disparity of Cult—due to a concern for members of the Body of Christ to be able to continue to practice and pass on the faith to their children, Church law prevents a Catholic from marrying an unbaptized person who is thus not a member of the Church (although a dispensation can be sought; CIC, c. 1086 §1).
- Sacred Orders—Church law prevents men who are already ordained deacons, priests, or bishops from getting married (CIC. c. 1087).
- Perpetual Vows of Chastity—Church law prevents those who have taken public vows of chastity in a religious order from marrying (CIC, c. 1088).
- Abduction—Church law prevents someone from kidnapping another for the purpose of marriage (CIC, c. 1089).
- Murder—Church law prevents a person from murdering his or her spouse in order to marry someone new, or from murdering the spouse of someone else in order to marry that person (CIC, c. 1090 §1, §2).
- Consanguinity—natural and Church law prevent couples from marrying when a blood relationship exists between the couple that makes them closer than second cousins (CIC, c. 1091 §1, §2).
- Affinity—Church law prevents marriages that involve in-law relationships in the direct line (e.g., upon the death of one's spouse marrying one's mother-in-law or father-in-law; CIC, c. 1092).
- Public Propriety—Church law prevents a person from seeking to marry a direct relative of someone with whom that person has been cohabiting (CIC, c. 1093).
- Adoption—Church law forbids a person from marrying someone with whom they have a family relationship established by adoption (CIC, c. 1094).

Any of these circumstances would impede, either by divine or Church law, a couple from freely surrendering themselves to each other, thus preventing them from speaking the "language of the body" in truth, which is the essential sign of the Sacrament of Marriage.

The Abiding Reality of the Sacrament

For the Sacrament of Marriage, the marital bond is the signifying and abiding reality (*res et sacramentum*) that is brought into being through the sacramental sign. Thus John Paul II said of the Christian married couple: "The sign they bring into being with the words of the conjugal consent is not merely an immediate and fleeting sign, but a sign that looks toward the future and produces a lasting effect, namely, the conjugal bond, one and indissoluble ('all the days of my life,' that is, until death)" (TOB 105:6). Far from being a "thing" or an abstract juridical reality, the bond should be understood as "a permanent union and communion of two persons."[15] Although no marriage in which the couple acknowledges the existence of God can be dissolved by the spouses' whims,[16] the bond of marriage is strengthened infinitely if both spouses are consecrated to Christ through Baptism.[17] Thus Baptism is the basis for the absolute indissolubility of Christian marriage,[18] and only sacramental marriage in Christ is absolutely indissoluble because the spouses are united *in Christ*.[19] As the *Catechism of the Catholic Church* states, the human communion of marriage "is confirmed, purified, and completed by communion in Jesus Christ, given through the sacrament of Matrimony" (CCC, 1644). The absolute indissolubility of this communion is the reality that is brought into being through the action of Christ in the efficacious sign of the consent of marriage. Once this bond is effected it exists as an ecclesial reality serving "the unity and growth of the whole Church."[20]

Discussing the bond of the Sacrament of Marriage is one way of highlighting the fact that sacramental marriage really does participate in the faithful and permanent love that Christ shares with his Church (CCC, 1647). In fact, as we have already seen, "the sacramentality of Marriage can only be understood in terms of the 'great mystery' of Christ giving himself up for his beloved spouse, the

---

15. Peter J. Elliott, *What God Has Joined*, 153.

16. Dietrich von Hildebrand, *Marriage: The Mystery of Faithful Love* (Manchester, NH: Sophia Institute Press), 56.

17. Ibid., 23.

18. Edward Schillebeeckx, *Marriage: Human Reality and Saving Mystery*, 2 vols., trans. N.D. Smith (New York: Sheed and Ward, 1965), 159.

19. Dietrich von Hildebrand, *Marriage*, 56.

20. Peter J. Elliott, *What God Has Joined*, 151.

Church."[21] The Letter to the Ephesians reveals the greatness of marriage when it compares the union of a husband and a wife to that of Christ and the Church (Eph 5:23–30), and makes it clear that Christian marriage is an effective sign of this permanent, undying love. It is the Holy Spirit, the eternal Person of love breathed forth by the Father and the Son, who in sacramental marriage effects this permanent bond between the married couple.[22] The *Catechism* explains that in the Sacrament of Marriage "the spouses receive the Holy Spirit as the communion of love of Christ and the Church. The Holy Spirit is the seal of their covenant, the ever available source of their love and the strength to renew their fidelity" (CCC, 1624). Thus the Holy Spirit bonds the couple together and gives them a special share in the love of the Trinity as they give and receive each other in the mutual surrender of their persons.[23]

The fact that the bond of Christian marriage is absolutely indissoluble is part of what it means for human love to be "caught up into divine love" (GS, 48). Thus the Sacrament of Marriage is a "concrete, earthly expression and incarnation of God's saving love for each of us."[24] In his conversation with the Pharisees about divorce (Mt 19:3–9) Christ showed that he had come to restore marriage as a sign of God's love (TOB 100:2). In his response to the Pharisees, when he reaffirmed the indissolubility of marriage, Jesus referred to marriage as "the primordial revelation of God's salvific will and action 'at the beginning' in the very mystery of creation" (TOB 100:1). Christ insisted on the indissolubility of marriage and "thereby *opens* marriage to the salvific action of God" (TOB 100:2). Jesus came to give married couples the graces they need to "overcome the consequences of sin and to build the unity of man and woman according to the Creator's eternal plan" (TOB 100:2), so that they may form "a communion of persons, according to the likeness with the union of divine Persons (see *Gaudium et Spes*, 24:3)" (TOB 100:1). As sacramental marriage experiences the grace of redemption, a grace of *"new creation"* (TOB 99:7) flowing

---

21. Ibid., 4.

22. Ibid., 148.

23. Marc Ouellet developed the understanding of how the Holy Spirit seals the couple's love and provides them a share in the love of the Trinity in "Chapter V—The Holy Spirit: Seal of the Conjugal Covenant," in *Divine Likeness*, 79–101.

24. Dietrich von Hildebrand, *Marriage*, xx.

from Christ's indissoluble love for his Church, this means that sacramental marriage too must be indissoluble. Christ's work of redemption "means *taking up all that is created* to express in creation the fullness of justice, equity, and holiness planned for it by God, and to express that fullness above all in man, created male and female 'in the image of God'" (TOB 99:7). Through the Sacrament of Marriage, the primordial sacrament of God's love is restored and spouses are made a perpetual sign of Christ's indissoluble love for the Church until they die (TOB 103:7).

The fact that Jesus Christ makes the bond of Christian marriage absolutely indissoluble realizes the deepest desires of conjugal love. The true lover who wants to be one with his beloved rejoices in the indissoluble nature of sacramental marriage as a fulfillment of conjugal love.[25] It is the fulfillment of a desire for an objective, permanent self-giving, an irrevocable gift of self. Thus, "all human will to marriage is therefore an imperfect realization of the mystery of Christ and his Church";[26] and it is this mystery that enters into and makes absolutely indissoluble the nuptials of Christian husbands and wives. Understanding the perfectly indissoluble bond as a gift that is effected by Christ in the Sacrament of Marriage leads one to understand why divorce is an abomination and a betrayal of this gift. Even though there are situations which dictate that continuing to live together would be "practically impossible" for spouses, separation and living apart does not sever the indissoluble bond of sacramental marriage (CCC, 1649; FC, 83; CIC, c. 1151–1155). Neither does civil divorce break the sacramental bond of marriage (CCC, 1650). Thus members of the Church who have been civilly divorced and remarried find themselves in the situation of committing adultery and cannot receive the Eucharist, which is the ultimate sign of Christ's self-giving love for the Church. These individuals should confess their sin in the Sacrament of Penance and commit themselves to living lives of continence with their civilly married spouse (CCC, 1650; FC, 84).[27] While some may think this impossible, it is not, because with the help of God's grace all things

---

25. Ibid., 59.

26. Walter Kasper, *Theology of Christian Marriage*, 80.

27. See also Pontifical Council for the Family, *The Pastoral Care of the Divorced and Remarried* and *Vademecum for Confessors Concerning Some Aspects of the Morality of Conjugal Life* (Boston: Pauline Books & Media, 1997).

are possible (Mt 19:26). As a friend of mine has expressed, the person whom I marry on my wedding day will change, and I do not know in what way my spouse will change; but regardless of that change, the Lord has bound my spouse to me and me to my spouse "in good times and in bad, / in sickness and in health . . . all the days of my life" (OCM, 62). As spouses are bound to each other their eternal salvation is bound up with each other; their ability to enter into communion with God will be determined by how faithful they were to the marital bond, according to which they promised to love and honor each other, come what may (OCM, 62).

The Grace of the Sacrament

Christ is not an onerous taskmaster. When Jesus came to restore God's original plan for marriage, "he himself gives the strength and grace to live marriage in the new dimension of the Reign of God" (CCC, 1615). Sacramental marriage, therefore, "is an efficacious expression of the saving power of God" (TOB 101:1). The grace (*res tantum*) that Christ offers to spouses through the Holy Spirit in the Sacrament of Marriage is the ongoing participation "in the salvific love of Christ" (TOB 102:2), the nuptial love that he shares with his Church. Thus a solemn blessing at the end of *The Order of Celebrating Matrimony* prays for the couple: "May he, who loved the Church to the end, / unceasingly pour his love into your hearts" (OCM, 250).

I have frequently told couples that we often talk about Christian marriage being a sign of Christ's love for his Church, but we neglect to stress that Christian marriage is an *effective* sign of this love. In other words, in the Sacrament of Marriage, Christ's love for the Church is made present in the love of the human spouses, and they are empowered through the Holy Spirit to love each other with Christ's love (CCC, 1661). In sacramental marriage Christ seeks to empower couples to love each other with a love that is unconditionally accepting of the other, completely dedicated, totally faithful, of untiring service, and uncompromising with regard to living up to marriage's demands.[28] The Second Vatican Council stated, Christ "encounters Christian spouses through the sacrament of marriage" and "abides with them" (GS, 48). In short, through the Sacrament of Marriage Christian

---

28. Dietrich von Hildebrand, *Marriage*, xxi.

spouses are empowered to love each other with a sacrificial love because that is how Christ loved the Church. When a Christian couple looks at a crucifix they should be reminded of the nuptial love that they are called and empowered to offer to each other.

It is the gift of grace offered in sacramental marriage that empowers a couple to love with redemptive love, a love that shares "in the love of the pierced heart of the Bridegroom."[29] The grace of the sacrament assists spouses in rediscovering the freedom of being a gift (TOB 32:6, 43:6, 101:5) so that they can exist as a communion of persons (GS, 12; TOB 9:2), participating in the love of the Trinity.[30] Furthermore, the grace of the Sacrament of Marriage is not just available on the couple's wedding day. The grace that Christ offers to the couple through the Holy Spirit is continually operative while both spouses are alive, helping them to live their married life as a reflection of Christ's love for his Church and making that love present. As John Paul II stated, "The gift of Jesus Christ is not exhausted in the actual celebration of the sacrament of marriage, but rather accompanies the married couple throughout their lives" (FC, 56). This is truly wonderful news!

At the end of chapter 4 we mentioned that when the conjugal love that spouses share is transformed by God's love, *agape*, it becomes conjugal charity, "a spousal form of *agape*,"[31] and thereby "reaches that fullness to which it is interiorly ordained" (FC, 13). In the Sacrament of Marriage "married love is caught up into divine love" (GS, 48), and conjugal love is transformed by *agape* to enable couples to realize the model of Christian married love that is presented in Ephesians 5. "Through the sacrament of matrimony Christ himself is present in the Christian family and transforms the flesh and blood love of the partners into an unconditional self-giving, so that, gradually, their love for each other will lead them close to Christ himself."[32] It is sacramental marriage that assures the couple of this gift of God's grace and that elevates conjugal love to the mysterious communion of love and life,

---

29. Peter J. Elliott, *What God Has Joined*, 42.

30. United States Conference of Catholic Bishops, *Marriage: Love and Life in the Divine Plan* (Washington, DC: 2009), 35.

31. Peter J. Elliott, *What God Has Joined*, 63.

32. Roch Kereszty, *Jesus Christ: Fundamentals of Christology*, 3rd ed., rev. and updated (Staten Island, NY: Alba House, 2002), 84.

in and for Jesus. Sacramental marriage brings together human and divine love that "leads the partners to a free and mutual self-giving, experienced in tenderness and action, . . . permeating their entire lives" (GS, 49).

In the Sacrament of Marriage, Christ transforms the spouses' conjugal love with his love. Transforming their love with his grace, Christ empowers the Christian couple to see each other as images of God, in ways that God sees them, as members of Christ's Mystical Body, and to see Christ in each other.[33] Empowered by grace, Christian conjugal love takes on new depths of purity and unselfishness.[34] This conjugal charity ultimately desires the eternal happiness of the beloved, and Christian spouses realize that the salvation of their beloved concerns them in a particular way.[35] Empowered by Christ's love, Christian spouses become concerned with collaborating in each other's sanctification because they realize their goal is to help each other grow in their union with Jesus.[36] The spiritual fruitfulness of Christian conjugal love provided in the Sacrament of Marriage consists of fostering the beloved's transformation in Christ.[37] In conjugal charity, the more the spouses grow in love for each other, the more they grow in love for Jesus, because he lives in their love.[38] Thus together, in the Sacrament of Marriage, spouses live for Jesus through each other.[39] This means that in sacramental marriage the spouses continually encounter Christ through each other. In truth, only the grace of the Sacrament of Marriage can enable marriage to attain the eternal union with the Bridegroom for which conjugal love longs.[40]

It should be noted that it is possible for a married couple in a state of mortal sin to thwart the ability for Christ to enliven and empower their love with his grace. However, their state of sinfulness does not extinguish the Sacrament of Marriage, nor does it extinguish the grace that Christ offers them. In fact, a couple can even get

---

33. Dietrich von Hildebrand, *Marriage*, 45.
34. Ibid., 46.
35. Ibid.
36. Ibid.
37. Ibid., 48.
38. Ibid., 75.
39. Ibid., 10, 45–46.
40. Ibid., xiii–xiv.

married in a state of mortal sin and administer the Sacrament of Marriage validly to each other, even though the grace of the sacrament will be rendered unfruitful in its effects upon them as individuals. The reason that a couple finding themselves in this situation can still validly administer the sacrament is that by virtue of the indelible character of their Baptism, they are united to each other by Christ *ex opere operato*. Thus, even though one or the other spouse may be in a state of serious sin, an indissoluble bond (*res et sacramentum*) is still forged between them that has a real effect on the life of the Church. Additionally, should the couple repent of their sin and receive Christ's healing in the Sacrament of Penance, the grace of the Sacrament of Marriage will "revive" in them due to the abiding bond that was effected between them by Christ.[41] Thus, even though through sin a couple can at any time in their married life render unfruitful this special share in Jesus' love, this love can be reenlivened throughout the course of the couple's life together. Even if the sacrament is not fruitful for the individual recipients at a given point in time, the sacrament still has an effect on the Church because it "is truly a ritual prayer of Christ and his Church"[42] that expresses her faith and that has indelibly united two members of the Body of Christ. This highlights the fact that marriage is an ecclesial and not a private reality, having an impact for good or ill on the life of the entire Church. Thus, couples should always remember that their marriage is never just about them.

Finally, one may ask for evidence that grace is at work in the marriage of Christians in a way that makes them different from other marriages. A response to this question begins by noting that the Sacrament of Marriage does not immune couples to or inoculate them against the difficulties that all marriages are destined to face in a fallen world. That Christ offers the Christian couple grace to live out their joint life also "does not release married couples from their duty

---

41. In chapter 10, I noted that, according to St. Augustine, the grace of certain sacraments, which are received in an unfit state and thus with no effect on their recipient, can revive and have an effect on the recipient after repentance takes place (see *On Baptism, Against the Donatists*, I.12.18–20). Other sacraments in which the "reviviscence" of grace is possible are Baptism, Confirmation, Holy Orders, and Anointing of the Sick. For further comments on "reviviscence" see Bernard Leeming, *Principles of Sacramental Theology*, 266–267, 278–279, as well as Edward Schillebeeckx, *Christ the Sacrament*, 147–152.

42. Edward Schillebeeckx, *Christ the Sacrament*, 82.

to *work* diligently at their marriages; indeed, it *requires* it!"[43] John Meyendorff noted that "a sacrament is not an imaginary abstraction. It is an experience where man is not involved alone, but where he acts in communion with God. In a sacrament, humanity participates in the higher reality of the Spirit, without, however, ceasing to be fully humanity."[44] This means that far from becoming a different reality, in the Sacrament of Marriage "married life is transformed from within by . . . communion with Christ."[45] John Paul II explained the transformation worked by the Holy Spirit in the hearts of spouses when he stated:

> The love of God . . . molds—in a completely unique way—the love of husband and wife, deepening within it everything of human worth and beauty, everything that bespeaks an exclusive gift of self, a covenant between persons, and an authentic communion according to the model of the Blessed Trinity.[46]

However, in order to achieve this love the couple must open themselves up to and rely upon the grace that Christ makes available to them continuously in their lived sacrament. "Without his help man and woman cannot achieve the union of their lives for which God created them 'in the beginning'" (CCC, 1608). With this help, they will give evidence to the world that Jesus is empowering them to love each other no matter what.

The impact of grace on the life of a married couple is perhaps most evident during times of turmoil. I encountered the most power-ful evidence of the grace that is operative in the Sacrament of Marriage in a couple who had experienced serious marital trouble. This couple reported that they had emotionally and psychologically tortured each other, and each had been unfaithful to the other through extramarital affairs. They were on the verge of divorce when after a long absence they went to Mass together, heard the Gospel reading, and were convinced that they needed to seek forgiveness from God and each other to heal their broken marriage. They sought help from

---

43. Paul Gondreau, "The Redemption and Divinization of Human Sexuality," 406.

44. John Meyendorff, *Marriage: An Orthodox Perspective*, 2nd expanded ed. (Crestwood, NY: St. Vladimir's Seminary Press, 1975), 21.

45. Edward Schillebeeckx, *Marriage*, 168.

46. John Paul II, Apostolic Exhortation *Redemptoris Custos* (Guardian of the Redeemer) (Boston: Pauline Books and Media, 1989), 19.

Retrouvaille (French for "recovery"),[47] a ministry that focuses on helping troubled marriages, and through a long process the couple recovered their marriage. When they tell their story this couple says, in retrospect, that it is a miracle that they remained together through all of their mutually inflicted pain. They are also aware that the one who worked this miracle in them was Jesus. They were weak and had hurt each other severely, but Jesus had bound them together and was constantly offering them the grace they needed to heal their wounds—they just had to accept it. Although the wounds they inflicted on each other will never fully go away, this couple has learned to love each other again by giving and receiving forgiveness. They are a testimony to the grace of the Sacrament of Marriage.

The Threefold Purpose of the Sacrament

The purpose of the sacraments is that they communicate Jesus Christ's saving work to us in a way that is appropriate to our human nature. If we ask how Jesus' saving work becomes ours, the answer is through faith, which is the adherence of the whole person to Christ (CCC, 150), and through the sacraments. This answer includes both faith *and* the sacraments because Christ wants to transmit the grace of salvation to us in a way that is truly human. During his earthly ministry we see Jesus offering the grace of salvation to people by using outward signs. He could have worked his miracles without external signs, but he chose to touch (Mt 8:15; 9:20, 25, 29; 14:36; 20:34; Lk 4:40; 5:13; 7:14; 22:51), call out (Mt 8:26; Mk 1:25; 8:34; Lk 4:35, 39; 7:14; 8:24, 43; 9:42; 13:13; Jn 11:43), spit and stick his fingers in a man's ears (Mk 7:33), and smear mud in another man's eyes (Jn 9:6), in order to offer healing in a truly human way. Likewise, it is through the sacraments that Christ continues to touch us, speak to us, and offer us his grace in a truly human way.

Christ's "humanity united with the person of the Word was the instrument of our salvation" (SC, 5). "The humanity of Christ in all its reality, physical as well as spiritual, has become the instrument through which the grace-giving Spirit is sent into the world."[48]

---

47. For information on the *Retrouvaille* ministry see www.retrouvaille.org.

48. Colman O'Neill, *Meeting Christ*, 24.

Therefore, Jesus' humanity is the direct cause of our sanctification.[49] This means that anything we do that has pertinence for our salvation must be offered to God through the humanity of Christ, by which he is one with us and by which he is our Mediator. Through the sacraments we are able to unite ourselves, body and soul, to the humanity of Christ, by which he is one with us. Uniting our humanity with the humanity of Jesus, we are then able to offer ourselves back to the Father in union with him. Christ's humanity has been perfectly conformed to the life of the Trinity,[50] and to share in the life of the Trinity, all of the members of the Mystical Body of Christ must be perfectly conformed to Christ's glorified humanity.[51] "The complete humanity of Christ, glorified body as well as soul, is active in all the sacraments,"[52] and he wants us to unite ourselves to him. By uniting ourselves to Christ's humanity we are also united to his divinity and thereby become partakers in the divine nature (CCC, 1129; 2 Pet 1:4). Thus the sacraments unite us with and conform us to Jesus (CCC, 1129). This means that the sacraments are not impersonal mechanisms by which grace is "'put into us' automatically."[53] Instead, the sacraments are truly personal encounters with the God-man Jesus Christ, in his Mystical Body, the Church, through which he seeks to allow his saving work to become ours.[54] In truth, the sacraments are not "things" to be described but mysterious encounters with the risen Lord in the fullness of his humanity and his divinity.

As we consider the sacraments as encounters with Jesus, it is possible to distinguish three aspects of Christ's overall purpose of communicating his saving love to us through the sacraments. In accomplishing the overarching goal of communicating saving love, the sacraments have the threefold purpose of:

1. remedying sin and sanctifying us;
2. building up the Church as the Mystical Body of Christ; and
3. giving worship to God (CCC, 1123).[55]

---

49. Ibid., 81–82.
50. Ibid., 24–25.
51. Ibid., 83.
52. Ibid., 39.
53. Edward Schillebeeckx, *Christ the Sacrament*, 3, 43–45.
54. See ibid., 92, 133.
55. Also see *Sacrosanctum Concilium*, 59.

The sacraments remedy sin and sanctify us because in the process of communicating his saving work to us and conforming us to himself, Christ ministers to our bodily and fallen condition. In a fallen world, subject to the tendency to sin called concupiscence, we are prone to become inordinately attached to created realities and even worship them in place of God. In the sacraments Christ comes to heal our disordered attachments and provides us instead with a healthy attachment to created realities. By remedying sin in the individual recipient of the sacraments, the sacraments simultaneously build up the Church because each individual believer is a living cell in the Mystical Body of Christ. However, even if the individual recipient should thwart the effect of the grace offered to him in the sacraments, the celebration of the sacraments still serves to build up the Church because they are signs of the Church's faith that impact her life. By providing a remedy for sin and by providing external acts of worship offered by the whole Church, the sacraments also allow us to offer fitting worship to God. By accomplishing this threefold purpose the sacraments have an effect not only on the individual recipient of the sacraments, a grace effect, but also an effect on the Church, an ecclesial effect (CCC, 1134).

The purpose of the Sacrament of Marriage is that it allows spouses to continually encounter the saving work of Christ through each other in their married life. In every aspect of their day-to-day lives Christian spouses minister grace to each other.[56] Although it may often go unnoticed, this grace assists them in existing as mutual gifts for each other, and in coordinating the ends of marriage. The Sacrament of Marriage empowers spouses to bring up children as members of the Body of Christ and it assists them in supporting each other in their journey to salvation (LG, 41; GS, 48). In this way the primary and secondary ends of natural marriage, namely the procreation and education of children and the good of the spouses, are elevated by the grace offered to the spouses in the Sacrament of Marriage. Thus the natural ends of marriage are "supernaturalized" and oriented toward salvation. Therefore, it is proper to say that "the primary end of sacramental marriage is supernatural: it consists in the sanctity of conjugal love called to reproduce and incarnate the spousal love of

---

56. Peter J. Elliott, *What God Has Joined*, xiii.

Christ and the Church (Gen 2:24; Eph 5:21–23)."[57] I have often said
to students that while the natural ends of marriage are the procreation
and education of children and the good of the spouses, the supernatural purpose of marriage is the spouses getting each other to heaven,
which involves placing their children on that same path. To paraphrase
a well-known old television show that was made into a movie, this is
the mission of the sacramentally married couple, should they choose to
accept it. However, their mission is far from impossible, because they
are empowered by Christ who through the Sacrament of Marriage
communicates his saving love to them. To assist them in accomplishing their mission, Jesus offers the sacramentally married couple the
grace to remedy sin, build up the Church, and offer worship to God.

How the Sacrament Remedies Sin and Sanctifies

In chapter 3 we discussed the effects that sin had on the relationship
between man and woman in marriage. When Jesus proclaimed
the indissolubility of marriage and condemned divorce (Mt 19:3–9),
he simultaneously exhorted men and women to participate in the
grace of redemption and experience moral conversion (TOB 100:2).
Thus he presented marriage as a call to holiness. However, "to heal the
wounds of sin, man and woman need the help of the grace of God"
(CCC, 1608). It is sacramental marriage that gives couples a new
capacity, a "supernatural strength" through grace to grow in holiness
in every aspect of their life together.[58] The Sacrament of Marriage
serves as a remedy for sin by providing couples the grace to resist
temptations particular to married life. While God can make his grace
available to couples who are not able to avail themselves of the sacramental order, the Sacrament of Marriage assures couples of the grace
to combat the temptations to "self-absorption, egoism, pursuit of one's
own pleasure" (CCC, 1609), selfishness, and even the temptation to
succumb to sexual concupiscence. "Only sanctifying grace, God's
supernatural assistance, can give husband and wife the power to overcome their selfish tendencies and moral shortcomings."[59] As they rely
upon God's grace there will grow in the spouses' hearts a deepened

---

57. Marc Ouellet, *Divine Likeness*, 93.

58. Alice von Hildebrand, "Introduction," in *Marriage: The Mystery of Faithful Love*, xiii.

59. Paul Gondreau, "The Redemption and Divinization of Human Sexuality," 402.

sense of each other's dignity "in conjugal life together and in every other sphere of reciprocal relations" (TOB 101:1).

We have discussed marriage as a "remedy for concupiscence" (1 Cor 7: 2–3, 9) in our discussion of natural marriage, as well as in the chapters covering the development of the theology of marriage. As has already been noted, the proper way to understand sacramental marriage as a "remedy for concupiscence" is to realize that the Sacrament of Marriage elevates the spouses' sexual union through grace.[60] This means that far from merely providing a sexual outlet, sacramental marriage provides a "remedy for concupiscence" by providing spouses the grace to combat selfish sensuality and to order their sexual desire in service to the threefold good of marriage.[61] Sacramental marriage provides the grace to assist the couple in directing their sexuality toward being a total gift of self that is absolutely permanent, faithful, and fruitful. Receiving the grace to serve the triune good of marriage includes receiving the assistance to coordinate the procreative power of sexual intercourse with self-giving love, so that love and life are never separated (TOB 101:6). It is the Sacrament of Marriage that allows spouses to live a life "according to the Spirit" (Rom 8:4–5; Gal 5:25) so they can "master the concupiscence of the flesh" (TOB 101:4), discover the true freedom of being a gift through the spousal meaning of the body, and form a life-long communion of persons (TOB 101:4–5). The grace of the Sacrament of Marriage assists spouses in speaking the "language of the body" in truth so that their one-flesh union might be a "'sacramental' expression, which corresponds to the communion of persons" (TOB 31:2). Thus in the Sacrament of Marriage, sexual intercourse itself can be a means of growing in grace. This is what it means to say that the Sacrament of Marriage offers a "remedy for concupiscence" (TOB 101:1–4), an integral part of the sanctification that Christ offers to spouses through the sacrament.

How the Sacrament Builds Up the Church

The Sacrament of Marriage serves the purpose of building up the Church by giving the Christian couple the privilege of enfleshing Christ's love for his Church in new members of the Mystical Body,

---

60. Peter J. Elliott, *What God Has Joined*, xxxv.

61. Ibid., 70–71.

thereby perpetuating and expanding the Church and the Kingdom of God. As Matthias Scheeben noted, when two baptized Christians contract marriage they are "not merely two human beings, or even two persons simply endowed with grace, but two consecrated members of Christ's body [who] enter into union for the purpose of dedicating themselves to the extension of this body."[62] Thus the Christian family introduces each of its members not just into the "human family" but also "into the 'family of God,' which is the Church" (FC, 15).

If "the Church is nothing other than 'the family of God'" (CCC, 1655), the Sacrament of Marriage builds up this family by constituting the married couple as a "domestic church." When Christian spouses consent to marriage they also consent to forming a "domestic church."[63] They consent not only to give and receive each other, but also to receive children from God so that their household may become the building block of the greater family of God. This means that every Christian couple, by being open to life-giving love (whether or not they have children), "is a small communion of persons that both draws its sustenance from the larger communion that is the whole Body of Christ, the Church, and also reflects the life of the Church so as to provide a kind of summary of it."[64] To call the Christian home a "domestic church" means that "the family is a living image and historical representation of the mystery of the Church" (FC, 49). Thus "the couple is rightly called a domestic Church, *ecclesia domestica*, because it incarnates the nuptial relationship between Christ and the Church."[65] John Paul II helped to explain what it means to call the family a "living image" of the nuptial relationship between Christ and the Church when he stated:

> The family itself is the great mystery of God. As the "domestic church," it is the *bride of Christ*. The universal Church, and every particular Church in her, is most immediately revealed as the bride of Christ in the "domestic church" and in its experience of love: conjugal love, paternal and

---

62. Matthias Scheeben, *The Mysteries of Christianity*, trans. Cyril Vollert (St. Louis, MO: B. Herder Book Co., 1946), 599.

63. Peter J. Elliott, *What God Has Joined*, 140.

64. United States Conference of Catholic Bishops, *Marriage: Love and Life in the Divine Plan*, 38.

65. Marc Ouellet, *Divine Likeness*, 213.

maternal love, fraternal love, the love of a community of persons and of generations. (LF, 19)

If the family is truly the "living image" of the Church in its experience of love this means that the family is more than just a miniature model of the Church. "The family is not only an image of this relationship [of Christ and the Church] but also its concrete realization, founded on the truth of the sacrament of marriage."[66] As a living image and concrete realization of the Church, marriage and family life must "make an active contribution to the building up of the Church."[67] As John Paul II stated, "The family is placed at the service of building up the Kingdom of God in history by participating in the life and mission of the Church" (FC, 49). Due to the Sacrament of Marriage "the couple's whole being in all its dimensions . . . is to be seen as an ecclesial being."[68] This means that the family is not just a recipient of the pastoral activity of the Church, but it is also an active agent that contributes to accomplishing the Church's mission of bringing the love of Christ to all.

The family participates in the life and mission of the Church by sharing in the threefold office of Christ as prophet, priest, and king (FC, 50). Having been baptized into Christ, Christian spouses share in this threefold office (CCC, 783), and they exercise it in a way unique to their state in life as a married couple both in the context of their home life and in the larger context of the Church and society.

The "domestic church" fulfills its prophetic role as "a believing and evangelizing community" (FC, 50, 51–54), "*by welcoming and announcing the word of God*" (FC, 51). This means that inside the home "parents are, through the witness of their lives, the first heralds of the Gospel for their children" (FC, 39). As "*the first and most important educators* of their own children" (FC, 16), when parents provide a religious education to their children they share in the Church's mission of evangelization (FC, 16) and help the Church to grow. In this way parents serve as prophets when "by word and example" (CCC, 1656), they assist their children to grow in their knowledge of Christ, to grow in Christian virtue, and to discern their own vocations

---

66. Ibid., 213.
67. Walter Kasper, *Theology of Christian Marriage*, 38.
68. Marc Ouellet, *Divine Likeness*, 216.

(CCC, 1656). John Paul II pointed to the "domestic church" as the first agent of evangelization when he stated that "the Christian family, in fact, is the first community called to announce the Gospel to the human person during growth and to bring him or her, through a progressive education and catechesis, to full human and Christian maturity" (FC, 2). Outside the home, the "domestic church" acts as prophet by evangelizing society by word and example.[69] This prophetic witness occurs first and foremost in the "everydayness" of family life.[70] The fidelity, fruitfulness, and indissolubility of sacramental marriage itself is a prophetic sign of Christ's love in the world. Additionally, the family can fulfill its "evangelizing and missionary task" (CCC, 2205) by courageously proclaiming the love of Christ in a myriad of public venues in a myriad of ways. So crucial is this prophetic role of the Christian family that John Paul II said that "the future of evangelization depends in great part on the Church of the home" (FC, 52, 65).[71]

The "domestic church" fulfills its priestly role as "a community in dialogue with God" (FC, 50, 55–63). Inside the home this priestly mission is centered around "the sacraments, through the offering of one's life, and through prayer" (FC, 55). Nourished by the Sacraments of Reconciliation and Eucharist the family is enabled to make of its daily life an acceptable offering of sacrifice to God (FC, 59). Realizing that the strength they need to live out their vocation comes from God and not from themselves, married couples must draw from the strength of these sacraments if they are to love and honor each other all the days of their lives (OCM, 62). Dialoguing with God in prayer allows the family to discover who it is and gives it the power to live out this identity (LF, 4; FC, 59–62). For spouses, part of their priestly offering is that of their one-flesh union in their marriage bed wherein they offer their love-making to God in accord with his design for the marital act. Outside the home, the "domestic church" serves its priestly role by providing everyday examples of prayer and sacrifice as a family. Even praying over a meal in public as a family is a way of exercising the domestic church's priestly role, helping to sanctify the world and give glory to God (1 Cor 10:31).

---

69. Peter J. Elliott, *What God Has Joined*, 226.

70. Ibid., 227–229.

71. For further comment on the central role of the family in evangelization, see Perry J. Cahall, "The Nucleus of the New Evangelization," *Nova et Vetera*, English ed., 11.1 (2013): 39–56.

Both inside and outside of the home, the Christian family is "called to partake of the prayer and sacrifice of Christ" (CCC, 2205).

The "domestic church" fulfills its kingly role as "a community at the service of man" (FC, 50, 63–64). Inside and outside the home this role entails service to life and love.[72] Inside the home spouses serve the good of each other and the good of their children in innumerable ways. Children also provide their own service to the good of the family. Outside the home the family's royal mission is that of service to life and love in society, always upholding and defending the dignity of the human person. Each family should seek to go out of itself and serve the larger community, in any number of ways. In short, the kingly mission of the "domestic church" means that it must be a "sanctuary of life and love,"[73] both inside and outside the walls of the home.

The Holy Spirit dwells in this "domestic church"[74] to enable it to fulfill its roles as prophet, priest, and king, and in so doing the Spirit empowers the family to live as a "communion of persons" that finds its model in the Trinitarian communion of God (LF, 6, 7). Relying upon God's grace, "the 'communion of persons' in the family should become a preparation for the 'communion of saints'" (LF, 14). In this way the family, as a community of life and love (FC, 50), becomes a "*saving* community" (FC, 49), truly building up the Church.

How the Sacrament Enables Spouses to Offer Fitting Worship

The Sacrament of Marriage empowers Christian spouses to offer fitting worship to God in a manner particular to their state as a married couple. The Second Vatican Council taught that through the Sacrament of Marriage, husbands and wives "are fortified and, as it were, consecrated, for the duties and dignity of their state" (GS, 48). Ultimately, the worship that spouses offer is their daily life as a couple. All of their prayers, works, joys, and sufferings as a couple and as a family form the substance of their worship. As the spouses "continually

---

72. Peter J. Elliott, *What God Has Joined*, 226.

73. John Paul II, "Message for the 43rd Italian Catholic Social Week," no. 6, accessed April 18, 2013, www.vatican.va/holy_father/john_paul_ii/speeches/1999/november/documents/hf_jp-ii_spe_16111999_week-cath_en.html.

74. Peter J. Elliott, *What God Has Joined*, 150.

minister Grace to one another in daily life,"[75] the Trinity imparts a special share of his life and love to them, so that they are able to "put into action what he intends their union to signify."[76] This gives them the ability to offer their entire married life back to him in an act of worship. Thus the bishops at Vatican II stated that "spouses are penetrated with the spirit of Christ and their whole life is suffused by faith, hope, and charity; thus they increasingly further their own perfection and their mutual sanctification, and together they render glory to God" (GS, 48). Providing this empowerment, "the same sacrament confers on them the grace and moral obligation of transforming their whole lives into a 'spiritual sacrifice'" (FC, 56). This worship includes the spouses sharing a common life together "'til death do they part," living faithfully as one flesh according to God's design for sexuality, and fulfilling their vocations as parents. The domestic church unites its offering to the public worship of the Church, especially in the Eucharist, and draws strength from this worship to be able to make its own daily sacrifice.

THE SACRAMENT AND THE PASCHAL MYSTERY

The last topic to note is the relationship of the Sacrament of Marriage to Christ's Paschal Mystery: his Passion, Death, Resurrection, and Ascension. The whole "'sacramental economy' . . . is the communication (or 'dispensation') of the fruits of Christ's Paschal mystery" (CCC, 1076). As such, each sacrament has its source in and memorializes the Paschal Mystery of Christ that occurred in the past, unites us to Christ's saving action in the present, and pledges future glory.[77] John Paul II called these three dimensions of the sacraments "memorial, actuation, and prophecy" (FC, 13), and he noted of the Sacrament of Marriage:

> As a memorial, the sacrament gives them [the married couple] the grace and duty of commemorating the great works of God and of bearing witness to them before their children. As actuation, it gives them the grace and duty of putting into practice in the present, towards each other and

---

75. Ibid., xvii.
76. Ibid., 63.
77. ST III, q. 60, a. 3.

their children, the demands of a love which forgives and redeems. As prophecy, it gives them the grace and duty of living and bearing witness to the hope of the future encounter with Christ. (FC, 13)

In each of these three dimensions the Sacrament of Marriage derives its efficacy from Christ's Paschal Mystery. As a memorial, first signified in their exchange of consent (*sacramentum tantum*) marriage "'re-calls' and makes present Christ's espousal of his Church in the Incarnation and his self-immolation for his beloved spouse on the Cross."[78] "As 'actuation,' Marriage consent and consummation establishes the abiding reality, the indissoluble bond [*res et sacramentum*], 'that which God has joined.'"[79] As prophecy, empowered by grace (*res tantum*) marriage testifies to the sanctification that the Holy Spirit works in the couple in this life which leads to eternal life with God.[80]

The introduction to *The Order of Celebrating Matrimony* notes how marriage relates to the Paschal Mystery when it states, "The Savior of the human race offers himself to the Church as Spouse, fulfilling his covenant with her in his Paschal Mystery" (OCM, 6). St. Thomas Aquinas pointed out that the Sacrament of Matrimony has its origin in Christ's Passion not by way of suffering but by way of love.[81] The Passion of Christ is the ultimate nuptial offering of the bridegroom for his bride. As John Paul II noted, "The 'sincere gift' contained in the Sacrifice of the Cross gives definitive prominence to the spousal meaning of God's love" (MD, 26). Thus the Cross of Christ shows us that true nuptial love is willing to bear sacrifice and suffering for the sake of the beloved, aspects of married life we will explore in chapter 18.

Paul Gondreau pointed out that part of the mystery of sacramental marriage is that "the sacrament of matrimony allows man and woman to join themselves, in their very spousal union, not simply to the Person of Christ, but specifically to the Person of Christ *on the Cross*."[82] Thus John Paul II could say that the Christian married couple becomes a "permanent reminder to the Church of what happened on

---

78. Peter J. Elliott, *What God Has Joined*, xix–xx.
79. Ibid., xx.
80. Ibid.
81. ST Suppl, q. 42, a. 1, ad 3.
82. Paul Gondreau, "The Redemption and Divinization of Human Sexuality," 388.

the Cross" (FC, 13). Theodore Mackin noted that because the Sacrament of Marriage has its origins in the Passion of Christ, "the spouses can co-work with him only sacrificially. The sacrament calls to the spouses to enter into the mystery of the cross, into Christ's self-giving death. . . . Their sacrament takes all the spouses' suffering into Christ's suffering."[83] Thus, when they get married, Christian spouses "enter in a new way into the passion of Christ"[84] *with each other*. It can be no other way, since in the love he offers to his spouse, Christ shows us that the measure of true love is sacrifice. Yet this sacrifice allows us to rise to new life, to experience joy even amidst suffering, and to abide in love for all eternity.

The "Great Mystery"

One of the prefaces in the rite of marriage prays:

> In the union of husband and wife
> you give a sign of Christ's loving gift of grace,
> so that the Sacrament we celebrate
> might draw us back more deeply
> into the wondrous design of your love. (RM, "Preface B")

Thus it is through this sign, which is effective of grace, that Jesus Christ elevated marriage to be "the visible embodiment of his love for the Church."[85] The Sacrament of Marriage "is a 'great mystery' [precisely] because it expresses *the spousal love of Christ for his Church*" (LF, 19). Marriage "is holy because it both symbolizes and makes present in the world the life-giving, love-giving, grace-giving, union of Christ with his Church."[86] The Sacrament of Marriage not only has the effect of uniting the Christian couple's love to the "great mystery" of Christ's love for the Church, but it also has the effect of making Christ's love present to the whole Church, a living embodiment of the nuptials of the Bridegroom and his Bride. Thus Marriage,

---

83. Theodore Mackin, *The Marital Sacrament*, Marriage in the Catholic Church (New York: Paulist Press, 1989), 605–606.

84. Colman O'Neill, *Meeting Christ*, 250.

85. United States Conference of Catholic Bishops, *Marriage: Love and Life in the Divine Plan* (Washington, DC: 2009), 30.

86. William E. May, *Theology of the Body in Context: Genesis and Growth* (Boston: Pauline Books & Media, 2010), 163.

like all of the sacraments, is intended not just for its recipients but for the whole Church. In the Sacrament of Marriage, Christian spouses are incorporated into the nuptials of Christ and the Church, and are given both the dignity and the incredible task of being living signs of the "great mystery" of God's saving love. Part 6 of this book will discuss how Christian married couples can view their daily life as united to Christ and live out this dignified task, by relying upon the grace of the Sacrament of Matrimony.

Part VI

Living the Mystery of Marriage

This final part of this book presents key aspects of a spirituality of marriage, an overview of sexual morality with an emphasis on responsible parenthood, and an explanation of the complementary relationship between the vocation of marriage and the vocation of consecrated celibacy. All of the chapters in part 6 are grounded in the sacramental reality of marriage, and together they focus on articulating how Christian spouses can live the mystery into which they enter when they exchange their consent to become a living sign of Christ's redemptive love as husband and wife.

Chapter 17

Approaching Married Spirituality

INTRODUCTION

The spirituality of married and family life remained underdeveloped for centuries while attention was given to the spirituality of consecrated virgins and celibates.[1] Oftentimes, because consecrated celibacy is a higher calling than marriage, the spiritual growth of married couples was addressed simply by discouraging sin or by encouraging them to adopt a variant of monastic spirituality.[2] With the Second Vatican Council's universal call to holiness (LG, 40–41) and St. John Paul II's insistence that "in God's plan, all husbands and wives are called in marriage to holiness" (FC, 34), married spirituality has received renewed and much needed attention in the life of the Church.

There are now scores of books available that deal with living one's Christian faith in the vocation of marriage. As a spirituality of marriage is still under development in the life of the Church, it would be presumptuous to attempt to present a definitive or comprehensive understanding of married spirituality. Instead, what follows is an attempt to identify some of the foundational and key elements of married spirituality that have been elucidated in the postconciliar era, focusing especially on elements of married spirituality that might be overlooked.

---

1. Marc Ouellet, *Divine Likeness: Toward a Trinitarian Anthropology of the Family*, trans. Philip Milligan and Linda M. Cicone (Grand Rapids, MI: William B. Eerdmans Publishing Company, 2006), 99.

2. John S. Grabowski, *Sex and Virtue: An Introduction to Sexual Ethics* (Washington, DC: Catholic University of America Press, 2003), 65–66.

Before proceeding, I would like to briefly discuss the meaning of "spirituality." For many this can be a difficult or elusive word to define and understand. Often in a discussion of spirituality the focus is placed on prayer and other spiritual practices. However, these spiritual practices are often not integrally connected to other aspects of Christian existence, such as the Christian moral life or the ecclesial context within which one lives out one's call to discipleship. This is unfortunate as Scripture does not support a dichotomy between spirituality and morality, or a dichotomy between a life of personal prayer and existence in the larger community of the Church. Instead of a personal prayer life disconnected from other aspects of existence, *authentic Christian spirituality is the all-encompassing effort to conform one's life more perfectly to the Person of Jesus Christ, under the guidance and influence of the Holy Spirit in the context of the ecclesial community.* With this holistic understanding of spirituality in mind, this chapter and the next chapter will outline an approach to married life in which Christian spouses attempt to allow themselves to be conformed to the Person of Christ, in the context of the ecclesial community, by relying upon the grace that the Holy Spirit offers them in the Sacrament of Marriage. Thus what follows is an identification of key aspects of an approach to the mystery of married life that will enable spouses to see and live their daily life in the light of Jesus Christ, growing in intimacy with him and each other.

MARRIAGE AS A VOCATION TO HOLINESS

To say that marriage is a vocation (from the Latin *vocare* meaning "to call") means that it is a call that God issues to embrace a specific way of life. John Paul II (Karol Wojtyla) explained that to talk about "'vocation' indicates that there exists a proper direction of every person's development through commitment of his whole life in the service of certain values."[3] Often, within the Catholic Church, when we hear the word "vocation" we think only of those who have received a call from God to embrace the priesthood or the consecrated religious life. The reality of a vocation applies not only to those who embrace priesthood or religious life; marriage is itself a vocation, a way of life that

---

3. Karol Wojtyla, *Love and Responsibility*, trans. Grzegorz Ignatik (Boston: Pauline Books & Media, 2013), 242.

God calls the majority of people in the Church to embrace. In fact, one can argue that if there is a current "vocations crisis" it is in the vocation of marriage.[4] As evidence for this claim, it is interesting to note that the percentage of diocesan priests who leave the priesthood is nowhere near the percentage of Catholic married couples who get divorced.[5] If marriage and consecrated celibacy progress and decline together (which we will discuss in chapter 21), is it any wonder that young men and women are hesitant to consider entering into a committed relationship with a Spouse whom they cannot see, when in many of their homes there has been no evidence that it is possible to live a lifelong covenant with a spouse whom they can see? Furthermore, we are at a time in our societal evolution (or devolution) in which few relationships are seen as permanent and the reality of marriage itself is being challenged. This, by anyone's definition, constitutes a "crisis" and it is a crisis to which the Catholic Church must respond.

It must be remembered that "both marriage and virginity are vocations."[6] By calling a man and a woman to the vocation of marriage, God calls them to establish a lifelong covenant with each other that is ordered toward the procreation and education of children and the good of the spouses (CCC, 1601; CIC, c. 1055 §1). As Christ has elevated marriage to the level of a sacrament (CCC, 1601; CIC, c. 1055 §1), this vocation is also a call to holiness for baptized spouses that brings with it a particular gift of grace (TOB 84:8). Thus Christian marriage is one particular way in which Christ seeks to realize the universal call to holiness that he issues to all the members of his corporate bride, since the love he offers his bride seeks nothing but her

---

4. Cardinal Archbishop Timothy Dolan of New York confirmed this insight in an August 13, 2009, interview in which he called the instability of marriage in the United States of America "the real vocation crisis." He stated, "We have a vocation crisis to life-long, life-giving, loving, faithful marriage. If we take care of that one, we'll have all the priests and nuns we need for the church" ("N.Y. Archbishop Takes Stock of Challenges in American Catholic Church," *Catholic News Agency*, August 13, 2009, accessed June 12, 2013, www.catholicnewsagency.com/news/n.y._archbishop_takes_stock_of_challenges_in_the_american_catholic_church/).

5. An article published in 2011 by *Our Sunday Visitor* reported that 23% of Catholic marriages end in divorce (Emily Stimpson, "The Church's Divorce Dilemma," OSV Weekly, May 22, 2011). By comparison, an article published in 2010 by *Our Sunday Visitor* reported that 0.38% of diocesan priests leave the priesthood each year (Mark Gray, "Facing a Future with Fewer Catholic Priests," OSV Weekly, June 27, 2010). Both articles used data compiled by the Center for Applied Research in the Apostolate (CARA) at Georgetown University; this website can be found at cara.georgetown.edu.

6. Karol Wojtyla, *Love and Responsibility*, 242.

sanctification (TOB 91:6). In the previous chapters we already discussed how spouses are united to each other through Christ in the Sacrament of Marriage, and that spouses continually meet Jesus and are united to him through each other. We also discussed how Christ continually offers spouses grace in their life together, providing a real path to sanctification. By responding positively to the call to marriage, the Christian couple is saying "yes" not only to each other but to the project of sanctification that Christ seeks to work in them through the power of the Holy Spirit. In this way they may be a living sign of Christ's love for his Church.

Christ calls married couples together to form a communion of persons in the Sacrament of Marriage so that they may be made fit to enter the eternal communion of Persons in heaven. However, we must remember that the Sacrament of Marriage is a "sacrament at the service of communion," meaning that the sacrament contributes to the salvation of the individual recipient only through service to others (CCC, 1534). This means that an individual spouse will be made fit for heaven only by: cooperating with the grace of the sacrament to promote the sanctity of his or her mate; raising up children "according to the law of Christ and his Church" (OCM, 60); and building up the Kingdom of God by participating in the Church's mission as a "domestic church." Thus a proper spirituality of marriage recognizes marriage as a vocation from Christ that is lived out in the context of his Mystical Body, the Church.

THE NEED FOR DISCERNMENT

St. John Paul II (Karol Wojtyla) asserted: "What is my vocation? This means: in which direction should the development of my personhood proceed in light of what I have in myself, what I can give of myself, what others—people and God—expect from me?"[7] If marriage is a call from God to embark upon a specific path toward holiness, this implies that a man and a woman who are contemplating marriage should thoughtfully and seriously discern the questions that John Paul II posed, and consider whether they are in fact being called to marriage. However, couples often fail to undertake this discernment because

---

7. Ibid., 243.

they are wrapped up in the emotions of being "in love."[8] In general, when we are discerning a vocation in life, we are using our intellects to reasonably consider the best way we can realize ourselves as self-giving gifts in response to Christ's great commandment to love God and neighbor (Mt 22:36–40; Mk 12:28–31). The direction one's life will take, and the particular state of life one embraces, will be the result of reasonably considering one's strengths and weaknesses, personality, and aptitudes. One must also be attentive to the movements of the Spirit in one's heart during prayer to determine one's most authentic desire. Additionally, discerning a vocation involves being attentive to external indicators, such as advice or confirmations received from other members of the Body of Christ.

There is no direct formula for discerning a vocation, and it is not often a neat and tidy business, but the process of discernment should be exciting. The excitement is due to the fact that by discerning a vocation, a person is entering into a dialog with God about the direction for one's life. We need to remember that the God whom we are engaging in this dialog loves us more than we love ourselves and wants our happiness even more than we want it! He wants to show us which path will make us happiest, and we have nothing to fear by engaging him in conversation about the path our lives should take. We need only do our best in discerning the true desire of our hearts, a desire which is authentic because it coincides with God's desire for us.

When we talk about discerning a vocation to married life, this can hardly be done in the abstract. We all have a natural inclination to make a nuptial gift of self, but as we will discuss in chapter 21, this can be accomplished in marriage or consecrated celibacy. The discernment of marriage really only begins when a relationship with another person emerges. As the relationship grows more intimate, the couple begins to ask, "Do I really want to marry this person?" Or, on a deeper level the question might be, "Would marrying this person be pleasing to God?" or "Would marrying this person promote the eternal salvation of both of us?" If the answers to each of these questions is "yes," the couple also needs to consider, "*Why* do I want to marry this person? *Why* do I think marrying this person would be pleasing to God?" and

---

8. A friend of mine who is a canon lawyer has often said that many couples, being swept away by the emotions of being "in love," are rendered blind, deaf, and dumb to the huge significance of the decision they are making when they commit to marriage.

"*Why* do I think marrying this person would promote our eternal salvation?" This type of reasonable discernment is necessary to help ensure that a person does not make a decision to enter into a lifelong commitment based primarily on emotion.

Dietrich von Hildebrand provided some helpful insights into what discerning marriage entails. First, he aptly noted that any big decision normally involves big risks, and that because of this fact a person should weigh heavily these risks before making such a decision. Obviously, marriage is a big decision with big risks and therefore "requires profound self-examination" and discernment.[9] As part of this self-examination a person should consider his or her motives for wanting to get married. As marriage is the most intimate personal union between two human beings, any utilitarian motive that is "not concerned with the other person as such"[10] is an inadmissible rationale for getting married. Examining oneself for the presence of such inappropriate motives would involve asking questions such as:

- Do I desire the other person as a mere object of sexual attraction and sensual pleasure?
- Do I desire the other as a means to achieve wealth, or power, or fame?
- Do I desire the other as a means to get away from home?
- Do I desire the support of the other person's family?
- Do I desire to be with the other person based on a fear of being alone or a fear that "No one else will want me?"
- Do I desire to treat the other person as a "project" to "fix" because no one better has come along?
- Do I desire to dominate the other person (or be dominated), possess the other person (or be possessed), or make the other person dependent (or be dependent)?
- Do I desire the other person primarily as a means to make me happy, expecting that he or she has the responsibility to make me happy?

Affirmative answers to any of the previous questions betray a motive that fails to treat the prospective spouse as an end in him or herself, but instead treats the person as a means to an end.

Once a person has examined himself or herself and has determined that none of the above unreasonable motives serve as the basis

---

9. Dietrich von Hildebrand, *Marriage: The Mystery of Faithful Love* (Manchester, NH: Sophia Institute Press, 1991), 63.

10. Ibid., 66.

for contemplating marriage to a prospective spouse, a further aspect of discernment is necessary. Dietrich von Hildebrand pointed out, as was noted in chapter 4, that the one right motive for entering into marriage is to discern whether the desire to share true conjugal love with each other really and truly exists.[11] A person must decide whether he or she has the desire to make a complete gift of self to the other in a lifelong covenant that is absolutely faithful and open to children, seeking the good of the other beyond his or her own good. In other words, the optimal response to the question, "Why do you want to get married to this person?" would be, "Because in this other person I have found a good to whom I want to give myself completely. I want to exist for this other person, and for this person alone. I want to spend the rest of my life serving this person's good, seeking his/her eternal salvation. And, God willing, I want our love to be incarnated in another human being." Such a response would evidence the existence of a desire to share true conjugal love. Even though few couples would ever articulate their desire to marry each other in exactly this manner, a couple who truly desires to share conjugal love with each other desires what is encapsulated in this response. Everyone who is called to marriage realizes that by embracing this vocation there is the opportunity to experience some type of personal fulfillment. However, this fulfillment comes not just from receiving from one's beloved but from giving to one's beloved, which is of the essence of conjugal love (see HV, 9). When discerning marriage, there should be a deep and profound appreciation for the mystery of the other person and a desire to put oneself at the service of this mystery.

Von Hildebrand rightly noted that discerning the willingness to share conjugal love with another person ultimately depends on "the qualities of the other's personality."[12] This highlights the fact that discerning marriage is not done in the abstract, but with reference to a particular person. Discerning the desire to share conjugal love with another includes asking questions such as:

- Is *this* person who he/she seems to be? Is *this* person loyal, faithful, and reliable?

---

11. Ibid., 67–69.
12. Ibid., 64.

- Do I share with *this* person a deep mutual respect for each other and each other's gifts?
- Do I share common interests with *this* person that are deep and profound?
- Do I want to make a free gift of myself in service to *this* person's good?
- Am I willing to sacrifice for *this* person?
- Will *this* person make a good parent?
- Can I see myself spending the rest of my life with *this* person?
- Do I delight in being with *this* person (and not who I hope he or she will become)?

Affirmative responses to all of these questions are positive indicators that there exists a desire to share conjugal love with a particular individual under consideration.

Finally, a person of faith who is pondering marriage should consider whether marriage to *this* particular person is pleasing to God and whether it will benefit the eternal welfare of the couple.[13] Discerning the potential impact of a prospective marriage on one's relationship with God might involve asking questions like:

- Has this relationship led me into vice and serious sin?
- Have I experienced spiritual and moral growth by being with this person?
- Am I a better man/woman when I am around this person?
- Do I experience a deep sense of joy and peace in this person's presence?
- Has this relationship led me into a more intimate relationship with Jesus?

Discerning the wisdom of a potential marriage also involves taking into account the opinion of others in the Church, especially one's family members and friends, perhaps asking the questions:

- What do my family and friends think about my relationship with this person?
- Do my family and friends think that this person is good for me? In other words, do they think that I am a better person when I am around this prospective spouse?

Discernment always has an ecclesial dimension, and others who know a couple well can often provide an objective assessment of

13. Ibid., 64, 68.

the relationship. Reasonable consideration of issues such as these will help a person discern whether it would be wise and prudent for a relationship to progress to marriage. All of the above considerations are aspects of discerning the one motive that is "completely adequate for marriage: *mutual love and the conviction that this union will lead to the eternal welfare of both spouses.*"[14] If marriage is truly a vocation to holiness, everyone who is contemplating marriage should want to undertake this type of discernment. Discernment is thus an essential element in a healthy spirituality of marriage.

THE NEED FOR PREPARATION

In addition to discerning a vocation to marriage, it is necessary to prepare to embrace this vocation. Many engaged couples seem to resent the fact that the Catholic Church requires a period of preparation, sometimes no longer than six months, before they can be married in the Church. Because I teach seminarians, I have at times reminded these engaged couples that a man who is preparing for ordination to the priesthood is required to undertake no fewer than four, but oftentimes as many as eight years of study to prepare to receive the Sacrament of Holy Orders. I remind these couples that similar to the Sacrament of Holy Orders, they too are preparing to receive a sacrament at the service of communion that entails a lifelong commitment of service to each other, to any children God may give them, and to the Church. I tell them that given the momentous step they are preparing to take in their lives by responding to this vocation from God, certainly a period of preparation is warranted, and they should be grateful to the Church for providing this period of preparation. Perhaps they should be grateful that it is a period of less than four years. If this does not convince couples that they need to prepare to embrace their marital vocation, it at least gives them pause.

St. John Paul II pointed out that preparing to embrace the vocation of marriage is a "gradual and continuous process" that "includes three main stages: *remote, proximate,* and *immediate* preparation" (FC, 66).[15] The Holy Father pointed out that *remote* preparation

---

14. Ibid., 64.

15. The Pontifical Council for the Family issued a wonderful document on May 13, 1996, titled *Preparation for the Sacrament of Marriage,* accessed June 13, 2013, www.vatican.va/roman

for marriage begins from early childhood (FC, 66), and I would even say from birth. John Paul noted that it is from an early age that children receive formation in the values and virtues that will shape and form their characters, and personalities, and consciences (FC, 66). It is during childhood that a person is socialized and educated in the faith (FC, 66). During this time children should learn the meaning of human sexuality in God's plan, and they should receive training in chastity. It is during this time of formation in the "domestic church," primarily through the teaching and example of their parents, that children learn how to find themselves through generously giving of themselves. Thus during the remote stage of preparation for the Sacrament of Marriage children should learn the meaning of true self-giving love.[16] It is during this remote period that children and adolescents learn "that marriage is a true vocation and mission, without excluding the possibility of the total gift of self to God in the vocation of priestly and religious life" (FC, 66). I have often said that if parents want to raise children to be happy adults, they should prepare them to be good fathers and mothers. If parents do this, they will help their children prepare to embrace either the vocation of marriage or the vocation to the consecrated religious life, because in either vocation they are called to be spouses as well as spiritual fathers or mothers (something we will examine further in chapter 21). Thus the foundational preparation for the vocation of marriage begins from the time a person is born.[17]

The second stage of preparation for marriage, the *proximate* stage, coincides with the engagement period during which couples receive more specific preparation for the Sacrament of Marriage (FC, 66). This period of preparation builds on the remote stage and

---

_curia/pontifical_councils/family/documents/rc_pc_family_doc_13051996_preparation-for-marriage_en.html, which elaborates the key aspects of the remote, proximate, and immediate stages of preparation.

16. For helpful guidelines in educating children about life and love, see Sacred Congregation for Catholic Education, *Educational Guidance in Human Love: Outlines for Sex Education*, November 1, 1983, accessed June 13, 2013, www.vatican.va/roman_curia/congregations/ccatheduc/documents/rc_con_ccatheduc_doc_19831101_sexual-education_en.html, and Pontifical Council for the Family, *The Truth and Meaning of Human Sexuality: Guidelines for Education within the Family*, December 8, 1995, accessed June 13, 2013, www.vatican.va/roman_curia/pontifical_councils/family/documents/rc_pc_family_doc_08121995_human-sexuality_en.html.

17. For more on the remote period of preparation, see Pontifical Council on the Family, *Preparation for the Sacrament of Marriage*, 22–31.

provides further, explicit instruction and formation regarding the nature of marriage, the sacramentality of marriage, conjugal morality, and the responsibilities inherent in forming a domestic church (FC, 66). This instruction, as all preparation for marriage, takes place within the family and within the larger ecclesial community (FC, 66). It is during this proximate stage of preparation that a person gains a renewed appreciation, or perhaps becomes more fully aware, of the beauty, dignity, and responsibilities inherent to the vocation of marriage.[18] It is during this time that engaged couples are catechized into a deeper understanding of marriage, perhaps receiving formation that was previously lacking. The couple should not only receive instruction on married life and the theology of marriage as a sacrament, but they should also be challenged to reflect on different aspects of their relationship and their own expectations for married life, pinpointing any difficulties that need to be resolved. The engagement period is the time for the couple to finalize their discernment regarding whether they truly want "to give themselves as a couple to Christ."[19] This time is analogous to the time that a young man spends in seminary discerning and preparing for the priesthood. Similar to time in seminary, this means that not every engagement period ends in marriage. Therefore, neither breaking off an engagement nor leaving seminary should be viewed as a sign of failure. Instead, this decisive change in one's course of action can be a real sign of maturity.

Finally, the *immediate* stage of preparation should take place in the months and weeks immediately preceding the wedding" (FC, 66). If during the engagement period a couple remains convinced that it will be truly good for them to marry, the immediate phase of preparation is the time for them to prepare to enter fully into the celebration of their wedding liturgy and to fully embrace everything God offers them in the vocation of marriage.[20]

John Paul II noted that in times past, and still today in some cultures, couples received preparation for the vocation of marriage from their own families who passed on "values concerning married and family life . . . through a gradual process of education and initiation" (FC, 66). However, the Holy Father pointed out that rapid changes in

---

18. For more on proximate preparation, see ibid., 32–49.

19. Ibid., 37.

20. For more on immediate preparation, see ibid., 50–59.

modern society have eroded the "ancient customs" that used to transmit a proper understanding of marriage (FC, 66). For this reason, the Church needs to provide "better and more intensive programs of marriage preparation" to try to assist couples in understanding the vocation to which they are being called, and to enable them to live out this vocation successfully (FC, 66).[21] This preparation should form engaged couples in a spirituality of marriage that enables them to understand marriage as a vocation to holiness. This preparation should also facilitate the discernment of this call, cultivate a desire to fully embrace it, and foster the adoption of a decisively Christian outlook to help spouses live it out. This outlook will be explored in the next chapter.

---

21. As part of the pastoral care that should be provided to those who are called to the vocation of marriage, the Code of Canon Law requires "personal preparation to enter marriage, which disposes the spouses to the holiness and duties of their new state" (CIC, 1063, 2º).

Chapter 18

Key Elements of Married Spirituality

A Spirituality of Tenderness

For several years I had been searching for a way to define the distinctive character of a spirituality of marriage, but could not formulate an appropriate term or phrase. Then I read a document of the Pontifical Council for the Family,[1] which specified "tenderness" as "*the soul of the sacrament of marriage*."[2] The document explained:

> Tenderness is a sentiment deeply engraved on a man and a woman's essence, which must be constantly recaptured, clarified and deepened throughout conjugal life. It requires constant, delicate attention towards the other and makes affectionate relations possible. It leads to wonder before the beauty of creation and all forms of life. It is a sign of the maturity of a couple's love, which is completed in renewed self-giving and welcoming the other. The Holy Spirit makes it possible to live the spirituality of tenderness fully.[3]

This idea of a spirituality of tenderness that serves as the soul of the Sacrament of Marriage struck me as the designation for which I had been looking. Designating the spirituality of marriage with the word "tenderness" coincides with what *Gaudium et Spes* taught about

---

1. The Pontifical Council for the Family, whose documents I have already cited, is an advisory body (referred to as a dicastery) that was instituted by Pope John Paul II in 1981 to assist the Church in providing pastoral ministry to Christian families.

2. Pontifical Council for the Family, "Conclusions of the XVI Plenary Assembly of the Pontifical Council for the Family: Vatican City, November 18–20, 2004," *Familia et Vita* 9.3 (2004): 218. Italics are in the original text.

3. Ibid.

conjugal charity when it stated: "A love like that, bringing together the human and the divine, leads the partners to a free and mutual self-giving, experienced in *tenderness* and action, and permeating their whole lives" (GS, 49; emphasis added). With the word "tenderness" the members of the Pontifical Council for the Family identified what is unique about married spirituality.

John Paul II (Karol Wojtyla) described the essence of tenderness as "the tendency to embrace the other's lived experiences and the states of the other person's soul with one's own affection."[4] This disposition is certainly required in marriage. Marriage does indeed require a delicate attention toward the other, being especially attuned to the other, in a way that is unique to this vocation. On a daily basis married couples must rely upon the grace that the Holy Spirit offers through the Sacrament of Marriage to help them be attuned to each other. They must also strive to clarify and deepen this tenderness throughout their lives together if they hope to grow in mutual affection. This delicate attention toward each other will prompt married couples to continually renew their self-giving and welcoming of each other, will allow them to wonder at the gift of new life that comes as a result of this mutual giving and receiving, and will help them to mature in their love.

What follows is an attempt to further specify five key aspects of a spirituality of tenderness: reverencing, sacrificing, suffering, repairing, and resurrection. This is certainly not an authoritative, nor an exhaustive, account of married spirituality. It is simply an attempt to more clearly delineate an approach to married life, an approach designated as a spirituality of tenderness that will enable spouses to see their daily life in the light of Jesus Christ and to grow in intimacy with him and each other.

Reverencing

The first and absolutely foundational aspect of a spirituality of tenderness is reverence. John Paul II stated that reverence is an essential aspect of married spirituality (TOB 132) and that it "must constitute *the basis* of the reciprocal *relations between the spouses*" (TOB 89:1).

---

4. Karol Wojtyla, *Love and Responsibility*, 186. Wojtyla provides a philosophical analysis of the basis of tenderness in affectivity and how tenderness relates to sensuality (*Love and Responsibility*, 185-192).

This reverence, or *pietas*, is referred to in Scripture as "fear of the Lord" (Ps 103:11; Prov 1:7; 23:17; Sir 1:11–16), designating reverential awe and wonder (TOB 89:1). In chapter 7 we mentioned that this reverence, for both God's plan for marriage and for each other, is evidenced by Tobias and Sarah in the prayer that they offer on their wedding night (Tb 8:4–9).

For Christian couples, this reverence which serves as the foundation of a marital spirituality of tenderness, *"springs from the* profound *consciousness of the mystery of Christ"* (TOB 89:1). Aware of the great love that Christ offers to his Church, a love in which they share, the Christian married couple's whole life together should be marked by reverence, as well as awe at what God has done for them and the beauty of the gifts he has given them. These gifts include: the gifts of their individual lives; the gift that each spouse is to the other; the gifts of their sexuality and God's plan for it; the gift of salvation won for them by Jesus Christ; and the gift of the special share in redemption that is offered to the couple through the Sacrament of Marriage.

Conscious of the mystery of Christ at work in their married life, the Christian couple is prompted to "be subject to one another out of reverence for Christ" (Eph 5:21). John Paul II stated that this passage from the Letter to the Ephesians shows that "the reciprocal relations of husband and wife must spring from their common relationship with Christ" (TOB 89:1), and from their reverence for him. Thus, as was pointed out in chapter 8, the mutual subordination/ subjection to which the couple is exhorted in Ephesians 5 flows out of reverence for Christ. Out of reverence for Christ, whose marvelous love has redeemed both of them and restored their dignity as children of God, Christian spouses make a mutual gift of themselves, and both husband and wife submit themselves in loving service to each other (TOB 89:4). Thus John Paul II stated, "Penetrating their hearts, kindling in them that holy 'fear of Christ' (that is, *pietas*), the mystery of Christ must lead them to 'be subject to one another': the mystery of Christ, that is, the mystery of the election of each of them from all eternity in Christ 'to be adoptive sons' of God" (TOB 89:2). Out of reverence for Christ, who in his infinite goodness has not only granted the spouses the gift of redemption but has also given them the gift of each other to form a family, each spouse realizes that his or her life is no longer about himself or herself. In the love that they share they are called to a life of mutual submission out of reverence for Christ, who submitted himself to the Paschal Mystery out of love for his bride. Thus the "family" that Christian spouses are called to form becomes an apt acronym for, "Forget About Me, I Love You."[5]

In the daily life of a married couple, mutual subjection out of reverence means "to take into account the wishes, opinion and sensitivity of one's spouse; to discuss, not to decide on one's own; to be able to give up one's own point of view." [6] In other words, mutual submission out of reverence means that spouses must always seek to be delicately attentive to each other. This same attentiveness and submission out of reverence must also be exhibited by spouses in what they do in the bedroom and by how they treat each other in their marriage bed (see TOB 117b:4). They must revere God's plan for sexuality (TOB 132:1) in order to speak the "language of the body' in truth (TOB 132:2), and in order to prevent their conjugal relations from becoming habitual (TOB 132:3), lacking affection and sensitivity. Showing this reverence in the bedroom will assist spouses in remaining attentive to each other in their conjugal relations (TOB 132:5), allowing them to renew their giving and welcoming of each other as persons.

Thus reverence as the foundation of a spirituality of tenderness means loving one's spouse "not for any qualities he or she may possess, but for his or her inherent and unrepeatable value as a person."[7] Reverence means subjecting oneself in delicate attention to the good of one's spouse in all aspects of married life. Without this reverence, which the Holy Spirit gifts to the couple in the Sacrament of Marriage, a couple's love will not deepen or mature. On the other hand, if spouses rely on grace to revere and submit to each other out of reverence for Christ, they will be able to realize the "communion of persons" that God calls them to form (TOB 89:6).

---

5. I thank Fr. Monte Hoyles, a priest of the Diocese of Toledo, Ohio, for sharing this acronym with me.

6. Raniero Cantalamessa, "Father Cantalamessa on Marital Submission: Pontifical Household Preacher on This Sunday's Gospel," August 25, 2006, trans. ZENIT news agency, accessed May 9, 2013, www.zenit.org/en/articles/father-cantalamessa-on-marital-submission. Fr. Cantalamessa is a Franciscan priest and served as preacher to the papal household under Pope John Paul II, Benedict XVI, and Francis.

7. Peter J. Elliott, *What God Has Joined: The Sacramentality of Marriage* (Staten Island, NY: Alba House, 1990), 189.

Sacrificing

We have established that a marital spirituality of tenderness is founded in a reverence for the Lord that leads to mutual subjection between spouses. Thus in Christian marriage each spouse makes an unreserved gift of self, mutually subjecting themselves in service to the other's good. This is consistent with conjugal charity that seeks to exist for the other without counting the cost. This gift of self means willing the good of the other to the point of sacrificing one's very self for that good. Jesus teaches us by word and example that the true measure of love is sacrifice (see Jn 15:13). His oblation of self on the Cross shows us that spousal love reaches its fulfillment in self-sacrifice. The insepa-rable connection of sacrifice and Christian spousal love is evidenced in the *Order for Celebrating Matrimony* which prays to the Father:

> Through Christ's paschal sacrifice,
> by which he loved the Church
> and presented her to you washed clean in his Blood,
> you mystically foreshadowed the fullness of wedded love
> in the Sacrament of Matrimony (OCM, 265)

It should be noted that Christ's sacrifice out of love for his bride, which is the source of the conjugal charity of the Sacrament of Marriage, is not a sacrifice of desolation, but a sacrifice of oblation, pouring himself out in love. In truth, spouses will only experience happiness in marriage to the degree that they are willing to undertake sacrificial giving for each other, pouring themselves out in love for each other. As John Paul II stated, "Sacrifice cannot be removed from family life, but must in fact be wholeheartedly accepted if the love between husband and wife is to be deepened and become a source of intimate joy" (FC, 34).

This sacrificial giving begins with spouses sacrificing their own individual agendas in service to their marriage. Spouses must be willing to sacrifice their self-centeredness in order to focus on the beloved. They need to embrace a life of asceticism, self-discipline, and self-denial in order to be gift for each other. Spouses must also embrace and live the evangelical counsels (CCC, 1973–1974, 2053) of poverty, chastity, and obedience, in a manner that is appropriate to married life, in order to be gift for each other. These are not popular concepts in an overly

indulgent, "Just do it!" culture that is focused on the immediate gratification of any and all desires, but they are necessary aspects of living
a sacrificial life that will renew a couple's love and bring it to maturity.

How many times do marriages fail because spouses are unwilling to sacrifice their professional or personal goals for the good of their
family? How many times do spouses cite "irreconcilable differences"
because one or the other of them is unwilling to sacrifice a want in
deference to the other's needs? When a man and woman get married
each of them needs to realize that they no longer belong to themselves.
Each spouse's life, including one's time, one's money, and one's body
belongs to the beloved. This is the sacrificial offering of married love
according to which the couple has truly surrendered themselves to each
other. Living a spirituality of tenderness in marriage means not only
living in constant, delicate attention to the needs and desires of one's
beloved, but it also means being willing to sacrifice one's own wants and
sometimes even needs for the sake of the beloved. As a couple grows
in conjugal charity, they shift from asking, "What more can my
husband/wife do for me?" to asking, "What more can I do for my
husband/wife which I still have not done?"[8] This type of mutual
self-sacrifice must be undertaken if spouses are to live no longer as two,
but as one. Far from leaving a married couple empty, undertaking this
mutual sacrifice breaks the spouses out of isolation, solipsism, and
self-centeredness and fills both of them with the joy of realizing themselves in the freedom of the gift, which is the goal of their humanity.

Living a spirituality of tenderness also involves spouses sacrificing their joint agendas and submitting to the project of reconstruction
that the Holy Spirit wants to work in them as a couple. Through Baptism
each spouse belongs to Christ as an individual, but in the Sacrament
of Marriage Jesus has indissolubly bound the couple together and has
consecrated them *together* for his own purposes. Jesus has a plan for
each married couple that he binds together in his Mystical Body, and
each couple needs to constantly engage the Lord in prayer about his
plan for their lives. The Christian married couple needs to relinquish
the façade of control over their lives, and enter into dialog with Jesus
about his desires for them. These desires include those related to the
couple's work, the management of their finances, and their family size.

---

8. Raniero Cantalamessa, "Father Cantalamessa on Marital Submission."

In jointly sacrificing their own agendas in deference to the Lord's plan, the couple should always be mindful of the fact that the Lord will not be outdone in generosity.

A Christian married couple needs to realize that by joining or "yoking" (from the Latin *[con]iungere*, from which we get the English "conjugal") them together in the Sacrament of Marriage to be a living sign of his love for his Church, Jesus seeks to live his life over again in them *as a couple*. This means that if married love is to be an effective sign of the love of the heavenly bridegroom for his bride, then this living sign will *necessarily* involve sacrifice. The essence of sacrifice is making an offering of something precious out of love to show reverence and devotion to another. We can also say that the measure of true love is the willingness to sacrifice for the beloved. This is why Benedict XVI could state that it is from the pierced side of Christ on the Cross that the definition of love must begin (DCE, 12). Jesus' sacrifice on the Cross was the full manifestation of his loving obedience to the Father and his love for humanity, because in this complete offering of self, he went to the limits of love in order to reconcile man with God. One could say that while the *foundation* of a marital spirituality of tenderness is reverence, the *essence* of marital tenderness is the true gift of spouses to each other, to their family, and to the Lord in a spirit of self-sacrifice. This spirit of joyful sacrifice should permeate the couple's entire life as they offer all of their daily tasks, however pleasant, difficult, irksome, or mundane, in love to the Father. Whether it is enjoying a day playing outside with one's children, working at a less than ideal job in order to support a family, performing household tasks that one would rather avoid, or any of the myriad of other forms of service to the family that is required of spouses, all of the couples' prayers, works, joys, and sufferings can be offered to God as a sacrifice of praise. This is the living sacrifice and the daily worship that Christian spouses are called to offer as a living sign of Christ's love for his Church.

Since being able to embrace sacrifice is so central to living a happy, successful marriage, in sacramental marriage the spouses' love will be deepened by sharing in the Eucharist together (CCC, 1644). The Eucharist is "the source and summit of the Christian faith" (LG, 11) and "the sum and summary of our faith" (CCC, 1327) because "it *re-presents* (makes present) the sacrifice of the cross" by which the

Lord Jesus accomplished our salvation (CCC, 1366). In the Eucharist, Jesus is present body, blood, soul, and divinity (CCC, 1374) to make "it possible for all generations of Christians to be united with his offering" (CCC, 1368). "The Eucharist draws us into Jesus' act of self-oblation" (DCE, 13).

We must remember that the sacrificial offering that Christ made of himself on the Cross, which is re-presented in an unbloody manner at every Mass, is a nuptial offering of the bridegroom for his bride.[9] We may even say that Christ's nuptial union with his bride is "consummated" in his sacrifice on the Cross and that in the Sacrament of the Eucharist Christ continues this act of consummation.[10] It is in the Eucharist that the bridegroom offers himself completely for his beloved bride,[11] nourishing and feeding her with his very Body and Blood (TOB 92:8). This is why "the Eucharist and marriage are two inseparable and complementary expressions of the mystery of the covenant between God and his people."[12] John Paul II stated that the Eucharist is in fact *the Sacrament of the Bridegroom and the Bride*" (MD, 26), and he explained the intimate connection between the Sacrament of Marriage and the Eucharist when he wrote:

> The Eucharist is the very source of Christian marriage. The Eucharistic Sacrifice, in fact, represents Christ's covenant of love with the Church, sealed with His blood on the Cross. In this sacrifice of the New and Eternal Covenant, Christian spouses encounter the source from which their own marriage covenant flows, is interiorly structured and continuously renewed. As a re-presentation of Christ's sacrifice of love for the Church, the Eucharist is a fountain of charity. (FC, 57)

Thus, to begin to drink from this fountain of charity together it is fitting that a Christian husband and wife be joined in marriage during the communal celebration of the Mass (OCM, 29), which makes present Christ's sacrificial offering of himself in spousal union with the Church. The *Catechism of the Catholic Church* explains:

---

9. See Marc Ouellet, *Divine Likeness*, 154–167; see also Angelo Scola, *The Nuptial Mystery*, trans. Michelle K. Borras (Grand Rapids, MI: William B. Eerdmans, 2005), 268, 296–297.

10. Peter J. Elliott, *What God Has Joined*, xxiv; see also Livio Melina, *Building the Culture of the Family: The Language of Love* (Staten Island, NY: Alba House, 2011), xxiv–xxv, 88, 151.

11. Peter J. Elliott, *What God Has Joined*, 24.

12. Marc Ouellet, *Divine Likeness*, 216.

In the Eucharist the memorial of the New Covenant is realized, the New Covenant in which Christ has united himself for ever to the Church, his beloved bride for whom he gave himself up. It is therefore fitting that the spouses should seal their consent to give themselves to each other through the offering of their own lives by uniting it to the offering of Christ for his Church made present in the Eucharistic sacrifice, and by receiving the Eucharist so that, communicating in the same Body and the same Blood of Christ, they may form but "one body" in Christ. (CCC, 1621)

The rite of marriage prays that newly joined spouses may be made "one heart in love / by the Sacrament of Christ's Body and Blood" (RM, "Nuptial Blessing A"). John Paul II even stated: "The liturgical crowning of the marriage rite is the Eucharist, the sacrifice of that 'body which has been given up' and that 'blood which has been shed,' which in a certain way finds expression in the consent of the spouses" (LF, 11). By celebrating the rite of marriage in the context of the Eucharistic liturgy, the Christian couple is reminded from the start that their one-flesh union is indissolubly united to Christ's Paschal Mystery. As Peter Elliott wrote, "The Nuptial Mass and first Communion shared as husband and wife brings them into communion with the Sacrifice which they are called to live out each day as Christian spouses."[13] Thus the sacrifice of married life should be Eucharistic.

From the moment Jesus joins a married couple in the Sacrament of Marriage, the couple is called to enter into Christ's Paschal act of self-donation and become a living sign of his sacrificial giving of himself to his Church. In the Eucharist, Christian spouses encounter the love of the Bridegroom who purifies their love with his sacrifice. This is why John Paul II stated that there is no greater power or wisdom in which the family can be educated than that of the Eucharist (FC, 18). For Christian spouses the Eucharist is "the primary path of *education in the gift*, and therefore of education in how to live reality."[14] There can be no more delicate attention shown to a spouse than the tender care that Christ provides to his bride by nourishing her with his very flesh (Eph 5:29). Therefore, receiving the Eucharist together throughout

---

13. Peter J. Elliott, *What God Has Joined*, xxiii.
14. Angelo Scola, *The Nuptial Mystery*, 302.

their life in the heart of the ecclesial community is central to Christian spouses living a spirituality of tenderness.

Suffering

True love involves compassion, a willingness to suffer with and for one's beloved. St. Paul taught this when he stated that love bears and endures all things (1 Cor 13:7). Spouses promise this when they pledge to be faithful "in good times and in bad" (OCM, 62). Reverencing Christ, the gift of one's spouse, and the gift of marriage, spouses who are willing to sacrifice for each other in a Eucharistic manner are also willing to suffer for the good of each other and for the good of their marriage. There are two main ways in which spouses can express love for each other: giving gifts to each other and suffering for each other.[15] These ways of expressing love correlate with the two main ways God has revealed his love for us. In the beginning God blessed us with the many gifts of creation, and then, in the fullness of time, he revealed the depths of his love by suffering and dying for us on a Cross. In the beginning of their marriages newlyweds express love by giving gifts to each other, but eventually these gifts are not sufficient. In the end, it is suffering with and for another that reveals the depths of one's love. The willingness of spouses to endure suffering *with* the beloved, even when there is nothing that he or she can do to alleviate the suffering, is true compassion. Furthermore, the willingness to endure suffering *for* one's beloved, to take burdens on oneself in order to free the beloved from oppression, is a Christ-like offering of self that lifts spousal love to new heights. It is possible for spouses to experience an intimacy beyond words when they endure suffering together out of love.

It is important to note that conjugal charity will prompt spouses to suffer for each other even when it is one spouse who causes suffering for the other. Spouses learn this reality of marital tenderness as they contemplate the Cross. Jesus came to offer himself for the salvation of the world, and in doing so he invited everyone to become part of his Mystical Body. However, he was betrayed by one of his closest followers (Jn 13:2), abandoned by those whom he loved to the end (Jn 13:1),

---

15. The following comments on love expressed through gifts and suffering are based on Raniero Cantalamessa, "Father Cantalamessa on Marital Submission."

and tortured and then killed by those to whom he offered forgiveness with his final breaths (Lk 23:34). All of these individuals, and all members of the Church who betray Jesus through sin, are his corporate bride for whom he made a sacrificial gift of self, enduring the worst suffering imaginable. No human spouse could ever suffer at the hands of his or her beloved more than Jesus. When husbands or wives experience suffering that is caused by their spouse, whether it be through callousness, mean-spiritedness, infidelity, indifference, or abandonment, they must remember that Christ calls them to bear this suffering for the sake of their beloved. Bearing this suffering assumes, of course, that the spouses are bound to each other in a valid sacramental marriage and that the suffering is not the result of outright spousal abuse.[16] Spouses should remember that if their marriage is a valid sacrament it is a gift from God that he will use to draw them closer to him.[17] Even if spouses experience suffering because they think they are "poorly matched" or because they think they made a mistake in choosing to get married, in his providence God permitted this "mistake" because he will promote the good of both of the spouses through their marriage if they avail themselves of the graces he offers them.[18]

As part of a spirituality of tenderness, spouses need to understand something about a Christian theology of suffering to know that when they experience suffering in their marriage, it does not signal the end of marriage or married love. Many couples getting married have imbibed the lie that marriage is supposed to be "happily ever after." As they have based their marriages on this myth, when suffering comes, spouses start to wonder whether getting married was a mistake. Assuming that their marriages were valid, this could not be

---

16. Nothing that is stated here would ask a spouse to stay in an abusive relationship. Many people misconstrue the Catholic Church's teaching on the indissolubility of marriage and the inadmissibility of divorce to imply that the Catholic Church would force abused spouses to submit themselves to mistreatment. This is simply not the case. In a truly abusive relationship the abused spouse has the right, and the obligation, to remove herself or himself and any children from the abusive situation. Thus separation, and even civil divorce to disentangle household finances, is sometimes required. God does not require anyone to be a masochist. In addition, abuse may be an indicator that the abusing spouse was incapable of offering the consent that is necessary to contract a valid marriage, possibly leading to an annulment.

17. Joseph E. Kerns, *The Theology of Marriage: The Historical Development of Christian Attitudes Toward Sex and Sanctity in Marriage* (New York: Sheed and Ward, 1964), 218.

18. Ibid.

farther from the truth. It is true that no one gets married with the intention of causing themselves suffering, and even St. Thomas Aquinas stated that the Sacrament of Matrimony has its origin in Christ's Passion not by way of suffering but by way of love.[19] However, in a fallen world, loving another with sacrificial love always carries with it the risk of suffering.

In giving yourself completely to another there is always the possibility that your gift will not always be appreciated, that some terrible calamity will befall your beloved, or that death will tear him or her away before you are ready to say goodbye. However, a person who seeks to avoid suffering at all costs will never know the joy of love.[20] First of all, Jesus made it clear that if we want to experience the joy of the resurrection we cannot escape the cross of suffering in this fallen world (FC, 34.5). He bids each of us to bear our cross out of love for him (Mt 10:38) so he can give us the fullness of joy (Jn 15:11). Also, because Christian spouses are taken up into the Paschal Mystery *together* they will experience the pain of suffering together, a pain that will serve to purify and refine their love. In the love that they share with each other, spouses will be introduced to Christ on a deeper level and will come to know each other more deeply through what they suffer together. Instead of fleeing from this suffering, they must walk through it *together*, trusting that Jesus himself will bear the load with them (see Mt 11:30) and lead them into the new life he has promised. Thus one of the nuptial blessings in the rite of marriage prays for the newly married couple: "In happiness may they praise you, O Lord, / in sorrow may they seek you out; / may they have the joy of your presence / to assist them in their toil, / and know that you are near / to comfort them in their need" (RM, "Nuptial Blessing C").

It is worth pointing out that one's spouse is rarely the main cause of suffering in marriage. Instead, the main suffering of marriage is suffering the process of conversion that the Holy Spirit wants to work in oneself. In his plan, God intends marriage, and especially sacramental marriage, to foster the spouses' growth in virtue and their ability to be self-gift through self-denial, by calling them to focus on serving the good of each other and their family. This means that the

---

19. ST Suppl., q. 42, a. 1, ad 3.
20. See Dietrich von Hildebrand, *Marriage*, 61.

real laying down of one's life in marriage is in the moral and spiritual life,[21] and the real suffering of marriage is suffering a death to self for the sake of one's beloved. Selfishness in all of its forms is the enemy of love (LF, 14), and in the end it is selfishness, not one's spouse, that causes the most suffering in marriage. Spouses must struggle against this selfishness to win a victory over self for the sake of the beloved.[22] This is part of the demanding nature of love, and as John Paul II pointed out, "Only the one who is able to be demanding with himself in the name of love can also demand love from others" (LF, 14).

Spouses must allow themselves to experience the agony and the demands of love if they want to experience the freedom of love, not "free love," which is mutual use of another. The problem is that we tend to see love and its demands as threatening because they entail the death of self-centeredness and selfish inclinations. Due to human weakness all spouses fear this death to self, and perhaps think to themselves regarding the demands of married love, "This is going to kill me!" However, this is precisely Jesus' purpose for marriage—a death to self that raises us to new life! We can even go so far as to say, as a friend of mine has said to engaged couples, "You have chosen to get married. Now, prepare to die."[23] Throughout marriage spouses struggle to accept this death to self. However, we need to realize that dying to self is not a work of senseless suffering and desolation, but a work of life, beauty, and joy.[24] In fact, learning to die to self is learning the language of true love because spouses cannot say "yes" to each other if they are not able to say "no" to themselves.[25]

As spouses suffer individually to overcome selfishness in their hearts, they will also be called to suffer the conversion of each other.[26] At the beginning of marriage, spouses will inflict suffering upon each

---

21. I borrow this insight from Deacon James Keating, director of theological formation at the Institute for Priestly Formation in Omaha, NE. See his book *Spousal Prayer* (Omaha: IPF Publications, 2013).

22. Alice von Hildebrand, "Introduction," in *Marriage: The Mystery of Faithful Love* (Manchester, NH: Sophia Institute Press, 1991), xii.

23. This statement is taken from Deacon James Keating.

24. Raniero Cantalamessa, "The Language of Love: Gospel Commentary for 22nd Sunday in Ordinary Time," August 29, 2008, trans. ZENIT news agency, accessed May 14, 2013, www.zenit.org/en/articles/the-language-of-love.

25. Ibid.

26. I borrow this insight from Deacon James Keating.

other, as they struggle to lay down their former single lives in order to truly become one. When children come along the couple will experience suffering together, as they realize that their lives must not just shift to accommodate this new little person but must be reoriented around the good of this person. Throughout married life, as Christ seeks to make them fit for eternity with him, spouses will experience suffering at each other's hands as each of them struggles to overcome selfishness in its many forms. However, bearing this suffering will bond them closer together in intimacy.

Sadly, in this life, it is true that we will hurt those whom we love the most. This is because our callous words and hurtful actions sting harder those who are closest to us. It is important for couples to know that because they are both sinners living in a fallen world, it is inevitable that they will cause suffering to each other. However, the real question is what couples do after they have hurt each other. Will they bear this suffering in tenderness or will they retreat from their relationship? In the Sacrament of Marriage, Jesus offers couples the grace to bear this suffering so that they may overcome sin through each other.

When I became engaged to be married I received a congratulations card from a married friend of mine, a card that I found quite curious at the time. The card had no words on the front of it, but instead it had a beautiful painting of the Crucifixion. On the inside of the card my friend had written, "Congratulations on your engagement! Welcome to the 3 rings of marriage—the engagement ring, the wedding ring, and the suffering." At the time, I found this card to be somewhat dark and wondered if my friend was implying something about his lack of satisfaction with his own marriage. After being married for a while I soon realized that he meant nothing of the sort. He meant to prepare me for the project of self-purification that the Lord would begin working in me, as he called me to let go of my self-centeredness so that I could focus on my bride.

If true love cannot be experienced without the suffering of the cross, spouses will do well to hang a crucifix prominently in their home, and to spend time together praying before it. In fact, some friends of mine have even suggested that spouses focus more precisely on the feet of the crucified Jesus. On the Cross we see in Jesus' feet two members of his body bound by the nail of suffering.[27] In some ways there can be no better image upon which Christian spouses can reflect. Come what may, they are bound together, and it is through their shared suffering that their love will be clarified and deepened as they grow in delicate attention to each other. Furthermore, a Christian couple can be assured that none of the suffering they experience in their marriage will be meaningless. The Cross of Christ should remind them that whatever the cause of their suffering, Jesus will draw good out of it and use it to redeem their love—this is his promise!

Repairing

With reverence as the foundation of a spirituality of tenderness, Christian married couples will be prompted to sacrifice and suffer for each other. They will also seek to constantly refine, improve, and repair their love for each other. They will want to practice what Fr. Raniero Cantalamessa has called the "art of repairing."[28] Given that we live in the "throw away and replace it" culture of rampant consumerism, married couples need consciously to cultivate the art of repairing. This art should not be confused with repairing or fixing one's spouse, as if one's spouse is a project to work on, or as if it is always the other's fault when difficulties arise. Instead, the art of repairing is about exerting the effort to be constantly attentive to and maintaining the relationship. This art is implied in the Letter to the Ephesians when husbands are exhorted to love their wives as Christ loves the Church, "that he might sanctify her, . . . that he might present the Church to himself in splendor, without spot or wrinkle or any such thing, that she might be holy and without blemish" (Eph 5:26–27).

Part of the art of repairing involves repairing damage that results from "deferred maintenance" or neglect. This is a situation which calls for the art of repairing, healing damage that is caused due to a lack of attentiveness to one's spouse. A husband, taking Christ as his model, can repair this situation by showing his wife in word and

---

27. I thank Mrs. Gina Switzer, a religious artist in Columbus, OH, and Deacon James Keating for this wonderful insight.

28. Fr. Cantalamessa's comments on the "art of repairing" may be found in Raniero Cantalamessa, "Father Cantalamessa on Marriage: 'Rediscover the Art of Repairing!' Says Pontifical Household Preacher," October 6, 2006, trans. ZENIT news agency, accessed May 9, 2013, www.zenit.org/en/articles/father-cantalamessa-on-marriage.

deed how much he appreciates her as an irreplaceable gift in his life. Likewise, a husband can grow weary of his work, lose enthusiasm, and close in on himself when he feels that he is unappreciated and that his efforts serve no purpose. In this situation, a wife can practice the art of repairing by showing her husband that she is proud of him, that she esteems him, and that she admires him. Thus part of the art of repairing involves spouses being attentive to each other by expressing mutual appreciation and esteem. Spouses can repair their relationship by reminding each other that they are cherished as the apple of each other's eye (see Dt 32:10; Ps 17:8). They can practice the art of repairing when through word and deed they let each other know "it's good that you are here; how wonderful that you exist!" [29]

Spouses must also practice the art of repairing during times in married life that are emotionally arid or sterile, lacking any affective consolation or feelings of closeness with one's spouse. It is not necessarily the wrongdoing or faults of the spouses that cause these "dark nights" of the emotions. [30] Instead, these times are due to the fickleness of human emotions. Eventually, every marriage will struggle with a lack of excitement and will experience this "dark night of the senses."[31] The jubilation and ecstasy of the newlywed phase wanes and the couple experiences an emotional dryness or emptiness in their relationship. Lacking feelings of consolation, it is at this point that the couple must make a conscious choice to continue loving each other, serving each other's good even when they may not feel like doing so. They proceed based upon an act of the will. On their wedding day couples should be mindful of the fact that they will not be able to predict how they will feel about each other five, or ten, or fifty years from that day, but they will be able to promise that they will love each other no matter how long they are married. This is because love, as we discussed in chapter 4, is a choice, an act of the will. Love is not

---

29. Josef Pieper, *Faith, Hope, Love* (San Francisco: Ignatius Press, 1997), 170.

30. Raniero Cantalamessa, "Father Cantalamessa on Marriage." The image of the "dark night" comes from the Christian mystical tradition, and more precisely, St. John of the Cross (1542–1591) who wrote a treatise titled *Dark Night of the Soul* in which he speaks of a "dark night of the senses" and a "dark night of the spirit." The "dark night of the senses" involves times of aridity and sterility in the spiritual life, in which prayer brings no emotional consolation and God seems distant and aloof. The "dark night of the spirit" involves times in which the believer, lacking any sense of God's presence, is tempted to doubt.

31. Ibid.

primarily a feeling, and consenting to marriage is not consenting to a relationship of emotional consistency. Marriage is not a promise of "happily-ever-after" but of "committed-ever-after," and this commitment endures regardless of the ebbs and flows of one's emotions.

Married couples can also experience a deeper spiritual struggle, or a "dark night of the spirit." This is when spouses experience not just emotional dryness but intellectual temptations. They may doubt whether they married the right person, wondering whether they have made a mistake. They may experience the temptation to lose focus on the life and the path they have chosen together, and instead dream about other potential paths that each of their lives could have taken. At these times they need to remember that Christ stated, "No one who puts his hand to the plow and looks back is fit for the kingdom of God" (Lk 9:62). In other words, they need to realize that they have made a choice for each other that has provided direction and shape to their lives, giving them a particular "row to plow" together in God's vineyard. They need to remember that they cannot make progress towards the Kingdom by constantly looking back. When intellectual doubts and temptations come, the couple must fight these temptations and move forward in the darkness, persevering in faith: faith in each other, faith in the commitment they have made, and most importantly, faith in Jesus Christ. In order to get through these spiritual temptations the couple needs to pray with even more intensity and rely upon the grace of the Sacrament of Marriage to help them remain faithful to the choice they have made. Again, on their wedding day a couple cannot predict what thoughts may cross their minds any number of years down the road, but they can guarantee that they will love each other, because love is an act of the will.

As the couple moves forward in faith, instead of being paralyzed by the darkness, they realize that these dark nights of the senses and of the spirit serve to purify their love by making it more selfless than it was in the beginning.[32] When spouses love each other even when there are no feelings, and when they love in the face of intellectual darkness and temptations, they truly love for the sake of the other and not for any self-satisfaction or gratification. They love simply to give, not to take anything from the beloved. In a miniscule manner

---

32. Ibid.

they are participating in the darkness that Christ experienced during his Passion, but during which he still chose to love to the end. When a couple has persevered through the dark nights that occur during the course of their married life, they realize that "they love one another a bit more with a love of tenderness, free of egoism and capable of compassion; they love one another for the things they have gone through and suffered together."[33]

Even when a married couple experiences dark nights in their life together they must continue to practice the craft of repairing. Spouses must invite Jesus into their marriage because it is Christ himself who will do the repairing—and he wants to do the repairing! He wants to use the couple's dark nights to draw them into a new dawn for their love. The Christian married couple must throw themselves into Christ's arms, and relying upon and cooperating with the grace that he promises them in the Sacrament of Marriage, allow him to help them do the necessary repairs.

Certainly the art of repairing involves making reparation for wrongs that spouses commit against each other, either by action or omission. Each spouse must seek to heal damage that each has done to their relationship. The art of repairing also involves practicing the art of forgiving. I have often told engaged couples that in order to make a marriage work they need to hone three skills: the ability to communicate well with each other, the ability to sacrifice for each other, and the ability to forgive each other. Communicating well is itself a form of constantly tending to and repairing a marriage. However, the ability and willingness to give and receive forgiveness is necessary when one spouse causes suffering to the other. Holding grudges and "keeping score" is a recipe for marital ruin. Each spouse must make it a regular practice to examine his or her conscience and to be ready to say, "I'm sorry," or, "I forgive you," as a result of this examination.

There is great wisdom for spouses in the biblical injunction not to let the sun go down on one's anger (Eph 4:26), especially if the married couple is angry with each other. Part of living a spirituality of tenderness entails always being ready to offer forgiveness, even if it means offering it "seventy times seven times" (Mt 18:22). The Letter to the Ephesians even associates forgiveness with tenderness when it

---

33. Ibid.

instructs Christians to "be kind to one another, *tenderhearted*, forgiving one another, as God in Christ forgave you" (Eph 4:32; emphasis added). There is no greater example of tender love than that of Jesus who forgave his bride from the Cross to which she had pinned him, offering this forgiveness even before it was requested. Christian spouses are called to rely upon the grace of the Sacrament of Marriage to practice forgiving each other, as Christ forgave his bride with infinite tenderness from the Cross. In so doing they will experience the "continual renewal of their mutual self-gift, by means of the *experience of forgiveness.*"[34]

However, couples will be able to ask for and receive forgiveness and tender mercy from each other only if they ask for and receive forgiveness and mercy from Jesus in the Sacrament of Penance. Here again, as with reliance on reception of the Eucharist, it becomes obvious that authentic married spirituality is not an isolated spirituality, but a spirituality integrated into the larger ecclesial community. John Paul II commented on the necessity of Penance and the Eucharist for married and family life when he stated, "Participation in the sacrament of Reconciliation and in the banquet of the one Body of Christ offers to the Christian family the grace and the responsibility of overcoming every division and of moving towards the fullness of communion willed by God" (FC, 21.6). The more spouses are able to approach the Sacrament of Penance to receive forgiveness from the Bridegroom, the easier they will find it to ask for and offer forgiveness to each other. John Paul II aptly described how the Sacrament of Penance impacts married life when he stated:

> The celebration of this sacrament acquires special significance for family life. While they discover in faith that sin contradicts not only the covenant with God, but also the covenant between husband and wife and the communion of the family, the married couple and the other members of the family are led to an encounter with God, who is "rich in mercy," who bestows on them His love which is more powerful than sin, and who reconstructs and brings to perfection the marriage covenant and the family communion. (FC, 58)

Thus, in the Sacrament of Penance spouses will learn that true love can heal and repair wounds through forgiveness and reconciliation,

---

34. Angelo Scola, *The Nuptial Mystery*, 269.

and they will be empowered to offer this healing to each other (LF, 14). From the Sacrament of Penance spouses will learn to be merciful with each other until death parts them, because they will receive unbounded and endless mercy from God who never ceases to forgive them.[35] They will receive from the Sacrament of Penance the grace they need to repair and regenerate their love and rebuild their communion.[36]

There is no greater way for a married couple to be tender with each other than to offer forgiveness and mercy to each other. When a spouse knows he or she has wronged the beloved, nothing gives the spouse new life like hearing the beloved speak the words, "I forgive you!" When couples rely upon God's grace to grow in their facility to be forgiving and merciful, they renew their love and give each other new life. Cooperating with Christ to practice the art of forgiveness is an essential aspect of the art of repairing. By seeking to improve, refine, and repair marital love, yet another hallmark of marital tenderness is displayed.

Resurrection

If Christian spouses cooperate with the grace that Christ offers them in the Sacrament of Marriage to practice a spirituality of marital tenderness by revering, sacrificing, suffering, and repairing, Jesus will allow them to experience the resurrection of their love. If spouses are willing to revere Christ and each other, sacrifice for each other, suffer for and with each other, and repair their love for each other, they will experience the joy of true marital intimacy and rise to new life together. Each spouse will know the other and be known on a deep level, and at the same time they will experience deeper intimacy with God. They will love more tenderly, truly attentive to each other with a clearer and deeper vision of each other and of the love that they share. They will be filled with wonder at all the Lord has done in them and for them, and as their love matures, they will be able to renew the self-giving and welcoming of each other that joined them in marriage because they have allowed themselves to be drawn deeper into the tender heart of Jesus.

It is the Holy Spirit who empowers spouses to fully live this spirituality of tenderness and experience the joy of the resurrection of

---

35. Peter J. Elliott, *What God Has Joined*, 185.
36. See Livio Melina, *Building a Culture of the Family*, 23–40.

their love. In truth, as John Paul II pointed out, "Love can be deepened and preserved only by love, that love which is 'poured into our hearts through the Holy Spirit which has been given to us' (Rom 5:5)" (LF, 7). Therefore, to live a spirituality of tenderness, couples must ask for this love through prayer. They must ask for this grace not only individually, but as a couple. If they want to experience the resurrection of their love and an intimacy in the Lord, spouses need to take the time to pray together, expressing aloud their praise, thanksgiving, reparation, and petitions. Through this prayer the Holy Spirit will teach spouses how to reverence, sacrifice, suffer, and repair so that they may live tenderly with each other, seeing more clearly the "great mystery" they are called to live.

THE SPIRITUALITY OF NONSACRAMENTAL MARRIAGES

At the end of this chapter on married spirituality, a word needs to be said about marriages between Catholics and non-Catholics and how these spouses can live a spirituality of tenderness.

There are two situations to address: mixed marriages, which involve marriages between a Catholic and a baptized non-Catholic, and disparity of cult marriages, which are marriages between a Catholic and a nonbaptized person.

Mixed marriages are fully sacramental unions, because both spouses are validly baptized. By virtue of the spouses' Baptisms, Christ acts through the couple's mutual exchange of consent to bind them together for life, offering them a share in the love he shares with his Church. However, because in mixed marriages spouses do not share the same faith, the Catholic Church counsels its faithful to exercise great caution before entering into such unions. It requires Catholics to receive permission from the local Church authority before entering into a mixed marriage (CCC, 1633–1635; CIC, c. 1124). This permission is required so that pastors may help couples discern potential difficulties in their proposed life together, and whether any of these difficulties may pose insurmountable barriers to living a common life.

A couple who is discerning a mixed marriage needs to consider whether their lack of unity in faith will lead to disunity, tension, or conflict in the home (CCC, 1634). Additionally, many non-Catholic Christians do not share an understanding of marriage that coincides with the teaching of the Catholic Church. As was noted in the chapters dealing with the development of the theology of marriage, most Protestant churches do not believe that marriage is a sacrament, nor do they believe that marriage is necessarily indissoluble. This can pose significant difficulties in a shared vision of married life, and could even pose barriers to a valid exchange of consent if the non-Catholic spouse does not intend a permanent union or formally rejects what the Catholic Church intends to do in the celebration of marriage. Although the Orthodox Church believes in the sacramentality of marriage, we have noted how it holds that the priest, and not the couple, is the minister of the Sacrament of Marriage. We have also noted that the Orthodox allow for the practice of divorce. There can also be significant differences in the understanding of sexual morality between Catholics and non-Catholic Christians, a topic which we will address further in the next chapter. Even given the potential differences that can exist between a couple who is considering a mixed marriage, by giving permission to contract these unions the Catholic Church acknowledges that these marriages can be God's will for the couple. It is even possible for a couple in a mixed marriage to live a spirituality of tenderness with each other if they place "in common what they have received from their respective communities, and learn from each other the way in which each lives in fidelity to Christ" (CCC, 1634).

As the non-Catholic spouse is not baptized, couples entering into disparity of cult marriages do not receive the Sacrament of Marriage.[37] Since marriage always has social ramifications, and because disparity of cult marriages involve a member of the Body of Christ uniting with someone who does not believe in Jesus, the Catholic Church considers this difference in faith to be an impediment that invalidates the marriage unless a formal dispensation is sought

---

37. However, if at some point during their married life the nonbaptized spouse (or two unbaptized spouses) receive Baptism, the marriage becomes a sacrament at the moment of the Baptism without the couple needing to reprofess their consent to each other. Having already pledged themselves to each other in the covenant of marriage, Christ works in and through this covenant once both spouses have been incorporated into him, elevating their natural union to the level of a sacrament.

from the local bishop (CCC, 1635; CIC, c. 1086). Similar to the couple entering a mixed marriage, a couple in this situation should carefully discern what difficulties may be introduced into their home because of their lack of shared faith. The nonbaptized spouse's understanding of the nature and properties of marriage and his or her understanding of sexual morality should also be ascertained. Nonetheless, by being willing to grant a dispensation to disparity of cult marriages, the Church is able to recognize that God may in fact call two such people together. Peter Elliott pointed out that disparity of cult unions can be instances of Christ extending his salvific will to the non-Christian spouse through the Christian spouse, and in return by loving the Christian spouse the non-Christian spouse implicitly loves Jesus. [38] St. Paul himself stated that "the unbelieving husband is consecrated through his wife, and the unbelieving wife is consecrated through her husband" (1 Cor 7:14). [39] However, the Church emphasizes the special task and responsibility that falls to the Catholic spouse in a disparity of cult marriage (CCC, 1637). Through prayer, example, and love, the Catholic spouse can prepare the non-Christian spouse to accept the grace of conversion (CCC, 1637). By taking the lead in revering, sacrificing, suffering, and repairing, the Catholic spouse can invite his or her unbaptized spouse into a life of tenderness, opening up the possibility of a relationship with Jesus for the non-Christian.

When dealing with mixed and disparity of cult marriages it should be noted that the burden of discerning these unions, as with all marital unions, ultimately rests with the couples themselves. Couples in these situations should consider all of the questions that were discussed in the section of the previous chapter dealing with discernment. Additional issues should also be considered. First of all, when there is a difference of faith between spouses there needs to be a deep

---

38. Peter J. Elliott, *What God Has Joined*, 201–202. As the nonbaptized spouse has become associated with the great mystery of salvation by joining in one flesh with the baptized spouse, Peter Elliott posited that disparity of cult marriages, while not fully sacraments, are more than just primordial signs of God's covenantal love for humanity (201–203).

39. It should be noted that the "Pauline Privilege" (1 Cor 7:13–16) that was discussed in chapter 8 cannot be invoked in a disparity of cult marriage that is entered into according to Church law, or that results from the conversion of one spouse to the Catholic faith while the other spouse agrees to live peaceably with the newly converted spouse (Peter J. Elliott, *What God Has Joined*, 199).

mutual respect for each other's respective confessions. The harmony of a home will most certainly break down if one spouse views the other's beliefs with disrespect or animosity. Additionally, spouses in a mixed or disparity of cult situation should ask themselves if they are willing to go through life together if their difference in faith persists. Too often a spouse counts on his or her mate converting to his or her faith at some time in the future. Couples need to realize that conversion is a free decision that is ultimately between an individual and the grace of God. To count on this conversion occurring is nearly tantamount to placing a condition on the marriage.

Perhaps most importantly, when a Catholic marries a non-Catholic, baptized or not, the Catholic spouse must promise to continue practicing the Catholic faith and to do everything he or she can to baptize and raise his or her children in the Catholic faith (CCC, 1635; CIC, c. 1125). The Catholic faith is the greatest gift that a member of the Body of Christ has received and the greatest inheritance that can be bequeathed to his or her children. As this promise is required of the Catholic, a promise that he or she should desire to make without being asked, the couple needs to discuss how they envision practicing their respective faiths, and how they will raise their children. Since they intend to become one flesh, forming one life together, the practice of their faiths and the raising of their children should be done together or else these issues will become a source of division in the home.

Couples should mutually support each other in practicing their respective faiths by encouraging each other in prayer and worship. They should also pray and worship together, even if they cannot fully participate in each other's ecclesial gatherings. Regarding children, some couples intend to expose their children to the Catholic faith and another faith simultaneously, intending to allow the children to choose which faith they want to practice when they reach a certain age. This is not a good idea on two counts. First of all, by sending the message that each faith is equally valid, religious indifference may arise (CCC, 1634). Children might infer that religion is just a matter of taste and preference instead of a matter of truth. Secondly, because the two faiths that the children experience are each associated with a different parent, asking children to choose a religion is tantamount to asking them to choose between their parents. This is a psychological burden that parents should avoid placing on a child. When faced with such a decision a child might easily choose to be nonreligious. This does not mean that children cannot be exposed to aspects of different faiths, but given the Catholic spouse's promise to do everything possible to raise the children Catholic, it would be preferable to invite the non-Catholic spouse to cooperate, to whatever extent he or she feels comfortable, in raising the children in the Catholic faith.[40] In this way the education of the children in the faith is a joint effort, instead of appearing to the children that one parent is sidelined in this endeavor. However, in order for this joint effort to occur, it implies that instead of just a tolerance for Catholicism, the non-Catholic spouse should have a respect for and a resonance with the Catholic faith, seeing in Catholicism a heritage that he or she is happy to facilitate handing on to children.

Raniero Cantalamessa summed up the responsibility of Catholic spouses who are in mixed or disparity of cult marriages when he stated:

> Married couples are not always in the same place, religiously speaking. Perhaps one of them is a believer and the other is not, or at least not in the same way. In this case, the one who knows Jesus should invite him to the wedding and do it in such a way—with kindness, respect for the other, love and coherence of life—that Jesus soon becomes the friend of both. A "friend of the family!"[41]

By lovingly inviting Jesus into the home and making Jesus a friend of the family, even spouses in mixed or disparity of cult marriages can journey into a spirituality of tenderness together.

---

40. It should be noted that the Catholic spouse in a mixed or disparity of cult marriage does not promise that the children will in fact be raised Catholic, but instead promises "to do all in his or her power so that all offspring are baptized and brought up in the Catholic Church" (CIC, c. 1125 §1). The Catholic spouse would be fulfilling this promise even if the non-Catholic spouse prevented the Catholic spouse from having the children baptized in the Catholic Church or from raising them in the Catholic faith. In this instance for the Catholic spouse to do "all in his or her power" would mean exposing the children to the Catholic faith in other ways. Certainly, this would not be ideal, and would need to be seriously discerned before entering marriage.

41. Raniero Cantalamessa, "Father Cantalamessa on Christ at Cana: Pontifical Household Preacher Comments on Sunday's Readings," 12 January 2007, translated by ZENIT news agency, www.zenit.org/en/articles/father-cantalamessa-on-christ-at-cana (accessed May 9, 2013).

Summary

Marriage should be seen as a vocation to holiness that requires discernment and preparation before a couple embraces this vocation. It is a vocation in which Christ invites couples to live a spirituality of tenderness, empowered by the grace that they receive in the Sacrament of Marriage. This tenderness is founded on reverence and is willing to sacrifice and suffer for the beloved, as well as to repair marital love in an ongoing manner. Practicing this spirituality of tenderness under the guidance of the Holy Spirit in the context of the ecclesial community can lead couples to experience the ongoing renewal and resurrection of their love as they allow themselves to be conformed more completely to Jesus. Furthermore, this tenderness can pervade all aspects of married life, including what spouses do in their marriage bed, which is the focus of the next two chapters.

Chapter 19

Key Principles
of Sexual Morality

Introduction

This chapter applies what has been written about marriage up to this
point in the book, and explains how the mystery of marriage is experienced in the intimacy of sexual intercourse. While the principles of
sexual morality covered in this chapter apply to all marriages, this
chapter is also a continuation of the previous chapters on married
spirituality. If Christian spirituality is the all-encompassing effort to
conform one's life to the Person of Jesus Christ, then for spouses this
effort incorporates the intimacy of sexual union. Since the commitment
of faith informs the entirety of one's Christian existence, a spirituality
of marital tenderness should enter into the marriage bed. A married
couple's sexual intimacy should be suffused with tenderness that is
marked by reverence, sacrifice, a willingness to suffer, and a willingness to exert effort to repair their relationship. Christian spouses
should rely upon the grace of the Sacrament of Marriage and welcome
the presence of the Holy Spirit into their bedroom to enable them to
practice this spirituality of tenderness. Therefore, they can maintain
delicate attention to each other in their love-making and renew their
self-giving and welcoming of each other in the conjugal act. Living a
spirituality of tenderness allows married couples to experience wonder
before the creation of new life that God brings into existence through
their love-making, and it helps them to recapture, clarify, and deepen
their love as they mature as a married couple and experience the
resurrection of their love. Sexual morality cannot be separated from

spirituality because one's commitment of faith should pervade one's entire life. Thus the principles of sexual morality that are discussed in this chapter are placed in the context of a marital spirituality of tenderness and in the context of the sacramental theology of marriage, since it is the consecration that spouses receive in the Sacrament of Marriage that empowers them to live tenderly with each other.

FOUR PRINCIPLES OF SEXUAL MORALITY[1]

There are four basic principles of sexual morality that can be used to present Catholic teaching on sexuality. I have drawn these four principles of sexual morality from John Paul II's *Theology of the Body*. These principles are not explicitly stated by John Paul II; rather, I have extrapolated them from his text. I am not suggesting that these are the only four important principles upon which the *Theology of the Body* is built, nor are these necessarily John Paul II's most important insights. They are simply four principles that help us understand sexual morality and God's design for human loving. These four principles are:

1. We are not our own.
2. Sex is about a union of persons, not merely bodies.
3. Sex is about giving and receiving, not taking.
4. Sex is meant to give and receive life and love.

These principles exist in a hierarchy with each subsequent principle depending on the previous principle(s). Each of these four propositions is necessary in order to understand Catholic teaching on sexual morality and together they exist as a unified whole.[2]

---

1. The following treatment of the four principles of sexual morality as well as other portions of this chapter represent a revised and expanded version of Perry J. Cahall, "Preaching, Teaching, and Living the Theology of the Body," *The Linacre Quarterly* 73.3 (Aug. 2007): 213–29. Copyright © Catholic Medical Association, reprinted by permission of Taylor & Francis Ltd., www.tandfonline.com on behalf of the Catholic Medical Association.

2. For reliable and more extensive treatments of Catholic teaching on sexual morality see: John S. Grabowski, *Sex and Virtue: An Introduction to Sexual Ethics* (Washington, DC: The Catholic University of America Press, 2003); Ronald Lawler, Joseph Boyle, and William E. May, *Catholic Sexual Ethics: A Summary, Explanation, and Defense*, 2nd ed. (Huntington, IN: Our Sunday Visitor, 1996); William May, *Marriage: The Rock on Which the Family is Built* (San Francisco: Ignatius Press, 2009); William E. May, *Sex, Marriage, and Chastity: Reflections of a Catholic Layman, Spouse and Parent* (Chicago: Franciscan Herald Press, 1981); Alexander Pruss, *One Body: An Essay in Christian Sexual Ethics* (Notre Dame, IN: Notre Dame University Press, 2013); Paul M. Quay, *The Christian Meaning of Human Sexuality* (San Francisco: Ignatius Press, 1985). For further treatment of issues concerning reproductive technologies, see William E. May,

We Are Not Our Own

The first, and in many ways most important, principle of sexual morality is, "We are not our own." This principle comes from St. Paul's First Letter to the Corinthians. St. Paul states clearly, "The body is not meant for immorality, but for the Lord, and the Lord for the body" (1 Cor 6:13). After making the point that the bodies of Christians have become members of Christ, St. Paul asks whether it is lawful for a Christian to have sexual relations with a prostitute (1 Cor 6:15). He then provides the response to this question by saying, "Shun immorality. Every other sin which a man commits is outside the body; but the immoral man sins against his own body. Do you not know that your body is a temple of the Holy Spirit within you, which you have from God? You are not your own; you were bought with a price. So glorify God in your body" (1 Cor 6:18–20).

Commenting on St. Paul's inspired insights, John Paul II emphasized that Christ brought redemption to the entire person—including our bodies! John Paul stressed the fact that because the human body has been joined to God in Christ, it has received "a new dignity" and a "supernatural elevation" (TOB 56:4). The fact that the body is destined to be resurrected and participate in ultimate happiness also shows how seriously God takes the human body, and that eschatological happiness "cannot be understood as a state of the soul alone, separated . . . from the body" (TOB 66:6). All of this means that our bodies are holy, that God has reclaimed our bodies for himself by making us temples of the Holy Spirit through Baptism, and that our bodies are destined to participate in the love of the Trinity for all eternity! Therefore we should not turn the human body into an object or a thing, but instead must keep our bodies "with holiness and reverence" (TOB 57:2; see 1 Thes 4:3–5), because God has claimed them for himself.

The fact that we are not our own, that we belong to God soul *and* body, is a principle of sexual morality that should be embraced by

---

Catholic Bioethics and the Gift of Human Life, 2nd ed. (Huntington, IN: Our Sunday Visitor, Inc., 2008), and William E. May, *Catholic Bioethics and the Gift of Human Life*, 2nd ed. addendum (Huntington, IN: Our Sunday Visitor, Inc., 2010).

a marital spirituality of tenderness that has reverence as its foundation.[3] Married couples should stand in reverential awe at the gifts of each other, their bodies, and their complementary sexuality, which belong to God before belonging to them. In fact, everything we have and everything we are comes to us as gifts from God. We cannot claim to have made ourselves or to have acquired anything apart from the gifts and abilities that God has bestowed upon us. When spouses realize their complete and utter dependence on God, they realize that they are not their own and that they should be prompted to revere the gifts they have been given: the gifts of their lives, each other, their marriage, and their sexuality, all of which have been transformed by the gift of redemption, and which are elevated by the grace of the Sacrament of Marriage. When we realize we are not our own we should want to understand God's plan for us, including his plan for human sexuality.

It was pointed out in chapter 2 that John Paul II began his *Theology of the Body* by highlighting a question that the Pharisees asked Jesus about divorce, to which Jesus responded by taking them back to "the beginning" (Mt 19:3ff.; TOB 1). John Paul noted that in this conversation with the Pharisees, Jesus challenges us "to reflect on the way in which, in the mystery of creation, man was formed" (TOB 1:4), in order to teach us about marriage and what it means to be made male and female. As we discussed in chapter 3, God created the human person, both male and female, in his image (Gen 1:26–27). In fact, the body and the duality of the sexes is a revelation of God's love inscribed in creation. The human person is a unity of body and soul, and in this totality images God. This means that every man and woman should accept his or her male or female sexuality, because sexuality is a gift that we receive from God (CCC, 2333). Sexuality affects all aspects of the person in the unity of body and soul, determining our affectivity, how we can relate interpersonally, and our capacity to love and procreate (CCC, 2332; TOB 10:1). Being male and female governs the way in which we form bonds of communion with other people, and makes communion possible (CCC, 2332; TOB 10:2–3).

The *Catechism of the Catholic Church* states: "God is love and in himself he lives a mystery of personal loving communion. Creating

---

3. For an excellent discussion of how reverence as the core of spirituality ensures respect for God's design for sexuality, see Mary Shivanandan, "Conjugal Spirituality and the Gift of Reverence," *Nova et Vetera*, English ed., 10.2 (2012): 485–506.

the human race in his own image . . . God inscribed in the humanity of man and woman the *vocation*, and thus the capacity and responsibility, of *love* and communion" (CCC, 2331). This means that only in the distinction between masculinity and femininity can love be realized through the body and the love of the Trinity be fully imaged (TOB 9:3). Thus our bodies play a part in expressing and reflecting the image of the Trinity in which we were made, by making it possible for us to enter into a body-soul communion of persons.

John Paul II stated, "Man, whom God created 'male and female,' bears the divine image impressed in the body 'from the beginning'; man and woman constitute, so to speak, two diverse ways of 'being a body' that are proper to human nature in the unity of this image" (TOB 13:2). The human body is meant to make God's love visible in the world, and the human body is the only body in the created order that can express love. It is sexual difference that allows man and woman to unite in a communion of persons in marriage, to express love through a body, and to imitate "in the flesh the Creator's fecundity and generosity" (CCC, 2335). John Paul II asserted, "The [human] body, in fact, and only the body, is capable of making visible what is invisible: the spiritual and the divine. It has been created to transfer into the visible reality of the world the mystery hidden from eternity in God, and thus be a sign of it" (TOB 19:4). This mystery is the mystery of God's saving love for man as well as the mystery of God's own life of love. This means that the masculinity and femininity of human persons are visible signs of the inner life of God[4] who is the infinitely intimate communion of Persons (see also TOB 100:1). Therefore, it is accurate to say that John Paul II posited a sacramental quality of the human body according to which masculinity and femininity are meant to be visible signs of the invisible love of the Trinity.

Thus we belong to God completely, body and soul, and in and through our bodies we are meant to image the very love that is God. This necessarily means that the manner in which we conduct ourselves as embodied persons is part of the worship we offer to God. We must take this into account in our behavior with regard to how we treat our own bodies and how we treat others' bodies. St. Paul made it clear in his First Letter to the Corinthians that what we do with our bodies is

---

4. As has been already stated, this does not imply that God's inner life is gendered, as gender does not apply to the divine nature.

part of our response of faith. He impressed upon his readers that because Christ claimed us for himself we do not have the right to do with ourselves as we please.

To the modern world this last statement is hard to swallow. It flies in the face of the radical individualism and libertine mentality of our age that equates freedom with the ability to do whatever we want to do, whenever we want to do it. John Paul II recognized that the lack of understanding of human sexuality and marriage stems from this misunderstanding of freedom, (see especially FC, 6), which we discussed in chapter 3. A concept of freedom that claims to be absolute (i.e., doing whatever one wants) ends up treating the human body as raw datum or a tool for pleasure. Contrary to this counterfeit freedom, which ultimately denigrates the human body and human sexuality, John Paul II stressed that we are only free to the extent that we embrace the truth that comes from God. True freedom is contingent upon the truth about our nature that comes from God and can *never* be separated from that truth. Freedom is not the ability to do whatever we want to do. Instead, freedom is found in living in accord with the truth of human nature created by God, seeking to grow in our likeness to the God of love in whose image we are made.

The fact that we are not our own and that we therefore do not have the right to do with ourselves as we please is not harsh or limiting of authentic freedom when we realize that the God to whom we belong loves us more than we love ourselves, wants our happiness more than we want it, and knows with absolute certainty what will make us happy because he made us. Jesus Christ came to redeem humanity and the fullness of the human condition. The Incarnation shows that God intends to redeem the human person to the core. Our bodies and our sexuality are not bracketed off in this work of redemption (see Rom 8:23; TOB 49). As faith is the adherence of the *whole* person to God (see CCC, 150), Jesus asks us and empowers us to abandon ourselves to the Creator's design for our sexuality; a design which is for our happiness and which he has given us the ability to understand with the light of human reason. In his invitation to follow him, Jesus asks for *all* of us, nothing more and nothing less. He promises to lead us to experience happiness with him not only in the next life, but here, even amidst difficulties and struggles. If we wish to experience true sexual freedom we must come to the point where we trust that we can experience this freedom only by living in accord with God's design, because he created all of us, including our sexuality. The Catholic Church's teachings on sexual morality guide us into the intimate love for which we all long, because her teachings simply safeguard God's plan and call us to remember that we are not our own. This *is* good news because the one to whom we belong loves us more than we love ourselves, wants our happiness more than we want it, and knows what will make us truly happy, even in the sexual arena.

If we look into our hearts and are honest with ourselves, we know we are not our own. God has fashioned us in such a way that our hearts' deepest desires are meant to point us to him, who alone can satisfy these desires. In the opening chapter of this book we pointed out the desire that each of us has to experience intimacy with another, to enter into the personal mystery of another and to allow the other to enter into the mystery of our person. In chapter 4 we pointed out that the deepest and most basic desire of the human heart is the desire to love and be loved. In accord with the "spousal meaning" of the body, that was discussed in chapter 3, every man and woman longs to make a nuptial gift of self and experience a love that is faithful, fruitful, and forever. Thus to be human means that we long to experience the intimacy of nuptial union in which we give a total gift of self to the beloved, and receive the gift of the beloved in return. We long for the intimacy of mutual indwelling.[5] Each of us longs to be cherished by and united to another from deep within our being where we are most ourselves. We long to be known, loved, and treasured as if we are the only one in the world in the other's eyes. We long to "let down our guard" and be completely open with our beloved, giving ourselves completely and receiving the same gift from our beloved.

We pointed out in chapter 1 that we have this desire, this yearning, because we have been created by a God who is himself an intimate communion of love. The Trinity—Father, Son, and Holy Spirit—is love. This God of love seeks to share his intimate life of love with us and calls us to enter into intimate communion with him. God wants every single human person to experience nuptial union with

---

5. Thomas Aquinas commented on how friendship-love, which he saw as the highest form of human love, desires mutual indwelling in ST I-II, q. 28, a. 2. Thus while Aquinas' focus was on friendship and John Paul II's focus was on nuptial love, they both saw that the love for which we long desires mutual indwelling.

him, to feel cherished by him, and to be intimately united to him with the entirety of our being. The Triune God of love loves us so much that he wants us to experience intimacy not only with him, but with other human persons. God intends our interpersonal intimacy to be a sign of his love for us. Our human intimacy is supposed to open us up to intimacy with God and show us that we are not our own, that we are meant to give ourselves away in love to another, and to receive their love in return. As this personal union, a nuptial union, is made possible by God, we will be able to experience this intimacy when we have given ourselves over, body and soul, to God, his love, and his plan for us; when we realize our complete and utter dependence on him, when we realize that we are not our own.

The problem is that our culture has confused the intimacy of nuptial love with genital activity.[6] In our ache to be loved and cherished, to belong to and to receive another, we can mistake genital activity for intimacy and use it as a substitute for true loving communion. We need to remember that God designed the conjugal act to be the sacred sealing of a marriage covenant between a husband and a wife. Therefore, true sexual intimacy can be experienced only in marriage, because only in this context is sexual union in "conformity with the objective truth of the man and woman who give themselves" (LF, 12). We find by our own sad experience that when we engage in sexual activity outside of the context of the marital covenant, sex becomes a substitute for and the enemy of real personal intimacy. Many of our relationships fail because we are acting out of our unmet needs and because we look for the answer to our ache for intimacy in nonmarital sex. Relationships that involve genital activity outside of marriage end up hurting us because we act out of unhealed wounds or unmet needs for security and affection, thinking that this activity will somehow heal our wounds and fulfill our needs. We may even have a succession of relationships that involve sexual activity, none of which proves to satisfy our deepest longings. Instead of experiencing the intimacy we seek, we can end up going from relationship to relationship, suffering a great loneliness because we are confusing genital activity with the intimacy of nuptial love. We may even enter into and

---

6. For a thoughtful analysis of the effects of the sexual revolution which fostered this confusion, see Mary Eberstadt, *Adam and Eve after the Pill: Paradoxes of the Sexual Revolution* (San Francisco: Ignatius Press, 2012).

stay in relationships that do not make us feel cherished, but rather make us feel used, worthless, and horrible about ourselves all in a search for the love that satisfies. Spouses also find that disobeying God's design for sexuality within marriage leads to fragmentation and estrangement instead of the intimacy they seek.

Only God can fill the bottomless canyon of the human heart. Intimacy with the Trinity is the source of all true intimacy between human persons, including spouses. The great paradox of intimacy and conjugal love is that we will be able to receive the gift of love that God wants us to experience with another human person when we are secure in our relationship with the Trinity. When we receive God's love we will be free enough not to be a needy person who primarily takes from others without ever giving. We will be secure because we will know we are loved and cherished, and we will know who we are—a beloved of God! The more intimate we become with the Father, Son, and Holy Spirit, the more open we become to the persons the Trinity gives us to love. This is why the source of true human intimacy, including intimacy between spouses, is intimacy in prayer, which is time spent with the Trinity of love. It is the Trinity alone who loves us as we long to be loved: with an infinite gift of self, not needing anything from us, loving us unconditionally with a love that can never be broken, with a love that will never betray us, and a love that will satisfy us completely. Thus our ability to enter into truly loving relationships is not drawn primarily from each other, but from God. Being in love with God means always having love to give. To experience the love for which we all long we must receive each other as gifts from God and give God's love to each other, loving as he loves. However, we cannot do this unless we die to ourselves and acknowledge that we are not our own. Only when we drink in this truth and allow it to penetrate the very core of our being will we be able to experience the truth of our sexuality, true personal intimacy, and the truth of conjugal love.

Catholicism is a religion of the most profound intimacy: intimacy with the divine Persons of the Trinity and intimacy with one another. The Church's teachings on sexual morality guide us into the intimacy and the nuptial union for which we all long because her teachings simply safeguard God's plan and remind us that we are not our own. The Church's teachings remind us that we need to give ourselves to God and his plan for human love[7] if we want to receive the intimacy of nuptial union that he desires for us, in whatever vocation he calls us to embrace. We will say more about this in the final chapter of this book.

Therefore, if we want to experience sexual fulfillment we need to embrace and reverence God's design for human love. This design precedes us. It is objective. No amount of self-will or rationalization can alter this design. A sane person lives in accord with reality. So much of the sexual libertinism of our age is, quite simply, insanity, because it refuses to live in accord with the objective nature of human sexuality. Modern sexual libertines do not want to acknowledge that there is anything objective and unchangeable about human sexuality. Sex, and the human body, have been emptied of their meaning and are constantly manipulated by a distorted idea of freedom. Yet, human sexuality does have objective features, ingrained in our nature by God. The next three principles, all of which are ascertainable through natural law reasoning, recall these features.

Sex Is about a Union of Persons, Not Merely Bodies

The first objective feature of sexual intercourse is that sex is about a union of persons, not just a union of bodies or body parts or biological material. Sexual intercourse is about a union of persons because human sexuality affects the entirety of the human person. As was pointed out in chapter 3, we are an intimate union of body and soul (CCC, 364–65)—embodied spirits. The body expresses the person and in this way is a sacrament of the soul, a visible sign of an invisible reality. In the *Theology of the Body* John Paul II stated that "the body is the expression of the spirit and is called, in the very mystery of creation, to exist in the communion of persons 'in the image of God'" (TOB 32:1). John Paul stressed over and over again that sexuality involves the entire person, body and soul.

If sexuality affects all aspects of the human person in the unity of body and soul (CCC, 2332; TOB 10:1), then this means that sexuality is not just about "parts" but instead sexuality affects all aspects of

---

7. Remember that at the end of what has come to be known as the *Theology of the Body*, John Paul II stated the whole work could be called "'Human Love in the Divine Plan' or with greater precision, 'The Redemption of the Body and the Sacramentality of Marriage'" (TOB 133:1).

the person. "Sexuality . . . is not something simply biological, but concerns the innermost being of the human person as such" (FC, 11; CCC, 2361). Man and woman are both created in God's image and thus possess equal personal dignity (CCC, 2334; TOB 9). However, their equality does not mean identity or sameness. "Each of the two sexes is an image of the power and tenderness of God, with equal dignity though in a different way" (CCC, 2335). Man and woman each image God in their own distinctive way and their sexual difference is directed towards personal complementarity in a "communion of persons" (TOB 9:2–3; see also CCC, 2333).

If we are embodied spirits created to enter into a communion of persons, then sexual intercourse is always a personal act, never just a bodily act (TOB 10:2–5; see also HV, 9). The Old Testament uses the language of "knowing" (*yada* in Hebrew) to refer to sexual intercourse (e.g., Gen 4:1–2; TOB 20:2). In the New Testament, when Paul discusses sexual immorality (see 1 Cor 6:13–20 cited above) he "understood 'body' [*soma* in Greek] as the whole person considered under the aspect of his or her physical dimension."[8] For Paul this meant that the whole person, and not just the person's genitals, is involved in sexual activity because it is the activity of the person.[9] Thus it is through the body that a man and a woman come "to know" each other personally, because "they reveal themselves to one another with *that specific depth of their own human 'I,' which precisely reveals itself also through their sex*, their masculinity and femininity" (TOB 20:4). In sexual intercourse, "Man and woman express . . . the whole truth of their persons" (TOB 123:4) and become one, in all of their complementarity and complexity (TOB 20:5). This is why John Paul II emphasized that sexual union should always be about the person and should never treat the person as a means to an end (LF, 12).

Since we are embodied spirits, this means that what we do with our bodies in sexual intercourse we do with our persons. However, our society acts as if this is not so. Too often our culture acts as if sexual intercourse is just about two bodies coming together to derive as much pleasure from each other as possible. The fact that terms like "casual sex," "recreational sex," or "one-night stands" have entered our common

---

8. Francis Martin, "Marriage in the New Testament Period," in *Christian Marriage: A Historical Study*, ed. Glenn W. Olsen (New York: The Crossroad Publishing Company, 2001), 81.

9. Ibid.

vocabulary shows how depersonalized sexual intercourse has become in our culture. The idea that one can engage in sexual activity as some type of pastime or personal amusement that involves no personal investment or commitment beyond a fleeting encounter, betrays a complete instrumentalization of the body and as such, the degradation of the human person. The phenomenon of "friends with benefits" is another instance of two people mutually instrumentalizing each other for the purpose of pursuing periodic genital pleasure without any commitment to each other. The reality is that none of these supposedly liberating experiences of sexual intercourse will fill the deep yearning for intimacy in the human heart. Instead, these behaviors treat our bodies as pleasure tools, leave us hollow, and turn us into slaves of lust. They also damage us and blind us to the love that can offer fulfillment.

Another instance of divorcing the body from the person can be seen with the advent of certain procedures of reproductive technology that separate the procreation of a child from the conjugal act. We have now stepped into the "brave new world"[10] in which the procreation of a human person is sometimes viewed as no more than a form of production that results from the joining of egg with sperm. There is no longer any reverence shown for God's design for how these gametes are supposed to come together; through a personal act of mutual self-donation between a husband and wife. When we separate the power to create a human life from the conjugal act, we have made ourselves the "lords of life" and have truly instrumentalized our sexuality and our bodies, seeing them as no more than sources of necessary biological material. Our culture has therefore adopted a dualistic view of the human person in which the body has been separated from the soul.

According to God's design the conjugal act is meant to be the sacred sealing of a personal covenant. As discussed in chapter 5, the very essence of a covenant is a mutual exchange of persons that involves a total self-giving of one person to another (TOB 104). Sexual intercourse is designed by God to enact the wedding vows throughout the

---

10. This novel written by Aldous Huxley in 1932 is still worth reading. Many aspects of the imaginative future world that Huxley described, in which the production of human life was separated from the conjugal act and children were produced in an industrial setting for eugenics purposes, have become reality.

entirety of married life.[11] It is meant to be "the regular *sign* of the communion of persons" of the spouses (TOB 37:4). Furthermore, the marriage covenant and the personal act which seals this covenant are meant to be living signs of the covenantal love between God and his people, which culminates in Christ's self-oblation of love offered to his bride, the Church. Thus sexual intercourse is most correctly referred to as the "marital act" or the "conjugal act" because sexual intercourse is a gift given to spouses that is supposed to speak the language of the covenant through the body, a language of self-donation that is authored by God (TOB 105:5), and which spouses must choose to read and speak in truth (TOB 105:6).

Marriage is the only context in which it is possible to speak the language of sexual intercourse in truth. Only in marriage can sexual union be an expression of a communion of persons, because only in marital consent have spouses proclaimed that they have handed themselves over to each other completely and permanently through a solemn act of their wills (see TOB 105:3). Since sexual intercourse is designed to be the ultimate expression or sealing of the mutual consent of the spouses through the body, this means that only spouses have the right to express their love in this way. This is why Scripture and the Church teach that sex outside of marriage is a false substitute for true intimacy of heart and soul.

As mentioned earlier in this chapter and in chapter 4, in sexual activity outside of marriage something is always being held back because people are trying to share their bodies without fully sharing their hearts and souls. An unmarried couple who is engaged usually thinks they are expressing true love for each other by engaging in sexual intercourse. The reality is that they cannot express true love in this act because sex outside of the marriage bond cannot be the ultimate expression, through the body, of the mutual consent of the couple to give and receive each other completely. There is a world of difference between a faithful and lifelong commitment that is open to children, and a relationship of mutual convenience. Nonmarital sex is (at best) the mutual use of each other's bodies because it promises nothing except what is done in the moment. God calls married couples and only married couples to a life of personal union that

---

11. John S. Grabowski, *Sex and Virtue*, 46.

includes sexual intercourse, the most intimate expression of love that can be shared between two people. Our society's attempt to separate sexual activity from a union of persons in the marriage bond has led to the disintegration of persons and the family.[12] Reverencing this link between sex and marriage is the only way to experience true sexual liberation, because it is the only way to experience a true "communion of persons."

Sex Is about Giving and Receiving, Not Taking

As we discussed in chapter 4, true love is self-giving, and never self-seeking. True love seeks to give in order to serve the true good of the beloved, even if this service involves sacrifice or even suffering as was mentioned in chapter 18. True love also desires to receive the gift of the other person. John Paul II emphasized repeatedly throughout his pontificate (following the lead of GS, 24) that the human person finds meaning in life and comes to a full understanding of his or her humanity only through making a sincere gift of self to others and to God (see TOB 15). Thus, as was discussed in chapter 3, the person is a being-gift and freedom is the fundamental characteristic of the person that allows us to live out our being-gift and enter into communion with others. If we seek the meaning of freedom and why God gave it to us, we see that it is our capacity for giving and that God gave it to us to be able to give. True freedom is found to the extent that we accept ourselves as gifts from God and experience ourselves as self-giving gifts. Thus true freedom is being a gift according to the truth that comes from God. Also, true personal intimacy is experienced when we give ourselves as gifts in an act of true freedom, and receive the gift of other persons in accord with the truth about ourselves and others.

The concept of "gift" is in many ways the key to understanding human sexuality and Catholic sexual morality (see LF, 12). God gifts us with our sexual identity. Sexuality itself is intended to provide us with the power of creative self-giving. John Paul II stated that the complementarity of the male and female bodies reveals to us that we are made to be gifts, to express love for one another, and to exist for

---

12. As evidence of this disintegration, in 2007 nearly four in ten US births were to unmarried women. See Stephanie J. Ventura, "Changing Patterns of Nonmarital Childbearing in the United States," *National Center for Health Statistics Date Brief*, no. 18 (May 2009):1, accessed June 14, 2013 www.cdc.gov/nchs/data/databriefs/db18.pdf.

someone (TOB 14; see also TOB 17). This is what John Paul referred to as the "spousal meaning of the body" (TOB 14:15), an understanding of which John Paul II said is essential for understanding the purpose of human existence (TOB 18:4). The gendered human body with its spousal meaning is a gift-sign, revealing to us our capacity for love and communion. Consistent with the person-as-gift and the body as a gift-sign, sexual intercourse is meant to be an expression of the complete mutual self-giving of spouses to each other. Thus John Paul II asserted:

> Every man and every woman fully realizes himself or herself through the sincere gift of self. For spouses, the moment of conjugal union constitutes a very particular expression of this. It is then that a man and a woman, in the "truth" of their masculinity and femininity, become a mutual gift to each other. All married life is a gift; but this becomes most evident when the spouses, in giving themselves to each other in love, bring about that encounter which makes them "one flesh" (Gen 2:24). (LF, 12)

Therefore, for sexual intercourse to be an expression of true intimacy it must be an act of self-gift, seeking the good of the other in the context of marriage, in which the two really have become one. As the ultimate expression of conjugal love, the conjugal act is designed to express a mutual gift of self that is free, irrevocable, faithful, and fruitful.

In several places within this book we have already discussed how John Paul II wrote about a language of the body in the *Theology of the Body*. We are all familiar with the term "body language" but John Paul II was speaking of more. He noted that the human person needs a body to fully express himself or herself. Acts performed with the human body have an objective meaning even if we do not believe that they do. John Paul pointed out that in sexual intercourse the body speaks a language that is objective, and that this language is one of complete mutual self-donation and self-gift. It is through this language that spouses receive each other's person (TOB 108; TOB 111–113). Marriage is the only context within which the body can speak this language in truth. In fact, we discussed in chapters 14 and 15 that John Paul II explained the essential sign of the sacrament of marriage as the "language of the body" spoken in truth.

Any attempt to engage in sexual intercourse outside of marriage is equivalent to speaking a lie with the body. Premarital sex, which Scripture calls fornication, falsifies the language of mutual self-gift because the intention of an unmarried man and woman engaging in sexual intercourse cannot coincide with the objective language of the body. As we discussed in chapter 4, in premarital intercourse, even intercourse during the engagement period, the body is trying to speak a language of complete mutual self-donation, but it cannot speak this language since the couple has withheld this consent from each other. An engaged couple having premarital sex may convince themselves that they are "committed" to each other and that they are "gifting" themselves to each other by engaging in sexual intercourse. The ecstatic (from the Greek *ekstasis* which literally means standing [*stasis*] outside [*ek*]) experience of sexual intercourse that allows them to transcend themselves may even lead them to think that they are experiencing true intimacy with each other. However, while an engaged couple is able to "stand outside" themselves in a sexual encounter, they cannot experience the intimacy of personal communion with each other because they have not given themselves to each other in the exchange of marital consent. The two cannot become truly one through this act, and deep down the couple knows this. The couple is putting themselves in the situation of speaking a lie to each other through their bodies.

Since they are speaking a lie to each other through their bodies when they have sexual intercourse, unmarried couples, even if they are engaged, cannot experience the intimacy that they seek. Even though they want to experience intimacy through their love-making, unmarried couples sow seeds of distrust in their relationship because their bodies are speaking untruth to each other. This became evident to me in a conversation with a friend who had been married only after having premarital sex with her spouse. She explained to me that for the first few years of her married life she was constantly suspicious of her husband, worrying that he would cheat on her or have an affair with another woman. She confided that she had no reason to suspect her husband of infidelity, yet her anxiety persisted. She then explained that one day she had an epiphany. She reported that she realized why she was worried about whether or not her husband would remain faithful to her, and she explained her revelation in these words:

"I realized that my husband had already had sex with someone who was not his spouse, so why wouldn't he do it again?" My friend went on to explain that she viewed this realization as a moment of grace. She and her husband realized that by having premarital sex they had, in many ways unwittingly, sown seeds of distrust in their relationship that had burdened their marriage up to that point. With this realization they proceeded to ask for and receive forgiveness from each other and from God, putting their marriage on a much firmer foundation. Living through the anxiety of the early years of her marriage, which by the grace of God is now in its thirtieth year, my friend realized that only spouses can speak the language of the body in truth and experience true personal communion.

In commenting on Ephesians 5, John Paul II pointed out St. Paul's teachings that the bodies of husbands and wives are sacred in their one-flesh union. Husbands are exhorted to love their wives as they love their own bodies (Eph 5:28), showing "the dignity of the body and the moral imperative to care for its good" (TOB 92:8). John Paul asserted that for Christian spouses, rereading the language of the body in truth forms "the content and principle of their new life in Christ and in the Church" (TOB 105:2). Thus speaking the language of the body in truth is part of how spouses keep God's commandments, which is prayed for in one of the nuptial blessings of the rite of marriage:

> And now, Lord, we implore you:
> may these your servants
> hold fast to the faith and keep your commandments;
> made one in the flesh,
> may they be blameless in all they do.
> (RM, "Nuptial Blessing A").

We need to remember that the language of the body spoken in truth is the essential sign of the Sacrament of Marriage. This means that the conjugal act is meant to be an efficacious sign of the gift of one's whole self to the other, and a reception of the gift of the other. Additionally, in the Sacrament of Marriage the body becomes an efficacious sign of grace, and sexual intercourse in marriage can be an opportunity to grow in grace (TOB 87:5).[13] In sacramental

---

13. See also John S. Grabowski, *Sex and Virtue*, 68.

marriage Christ gives grace to spouses to discover the true freedom of being a gift through the spousal meaning of the body, in order to form a life-long communion of persons that images "the self-giving that is the basis of Trinitarian communion."[14] Therefore, through grace the language of the body spoken in sexual intercourse is meant to participate in the total self-giving love of the Trinity, as well as the total self-giving love of Christ for his Church which reveals the inner love of the Trinity.

In chapter 14 we discussed how John Paul II stated that the language of the body that spouses speak to each other in the conjugal act is linked to the language of the liturgy (TOB 114–117b). The language of the body is a language of praise and worship in which the couples speak through their bodies the language that they first verbalized in the exchange of their marital consent. John Paul even explained that "conjugal life in some sense becomes liturgy" (TOB 117b:6). This means that the language of the body that spouses speak to each other in the conjugal act is taken up into the daily worship that they offer to God as a couple, forming an essential aspect of the spirituality of marriage (TOB 117b:3). This spirituality is based in reverence, understood as "*a spiritually mature form* of that reciprocal *fascination* . . . of the man for femininity and of the woman for masculinity" (TOB 117b:4). Filled with fascination, awe, and reverence for the God who made them, spouses are prompted to revere each other in their sexual union.

Moreover, the reverence that spouses show to each other in conjugal relations can be analogized to a eucharistic offering. This act of self-donation in which spouses surrender themselves to each other out of love to become one flesh is analogous to the Eucharist, in which Christ offers his own flesh to build up and nourish his bride the Church (see TOB 92:8; 99:1).[15] John Paul II explained that Christ gives the fruits of redemption and his very self to the Church in an act of spousal donation, "according to the likeness of the spousal relationship between husband and wife" (TOB 94:5). The ultimate goal of spouses is to cooperate with the grace offered them in the Sacrament of Marriage, to love each other in every aspect of their marriage as Christ loves the

---

14. Ibid., 70.
15. See also John S. Grabowski, *Sex and Virtue*, 65.

Church; Christ continues to offer his love to his spouse through the gift of himself in the Eucharist.

"Each act of sacramentalized spousal union is thus a sign of the self-giving of Christ the Bridegroom,"[16] a gift in which Christ gives all of himself "without reserve."[17] As in the Eucharist, a married couple's conjugal union recalls and makes present their covenant of love.[18] If spouses draw upon the gift of Christ's love in the Eucharist they will grow in their ability to be gifts of love in every aspect of their marriage, including their ability to offer themselves to each other in their marriage bed.[19] They will be able to grow in their ability to speak a language of thanksgiving in their marriage bed which says to each other and to God, "This is my body given up for you." In the Sacrament of Marriage, spouses receive the grace to assist them in incorporating their love-making into the daily worship that they offer to God as a couple.[20]

It should be noted that approaching the conjugal act as part of the worship that spouses offer to God does not ensure that every instance of sexual union between a husband and a wife will be subjectively satisfying. The idea that every sexual encounter will be an experience of ecstasy is a fallacy that exists only in movies, television, and lewd commercials that tempt couples to "buy better sex." John S. Grabowski aptly stated:

> A common objection to such a view of sexual intimacy as a bodily self-gift that recalls a couple's wedding vows is that it creates an unrealistic and overly romantic view of sex far removed from the everyday experience of most couples. But to describe sex as liturgical and analogous to worship is not to suggest that every conjugal act will approximate mystical experience, any more than liturgical prayer always involves ecstasy. It simply means that spouses give themselves to each other as they are (joyous, anxious, tired, energetic, preoccupied, attentive, etc.) and in so doing symbolically enact their vows to one another. The "objective" meaning

---

16. Peter J. Elliott, *What God Has Joined*, 156.

17. Angelo Scola, *The Nuptial Mystery*, trans. Michelle K. Borras (Grand Rapids, MI: William B. Eerdmans Publishing Company, 2005), 370.

18. John S. Grabowski, *Sex and Virtue*, 54.

19. Peter J. Elliott, *What God Has Joined*, 156.

20. Ibid., 158.

of the bodily language they speak may or may not be fully assimilated in the couple's "subjective" experience at any given moment.[21]

In other words, striving to speak the language of the body in truth does not guarantee that couples will always have "great sex." At times, when they speak this language they may stutter or stammer, and these instances may be less than satisfying or even frustrating. However, the important aspect is that the couple speaks truth by trying as best they can to be gift to each other and to receive each other's gift.

Lust, or "adultery of the heart" (Mt 5:27–28), is the antithesis of liturgical language and conjugal spirituality founded in reverence because it is a violation of the meaning of sexuality as self-gift (see TOB 24–59; esp. 31, 32, 33, 40). Instead of reverencing and receiving the other as gift and offering oneself as a gift, lust turns the other into an object of sexual gratification (TOB 40). Lust is a disordered desire for sexual pleasure that selfishly seeks sexual gratification apart from true love as a sincere gift of self (CCC, 2351). Lust violates the person as gift and distorts the spousal meaning of the body. In a world consumed by lust, people too easily bypass giving and focus on taking. Instead of focusing outward and offering ourselves in generous love we turn in on ourselves and focus on satisfying our own selfish desires. This lust or adultery of the heart can even infiltrate marriage and cause spouses to use each other (TOB 42:7).

As was noted in chapter 3, after the Fall, lust almost destroyed the communion of persons that existed between man and woman. Before the Fall, the original man and woman were integrated persons experiencing harmony between their bodies and their souls (see TOB 18:1–3). This made a full communion of persons—body and soul—between them possible and enabled them to be gift for each other (see TOB 18:5). After the Fall, man and woman each lost their internal peace, which had been signified by being naked without shame (Gen 2:25), and they felt the need to cover their nakedness as a result of this internal disquiet (Gen 3:7; see TOB 26:5). Their communion of persons was threatened and wounded by a new desire to dominate the other through lust (one should note Gen 3:16 which speaks about

21. John S. Grabowski, *Sex and Virtue*, 69.

the woman's desire being for her husband and her husband ruling over her; TOB 31:1).

However, we are not destined to be overcome by lust in this fallen world. John Paul II pointed out that if we do not want to be dominated by lust we must grow in self-mastery (TOB 49:3–6). As John Paul stated, "Purity is a requirement of love" (TOB 49:7). We must exert the effort to control our desires or they will end up controlling us. We are created in God's image by being given the capacity to act as his representatives (Gen 1:28, dominion in the garden) through self-consciousness (reason) and self-determination (will). We can become like God, and perfect our freedom, image, and nature, insofar as we master ourselves through reason and will with the help of God's grace, and exercise our dominion through self-giving. In order to be self-gift we must master ourselves first (TOB 123:5; 125:4; 127:5; 130:4; see also CCC, 2338–2347), because no one can give what he or she does not have. By mastering themselves according to truth and speaking this truth through their bodies, man and woman can form a communion of persons (TOB 123:7). This will involve ongoing conversion and lifelong effort, but the grace of redemption won for us by Christ makes this transformation possible. Furthermore, it is worth the effort in order to realize the deepest desire for intimacy in the human heart. As we pointed out in the previous chapter, in this life there is no resurrection without the cross. Christian spouses are called and empowered by Christ in the Sacrament of Marriage to reverence and receive each other as gifts from God and give God's love to each other, loving as he loves. They are empowered to live an authentic married spirituality that embraces self-sacrifice, and even suffering, dying to themselves to experience true intimacy and the true meaning of sexuality.

Dominion in the realm of sexual desire involves growing in the virtue of chastity because chastity promotes the self-mastery that enables us to be gift (CCC, 2337, 2395). Chastity is often misconstrued as mere abstinence from sexual intercourse or it is equated with sexual repression. In reality, the virtue of chastity is the practice of controlling sexual desire according to will and reason, and integrating sexuality within ourselves so we can become self-gift (CCC, 2337–2338). Far from being primarily an experience of repressing sexual passion, chaste living is a positive experience of joy, growing in purity of heart and fully possessing oneself in true freedom to become self-gift

(TOB 58:7). Chastity frees us to love (TOB 128:3). It is the virtue that enables us to express true love in all of our physical displays of affection. Living chastely does mean saying no to all illicit genital stimulation and controlling the desire for illicit sexual pleasure. The term "illicit" refers to all sexual pleasure that cannot be fulfilled in sexual intercourse within the confines of marriage, which is the only place where a total act of self-giving conjugal love is possible (see CCC, 2351–2356). Out of reverence for the gift of the person and the gift of sexuality, chastity says no to actions that play with our senses and our bodies. However, chastity is not a mortification of love, but a condition for true love (see TOB 129:5). Chaste living says yes to receiving the other person, and always affirms the other person through this reception. Chastity says no to selfish behavior that ignores the person because "it feels good," but chaste living ultimately says yes to loving without regrets. The virtue of chastity frees us from aggression, selfishness, self-centeredness, and self-seeking. Chastity promotes self-respect, as well as respect and reception of others as persons who are made in God's image. As chastity is about respecting and receiving ourselves and others as gifts and living our sexuality according to God's plan, it is at the heart of a married spirituality that is founded on "*reverence for what comes from God*" (TOB 131:2). In fact, John Paul II stated, "The reverence born in man for everything bodily and sexual, both in himself and in every other human being, male and female, turns out to be the most essential power for keeping the body 'with holiness'" (TOB 54:4). Reverencing God's gift of sexuality through chaste living gives us joy and peace because it makes us truly free to be what a person is meant to be—self-gift.

Since chastity is necessary in order to experience true freedom and happiness (CCC, 2342), it is a necessary virtue throughout life and in all states of life (see CCC, 2348–2350). Chastity *before* marriage is necessary to be able to give oneself as a gift, free from the domination of passions. Chaste living is the only true preparation for marriage. Before marriage, chastity takes the form of abstinence from all willful genital stimulation and sexual pleasure, because engaging in these activities cannot be aimed at true self-giving outside of marriage. Abstaining from sex and from willful genital stimulation before marriage shows that we love the other person for who he or she is, and not for how he or she performs in bed or how he or she makes us feel.

Chastity is necessary *during* marriage to be able to give oneself as a gift, free from domination of passions. Due to the fact that lust or adultery of the heart can exist in marriage, spouses should never seek to sexually excite each other unless they intend to engage in the conjugal act. To do otherwise would amount to using the body and the person as a plaything. There is also the virginal chastity of the consecrated religious (see CCC, 1618–1620). As we will discuss in the final chapter, the free choice to give oneself in love in complete body-soul self-donation is what makes celibacy a legitimate vocation from God, a vocation that is a sign of the resurrected life when we will neither marry nor be given in marriage (see Mt 22:30). Chastity manifested in a life of celibacy testifies to the truth of the person as gift (TOB 15:5; 80:1, 6). Thus, as we will see in chapter 21, consecrated celibacy and marriage give meaning to each other because they are both forms of spousal love lived *for* another (see TOB 76,78, 81), but neither can be lived without the virtue of chastity.

Only by embracing and living a life of chastity can one rediscover the spousal meaning of the body. Only by living chastely can a person be truly free, truly able to give oneself as a gift in whatever vocation God calls one to, truly living and growing as an image and likeness of God. John Paul II stated, "The inner man must open himself to life according to the Spirit, in order to share in evangelical purity of heart: in order to find again and realize the value of the body, freed by redemption from the bonds of concupiscence" (TOB 58:5). Living unchastely desensitizes us to love, making us takers rather than givers and receivers. We are not our own, but giving in to lustful passions is acting as if we have the right to manipulate the human body, our own and others, for our own ends.

In his words about "adultery of the heart," Jesus tells us that we must undertake self-mastery to control our desires instead of allowing our desires to control us. John Paul II stated that we are not to fear Christ's words, which call us to conquer lust in our hearts (Mt 5:28), but instead we should have confidence in their salvific content and power (TOB 43:7). Christ came to liberate us from lust so that we can experience the freedom of love (see TOB 52, 53). Through an ongoing conversion of heart, empowered by the Holy Spirit, we can experience the redemption of our sexuality. Christ wants to redeem *all* of us, body and soul (see TOB 46). He wants to redeem our love by incorporating us into his union with his Church and nourishing us through his sacraments. He makes it possible for us to live a life of self-gift for the other in order to come to a full understanding of our humanity. This is truly good news, and we must not empty the Cross of Christ of its power (1 Cor 1:17). If we want to experience true sexual freedom we must allow our lust to be crucified and invite Christ in to transform, redeem, and purify our hearts. Christ's love must enter the inner sanctuary of our hearts to enable us to be gift for each other and to receive each other as gifts.

Sex Is Meant to Give and Receive Life and Love

According to God's design ingrained in human nature, the total mutual gift of self that occurs through the union of persons in the conjugal act is designed to give and receive life *and* love. In his encyclical letter of 1968, *Humanae Vitae*, Pope Paul VI pointed out that natural law shows us there are two purposes of the sexual act that anyone can see just by examining it with human reason: procreation (life) and union (love) (HV, 12; see John Paul II's comments in TOB 119). Paul VI noted that God established an "inseparable connection . . . between the unitive significance and the procreative significance which are both inherent to the marriage act" (HV, 12). Thus, anything that intentionally opposes or prevents one or the other of these ends of sexual intercourse, as they are ingrained in our nature, is contrary to God's design, harmful to us, and, if done knowingly and willingly, is sinful. This is the shorthand guide and the "relevant principle of conjugal morality" (TOB 121:6) for coming to a moral judgment about any particular sexual act.

Hopefully the principles of sexual morality that have been outlined thus far in this chapter, as well as material covered in chapters 4 and 5, make it clear why sexual acts that oppose the life-giving or love-giving aspects of sexual union are opposed to "an integral conception" of the human person, created as an intimate unity of body and soul, and the reality of conjugal love, which seeks complete mutual self-giving (TOB 121:4; see HV, 7–9). Examples of sexual acts that oppose the life-giving potential of sexual intercourse would include: bestiality, homosexual intercourse (see CCC, 2357–2359), all forms of contraception (withdrawal, direct sterilization procedures, barrier methods, oral, transdermal, or injected hormonal agents, intrauterine devices, spermacides; see CCC, 2370), and masturbation (solitary or with a partner; see CCC, 2352). Examples of sexual acts that oppose loving union would include: rape or forced intercourse (which can occur between spouses; see CCC, 2356), incest (violating the loving trust of a family member; see CCC, 2356, 2388), molestation (violating the loving trust of a child; CCC, see 2356, 2389), adultery (violating the covenantal love of marriage; see CCC, 2380–2381), polygamy or polyandry (violating the exclusive nature of the gift of self in sexual intercourse; see CCC, 2387), prostitution (treating sex as a commodity; see CCC, 2355), pornography (objectifying another person as "eye candy"; see CCC, 2354), premarital sex/fornication/ "trial" marriages (pretending committed love; see CCC, 2353, 2390–2391), and certain reproductive technologies that intend to make or produce a child apart from an act of loving sexual union between spouses (e.g., artificial insemination, whether heterologous, when sperm and/or egg are donated by someone other than the married couple, or homologous, when the sperm and egg belong to the married couple; *in vitro* fertilization; surrogate motherhood; cloning; see CCC, 2376–2377). It should be noted that aspects of reproductive medicine that seek to promote the health of a couple so that they can conceive a child through the conjugal act are morally legitimate. Thus there is a difference between *assisting* the couple to conceive through conjugal intercourse and *replacing* that act with a procedure.[22]

Interestingly, if we examine them, any sexual act that opposes life also opposes loving union (TOB 123:6). Bestiality precludes loving personal union, because it is an attempt to sexually unite with a nonperson. Homosexual intercourse precludes a true sexual union of persons because two people of the same gender lack the differences that make the reception of the other person's gift possible. Contraception, in all of its forms, precludes the fullness of loving personal union because a couple who engages in this behavior withholds

---

22. For a good, brief discussion of the morality of reproductive technologies, see USCCB Committee on Pro-Life Activities, *Life-Giving Love in an Age of Technology* (Washington, DC: United States Conference of Catholic Bishops, 2009). See also Congregation for the Doctrine of the Faith, *Donum Vitae* (Instruction on Respect for Human Life in Its Origin and on the Dignity of Procreation Replies to Certain Questions of the Day), 1987, accessed February 26, 2016, www.vatican.va/roman_curia/congregations/cfaith/documents/rc_con_cfaith_doc_19870222 _respect-for-human-life_en.html.

their fertility from each other and therefore fails to give and receive the fullness of each other's person. Masturbation seeks the pleasure of genital stimulation without the fullness of sexual union.

John Paul II explained more clearly why a sexual act that opposes the procreative end of sexual intercourse also opposes the unitive end. John Paul highlighted the fact that the unitive (loving) and procreative (life-giving) aspects of sexual intercourse are both aspects of the "self as gift" (FC, 32) and cannot be separated from each other in an act of sexual intercourse without doing harm to the integrity of both the act and the persons involved (TOB 118:5–6). Therefore, the morality of the marriage act is determined by the nature of the act and the personal dignity of the spouses (HV, 13). John Paul noted that a conjugal act artificially deprived of fecundity ceases to be an act of love because the act has been deprived of its full truth (TOB 123:6). Although bodily union occurs, a communion of persons cannot (TOB 123:7). Thus, any act that opposes the procreative end of sexual intercourse also opposes its unitive end. This behavior is contrary to human nature as an intimate unity of body and soul, as well as the nature of the conjugal act; it does not promote true freedom and, if done with full knowledge and free consent, is sinful. These actions, examples of which appear above, violate the true meaning of conjugal love and thus the ability to give oneself completely and freely as a gift, and to receive the totality of the gift of the other in a communion of persons.

John Paul II stated that his whole catechesis on the *Theology of the Body* can be seen as a commentary on *Humanae Vitae* (TOB 119:5; 133:2). John Paul grounded the teaching of *Humanae Vitae* in the gift of self and the language of self-gift that the body is designed to speak in order to form a communion of persons. In their exchange of marital consent spouses pledge to give and receive each other in their totality. This is encapsulated in the language, "I take you to be my wife / my husband" (see OCM, 62); see TOB 103:1–2). John Paul II pointed out that spouses must be aware that by these words they are pledging to give and receive each other in all of their masculinity and femininity to constitute a lifelong "communion of persons" (TOB 103:5). Furthermore, these vows spoken in the liturgy presuppose a "language of the body" by which the spouses become mutual gift (TOB 103:6). The words they vocalize are fulfilled through conjugal intercourse (TOB 103:2–3; 105:6).

John Paul noted that if spouses are truly giving and receiving each other completely in the conjugal act, then they are giving and receiving *all* of themselves, including their fertility (TOB 123:6). If spouses are truly expressing love for each other in sexual intercourse they will maintain the conjugal act's "intrinsic relationship to the procreation of human life" (HV, 11). By maintaining the conjugal act's intrinsic relationship to life, a husband and wife communicate the fullness of themselves to each other and, if conditions are right, the possibility exists for them to come to a deeper knowledge of each other and grow in intimacy with each other by receiving the gift of a child. As John Paul II stated, "Procreation brings it about that 'the man and the woman (his wife)' *know each other reciprocally in the 'third,' originated by both*" (TOB 21:4). In contrast, if spouses engage in sexual intercourse and refuse life by opposing or preventing the conjugal act's intrinsic relationship to life, they are in some way opposing or preventing love because they are preventing complete mutual self-donation and short-circuiting the language of the body. They are refusing to give part of themselves and refusing to receive a part of their spouse. Therefore, rejecting one's fertility or the complementary fertility of the beloved not only prevents life, but it also prevents a total gift of self and thus also prevents the fullness of loving union (TOB 123:6).

In God's design the union of persons that occurs through a total mutual gift of self in the conjugal act has the twofold end of giving life and love because this spousal union is supposed to be a sign of how God loves us. We already discussed, especially in chapter 6, that God created marriage as the primordial sacrament to be a sign of his covenantal love for humanity. This love is free, faithful, forever, and fruitful. God gives himself to humanity, a gift that culminates in the sacrifice of Jesus on the Cross, loving us unconditionally and with utmost fidelity to bring us new life as we receive his gift. Called to image this love in the covenant of marriage, spouses are to make a complete, mutual, and faithful gift of themselves in the conjugal act that retains the act's "intrinsic relationship to the procreation of human life" (HV, 11). In the Sacrament of Marriage spouses are empowered to love as Christ loves and make such a gift.

SUMMARY

In his *Theology of the Body* John Paul II provided a context within which we can understand the Catholic Church's teachings on sexuality (TOB 59). Embracing this teaching is essential if we are to realize the dignity of marriage, sexuality, and ourselves. Living the theology of the body is not a program for "great sex" in the worldly sense. However, even if spouses stutter at times in speaking truth through the language of the body, they can experience the personal intimacy for which their hearts so desperately long. John Paul II exhorted all "who seek the fulfillment of their own human and Christian vocation in marriage . . . to make of this 'theology of the body,' . . . the content of their lives and behavior" (TOB 23:5). If we live this theology of the body we can fulfill the words of St. Paul in his letter to the Romans, who implores us "to offer your bodies as a living sacrifice, holy and pleasing to God, your spiritual worship" (Rom 12:1).

The discussion of the above four principles of sexual morality that are drawn from the *Theology of the Body* should help people to understand why the Catholic Church teaches what it does in the area of sexual morality. The first principle highlights that we did not make ourselves, that we belong to a God of love, and that we need to allow God to be God by reverencing the plan for human love that he has ingrained in our sexuality. The second principle stresses that according to God's design the true freedom of sexual intercourse can only be experienced in the union of persons within marriage. In marriage spouses are donating the entirety of themselves to each other, body and soul, through their covenantal consent. Marriage is a call to committed and unconditional love, the way God loves. Each spouse makes a complete donation of self to the other, but also pledges to receive the other unconditionally in his or her totality. Thus the third principle points out that the language of the body in sexual intercourse should always be a physical expression of the wedding vows, the essence of which is complete mutual self-donation and self-gift. True spousal love is ordered towards giving oneself completely and receiving the other completely, including, according to the fourth principle, one's capacity not only to express love but also to generate new life. In short, sexual intercourse is meant to be a free, loving, life-giving gift of one's whole self to the other—a Eucharistic offering of thanksgiving. Anything short of this language is a lie. This plan for our sexuality that God ingrained in our very bodies is for our good and our happiness, and we can overcome any difficulties in living out this plan with the help of God's grace. In fact, Christ came to give us the graces needed to "overcome the consequences of sin and to build the unity of man and woman according to the Creator's eternal plan" (TOB 100:2). This means that we *can* direct our sexuality to express true love and experience true sexual freedom, loving responsibly and speaking the "language of the body" in truth. As speaking this language is "the content and principle of their new life in Christ and in the Church" (TOB 105:2), the next chapter will discuss in more detail how spouses can responsibly speak this language to plan their family and serve the ends of marriage.

Chapter 20

The Church's Teaching on the Mission to Responsible Parenthood: At the Service of Life and Love

INTRODUCTION

When a man and a woman embrace the vocation of matrimony they embrace the vocation to possible parenthood. In fact, "matrimony" is a word derived from the Latin words *mater*, meaning "mother," and *munus*, meaning "mission," "duty," or "office," thus connoting an institution which has the potential of conferring upon a woman the mission, duty, and office of motherhood. The call to parenthood is explicit in the rite of marriage when the couple is asked, "Are you prepared to accept children lovingly from God / and to bring them up / according to the law of Christ and his Church?" (OCM, 60). This call to parenthood is an exalted vocation that should be exercised responsibly.

"Responsible parenthood" is the term that Pope Paul VI used to refer to the morally upright way in which spouses regulate the birth of children, in fulfillment of their God-given mission to transmit new life (HV, 10).[1] Unfortunately, the Catholic Church's teachings on the mission to responsible parenthood are misunderstood by non-Catholics and many Catholics. Sadly, this is because these teachings are often presented poorly by pastors and others who are in charge of

---

1. The Second Vatican Council similarly referred to the "responsible transmission of life" (GS, 51).

teaching the faith in parishes. In addition, our culture has lost sight of the meaning of the truly responsible transmission of life.

In order to fulfill their mission to truly responsible parenthood, spouses must continually speak the language of the body in truth in order to abide by the "relevant principle of conjugal morality" (TOB 121:6). A clear understanding of the Church's teaching on the mission to responsible parenthood makes it possible to understand every Catholic teaching dealing with sexual morality. For this reason, and because the mission to be parents is intrinsic to the vocation of marriage, this chapter is devoted to discussing the Catholic Church's teaching on responsible parenthood. This discussion is placed in the context of married spirituality and the sacramental reality of marriage, presupposing the principles of sexual morality discussed in the previous chapter as well as the principles of natural law discussed in chapter 5.

RESPONSIBLE PARENTHOOD, CONTRACEPTION, AND NATURAL FAMILY PLANNING

Being married and sharing conjugal love means being aware of the mission and vocation to become parents (CCC, 2367). This mission is an incredible privilege since by procreating and educating children, parents participate in "the Father's work of creation," and the family that they form "is a communion of persons, a sign and image of the communion of the Father and the Son in the Holy Spirit" (CCC, 2204). However, in calling spouses to be parents God calls married couples to embrace this mission responsibly (see HV, 10; CCC, 2368). "In particular, responsible fatherhood and motherhood directly concern the moment in which a man and a woman uniting themselves 'in one flesh,' can become parents" (LF, 12). As this particular expression of married love carries with it an inherent life-giving potential, couples "are responsible for their potential and later actual fatherhood and motherhood" (LF, 12). In other words, when a married couple decides to engage in the conjugal act, they must be cognizant of the potential for this unique expression of their love to generate a new human life. The couple agreed to accept this potential gift on their wedding day (see Introduction). By responding yes to the question about the willingness to accept and raise children, a married couple pledges an oath before God and the assembled community to accept the mission and vocation to responsible parenthood, if God should gift them with children. As spouses are called to speak the language of the liturgy through the language of the body, their mission and vocation to responsible parenthood is realized precisely through the marital act.

However, truly responsible parenthood cannot be about manipulating or dominating reproductive potential (TOB 123:1), which would betray a lack of reverence for what God has made. In addition, responsible parenthood cannot only be about a married couple unreasonably limiting the size of their family (TOB 125:3). Instead, truly responsible parenthood is a vocation of service to love *and* life, involving a complete gift of self in personal union that takes place in dialogue with God, preserving his plan for sexual intercourse (TOB 129:2). As John Paul II stated:

> In the conjugal act, husband and wife are called to confirm in a responsible way the mutual gift of self which they have made to each other in the marriage covenant. The logic of this total gift of self to the other involves a potential openness to procreation: in this way the marriage is called to even greater fulfillment as a family. (LF, 12)

Thus the language of the body that is spoken in the conjugal act should be the language of covenant. As we discussed in the previous chapter, we are not our own, including our sexuality. Furthermore, sexual intercourse is about a union of persons and not just bodies, giving and receiving both life and love. Thus, spouses have the responsibility of maintaining the full meaning of *every* act of sexual intercourse in *both* its procreative and unitive dimensions (CCC, 2366). In this way the language they speak to each other in each act of sexual union is the language of truth (TOB 105:6; TOB 118:4–6).

However, before proceeding it is necessary to dispel a misconception. Regardless of past misguided theological opinions, the Catholic Church does *not* teach that every time a married couple engages in the conjugal act that they must intend to conceive a child. The Church does *not* say that a couple must have as many children as is physically possible until they exhaust themselves physically, emotionally, psychologically, or financially. The Church does teach, however, that couples should be *truly* responsible parents, transmitting life responsibly (GS, 51). In his encyclical *Humanae Vitae*, Paul VI stated that truly responsible parenthood is based on a hierarchy of duties or responsibilities (HV, 10; see also TOB 121:6; 125:3). Truly responsible parents are responsible primarily toward God who created marriage and the marital act, ordering them toward the procreation and education of children and the good of the spouses. Second, spouses must be responsible toward each other, respecting each other as another self (Eph 5:28). Next, spouses must be responsible toward the members of their already existing family. Finally, couples must be responsible toward the society of which the family is the foundational unit. Paul VI taught that based upon this hierarchy of responsibilities, and taking into account physical, economic, psychological, and social conditions facing a married couple, it may be incumbent upon a couple to have many children or, for just reasons, a couple may decide not to have another child for a definite or indefinite period of time (HV, 10).[2] John Paul II noted, "If we assume that the reasons for deciding not to procreate are morally right, the moral problem of the way of acting in such a case remains" (TOB 122:3). In other words, how do spouses act truly responsibly when they realize that they cannot prudently welcome another child into the world?

Responsible parenthood can be accomplished only with an upright conscience in accord with the truth of the objective moral order (GS, 51). According to this moral order, which has been established by God and which we can ascertain through the use of human reason, sexual intercourse is about a union of persons in which a husband and wife give a full gift of self in service to life and love. "The two dimensions of conjugal union, the unitive and the procreative, cannot be artificially separated without damaging the deepest truth of the conjugal act itself" (LF, 12). Therefore, morally wrong is "any action which either before, at the moment of, or after sexual intercourse, is

---

2. At one point in *Humanae Vitae* Paul VI stated that a married couple may avoid having another child for "serious reasons" (*seriis causis*; HV, 10). Later in the document he spoke of "just causes" (*justae causae*) and "just reasons" (*justas rationes*) for spacing births (HV, 16). The Vatican website translates the latter two phrases as "well-grounded reasons" and "reasonable motives" respectively (the Latin and English texts, accessed February 26, 2016, can be found at w2.vatican .va/content/paul-vi/en/encyclicals.index.html). "Serious" and "just" should not be seen as opposed to each other. Rather, in the context of the entirety of the document "serious" is most properly understood as "reasonably justifiable" as opposed to "trivial" or "frivolous." Janet E. Smith supports this position in "The Moral Use of Natural Family Planning," in *Why "Humanae Vitae" Was Right: A Reader*, ed. Janet Smith (San Francisco: Ignatius Press, 1993), 447–471, especially pp. 461–462.

specifically intended to prevent procreation—whether as an end or as a means" (HV, 14). This is the definition of a contraceptive act. On the other hand, responsible parenthood means observing "the fundamental nature of the marital act" and "the inseparable connection, established by God, which man on his own initiative may not break, between the unitive significance and the procreative significance which are both inherent to the marriage act" (HV, 12).

For several years I taught a course on marriage to college undergraduates. When it came time to discuss sexual morality, I used to lead the students in an exercise of natural law reasoning by asking them, "What is sex for?" Without fail, the first response to my question was always, "Babies." I would point out to the students that no matter how much our culture wants to pretend that sex no longer has anything to do with babies, it is obvious that babies are the primary end of sexual intercourse, meaning that the baby-making potential of sexual intercourse is what distinguishes this act from all other human activities and thus most clearly defines it. Then, I would ask the students if there is any other purpose for sexual intercourse. Always, without fail, someone in the class would respond that sex also seems to serve the purpose of expressing love between a married couple. I would then affirm that expressing love is the secondary end of the conjugal act, explaining that "secondary" does not mean less important (as was explained in chapter 5), only that expressing love does not distinguish the act the way baby making does, because a married couple can express love for each other in any number of ways that do not carry with them a procreative potential. I would then ask if there are any other purposes of sexual intercourse besides babies and bonding the couple in love.[3] Without fail, it was always a young man in the classroom who would raise his hand and say something such as, "I think another purpose of sex is pleasure." I would respond by asking the class, "Does anyone see anything wrong with saying that pleasure is one of the purposes or ends of sexual intercourse?" Always, without fail, a young woman would raise her hand to refute this claim. One of the brightest, and most blunt, students I ever had in class once responded by stating, "I think there *is* something wrong with saying that the

---

3. I borrowed the terms "babies and bonding" to refer to the "procreative and unitive" ends of sexual intercourse from Janet Smith's audio recording, "Contraception, Why Not?" (Dayton, OH: One More Soul, 2006).

purpose of sex is for pleasure. If that were the purpose, I wouldn't need anyone else for that. If that were the purpose of sex the other person would just fade away."

This image of "fading away" is an image that has always stayed with me, because in fact that young woman was correct. If the goal or end (*finis operis*) of sex is pleasure, then the other person with whom one engages in sexual intercourse becomes a mere instrument of pleasure, and the reality of forming a communion of persons through sexual intercourse is short-circuited and rendered impossible. I would pursue this exercise in natural law reasoning with the students by affirming the insight that the purpose of sexual intercourse is not pleasure, although there is obviously intense pleasure associated with the conjugal act. I would explain that God is so good that he attached pleasure to every activity that is necessary for us to survive as individuals or as a human species. It is almost as if God said, "Just so you don't forget to do these things that are necessary for your continued existence, I will make them pleasurable for you." How generous and good God is! I would give the example of eating, explaining that when we are hungry we experience a discomfort in our stomachs, which is a cue that we need to nourish our bodies. When we eat to satisfy our hunger there is a pleasure that comes with satiating our appetite. It is certainly appropriate to enjoy a good meal, and we can legitimately enjoy eating without explicitly intending to nourish our bodies. However, if we mistakenly convince ourselves that pleasure is the goal or end of eating, we can end up indulging our appetite in such a way that our eating causes us ill health instead of promoting our well-being. I would then point out to the students that we have a word for someone who eats solely for pleasure regardless of their hunger cues, and I would ask them if they knew the word for such a person. More than one student would respond, "A glutton." I would then compare the example of eating to sexual intercourse. I would make it clear that it is certainly not wrong for spouses to enjoy the pleasure of the conjugal act, nor is it wrong for them to pursue this pleasure together without explicitly intending the ends of babies and bonding (CCC, 2362–2363).[4] However, I would then point out that if husbands

---

4 In this case the couple engages in sexual intercourse with a subjective intention/purpose (*finis operantis*) that does not explicitly coincide with the twofold end (*finis operis*) of the conjugal act, but their intention does not contradict the ends, and therefore the nature, of the act.

and wives indulge in sexual intercourse solely for the pleasure, while preventing or opposing the purposes of babies or bonding, they become sexual gluttons.[5] By acting as gluttons the other person "fades away" from the act, spouses betray God's design for sexual love, and they end up doing something that is unhealthy for them. As John Paul II stated: "The person can never be considered a means to an end; above all never a means of 'pleasure.' The person is and must be nothing other than the end of every act. Only then does the action correspond to the true dignity of the person" (LF, 12).

Thus maintaining the unitive and the procreative dimensions of each act of sexual intercourse is a principle of natural law and, as pointed out in the last chapter, it is *the* "relevant principle of conjugal morality" (TOB 121:6). This is the principle of conjugal morality that was taught by Vatican II in *Gaudium et Spes* (GS, 51) and by Paul VI in *Humanae Vitae* (HV, 12; see TOB 122:1). We are not our own, and God has ingrained his plan for sexual intercourse in our nature in such a way that we cannot escape it. Therefore, responsible parenthood is a vocation of service to life-giving love, and it involves a holistic and integral vision of the human person (HV, 7). Truly responsible parenthood involves a couple dialoging with God about their intention (*finis operantis*) to achieve or avoid the conception of another child, and truly responsible parenthood must preserve God's plan for sexual intercourse (*finis operis*) regardless of the couple's intention for the act (GS, 51; FC, 32). If we hope to achieve true sexual freedom, we need to see God's plan for our sexuality, trust that this plan is for our good and our happiness, reverence the two inseparable meanings of the conjugal act (TOB 131:4–5), and live in harmony with this design, even when it involves sacrifice.

Natural Methods of Regulating Fertility

Living in accord with God's plan for sexual union means that if for just reasons a married couple needs to postpone having a child or to limit their number of children, a couple may undertake periodic continence to avoid pregnancy by abstaining from sexual intercourse during times when they are most fertile and therefore most likely to

---

5. In this case the couple's subjective intention (*finis operantis*) directly contradicts the twofold end (*finis operis*) of the act, and therefore its nature.

conceive. Alternatively, if they desire to have a child, a couple may target fertile times for their lovemaking. In this way the couple works with and reverences God's design for sexuality instead of trying to change or oppose this design (TOB 122:1–2). This is a practice commonly referred to as natural family planning or NFP.[6] Natural family planning is "natural," not because it uses no artificial devices or drugs, but because it conforms to God's plan for the nature of the conjugal act and his plan for the nature of the human person (TOB 125:1; 130:4).

NFP respects the nature of the marital act because it maintains the connection between the procreative *and* unitive meanings of each act of sexual intercourse, never placing a barrier to life or to love. When a couple avoids a pregnancy by practicing periodic continence they never attempt to engage in the conjugal act and distort it by opposing its procreative potential. Rather, they abstain from intercourse during fertile times and engage in the conjugal act at a time when the generation of life, which they cannot for just reasons now pursue, is not possible. Since the couple using NFP to avoid a pregnancy does so by abstaining, NFP does not work contra conception. Moreover, acts of intercourse during infertile times are simply nonconceptive, not contraceptive. Even if a husband and wife avoid conception by having intercourse only during infertile times, the fertility of each of them is fully accepted and revered, and each conjugal act's intrinsic relationship to life is maintained. Thus, methods of natural family planning recognize fertility as a healthy condition and revere fertility as something sacred. NFP treats sexual intercourse and its procreative potential as "holy ground,"[7] respecting the sanctity and integrity of the conjugal act.

---

6. The moral liceity of avoiding a pregnancy by reserving the conjugal act for infertile periods was taught by Pius XI in *Casti Connubii* (59) and reiterated by Paul VI in *Humanae Vitae* (16) and by John Paul II in *Familiaris Consortio* (32), as well as by the *Catechism of the Catholic Church* (2370). It should be noted that modern methods of NFP are scientifically researched and therefore are not the same as the "rhythm method" of the early twentieth century. The rhythm method was based on a monthly calendar, assumed every woman's menstrual cycle was predictable, and instructed women to count a certain number of days relative to her period to determine the most fertile time of her cycle. Modern methods of NFP are based on day-to-day observations that a woman makes of biological fertility markers, including cervical mucus and basal body temperature, so that she can assess her fertility on any given day.

7. I borrow this image from Janet E. Smith, "Contraception, Why Not?"

Practicing natural family planning also respects and reverences the nature, dignity, integrity, and sanctity of the human person. NFP respects the dignity of the spouses, who are an integral unity of *body and soul*, and assists couples in *fully* giving and receiving each other as gifts. By reverencing and maintaining the inseparability of the procreative and unitive ends of the conjugal act, natural family planning reverences the unity of body and soul in the human person. As John Paul II noted: "To accept the [woman's] cycle and to enter into dialogue means to recognize both the spiritual and corporal character of conjugal communion" (FC, 32). Thus, practicing NFP implicitly recognizes, accepts, and reveres one's fertility as an inseparable aspect of one's person.

Far from a method of dominating nature (HV, 2), natural methods of birth regulation promote self-mastery (HV, 21) through the practice of chastity to control sexual desire and therefore respect the nature of the human person (see TOB 123:1). Exercising the virtue of chastity by practicing periodic continence *is* in accord with human nature because it subjects the body and bodily passions to control of reason and will, and does not treat bodily urges as *the* defining aspect of the person. In a fallen world either we master our desires according to virtue or they will master us (CCC, 2339). Natural family planning facilitates the mastery and integration of sexual desire according to the virtue of chastity, and helps a couple to learn that they can engage in the conjugal act in true freedom only if they are able to abstain from it. By promoting self-mastery through the practice of periodic continence, NFP helps spouses to overcome lust and experience the freedom of being a gift by speaking the language of the body in truth (TOB 123). Practicing self-mastery through periodic continence is necessary for couples to treat each other with tenderness, and to avoid simply using each other to satisfy sexual urges.[8] Thus, natural family planning recognizes the truth of the human person as *body and soul*, and by reverencing what God has made, NFP promotes tender attention to and acceptance of the person (TOB 132:5; FC, 32). Practicing natural family planning allows couples to grow in their humanity and thus to love each other with a truly human and tender love.

---

8. Karol Wojtyla, *Love and Responsibility*, trans. Grzegorz Ignatik (Boston: Pauline Books & Media, 2013), 188.

Contraception

Beginning in part 2 of this book, we have already pointed out how contraception is contrary to the nature of marriage and married love. Now we are in a position to explain the disordered nature of contraceptive behavior in more detail. In contrast to practicing periodic continence, contraceptive behavior does not respect the nature of the marital act or the person. First of all, by engaging in the conjugal act and simultaneously attempting to make procreation impossible, the couple opposes one of the ends (*finis operis*) of the conjugal act that God has ingrained in the act itself. Contraception tries to exclude the procreative dimension of the marital act, treating fertility as if it were some type of a disease instead of a gift from God.[9] Contraception shows a lack of trust in God's design for the conjugal act, and seeks to change the nature of this act to suit the purposes (*finis operantis*) of the couple, thereby usurping God's authority as Creator. If the avoidance of children is necessary, choosing contraceptive behavior also shows a lack of trust in God's ability to grant the grace to sustain the couple in continence.[10] Thus contraception is a sin against faith,[11] and by failing to reverence the work of God, contraception is "the antithesis of conjugal spirituality" (TOB 132:2).

Additionally, contraception turns the human person into "*an object of manipulation*" (TOB 123:1), failing to revere the person as an intimate union of body and soul. Contraception treats a person's fertility as if it is a "thing" that can be separated from the person, and therefore promotes a dualistic vision of the person wherein the body is separated from the "real me." Contraceptive behavior therefore prevents a full gift of self, body and soul. Instead of promoting the practice of virtue, contraception makes it easy for a couple to give in to sexual concupiscence, succumb to lust, and treat each other as objects of sexual gratification. Instead of fostering true sexual freedom and tenderness through self-mastery, contraception can lead couples to be slaves to passion, dehumanizing their love. Thus contraception is truly unnatural.

---

9. This insight is borrowed from Janet E. Smith, "Contraception, Why Not?"

10. Peter J. Elliott, *What God Has Joined: The Sacramentality of Marriage* (Staten Island, NY: Alba House, 1990), 213.

11. Ibid.

Barrier methods of contraception are often used outside the context of marriage in an attempt to avoid the transmission of sexually transmitted diseases and thus to practice "safe sex." However, John Paul II noted that "safe sex" endangers the person and the family, and thus all of society, because it risks a loss of the truth about the person, the family, freedom, and love (LF, 13). He noted that "safe sex" is ultimately about satisfying concupiscence and leads persons to mutually use each other, making them *slaves to their weaknesses*" (LF, 13). It is possible to make the same claim about all forms of contraception, whether they are used in the context of marriage or not.

In highlighting the difference between contraception and natural family planning, it should be emphasized that practicing NFP well is to practice truly responsible parenthood. Therefore NFP is *not* to be viewed primarily as a means of avoiding pregnancy. Unlike contraception, natural family planning is true family planning because it can also be used to conceive life. As methods of NFP allow a woman to track her symptoms of fertility, NFP can be used to target the most fertile times of a woman's cycle, and thus help married couples achieve a pregnancy. Natural family planning can even be used with great benefit to assist couples who have problems with their fertility to conceive. Thus, NFP can be used to *fully* cooperate with God's creative power—something contraception cannot do.

Additionally, NFP can be used as a way of promoting overall reproductive health for the woman and the couple, and as such it is good medicine![12] Medicine is practiced to promote the health of the person. I have often pointed out to students that contraception and its more permanent form, sterilization, are the only areas of modern "medicine" in which the purpose of the "treatment" is to target a perfectly functioning system of the body, namely the reproductive system, and to interfere with that system so that it no longer functions properly. Shouldn't we expect negative outcomes if this is the action we are

---

12. For the medical benefits of natural family planning and a discussion of its effectiveness in helping couples to achieve or avoid pregnancy, see Thomas W. Hilgers, *The NaProTechnology Revolution: Unleashing the Power of a Woman's Cycle* (Omaha, NE: Pope Paul VI Institute Press, 2010), as well as *Creighton Model FertilityCare™ System: An Authentic Language of a Woman's Health and Fertility—An Introductory Booklet for New Users*, 5th ed. (Omaha, NE: Pope Paul VI Institute Press, 2003), especially pages 39–51 and 53–56. Dr. Hilgers is one of the leading experts in medical research on natural family planning, having developed the Creighton Model FertilityCare™ System. He has shown very convincingly that NFP promotes total health, in contrast to the many dangers of methods of artificial contraception.

choosing? Wouldn't people think it ludicrous if a cardiologist said, "You have an incredibly healthy and well-functioning heart. So, I would like to give you a medication that will cause your heart to beat irregularly." However, this is exactly what contraception does to the female reproductive system. In contrast, natural family planning is truly good medicine because, along with having no negative physical side effects, NFP actually promotes the overall health of a woman by heightening her awareness of irregularities in her cycle that might be indicative of larger health problems. This is one more way in which practicing NFP promotes reverence not only for the nature and dignity of the conjugal act, but also for the nature and the dignity of the person. As John Paul II said, the difference between contraception and natural family planning is a difference that "involves in the final analysis two irreconcilable concepts of the human person and of human sexuality" (FC, 32).

In 1968, Pope Paul VI predicted what would happen if the unnatural practice of contraception were to take hold in society. He predicted that there would be an increase in conjugal infidelity and a general lowering of morality, a loss of respect for women who would be viewed as objects, the imposition of population control policies by government authorities, and the further domination of the human body and its functions, treating our bodies as machines (HV, 17). Sadly, all of these predictions have been realized.[13]

In many ways contraception is the paradigmatic issue in sexual morality. Contraceptive behavior represents an acceptance of the premise that it is morally legitimate to separate the baby-making and the love-making dimensions of the conjugal act. Once this premise is accepted it leads to other distortions of the conjugal act and of the human person.

As the practice of contraception denies that sexual intercourse is intrinsically designed for babies, sexual activity is easily taken out of the context of marriage. Both married and unmarried men and women convince themselves that they can have as much sex as they want without ever countenancing having a baby. Once the link between sex and babies is severed, the link between sex and fidelity or permanent

---

13. For further comments on how Paul VI's predictions have come true see Janet E. Smith, "Paul VI as Prophet," in *Why "Humanae Vitae" was Right: A Reader*, ed. Janet E. Smith (San Francisco: Ignatius Press, 1993), 519–531.

commitment is also weakened, paving the way for the pursuit of sex just for pleasure. In this way the acceptance of the contraceptive principle leads to an increase in premarital intercourse, cohabitation, promiscuous and adulterous behavior, masturbation, and pornography.

A contraceptive mentality can lead to the practice of abortion because if contraceptive measures fail, children may be viewed as "accidents." Contraception fosters the lie that sexual intercourse has nothing to do with babies, and as a result even married couples begin to view children as "intrusions" into their relationship. As choosing contraceptive behavior is choosing to oppose life, the failure of contraceptive measures to prevent life from occurring can lead to choosing more extreme measures to oppose life, such abortion, once life has been unintentionally conceived through the failure of contraception.[14]

The acceptance of contraception also leads to the practice of reproductive technologies that attempt to manufacture human beings apart from the conjugal act, such as artificial insemination, *in vitro* fertilization, surrogate motherhood, or cloning. These procedures are the inverse of contraception because they attempt to produce babies without having sex. The *Catechism of the Catholic Church* states that any act that dissociates husband and wife in their act of procreation or any act that dissociates the sexual act from the procreative act is immoral

---

14. It is interesting to note that in 1973, in deciding the cases of Roe v. Wade and Doe v. Bolton, the United States Supreme Court noted a link between contraception and abortion. In the decision of Roe v. Wade, the court commented on Doe v. Bolton stating, "We thus have as plaintiffs a married couple who have, as their asserted immediate and present injury, only an alleged 'detrimental effect upon [their] marital happiness' because they are forced to 'the choice of refraining from normal sexual relations or of endangering Mary Doe's health through a possible pregnancy.' Their claim is that sometime in the future Mrs. Doe might become pregnant because of possible failure of contraceptive measures, and at that time in the future she might want an abortion that might then be illegal under the Texas statutes" (United States Supreme Court, *Roe v. Wade*, annotated by Bo Schambelan [Philadelphia: Running Press, 1992], 19). In rendering the decision in Doe v. Bolton the court stated of Mrs. Doe, "she was forced either to relinquish 'her right to decide when and how many children she will bear' or to seek an abortion that was illegal under the Georgia statutes. This invaded her rights of privacy and liberty in matters related to family, marriage, and sex, and deprived her of the right to choose whether to bear children" (ibid., 54). The court was even more explicit about the link between contraception and abortion in its adjudication of Planned Parenthood v. Casey in 1992. In this case the majority opinion stated, "Abortion is customarily chosen as an unplanned response to the consequence of unplanned activity or to the failure of conventional birth control. . . . [F]or two decades of economic and social developments, people have organized intimate relationships and made choices that define their views of themselves and their places in society, in reliance on the availability of abortion in the event that contraception should fail" (accessed February 26, 2016, www.law.cornell.edu /supremecourt/text/505/833).

(CCC, 2376–2377). This means that procedures that are designed to manufacture a child apart from the conjugal act violate the dignity of the newly created child by treating him or her as an object that can be manipulated into existence apart from a loving act of mutual self-donation between a husband and a wife. These procedures represent "the domination of technology over the origin and destiny of the human person" (CCC, 2377, quoting *Donum Vitae*, II, 5). Instead of welcoming children as gifts from God (LF, 9; CCC, 2378), through these procedures couples make themselves the lords of life, treating human beings as manipulable objects. Married couples who suffer with infertility have a painful and sorrowful cross to bear, and no one should make light of this cross (CCC, 2374). However, we cannot avoid suffering at all costs. When a couple gets married there is no guarantee that they will be able to have children, and no amount of desire to have a child, no matter how intense, gives a couple a right to a child. A child is always and everywhere a *gift*, and by definition no one has a right to a gift. In fact, by virtue of his or her innate dignity as a person created in the image and likeness of God, "only the child possesses genuine rights: the right 'to be the fruit of the specific act of the conjugal love of his parents,' and 'the right to be respected as a person from the moment of his conception'" (CCC, 2378, quoting *Donum Vitae*, II, 8). It should be noted that children who are conceived via immoral reproductive procedures are no less human than anyone else, and being made in God's image and likeness they possess the same dignity as any other human person. God has arranged the natural order so that he will ensoul a human being when the biological conditions for the creation of a new human life are present. However, we can bring about those conditions either morally, through the conjugal act in the context of marriage, or immorally, by manipulating the combination of sexual gametes apart from the conjugal act.

By being manipulated into existence it is the child's dignity that has been violated, whether inside or outside of marriage. This became clear to me in the first course that I ever taught. After discussing sexual morality and the morality of certain reproductive procedures in class one day, a young woman stayed after class to talk with me. She told me that she wanted me to know that the class discussion had special importance for her because she was the result of heterologous artificial insemination, her mother having been inseminated by donor sperm. I assumed this young lady was going to express anger with me. However, to my surprise, with tears in her eyes she expressed gratitude. She explained that ever since her parents had told her how she had been conceived, she had wondered whether God really wanted her here. However, hearing that every human person, no matter how he or she is conceived, is made in the image and likeness of God and possesses innate dignity, she realized that God loves her. This student is evidence of how certain reproductive procedures violate the dignity of the child. This young woman knew she was not the result of a loving act of mutual self-donation between her father and her mother, and she did not know the identity of her biological father. She lived with the burden of wondering whether her origins meant that God did not really want her here because she felt she had been manipulated into existence. I found myself wondering why this young woman's parents had placed this burden on her by telling her how she had been conceived. Perhaps one reason they would do so is that deep down they realized they had contravened God's design for human love and they felt that somehow they could pacify their consciences by telling their daughter of her origins with the intention of eliciting gratitude from her. This is far from what happened. This young woman realized that she needed to be grateful to God for her life, but she also realized that she needed to move toward forgiving her parents for conceiving her in a way other than how God intended.

As the acceptance of the contraceptive principle has led to the acceptance of reproductive technologies that separate baby making from love making, it has also lead to an acceptance of eugenics practices. Once children are manufactured apart from the conjugal act, instead of welcoming each new human being as a gift, it becomes a temptation to produce a child who has desirable traits and characteristics while destroying at an embryonic stage those children who have undesirable characteristics, deformities, or deficiencies. These decisions take us further down the path of Huxley's *Brave New World*.

Finally, the acceptance of the contraceptive principle inevitably leads to the acceptance of homosexual activity.[15] Once a

---

15. Homosexual activity is to be distinguished from homosexual orientation or tendencies. The *Catechism of the Catholic Church* explains that homosexual acts cannot be approved because they "do not proceed from a genuine affective and sexual complementarity" (CCC, 2357).

culture separates baby making from love making and treats sexual intercourse as a completely private act pursued for pleasure and personal fulfillment with no pertinence to the larger social order, homosexual behavior logically fits into that category. If heterosexual couples can be considered "married" just because they pledge to live together faithfully even though they view children as an intrusion into their union and permanently contracept in an effort to prevent procreation, then homosexual couples who pledge to live together faithfully can rightly ask why they cannot be considered "married." If marriage and conjugal intercourse are not intrinsically related to baby making, then engaging in sexual activity with a person of the opposite sex becomes arbitrary. If the potential for procreating is ruled out as a criterion for morally engaging in the conjugal act, then the only consideration that is left is one's own preference for genital stimulation and the convenience of an available and willing sexual partner.

These and other distortions of human sexuality and the human person can only be widely accepted and mainstreamed in society because of the acceptance of the contraceptive principle. Truly, this principle is the foundation upon which the "brave new world" is built.

The Moral Difference between Contraception and Natural Family Planning[16]

At times in the past I have had students who have asked, "Isn't natural family planning just Catholic contraception or a 'natural' form of contraception?" Hopefully what has already been discussed in this chapter about natural family planning and contraception has helped

However, the *Catechism* goes on to explain that men and women who have homosexual tendencies do not choose their condition and "must be accepted with respect, compassion, and sensitivity. Every sign of unjust discrimination in their regard should be avoided" (CCC, 2358).

16. For a collection of twenty-two different essays that contribute to explaining the intrinsic evil of contraception and the difference between contraception and natural family planning, see Janet E. Smith, ed., *Why "Humanae Vitae" was Right: A Reader* (San Francisco: Ignatius Press, 1993). See also Germain Grisez, Joseph Boyle, John Finnis, and William E. May, "'Every Marital Act Ought to be Open to New Life': Toward a Clearer Understanding," *The Thomist* 52.3 (July 1988): 365–426; William F. Murphy Jr., "Forty Years Later: Arguments in Support of *Humanae Vitae* in Light of *Veritatis Splendor*," *Josephinum Journal of Theology* 14.2 (Summer/Fall 2007): 122–167; and Martin Rhonheimer, *Ethics of Procreation and the Defense of Human Life: Contraception, Artificial Fertilization and Abortion*, ed. William F. Murphy Jr. (Washington, DC: Catholic University of America Press, 2010). For a good, brief presentation of the difference between contraception and NFP, see USCCB Committee on Pro-Life Activities, *Married Love and the Gift of Life* (Washington, DC: United States Conference of Catholic Bishops, 2006).

the reader to distinguish between the two types of behavior. However, I always saw this question as incredibly important to address directly, because answering it allowed me to clearly delineate the moral difference between contraceptive behavior and natural family planning. I always responded to this question by noting that it is important to ponder what may lead some people to ask this question. I think people ask this question because they understand that NFP and contraception can both be used to evade the conception of a child. Therefore, many people think that because the result of both behaviors can be the same, the behaviors themselves must be morally equivalent. However, judging the moral quality of an act based upon its outcome is never a good method of moral reasoning.[17] A simple example makes this point.[18] As a husband and a father I have the responsibility of helping to provide for the material well-being of my family. I can do this in one of two ways. I can put in an honest day's work for an honest day's pay and bring home a paycheck that helps me provide for my family. Or, I can rob a bank to get the money I need to provide for my wife and children. Either type of behavior allows me to achieve the goal of providing for my family, but clearly one type of behavior is morally good and the other is morally evil. This is an example which shows that we cannot judge the moral quality of an act by its outcome, and that a good end never justifies an evil means (CCC, 1753; HV, 14).

If we apply this bank robbery example to the difference between contraception and natural family planning, we can say that contraception robs a conjugal act of its procreative meaning by opposing its life-giving potential, and it robs a conjugal act of its unitive potential by preventing a full gift of self. Natural family planning opposes neither the procreative nor the unitive end of any act of marital intercourse and robs it of nothing. Therefore, contraception and periodic continence represent two morally different means of realizing the same end or goal of avoiding a pregnancy. However, more needs to be said to explain why natural family planning is not Catholic or "natural" contraception.

---

17. Judging the morality of an act based upon its outcome or consequence is a method of moral reasoning referred to as consequentialism. This method of moral reasoning has been condemned by John Paul II in *Veritatis Splendor* (75).

18. Janet E. Smith used the same example that follows in *Humanae Vitae: A Generation Later* (Washington, D.C.: CUA, 1991), 120.

First of all, there is no such thing as "natural" contraception. Contraception is not immoral because it uses artificial devices, chemicals, additives, or preservatives to render the generation of life impossible. It bears repeating that contraceptive behavior includes "*any* action which either before, at the moment of, or after sexual intercourse, is specifically intended to prevent procreation—whether as an end or as a means" (HV, 14; emphasis added). Thus, *all* ways of engaging in the marital act and preventing the procreative (or the unitive) aspect of that act are artificial and as such they are contrary to the nature of the conjugal act and human nature.[19] These actions turn the marital act, which is supposed to be an act of total self-giving love, into an artificial expression of affection devoid of its true meaning. The oldest form of contraceptive behavior known to man is the "withdrawal" method, which involves no devices, chemicals, additives, or preservatives in an attempt to render procreation impossible while engaging in the conjugal act.[20]

The fact that withdrawal is a form of contraceptive behavior shows that *the* moral difference between using contraception and using NFP to regulate births is precisely that contraceptive behavior is an act of engaging in sexual intercourse and directly intending to oppose the life-giving potential of that act of sexual intercourse, while using NFP to avoid a conception is the act of abstaining from sexual intercourse during times of fertility, thereby intending to avoid conception

---

19. Pertaining to contraception being contrary to the nature of the conjugal act and to the nature of the human person, the Second Vatican Council noted, "When it is a question of harmonizing married love with the responsible transmission of life it is not enough to take only the good intention and the evaluation of motives into account: objective criteria must be used, criteria drawn from the nature of the human person and human action, criteria which respect the total meaning of mutual self-giving and human procreation in the context of true love" (GS, 51). Paul VI stated that "the fundamental nature of the marriage act, while uniting husband and wife in the closest intimacy, also renders them capable of generating new life—and this as a result of laws written into the actual nature of man and of woman" (HV, 12). Commenting on this passage from *Humanae Vitae*, John Paul II stated, "The encyclical leads one to look for the foundation of the norm determining the morality of the actions of man and woman in the conjugal act, in the nature of this act itself and more deeply still in the nature of the acting *subjects themselves*" (TOB 118:5; see also TOB 125:1).

20. In the Bible, the withdrawal method is used by Onan (Gen 38:8–10), who married his brother's widow following the custom of levirate marriage. However, because Onan did not want to raise children that would be considered his brother's heirs "when he went in to his brother's wife he spilled the semen on the ground" (Gen 38:9). The Lord was so displeased with Onan that he was struck dead for his sin (Gen 39:10). For an account of how the sin of Onan has been treated in Christian tradition, see Alexander Pruss, *One Body: An Essay in Christian Sexual Ethics* (Notre Dame, IN: University of Notre Dame Press, 2013), 280–283.

(TOB 122:1–2). Contraceptive behavior is a choice to engage in the conjugal act and deliberately work against (contra) conception. By choosing this behavior spouses make themselves the "lords of life" and they falsify the language of the body that is spoken in the conjugal act. In contrast, properly using NFP to avoid a conception is a choice to revere and work with God's design for sexuality. Instead of trying to prevent the primary end of an act of sexual intercourse, spouses using NFP choose to avoid sexual intercourse altogether when the natural consequence of this expression of love, namely a child, cannot responsibly be welcomed. By using NFP neither the woman's nor the man's fertility is rejected, and a total mutual giving of self is preserved in each conjugal act, even if a particular act is nonconceptive. When a couple uses NFP to avoid a pregnancy for just reasons they are not choosing to engage in the conjugal act and prevent its primary end, as in contraception. Instead, the object of their choice is to refrain altogether from speaking the language of the body in sexual inter-course. [21] However, when they do choose to speak this language they speak it in truth. Thus, when a couple needs to avoid having a child, the moral difference between using contraception versus NFP is in the difference between the deliberate choice to engage in the conjugal act and prevent the life-giving potential of that act, versus the deliberate choice to abstain from the conjugal act during fertile times to avoid a conception.

There are times in life when a good cannot be pursued and should in fact be responsibly avoided. [22] However, a good cannot ever be formally prevented or opposed. For instance, a married couple could provide many different goods, fulfilling their responsibility of providing for their family. However, because their resources are limited they

---

21. For an understanding of the moral object of an action versus the intention with which an action is performed see CCC, 1750–1752. In brief, the object of a moral action is what type of action a person chooses to perform, coinciding with the nature of the act as determined by its ends (*finis operis*), while the intention is the motive for which the action is performed (*finis operantis*). The object deals with *what* type of behavior is chosen, while the intention deals with *why* this kind of behavior is chosen. "In contrast to the object, the *intention* resides in the acting subject" (CCC, 1751).

22. Paul VI noted the legitimacy "for acceptable reasons" of the "intention to avoid children and wish to make sure that none will result" (HV, 16). However, doing so through the use of natural family planning, which avoids children by avoiding sexual intercourse during fertile times, is morally acceptable, while accomplishing this intention through the use of contraception, which avoids children by preventing the life-giving potential of the conjugal act, is immoral.

must discern which goods to pursue for the sake of their family while forgoing others. While it may provide relaxation and refreshment to go on a family vacation, the family must first be provided with adequate food, clothing, and shelter. Thus the couple must responsibly choose some goods and forgo or avoid others. However, what the couple cannot do, and what would be immoral, would be to try to provide for some members of their family while starving another member of their family. In this way they would be choosing to oppose or prevent the good of the individual who is starved, as well as the good of their entire family. The choice between using contraception or using NFP to avoid a pregnancy is whether to engage in the conjugal act and oppose its nature and the nature of the human person, or to avoid the good of the conjugal act out of reverence for its nature and human nature. In short, the choice, as John Paul II stated, is whether to speak the language of the body in truth. Contraception is the choice to falsify this language by preventing life in an act of intercourse, simultaneously preventing a full gift of self.[23] NFP speaks the language of the body in truth by respecting and maintaining the nature of the conjugal act as a complete gift of self, including one's fertility, every time the language is spoken.

Natural Family Planning, Contraception, and the Language of the Body

It is important to understand clearly how natural family planning and contraception relate to the language of the body that sexual intercourse is supposed to speak. Remember that John Paul II stated that the moral norm for the marital act is rereading the language of the body in truth (TOB 119:2). He therefore grounded the Church's teaching on the responsible transmission of life in an understanding of the language of self-gift that God designed the body to speak in the conjugal act (TOB 118:4–6). John Paul II stated that "every believer, and in particular every theologian, should reread and understand ever more deeply the moral teaching of the encyclical [*Humanae Vitae*] in this integral context" (TOB 119:5).

---

23. Paul VI notes that a couple using contraception may have the same intention as that of a couple using NFP, namely to avoid a pregnancy (HV, 16). However, the couple using contraception chooses a type of behavior that is intrinsically opposed to and prevents life by short-circuiting the conjugal act's "intrinsic relationship to the procreation of human life" (HV, 11).

Applying the language of the body to contraceptive behavior allows us to see that an act of contraceptive intercourse says "no" not only to giving life, but "no" to a full act of self-donating love. The language of contraception says, "I want to receive all of you . . . but that," or, "I want to give all of myself to you . . . but this."[24] If we explain the content of "this" and "that," they are a husband's and a wife's fertility; a fertility that each of them acts as if it is not part of their persons. If the spouses are trying to unite in the conjugal act without giving and receiving each other's fertility then the spouses are not giving and receiving the fullness of each other. In fact they are rejecting a dimension of each other's personal identity, a dimension that most clearly distinguishes them as male and female in their bodily complementarity. Thus by rejecting each other's fertility, a contraceptive act of intercourse separates the body from the person and does not result in a true union of persons. By rejecting each other's fertility a couple rejects the primary end of the conjugal act and, by doing so, rejects a total gift of self. Thus, John Paul II stated:

> When couples, by means of recourse to contraception, separate these two meanings that God the Creator has inscribed in the being of man and woman and in the dynamism of their sexual communion, they act as "arbiters" of the divine plan and they "manipulate" and degrade human sexuality—and with it themselves and their married partner—by altering its value of "total" self-giving. (FC, 32)

The language of contraception contradicts the wedding vows that the couple exchanged, in which each of them pledged to make a total gift of self to the other.[25] Contraception falsifies the language of the body (TOB 123:6) and prevents a communion of persons (TOB 123:6). Therefore, John Paul II pointed out that a conjugal act artificially deprived of fecundity ceases to be an act of love because the act has been deprived of its full truth (TOB 123:6). Regarding the language of contraception he explained:

---

24. I borrow this language from Janet Smith, "Contraception Why Not?"

25. Due to the fact that contraceptive intercourse prevents a full gift of self, it is legitimate to question whether a contracepted act of intercourse constitutes a true conjugal act and therefore whether such an act truly consummates a marriage. For a good discussion of this question, see William E. May, "The Significance of the Consummation of Marriage, Contraception, Using Condoms to Prevent HIV, and Same-Sex Unions," *Josephinum Journal of Theology*. 14.2 (Summer/Fall 2007): 207–217.

Thus the innate language that expresses the total reciprocal self-giving of husband and wife is overlaid, through contraception, by an objectively contradictory language, namely, that of not giving oneself totally to the other. This leads not only to a positive refusal to be open to life but also to a falsification of the inner truth of conjugal love, which is called upon to give itself in personal totality. (FC, 32)

With the above quote John Paul responded to someone who might object, "Why do I have to give all of myself in marital relations with my spouse?" It is the "inner truth of conjugal love" that dictates a complete giving of self. True love holds nothing back, and in marriage the spouses give themselves totally to each other. Similarly, in the conjugal act they are to give all that they have to offer each time they engage in the conjugal embrace, which includes their fertility. If one thinks that it should be morally acceptable to give a partial gift of self in the conjugal act then he or she does not understand the nature of conjugal love. Furthermore, the fact that Christian spouses are supposed to reflect and participate in Christ's spousal love for the Church, dictates that they make a total gift of themselves in sexual union. After all, it is hardly conceivable and in fact fallacious to think that Jesus, who loved to the end (Jn 13:1), would give anything less than a total gift of himself to his bride.

It should be clarified that when John Paul II taught that contraception opposes loving union, he was not accusing couples who practice contraception of not loving each other. Instead, he was pointing out that by using contraception, couples are not allowing themselves to experience the fullness of love that God wishes them to communicate in the marital act. Contraception impedes what is supposed to be the most intimate communication of love between a husband and a wife. Additionally, because contraception presents the danger of one spouse using the other for sexual pleasure, contraceptive sex can lead to the other person "fading away" from this most intimate expression of love. Thus contraception can result in a form of mutual masturbation, a form of unchaste behavior that opposes both life and love in the mere quest for genital stimulation (CCC, 2352).

Unlike contraception, natural family planning allows spouses to speak the language of the body in truth by allowing a "man and woman [to] express . . . the whole truth of their persons" in the conjugal act (TOB 123:4). By practicing NFP, a couple always gives the fullness of themselves—they give everything they have to give—in each act of sexual intercourse, never short-circuiting the communication of their persons through their bodies, and never preventing, opposing, suppressing, or impeding the life-giving potential of an act of sexual intercourse as is the case with contraception. Comparing natural methods of regulating fertility to contraception John Paul II stated:

> When, instead, by means of recourse to periods of infertility, the couple respect the inseparable connection between the unitive and procreative meanings of human sexuality, they are acting as "ministers" of God's plan and they "benefit from" their sexuality according to the original dynamism of "total" self-giving, without manipulation or alteration. (FC, 32)

While the language of contraception says, "I don't want your fertility. I just want to have sex with you," the language of NFP says, "I accept all of you, and I am willing to have a baby with you."[26] By speaking this language through the body, natural family planning thereby allows the couple to rejoice in the truth (1 Cor 13:6).

The Misuse of Natural Family Planning

In trying to morally distinguish contraception from natural family planning, many people may ask, "Isn't it possible to misuse NFP?" The short answer is, "Yes, it is possible to use NFP in an immoral manner, just as it is possible to misuse any good for an immoral end."[27] However, a more complete answer to this question involves returning to a proper understanding of responsible parenthood. We should remember that responsible parenthood *cannot* always avoid or not welcome children if there is no just reason for doing so. Responsible parenthood cannot focus only on limiting children, but should include a willingness to accept a larger family. Always choosing to avoid a child, without a sufficient reason, is not practicing good stewardship

---

26. Janet E. Smith uses similar language to explain the "language of the body" in *Humanae Vitae: A Generation Later*, 112–114.

27. For instance, human intelligence is a created good. However, we can use our reason to choose to perform evil actions. Or, to use an example from a previous chapter, the field of medicine is a good designed to promote the health of the human person. However, a sadistic doctor can practice medicine to do harm rather than good.

of a couple's gift of fertility. To practice truly responsible parenthood, couples should be generous with themselves and be receptive to a child unless they have a just reason to avoid a conception. Thus John Paul II noted, "The use of 'infertile periods' in conjugal shared life can become a source of abuses if the couple thereby attempt to evade procreation without just reasons, lowering it below the morally just level of births in their family" (TOB 125:3). In other words, because the conjugal act is designed for both love *and* life, a couple should not avoid life without a just reason.

For a married couple, even the periodic continence of natural family planning cannot be about maintaining absolute control of their fertility without discerning God's will. The question a Christian married couple needs to ask throughout their fertile years is, "Does Jesus want us to have another child?"[28] The answer is sought in dialogue with Jesus as a couple. First, a couple should always strive to be generous with themselves in fulfilling their God-given mission to bring forth new life, avoiding selfish excuses for limiting their family size that might be based in comfort or convenience (CCC, 2368).[29] Then, as they discern whether or not to have a child, or another child, a couple should consider their obligations to God, to each other, to their already existing family, and to society (HV, 10).[30] After taking these obligations into account, if a couple can envision placing themselves before Jesus and saying to him, "Lord, we are not able prudently to welcome another child into our lives right now because . . . ," and they have something to add after the "because" which is a reasonably just motive for not pursuing or avoiding a conception, then they are using NFP in a morally upright manner. Examples might include, "because we are dealing with a health condition," or "because we are having financial difficulties," or "because we are emotionally and psychologically stressed right now with our current family." A reason to avoid or not pursue the conception of a child is qualified as "just" if it reflects the need to fulfill other moral obligations which could not be fulfilled, or to tend to other goods which would not be cared for, or could even be harmed,

---

28. E. Christian Brugger, "Just Cause and Natural Family Planning: Spacing Children Requires Discernment, Discussion," January 10, 2010, ZENIT new agency, accessed May 25, 2013, www.zenit.org/en/articles/just-cause-and-natural-family-planning.

29. See also Janet E. Smith, "The Moral Use of Natural Family Planning," 462.

30. A similar discernment is necessary when a couple is considering the adoption of a child.

by pursuing another child. There could be many just reasons that would make it wise or prudent to use NFP to avoid a pregnancy. However, if the couple cannot identify a reason why they need to avoid a conception, or their reason is clearly selfish, such as, "We would like a speed boat, or a third car, or a vacation home, or additional money for a more comfortable retirement, more than we would like another child," then the couple is using NFP inappropriately and selfishly and needs to challenge themselves to be generous in having another child. These unjust reasons to forego a child do not concern the need to fulfill other moral obligations or to tend to other goods, and therefore they do not justify the couple's choice to avoid the generation of life.

However, even in the event that a couple uses NFP selfishly I maintain that they are not guilty of the sin of contraception.[31] This is because the act of abstaining, which avoids a conception by avoiding sexual intercourse, is different than the act of contracepting, which prevents a conception while engaging in sexual intercourse. In choosing to abstain during fertile times, a couple chooses to avoid the conjugal act because they are not ready to have a child (which could be for either just or unjust reasons). In choosing to contracept, although their intention may also be to avoid having a child (for the same just or unjust reasons), a couple chooses to engage in sexual intercourse and oppose the nature of the conjugal act and the nature of each other.

Commenting on contraception and the misuse of the recourse to periodic abstinence, John Paul II noted that the couple who has recourse to the natural regulation of fertility without just cause "constitutes *a separate ethical problem* when one treats of the moral sense of 'responsible fatherhood and motherhood'" (TOB 122:3). A reasonable interpretation of this statement is that even if a married couple misuses NFP by unreasonably restricting their love-making to infertile periods when there is no just reason to do so, they are still not choosing an action that is intrinsically contraceptive. The object (*finis operis*) of

---

31. Some Catholic moral theologians operating within the tradition of the Church hold that misusing NFP should be qualified as the sin of contraception, but others do not. In what follows I will explain how I see a misuse of NFP as an act of selfishness that is distinct from an act of contraception. Further support for the position taken here can be found in E. Christian Brugger, "Just Cause and Natural Family Planning," and William H. Marshner, "Can a Couple Practicing NFP Be Practicing Contraception?" *Gregorianum* 77.4 (1996): 677–704. Marshner explains why some moral theologians view every misuse of NFP as contraception. Thus, while all of these theologians agree that it is possible to misuse NFP, they differ regarding what this sin should be called.

their choosing is not a type of behavior "which either before, at the moment of, or after sexual intercourse, is specifically intended to prevent procreation—whether as an end or as a means" (HV, 14).[32] Instead, even though this couple is choosing to avoid a pregnancy without just reason, the object of their choosing is to abstain from the conjugal act altogether during fertile times. Although this couple may be acting unjustly and selfishly, they still do not choose to engage in the conjugal act and violate its procreative and unitive dimensions.

I once spoke with a young married couple who was practicing natural family planning, and in the course of our discussion I mentioned the need to have a just reason to use NFP to avoid the conception of a child. This couple expressed surprise that they needed a reason not to have a child. When I asked them why they were using NFP to avoid a pregnancy they responded that they were waiting until "the time is right." I then asked what would indicate when the time is right, and I asked further why the current time was not "right." "In other words," I said, "what reasons can you present to God that would prevent you from welcoming another child into the world?" The couple clearly had not thought about this, and they left our conversation with something to ponder.

Even though this couple seemed to lack a just reason for using NFP to avoid a pregnancy, I do not think this couple was guilty of contraceptive behavior. They did not want to engage in the conjugal act and "either before, at the moment of, or after sexual intercourse . . . prevent procreation" (HV, 14). In fact, they practiced NFP because they wanted to revere God's design for sex. They did not want to oppose or prevent life while engaging in sexual intercourse, but they were choosing unreasonably to abstain from intercourse during fertile times. Therefore, I think that their unreasonable and unjust behavior was distinct from an act of contraception. This couple was guilty of selfishness, but not of contraception. I think that the example of this couple shows that spouses can be guilty of a sin (if they act freely with full knowledge of the wrongfulness of what they are doing) of selfishness, even serious selfishness, by using NFP to unjustly avoid having a child. However, in this case they are not guilty of choosing a type of

---

32. Thus Janet E. Smith noted that a contraceptive act always pertains to an act of intercourse (*Humanae Vitae: A Generation Later*, 366), as does E. Christian Brugger, "Just Cause and Natural Family Planning."

behavior (a moral object) which by its very nature prevents the life-giving potential of an act of conjugal intercourse, while simultaneously engaging in this embrace. The latter would be a contraceptive act.[33] However, it is important to note that the virtue required to practice natural family planning, and the communication it promotes between the couple, mitigates against using it selfishly. People instinctively recognize that there is a difference between practicing NFP and practicing contraception, and they realize that the difference involves the effort and self-discipline that must be exerted. I have found this to be the case when in response to the question, "Aren't contraception and NFP the same thing?" I reply, "Well if they are the same thing, why don't you just practice NFP?" Sometimes the hesitance to embrace natural family planning is due to a couple's fear that NFP will not be effective at helping them space their children. However, once they learn that modern methods of natural family planning are as effective as any contraceptive agent on the market at helping a couple to space their children, often they are still reluctant to try NFP. This reluctance comes from the intuitive realization that NFP requires something that contraception does not—self-mastery through the practice of virtue.

---

33. Janet E. Smith agrees that couples using NFP for selfish reasons are guilty of the sin of selfishness and not the sin of contraception (ibid., 369), as does E. Christian Brugger when he states:

If NFP is chosen wrongly, the wrongness lies in the fact that it is chosen without "good reason" and therefore usually selfishly. The sin here (presuming a person knows what he is doing and freely does it) is the sin of selfishness. (For a Catholic, it can also be the sin of disobedience to authoritative Church teaching.) But choosing NFP selfishly is not the same as contracepting. Strictly speaking, persons can only contracept if they also choose intercourse: a contraceptive act renders sterile an act of intercourse (recall the famous definition from *Humanae Vitae*, No. 14: "Any action which either before, at the moment of, or after sexual intercourse, is specifically intended to prevent procreation—whether as an end or as a means."); a contraceptive act always relates to some act of sexual intercourse; it is an act contrary to conception (literally contra-conception).

If there is no act of intercourse between a potentially fertile heterosexual couple, there is no potential conception to act contrary toward. Those who choose not to have intercourse, that is, choose abstinence (as NFP practitioners do when they want to avoid pregnancy), cannot act contrary to any conceptive-type of act, since they are specifically avoiding such acts. Therefore, those who choose NFP wrongly, although they do wrong, they do not do the same thing as those who contracept. Strictly speaking, they do not, indeed cannot, have a "contraceptive intention," although their frame of mind might be characterized by what John Paul II called a "contraceptive mentality" (by which I take him to mean, a mentality that sees the coming to be of new life as a threat, something rightly to take measures against). [Note: some moral theologians would disagree with me here; they believe that NFP can be chosen with a 'contraceptive intention' and therefore constitute for some couples a form of contraception.] ("Just Cause and Natural Family Planning")

It is very difficult, if not almost impossible, to maintain prolonged use of NFP with a selfish mentality because practicing natural family planning involves being willing to exercise self-mastery through chastity in order to practice periodic abstinence. Practicing this abstinence means being willing to sacrifice the opportunity to engage in the conjugal act out of reverence for what God intends for that particular expression of marital love. For a couple who is opposed to life, or who uses NFP for selfish reasons, this sacrifice will be too inconvenient and will prove to be too much for them to tolerate. Eventually, spouses who use NFP with a selfish mentality will either change this mentality and become receptive to life, or they will abandon their use of NFP. Thus, practicing natural family planning has the potential to work selfishness out of a couple's relationship, enabling their love to mature.

Natural Family Planning and Married Spirituality

The fact that Natural Family Planning can help spouses overcome selfishness highlights the fact that NFP, unlike contraception, can foster a married spirituality of tenderness in all its dimensions. Having recourse to natural means of regulating fertility incorporates the conjugal act into a couple's life of faith, reverencing the conjugal act as God created it and thereby reverencing the work of God (TOB 132:1, 3–5). In this way practicing natural family planning "*is part of* Christian *conjugal and family spirituality*" (TOB, 131:6) that has reverence as its foundation.

Often couples are hesitant to practice this reverence because they fear that natural family planning will reduce their sexual intimacy, and somehow they see this as "unnatural." It is true that if a couple needs to use NFP to avoid a pregnancy they may not be able to engage in the marital act at times when they might be most desirous of it. However, this is not unnatural, even if it might be difficult. What is unnatural is manipulating mainly the woman's reproductive system, often by making her temporarily infertile through the use of chemicals, so that a couple can have "sex-on-demand." The reality is that, at least in the United States of America, we live in one of the most oversexed, overweight, most in-debt cultures on the planet. In our self-indulgent lifestyle we have lost sight of the fact that frequency of genital stimulation does not equate with personal intimacy.

Instead, true intimacy can only be experienced by embracing a spirituality of tenderness that includes sacrificing and suffering for the beloved. This willingness to sacrifice should include a married couple's efforts to plan their family. As John Paul II stated:

> Accordingly, the function of transmitting life must be integrated into the overall mission of Christian life as a whole, which without the Cross cannot reach the Resurrection. In such a context it is understandable that sacrifice cannot be removed from family life, but must in fact be whole-heartedly accepted if the love between husband and wife is to be deepened and become a source of intimate joy. (FC, 34)

Embracing the cross as responsible parents means that if a married couple needs to avoid a pregnancy, and therefore needs to abstain from sexual intercourse, they can embrace this abstinence as a loving sacrifice offered to each other and to God. Together, the couple can embrace the ascetic discipline of periodic continence because they are concerned with what is truly good for each other (TOB 125:2). Natural family planning, unlike contraception, acknowledges that abstinence can be an expression of love in service to the good of one's spouse and that it should not be feared. Suffering this abstinence can draw a couple closer together as they learn how to be intimate with each other in nongenital ways.

Natural family planning can intensify the intimacy of sexual intercourse itself in at least three ways. First, NFP promotes communication between spouses. A couple practicing contraception is rarely forced to discuss their sex life. They simply need to know, "Did you take the stuff?" or "Do you have the stuff?" However, a couple practicing NFP must actually talk about their lovemaking with each other and with God on an ongoing basis. As couples foster good communication skills they are better able to practice the art of repairing that is so essential to married life. Secondly, a couple practicing NFP can know more precisely when they are participating in God's creative power to allow their love to take on flesh. Actively pro-creating a new life with God can bring about immense joy for the couple, and can enhance *both* the procreative and the unitive aspects of the conjugal act. Therefore, natural family planning can actually enhance the intimacy of the conjugal act in a way that contraception never can. Finally, NFP enhances the intimacy of the conjugal act by promoting growth in pure and chaste love. It is the virtue of chastity that allows couples to be gift for each other in their sexual intimacy. NFP requires the exercise of chastity and trains the couple to control their desire for sexual pleasure according to reason. In this way practicing natural family planning helps the couple to combat lust in their hearts. It prevents the couple from adopting the "sex-on-demand" mentality that causes them to look upon each other as objects of use. By promoting chaste behavior, NFP helps the couple to integrate sexual desire so they are free to give themselves fully in the conjugal act as the result of a conscious choice of "mature spontaneity" (TOB 48:2, 4–5), instead of being driven by a selfish desire for pleasure. Thus the discipline that periodic continence requires can actually enhance and enrich a couple's sexual intimacy (TOB 128:3). The couple can be truly attentive to each other as persons, renewing the self-giving and welcoming of each other in true tenderness (see FC, 32).

Along with enhancing the intimacy of sexual intercourse, natural family planning can also help a couple to realize that genital intimacy is not the only form of intimacy that is important for a healthy marriage. NFP helps a married couple to avoid overemphasizing genital activity in their relationship (see TOB 125:6; 128:6). As NFP requires the practice of virtue and the use of the entirety of the couples' faculties, body and soul, it is harder for the couple to conveniently ignore the nongenital aspects of marital intimacy. Natural family planning promotes a more holistic understanding of marital intimacy, which includes its spiritual, physical, intellectual, creative, and emotional dimensions. In a very real sense NFP adds S.P.I.C.E. to marriage.[34]

When couples judge that they should not engage in the conjugal act because they cannot responsibly welcome another child, they can learn to share *Spiritual* intimacy with each other through prayer. Hearing each other express their hopes, disappointments, thanks, and needs to God in prayer can give spouses insight into each other's souls and promote true "in-to-me-see" (intimacy). Spiritual

---

34. This acronym was developed and copyrighted by Dr. Thomas W. Hilgers and is explained in Creighton Model FertilityCare™ System, 5–6, 35–38. More information on the Creighton Model FertilityCare™ System can be found at www.popepaulvi.com.

intimacy can also be experienced in shared suffering. NFP helps couples to realize that P*hysical* intimacy includes more than just genital contact. Couples learn that physical intimacy can be experienced through tender touches, hugs, caresses, kisses, and holding that express respect and care for each other's bodies and offer tender, gentle expressions of love. Physical intimacy can also be experienced by tenderly caring for each other's physical health. Couples can share I*ntellectual* intimacy by communicating about important topics and issues of common interest and concern. Without this open and honest communication on the intellectual level a marriage will not be healthy. As was already noted, NFP requires couples to communicate about their fertility, and if they can communicate openly and honestly about their fertility then there is little they cannot talk about. As NFP facilitates this intellectually honest communication it "facilitates the solution of other problems" (TOB 125:6), helping them to maintain and repair other aspects of their relationship. NFP fosters growth in C*reative* intimacy by fostering positive energy around common goals that do not include sexual intercourse. A couple learns that having fun together and enjoying each other in shared activities is an experience of authentic intimacy. Finally, couples practicing NFP learn to grow in E*motional* intimacy. Practicing natural family planning well means expressing and respecting each other's feelings, including feelings of frustration, and empathizing with each other on a deep level. It means being willing to be vulnerable in sharing one's feelings with one's spouse, and it "favors attention to one's partner" (TOB 125:6). If a couple uses natural family planning and challenges themselves to grow in a holistic approach to intimacy, when they need to abstain from sexual intercourse it will make coming together again in sexual union all the more joyful, because they will have grown in tenderness for each other in other ways.

A healthy marriage needs all of the aspects of intimacy designated by S.P.I.C.E., and different situations and stages in life can necessitate focusing more on some types of intimacy than on others. NFP assists a couple in developing true intimacy in all of these areas instead of simply equating intimacy with sexual intercourse (see TOB 128:6). Restricting intimacy to the conjugal act will ultimately lead to a fragmented relationship. Practicing NFP prevents sex from becoming a Band-Aid solution for a couple's problems. It enriches a couple's relationship, and therefore, the couple should not fear the effort and mutual sacrifice needed to practice NFP. I have often pointed out to couples that the average window of fertility in a woman's menstrual cycle is seven to ten days. I have noted that if they have a need to avoid a pregnancy, and they cannot undertake seven to ten consecutive days of abstinence from sexual intercourse without it causing them severe marital strife, then there is something more deeply wrong with their marriage, and they are merely using sex as a patch. Practicing natural family planning mitigates against this patchwork approach to marriage.

Thus John Paul II noted that embracing natural methods of regulating fertility promotes truly human growth. As the couple grows in marital chastity they experience the fruits of self-mastery (HV, 21), which include "serenity and peace" (TOB 125:6). Practicing NFP "helps the spouses to drive out selfishness, the enemy of true love" (HV, 21; TOB 125:6). Practicing NFP "deepens their sense of responsibility" to God, each other, their family, and society (HV, 21; TOB 125:6). Natural family planning aids a married couple in growing in true freedom by helping them give and receive each other as gifts. Through the discipline of natural family planning "parents acquire the capacity of having a deeper and more efficacious influence in the education of their offspring," because the parents have mastered themselves in the service of life and love (HV, 21; TOB 128:6). Thus exerting the effort and embracing the sacrifice needed to speak the language of the body in truth contributes to the good of the spouses and the whole family (TOB 124:3), as an integral aspect of a spirituality of tenderness.

Certain pragmatic personalities may still ask, "But is natural family planning really practical?" John Paul II answered this question by first noting that when Pope Paul VI reiterated the Catholic Church's teaching on responsible parenthood in *Humanae Vitae*, he was motivated by pastoral concern for spouses, and as such this teaching is immanently practical and concrete (TOB 120:6). John Paul stated, "Pastoral concern means seeking the *true* good of man, promoting values impressed by God in the human person" (TOB 120:6). In other words, true pastoral concern directs us towards fulfilling God's plan for human love; it does not fail to uphold this plan or present it as unattainable.

The reason why some people judge this plan to be impractical or unrealistic is that they fail to realize that true love *always* involves effort and sacrifice (see TOB 127:4). True love and authentic married spirituality will always involve the effort of growing in self-mastery to overcome selfish desire and lust in the heart (see TOB 127:5). Natural family planning helps couples to realize that this self-mastery involves living the virtue of chastity and practicing periodic continence in order to practice responsible parenthood and speak the language of the body in truth. Ensuring the truth of the language of the body will involve asceticism, and practicing responsible parenthood will entail effort, commitment, and self-denial (see HV, 21; TOB 125:2). However, exerting the self-discipline and the self-denial necessary to regulate births through the practice of periodic continence transforms love and the persons involved by truly humanizing their love.

Traveling this way of love *is* realistic, especially from a Christian perspective (TOB 126:4), and it is essential to an authentic married spirituality. Every moral law that God gives is for the purpose of making us happy, and he gives the grace to accomplish each law (TOB 120:5). Reverencing this law does not lead to enslavement but to true freedom (Jas 1:25). St. Paul tells us that the grace of Christ has been poured into our hearts through the Holy Spirit (Rom 5:5; see HV, 25; TOB 126:4) to enable us to live in accord with this law of freedom. In the Sacrament of Marriage, the Holy Spirit offers Christian spouses additional graces to empower them to fulfill the vocation of service to life and love to which God has called them. Through the consecration they receive in the Sacrament of Marriage spouses belong to Christ and are empowered to love as Christ loves, which means being empowered to always give a total gift of self. Additionally, Christian spouses can "draw grace and love from the ever-living fountain of the Eucharist" and "overcome their own faults and sins in the sacrament of Penance" (TOB 126:5). Relying upon all of these graces, spouses can embrace truly natural means of regulating their fertility and be truly responsible parents, reverencing the works of God, embracing sacrifice and suffering, and practicing the art of repairing to experience the renewal and resurrection of their love. In this way a spirituality of tenderness enters the spouses' bedroom, allowing them to: practice delicate attention to each other; recapture, clarify, and deepen their love; stand in wonder and awe before creation and life; allow their love to mature; and renew the mutual giving and receiving of their persons all under the influence of the grace of the Holy Spirit.

SUMMARY

This chapter has focused on discussing what it means for a married couple to practice truly responsible parenthood, which is an inherent aspect of the vocation to marriage as a call to serve life and love. We have delved into the difference between contraception and natural family planning, drawing upon the insights of St. John Paul II, explaining how natural family planning is truly responsible and why contraception is not. Practicing truly responsible parenthood, even if it involves sacrifice and suffering, is necessary in order to reverence the nature of the human person, the nature of conjugal love and marriage, and the nature of the conjugal act, all of which are works of God. As practicing truly responsible parenthood fosters communication, it helps couples to develop facility in maintaining and repairing their relationships, and it is necessary for marriage to be a living sign of God's life-giving love for man and Christ's life-giving love for the Church. In the Sacrament of Marriage, Christ gives couples the grace to combat concupiscence and coordinate the life-giving and love-giving ends of the conjugal act, so they can consistently speak the language of the body in truth to form a communion of persons. In this way spouses allow a spirituality of tenderness to pervade every aspect of their marriage, and they incorporate what they do in their marriage bed into the daily worship that they offer to God as a couple, a living sacrifice that they ask him to make acceptable and pleasing.

Chapter 21

Marriage and Continence for the Kingdom—"A Living Sign of the World to Come"

INTRODUCTION

In order to understand fully the mystery of marriage and see it in its proper perspective it is necessary to end this book with a discussion of consecrated celibacy. This may seem ironic to many people because for them consecrated celibacy is a sign of contradiction. We live in a world that has separated sexual intercourse from marriage and that mistakenly sees genital activity as a necessary means of self-expression in a misguided attempt to experience intimacy. In this context many people think that making a lifelong commitment of celibacy is unnatural. Additionally, many people ask, "How can the Catholic Church claim to uphold the dignity and goodness of marriage and sexual intercourse when it encourages people to think about forgoing marriage and sex altogether?" We have already seen in part 4, "The Development of the Theology of Marriage," that from the earliest days of the Church consecrated celibacy has been consistently upheld as a "higher" state of life than marriage. It is important to understand why this is the case. In this chapter we will explain the origins of the celibate vocation in Sacred Scripture and explain how, far from contradicting each other, marriage and celibacy actually complement and help to explain each other. Finally, we will present the virginal marriage of Mary and Joseph as the preeminent example of the complementary relationship between marriage and celibacy, and a living sign of the world to come.

JESUS' TEACHING ON MARRIAGE AND CELIBACY

In the course of reasserting God's original plan for the "primordial sacrament" of marriage, Jesus presented his disciples with the vocation to celibacy. In Matthew's Gospel, after hearing Jesus' response to the Pharisees' question about divorce, the disciples engaged Jesus in their own dialogue:

> The disciples said to him, "If such is the case of a man with his wife, it is not expedient to marry." But he said to them, "Not all men can receive this saying, but only those to whom it is given. For there are eunuchs who have been so from birth, and there are eunuchs who have been made eunuchs by men, and there are eunuchs who have made themselves eunuchs for the sake of the kingdom of heaven. He who is able to receive this, let him receive it." (Mt 19:10–12)

In the above passage, after hearing Jesus' teaching about the indissolubility of marriage and the inadmissibility of divorce, the disciples reacted by saying that if the bond of marriage is so indelible, it would be more expedient not to marry. Jesus' response is somewhat astounding. First of all, he in no way refuted the disciples' insight that it is not expedient, or easy to live a faithful married life in which one is permanently bound to one's spouse. In fact, Jesus' response seemed to implicitly acknowledge that one should weigh the seriousness of marriage before making such a permanent commitment. Therefore he pointed to the need for thoughtful discernment of the vocation of marriage, something we discussed in chapter 17. Secondly, in his response to the disciples, Jesus revealed a way of living for and devoting one's life to God that does not involve marriage. Jesus mentioned "eunuchs." A eunuch is a male who is unable to get married because he is unable to engage in sexual intercourse, a necessary prerequisite for marriage. Jesus spoke of eunuchs who are so from birth (due to some type of physical abnormality), and eunuchs who have been made so by others (because they have been castrated). Then he mentioned eunuchs who have made themselves so, not by some form of physical mutilation, but by the choice to radically commit their lives to the service of the kingdom of heaven. He said, "Not all men can receive this saying, but only those to whom it is given" (Mt 19:11), acknowledging that God issues a call to some people to a life of celibacy in service to his kingdom.

This statement of Jesus would have been surprising to his disciples, because it would have gone "against the whole tradition of the Old Covenant, according to which . . . marriage and procreation were religiously privileged" (TOB 76:5). The people of the Old Testament strove for marriage because it was seen as a way of serving God's covenant made with Abraham to bring forth numerous descendants (TOB 74:3). Therefore, Jesus' affirmation that it is not expedient for some to marry would initially have been difficult for the disciples to understand. I suspect that two millennia later, in a society that is obsessed with the pleasure of sexual activity, Jesus' affirmation of a life of celibacy is still hard for many people to understand. Since we have highlighted and stressed the crucial importance of marriage as the "primordial sacrament" of God's love, one might wonder what possible role celibacy can have in God's plan and what the vocation of celibacy has to do with marriage.

All married couples know that continence, at least periodic continence, and marriage are not mutually exclusive. Circumstances will require every married couple to embrace periods of continence in their marriage. These circumstances include: certain times during pregnancy, postpartum periods, times of illness or injury, periods of separation due to travel, etc. During these periods of continence spouses do not cease to share conjugal love with each other and, as the previous chapter highlighted, their relationship is not devoid of intimacy. They simply experience intimacy in different ways. This lived reality should help people understand why the vocations of marriage and celibacy might have something to say to each other.

In trying to understand the relationship between the vocation of marriage and the vocation of continence for the kingdom, we must remember that when Jesus affirms the vocation of continence for the kingdom, he had just finished affirming God's original design for marriage from the beginning (Mt 19:3–9). Furthermore, by his statement, "He who is able to receive this, let him receive it" (Mt 19:12), Jesus made it clear that embracing a life of celibacy for the kingdom is an exception to the state in which man was called to exist from the beginning (TOB 73:5). Thus, choosing celibacy or "continence for the kingdom" is a particular and "exceptional vocation," while the vocation to marriage is "universal and ordinary" (TOB 76:4), meaning that all people have a natural inclination to marriage but God grants certain people the special charism of celibacy. In his discussion with his disciples, Jesus implied that the choice of a celibate life is the result of responding to a particular movement of God's grace in one's heart (TOB 73:4), and it is based upon this grace that one finds "an adequate resonance in the human will" (TOB 76:4). Embracing continence for the kingdom in response to this grace means embracing a life that "carries *above all the imprint of likeness to Christ* who himself, in the work of redemption, made this choice 'for the kingdom of heaven'" (TOB 75:1). Therefore, in Matthew 19 we see Jesus affirming the universal call to marriage while simultaneously presenting a new and exceptional call for some to follow him in a life of celibacy lived for God's kingdom.

We need to examine how this life of celibacy for the kingdom can be congruous with the reality discussed in chapter 3; namely, that the human person finds his or her fulfillment only by making a sincere gift of self to others (GS, 24). On this score, some might see conse-crated celibacy as a sign of contradiction. However, a way of life that involves single-hearted devotion to the service of God's kingdom cannot be a way of avoiding self-giving, but must be an alternative way of realizing oneself as a gift in accord with the "spousal meaning of the body," that reveals our call to loving communion. Otherwise, if celibacy was not consistent with the body's spousal meaning and the person as gift, it would violate "the fundamental component of human existence in the world" (TOB 15:5). Thus John Paul II noted that a call to a life of continence must respect the masculinity or femininity of the human person as well as our call to form a communion of persons (TOB 77:1). In other words, continence for the kingdom must pro-claim the full truth of humanity.

Certainly no one would accuse Jesus, who lived a celibate life, of failing to give himself. On the contrary, he gave himself in love "to the end" (Jn 13:1). He is the bridegroom who makes the ultimate spousal offering of himself for his beloved, yet he does so by embrac-ing a life of celibacy. Thus, in Jesus, we should be able to see that embracing celibacy does enable a person to realize himself or herself as a gift in a spousal way. John Paul II stated:

While Christ reveals to man and woman another vocation, above the vocation to marriage, namely, renouncing marriage in view of the kingdom of heaven, he highlights the same truth about the human person with this vocation. If a man or a woman is capable of making a gift of self for the kingdom of heaven, this shows in turn (and perhaps even more) that the freedom of the gift exists in the human body. This means that this body possesses a full "spousal" meaning. (TOB 15:5)

Thus Jesus revealed a way of realizing oneself as a complete gift for others, body and soul, that exists alongside God's institution of marriage. As John Paul II stated: "Christian revelation recognizes two specific ways of realizing the vocation of the human person, in its entirety, to love: marriage and virginity or celibacy" (FC, 11).

Contrary to popular belief, Jesus' call to embrace continence for the kingdom does not frustrate some "sexual instinct" in the human person as if we are no different from animals (TOB 80:4). In order to understand the celibate vocation, we must recall that there is a difference between sexuality and sexual intercourse. While sexual intercourse is designed by God to be the sacred sealing of a marital covenant in a one-flesh union, sexuality (gender) is about the person's identity as a man or a woman that provides the power to love and to be self-gift in a male way or a female way. In addition, loving with the fullness of one's masculinity or femininity does not mean that we must necessarily engage in sexual intercourse. As we have noted, experiencing human intimacy as a man or a woman cannot and should not be reduced to genital activity. There are many ways of experiencing intimacy and entering into personal communion with others that do not involve stimulating one's genitals. As was discussed in the previous chapter, true intimacy can be experienced on the spiritual, physical (and non-genital), intellectual, creative, or emotional levels.[1] All of these forms of intimacy are truly human ways of experiencing communion with another that are sorely undervalued in today's society.

Understanding the distinction between sexuality and sexual intercourse should also help us to see that those who embrace continence for the kingdom do not renounce their sexuality, nor are they

---

1. Spiritual, physical, intellectual, creative, and emotional intimacy, with the acronym S.P.I.C.E., are discussed in Thomas W. Hilgers, *Creighton Model FertilityCare System: An Authentic Language of a Woman's Health and Fertility—An Introductory Booklet for New Users*, 5th ed. (Omaha, NE: Pope Paul VI Institute Press, 2003), 5–6, 35–38.

asexual. We are all sexual beings because sexuality is about who we are and encompasses our ability to love as a man or a woman in both genital and nongenital ways. The question for each of us is how we can live out our sexuality in accord with the "spousal meaning of the body" to become self-giving gifts.

Married couples mutually surrender themselves to each other through the gift of their complementary genders to form a communion of persons that includes the conjugal act. However, those who embrace continence for the kingdom also take part in a spousal giving that involves offering the entirety of the self, including the body, to Christ (TOB 80:5). Thus continence for the kingdom is "*a particular response to the love* of the Divine Bridegroom" (TOB 79:9), and as a way of answering in a particular way the Redeemer's spousal love, continence for the kingdom acquires "*the meaning of an act of spousal love*" (TOB 79:9). It is "a profound 'yes' in the spousal order: the gift of self for love in a total and undivided manner" (MD, 20). It is a spousal offering of self that involves "*renunciation . . . out of love*" (TOB 79:9). Thus John Paul II maintained that a true choice of continence involves understanding the "spousal meaning of the body", embracing it, and freely giving oneself in accord with the meaning of masculinity and femininity (TOB 80:5–7). Paradoxically, by renouncing marriage and embracing a life of continence for the kingdom, a disciple of Jesus confirms the meaning of marriage as well as the spousal meaning of the body through the realization of the self as a gift (TOB 81:3, 6).

Far from having contempt for the gift of their sexuality, those who embrace continence for the kingdom willingly choose to forego the good of marriage out of a desire to give themselves wholly *to God*, and wholly in service to others for God's sake. Living a life of celibacy is not a refusal to give oneself, but a willingness to be a total gift for the kingdom, body and soul, thus realizing one's humanity. It is a gift that forgoes marriage to be a gift in another way. In fact, the celibate, because of the nonexclusive love that is embraced, "can realize himself 'differently,' and in some sense 'more' than in marriage, by becoming 'a sincere gift for others' (*Gaudium et Spes* 24:3)" (TOB 77:2). Living a life of celibacy clearly involves temporal renunciation, particular demands, and self-sacrifice, but it is precisely this renunciation, these demands, and this sacrifice that make continence for the kingdom a powerful and convincing sign of self-giving love (TOB 77:3; 79:8). By sacrificing marriage, those who embrace continence for the kingdom present the world with a unique and living sign of sacrificial love. It is also this sacrifice that allows the celibate to bear fruit for the kingdom as a spiritual father or mother (TOB 78:5; FC, 16). In the end, "marriage and virginity or celibacy are two ways of expressing and living the one mystery of the covenant of God with His people" (FC, 16). They are both ways of affirming the human person's call to be self-gift through a spousal donation of self (TOB 78:4).

The relationship of celibacy to marriage can be more clearly understood when we look at how Jesus explained the relationship of marriage to the resurrection. In Matthew's Gospel we are told of a conversation that Jesus had with the Sadducees, who were among the Temple elite in Jesus' day, and who did not believe in the resurrection from the dead that many Jews in Jesus' time believed would occur at the end of the world. Matthew's Gospel states:

> The same day Sadducees came to him, who say that there is no resurrection; and they asked him a question, saying, "Teacher, Moses said, 'If a man dies, having no children, his brother must marry the widow, and raise up children for his brother.' Now there were seven brothers among us; the first married, and died, and having no children left his wife to his brother. So too the second and third, down to the seventh. After them all, the woman died. In the resurrection, therefore, to which of the seven will she be wife? For they all had her." But Jesus answered them, "You are wrong, because you know neither the scriptures nor the power of God. For in the resurrection they neither marry nor are given in marriage, but are like angels in heaven."[2] (Mt 22:23–30)

In the above passage, the Sadducees were referring to the practice of levirate marriage (Dt 25:5–10), which we discussed in chapter 7, in an attempt to disprove the resurrection. In response, Jesus corrected the Sadducees both for their lack of understanding of Scripture and for their lack of understanding of the resurrection. By stating that there is no marriage in the resurrection, Jesus "indicates that there is a condition of life without marriage in which man, male and female, finds . . . the fullness of personal giving and of the intersubjective communion of persons" (TOB 73:1). It is for this reason that in

---

2. Mk 12:18–27 and Lk 20:27–36 also contain accounts of Jesus' dialogue with the Sadducees that are nearly the same as Matthew's account.

Jesus' response to the Sadducees, which deals with our resurrected existence, John Paul II saw the third of the three words of Jesus that provide us with a theology of the body. We discussed the first two of these words in chapter 3 in our discussion of theological anthropology. By allowing Jesus to teach us in his three words about (1) original humanity (Mt 19:3–9), (2) historical humanity (man after the Fall; Mt 5:27–28), and (3) resurrected humanity (Mt 22:23–30), we can come to a more complete understanding of what it means to be made male and female in God's image. We can also come to a more complete understanding of marriage in God's plan.

Jesus' conversation with the Sadducees points to the fact that the fulfillment of the redemption of the body (see Rom 8:23) will occur in the general resurrection, of which Christ's Resurrection is a preview. The resurrection is the fulfillment of God's plan of redemption, which will include the perfect integration of men and women as embodied spirits made in the image and likeness of God (TOB 66:1). It is important here to comment on Christ's remark that in the resurrection we will be "like angels" (Mt 22:30). Too many people misunderstand this verse to imply that we will *become* angels, perhaps sprouting wings and becoming chubby little cherubs. This is impossible, and it is bad metaphysics (see TOB 66:5). It is true that because they possess rational souls, angels, like humans, are persons. However, a key difference between an angelic person and a human person is that human persons have bodies. Jesus affirmed the understanding of the human person as an embodied person in his own Resurrection and in what he said about the general resurrection. By saying we will be "like angels" (Mt 22:30), Jesus was saying that in the resurrection our bodies will be submitted to our spirits in a different and even more perfect way than was experienced by original man and woman (TOB 66:5). This is confirmed in Christ's own resurrected existence in which his body is so perfectly subject to his spirit, glorified or "spiritualized" (TOB 66:5; 67:1), that he can do things such as appear and disappear before the disciples' eyes (see Lk 24:31–43; Jn 20:19–23). Nonetheless, the resurrected Jesus has a real body, and he will have this body for all eternity.

In addition, John Paul II noted that Christ's words about us being neither married nor given in marriage in the resurrection (Mt 22:30), "seem to affirm . . . that human bodies, which are recovered and also renewed in the resurrection, will preserve their specific masculine or feminine character and that the meaning of being male or female in the body will be constituted and understood differently in the 'other world' than it had been 'from the beginning' and then in its whole earthly dimension" (TOB 66:4). John Paul explained that in the final state of humanity in the resurrection, sexuality, being made male or female, will be understood fully in all of its significance. The resurrected life will therefore be the full realization of the "spousal meaning of the body" (TOB 67:5), with the gendered human body clearly revealing the person as gift. The spousal meaning of the body will be realized in the perfect communion of persons that exists among the saints (TOB 68:4). Furthermore, the human body will partake in ultimate happiness, which is personal union with God in the ultimate communion of persons (TOB 69). God will gift himself fully to man and woman, "divinizing" us (TOB 67:3), and in return man and woman will fully gift themselves to God in soul and body (TOB 68:3).

Embracing a life of continence for the kingdom in this life is a sign of the resurrected existence in which we will exist in body-soul communion with God and each other in a manner that will not involve marriage or the marital act. For this reason those called to live continence for the kingdom of heaven help to reveal the meaning of our bodies and our ultimate destiny (TOB 74:1). Continence for the kingdom is a sign that is charismatic, meaning a particular sign of the work of the Holy Spirit, and eschatological, meaning a sign of the "end-time" (*eschaton* in Greek) (TOB 75:1). Celibacy is "a testimony among men that anticipates the future resurrection," in which people will no longer marry (Mt 22:30) "because God will be 'all in all'" (1 Cor 15:28; TOB 75:1). In the resurrection, we will all exist in a state of "eschatological 'virginity' . . . in which . . . the absolute and eternal spousal meaning of the glorified body will be revealed in union with God himself . . . in the mystery of the communion of saints" (TOB 75:1). Thus those who embrace continence for the kingdom are living in accord with their masculinity or femininity by embracing what sexuality is meant to point us to—nuptial union with God. "The celibate person thus anticipates in his or her flesh the new world of the future resurrection" (FC, 16). In the midst of a society that has lost the sense of the transcendent, the witness of consecrated celibacy reminds us that the true wedding day for all of us is the day of the resurrection. Thus consecrated celibacy is the clearest sign of our final home in which God will be everything to everyone; Jesus calls some to a state not involving marriage in this life as a foreshadowing and a sign of this resurrected existence.

The fact that continence for the kingdom is an eschatological sign is precisely why in the Catholic tradition celibacy is referred to as a "higher" call than marriage. Sometimes this language has been misunderstood. John Paul II explained: "The *'superiority' of continence to marriage never means, in the authentic tradition of the Church, a disparagement of marriage* or a belittling of its essential value" (TOB 77:6). Instead, the superiority of continence rests in "the motive of the kingdom of heaven," which takes nothing away from the dignity of marriage (TOB 77:6). Christ did not propose celibacy to his disciples because there is somehow something wrong with marriage, but instead he presented celibacy to them because of its particular relationship to the kingdom of heaven (TOB 78:1). Marriage and continence do not oppose each other and the Christian community is not divided into the "perfect" who are continent and the "imperfect" who are married (TOB 78:2). After all, we must remember that, "*The perfection of Christian life is measured . . . by the measure of love*" (TOB 78:3).[3] What makes celibacy a "higher" calling is that in some way it is heaven breaking into earth (I use "higher" here because it is the standard language in the tradition, and it is language that John Paul II explained).

Having a particular relationship to the kingdom of heaven, celibacy is "a living sign of the world to come."[4] This is why when students in the past have objected that the commitment of celibacy seems unnatural, I have replied, "Well, in some ways you're right—it's supernatural." It is supernatural because it is done "for the kingdom of heaven" (TOB 74:1), and it is made possible by a special grace.

As was noted at the beginning of this chapter, understanding celibacy helps us to understand marriage and put it in its proper perspective. In fact, "it is not possible to define Christian marriage without

---

3. St. Augustine expressed this same insight in *Holy Virginity*, trans. J. McQuade, FOC, vol. 27 (1955), 47.

4. Second Vatican Council, *Presbyterorum Ordinis*, Decree on the Ministry and Life of Priests, in *The Basic Sixteen Documents: Vatican Council II: Constitutions, Decrees, Declarations*, ed. Austin Flannery, OP (Northport, NY: Costello Publishing, 1996), no. 16.

at the same time referring to the eschatological call to abstinence."[5]
Jesus made it clear that there is no marriage in the resurrection. First
of all, in heaven the primary natural end of marriage serves no purpose, since there is no more need to populate creation with more little
images and likenesses of God (TOB 66:2). In addition, marriage does
not exist in the resurrection because spouses have accomplished their
supernatural purpose of getting each other to heaven, in which the
only exclusive union is between God and each individual person. This
is the one marriage to which we all are called, and to which our earthly
marriages point. Once we experience the fullness of God's love for
man we no longer need the sign of marriage to point us to this love.

Married people may ask, "What will become of my love for
my spouse in the resurrection?"[6] As "love never ends" (1 Cor 13:8) it is
safe to say that the love that spouses share will not be obliterated, and
that they will not develop "amnesia" regarding the relationship that
they shared with each other in their earthly life together. However,
the reality is that (assuming spouses truly loved each other in this life)
their love for each other will be perfected in their love for God, but
their love will not be exclusive as it was in this life. In the resurrection
spouses will experience the perfection of the conjugal love they had
for each other. This perfect knowing of the other, however, will not
involve sexual intercourse. The love of earthly spouses will be perfectly
subordinated to the one spouse who alone can perfect their love for
each other. Husbands and wives will see the glory of each other fully
revealed in the light of Christ, but instead of focusing on each other,
they will be drawn deeper into the mystery of the Trinity as they see
God's love refracted through the person who was their earthly spouse.
They will see each other in ways that God sees them and the fullness
of each other's finite mystery will be laid bare before their eyes,
illuminated by the ineffable light of the Beatific Vision. Spouses will
see each other as they never saw each other before and they will know
each other in a way that they cannot now fathom. They will reverence
each other, body and soul, in the Lord and eternally thank God for

---

5. Edward Schillebeeckx, *Marriage: Human Reality and Saving Mystery*, trans. N. D. Smith,
2 vols. (New York: Sheed and Ward, 1965), 206.

6. Much of the text in the next two paragraphs has been modified from Perry J. Cahall,
"Toward Understanding the Holy Family of Nazareth as a Model of Married and Family Life,"
Anthropotes 24.2 (2008): 291.

the beauty that the other embodies. God's radiance shining through the former earthly spouses to each other will be the greatest and only gift they can have a part in giving to each other in eternity where God will be all in all (1 Cor 15:28).

Thus in the resurrection the conjugal love of spouses will be fulfilled, as they will finally be able to be fully and definitively gift for each other in the Lord, realizing that each belongs totally to him. In the resurrection the only nuptial union that will exist is that between created persons and God, a union that is signified by earthly marriage and of which those who embrace continence for the kingdom in this earthly life experienced a foretaste. Thus the resurrection is the fullness of nuptial union in which the bridegroom takes his bride to the place he has prepared for her in his Father's house (Jn 14:2–3).[7] In heaven this one nuptial union with God marked by permanence, fidelity, and infinite spiritual fecundity will be shared in communion with others. In the resurrection the mutual interchange of love between earthly spouses will have a uniqueness about it (as does any love between two unique individuals), but in eternity they will no longer be married because their love will be subordinated to the one marriage between the Triune God and the communion of saints. Earthly spouses will see each other anew through the one heavenly spouse.[8]

PAUL'S TEACHING ON MARRIAGE AND CELIBACY

After what Jesus said about marriage and celibacy in the Gospels, the most important teachings on these vocations are found in the Pauline letters. In his writings, St. Paul discussed the difference between marriage and celibacy from a more practical, and one might say "human and realistic" (TOB 84:5) perspective. In his First Letter to the Corinthians St. Paul responded to questions that were posed to him by the members of the church in Corinth about abstaining from sexual intercourse in different situations. St. Paul stated:

> Now concerning the matters about which you wrote. It is well for a man not to touch a woman. But because of the temptation to immorality, each

---

7. Peter J. Elliott, *What God Has Joined: The Sacramentality of Marriage* (New York: Alba House, 1990), 35.

8. This would apply to people who had more than one earthly spouse (e.g. remarrying after the death of a spouse).

man should have his own wife and each woman her own husband. The husband should give to his wife her conjugal rights, and likewise the wife to her husband. For the wife does not rule over her own body, but the husband does; likewise the husband does not rule over his own body, but the wife does. Do not refuse one another except perhaps by agreement for a season, that you may devote yourselves to prayer; but then come together again, lest Satan tempt you through lack of self-control. I say this by way of concession, not of command. I wish that all were as I myself am. But each has his own special gift from God, one of one kind and one of another. (1 Cor 7:1–7)

Some may be prone to read the above passage as a rather negative judgment on marriage and marital intercourse. However, we should look a little closer at what Paul said. First, Paul responded to the Christians in Corinth who hold that it is "well for a man not to touch a woman" (1 Cor 7:1). Apparently the Corinthians thought it was ideal for husbands and wives to abstain from sexual relations.[9] In response to this opinion, Paul affirmed that "because of the temptation to immorality" it is good to marry and that in marriage spouses should render to each other their conjugal rights (1 Cor 7:2–4). The language of 1 Corinthians 7:2–3, and some of the following passages in the same chapter (see 1 Cor 7:5, 9) led to the traditional reference to marriage as a "remedy for concupiscence" (*remedium concupiscentiae*; see TOB 84:8; 101:2–3). While we already addressed a proper understanding of marriage as a "remedy for concupiscence" in chapters 5 and 14, St. Paul was not counseling couples to see each other as outlets for satisfying sexual urges. Instead, Paul affirmed the goodness of conjugal relations and presented marriage as the context within which a husband and a wife can direct and order their sexual desires, thus battling sexual concupiscence and growing in self-mastery according to "life in the Spirit" (see Gal 5:16–17; TOB 50–53).

Paul clarified that spouses have a mutual obligation to support each other through conjugal intercourse (1 Cor 7:3). It is this text that is the origin of traditional discussions of a "conjugal debt" (*debitum coniugum*) owed by the spouses to each other.[10] The language of

---

9. Raymond E. Brown, Joseph A. Fitzmyer, and Roland E. Murphy, eds., *The New Jerome Biblical Commentary* (Englewood Cliffs, NJ: Prentice Hall, 1990), 804.

10. Based upon the Latin Vulgate, "*uxori vir debitum reddat similiter autem et uxor viro*," 1 Cor 7:3 is sometimes rendered: "Let the husband render the debt to his wife, and the wife also in like manner to the husband" (Douay-Rheims Bible).

"conjugal debt" was addressed in chapter 5 in the section that dealt with marriage as a covenant; St. Paul stressed to spouses the necessity of realizing that each of them has the obligation to support their mate, soul *and* body. Paul emphasized this point by noting that spouses mutually surrender rights over their bodies to each other (1 Cor 7:4). Again, we should understand St. Paul's exhortation to couples to render to each other their conjugal rights as an instruction to support each other in ordering and directing their sexual desires. We should not overlook the remarkable parity expressed here by Paul, giving the wife the same rights over her husband's body that her husband has over her. The wife is put on a radically equal footing with her husband with regard to the dignity of her person and her body.

Paul then addressed the question of a married couple who mutually agreed to abstain from sexual intercourse in order to devote themselves to prayer (1 Cor 7:5). On this topic, Paul referenced the temptation to immorality that can result from a husband and a wife trying to sustain long periods of abstinence, and counseled them to come back together after a time (1 Cor 7:5). This is realistic advice, given the struggle with concupiscence that each of us must deal with in a fallen world, and we need to realize that Paul was giving prudent pastoral advice to couples who desire to abstain from sexual intercourse. Again, Paul was counseling spouses to realize that they belong to each other body and soul, and that they have the responsibility of assisting each other in ordering their sexual desire within the context of their marital relationship. Furthermore, Paul was not mandating abstinence for a married couple (1 Cor 7:6). Instead, his advice implied that the couples' mutual decision to abstain "must be a fruit of the 'gift of God,' which is their 'own,'" (TOB 85:7; see 1 Cor 7:7), meaning that they must discern together whether, and for how long, they will abstain.

Paul's final words addressing the desire of a husband and a wife to abstain from sexual intercourse made it clear that Paul pre-ferred that all would embrace the call to celibacy ("I wish that all were as I myself am."). It is possible that Paul expressed this preference for celibacy because he expected that Jesus' return was imminent. In light of the end of the world, Paul was counseling people to lives of detach-ment.[11] Nonetheless, even in view of an imminent *parousia*, Paul did

---

11. *New Jerome Biblical Commentary*, 805.

not impose celibacy, but instead acknowledged that "each has his own special gift from God" (1 Cor 7:7). In this way Paul identified marriage as a gift with an assumed concomitant grace to help the couples live out their calling (TOB 101:2). This throws additional light on Paul's counsel to marry in order to avoid temptation (1 Cor 7:2, 9), because it presumes that trying to live a life of celibacy without receiving that particular gift would be impossible, and instead might present increased temptations to sin.

Paul's advice to the unmarried and widows is similar, expressing a preference for them to remain single, as he himself was (1 Cor 7:8). However, he stated that if they cannot remain abstinent, "it is better to marry than to be aflame with passion" (1 Cor 7:9). While his wording may sound negative, and even unattractive or unappealing, it is a different way of emphasizing the different gifts of marriage and celibacy, and that one needs to embrace the gift one is given. Paul reiterated his preference for the "higher" call of celibacy over marriage in his further advice to those who are not yet married (1 Cor 7:25–40). He stated that it was his opinion (1 Cor 7:25) that because "of the present distress" (1 Cor 7:26) and because "the form of this world is passing away" (1 Cor 7:31) it is better not to seek to marry (1 Cor 7:27), yet one does not sin if he or she does marry (1 Cor 7:28). Thus, although celibacy is the preferred calling, embracing marriage is a worthwhile and good choice.

Paul then noted that "those who marry will have worldly troubles" (1 Cor 7:28), explaining:

> I want you to be free from anxieties. The unmarried man is anxious about the affairs of the Lord, how to please the Lord; but the married man is anxious about worldly affairs, how to please his wife, and his interests are divided. And the unmarried woman or girl is anxious about the affairs of the Lord, how to be holy in body and spirit; but the married woman is anxious about worldly affairs, how to please her husband. I say this for your own benefit, not to lay any restraint upon you, but to promote good order and to secure your undivided devotion to the Lord. . . . So that he who marries his betrothed does well; and he who refrains from marriage will do better. (1 Cor 7: 32–35, 38)

Although some might see these comments of Paul as a negative assessment of married life, Paul was trying to provide a realistic and sober assessment of the "anxieties" of marriage, perhaps elaborating on why it might not be "expedient" for some to marry (Mt 19:10). He was also pointing out the benefits of securing one's undivided devotion to the Lord in a life of celibacy. There is a sober realism in Paul's advice, to which Joseph Kerns' comments relate when he stated:

> Work and worry do keep the eyes of a married couple on the world around them. So much time must be expended. So many errands and plans and emergencies clamor for attention. How shall they manage some time for God? How can they sustain interest in Him? For even when their gaze does turn from the world, it is toward each other. [12]

The answer to this dilemma is that spouses can sustain their interest in God by doing their errands *for* God, however mundane these errands may be. Instead of trying to maintain a life of prayer or meditation that runs parallel to their familial responsibilities and subsequently viewing their daily lives as somehow getting in the way of their prayer lives, spouses should instead see their daily responsibilities as part of their prayer; whether these responsibilities entail going to work, cleaning and fixing things around the house, making meals, changing diapers, or any other task that needs to be performed for the good of the family. Nonetheless, Paul noted that consciously offering these tasks as part of one's daily worship takes effort.

Paul's realistic perspective also sounded a "warning for those who think . . . that conjugal union and life should bring them only happiness and joy" (TOB 83:3). This is certainly a necessary warning in an age in which all too many newlyweds buy into the myth of "happily ever after." Paul's point regarding a life of continence was that one who is "unmarried . . . can completely dedicate his thought, his effort, and his heart" in service to the kingdom (TOB 83:7). One need only think of an example like Blessed Mother Teresa of Calcutta to see an instance of such service. Mother Teresa's example showed that someone who embraces service to the kingdom does not "close himself in himself, but opens himself to the world, to everything that is to be led back to Christ" (TOB 83:10). Again, "The spousal character of 'continence for the kingdom of God' becomes . . . apparent" when Paul stated that "the one who is not married is anxious about

---

12. Joseph E. Kerns, *The Theology of Marriage: The Historical Development of Christian Attitudes toward Sex and Sanctity in Marriage* (New York: Sheed and Ward, 1964), 256.

how to please God, while the married man must be anxious also about how to satisfy his wife" (TOB 84:1). In addition, lest we think that Paul was degrading marriage, he stated that the one who marries does well, while the one who embraces a life of celibacy does better. Thus Paul clarified: "It is not a question *of discernment between 'good' and 'evil,' but only between 'good' and 'better'*" (TOB 82:6). All of this more "human and realistic" (TOB 84:5) advice regarding marriage and celibacy must be understood in light of what has already been said about why the Catholic tradition refers to celibacy as a "higher" calling than marriage.

THE COMPLEMENTARITY OF MARRIAGE AND CELIBACY

Although many may see marriage and celibacy as somehow contradicting each other, John Paul II pointed out the complementarity of these two vocations. He noted that in Jesus' dialogue with the Pharisees, followed immediately by his conversation with his disciples (Mt 19:3–12), Jesus affirmed marriage as inherent to the original constitution of the human person in the beginning while also proposing the way of continence for the kingdom (TOB 76:5). John Paul pointed out that in Jesus' response to the disciples' statement about it not being expedient to marry (Mt 19:10), Jesus did not render a negative judgment on marriage or set continence for the kingdom of heaven in opposition to marriage (TOB 73:3). Instead, Jesus pointed to the particular value of celibacy, precisely because it is the result of a conscious choice to live "for the kingdom" as an eschatological sign (TOB 73:5). By addressing marriage and celibacy in the same discussion begun by the Pharisees, Christ showed us that marriage and continence help to explain each other (TOB 76:6). The two vocations of marriage and celibacy are complementary; they actually need each other and "complete each other" in the service that each provides to the kingdom of heaven (TOB 78:2).

First of all, both vocations complement each other because both help us to understand what it means to be a human person, made male or female, who realizes himself or herself through a spousal gift of self. Before becoming pope, John Paul II stated, "A need for spousal love dwells in man, a need to give himself to another person."[13] Both marriage and consecrated celibacy respond to this need because the essence of the choice of marriage or celibacy is "gift" (TOB 80:6). In marriage, "man and woman . . . become a reciprocal gift to each other through their masculinity and femininity, also through their bodily union" (TOB 77:3). By embracing continence for the kingdom, a person is called to participate in a particular way in the establishment of the kingdom by giving himself or herself totally to Christ in service to others. Each of these vocations must be chosen for the values that each has in God's plan (TOB 79:6). Those who get married must live out their vocation according to God's plan for marriage present "from the beginning" (TOB 79:6). Those who embrace continence for the kingdom must embrace a way of life that highlights renunciation of self and taking up the cross to follow Christ (Lk 9:23) in a particular way to serve the kingdom (TOB 79:3).

However, both vocations are calls to spousal love that complement each other in revealing the "spousal meaning of the body" and the universal human vocation to self-giving love. As John Paul II explained:

> These two dimensions of the human vocation are not opposed to each other, but complementary. Both provide a full answer to one of man's underlying questions: namely, the question about the meaning of "being a body," that is, the meaning of masculinity and femininity, of being "in a body" a man or a woman. (TOB 85:9)

Both married love and celibate love are "spousal," being expressed through the complete gift of self. "The one as well as the other love tends to express that spousal meaning of the body, which has been inscribed 'from the beginning' in the personal structure of man and woman" (TOB 78:4). This is why Christ's spousal relationship with his Church described in Ephesians 5:25–33 is important for both the married and the continent (TOB 79:7). This passage applies to Christian spouses, but it also concretizes what Christ invited his disciples into when he spoke of continence for the kingdom (TOB 79:7).

In reality, both marriage and consecrated virginity arise out of a desire to give oneself in conjugal love. Both vocations arise out of the desire of a true lover to make an objective, total gift of self to the

---

13. Karol Wojtyla, *Love and Responsibility*, trans. Grzegorz Ignatik (Boston: Pauline Books & Media, 2013), 239.

beloved. Both vocations desire to make a gift of self that is faithful, permanent, and fruitful. We must remember that we are made in the image of the Trinitarian God of love and therefore we are called to exist in a relation of self-giving love with God and with others. This is why in each of us is an "ache" for conjugal love, aching to experience intimacy and to be loved as the apple of someone's eye in a totally faithful, absolutely permanent, and completely fruitful manner.[14] Thus we are all called to be spouses and parents through a nuptial gift of self, and each of us in our heart of hearts is willing to take a risk in giving ourselves to another to experience nuptial union. "Christian revelation recognizes two specific ways of realizing the vocation of the human person, in its entirety, to love: marriage and virginity or celibacy" (FC, 11).

There is a second way in which marriage and celibacy complement each other beyond highlighting different ways in which we can achieve the common human vocation of realizing ourselves as gifts. Both vocations point us toward our ultimate calling in different ways. While continence for the kingdom is a sign of the resurrected life in which God will be all in all, marriage remains the "primordial sacrament" of God's covenantal love, providing a constant reminder of God's eternal desire to draw us into his life of love. The complementarity of these two vocations in God's design was articulated well by Cardinal Jose Medina Estévez when he wrote:

> Celibacy for the sake of the kingdom of heaven *makes present that which is everlasting*, whereas marriage bears the marks of transitory realities. Yet marriage is also a sign of what is most permanent in God's plan: his spousal love for his people, and from this perspective, above and beyond the life of conjugal intimacy, it *points to that which will never pass away*.[15]

Thus while celibacy reminds us that our ultimate destiny is life with God, marriage is a reminder that this life involves nuptial intimacy. In this manner, each in their own way, both marriage and virginity are reminders that we are meant to give ourselves fully to the

---

14. I borrow this insight from Sr. Mary Ann Fatula, Dominican sister and former professor of theology at Ohio Dominican University, who as a bride of Christ has taught her students for decades by word and example what it means to love God and others with a nuptial gift of self.

15. Jose Cardinal Medina Estévez, *"Male and Female He Created Them:" On Marriage and the Family*, trans. Eladia Gomez-Posthill and Michael J. Miller (San Francisco: Ignatius Press, 1997), 36.

one spouse, Jesus Christ. Everyone is called to nuptial union with Christ[16] as a member of the Church, his bride, and through Baptism Jesus weds himself to each of his followers (see CCC, 1617), beginning the process of making them "holy and without blemish" (Eph 5:27).

The celibate *and* the married vocations are both indispensable in building the Kingdom of God. This is so not only because those who embrace these vocations offer different and complementary forms of service to the Church, but also because each vocation complements the other by demonstrating the other's meaning. Thus John Paul II stated that "the values proper to the one and the other state [marriage and celibacy] . . . *complete each other and in some sense interpenetrate*" (TOB 78:4). In fact, history shows that when one of these vocations is esteemed and flourishes, the other flourishes, and when one of these vocations is undervalued and suffers the other is undervalued and suffers.[17] As Walter Kasper has stated regarding marriage and consecrated celibacy, "Each stands or falls with the other."[18] This can be explained by noting that when marriage is esteemed as a great gift from God, the value of celibacy is elucidated. Likewise, when celibacy is esteemed, marriage will be seen in its proper relationship to eternity and spouses will be freed from the disappointment that results when "exaggerated expectations are projected onto marriage."[19] However, if marriage is not esteemed and the ability to live a love that is faithful, fruitful, and permanent is doubted, consecrated celibacy will not even seem possible. Likewise, if consecrated celibacy is not esteemed then spouses will be tempted to absolutize their marriages and will inevitably succumb to the distorted expectation that they can give each other "heaven on earth."[20] The next two sections will explain further the interpenetration of these two vocations and how each of them helps to explain the other.

---

16. Peter J. Elliott, *What God Has Joined*, 224.

17. Ramón García de Haro, *Marriage and the Family in the Documents of the Magisterium: A Course in the Theology of Marriage*, trans. William E. May, 2nd ed. (San Francisco: Ignatius Press, 1993), 230.

18. Walter Kasper, *Theology of Christian Marriage* (New York: The Seabury Press, 1980), 44.

19. Ibid., 43.

20. Ibid.

Marriage Demonstrates the Nuptial Dimension
of Continence for the Kingdom

The motivation for embracing a life of permanent continence for the kingdom is to live a life of love in imitation of Christ, who is both fully consecrated and fully spouse. As we have seen, the ecclesial and earthly reason for consecrated celibacy and virginity is to provide a special service to the kingdom with an undivided heart. However, the higher purpose for embracing continence for the kingdom is to enter into spousal unity with Christ through a nuptial gift of self. In making this gift, the celibate or the virgin forms a new family in Christ. In this way celibacy serves as the greatest sign of the eschaton when we will exist in nuptial union with the one spouse in a state of eschatological virginity.

Marriage, as a sign of God's covenantal love for humanity and of Christ's love for the Church, is thus a reminder of the spousal love that the virgin or celibate has embraced as an earthly sign of the resurrection. As living signs of Christ's union with the Church, married spouses remind celibates of the nuptial dimension of their union with Christ. They serve to remind the celibate that the union with Christ to which everyone is called is a nuptial union. The consecrated virgin, as a bride of Christ, is married to Jesus himself, foreshadowing the destiny of every human soul. By embracing a life of consecrated virginity a young woman sacrifices the noblest of earthly goods, marriage, to achieve the status of direct marriage to Christ.[21] Men who embrace a life of consecrated celibacy are living reminders of Christ's celibate and nuptial gift of self in union with his Church. Men who receive ordination to the priesthood become effectual signs of Jesus the bridegroom, laying down his life for his beloved spouse the Church.[22]

---

21. Dietrich von Hildebrand, *Marriage: The Mystery of Faithful Love* (Manchester, NH: Sophia Institute Press, 1991), 75.

22. Peter J. Elliott, *What God Has Joined*, 223. Elliott also noted, "At the level of sacramental sign, we see that only a man can be a priest, for the bride cannot be the bridegroom, and gender is inscribed into our very human nature in creation—and more wondrously elevated in the 'great mystery' of Christ and the Church" (ibid.). Thus Elliott pointed out that the reason women cannot be priests is due to the sacramental nature of the priesthood. The masculinity of the priest is a necessary aspect of the "matter" of the sign of the Sacrament of Holy Orders, which signifies Christ the bridegroom in his nuptial relationship with his Church. The priesthood is not primarily a function, but a sacrament. Being unable to distinguish between a sacrament and a functionary office is the main reason why many in contemporary society, including many Catholics, are unable to understand why women cannot be ordained priests. To maintain that a woman cannot

Those who have embraced continence for the kingdom need the witness of holy married couples to remind them of the intimate love that Jesus wishes to share with them and that he wishes them to share with the Church. Christian spouses show the consecrated celibate that his or her life "should not imply a flight from the world, but is in fact a special form of service in the world and for others."[23] Holy spouses and domestic churches show consecrated celibates how to spend time with their spouse and their spiritual family. This is how marriage helps to reveal the nuptial dimension of celibacy as a union with the one spouse, Jesus Christ. Thus without an esteem for marriage as a great gift from God, consecrated virginity or celibacy cannot exist (FC, 16). John Paul II stated, "*One cannot correctly understand virginity . . . without referring to spousal love*" (MD, 20). This is because as we have seen, "It is through this kind of love that a person becomes a gift for the other" (MD, 20). Thus, those who embrace consecrated virginity need earthly marriage to reveal the fullness of the nuptial dimension of their calling.

Orthodox Bishop Kallistos Ware has written, "Monastics and lay people not called to matrimony, if they are to be authentically human, need to realize in some other way the capacity for mutual love which finds its primary expression through the man-woman relationship within marriage."[24] Furthermore, John Paul II affirmed that all spousal love, whether it finds its expression in marriage or in consecrated celibacy, must lead to spiritual fatherhood and motherhood (TOB 78:5). This is why on many occasions I have reminded seminarians in my classes that every human being is called to be not only a spouse, but also a parent.[25] As we are all called to realize ourselves as spiritually fruitful through a nuptial gift of self, it is quite possible that when we meet God he will ask us two questions: "Did you love

---

be a priest says nothing negative about womanhood. It simply says that a woman cannot be a bridegroom. However, by embracing a life of consecrated virginity a woman can be a living sign of Christ's bride, the Church—certainly a dignified and exalted vocation.

23. Walter Kasper, *Theology of Christian Marriage*, 44.

24. Kallistos Ware, "The Sacrament of Love: The Orthodox Understanding of Marriage and Its Breakdown," *Downside Review* 109 (1991): 79–93.

25. For further comments on the necessity of women realizing themselves as spouses and mothers, see MD, 20–21. For further comments on the necessity of men realizing themselves as spouses and fathers, see Perry J. Cahall, "Spiritual Fatherhood and Generativity," *Downside Review* 129 (Apr. 2011): 77–88.

your spouse?" and "Where are your children?" It is marriage that reminds the consecrated celibate that at life's end he or she must be ready to answer these questions.

Continence for the Kingdom Demonstrates the Consecrated Dimension of Marriage

Not only does married life help to reveal the nuptial dimension of consecrated celibacy, but consecrated celibacy simultaneously reveals a consecrated dimension of the Sacrament of Marriage. In the nineteenth century Matthias Scheeben wrote about a consecration that Christian spouses receive in the Sacrament of Marriage.[26] Similarly, the Second Vatican Council spoke of a consecration that spouses receive in sacramental marriage (GS, 48, 49). In one of the prefaces to the Eucharistic Prayer, the rite of marriage even states: "And so, the Sacrament of holy Matrimony, / as the abiding sign of your own love, / consecrates the love of man and woman, / through Christ our Lord" (RM, "Preface C," 1040). In order to understand this marital consecration we need to remember that the individual goal of every human person is making a complete gift of himself or herself to God.[27] Thus each and every human person is ultimately called to consecrate his or her life to God. By joining to become one flesh in marriage Christian spouses not only consecrate themselves to each other, but they also make a promise to consecrate themselves for service to Christ and his Church.[28]

However, the consecration of the Sacrament of Marriage has a dimension beyond the spouses promising themselves to Christ. By joining two people in the Sacrament of Marriage, Christ himself has jointly consecrated the spouses to him. Thus, while consecrated religious men and women are consecrated to Christ by virtue of their own solemn commitment (*ex opere operantis*), in the Sacrament of Marriage, Christian spouses are consecrated to Christ by virtue of his action in and through their mutual consent (*ex opere operato*).[29] In

---

26. Matthias Joseph Scheeben, *The Mysteries of Christianity*, trans. Cyril Vollert (St. Louis: B. Herder Book Co., 1946), 598.

27. Peter J. Elliott, *What God Has Joined*, 157.

28. Dietrich von Hildebrand, *Marriage*, 50.

29. Peter J. Elliott, *What God Has Joined*, 68.

other words, through their consent, Christ himself sets the spouses apart for each other, and he sets them apart as a couple to accomplish his own holy purposes in and through their union.[30] As Dietrich von Hildebrand stated, the Sacrament of Marriage "does not only mean that spouses give themselves to each other in God; they give themselves anew to Christ in the other."[31] Through the spouses' consent Christ brings a new reality into being and consecrates it for his own purposes, empowering the couple through this consecration to accomplish his purposes (see TOB 127:3). Thus the indissoluble marriage bond that Christ effects between the couple through the Holy Spirit belongs to him, and the spouses have the responsibility of living and sacrificing for this new reality in order to preserve and cherish it.[32]

Those who have embraced a life of continence for the kingdom are a sign to those who are married that they belong to Christ, and that they are consecrated to him for his purposes. Celibacy is a clear sign to married couples that they are not their own but that they belong body and soul to the Lord.[33] The witness of the consecrated celibate reminds the married couple that through their Baptism they have already entered into the nuptial mystery of the union of Christ with his Church (CCC 1617), and that by getting married their promise to each other is also a promise to Christ to live out their baptismal commitment together as a couple in union with him. Those who have embraced continence for the kingdom remind earthly spouses that Jesus is the one, true spouse. The witness of consecrated celibacy reminds married persons that everyone is meant to be in a nuptial relationship with Christ in which they receive Christ and give themselves to him.[34] If married couples show consecrated celibates how to live intimately with their spouse in the world, consecrated celibates show married spouses how to subordinate and consecrate their love to Christ. Continence for the kingdom is a sign to those who are married of the eschatological existence they are ultimately

30. Ibid., 152.

31. Dietrich von Hildebrand, *The Mystery of Marriage*, 50.

32. Ibid. See also Marc Ouellet, *Divine Image: Toward a Trinitarian Anthropology of the Family*, translated by Philip Milligan and Linda M. Cicone (Grand Rapids, MI: William B. Eerdmans Publishing Company, 2006), 97-98.

33. John S. Grabowski, *Sex and Virtue: An Introduction to Sexual Ethics* (Washington, DC: Catholic University of America Press, 2003), 64.

34. Peter J. Elliott, *What God Has Joined*, 14.

called to—spousal union with Christ. Thus consecrated celibacy reminds married couples that the ultimate goal of their marriage is to prepare them for heaven, and that the conjugal charity they share in this life, according to which they desire each other's fulfillment in Christ, will find its fulfillment in the eschatological virginity of the next life.[35] They are reminded that their purpose as spouses is to "enter, God willing, into the eternal saving union with God which will replace the union of the earthly sacrament which signified and even foreshadowed it."[36]

Thus, "although continence 'for the kingdom' is a renunciation of marriage . . . continence indirectly *serves to highlight* what is most lasting and most profoundly personal in the conjugal vocation": personal gift and the spousal meaning of the body (TOB 81:6). Practically, the witness of consecrated celibacy shows married couples that intimacy and self-gift go beyond sexual intercourse. It also shows that in order to achieve nuptial union one must practice renunciation of self (TOB 81:3). Additionally, the witness of continence for the kingdom shows Christian spouses that their spousal love can only find fulfillment through self-donation to Jesus, the one spouse. Human spouses must recognize that they cannot fill each other up completely, and they must instead call each other to realize that Jesus is their one, true spouse. Ultimately, every human spouse is "sweet bait" for the Lord, which he uses to draw the other into deeper nuptial union with him.[37] Married couples need the witness of consecrated virgins to remind them that they need the one spouse, that he alone can grant them the love that is enough for the human heart, and that the first priority of this life is to belong to him.

35. For further comments on how nuptial love finds fulfillment in the detachment of virginity, see Angelo Scola, *The Nuptial Mystery*, trans. Michelle K. Borras (Grand Rapids, MI: William B. Eerdmans Publishing Company, 2005), 269–271.

36. Peter J. Elliott, *What God Has Joined*, xvii.

37. I borrow this phrase from Sr. Mary Ann Fatula, OP.

THE MARRIAGE OF MARY AND JOSEPH

The complementarity of marriage and celibacy are fully revealed to us in the marriage of Mary and Joseph (see TOB 75:2–3).[38] Mary and Joseph were called to live the mystery of conjugal love in both its married and virgin/celibate forms. As John Paul II noted, *"The marriage of Mary with Joseph . . . conceals within itself,* at the same time, *the mystery* of the perfect communion of the persons, of the Man and the Woman in the conjugal covenant and at the same time the mystery of this *singular 'continence for the kingdom of heaven'"* (TOB 75:3). Since Mary and Joseph were given the vocation of raising God the Son, we should expect their union to be unique. We perhaps arrive at a stumbling block in coming to know that their marriage was perfectly continent.[39] On this point Mary Shivanandan noted:

> While conjugal union, the total gift of self, consummates a sacramental marriage, something new entered history with the Incarnation, the total bodily gift of self to God in Christ. Joseph and Mary were uniquely called to this total bodily gift to God in Christ within their marriage. In every way apart from the conjugal act, theirs was a true marriage.[40]

It is interesting to note that the early Fathers of the Church saw evidence of the continent nature of the marriage of Mary and Joseph in the canonical Gospels. In Luke's Gospel we find the account of the Annunciation of Gabriel to Mary. In this encounter, after Gabriel revealed to Mary that she was to bear the "Son of the Most High" (Lk 1:32), Mary asked, "How shall this be, since I have no husband?" (Lk 1:34). St. Augustine noted that at the moment Mary asked this question she was betrothed to Joseph and should

---

38. The text of this section is taken, with some modifications, from Perry J. Cahall, "Toward Understanding the Holy Family of Nazareth," 275–312.

39. Mary and Joseph lived a continent marriage. From the beginning, the Catholic Church has consistently taught that the reference to Joseph not having relations with Mary "until she had borne a son" (Mt 1:25) does not (unlike modern English) imply that Joseph and Mary had relations after Jesus was born (see Raymond E. Brown, Joseph A. Fitzmyer, and Roland E. Murphy, eds., *The New Jerome Biblical Commentary* [Englewood Cliffs, NJ: Prentice Hall, 1990], 635). Also, the New Testament references to Jesus' "brothers and sisters" (see Mt 12:46; 13:55; Mk 3:31; 6:3; Lk 8:19) refer to kinsmen in general, or they could refer to step-siblings if Joseph had been previously married (see *The New Jerome Biblical Commentary*, 657).

40. Mary Shivanandan, "Conjugal Spirituality and the Gift of Reverence," *Nova et Vetera*, English ed. 10.2 (2012): 489.

have expected to have marital relations with him in the near future.[41] It is also important to note that in the first century, "according to Jewish custom, marriage took place in two stages: first, the legal, or true marriage was celebrated, and then, only after a certain period of time, the husband brought the wife into his own house. Thus, before he lived with Mary, Joseph was already her 'husband.'"[42] This reality must be understood when we read in Matthew's Gospel that, "when his mother Mary was *betrothed* to Joseph, but before they lived together, she was found with child through the Holy Spirit" (Mt 1:18; emphasis added). Hence, Augustine stated that Mary's question to the angel, in Luke 1:34, reveals that she and Joseph had already pledged to live a continent marriage.[43] Otherwise, Augustine observed, her question would not make sense since she would have assumed that she would become mother of the "Son of the Most High" through normal marital relations with her betrothed husband. John Paul II seemed to confirm Augustine's insight when he said that Mary was the first to express an awareness of the new eschatological Kingdom, "for she asks the Angel: 'How can this be since, I have no husband?' (Lk 1:34). Even though she is 'betrothed to a man whose name was Joseph' (cf. Lk 1:27), she is firm in her resolve to remain a virgin" (MD, 20).

It is also possible, however, that the question that Mary posed to Gabriel in Luke 1:34 does not imply what Augustine and other Fathers and Doctors of the Church inferred.[44] It is possible that at the moment of Gabriel's annunciation to Mary, while she was betrothed to Joseph but before they "knew" each other, the couple intended to

---

41. Augustine, *Holy Virginity*, 4.

42. John Paul II, *Redemptoris Custos*, Apostolic Exhortation (Boston: St. Paul Books and Media, 1989), no. 18. In this passage John Paul II outlined the Jewish marriage ritual that Mary and Joseph would have followed. See also Raymond E. Brown, *The Birth of the Messiah: A Commentary on the Infancy Narratives in Matthew and Luke* (Garden City, NY: Doubleday, 1993), 123–124.

43. Augustine, *Holy Virginity*, 4. Thomas Aquinas, following Augustine, read Luke 1:34 as showing that Mary and Joseph must have mutually consented to take a vow of virginity after they were married (see ST III, q. 28, a. 4). St. Bernard of Clairvaux (1090–1153) and St. Francis de Sales (1567–1622) shared Aquinas's position (see Joseph F. Chorpenning, "The Guidance and Education of His Divine Infancy," in *The Holy Family in Art and Devotion*, ed. Joseph F. Chorpenning [Philadelphia: Saint Joseph's University Press, 1998], 43). Modern biblical scholars, however, tend to disagree with the treatment of Luke 1:34 by Augustine et al. For an example see Raymond E. Brown, *Birth of the Messiah*, 303–309.

44. Benedict XVI pointed this out in *Jesus of Nazareth: The Infancy Narratives* (New York: Image, 2012), 34–35.

consummate their marriage once Joseph did take his new bride into his home. In this scenario, it is the angelic appearances regarding the Incarnation, first to Mary and then to Joseph (Mt 1:20–25), that changed everything as far as their marriage was concerned, as it did with all human events and all of human history. The Incarnation radically reoriented the lives of those who were most intimately touched by it; Mary and Joseph would have intuitively understood their call to perpetual continence out of reverence for the work of the Lord of Hosts in the womb of Mary.

In order to understand the continent marriage of Mary and Joseph, we must remind ourselves that the conjugal act is not the essence of marriage and cannot be equated with married/conjugal love. We must recall that conjugal love "aims at a deeply personal unity, a unity that, beyond union in one flesh, leads to forming one heart and soul" (CCC, 1643). The conjugal act is the covenantal sealing and consolidation of the mutual consent of the spouses through their bodies. Only spouses have a right to this act, because only spouses have consented to mutually donate themselves to each other. A union of bodies can legitimately occur only because a husband and wife have already entered into a union of hearts. Spouses, however, can mutually agree to forego the rights to each others' bodies that they gain through exchanging marital consent. We saw that St. Paul counseled such continence for the sake of prayer in 1 Corinthians 7:5. Following St. Augustine, we saw that St. Thomas Aquinas explained, "the form of matrimony consists in a certain inseparable union of souls, by which husband and wife are pledged by a bond of mutual affection that cannot be sundered."[45] Therefore, Aquinas noted:

> Marriage is not essentially carnal union itself, but a certain joining together of husband and wife ordained to carnal intercourse . . . in so far as they each receive power over the other in reference to carnal intercourse, which joining together is called the nuptial bond. Hence . . . to consent to marry is to consent to carnal intercourse implicitly and not explicitly.[46]

Commenting on the union of Mary and Joseph, Aquinas asserted that they were truly married "because both consented to the

---

45. ST III, q. 29, a. 2.
46. ST Suppl., q. 48, a. 1.

nuptial bond, but not expressly to the bond of the flesh, save on the condition that it was pleasing to God."[47]

The comments of Peter Elliott are also helpful in assisting spouses today to see more clearly and relate to the mystery of the marriage of Mary and Joseph. He explained:

> As in the Marriage of Our Lady and Saint Joseph, a man and woman, by mutual consent, can refrain from consummation and any spousal union in their Marriage. Only if we place this within the ultimate "nuptial meaning of the body" can we understand how this can be a Marriage. Our common calling is to give ourselves completely to God. Within that universal vocation we may discern two specific vocations: the chaste self-giving of Marriage, and the chaste self-giving of virginity. Our Lady and Saint Joseph combined both vocations. They gave themselves to one another by mutual nuptial consent, and by a mutual consent they shared the gift of their virginity, offering themselves to God. That gift was embodied, in shared lives lacking only spousal union, but imbued with tender love. This way of love by consenting not to exercise that mutual right over one another for spousal union is understood well today by many couples using natural means of planning their families. They share in something of the love between Our Lady and Saint Joseph, a love which points to the ultimate nuptial meaning of our bodies, union with God forever in his Kingdom.[48]

At this point a few questions might be helpful. Could it be possible that any two spouses could love each other more than Mary and Joseph? Could it be possible that any wife could love her husband more than the New Eve could love her bridegroom? Could it be possible that any husband could love his wife more truly than the "just man" (Mt 1:19) could love his bride? Could it be possible that any couple's love could equal that of the couple through whom God incarnate began his work of redeeming marriage? Mary and Joseph could have held nothing back from each other and would have experienced the deepest personal intimacy. In a perfectly continent marriage they were complete gift to each other and together offered their union as gift in loving service to Christ and his Kingdom. For all couples Christ is the source of truest intimacy. In the case of Mary and Joseph, they were united to each other through Christ in an unparalleled

---

47. ST III, q. 29, a. 2.
48. Peter J. Elliott, *What God Has Joined*, 157.

manner. "In other human couples it is the mutual love of husband and wife expressed in their vows and consummated in sexual relations that creates their unity and brings forth the child. . . . In the case of the Holy Family, the child himself (who is God's gift to Mary first and then along with Mary to Joseph) brings about the close intimacy between Mary and Joseph."[49]

If continence in marriage strikes us as somehow offensive, we are falling prey to the arithmetic that equates love and intimacy with sexual activity. Although sexual intercourse finds its rightful place only in marriage, the essence of marriage is not reducible to sexual acts; instead it involves self-donation through conjugal love, and it is the marriage of Mary and Joseph that fully reveals this truth. Although to enter into a marital covenant I must be willing and able to hand my body over to my spouse in the conjugal act, to exist in a state of self-donation toward my spouse does not mean that we must engage in sexual intercourse. In fact, in some instances, such as illness or the legitimate need to avoid a pregnancy, it means that we should not.[50] If spouses are honest, they will probably admit that some of the most intimate moments that they have shared with each other did not involve the conjugal act. The truth is that true love can be experienced only when earthly passions are crucified to themselves (Gal 5:24). Pope Benedict XVI noted that as love is purified it increasingly seeks

---

49. Roch Kereszty, *Jesus Christ: Fundamentals of Christology*, 3rd ed. (Staten Island, NY: Alba House, 2011), 89.

50. It is interesting to note that canon law anticipates the possibility that a given marriage might not be consummated, without giving any specific reasons why. The code states, "For a just cause, the Roman Pontiff can dissolve a nonconsummated marriage between baptized persons or between a baptized party and a non-baptized party at the request of both parties or of one of them, even if the other party is unwilling" (CIC, c. 1142). However, the code recognizes the validity of a nonconsummated marriage. Such a union is called a "ratified" marriage (CIC, c. 1061§1), assuming that valid consent was exchanged. It should be noted, however, that a mutual pledge to live a continent marriage on the part of the spouses cannot be presented as a precondition by one or both spouses for entering into marriage. This means that the couple must understand that through their marital vows they are handing themselves over to each other body and soul. At the point of the valid exchange of consent the couple is married and they have given rights to their own bodies to each other. They may mutually decide not to exercise these rights over each other for a period of time or perpetually, but if after making a mutual personal pledge of continence one of the spouses could not live out this pledge, the other spouse would be obligated to consummate the union because their marriage vows take precedence. It must also be noted that a desire to live a continent marriage must not bespeak selfishness or a lack of openness to children, but could conceivably only be done to devote themselves to prayer (1 Cor 7:5). I thank Sr. Elizabeth McDonough, OP, former Bishop Griffin Chair of Canon Law at the Pontifical College Josephinum, for discussing these canons with me and providing me with some helpful insights.

the good of the beloved and in doing so embraces renunciation and sacrifice (DCE, 6). Thus the fact that the marriage of Mary and Joseph was perfectly continent, while unique, takes nothing away from their experience of the conjugal love and intimacy that they shared. They ordered their passions in perfect continence to see each other as complete gift.

In their earthly marriage, Mary and Joseph gave themselves completely to each other through Christ, thus fulfilling conjugal love and foreshadowing the resurrected existence in the communion of saints. As continent spouses they anticipated in their "flesh the new world of the future resurrection" (FC, 16) in which we will all exist in virginal union with God and each other (TOB 68:3–4). As a married couple Mary and Joseph were a sign of God's covenantal love made manifest in Christ's union with the Church. However, by jointly embracing continence for the kingdom they already participated in the heavenly marriage with the one bridegroom. In a unique way, the marriage of Mary and Joseph laid the foundation for "the communion of persons in the family [that] should become a preparation for the communion of saints" (LF, 14). Mary and Joseph are thus clear evidence that it is "the mystery of the Incarnation which elevates our human potentialities by penetrating them from within."[51] In the marriage of Mary and Joseph, eternity truly broke into time.

This elevation of the marriage of Mary and Joseph to the level of a preeminent eschatological sign means that Mary and Joseph presented us with the archetype of marriage. They embodied and fulfilled the "great mystery" (Eph 5:32) of marriage as a sign of Christ's union with his Church. John Paul II noted, "What St. Paul will call the great mystery found its most lofty expression in the Holy Family" (LF, 20). The ability of Mary and Joseph to express the great mystery in the most exalted manner is due to the special graces with which the Lord endowed each of them individually. Mary, as "full of grace" (Lk 1:28), possessed a plenitude of God's love from the first moment of her existence, making her free from any trace of sin and as such the most perfect creature that God created. This is the reality of the Immaculate Conception (CCC, 491). Joseph, while not equal to Mary in fullness of grace, is poignantly referred to in Sacred Scripture as

---

51. Pope Paul VI, "Christian Witness in Married Life: Address of Pope Paul VI to the Teams of Our Lady," in *The Pope Speaks* 15 (1970): 123.

"the just man" (Mt 1:19). St. John Chrysostom pointed out succinctly that this title means that St. Joseph was "virtuous in all things."[52] Pope Leo XIII in his encyclical on St. Joseph, *Quamquam Pluries* (1889), said of Joseph, "There can be no doubt that more than any other person he approached that supereminent dignity by which the Mother of God is raised above all created natures."[53] Thus God gifted these two individuals with the grace necessary to realize the "great mystery" in a preeminent way in their marriage.

Being the most lofty expression of the "great mystery," however, does not mean that the marriage of Mary and Joseph was necessarily a sacrament.[54] I could find no magisterial text that referred to the marriage of Mary and Joseph as the first example of the sacrament of Christian marriage.[55] It does not seem appropriate to call the marriage of Mary and Joseph a sacrament, as their marriage seems to go beyond presenting us with a sign of Christ's union with the soul or his union with the Church. For Mary and Joseph the distinction between the outward sign and the inner spiritual reality that is proper to the Sacrament of Marriage does not seem to hold; in fact they seem to be one and the same reality. In this way, their marriage seems to be a uniquely unrepeatable earthly foretaste of the resurrection, as was stated above. Thus Mary and Joseph did not experience something less than the Sacrament of Marriage; on the contrary, they experienced

---

52. John Chrysostom, *Homily IV on the Gospel of Matthew*, NPNF, vol. 10, First Series, 7.

53. Quoted in Joseph F. Chorpenning, "The Holy Family as icon and model of the civilization of love: John Paul II's Letter to Families," *Communio* 22 (Spring 1995): 97.

54. I thank Fr. Joseph Murphy, sj, associate professor of moral and systematic theology at the Pontifical College Josephinum, for prompting me to consider this point.

55. There are theologians who maintained that the marriage of Mary and Joseph was in some sense a sacrament, such as Hugh of St. Victor (see Hugh of St. Victor, *Hugh of Saint Victor on the Sacraments of the Christian Faith (De Sacramentis)*, trans. Roy J. Deferrari [Eugene, OR: Wipf and Stock Publishers, 2007], II.11.5), Jean Gerson (1363–1429) (see Joseph F. Chorpenning, "Icon of Family and Religious Life: The Historical Development of the Holy Family Devotion," in *The Holy Family as Prototype of the Civilization of Love: Images from the Viceregal Americas* [Philadelphia: Saint Joseph's University Press],14), and St. Thomas Aquinas (see ST III, q. 29, a. 2). Recall that Hugh of St. Victor and Thomas Aquinas taught that a nonconsummated marriage is a sign of Christ's union with the soul, which happens through grace; while a consummated marriage is a sign of Christ's union with the Church, which occurs as a result of the Word becoming enfleshed. Recall also that St. Thomas considered the nonconsummated marriage to be dissolvable, since the union of Christ and the soul can be broken by sin, while he considered the consummated union to be indissoluble, since Christ indelibly united himself with the Church in one flesh. It does not, however, seem appropriate to say that the marriage of Mary and Joseph could theoretically be dissolved since they were called together and united in a unique way by Christ.

something more. We must remember that the sacraments were not fully established "in power" until Christ accomplished our salvation through his Death and Resurrection.[56] Moreover, during Jesus' earthly life the sacraments were not needed because it was still possible to have immediate contact with him.[57] Thus Mary and Joseph realized the "great mystery" of marriage in a way that surpasses the realization of the mystery of Christ's union with his Church in the efficacious sign of the Sacrament of Marriage. The Sacrament of Marriage, which Christ gave to the Church, is an effective sign of Christ's love for the Church, through which Christ empowers the spouses to love as he loves and thus allows them to experience union with him through each other and union with each other through him. Mary and Joseph experienced this presence of Christ in their marital union in a way that is unparalleled. Their marriage is a reality above that of a sacrament because in their union Christ is uniquely present, giving them a foretaste in this life of resurrected life with him. There can be no earthly marriage that approaches that of Mary and Joseph, in whom marriage itself is recapitulated in Christ. However, the paradox is that their marriage is the earthly archetype of marriage, and it is the Sacrament of Marriage that allows other Christian spouses to participate in the reality that they lived, a reality in which they experience a nuptial love that consecrates them to Christ.

Thus in contemplating the marriage of Mary and Joseph we are led to see that they lived the consecrated aspect of marriage and the nuptial aspect of celibacy to the fullest degree possible, showing the complementarity of these two vocations in the universal call to spousal love. The virginal marriage of Mary and Joseph revealed in a unique way the consecrated aspect of married love. The common goal of spouses, and the individual goal of every human person, is a complete giving of themselves to God.[58] Thus each and every human person is called to consecrate his or her life to God, whether married or not. Mary and Joseph lived the consecrated aspect of marriage to its fullest and thus accomplished the goal of marital giving, which is sanctification and salvation. They jointly consecrated their marriage in

---

56. Edward Schillebeeckx, *Christ the Sacrament of the Encounter with God* (New York: Sheed and Ward, 1963), 118.

57. Ibid.

58. Peter J. Elliott, *What God Has Joined*, 157.

undivided service to the Word made flesh. As a result of this radical consecration, Mary, through her virgin motherhood, and Joseph, through his continent spousehood, partook in a fruitfulness of redemption that was different from the fruitfulness of mere flesh (TOB 75:3). Their continence was perfectly fruitful, experiencing the Incarnation of love himself in their midst.

Likewise, the continent marriage of Mary and Joseph revealed in a unique manner the nuptial aspect of celibacy. "Mary and Joseph entered the realm of fairest love by the gift of self that they made in service of the Incarnation and Redemption."[59] By mutual consent they shared their virginity, offering themselves completely to God.[60] They desired only to help each other fulfill God's will for their lives. The fact that they remained continent was not selfish. Instead, they gave the totality of themselves to each other for the purpose of assisting each other to grow in union with Christ. As a result of this total mutual self-giving, their marriage experienced the fullness of conjugal love,[61] and participated fully in the triune marital good of fidelity, indissolubility, and fruitfulness.[62]

The Holy Family of Nazareth was typified by the word *gift*. Mary and Joseph emptied themselves and put themselves wholly at the service of God's plan and the good of their family. Due to their reception of each other as gifts and their offering of themselves as gifts back to the God who gave them to each other, as individuals and as a family they were *truly and fully* human. As they lived as gift, the Holy Family is the model of fairest love (LF, 21). In contemplating the Holy Family at Nazareth we gaze upon a family that is the closest approximation to an earthly model of the love of the Trinity. In fact, before Jesus, Mary, and Joseph were referred to as the "Holy Family," they were referred to as the "earthly trinity," a term first used by Jean Gerson (1363–1429).[63] St. Francis De Sales (1567–1622) noted that in the Holy Family we see "the mystery of the most holy and adorable Trinity. . . . It was a trinity on earth representing in some sort the

---

59. Joseph F. Chorpenning, "The Holy Family as Icon," 88.

60. Peter J. Elliott, *What God Has Joined*, 157.

61. Augustine, *Sermon* 51, trans. Edmund Hill, WSA, part 3, vol. 3 (1991), 21.

62. Augustine, *Marriage and Desire*, trans. Roland J. Teske, WSA, part 1, vol. 24 (1998), I,11,13.

63. Chorpenning, "The Holy Family as icon," 84 and 85, fn. 6.

most holy Trinity. Mary, Jesus, and Joseph—Joseph, Jesus, and Mary—
a trinity worthy indeed to be honored and greatly esteemed."[64] All
Christian married couples, in forming a domestic church, are called
and empowered by Christ in the Sacrament of Marriage to reflect the
love of the Triune God. As Pope John Paul II stated, "Christian
families exist to form a communion of persons in love. As such, the
Church and the family are each in its own way living representations
of the Most Holy Trinity."[65] As the preeminent example of the earthly
communion of persons effected by Christ, Mary and Joseph allowed
themselves to be molded by God and led to heaven through the tender
love they shared with each other, a love which had its origin in Jesus
and in which Jesus was present and active. Relying upon the grace of
the Sacrament of Marriage and Christ's active presence in their union,
every Christian couple must seek to grow in tender love and cooperate
with God's plan to mold them into a communion of persons and
a living sign of Christ's love for his Church.

---

64. *The Spiritual Conferences of St. Francis de Sales*, trans. F. Aidan Gasquet, OSB, and Henry
Benedict Mackey, OSB (Westminster, MD: Newman Press, 1962), 373–74, quoted in Joseph
Chorpenning, "'The Guidance and Education of His Divine Infancy': The Holy Family's Mission
in St. Francis De Sales," in *The Holy Family in Art and Devotion*, ed. Joseph Chorpenning
(Philadelphia: Saint Joseph's University Press, 1998), 41.

65. John Paul II, Address at Columbia, South Carolina, September 11, 1987, in *The Wisdom
of John Paul II: The Pope on Life's Most Vital Questions*, compiled by Nick Balakar and Richard
Balkin (New York: HarperSanFrancisco, 1995), 32.

Conclusion

In his book *Nuptial Mystery*, Cardinal Angelo Scola pointed out that every age can be interpreted by looking "at how it regards marriage and the family," because without understanding the reality of marriage and the family "it is impossible to understand man."[1] The reality of marriage and its essential characteristics that are ingrained in human nature by our Creator used to be taken for granted. Today, however, none of these characteristics are widely accepted, and as a result, we are forgetting who we are. Through the practice of divorce, modern society questions the idea that marriage must be permanent. Through the pervasive use of contraception, the increasing use of reproductive technologies that separate baby making from the conjugal act, and through the increase in out-of-wedlock births, modern society questions the idea that marriage has anything essentially to do with children. Through the widespread and now largely culturally accepted practice of cohabitation, modern society calls into question the absolute fidelity of marriage that excludes "trying someone out" and even calls into question the very usefulness of marriage. We have now reached the point at which the reality that marriage must be between a man and a woman is receiving ever increasing opposition. Perhaps this last issue, more than any other, shows how thoroughly confused our culture is regarding marriage and the human person.

What was once assumed or taken for granted is now being challenged; namely the unique complementarity of a man and a woman that allows them to be "yoked together" in conjugal love to form a unique human relationship we call marriage. On many levels of society, the question is being raised as to whether two people of the same gender can now lay claim to the state of matrimony, a word, which we have already noted, means to bestow upon a woman the office of a

---

1. Angelo Scola, *The Nuptial Mystery*, translated by Michelle K. Borras (Grand Rapids, MI: William B. Eerdmans Publishing Company, 2005), 337.

mother. [2] Those who oppose the "redefinition" of marriage to include couples of the same gender are labeled "mean-spirited," "intolerant," or "homophobic." Sadly, this issue has transgressed beyond civil discourse and reasoned debate. In fact, any attempt to defend the "traditional" vision of marriage is simply shouted down while avoiding true, reasoned engagement based upon natural law. As Angelo Scola noted, "Today . . . thought's elementary capacity to relate to reality is very often ignored. I am convinced that conversion (*metanoia*) *is* necessary . . . in this respect. I am referring to the urgency of turning (*cum-vertere*) to things just as they are, to reality in itself. What we need today is a conversion 'to the real.'"[3] If this conversion does not occur, Scola noted, "Modern society, deeply confused about the fundamental terms both of man and woman and of marriage and the family such as God conceived them, runs the risk of the 'abolition of man.'"[4] The confusion that leads to the danger of abolition is ultimately sown by the Father of Lies who, seeking to obscure God's love for humanity, has sought from the beginning to disrupt and obscure marriage as a "primordial sacrament" of God's love.[5] At this point in human history there is an urgent need to overcome our confusion and correct our vision lest we lose sight of the truth of God's love for us and the truth of ourselves.

The reality of marriage is so deeply ingrained in human nature that it is "the determining characteristic of a culture."[6] It is simply and profoundly true that "the history of mankind, the history of salvation, passes by way of the family" (LF, 23), which has its foundation in marriage. My sincere hope and prayer is that we may all come to see and appreciate the wonderful and awe-inspiring mystery of marriage, a mystery that is foundational to human existence. I wrote this book to be read and considered by "a culture which, in an ever

2. On June 26, 2015, the Supreme Court of the United States of America issued a decision in Obergefell et al. v. Hodges, Director, Ohio Department of Health, et al. that legalized same-sex "marriage" across the country.

3. Angelo Scola, *The Nuptial Mystery*, 90.

4. Ibid., 213. *The Abolition of Man* is a work written by C.S. Lewis. As part of this book Lewis argued for the recognition of unchanging truth that can be perceived through natural law reasoning.

5. Peter J. Elliott, *What God Has Joined: The Sacramentality of Marriage* (Staten Island, NY: Alba House, 1990), 9.

6. Angelo Scola, *The Nuptial Mystery*, 141.

more disturbing way, is in danger of losing sight of the very meaning of marriage and the family as an institution" (NMI, 10). Throughout this book I have relied upon the insights of St. John Paul II to help readers understand the centrality of the mystery of marriage to human existence, revealing God's love for us and his plan for us accomplished in Christ.

It is appropriate to note that now more than ever, to proclaim the truth about marriage as both a natural institution and a sacrament, is to "swim against the tide" of the current culture (LF, 12). As John Paul II noted, "The deep-seated roots of the 'great mystery,' the sacrament of love and life which began with Creation and Redemption and which *has Christ the bridegroom as its ultimate surety*, have been lost in the modern way of looking at things. The 'great mystery' is threatened in us and all around us" (LF, 19). Thus our modern culture needs to recover its roots and return to an outlook that will allow us to see the glorious mystery of marriage once again.

It is precisely in the face of this need for restorative vision that the Sacrament of Marriage has the potential to open people's eyes and serve "as a true beacon of hope."[7] Edward Schillebeeckx once aptly noted: "It is up to us as Christians to make the Church appear as visibly present to those people who are carried along by the current in this world, by providing the simple direct evidence of our Christian behavior and way of life. We can thus give them a real desire for salvation, and make it possible for them to come to believe."[8] In our current situation, which is experiencing the rapid breakdown of the fundamental cell of society (CCC, 2207)—marriage and family—it is Christian couples responding to the vocation of marriage who can provide a sign of hope. By the simple direct evidence of their Christian behavior and way of life, they can make the love of Christ visibly present to those "who are carried along by the current of this world." A solemn blessing in the rite of marriage even prays that the newly married couple will "be witnesses in the world to God's charity" (RM, "Solemn Blessing A").

---

7. Paul Gondreau, "The Redemption and Divinization of Human Sexuality through the Sacrament of Marriage: A Thomistic Approach," *Nova et Vetera*, English ed. 10.2 (2012): 413.

8. Edward Schillebeeckx, *Christ the Sacrament of the Encounter with God* (New York: Sheed and Ward, 1963), 210.

When Christ indissolubly unites a man and a woman together in the Sacrament of Marriage, he calls and empowers them to be witnesses to the love for which everyone longs. Jesus calls Christian spouses to "bear witness by their faithful love in the joys and sacrifices of their calling, to that mystery of love which the Lord revealed to the world by his death and resurrection" (GS, 52). As a living sign of Jesus' faithful, fruitful, and indissoluble love with which he loves us to the end (Jn 13:1), the Sacrament of Marriage is itself a living invitation to accept the love of the bridegroom. However, in order to be this living sign of Christ's love, Christian couples must cooperate with the grace that Jesus constantly offers them in the Sacrament of Marriage. They have received both a gift and a task. As John Paul II stated, "Only if husbands and wives share in that love [of Christ the bridegroom for his bride the Church] and in that 'great mystery' can they love 'to the end.' Unless they share in it, they do not know 'to the end' what love truly is and how radical are its demands" (LF, 19). If Christian spouses respond to their dignified calling and open themselves up to Christ's redemptive love, marriage can be seen and revered once again as a truly "great mystery," a mystery that, whether we have the eyes to see it or not, will always be at the foundation of human existence, revealing God's salvific love for us.

Selected Bibliography

The 1917 or Pio-Benedictine Code of Canon Law in English Translation. San Francisco: Ignatius Press, 2001.

Abelard, Peter. *Ethics.* Translated by D. E. Luscombe. Oxford: The Clarendon Press, 1971.

Ambrose of Milan. *Commentary of Saint Ambrose on the Gospel according to Saint Luke.* Translated by Íde M. Ní Riain. Dublin: Halycon Press, 2001.

_____. *Concerning Virginity.* NPNF. Second Series. Vol. 10

_____. *Letter 42 to Siricius, Bishop of Rome,* in *Saint Ambrose: Letters.* Translated by Sister Mary Melchior Beyenka. FOC. Vol. 26. 1954.

Anderson, Carl and Jose Granados. *Called to Love: Approaching John Paul II's Theology of the Body.* New York: Doubleday, 2009.

Aquinas, Thomas. *Summa contra Gentiles.* 4 vols. Translated by Vernon Bourke. Notre Dame, IN: University of Notre Dame Press, 1956.

_____. *Summa Theologica.* 5 vols. Translated by Fathers of the English Dominican Province. Reprinted, Allen, TX: Christian Classics, 1981.

Ashley, Benedict M. *Living the Truth in Love: A Biblical Introduction to Moral Theology.* New York: Alba House, 1996.

Athenagoras. *Plea.* In *Early Christian Fathers.* Translated and edited by Cyril C. Richardson. New York: Collier Books, 1970.

Augustine. *Adulterous Marriage.* Translated by C.T. Huegelmeyr. FOC. Vol. 27. 1955.

_____. *Answer to Julian.* Translated by Roland J. Teske. WSA. Part 1. Vol. 24. 1998.

_____. *Answer to the Two Letters of the Pelagians.* Translated by Roland J. Teske. WSA. Part 1. Vol. 24. 1998.

_____. *On Baptism, Against the Donatists.* Translated by J.R. King. NPNF. First Series. Vol. 4.

_____. *Concerning the City of God against the Pagans.* Translated by Henry Bettenson. London: Penguin Books, 1987.

_____. *Confessions.* Translated by Henry Chadwick. New York: Oxford University Press, 1991.

_____. *Continence.* Translated by M. F. McDonald. FOC. Vol. 16. 1952.

_____. *The Good of Marriage.* Translated by Charles T. Wilcox. FOC. Vol. 27. 1955.

_____. *On the Grace of Christ, and on Original Sin.* Translated by Peter Holmes and Robert Ernest Wallis. NPNF. Series 1. Vol. 5.

_____. *Holy Virginity.* Translated by J. McQuade. FOC. Vol. 27. 1955.

_____. *Letter 6*, 5; 8.* Translated by Robert B. Eno. FOC. Vol. 81. 1989.

_____. *Letter XCVIII.* Translated by J.G. Cunningham. NPNF. First Series. Vol. 1.

_____. *Letter CXXXVIII.* Translated by J.G. Cunningham. NPNF. First Series. Vol. 1.

_____. *The Literal Meaning of Genesis.* Translated by John Hammond Taylor. ACW. Vols. 41–42. 1982.

_____. *Marriage and Desire.* Translated by Roland J. Teske. WSA. Part 1. Vol. 24. 1998.

_____. *Retractations.* Translated by. M.I. Bogan. FOC. Vol. 60. 1968.

_____. *Sermon 9.* Translated by Edmund Hill. WSA. Part 3. Vol. 1. 1990.

_____. *Sermon 51.* Translated by Edmund Hill. WSA. Part 3. Vol. 3. 1991.

_____. *Sermon 299D.* Translated by Edmund Hill. WSA. Part 3. Vol. 8. 1994.

_____. *Sermon 354A.* Translated by Edmund Hill. WSA. Part 3. Vol. 11. 1997.

_____. *The Soliloquies.* Translated by Thomas F. Gilligan. FOC. Vol. 1. 1948.

_____. *Tractates on the Gospel According to St. John.* Translated by John Gibb and James Innes. NPNF. First Series. Vol. 7.

_____. *Tractates on the First Epistle of John.* Translated by John W. Rettig. FOC. Vol. 92. 1995.

_____. *The Trinity.* Translated by Edmund Hill. WSA. Part 1. Vol. 5. 1991.

_____. *Unfinished Work in Answer to Julian.* Translated by Roland J. Teske. WSA. Part 1. Vol. 25. 1999.

Basil the Great. *Letter 188.* In *Saint Basil: Letters Volume II (186–368).* Translated by Sister Agnes Clare Way. FOC. Vol. 28. 1955.

_____. *Letter 217.* In *Saint Basil: Letters Volume II (186–368).* Translated by Sister Agnes Clare Way. FOC. Vol. 28. 1955.

Beal, John P., Jams A. Coriden, and Thomas J. Green, eds. *New Commentary on the Code of Canon Law.* New York: Paulist Press, 2000.

Benedict XVI. Address to the Bishops of the Polish Episcopal Conference on their *Ad Limina* Visit. December 3, 2005. www.vatican.va/holy_father/benedict_xvi /speeches/2005/december/documents/hf_ben_xvi_spe_20051203_adlimina -polonia-ii_en.html.

_____. *Deus Caritas Est (God is Love).* Encyclical Letter. December 25, 2005. www. vatican.va/holy_father/benedict_xvi/encyclicals/documents/hf_ben-xvi _enc_20051225_deus-caritas-est_en.html.

_____. *Jesus of Nazareth: The Infancy Narratives.* New York: Image, 2012.

Bonaventure. *Breviloquium.* Translated by Dominic V. Monti. Vol. 9 of *Works of St. Bonaventure.* Saint Bonaventure, NY: Franciscan Institute Publications, 2005.

Book of Blessings. Study Edition. Collegeville, Minnesota: The Liturgical Press, 1989.

Bransfield, J. Brian. *The Human Person According to John Paul II.* Boston: Pauline Books & Media, 2010.

Brooke, Christopher N.L. *The Medieval Idea of Marriage.* Oxford: Oxford University Press, 1989.

Brown, Peter. *The Body and Society: Men, Women, and Sexual Renunciation in Early Christianity.* New York: Columbia University Press, 1988.

Brown, Raymond E., Joseph A. Fitzmyer, and Roland E. Murphy, eds. *The New Jerome Biblical Commentary.* Englewood Cliffs, NJ: Prentice Hall, 1990.

Broyde, Michael J. "The Covenant-Contract Dialectic in Jewish Divorce Law." In *Covenant Marriage in Comparative Perspective.* Edited by John Witte Jr. and Eliza Ellison. Grand Rapids, MI: William B. Eerdmans Publishing Company, 2005.

Brugger, E. Christian. "Just Cause and Natural Family Planning: Spacing Children Requires Discernment, Discussion," January 10, 2010. ZENIT news agency. www.zenit.org/en/articles/just-cause-and-natural-family-planning.

Brundage, James A. *Law, Sex, and Society in Medieval Europe.* Chicago: University of Chicago Press, 1987.

Budziszewski, J. *What We Can't Not Know.* Dallas: Spence Publishing Company, 2003.

Bullough, Vern L., and James A. Brundage. *Sexual Practices & the Medieval Church.* Buffalo, NY: Prometheus Books, 1982.

Burke, Cormac. *The Theology of Marriage: Personalism, Doctrine and Canon Law.* Washington, DC: Catholic University of American Press, 2014.

_____. *Covenanted Happiness: Love and Commitment in Marriage.* San Francisco: Ignatius Press, 1990.

Butler, Sara, MSBT. *Catholic Priesthood and Women: A Guide to the Teaching of the Church.* Chicago: Hillenbrand Books, 2007.

Buttiglione, Rucco. *Karol Wojtyla: The Thought of the Man Who Became John Paul II.* Translated by Paolo Guietti and Francesca Murphy. Grand Rapids, MI: Eerdmans, 1997.

Cahall, Perry J. "The Nucleus of the New Evangelization." *Nova et Vetera*, English ed., 11.1 (2013): 39–56.

_____. "Preaching, Teaching, and Living the Theology of the Body." *Linacre Quarterly* 73.3 (Aug. 2007): 213–229.

_____. "Saint Augustine on Conjugal Love and Divine Love." *The Thomist* 68 (2004): 343–73.

_____. "Saint Augustine on Marriage and the Trinity." *Josephinum Journal of Theology* 11.1 (Winter/Spring 2004): 82–97.

_____. "Spiritual Fatherhood and Generativity." *Downside Review* 129 (Apr. 2011): 77–88.

_____. "Toward Understanding the Holy Family of Nazareth as a Model of Married and Family Life." *Anthropotes* 24.2 (2008): 275–312.

_____. "The Trinitarian Structure of St. Augustine's Good of Marriage." *Augustinian Studies* 34:2 (2003): 223–232.

Calivas, Alkiviadis C. "Marriage: The Sacrament of Love and Communion." In *InterMarriage: Orthodox Perspectives.* Edited by Anton C. Vrame. Brookline, MA: Holy Cross Orthodox Press, 1997.

Calvin, John. *Institutes of Christian Religion.* Translated by Henry Beveridge. Grand Rapids, MI: William B. Eerdmans Publishing Company, 1979.

Cantalamessa, Raniero. "Father Cantalamessa on Christ at Cana: Pontifical Household Preacher Comments on Sunday's Readings." January 12, 2007. Translated by ZENIT news agency. www.zenit.org/en/articles/father-cantalamessa-on-christ-at-cana.

_____. "Father Cantalamessa on Marital Submission: Pontifical Household Preacher on This Sunday's Gospel." August 25, 2006. Translated by ZENIT news agency. www.zenit.org/en/articles/father-cantalamessa-on-marital-submission.

_____. "Father Cantalamessa on Marriage: 'Rediscover the Art of Repairing!' Says Pontifical Household Preacher." October 6, 2006. Translated by ZENIT news agency. www.zenit.org/en/articles/father-cantalamessa-on-marriage.

Catechism of the Catholic Church. 2nd ed. Washington, DC: Libreria Editrice Vaticana–United States Conference of Catholic Bishops, 2000.

Champlain, Joseph M. "Marriage, Liturgy of." In *New Dictionary of Sacramental Worship.* Edited by Peter E. Fink. Collegeville, MN: Liturgical Press, 1990.

Chorpenning, Joseph F. "The Guidance and Education of His Divine Infancy." In *The Holy Family in Art and Devotion.* Edited by Joseph F. Chorpenning. Philadelphia: Saint Joseph's University Press, 1998.

_____. "The Holy Family as Icon and Model of the Civilization of Love: John Paul II's Letter to Families." *Communio* 22 (Spring 1995): 77–98.

_____. "Icon of Family and Religious Life: The Historical Development of the Holy Family Devotion." In *The Holy Family as Prototype of the Civilization of Love: Images from the Viceregal Americans*. Philadelphia: Saint Joseph's University Press, 1996.

The Christian Faith in the Doctrinal Documents of the Catholic Church. 7th ed. Edited by J. Neuner and Jacques Dupuis. New York: Alba House, 2001.

Clement of Alexandria. *Stromateis*. In *Clement of Alexandria: Stromateis Books One to Three*. Translated by John Ferguson. FOC. Vol. 85. 1991.

Code of Canon Law: Latin-English Edition; New English Translation (Codex Iuris Cononici [CIC]). Washington, DC: Canon Law Society of America, 1998.

Collins, John J. "Marriage in the Old Testament." In *Marriage in the Catholic Tradition: Scripture, Tradition, and Experience*. Edited by Todd A. Salzman, Thomas M. Kelly, and John J. O'Keefe. New York: Crossroad, 2004.

Congar, Yves. *Lay People in the Church: A Study for a Theology of Laity*. Translated by Donald Attwater. 2nd rev. ed. Westminster, MD: Newman Press, 1965.

Congregation for the Doctrine of the Faith. *Considerations Regarding Proposals to Give Legal Recognition to Unions between Homosexual Persons*. June 3, 2003. www.vatican.va/roman_curia/congregations/cfaith/documents/rc_con_cfaith _doc_20030731_homosexual-unions_en.html.

_____. *Donum Vitae (Instruction on Respect for Human Life in Its Origin and on the Dignity of Procreation Replies to Certain Questions of the Day)*. February 22, 1987. www.vatican.va/roman_curia/congregations/cfaith/documents/rc_con_cfaith _doc_19870222_respect-for-human-life_en.html.

_____. *Instruction "Dignitatis Personae" On Certain Bioethical Questions*. September 8, 2008. www.vatican.va/roman_curia/congregations/cfaith/documents/rc_con _cfaith_doc_20081208_dignitas-personae_en.html.

_____. *Letter to the Bishops of the Catholic Church on the Collaboration of Men and Women in the Church and in the World*. May 31, 2004. www.vatican.va/roman _curia/congregations/cfaith/documents/rc_con_cfaith_doc_20040731 _collaboration_en.html.

_____. *Letter to the Bishops of the Catholic Church on the Pastoral Care of Homosexual Persons*. October 1, 1986. www.vatican.va/roman_curia/congregations/cfaith /documents/rc_con_cfaith_doc_19861001_homosexual-persons_en.html.

_____. *Persona humana (Vatican Declaration on Certain Questions of Sexual Ethics)*. December 29, 1975. www.vatican.va/roman_curia/congregations/cfaith /documents/rc_con_cfaith_doc_19751229_persona-humana_en.html.

Connery, John R. "The Role of Love in Christian Marriage: A Historical Overview." *Communio* 11 (1984): 244–257.

Cottier, George. "Reflections on Marriage and the Family." *Nova et Vetera*, English ed., 1.1 (2003): 11–25.

Creighton Model FertilityCare System: An Authentic Language of a Woman's Health and Fertility—An Introductory Booklet for New Users. 5th ed. Omaha, NE: Pope Paul VI Institute Press, 2003.

Crosby, John F. "The Estrangement of Persons from Their Bodies." In *Personalist Papers*. Washington, DC: Catholic University of America Press, 2004.

_____. "The Incommunicability of Human Persons." *The Thomist* 57 (1993): 403–442.

_____. "Karol Wojtyla's Personalist Understanding of Man and Woman." In *Personalist Papers*. Washington, DC: Catholic University of America Press, 2004.

Cutrone, Emmanuel J. "Sacraments." In *Augustine through the Ages: An Encyclopedia.* Edited by Allan D. Fitzgerald. Grand Rapids: Eerdmans, 1999.

de Haro, Ramón García. *Marriage and the Family in the Documents of the Magisterium: A Course in the Theology of Marriage.* 2nd ed. Translated by William E. May. San Francisco: Ignatius Press, 1993.

Eberstadt, Mary. *Adam and Eve after the Pill: Paradoxes of the Sexual Revolution.* San Francisco: Ignatius Press, 2012.

Elliott, Dyan. *Spiritual Marriage: Sexual Abstinence in Medieval Wedlock.* Princeton, NJ: Princeton University Press, 1993.

Elliott, Peter J. *What God Has Joined: The Sacramentality of Marriage.* New York: Alba House, 1990.

Enchiridion Symbolorum, Definitionum et Declarationum de Rebus Fidei et Morum (Compendium of Creeds, Definitions, and Declarations on Matters of Faith and Morals). Edited by Heinrich Denzinger and Adolphus Schönmetzer. 43rd ed. Edited by Peter Hünerman. Latin-English ed. Edited by Robert Fastiggi and Anne Englund Nash. San Francisco: Ignatius Press, 2012.

Epstein, Louis. *Marriage Laws in the Bible and the Talmud.* Cambridge, MA: Harvard University Press, 1942.

Estévez, Jorge Cardinal Medina. *"Male and Female He Created Them": On Marriage and the Family.* San Francisco: Ignatius Press, 2003.

Evdokimov, Paul. *The Sacrament of Love: The Nuptial Mustery in the Light of the Orthodox Tradition.* Translated by Anthony P. Gythiel and Victoria Steadman. Crestwood, NY: St. Vladimir's Seminary Press, 1985.

Fatula, Mary Ann. *Thomas Aquinas, Preacher and Friend.* Collegeville, MN: The Liturgical Press, 1993.

Fisher, Simcha. *The Sinner's Guide to Natural Family Planning.* Huntington, IN: Our Sunday Visitor, 2014.

Ford, John C. and Gerald Kelly. "The Essential Subordination of the Secondary Ends of Marriage." In *Marriage.* Readings in Moral Theology, no. 15. Edited by Charles E. Curran and Julie Hanlon Rubio. New York: Paulist Press, 2009. Originally published in *Contemporary Moral Theology.* Vol. 2, Marriage Questions. Westminister, MD: Newman, 1963.

Fox-Genovese, Elizabeth. *Marriage: The Dream That Refuses to Die.* Edited by Sheila O'Connor-Ambrose. Wilmington, DE: ISI Books, 2008.

Francis, Pope. *The Joy of the Gospel: Evangelii Gaudium.* Washington, DC: United States Conference of Catholic Bishops, 2013.

_____. *Lumen Fidei (The Light of Faith).* Encyclical Letter. June 29, 2013. www.vatican.va/holy_father/francesco/encyclicals/documents/papa-francesco _20130629_enciclica-lumen-fidei_en.html.

Gailardetz, Richard R. *A Daring Promise: A Spirituality of Christian Marriage.* New York: Crossroad Publishing, 2002.

George, Robert P., and Jean Bethke Elshtain, eds. *The Meaning of Marriage: Family, State, Market, and Morals.* Dallas: Spence Publishing Co., 2006.

Girgis, Sherif, Ryan T. Anderson, and Robert P. George. *What is Marriage? Man and Woman: A Defense.* New York: Encounter Books, 2012.

Gold, Penny S. "The Marriage of Mary and Joseph in the Twelfth-Century Ideology of Marriage." In *Sexual Practices & the Medieval Church.* Edited by Vern L. Bullough and James Brundage. Buffalo, NY: Prometheus Books, 1982.

Gondreau, Paul. "The Redemption and Divinization of Human Sexuality through the Sacrament of Marriage: A Thomistic Approach." *Nova et Vetera*, English ed., 10.2 (2012): 383–413.

Grabowski, John S. *Sex and Virtue: An Introduction to Sexual Ethics.* Washington, DC: Catholic University of America Press, 2003.

Gramunt, Ignatius. "The Essence of Marriage and the *Code of Canon Law*." *Studia Canonica* 25 (1991): 365–383.

Gray, Mark. "Facing a Future with Fewer Catholic Priests." OSV Weekly. June 27, 2010. www.osv.com/tabid/7621/itemid/6532/In-Focus-Facing-a-future-with-fewer -Catholic-prie.aspx.

Gregory of Nazianzen. *Oration XXXVII.* NPNF. Second Series. Vol. 7.

_____. *On the Making of Man.* NPNF. Second Series. Vol. 5.

_____. *On Virginity.* NPNF. Second Series. Vol. 5.

Grisez, Germain, Joseph Boyle, John Finnis, and William E. May. "'Every Marital Act Ought to Be Open to New Life': Toward a Clearer Understanding." *The Thomist* 52.3 (July 1988): 365–426.

Haas, John. "The Contemporary World." *Christian Marriage: A Historical Study.* Edited by Glenn W. Olsen. New York: Crossroad, 2001.

Hahn, Kimberly. *Life-Giving Love: Embracing God's Beautiful Design for Marriage.* Ann Arbor: Charis, 2001.

Harrison, Carol. "Marriage and Monasticism in St. Augustine: The Bond of Friendship." *Studia Patristica* 33 (1997): 94–99.

Harvey, John. *The Homosexual Person: New Thinking in Pastoral Care.* San Francisco: Ignatius Press, 1987.

_____. *The Truth about Homosexuality: The Cry of the Faithful.* San Francisco: Ignatius Press, 1996.

Healy, Mary. *Men and Women are from Eden: A Study Guide to John Paul II's Theology of the Body.* Cincinnati, OH: St. Anthony Messenger Press, 2005.

Heaney, Seamus. *The Development of the Sacramentality of Marriage from Anselm of Laon to Thomas Aquinas.* Washington, DC: Catholic University of America Press, 1963.

Hilgers, Thomas W. *The NaProTechnology Revolution: Unleashing the Power of a Woman's Cycle.* Omaha, NE: Pope Paul VI Institute Press, 2010.

Hitchcock, James. *History of the Catholic Church: From the Apostolic Age to the Third Millenium.* San Francisco: Ignatius Press, 2012.

Hogan, Richard M., and John M. LeVoir. *Covenant of Love: Pope John Paul II on Sexuality, Marriage, and Family in the Modern World.* San Francisco: Ignatius Press, 1985.

Hugh of St. Victor. *Hugh of Saint Victor on the Sacraments of the Christian Faith (De Sacramentis).* Translated by Roy J. Deferrari. Eugene, OR: Wipf and Stock Publishers, 2007.

Hunter, David. "Augustine, Sermon 354A: Its Place in His Thought on Marriage and Sexuality." *Augustinian Studies* 33.1 (2002): 39–60.

_____. "*Bono conjugali, De*." In *Augustine through the Ages: An Encyclopedia.* Edited by Allan D. Fitzgerald. Grand Rapids, MI: Eerdmans, 1999.

Ignatius of Antioch. *Letter to Polycarp (Ad Polycarpum).* In *Early Christian Fathers.* Translated and edited by Cyril C. Richardson. New York: Collier Books, 1970.

Irenaeus of Lyons. *Against Heresies.* ANF. Vol. 1.

Jerome. *Against Jovinian*. NPNF. Second Series. Vol. 6.

_____. *Commentary on Galatians*. Translated by Andrew Cain. FOC. Vol. 121. 2010.

John Chrysostom. "Homily 12: On Colossians 4:18." In *St. John Chrysostom on Marriage and Family Life*. Translated by Catherine P. Roth and David Anderson. Crestwood, NY: St. Vladimir's Seminary Press, 2000.

_____. "Homily 19: On 1 Corinthians 7." In *St. John Chrysostom on Marriage and Family Life*. Translated by Catherine P. Roth and David Anderson. Crestwood, NY: St. Vladimir's Seminary Press, 2000.

_____. "Homily 20: On Ephesians 5:22–33." In *St. John Chrysostom on Marriage and Family Life*. Translated by Catherine P. Roth and David Anderson. Crestwood, NY: St. Vladimir's Seminary Press, 2000.

_____. "Sermon on Marriage." In *St. John Chrysostom on Marriage and Family Life*. Translated by Catherine P. Roth and David Anderson. Crestwood, NY: St. Vladimir's Seminary Press, 2000.

_____. "On Virginity." In *John Chrysostom: On Virginity; Against Remarriage*. Translated by Sally Rieger Shore. Studies in Women and Religion. Vol. 9. New York: Edwin Mellon Press, 1983.

John Paul II. Address at Columbia, South Carolina. September 11, 1987. In *The Wisdom of John Paul II: The Pope on Life's Most Vital Questions*. Compiled by Nick Balakar and Richard Balkin. New York: HarperSanFrancisco, 1995.

_____. *Ecclesia in America* (*The Church in America*). Apostolic Exhortation. January 22, 1999. Boston: Pauline Books & Media, 1999.

_____. *Evangelium Vitae* (*The Gospel of Life*). Encyclical Letter. March 25, 1995. Boston: Pauline Books & Media, 1995.

_____. *Familiaris Consortio* (*The Role of the Christian Family in the Modern World*). Apostolic Exhortation. November 22, 1981. Boston: Pauline Books & Media, 1981.

_____. *God, Father and Creator*. A Catechesis on the Creed. Vol. 1. Boston: Pauline Books & Media, 1998.

_____. *Gratissimam Sane (Letter to Families)*. February 2, 1994. Boston: Pauline Books & Media, 1994.

_____. *Man and Woman He Created Them: A Theology of the Body*. Translation and introduction by Michael Waldstein. Boston: Pauline Books and Media, 2006.

_____. "Message for the 43rd Italian Catholic Social Week." www.vatican.va/holy _father/john_paul_ii/speeches/1999/november/documents/hf_jp-ii_spe _16111999_week-cath_en.html.

_____. *Mulieris Dignitatem* (*The Dignity of Woman*). Apostolic Letter. August 15, 1988. Boston: Pauline Books & Media, 1988.

_____. *Novo Millenio Ineunte* (*The Coming of the New Millenium*). Apostolic Letter. January 6, 2001. Boston: Pauline Books & Media, 2001.

_____. *Redemptor Hominis* (*The Redeemer of Man*). Encyclical Letter. March 4, 1979. Boston: Pauline Books & Media, 1979.

_____. *Redemptoris Custos* (*Guardian of the Redeemer*). Apostolic Exhortation, August 15, 1989. Boston: Pauline Books & Media, 1989.

_____. *Sources of Renewal: The Implementation of the Second Vatican Council*. San Francisco: Harper & Row, 1980.

_____. *Springtime of Evangelization*. San Francisco: Ignatius Press, 1999.

_____. *Veritatis Splendor* (*The Splendor of Truth*). Encyclical Letter. August 6, 1993. Boston: Pauline Books & Media, 1993.

Johnson, Maxwell E., ed. *Sacraments and Worship: The Sources of Christian Theology.* Louisville, KY: Westminster John Knox Press, 2012.

Joyce, George Hayward. *Christian Marriage: An Historical and Doctrinal Study.* New York: Sheed and Ward, 1933.

Justin Martyr. *First Apology.* In *Early Christian Fathers.* Translated and edited by Cyril C. Richardson. New York: Collier Books, 1970.

Kasper, Walter. *Theology of Christian Marriage.* Translated by David Smith. New York: Seabury Press, 1980.

Keating, James. *Spousal Prayer.* Omaha: IPF Publications, 2013.

Kereszty, Roch. *Jesus Christ: Fundamentals of Christology.* 3rd ed. rev. and updated. Staten Island, NY: Alba House, 2002.

Kerns, Joseph E. *The Theology of Marriage: The Historical Development of Christian Attitudes Toward Sex and Sanctity in Marriage.* New York: Sheed and Ward, 1964.

Kippley, John F. *Marriage is for Keeps: Foundations for Christian Marriage.* Wedding Edition with Marriage Rite and Readings. Cincinnati, OH: Foundation for the Family, Inc., 1994.

Kupczak, Jaroslaw. *Gift and Communion: John Paul II's Theology of the Body.* Translated by Agata Rottkamp, Justyna Pawlak, and Orest Pawlak. Washington, DC: Catholic University of America Press, 2014.

Kwasniewski, Peter. "St. Thomas on the Grandeur and Limitations of Marriage." *Nova et Vetera*, English ed., 10.2 (2012): 415–436.

Lasnoski, Kent J. *Vocation to Virtue: Christian Marriage as a Consecrated Life.* Washington, DC: Catholic University of America Press, 2014.

Lawler, Michael. *Ecumenical Marriage and Remarriage: Gifts and Challenges to the Church.* Mystic, CT: Twenty-Third Publications, 1990.

_____. "Marriage in the Bible." In *Perspectives on Marriage: A Reader.* Edited by Kieran Scott and Michael Warren. 3rd ed. New York: Oxford University Press, 2007.

_____. *Marriage and the Catholic Church: Disputed Questions.* Collegeville, MN: Liturgical Press, 2002.

_____. *Marriage and Sacrament: A Theology of Christian Marriage.* Collegeville, MN: Liturgical Press, 1993.

_____. *Secular Marriage, Christian Sacrament.* Mystic, CT: Twenty-Third Publications, 1985.

Lawler, Michael, and William P. Roberts, eds. *Christian Marriage and Family: Contemporary Theological and Pastoral Perspectives.* Collegeville, MI: Liturgical Press, 1996.

Lawler, Ronald, Joseph Boyle, and William E. May. *Catholic Sexual Ethics: A Summary, Explanation, and Defense.* 2nd ed. Huntington, IN: Our Sunday Visitor, 1996.

Leeming, Bernard. *Principles of Sacramental Theology.* Westminister, MD: Newman Press, 1956.

Levering, Matthew, ed. *On Marriage and Family: Classic and Contemporary Texts.* New York: Rowan and Littlefield Publishers, 2005.

Lewis, C.S. *The Four Loves.* New York: Harcourt, Brace and Co., 1988.

_____. *The Abolition of Man.* New York: HarperOne, 2009.

Lombard, Peter. *The Sentences—Book 4: On the Doctrine of Signs*. Translated by Giulio Silano. Mediaeval Sources in Translation 48. Toronto: Pontifical Institute of Mediaeval Studies, 2010.

Lowery, Mark. *Living the Good Life: What Every Catholic Needs to Know about Moral Issues*. Cincinnati, OH: Servant, 2003.

_____. "The Nature and Ends of Marriage: A New Proposal." *The Jurist* 65 (2005): 98–118.

Luther, Martin. *Babylonian Captivity of the Church*. Translated by A.T.W. Steinhäuser. Revised by Frederick C. Ahrens and Abdel Ross Wentz. In *Luther's Works*. Vol. 36. Edited by Abdel Ross Wentz. Philadelphia: Fortress Press, 1959.

_____. "The Estate of Marriage." Translated by Walter I. Brandt. In *The Christian in Society II. Luther's Works*. Vol. 45. Edited by Walther I. Brandt. Philadelphia: Fortress Press, 1962.

_____. *The Table Talk of Martin Luther*. Translated by William Hazlitt. London: G. Bell and Sons, 1902.

Lyons, James P. *The Essential Structure of Marriage: A Study of the Thomistic Teaching on the Natural Institution*. Dissertation. Studies in Sacred Theology, no. 40. Washington, DC: Catholic University of America Press, 1950.

Mackin, Theodore. *Divorce and Remarriage*. Marriage in the Catholic Church. New York: Paulist Press, 1985.

_____. *The Marital Sacrament*. Marriage in the Catholic Church. New York: Paulist Press, 1989.

_____. *What Is Marriage?* Marriage in the Catholic Church. New York: Paulist Press, 1982.

Makowski, Elizabeth M. "The Conjugal Debt and Medieval Canon Law." In *Equality in God's Image: Women in the Middle Ages*. Edited by Julia Bolton Holloway, Constance S. Wright, and Joan Bechtold. New York: Peter Lang, 1990. This essay was originally published in *The Journal of Medieval History* 3 (1977): 99–114.

Marshner, William H. "Can a Couple Practicing NFP Be Practicing Contraception?" *Gregorianum* 77.4 (1996): 677–704.

Martin, Francis. "Male and Female He Created Them: A summary of the Teaching of Genesis Chapter One." *Communio* 20 (1993) 240–65.

_____. "Marriage in the New Testament Period." In *Christian Marriage: A Historical Study*. Edited by Glenn Olsen. New York: The Crossroad Publishing Company, 2001.

_____. "Marriage in the Old Testament and Intertestamental Periods." In *Christian Marriage: A Historical Study*. Edited by Glenn Olsen. New York: The Crossroad Publishing Company, 2001.

May, William E. *Catholic Bioethics and the Gift of Human Life*. 2nd ed. Huntington, IN: Our Sunday Visitor, Inc., 2008.

_____. *Catholic Bioethics and the Gift of Human Life*, 2nd ed. addendum. Huntington, IN: Our Sunday Visitor, Inc., 2010.

_____. *Marriage: The Rock on Which the Family is Built*. San Francisco: Ignatius Press, 2009.

_____. *Sex, Marriage, and Chastity: Reflections of a Catholic Layman, Spouse and Parent*. Chicago, IL: Franciscan Herald Press, 1981.

_____. "The Significance of the Consummation of Marriage, Contraception, Using Condoms to Prevent HIV, and Same-Sex Unions." *Josephinum Journal of Theology* 14.2 (Summer/Fall 2007): 207–217.

_____. *Theology of the Body in Context: Genesis and Growth.* Boston: Pauline Books & Media, 2010.

Melina, Livio. *Building a Culture of the Family: The Language of Love.* Staten Island, NY: Alba House, 2011.

Meyendorff, John. *Marriage: An Orthodox Perspective.* 2nd expanded ed. Crestwood, NY: St. Vladimir's Seminary Press, 1975.

Murphy, William F., Jr. "Forty Years Later: Arguments in Support of *Humanae Vitae* in Light of *Veritatis Splendor.*" *Josephinum Journal of Theology* 14.2 (Summer/Fall 2007): 122–167.

Nichols, Aidan. *Holy Order: Apostolic Priesthood from the New Testament to the Second Vatican Council.* Oscott 5. Dublin: Veritas Publications, 1990.

Noonan, John T., Jr. *Contraception: A History of Its Treatment by the Catholic Theologians and Canonists.* New York: Mentor-Omega Books, 1965.

Norris, T. "Why Marriage is One of the Seven Sacraments." *Irish Theological Quarterly* 5.1 (1985): 37–51.

Nowak, David. "Jewish Marriage: Nature, Covenant, and Contract." In *Covenant Marriage in Comparative Perspective.* Edited by John Witte Jr. and Eliza Ellison. Grand Rapids, MI: William B. Eerdmans Publishing Company, 2005.

"N.Y. Archbishop Takes Stock of Challenges in American Catholic Church." August 13, 2009. Catholic News Agency. www.catholicnewsagency.com/news/n.y. _archbishop_takes_stock_of_challenges_in_the_american_catholic_church/.

Odozor, Paulinus Ikechukwu, ed. *Sexuality, Marriage, and Family: Readings in the Catholic Tradition.* South Bend, IN: University of Notre Dame Press, 2001.

O'Leary, Dale. *One Man, One Woman: A Catholic's Guide to Defending Marriage.* Manchester, NH: Sophia Institute Press, 2007.

Olsen, Glenn W. "Marriage in Barbarian Kingdom and Christian Court: Fifth through Eleventh Centuries." In *Christian Marriage: A Historical Study.* Edited by Glenn W. Olsen. New York: Crossroad Publishing Company, 2001.

_____. "Progeny, Faithfulness, Sacred Bond: Marriage in the Age of Augustine." In *Christian Marriage: A Historical Study.* Edited by Glenn W. Olsen. New York: Crossroad Publishing Company, 2001.

O'Neill, Colman. *Meeting Christ in the Sacraments.* Rev. ed. New York: Alba House, 1991.

Origen of Alexandria. *Commentary on the Gospel of Matthew.* ANF. Vol. 9.

_____. *Genesis Homily III.* In *Origen: Homilies on Genesis and Exodus.* Translated by Ronald E. Heine. FOC. Vol. 71. 1982.

Ouellet, Marc Cardinal. *Divine Likeness: Toward a Trinitarian Anthropology of the Family.* Translated by Philip Milligan and Linda M. Cicone. Grand Rapids, MI: Herder, 2006.

Paul VI. "Christian Witness in Married Life: Address of Pope Paul VI to the Teams of Our Lady." *The Pope Speaks* 15 (1970): 119–128.

_____. *Humanae Vitae (Of Human Life).* Encyclical Letter. July 25, 1968. www.vatican.va/holy_father/paul_vi/encyclicals/documents/hf_p-vi_enc _25071968_humanae-vitae_en.html (accessed June 18, 2013).

_____. *Matrimonia mixta* (*On Mixed Marriages*). Motu Proprio. October 1, 1970. www.vatican.va/holy_father/paul_vi/motu_proprio/documents/hf_p-vi_motu -proprio_19700331_matrimonia-mixta_en.html (accessed June 18, 2013).

_____. "Pope Paul VI to the Council Fathers." December 8, 1965. In *The Documents of Vatican II*. Edited by Walter M. Abbot. New York: Herder and Herder, 1966.

Peters, Edward. *Annulments and the Catholic Church: Straight Answers to Tough Questions*. West Chester, PA: Ascension Press, 2004.

Pieper, Joseph. *Faith, Hope, Love*. San Francisco: Ignatius Press, 1997.

Pierre, Teresa Olsen. "Marriage, Body, and Sacrament in the Age of Hugh of St. Victor." In *Christian Marriage: A Historical Study*. Edited by Glenn W. Olsen. New York: The Crossroad Publishing Company, 2001.

Pilon, Mark. *Magnum Mysterium: The Sacrament of Matrimony*. Staten Island, NY: Alba House, 2010.

Pinckaers, Servais. *Sources of Christian Morality*. Washington, DC: Catholic University of America Press, 1995.

Pius XI. *Casti Connubii* (*On Christian Marriage*). Encyclical Letter. December 31, 1930. w2.vatican.va/content/pius-xi/en/encyclicals/documents/hf_p-xi_enc _31121930_casti-connubii.html (accessed June 18, 2013).

Pontifical Council for the Family. "Conclusions of the XVI Plenary Assembly of the Pontifical Council for the Family: Vatican City, November 18–20, 2004." *Familia et Vita* 9.3 (2004): 217–224.

_____. *Family, Marriage, and "De Facto" Unions*. November 21, 2000. www.vatican.va /roman_curia/pontifical_councils/family/documents/rc_pc_family_doc _20001109_de-facto-unions_en.html.

_____. *The Pastoral Care of the Divorced and Remarried AND Vademecum for Confessors Concerning Some Aspects of the Morality of Conjugal Life*. Boston: Pauline Books & Media, 1997.

_____. *Preparation for the Sacrament of Marriage*. May 13, 1996. www.vatican.va /roman_curia/pontifical_councils/family/documents/rc_pc_family_doc _13051996_preparation-for-marriage_en.html (accessed June 13, 2013).

_____. *The Truth and Meaning of Human Sexuality: Guidelines for Education within the Family*. December 8, 1995. www.vatican.va/roman_curia/pontifical_councils /family/documents/rc_pc_family_doc_08121995_human-sexuality_en.html.

Pruss, Alexander. *One Body: An Essay in Christian Sexual Ethics*. Notre Dame, IN: University of Notre Dame Press, 2013.

Quay, Paul M. *The Christian Meaning of Human Sexuality*. San Francisco: Ignatius Press, 1985.

Ratzinger, Joseph Cardinal. *The Spirit of the Liturgy*. Translated by John Saward. San Francisco: Ignatius Press, 2000.

Regan, Augustine. "The Perennial Value of Augustine's Theology of the Goods of Marriage." *Studia Moralia* 21 (1983): 351–378.

Reynolds, Philip Lyndon. *Marriage in the Western Church: The Christianization of Marriage during the Patristic and Early Medieval Periods*. Supplements to *Vigiliae Christianae*. Vol. 24. New York: E.J. Brill, 1994.

Reynolds, Philip L. and John Witte, eds. *To Have and to Hold: Marrying and Its Documentation in Western Christianity, 400–1600*. New York: Cambridge University Press, 2007.

Rhonheimer, Martin. *Ethics of Procreation and the Defense of Human Life: Contraception, Artificial Fertilization and Abortion*. Edited by William F. Murphy Jr. Washington, DC: Catholic University of America Press, 2010.

Rite of Marriage. In *The Rites of The Catholic Church*. Volume One. New York: Pueblo Publishing Company, 1990.

Roman Catechism, The. Translated by Robert I. Bradley and Eugene Kevane. Boston, MA: St. Paul Editions, 1985.

Roman Missal, The. New Jersey: Catholic Book Publishing Corp., 2011.

Rubio, Julie Hanlon. *A Christian Theology of Marriage and Family*. New York: Paulist Press, 2003.

Sacred Congregation for Catholic Education. *Educational Guidance in Human Love: Outlines for Sex Education*. November 1, 1983. www.vatican.va/roman_curia /congregations/ccatheduc/documents/rc_con_ccatheduc_doc_19831101 _sexual-education_en.html.

Salzman, Todd A., Thomas M. Kelly, and John J. O'Keefe, eds. *Marriage in the Catholic Tradition: Scripture, Tradition, and Experience*. New York: Crossroad, 2004.

Scheeben, Matthias Joseph. *The Mysteries of Christianity*. Translated by Cyril Vollert. St. Louis: B. Herder Book Co., 1946.

Schillebeeckx, Edward. *Christ the Sacrament of the Encounter with God*. New York: Sheed and Ward, 1963.

_____. *Marriage: Human Reality and Saving Mystery*. Translated by N.D. Smith. 2 vols. New York: Sheed and Ward, 1965.

Schleck, Charles A. *The Sacrament of Matrimony: A Dogmatic Study*. Milwaukee: Bruce, 1964.

Schmitt, Émile. *Le mariage chrétien dans l'oeuvre de Saint Augustin. Une théologie baptismale de la vie conjugale*. Paris: Études Augustiniennes, 1983.

Scola, Angelo. *The Nuptial Mystery*. Translated by Michelle K. Borras. Grand Rapids, MI: Eerdmans, 2005.

Scott, Kieran, and Michael Warren, eds. *Perspectives on Marriage: A Reader*. 3rd ed. New York: Oxford University Press, 2007.

Second Vatican Council. *Gaudium et Spes* (*Pastoral Constitution on the Church in the Modern World*). In *The Basic Sixteen Documents: Vatican Council II; Constitutions, Decrees, Declarations*. Edited by Austin Flannery, OP. Northport, NY: Costello Publishing, 1996.

_____. *Lumen Genitum* (*Dogmatic Constitution on the Church*). In *The Basic Sixteen Documents: Vatican Council II; Constitutions, Decrees, Declarations*. Edited by Austin Flannery, OP. Northport, NY: Costello Publishing, 1996.

_____. *Presbyterorum Ordinis* (*Decree on the Ministry and Life of Priests*). In *The Basic Sixteen Documents: Vatican Council II; Constitutions, Decrees, Declarations*. Edited by Austin Flannery, OP. Northport, NY: Costello Publishing, 1996.

_____. *Sacrosanctum Concilium* (*Constitution on the Sacred Liturgy*). In *The Basic Sixteen Documents: Vatican Council II; Constitutions, Decrees, Declarations*. Edited by Austin Flannery, OP. Northport, NY: Costello Publishing, 1996.

Shepherd of Hermas. In *Marriage in the Early Church*. Edited and translated by David G. Hunter. Sources of Early Christian Thought. Edited by William G. Rusch. Minneapolis: Fortress Press, 1992.

Shivanandan, Mary. "Conjugal Spirituality and the Gift of Reverence." *Nova et Vetera*, English ed., 10.2 (2012): 485–506.

_____. *Crossing the Threshold of Love: A New Vision of Marriage in the Light of John Paul II's Anthropology.* Washington, DC: Catholic University of America Press, 1999.

Simkins, Ronald A. "Marriage and Gender in the Old Testament." In *Marriage in the Catholic Tradition: Scripture, Tradition, and Experience.* Edited by Todd A. Salzman, Thomas M. Kelly, and John J. O'Keefe. New York: Crossroad, 2004.

Smith, Janet E. "Contraception, Why Not?" Audio recording. Dayton, OH: One More Soul, 2006.

_____. *"Humanae Vitae": A Generation Later.* Washington, DC: Catholic University of America Press, 1991.

_____. "The Moral Use of Natural Family Planning." In *Why "Humanae Vitae" Was Right: A Reader.* Edited by Janet E. Smith. San Francisco: Ignatius Press, 1993.

_____. "Paul VI as Prophet." In *Why "Humanae Vitae" Was Right: A Reader.* Edited by Janet E. Smith. San Francisco: Ignatius Press, 1993.

Sokolowski, Robert. "What Is Natural Law? Human Purposes and Natural Ends." *The Thomist* 68 (2004): 507–529.

The Spiritual Conferences of St. Francis de Sales. Translated by F. Aidan Gasquet, OSB, and Henry Benedict Mackey, OSB. Westminster, MD: Newman Press, 1962.

Spiteri, Laurence. *The Code in the Hands of the Laity: Canon Law for Everyone.* New York: Alba House, 1997.

Stevenson, Kenneth. *Nuptial Blessing: A Study of Christian Marriage Rites.* New York: Oxford University Press, 1983.

Stimpson, Emily. "The Church's Divorce Dilemma." OSV Weekly. May 22, 2011. www.osv.com/tabid/7621/itemid/7889/The-Churchs-divorce-dilemma.aspx.

Stylianopoulos, Theodore G. "Toward a Theology of Marriage in the Orthodox Church." In *Intermarriage: Orthodox Perspectives.* Edited by Anton C. Vrame. Brookline, MA: Holy Cross Orthodox Press, 1997. This article was previously published in *Greek Orthodox Theological Review* 22.3 (1977): 249–283.

Tertullian. *An Exhortation to Chastity.* In *Tertullian: Treatises on Marriage and Remarriage.* Translated by William P. Le Saint. ACW. Vol. 13. 1951.

_____. *To His Wife.* In *Tertullian: Treatises on Marriage and Remarriage.* Translated by William P. Le Saint. ACW. Vol. 13. 1951.

_____. *On Monogamy.* In *Tertullian: Treatises on Marriage and Remarriage.* Translated by William P. Le Saint. ACW. Vol. 13. 1951.

United States Conference of Catholic Bishops. *Marriage: Love and Life in the Divine Plan.* Pastoral Letter. Washington, DC: USCCB Publishing, 2009.

United States Conference of Catholic Bishops Committee on Marriage and Family Life. *Between Man and Woman: Questions and Answers about Marriage and Same-Sex Unions.* 2003. www.usccb.org/issues-and-action/marriage-and-family /marriage/promotion-and-defense-of-marriage/questions-and-answers-about -marriage-and-same-sex-unions.cfm.

United States Conference of Catholic Bishops Committee on Pro-Life Activities. *Life-Giving Love in an Age of Technology.* Washington, DC: United States Conference of Catholic Bishops, 2009.

_____. *Married Love and the Gift of Life.* Washington, DC: United States Conference of Catholic Bishops, 2006.

United States Supreme Court. *Roe v. Wade.* Annotated by Bo Schambelan. Philadelphia: Running Press, 1992.

_____. Planned Parenthood of Southeastern Pennsylvania v. Casey. 505 U.S. 833 (1992). www.law.cornell.edu/supct/html/historics/USSC_CR_0505_0833 _ZO.html.

_____. United States v. Windsor. No. 12-307 (2013). www.law.cornell.edu /supremecourt/text/12-307#writing-12-307_OPINION_3.

Ventura, Stephanie J. "Changing Patterns of Nonmarital Childbearing in the United States." *National Center for Health Statistics Date Brief* 18 (May 2009): 1. www.cdc.gov/nchs/data/databriefs/db18.pdf.

Von Hildebrand, Dietrich. *Man and Woman: Love and the Meaning of Intimacy.* Manchester, NH: Sophia Institute Press, 1992.

_____. *Marriage: The Mystery of Faithful Love.* Manchester, NH: Sophia Institute Press, 1991.

Waite, Linda J., and Maggie Gallagher. *The Case for Marriage: Why Married People are Happier, Healthier, and Better Off Financially.* New York: Doubleday, 2000.

Ware, Kallistos. "The Sacrament of Love: The Orthodox Understanding of Marriage and Its Breakdown." *Downside Review* 109 (1991): 79–93.

Weigel, George. *Witness to Hope: The Biography of John Paul II.* New York: HarperCollins, 1999.

Welch, Lawrence J. *The Presence of Christ in the Church: Explorations in Theology.* Ave Maria, FL: Sapientia Press, 2012.

West, Christopher. *Good News about Sex and Marriage: Answers to Your Honest Questions about Catholic Teaching.* Ann Arbor, MI: Servant Publications, 2004.

_____. *Theology of the Body Explained: A Commentary on John Paul II's "Gospel of the Body."* Boston: Pauline Books and Media, 2007.

_____. *Theology of the Body for Beginners: A Basic Introduction to Pope John Paul II's Sexual Revolution.* West Chester, PA: Ascension Press, 2009.

Whitehead, Kenneth D., ed. *The Church, Marriage, and the Family.* Proceedings from the 27th Annual Convention of the Fellowship of Catholic Scholars, September 24–26, 2004. South Bend, Indiana: St. Augustine's Press, 2007.

_____. *Marriage and the Common Good.* Proceedings from the 22nd Annual Convention of the Fellowship of Catholic Scholars, September 24–26, 1999. South Bend, Indiana: St. Augustine's Press, 2001.

Witte, John, Jr. *From Sacrament to Contract: Marriage, Religion, and Law in the Western Tradition.* 2nd ed. Louisville, KY: John Knox Press, 2012.

Witte, John, Jr., and Eliza Ellison, eds. *Covenant Marriage in Comparative Perspective.* Grand Rapids, MI: William B. Eerdmans Publishing Company, 2005.

Wojtyła, Karol. *Love and Responsibility.* Translated by Grzegorz Ignatik. Boston: Pauline Books & Media, 2013.

Wrenn, Lawrence G. *The Invalid Marriage.* Washington, DC: The Canon Law Society of America, 1998.

Young, R.V. "The Reformations of the Sixteenth and Seventeenth Centuries." In *Christian Marriage: A Historical Study.* Edited by Glenn W. Olsen. New York: Crossroad Publishing Company, 2001.

Index